BLESSED ASSURANCE

MERCER
UNIVERSITY PRESS

Endowed by
TOM WATSON BROWN
and
THE WATSON-BROWN FOUNDATION, INC.

BLESSED ASSURANCE

The Life and Art of Horton Foote

Marion Castleberry

Mercer University Press | MACON, GEORGIA

35 Years of Publishing Excellence

MUP/ H892

Published by Mercer University Press, Macon, Georgia 31207
© 2014 by Mercer University Press
1400 Coleman Avenue
Macon, Georgia 31207
All rights reserved

9 8 7 6 5 4 3 2 1

Books published by Mercer University Press are printed on acid-free
paper that meets the requirements of the American National Standard
for Information Sciences—Permanence of Paper for Printed Library
Materials.

Library of Congress Cataloging-in-Publication Data

Castleberry, Marion, author.
  Blessed assurance : the life and art of Horton Foote / Marion
Castleberry.
      pages cm
  Includes bibliographical references and index.
  ISBN-13: 978-0-88146-505-1 (hardback : acid-free paper)
  ISBN-10: 0-88146-505-4 (hardback : acid-free paper)
  1. Foote, Horton. 2. Dramatists, American--20th century—
Biography. I. Title.
  PS3511.O344Z596 2014
  812'.54--dc23
  [B]
                                                2014015615

Contents

Preface

Horton Foote enjoyed a remarkable career. For more than seventy years, beginning in 1939 when he penned his first play, he wrote what he called personal dramas, timeless tales of family, home, and the mysterious resilience of the human spirit. He wrote more than a hundred works for theater, television, and film and was equally successful in all three mediums—a record of variety and productivity unmatched by any other American writer.

Like many people, I first encountered Horton Foote through his work. In 1963, when I was a twelve-year-old boy, my parents took me to see *To Kill a Mockingbird* at a movie theater in a small, East Texas town. I had seen only three movies at this stage of my life—*Old Yeller, Snow White*, and *Gone with the Wind*—so believe me when I say that *Mockingbird* was a revelation. Even as a child I knew I was experiencing something very special, and I can still remember my response to the film in vivid detail. On the screen was a familiar world filled with characters with whom I immediately connected; I, too, was born into an ordinary, hard-working family with limited cultural and economic resources, and I, too, had grown up in a small Southern community, just like the characters of Scout and Jem. A sheltered child, I knew little about social injustice or racism, and *To Kill a Mockingbird* opened my eyes in a profound way to a world far beyond my limited experience. The movie became a rite of passage for me, as it has been for many others, and because of it I would never again look at the world in the same way.

To Kill a Mockingbird was forever imprinted in my brain, and more than twenty years later I had the opportunity to see the movie again at a Galveston, Texas, film festival honoring Horton's work. This time, the writer I had so admired as a child was sitting directly in front of me, and as I sat there, awed by his presence and feeling immensely anxious, Horton suddenly turned to me and asked, "Marion would you mind doing me a favor? I would really enjoy a Dr. Pepper and a Hershey's almond bar. Could you get me one?"

I immediately jumped to my feet and ran, or rather limped, as quickly as I could to the nearest store, thinking nothing about the ankle operation from which I was still recovering. Unfortunately there were no Hershey's almond bars within a mile of the movie theater, and the film was about to start. Finally, by the grace of God, I was able to find one at a small convenience store and return to the theater in time to hear Kim Stanley's opening lines about having nothing to fear but fear itself. I handed Horton the candy bar, and he graciously thanked me. I was totally exhausted by my ordeal, but I felt honored to have had the opportunity to do something for my friend. When I finally told him, years later, of my struggle in finding that particular candy, he remarked, "Well Buddy, I didn't know," and then we laughed until we cried. Among his many other attributes, Horton also had a wonderful sense of humor.

In 1964, shortly after first seeing *Mockingbird*, I saw *Baby, the Rain Must Fall* for the first time. For a reason I cannot explain, I was deeply moved by the story of Henry, Georgette, and Margaret Rose. Little did I know that forty years later I would collaborate with Horton on the fiftieth anniversary production of the stage version of the story, *The Traveling Lady*. The newly created American Actors Company produced the play for the inaugural Horton Foote American Playwrights Festival at Baylor University, Texas, in 2004. Every day for a month, Horton and I worked together on the production, editing and fine tuning the script and guiding the actors to a memorable ensemble performance.

Horton was generous and supportive throughout the rehearsal period. It amazed me that he had written the play fifty years previously because, as he worked, he discovered a new love and respect for the story and was willing to make whatever changes were needed to ensure a successful production—almost as though he were working on a brand new play. As a result, he inspired everyone connected with the show.

As *The Traveling Lady* gained momentum, Horton arranged for the production to be performed at the Actor's Studio in New York and, later, at the Ensemble Studio Theatre. Horton was pleased with both productions, and when *The Traveling Lady* was nominated for a Drama Desk Award, he was the first to call and congratulate the cast. I will never forget that phone call or what Horton taught me during that time about the need for serious theater, about having passion for your work, and about the necessity of patience and steadfastness while dealing with a challenging and uncertain business. More importantly, Horton taught me how to be a better human being, how important family and faith are to one's happiness, and how to accept life's pitfalls and disappointments with courage and integrity. Horton always felt that his talent as a writer was a gift from God and that his real work was to discover deeper truths about life and, in doing so, to grow spiritually. I have never known anyone more devoted to their faith or more able to meet life's twists and turns with such grace.

I would be misleading you to say that Horton Foote was perfect. He wasn't. He had flaws like everyone else. He was obsessed with his writing; he was loyal to a fault; he had a temper; and he could be stubborn, especially about his work. James Houghton said it best in his memorial to Horton: "Beneath that sweet gentlemanly demeanor was a resilient, tough son of a gun who would always stand his ground, a sly fox who knew that a slow, steady path combined with defined determination and a gentle smile could win the day. And win it he did."[1] No, Horton Foote was not perfect but he was as close as they come.

When I first met Horton in the early 1980s he was in his late sixties and already a literary legend. He had been writing for more than forty years and had been awarded two Oscars and numerous other awards. I had expected him to be a bit distant and unapproachable. After all, he was a master playwright in the midst of an expensive film project, *The Trip to Bountiful*. But, to my great surprise, he was incredibly kind, gracious, and willing to take the time to greet an unknown college teacher and theater director. Our paths crossed again a few years later when Horton kindly agreed to be the subject of my doctoral dissertation. From 1985 to 1993, when I finally completed my study, I spent many wonderful hours with him, sitting with him on the front porch of his Wharton home, talking over a steaming plate of fried oysters, walking around the family graveyard, and visiting with those most dear to him: his wife Lillian, his Aunt Laura, cousin Nan Outlar, and high school theater teacher, Eppie Murphree. His family was a group of ordinary but very special people who loved him dearly, and whom he immortalized in numerous plays.

After 1993, I continued to pour over Horton's personal papers and writings and to interview members of his family, close friends, and others who had worked with him over the years. I spent many hours talking to Horton, and I visited his birthplace often, traipsing through the cemetery and town square, trying to imagine what Horton's childhood must have been like. I scoured the streets of New York, seeking out all the places he had lived during his career and the theaters in which he had worked. Following his footsteps was impressionistic

---

[1] James Houghton, "Memorial Essay," *Farewell: Remembering Horton Foote, 1916–2009*, ed. Marion Castleberry and Susan Christensen (Dallas TX: Southern Methodist University Press, 2011) 127.

research, to be sure, but it was the kind of enquiry that contributed to my sense of place in Horton's life and career. By the time I began writing this biography, I had in mind a rich and complex portrait of America's most endearing and enduring writer. As the years passed, Horton and I became very close friends; more than that, he became my mentor, my artistic father.

The last time I saw Horton was in 2007, at a performance of *Dividing the Estate* at Primary Stages in New York. Unfortunately, I could only spend a brief amount of time with him, but he was as loving and gracious as usual to my wife, Terri, and me, and he was extremely pleased with the reception the play received from New York audiences. Horton always amazed me with his thoughtfulness and his uncanny ability to keep up with the smallest details of the lives of those he cared about. What an amazing memory he had! What a gracious person he was!

I wrote this literary biography because I was dissatisfied with existing studies of Horton's writings. I felt that critics had made many glaring mistakes about his life and work and had tried too hard to place Horton in whatever particular theory or system they espoused, ignoring the beauty, simplicity, and truth of his dramas. This situation made me aware of the need for a factual and thorough foundation for all subsequent literary studies. My goal in writing this biography, therefore, was to concentrate on Horton Foote's life and art, to find out as much as possible about the circumstances that led to the writing of his plays and screenplays, to place those works within a framework of his daily life, and to examine the work itself in a straightforward way, taking into account a wide range of critical voices over the past seventy years. The sheer volume of plays and films written by Horton Foote prevents a thorough discussion of each and every play but I have tried to place all of his writing in biographical context.

My hope is that this book will become a useful tool for scholars of Horton Foote's writings and for artists interested in performing his plays, and that it will encourage more people to read his plays and see his films. I believe he is one of the truly great writers of our time, and while Horton does not need my championship, I trust this study will help convince others to arrive at the same conclusion. Hopefully, by tracing the artistic journey of this extraordinary man, readers will come to better appreciate his writing, joining others who have been inspired by Horton Foote's remarkable life and works.

Foreword

by Hallie Foote

I first remember really spending time with Marion Castleberry when he was working as a director with my father on his play, *The Traveling Lady*, at Baylor University, Texas, in 2004. It was to be part of The Horton Foote American Playwrights Festival that Marion had tirelessly advocated for many years. The play was a kind of culmination of all the hard work that he had put into making the festival happen. I got to Baylor and sat in on rehearsals and was so impressed. They had gotten some wonderful actors from New York to play the parts of Georgette and Henry Thomas and some other local actors in the other roles. I had been nervous for my father because sometimes things like that cannot go so well, but what I saw was really lovely. My father was in heaven. He was in rehearsal with a play he loved, with a director and a collaborator he admired, with actors that understood his play. My father seemed happy and energized, which meant things were going well creatively. I know that in that rehearsal process he made some changes to the play itself and that he felt it became a better play. It was not unusual for him to do this, and it was the value of rehearsal for him and why he loved it so. And he had Marion to thank for the experience because all the elements were there, the actors, the director, the production itself, and, because they were there, he had the ability to really hear and see the play and, in doing so, tune into places that needed to be worked on. And he did just that. It was a very happy time, and, at the end of it all, the play was seen by everyone who attended the festival that weekend, including some very distinguished actors and directors and designers—all kinds of people who had worked with my father before and who loved his plays. Very sophisticated people. And I think that they, too, were impressed.

Then on the last day of the festival, Marion made available a bus tour from Baylor University to Wharton, Texas, and anyone who wanted to go could tour my father's house in Wharton, the house my father was brought to when he was a year old. The town that he wrote some sixty plays about, but in those plays it was called Harrison. My father conducted the tour, and I have pictures of him on that day when he was really in his element. I remember thinking, "Marion is a remarkable man.

He gets the importance of my father and his work and has such a love of and an understanding of what he writes." I was so touched by how thrilled my father was to be able to share a piece of what really formed him as a writer. This place called Wharton, Texas.

Marion has known of my father since he saw as a young boy *To Kill a Mockingbird* in 1963. I know that movie and the subsequent movie *Baby, the Rain Must Fall* deeply affected Marion and made him curious about why they affected him so and who was behind what he saw. In 1984, Marion met my father on the set of *The Trip to Bountiful,* and they became fast friends.

The artistic path of a writer can be a lonely one, but the appreciation of scholars and critics who give it context and help deepen the understanding of his writing are invaluable. Marion was that for my father. Often my father would say to me, "I had no idea that's what it meant," and he would laugh about it. Marion was often shining a little light on the thing my father had created, illuminating it for him.

Marion's biography shows his devotion to my father's work as one of the leading scholars who has an astute and innate understanding of his writing. Marion led the charge that my father was not just a regional writer but also one who wrote of the universal human condition. Through his exhaustive research and endless curiosity about my father and the place about which he wrote—the fictional town of Harrison, Texas—Marion's rich and beautiful biography will be essential reading not just for scholars and artists, but also audiences as they continue to experience my father's plays and films and as they come to learn about American theater in the twentieth and twenty-first centuries.

For Terri, Colin, and Jerry Dale

"A family is a remarkable thing, isn't it?

—*Cousins*

Acknowledgments

This biography was made possible in part by a grant from the Clements Institute of Southwest Studies at Southern Methodist University, Texas, and a Faculty Research Leave from Baylor University. I want to express my appreciation to Russell Martin, II, director and curator of the DeGolyer Library at Southern Methodist University, Cynthia Franco, curator of photographs, and the other members of the library staff who were most helpful when I studied the Horton Foote Papers in the summers of 2002 and 2008. I also extend my gratitude to Baylor University for various kinds of assistance, including sabbaticals, released time, and grants, and to the administration, faculty, and staff for their support and encouragement, especially my colleagues, Dr. DeAnna Toten-Beard, Dr. David Jortner, and Dr. Stan Denman who covered my classes while I was on sabbatical.

I greatly appreciate the assistance of Dr. Marc Jolley and the staff of Mercer University Press, who offered expert advice and suggestions on publishing. I am indebted to Ann Whitaker and Rob Yoho, who read my manuscript with care and sensitivity and made the biography more accurate in spirit and fact. I also extend my gratitude to my graduate students Cason Murphy, Nick Hoenshell, and Amanda Lassetter for their help and my deepest appreciation to all those who over the years have contributed to my knowledge and understanding of the life and work of Horton Foote, including Dr. Bill Harbin, Michael Wilson, Devon Abner, Robert Duvall, Peter Masterson, Carlin Glynn, Lois Smith, Jean Stapleton, John Guare, Harris Yulin, Dr. Gerald Wood, Dr. Laurin Porter, Marian Burkhart, Wilborn Hampton, Dr. Charles Watson, Dr. Robert Haynes, Susan Christensen, Rebecca Briley, George Terry Barr, Merle Hudgins, Sheila Benson, Bruce Beresford, Crystal Brian, Ronald Davis, Robert Donahoo, Robert Ellerman, Alan Hubbard, Rochelle Oliver, Carol Goodheart, David Middleton, Buzz McCaughlin, Eppie Murphree, Nan Outlar, Charles Davis, Frank Girardeau, Barbara Hogenson, Romulus Linney, Roberta Maxwell, Matthew Modine, Myrtis Outlar, Wendy Phillips, Anne Rapp, Betty Joyce Sikora, Jerry Biggs, Joyce O'Connor, Jack Sbarbori, Shelly Shaver, Elizabeth Ashley, Jacques and Marguerite Barzun, Andre Bishop, Ellen Burstyn, William Carden, David Margulies, Caryn James, Marc Scott Zicree, Alice McLain, Estelle Parsons, Matthew Broderick, and Cameron Watson.

I am especially indebted to the Foote family—Hallie, Horton Jr., Walter, and Daisy—for their support of this project. Hallie was especially helpful during the writing of the biography as she read the manuscript, suggested important corrections in the text, and wrote the foreword to the biography. I want to thank Dianne Foote for her willingness to answer my questions and for her consent to use her personal collection of family photographs in the biography. I am also grateful to Michael Wilson and his associate David Alpert for all their help, and I appreciate the support and assistance of Lisa Pacino, Kathryn Kozlark, James (Tad) Hershorn, Susan Johann, Gregory Costanzo, Carol Rosegg, Joan Marcus, James Houghton at the Signature Theatre, and Philip Rinaldi at the Lincoln Center.

My deepest appreciation goes to my wife Terri for her unconditional love and support of this project. Her respect and affection for Horton Foote is equal to mine, and I cannot thank her enough for inspiring me with her patience, her understanding, her prayers, and her editing skills.

Finally, I want to express my love for Horton and Lillian Foote and my appreciation for Horton's friendship and support over the years. I cherish our time together.

Horton's family: Photo taken circa 1920. Seated from left Tom
Brooks; Daisy Brooks, Foote's grandmother, whom he called
Baboo, his uncle, Brother Brooks; another uncle, Speed Brooks,
and his Aunt Laura, in chair with Foote. Standing from left:
Foote's Uncle Billy, his Aunt Rose, and his mother and father,
Hallie and Horton Foote Sr.

Albert Horton Foote Sr., Horton's father. Photo taken circa 1910.

Harriet "Hallie" Gautier Brooks Foote, Horton's mother.
Photo taken circa 1914.

DeGolyer Library, Southern Methodist University, Dallas, Texas, A1992.1810

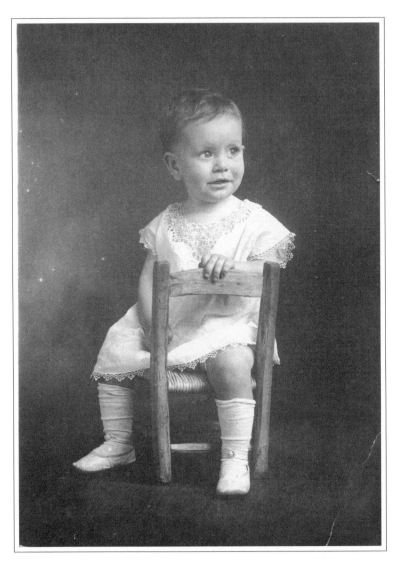

Albert Horton Foote Jr. Age one when his family moved into house on Houston Street.

DeGolyer Library, Southern Methodist University, Dallas, Texas, A1992. 1810

Horton and Lillian Foote. Photo taken circa 1945.

Horton and Lillian Foote with Albert Horton Sr. and Hallie
Foote. Photo taken circa 1940's.

Courtesy of Hallie Foote

From Left: Barbara Hallie, Daisy, Lillian, Horton Jr. and Walter posing with Horton Foote by the fireplace in their Nyack, NY home. Photo taken circa 1962.

DeGolyer Library, Southern Methodist University, Dallas, Texas, A1992.1810

Lillian Gish and Sheriff (Frank Overton) and Ticket Man (William Hansen) from *The Trip to Bountiful* (Television version, 1953)

DeGolyer Library, Southern Methodist University, Dallas, Texas, A1992.1810.

Lillian Gish as Carrie Watts in *The Trip to Bountiful.*

Courtesy of Hallie Foote

Robert Duvall and Horton Foote on the set of *Convicts,* 1989.

Photo taken by James Tad Hershorn, courtesy of DeGolyer Library, Southern Methodist University, Dallas, Texas, A1992.1810

Hallie Foote and Eddie Kaye Thomas in *Talking Pictures* at
Signature Theatre, 1994.

Photo by Susan Johann, courtesy of Signature Theatre

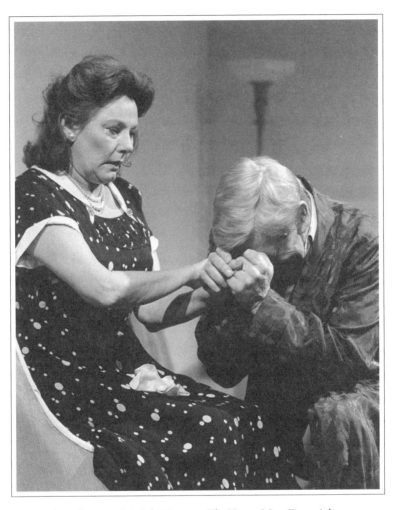

Carlin Glynn and Ralph Waite in *The Young Man From Atlanta*
at Signature Theatre, 1995.

Photo by Susan Johann, courtesy of Signature Theatre

Horton Foote, Michael Wilson, Jean Stapleton, Roberta Maxwell and Hallie Foote on the set of *The Carpetbagger's Children,* 2001.

DeGolyer Library, Southern Methodist University, Dallas, Texas, A1992.1810

Hallie Foote and Estelle Parsons in *The Last of the Thorntons* at Signature Theatre, 2000.

Photo by Susan Johann, courtesy of Signature Theatre

Horton Foote at Baylor University's inaugural Horton Foote
American Playwrights Festival, 2004.

Courtesy of Baylor University Theatre Department

Lois Smith, Devon Abner and Hallie Foote in *The Trip to Bountiful* at Signature Theatre, 2005.

Photo by Carol Rosegg, courtesy of Signature Theatre

Lynn Cohen, Margo White and Quincy Confoy in *The Traveling Lady* at Ensemble Studio Theatre, 2006.

Photo courtesy of Marion Castleberry

Dividing the Estate at Lincoln Center with Devon Abner,
Elizabeth Ashley, Penny Fuller, James DeMarse, Hallie Foote,
and Gerald McRaney, circa 2008.

Photo by Joan Marcus, courtesy of Lincoln Center

The Orphan's Home Cycle at Signature Theatre with Maggie Lacey
as Elizabeth and Bill Heck as Horace, 2010.

Photo by Gregory Costanzo, courtesy of Signature Theatre

Horton's children: Daisy Foote, Horton Foote Jr., Walter Foote and Hallie Foote at the DeGolyer Library during The Life and Works of Horton Foote Celebration in Dallas, Texas, 2011.

Photo courtesy of Diane Buglewizc Foote

Cast of the 60th anniversary production of *The Trip to Bountiful,*
including Cecily Tyson, Vanessa Williams, Cuba Gooding Jr.,
Tom Wopat and Condola Rashad, 2013.

Photo taken by Lisa Pacino, Under the Duvet Productions, NYC

Hallie Foote, William Converse Roberts (above), and
Matthew Broderick (below) in Horton Foote's *1918*.

Courtesy of Hallie Foote.

The production poster of Horton Foote's *The Orphans' Home Cycle.*

Courtesy of Michael Wilson

Part One

Genesis of a Playwright

Pretty soon it'll all be gone. Ten years…twenty…this house…me…you… But the river will be here. The fields. The woods. The smell of the Gulf. That's what I always took my strength from…we're part of all this. We left it but we can never lose what it has given us.

—Carrie Watts in *The Trip to Bountiful*

1

Origins
1821–1916

Albert Horton Foote, Jr., was born Tuesday, 14 March 1916, to Albert Horton Foote, Sr., and Harriet Gautier (Brooks) Foote, in a small rented room in Wharton, Texas. As Horton Foote recalled, his birthplace had a rich and extraordinary history, having been one of the first areas of Texas explored by Europeans in the sixteenth and seventeenth centuries. The land was inhabited as early as the Paleo-Indian period, and until the late eighteenth century, the fierce Karankawa Indians occupied the area that would become Wharton County. Spain controlled the territory until Mexico achieved independence in 1821, and Anglo-American colonization began under a program settled by the Mexican government in 1823, when Stephen F. Austin led three hundred white settlers to the south coast region.

The town of Wharton, which lies only forty-five miles inland from the Gulf of Mexico, was built on two leagues of land ceded by the Mexican government to William Kincheloe, a rancher and farmer in Austin's original colony. Named after two brothers, John and William Wharton, who were leaders in Texas's struggle for independence from Mexico, Wharton was officially placed on the geographic map in 1838 and later incorporated and named county seat in 1902. From the time Wharton was first settled in 1823 until its incorporation, it had only a few crude stores surrounded by plantations. Produce and goods were shipped up the river from the Gulf port of Matagorda some forty miles away, and boats carried the cotton, sugar cane, and corn back down to the river to ships waiting at the Gulf.[1]

Among the first settlers of the Texas Gulf Coast area were Horton Foote's maternal great-grandparents Dr. Peter William and Lucy Ann Gautier who, at the behest of their friend Stephen F. Austin, left their home of Judson County Florida to conquer the Texas wilderness. Within a decade, the Gautier's became one of the most prominent and respected

---

[1] Annie Lee Williams, *A History of Wharton County* (Austin TX: Van Boeckmann-Jones, 1964). I have drawn from this book for historical information on Wharton, Texas.

land-owning families in Texas. Peter William and Lucy Ann gave birth to four children—Harriet, Ariadne, Charles, and Lucy—who carried on the agricultural tradition of their forefathers. Peter William, also a medical doctor, was among those Texans who marched to turn back Mexican invading forces in 1842. He died in Velasco, Texas, in August 1850, and Lucy died three years later, on 23 November 1853, onboard the steamer "Mexico" on her passage from New Orleans to Galveston. Peter William and Lucy Gautier were buried in the historic Peach Point Cemetery in Brazoria County, Texas, the original burial ground of Stephen F. Austin.

In 1852, Peter and Lucy's daughter Harriet Gautier married John W. Brooks, Horton Foote's maternal great-grandfather, whose aristocratic ancestors immigrated to Virginia from Gloucester, England, in the 1600s. Legend has it that as a young girl, Harriet had gone to a fortune-teller and was told that she would marry a man who had come to Texas by boat and that he would want to build a brick house for them, but she must refuse and insist on a frame house, else she would have an unhappy and tragic life. John had come to Texas by boat from Virginia, and when he proposed to Harriet, he told her that after they married he would build her a brick house. Remembering the warning of the fortune-teller, however, Harriet refused to marry him unless he promised their home would be built of wood. He agreed, and following their wedding, the couple built an impressive wood-framed house on the banks of the Brazos River in Brazoria County, Texas, where they gave birth to five children—Nannie, Peter, Tom, Billy, and Laura.[2]

Historically, coastal southeast Texas was a westward extension of the Cotton Kingdom, and the Brooks family prospered as plantation owners until the Civil War, when the emancipation of the slaves and the post-war drop in cotton prices thrust the family into bankruptcy. John Brooks died on 4 October 1870, leaving his wife and children alone and penniless. Fortunately, Harriet Brooks was a strong matriarch who kept her family fed and instilled in her children a deep respect for their familial heritage. Her courage and resourcefulness during the difficult years of Reconstruction became legend in the family stories passed down to Horton Foote.

Born on 10 May 1865, Tom Brooks—Horton Foote's maternal grandfather—was only five when his father died but his mother's firm

---

[2] Horton Foote, interview by Marion Castleberry, 18 November 1988, Wharton, Texas.

guidance tempered the young Brooks's mathematical mind with moral steadfastness. He was especially concerned for the welfare of his family and was always ready to help the less fortunate. At the age of eighteen, Tom attended Texas A&M University, where he graduated with academic honors.

In 1886, Brooks moved to the rural community of Wharton, Texas, where he clerked in his uncle's grocery store. Later, he bought the store, turning it into a highly prosperous business, and in time became a rich and respected leader in Wharton and the Gulf Coast region, serving as county treasurer and vice president of a local bank. During this time, Brooks also served as an officer in the White Man's Union, an association created in 1889 to protect white interests and to limit black political participation during Reconstruction. The organization ensured that no person could file for public office without approval by the union, a policy that often caused serious conflict between blacks and whites of Wharton. The tension between the races eventually resulted in the politically motivated murder of a candidate for sheriff who supported the election of blacks to political offices. Many years later, Brooks's grandson, Horton Foote, would dramatize the effects of this tragic event on the lives of those involved with the murder in his 1969 novel, *Days of Violence*.

Even though Tom Brooks was, for a time, an active member of the White Man's Union, Horton Foote always admired his grandfather, and the town of Wharton shared his admiration. The Wharton newspaper described him as a man who combined "high ideals with a sound practical judgment…an affability of disposition and a saving sense of humor." He "exemplified the truest qualities of good citizenship" and "engaged in politics in its broader sense of duty as a citizen."[3] Brooks was also an imaginative speculator who, in the 1920s, embarked upon a business venture that brought his family immense wealth, while changing the face of Wharton forever.

When Tom Brooks arrived in Wharton in 1886, the old Southern plantation system had been largely abandoned, leaving thousands of acres of fertile soil idle and the five or six families who owned the land unsure of the future. With the profits from his grocery store, Brooks began buying up these plantations for very little money, dividing them into smaller farms, selling some of them for a sizable profit, and

---

[3] Horton Foote, *Farewell: A Memoir of a Texas Childhood* (New York: Scribner, 1999) 148.

managing others on a sharecropping arrangement. Although Brooks amassed a fortune from this endeavor, he must have been extremely generous because, as Horton Foote remembers, "For many years my family encountered people who had borrowed money in order to escape economic ruin."[4] Tom Brooks became Wharton's leading landowner and richest citizen, and in 1892, he opened a real-estate office in Wharton. He hired Wharton's first secretary, Daisy Speed, with whom he quickly fell in love and married a year later on 11 January 1893.

Daisy (1868–1954) was one of eight children born to John and Virginia Yerby Speed, who had come to Texas in the 1840s to manage a plantation in East Columbia, Texas, some thirty miles north of Wharton. Virtually self-educated, Daisy was an accomplished and intelligent young woman. After serving as governess on a large plantation, in 1884 she became, according to family stories, the first secretary to use a typewriter in the Wharton County courthouse. Miss Daisy was a fierce aristocrat with an enormous sense of family pride and a capacity for deep, unfaltering devotion to those she loved. Although her diminutive stature reflected softness, kindness, and gentility, to those who knew her Daisy Brooks was a Southern belle with a "backbone of steel and a mind of mercury."[5]

Tom and Daisy Brooks gave birth to eight children. Two daughters, Jennie and Daisy, died in infancy, while six others lived to be adults. They were Harriet (Hallie), the mother of Horton Foote, Jr. (1894–1974), Laura (1897–1992), Rosa (1900–1962), Thomas (1902–1950), John Speed (1904–1965), and William (1910–1969). All the children were reared in the family's impressive home on Richmond Road where, surrounded by their aristocratic neighbors, they lived in Southern elegance and adhered to the Protestant morality of their parents.

Unfortunately, as much as aristocratic pride and familial devotion upheld the Brooks family, Horton Foote's paternal ancestors—the Hortons and the Footes—were nearly overwhelmed by lost inheritance and personal rejection. Albert Clinton Horton—the playwright's great-great-grandfather and namesake—was born to William and Mary Horton in Hancock County, Georgia, on 4 September 1798. In 1829, Horton married Eliza Holliday, the daughter of a prominent Georgia businessman, and within three years of the marriage, he was elected to the Alabama state senate. Following his brief, one-year stint as senator in

---

[4] Horton Foote, interview by Marion Castleberry, 18 November 1988, Wharton, Texas.

[5] Ibid.

1834, Horton moved from Alabama to Texas in April 1835, quickly rising to economic and political prominence. At the outbreak of Texas's war for independence from Mexico, Horton joined his fellow statesmen in their struggle for autonomy, leading a cavalry unit known as the Mobile Greys in the revolution and fighting at the Battles of Goliad and San Jacinto. After the war, he was elected to the Congress of the Republic of Texas and appointed as commissioner to select the location for the capital of Texas. He helped frame the constitution of the new Republic and was a member of the State Constitutional Convention of 1845, which was called to consider annexation by the United States. When Texas joined the Union in 1845, Horton became Texas's first elected lieutenant governor, and when Governor James Pinckney Henderson left office on 19 May 1846 to command military forces in Mexico, Horton was made acting governor, a position he held until 1 July 1847.

By the time his political term ended, Albert Clinton Horton was rich and prosperous, owning both a home in Matagorda and the region's largest river valley plantation near Wharton, on which he built for his family a beautiful mansion, Sycamore Grove. The Hortons were Episcopalians, and Albert Clinton was elected vestryman and warden in 1839. A few years later, the family joined the Baptist faith, the largest denomination in Wharton, and Horton became one of the founders and Charter Trustees of Baylor University in 1845. Horton was regarded as one of the wealthiest men in the state, but the Civil War, which he passionately supported, served Horton no better than it had John Brooks. By 1865, Horton had lost his fortune, and in the fall of that same year, he died at his summer home in Matagorda. In the story of Governor Albert Clinton Horton, his great-great grandson, Horton Foote, discovered a compelling theme: the need for courage in the face of deprivation and loss.

Governor Horton and his wife Eliza gave birth to six children, but only two survived a yellow fever outbreak in the 1850s: Patience Louisiana Texas (born 21 September 1837) and Robert John (born 24 March 1844). In 1853, Patience married Colonel Isaac Newton Dennis, a law graduate of Harvard University in Cambridge, Massachusetts, and they gave birth to a daughter, Lida Horton Dennis. In 1861, four years before his death, Governor Horton had willed an equal amount of property and slaves to his daughter Patience and son Robert John, who had enlisted in the Confederate Army at age eighteen and was away at war. Patience died soon after, in 1863, leaving her inheritance to her daughter, Lida, who would later marry Judge Willie C. Croom.

In 1865, following his father's death, Robert John returned to Wharton and discovered that his niece had taken control of Sycamore Grove, and her father, Colonel Dennis, was managing the plantation. Ironically, Governor Horton's final will and testament was not entered into the Texas Probate files until August 1866, a year after his death, and by that time the slaves had been emancipated (1865) and the family's Confederate holdings had been deemed worthless.[6] Robert John was left with nothing from his father's estate, and although the Dennis family held onto Sycamore Grove for several more years, the plantation was sold off piece by piece by Patience's heirs. The mansion was finally demolished in 1960. Today, very little remains of Sycamore Grove. The cotton fields that once surrounded the mansion have been overrun by shopping centers and housing developments. All that is left of Albert Clinton Horton's magnificent plantation are two large sycamore trees and a small family graveyard.

The manner in which Sycamore Grove was divided became a source of tension and confusion among family members, and a number of stories grew up around the event. Although Robert John swore never to discuss the episode, his family, especially the Horton girls, continued to keep alive the story of how their father was unjustly cheated out of his inheritance. Horton Foote grew up with this story of duplicity passed down to him by his great-aunt Loula (Texas Louisiana Patience Horton) who, with great vigor and dramatic flair, told an unforgettable tale of intrigue and treachery. According to her, the plot to cheat her father was set in motion by Colonel Dennis and a mysterious figure named Phillips. The story goes that in the 1850s, when Robert John was about ten-years-old, Governor Horton had enrolled his son in a prestigious east coast boarding school. While there, Robert John was excessively teased about his Southern heritage and his habit of wearing long hair plaited in a queue. The young boy soon grew homesick for Sycamore Grove, and after only a few weeks Governor Horton arrived to take his son home. For their return trip, Governor Horton decided to take a boat from New York to Matagorda, and as they were boarding the vessel, they saw a young, orphaned bootblack on the dock. Having himself grown up without a father, and concerned that his son had no white companions to play with on the plantation, Governor Horton was immediately drawn to the boy, whom he adopted and educated as a lawyer. Because of his legal background, Phillips, the adopted son, was later put in charge of

---

[6] Merle Hudgins, unpublished essay on Albert Clinton Horton, June 2009.

the family holdings and expected to advise young Robert John. However, after the collapse of the Confederacy and Albert Clinton Horton's death, Phillips teamed up with Colonel Isaac Dennis who established himself as proprietor of Sycamore Grove. As a result, Robert John received nothing from his father's estate.[7]

This story fascinated Horton Foote as a child, and as an adult he sought to understand the reason his ancestors were deprived of their inheritance and social position. Unfortunately, the mystery remained unsolved for years, and Horton Foote passed away before he could uncover the truth about the event. What Horton did know, however, is that following Governor Horton's death the Horton family struggled to survive in a world that was often perilous and unfair.

On 12 September 1864, Robert John married Mary Hawes, the daughter of Judge Hugh Hawes, and after the war he tried to build a new life as a merchant in Matagorda, with little success. Economic conditions in southeast Texas were so bad during Reconstruction that he could not survive as a shopkeeper, and he was forced to take a job as a lighthouse operator on the Gulf Coast. He and his family lived on Saluria, an island port just off the coast of Texas, until a hurricane devastated the area, nearly drowning the family and leaving them homeless in 1886. Afterwards, Robert John and his wife, Mary Hawes, moved their family to Goliad, Texas, and then finally returned to Wharton where they lived until his death on 2 October 1904. Robert John and Mary Horton were the parents of six children: Albert Clinton, II (1875–1939), Mary (1873–1908), Loula (1871–1947), Reenie (1878–1927), Lida (1880–1961), and Corilla (1869–1940).

Corilla (Corrie) Horton married Albert Harrison Foote in 1889. Albert's family had moved to Texas from Virginia during the 1850s, bringing its own proud aristocratic history. His mother was Betty Elizabeth Roberdeau Foote (whose American heritage reached as far back as the Revolutionary War), and his father, Stephen Daniel Foote, had been a cotton broker in Galveston. Foote owned a fleet of ships and made a fortune buying and selling cotton for the Confederacy during the Civil War; but like so many in the South, the family lost their fortune by the end of the war. Stephen Daniel Foote died in 1870, leaving his wife and eight children bankrupt and destitute. They would have remained so if not for the kindness of William Alexander, a distant relative, who

---

[7] Horton Foote, interview by Marion Castleberry, 19 November 1988, Wharton, Texas.

took pity on the Foote clan. Alexander, a medical doctor and wealthy landowner, built the family a large house with his own hands on his Wharton plantation, and gave Elizabeth and her children one hundred acres of rich farmland to use as they pleased. Alexander also raised young Albert Harrison Foote (Horton Foote's paternal grandfather) as his own, trained him to be a lawyer, and made it possible for the rest of the Foote children to obtain an education. In his final will and testament, Alexander bequeathed, "Mrs. B.H. Foote and her children, Martha J. Foote, Henry S. Foote, Lilly Foote, Roberdeau Foote, Albert H. Foote, Cora Foote, Bettie Foote, and Stephen Foote…one hundred acres of land on which they now reside…to hold jointly during their lives, if they shall continue to reside on said land; But if either of them shall remove from said land or absent themselves from it for the space of two years, He or she shall forfeit all interest in this bequest. It is also my wish that none of the above mentioned legatee shall have power to alienate any part or all of this parcel of land until the youngest of them shall have become of lawful age."[8] Although Alexander's generosity was unprecedented and saved the family from excruciating poverty, his stipulation that the family members remain together or forfeit their share of the land and home helped bring about the dissolution of Albert and Corrie Foote's marriage.

As descendants understand it, the emotional and financial demands of the larger Foote family soured Albert Harrison and Corrie's otherwise promising union. Albert Harrison's brothers and sisters were not industrious, and Corrie, who cooked all the meals and cared for the family, began to feel resentful, her frustration often leading to quarrels with her proud mother-in-law. She grew distant and remote, and after the birth of her second child, Lilyan Dale, Corrie left Albert Harrison and returned to her mother and father. Albert Harrison began to drink heavily and died in 1902, only thirty-six years old. A year later, Corrie married Peter Earl Cleveland, a railroad engineer, and moved to Houston, abandoning her young son, Albert Horton (the playwright's father).

The harsh realities of family life weighed heavily upon Albert Harrison Foote's children. Albert Horton was twelve (1890) and Lily Dale (1889) was ten when their father died. Neither child was mature enough to understand the circumstances surrounding their parents' estrangement or their father's death. Lily Dale remained close to her

---

[8] W.F.S. Alexander, will dated 30 March 1879, Wharton County Courthouse, Wharton, Texas.

mother, and with time grew bitter towards her father and paternal family. Albert was devoted to his father, and neither time nor family scrutiny would ever diminish the love and respect he had for him. As the playwright explains, the death of Albert Harrison Foote haunted his son, Albert:

> I often questioned my father about the day my grandfather died, but he wouldn't say much except that it was a sad time, and his father was considered a brilliant lawyer. He told me that on the day of the funeral his father's best friend had taken him in his lap and told him that his father was a fine man and that he should always be proud of him. When my Grandfather Foote died, there was not enough money to buy a tombstone for his grave, and so it was unmarked until my father, when he was twenty-seven, married and with a child of his own, took his first savings and bought the tombstone for his father's grave.[9]

Albert Foote's relationship with his mother, Corrie, was further threatened when his stepfather refused to care for him. Cleveland offered to rear Lily as his own child—he doted on her, dressed her in the finest clothes, and paid for her music lessons, but he would not allow young Albert to live in his home, and he resented the child's occasional visits. Corrie appears to have done nothing to soothe her son's growing hatred of his stepfather, nor did she stop the humiliation to which he was subjected. Her grandson, Horton Foote, expressed the most revealing example of Corrie's relationship with her son:

> The classic story is that my father couldn't live with her, but she would give him breakfast each morning. But my father had to be out of the house each morning by five. He never put all this together until one morning he arrived at seven and his mother met him at the door. "Thank you son for buying me the eggs," she said, "I'm so grateful to you." My father thought she was unusually nervous and he looked over his shoulder and there sat Mr. Cleveland. His mother was not able to tell him the truth or to invite him inside. That's the kind of humiliation he went through. Afterwards, he never wrote his mother, and when he traveled to Houston, he never wanted to call her. He never ostensibly expressed hostility, but there was total indifference on his part. I know he could not bear the sight of the man she married.[10]

---

[9] Horton Foote, interview by Marion Castleberry, 18 November 1988, Wharton, Texas.

[10] Ibid.

Abandoned by his mother, Albert turned to his grandparents, aunts, and uncles for help. He spent his early years with his Grandfather and Grandmother Horton in Wharton, and, since all of the family members lived within a few blocks of one another, the boy developed a close bond with his aunts—Mary, Lida, and Reenie—as well as with his Uncle Albert. But it was his Aunt Loula who accepted the task of mothering him after the death of his grandparents and through her encouragement the young boy's emotional identification was nourished.

Young Albert always felt great affection and love from the Horton family; nonetheless, he never stopped searching for his own identity. His son, Horton Foote, would explain years later that his father was constantly reminded of his heritage, but aristocratic or not he had to fight for survival and live by his wits. He remained loyal to his family, but his sense of personal loss was great. He had been deprived of a father and rejected by his mother, but he seems never to have dwelled on the injustices done. As a consequence of this betrayal and rejection, Albert Horton's childhood was spent in pursuit of a single dream—"to belong to a family."[11] Years later, Horton Foote would faithfully reconstruct his father's quest in his literary masterpiece, *The Orphans' Home Cycle*.

When Albert Horton was in the sixth grade, he stopped going to school and began working around town doing anything to make a few dollars. He sold fish he caught in the river and empty whiskey bottles he found in the alleys behind the saloons and whorehouses. These were difficult times for a young boy to grow up in, and young Foote had been left adrift in an uncertain world. Gambling and drinking were much sought after pastimes. Public beatings and hangings on the courthouse square were a common occurrence. Ordinary men killed each other over the most trivial of matters, and young girls in Wharton carried guns with them to school, checking them in with the principal when they arrived and picking them up as they started for home. In an effort to restore cotton production after the Civil War, land owners established convict farms where a convict could work off his sentence at the rate of $7.50 a month. This practice saved money for the farmers but ultimately proved to be nothing more than a continuation of slavery, with the same kind of violence unleashed on the convict workers as had been used on the slaves.

---

[11] Ibid.

When Albert Horton was twelve years old, he moved out of his grandparents' house and went to work on his Uncle Albert's plantation near Lago, Texas, which was farmed by black convicts. The farm had a country store that catered to black sharecroppers, and the boy was often left in charge when his uncle was away gambling and drinking. After a few months, he left his uncle's house and moved in with a black couple, Martha and Douglas, with whom he spent most of his adolescent years. He would later admit that the time spent on the plantation was one of the happiest of his childhood.[12]

As the years passed, Albert Horton became a handsome, good-natured young man who dealt honestly and graciously with the public, and seldom went unemployed. He recognized at an early age that he could build a career around the merchandizing business. As a teenager, he managed a general store in Glen Flora, a rural community ten miles south of Wharton; in his twenties he traveled as a salesman to Arkansas, Alabama, Mississippi, and East Texas; and later he attended business school in Houston, where he began to think about opening his own store.

In 1913, Albert Horton bought a small cleaning and pressing shop in Wharton, where he also sold mail-order suits. During this time, Albert began to court Hallie Brooks. They went to movies, parties, and dances and began spending as much time together as they could. They had known each other since childhood, and Albert Horton remembered watching "the little girl with skinny legs as she and her friends passed the store in which he worked."[13] Now she had grown into a kind, generous, and beautiful young woman, and Albert fell deeply in love with her. Having searched for true companionship all his life, he soon proposed and Hallie accepted. However, Mr. Brooks did not favor the match: partly because her chosen mate had earned a reputation as somewhat of a hell-raiser and partly because he believed no man worthy of his daughter's hand in marriage. Tom Brooks appears to have been a moral and loving family man, but he was known to be domineering and strict. Horton Foote explained in his memoir, *Farewell*, that Mr. Brook's theories about the marriage of his daughters were simple and clear.

> Why should they marry when he could always provide for them? He could understand a man wanting to marry, but not a woman. He would point to all the unhappy marriages that were around them—women tied to worthless husbands with children to raise and care for, his sister

---

[12] Ibid.
[13] Ibid.

Nannie, forced by the early death of her husband to raise four children alone. That he had an extremely happy marriage himself seemed never to alter his views.[14]

Furthermore, Mr. Brooks strongly opposed his daughter's dating anyone who he believed practiced the sins of drinking, gambling, or dancing, and he refused to sanction her engagement. He forbade the couple to see each other, barred Albert Horton from coming to his house, and often sent Hallie away on lengthy trips to keep her away from Foote. Once before Mr. Brooks had refused to allow Hallie to marry a young man, Syd Joplin, and although she defied her father by seeing the boy, she finally succumbed to his wishes and refused the young man's proposal.

The family echoed Mr. Brooks's serious doubts about Foote and wondered why a young lady of Hallie's social standing wanted to marry a humble, ne'er-do-well merchant. As one family member recalled, "Not one in a hundred persons in Wharton would have given the marriage a chance but they were obviously wrong."[15] Few understood the love that Hallie felt for Albert Horton, and her parents were apparently insensitive to her feelings. She begged her father not to stand in the way of their marriage, but Mr. Brooks was unsympathetic to her wishes. Nevertheless, Hallie's devotion to Albert Horton was unshakable, and on Valentine's Day, 1915, the couple eloped and secretly married in the rented home of their friends, Allie and Arch Elmore, five blocks from the Brooks's house. Only the couple's closest friends were invited to the wedding for fear that word would get back to Hallie's parents.

The town's Methodist minister, who had been Hallie's pastor for many years, refused to marry them, but the Baptist preacher agreed to conduct the ceremony if Hallie would call her parents to let them know what she was about to do. Her mother wasn't home when she phoned, so she was forced to call her father at his office, ten minutes before the ceremony began. Mr. Brooks, of course, tried to talk his daughter out of marrying, but Hallie refused to listen. Consequently, Albert Horton Foote, age twenty-six, and Harriet Gautier Brooks, age twenty-two, were wed at five p.m. on 14 February 1915.[16]

---

[14] Foote, *Farewell*, 63–64.

[15] Nan Outlar, interview by Marion Castleberry, 16 November 1988, Wharton, Texas.

[16] Horton Foote, interview by Marion Castleberry, 19 November 1988, Wharton, Texas.

Although the marriage would last almost sixty years, the immediate cost of their elopement was high. Mr. Brooks severed all ties with his daughter for nearly a year, and the strained relationship between the proud father and son-in-law was never fully relieved. Brooks's anger toward his daughter and his distaste for Albert was partially soothed in time, but he apparently never completely forgave them for their deception.

Horton Foote admits in *Farewell* that he was always intrigued by the story of his mother clandestinely meeting and eloping with his father. Hallie's willingness to defy her parents in order to achieve individuation and realize her dream of love and companionship became one of the central themes in Foote's dramatic canon. Several of his plays, such as *Flight, Courtship,* and *On Valentine's Day* dramatize the courage and resourcefulness his mother showed that day.

The details of the early married life of Albert Horton and Hallie Foote from 1915 to 1916 may never be entirely known, but this much is certain: Albert Horton's entire world revolved around his bride. He was devoted to her, and she adored him. Throughout their marriage, Horton Foote's parents were deeply committed to each other, as is evident in their later correspondence. In a 1933 letter, Hallie wrote to Albert Horton, "Do you know you have never failed me *one* time…in any way?"[17]

The couple spent the first month of their marriage in a spare bedroom at the Elmore's house; later they rented a single room apartment in Mrs. Huston's boarding house on Burleson Street and took their meals next door at the home of Mrs. Walker, a family friend. They lived in the boarding house for two years while Albert Horton continued to work in his pressing shop and Hallie created a loving home environment to which her husband retreated each day from the frustrations and disappointments of the outside world.

To those who knew them, the Footes were, and would always be, a very private pair. Albert Horton did not seek the limelight of public office or desire any part of civic organizations (even though he was a passionate liberal "yellow dog" Democrat) but he was a well-liked and respected member of the Wharton community. He believed strongly in the value of hard work, and most of his waking hours were spent scratching out a modest living. Although he would never be a financial

---

[17] Hallie Foote to Albert Horton Foote, Sr., 23 October 1953. Letter in Horton Foote Papers, DeGolyer Library, Southern Methodist University, Dallas, Texas [hereafter cited as Horton Foote Papers].

giant like his father-in-law, Albert Foote would be remembered as an assiduous provider and devoted family man.

Hallie's world was equally self-contained. Having enjoyed the privileges to which her family status entitled her, she was often invited to prestigious parties and social gatherings but rarely accepted, choosing instead to spend the time with her husband. Relatives and friends remember that Hallie and Albert were totally absorbed in each other, and in all the years of their marriage, they were never separated for longer than one day. On 14 March 1916, Hallie gave birth to her first son and, from that time on, she dedicated her life to being a wife and a mother.

The birth of their son, Albert Horton Foote, Jr., was an important event for the family, primarily because it began a reconciliation process that reunited Hallie with her mother and father. For months after the elopement, the high-minded Mr. Brooks refused to speak to his daughter, and in fact both he and his wife Daisy went out of their way to avoid her. However, the estrangement ended as quickly as it had begun when the Brookses discovered that Hallie was expecting a baby. Horton Foote explained in *Farewell* that one morning in the summer of 1915 Hallie received a phone call from her mother, asking if she could visit Hallie at the boarding house. That afternoon Mrs. Brooks arrived, greeted her daughter, and began to talk as if nothing was wrong. No apologies were given and the topic of the elopement was never mentioned, then or ever. The next day, Mr. Brooks appeared, and as soon as he saw Hallie, he began to make plans to build the couple a house adjacent to his own. The house was a peace offering, one that helped mend the emotional scars left from the previous year. Although Albert Horton agreed to his father-in-law's plan, he never claimed ownership of the house, choosing instead to leave the property in Hallie's name.[18]

In 1917, the Foote family moved into a new six-room house at 515 North Houston Street. The house sat on three-quarters of an acre of land adjacent to the Brooks's stately Victorian home where Hallie grew up. It was in the Foote's house on North Houston Street that Horton Foote, future playwright, spent his childhood listening to tales about his family and watching the world unfold around him. After his parents' death in the 1970s, the house would become his permanent Texas residence, a place he would call "home" for more than ninety years, and where—

---

[18] Horton Foote, interview by Marion Castleberry, 18 November 1988, Wharton, Texas.

with his unique brand of humor, compassion, and sensitivity—he would continue to write plays depicting the heart of small-town America, plays that would have a profound and lasting effect on audiences for years to come.

2

A Texas Childhood
1916–33

Compared to his ancestors, Horton Foote enjoyed an ordinary, happy, and relatively uneventful childhood. His earliest recollections are of the enormous love of his extended family: his mother, father, aunts, uncles, great-aunts and great-uncles, grandfather and grandmother, and myriad cousins, all who doted over him endlessly. Horton apparently got all the attention he needed, which was probably more than that required by any child, for as he later revealed, "I was the only child and grandchild for over five and a half years. I knew that all the adults loved me. I was the center of the world."[1]

From all accounts, Horton was a tenderhearted, polite, and imaginative child, always intently observing everything around him. When he became old enough to wander outdoors, he began to take in all the sights and sounds around him—the smell of roses and honeysuckle vines, the melodies of the songbirds, the brilliantly colored wildflowers that appeared each spring, and the cotton fields that gilded the land. The rural days of his childhood left the boy with a profound feeling for the companionship of nature and an acute sensitivity to its moods.

Horton described the world of his early childhood as his "garden, his Eden," and he spent most of his early waking days, when not in school, roaming the confines of his parents' and grandparents' property.

> When I was a boy, our back yard was fenced in and we had a chicken house and a yard full of chickens. There was only one pecan tree then, and there were three fig trees and two chinaberry trees.... To the left of our yard was my grandfather's barn. When I was a very young boy, he kept a horse and a cow there. At the far end of this lot is a giant pecan tree, at least two hundred years old. I spent much time climbing this tree. I had to nail boards to the trunk to make a kind of ladder to help me reach its branches. To the right of our yard and across the street were cotton fields belonging to my grandfather and beyond them were cotton fields belonging to my great, great uncle. These cotton fields went right

---

[1] Horton Foote, interview by Marion Castleberry, 18 November 1988, Wharton, Texas.

up to the back edge of the town itself, to the livery stable and a section known as the "Flats" that had black restaurants and a black barber shop and pool hall…. The two houses directly across from my grandparents' had large acreages around them, too. In one of them lived a boy my age who became my best friend. His parents had come from Mississippi, and his father managed a cotton gin and oil mill. The land back of their house went down to the gin and my friend and I often went over to it climbing upon the platforms where the bales of cotton were kept, racing each other across them.[2]

Even though his parents were strict disciplinarians and very protective of their child, Horton was allowed to roam as much as he wanted, but he was warned not to go near the river. His parents cautioned him about the dangers there, often telling him about the ferocious suck holes beneath the water that could quickly seize the strongest swimmers and drown them. As Horton recalled, he often heard "the tolling of a bell, or the wail of a fire siren, announcing that someone had drowned."[3]

Horton and his friends spent many hours digging tunnels and caves; and, taking their inspiration from Huck Finn and Tom Sawyer, they formed endless clubs and secret societies. They climbed trees, and built clubhouses and tree houses. His parents' home and the surrounding land became a source of security and adventure for Horton. The freedom he felt as a child on Houston Street would eventually become a norm sought by all the characters in his plays.

In time, the town of Wharton also became a place of adventure and security for Horton. When he was born in 1916, the town had a respectable Main Street, replete with a number of dry goods and grocery stores, restaurants, drugstores, dollar stores, a picture show, and three hotels, all of which continued to survive in spite of economic uncertainty. The town boasted two banks, two bottling plants, two cotton gins, and an oil mill that made cottonseed cakes and produced a sweet pleasant odor that permeated the town during the summer and early autumn months. According to Horton, two of the drugstores had doctor's offices on their second floor, and when they were not busy, the doctors would sit or stand in front of their respective drugstores and talk

---

[2] Horton Foote, *Genesis of an American Playwright*, ed. Marion Castleberry (Waco TX: Baylor University Press, 2004) 18.

[3] Horton Foote, *Farewell: A Memoir of a Texas Childhood* (New York: Scribner, 1999) 122.

among themselves and to other men of the town, most of who owned land worked by the tenants. The men had ample time to visit, swap stories, remember the past, and play practical jokes. The post office was a busy place. Many people went to the Santa Fe train depot every day to meet the train, whether they were expecting someone or not. At least two of the hotels would have cars waiting to take the traveling salesmen or drummers, as they were called in the early 1900s, and their wares back to the hotel. The streets of Wharton were unpaved; at their best, they were filled with ruts and impossible to keep in repair. Horses, buggies, and wagons were still in great use among the country people, and torrential rain often made the roads impassable. On Saturdays the little sleepy town would come alive, and hundreds of people would fill the streets, coming from miles around to do their weekly shopping. Stores would open at seven in the morning and stay open until eleven at night. Horton's father, who owned a men's store downtown, would often keep his store open as late as twelve at night. "You couldn't walk down the street for people who worked the cotton fields coming to town," Horton recalled.[4]

During Horton's childhood, Wharton was a diverse community with an estimated population of three thousand. Among its inhabitants were aristocrats who could trace their ancestors' arrival to the 1830s, black families who came with them as slaves, Mexicans who immigrated during cotton-picking time, Jewish immigrants who arrived in the early 1850s, and Central Europeans who settled in America during the 1900s. The town was segregated—with separate churches, schools, and cemeteries for whites, blacks, and Mexicans—and operated according to Jim Crow laws and separatist principles. There was also a strong division between the social classes. Many townspeople considered themselves part of the Old South, and there was resentment between those who were aristocratic and those who were not. Horton explained that at least half of the residents were black and they lived mostly in two areas of town: "The larger of the two sections was known as the Quarters, and it was located across the railroad tracks outside the city limits. The other section, within the city limits, was called Freedman's Town. The white section of town began near the banks of the river and continued east and west for a number of blocks."[5] As a child, Horton was not fully aware of

---

[4] Horton Foote, *Genesis of an American Playwright*, ed. Marion Castleberry (Waco TX: Baylor University Press, 2004) 63.

[5] Ibid.

the social order of his home place or the set of hierarchies that governed life and death there, but he did recall how the sounds that permeated the night air—the music from a local church or a jukebox in a black restaurant, a waltz from a faraway Mexican dance hall or children calling to each other in the night as they began their after-supper games—had a lasting impact on him. He would later explore the effects of racism and social inequality in his plays and films.

Most evenings Horton's parents would spend time talking on the front porch; and since his bedroom faced the veranda, Horton often overheard their discussions about the day's events, dances his father had attended as a young man, or friends and family members who had died or moved away. He also heard their more serious talks about the life-or-death power of the weather and learned to accept the fact, as most children do, that life is sometimes a brutal struggle for survival. Horton's earliest memory of his father was walking out onto the porch with him and looking at the skies to see whether or not it was going to rain.

Horton seems to have acquired his father's obsessive interest in familial history, and he spent many hours listening to the compelling stories of his father's childhood. He later admitted: "Over half my plays are based on stories that my father told me. He loved to speculate about the past, what might have happened if this had happened or why did this happen this way. I know that's where I got my own curiosity and speculative nature."[6]

When Horton did leave his seemingly secure world, it was to go visiting with his mother and father in the evenings or on Sunday afternoons, often stopping by to spend time with his mother's childhood friends, his father's aunts, or his maternal grandparents. It was there that Horton learned to listen, a very valuable habit for a writer, especially a playwright.

At his great-aunts' houses, there was a great deal of talk about the past, most often about the Horton family. At his grandparents', he heard about the Brooks and Speed families and about the failures and accomplishments of their neighbors and friends. Horton's relatives were all very gifted storytellers, and he was a precocious listener. Unlike many boys his age, who preferred sports or outdoor activities, Horton loved stories, and as a youth he spent most of his time in the house listening to tales of the past.

---

[6] Horton Foote, interview by Marion Castleberry, 18 November 1988, Wharton, Texas.

The stories young Horton heard were often about individual courage, of relatives and neighbors who displayed extraordinary determination or sacrifice, or of undaunted family devotion. Most of the stories were about people who had lived before Horton's time, and yet, they became as real to him as if he had lived with them. He heard, in lurid detail, "stories of feuds, hurt feelings, suicide, jealousies, passions, scoundrels of all kinds," and he never grew tired of listening. No truth or speculation was withheld from him, and he was "never told to leave the room no matter how gruesome or unhappy the tale."[7]

One of the more shocking stories recounted frequently by both his aunts and grandparents was of a poor white man who lived alone with his mother and was having an alleged affair with their black cook. The Ku Klux Klan decided to make an example of him, grabbed him in broad daylight and tarred and feathered him, turning him loose on the courthouse square. Horton recalled that everyone had his or her own version of the story, and long after the poor man's death, sooner or later it would be told again as if it had happened the day before.

There were, of course, other tragic tales, like the lynching of a black man, a trustee from a prison farm who had been working in a neighbor's yard the day a white woman was raped and murdered; the story of cousin Mabel Horton, a celebrated beauty whose husband shot and unexpectedly killed himself on their honeymoon; and the tale of an aunt who was engaged to be married, but called it off only moments before the ceremony because she learned that her fiancé had fathered children with a black woman. He also recalled the bittersweet story of an aunt who wanted to marry her cousin but was forbidden by her father, and how afterwards the man would walk by her house every evening to see her, always tipping his hat and waving. Also part of an almost unending repository of stories was the baffling tale of Miss Minnie Mae, the prettiest girl in Wharton, who had been the belle of the ball, but who married a ne'er-do-well who never worked a day in his life. Miss Minnie Mae ended up a recluse, refusing to answer the door and seen only at night pacing to and fro in her garden, talking to herself.

During his childhood, Horton also visited the houses of black families, who were most often the servants of his grandparents and other white families in Wharton. He played with their children and listened to their stories, tales usually steeped in superstition and mysteries of the supernatural. One of Horton's favorite storytellers was Walter, a

---

[7] Foote, *Genesis*, 19.

yardman and chauffeur who worked for his Grandmother Brooks. Walter claimed to have the gift of second sight, which allowed him to see spirits visible only to him. He loved to tell about his experiences on a ship during World War I, how he had once seen mermaids rise out of the ocean, and how, when driving the Brooks family to church in their buggy one Sunday, the lead horse suddenly began to rear and pitch. No one could understand the horse's odd behavior except Walter and his sister, Eliza, who claimed the horse was scared by a fiery chariot in the middle of the road. Walter and Eliza insisted they couldn't go a step further until the chariot disappeared.[8]

These tales, and others like them, would, in time, provide the grist for Foote's many plays and films. Beyond the stories themselves, Horton was fascinated with how the events of the past were constantly reorganized and shaped by the storyteller's imagination. He especially enjoyed listening to his Aunt Loula's dramatic tales. Horton recalled that she was a tall, regal woman with dyed black hair and a fondness for the color red. Extremely loyal to her family, she kept the Horton family stories alive, not always with great accuracy, but with imagination, vividness, and gusto. Horton recalled the tales, "growing more lurid through the years." As she told them, "she would cock her head to one side, close her eyes slightly and her voice would take on a heightened quality, almost a chant as she recounted the history of her family, and she never tired of telling it to any of the nieces and nephews that would listen."[9]

Horton would often ask his Aunt Loula to describe an event and then have another relative tell the same story. "The story would be like a theme of music," he remembered, "except I would hear a variation on that theme."[10] In the process, the young boy learned an important lesson about the subjectivity of memory and how accepted truths often change with time and circumstance: "I've learned that you can hear the same story told by six or seven people, and even though they think it's the same story, it's not. Every version is personal, it's subjective and all of them are telling the truth as they see it."[11] In such multiple narratives, the future playwright discovered a way to reveal the inner lives of his

---

[8] Foote, *Farewell*, 77.

[9] Foote, *Genesis*, 23.

[10] Horton Foote, interview by Marion Castleberry, 19 November 1988, Wharton, Texas.

[11] Ibid.

characters and the drama between speakers. Foote scholar, Laurin Porter, points out that Horton's characters are all storytellers of one kind or another; they delight in anecdotes, family legends, and local gossip. Creating characters that are tellers of tales, a long-standing tradition in Southern literature, is regarded by scholars and critics as one of Horton Foote's most Southern characteristics.

Horton admitted there were also demands that came from being part of such a family. There was always fear of scrutiny, and in a large extended family like his, where a sixth or seventh cousin is kin, the possibility one might not like a certain relative, or might be in competition with him, always existed. Horton recalls the day a descendent of Lida Horton Dennis—a niece Aunt Loula claimed stole the family's house and lands—entered his father's store. "My father greeted him by calling him cousin, and he bought a hat and they talked together for a while about the weather and the crops. When he left and I was told who he was and that he lived on the Horton plantation, I said hotly, 'How could you talk to him, cousin or not?' My father said, 'Don't fill your head with all that. That's done. Forget it. Have you forgotten it?' I asked, 'Yes, I have,' he said, 'That and a lot more. You have to too, if you don't want to be swallowed up in bitterness.'"[12] Horton would later write a similar scene in his play *Cousins*, where two characters discuss how their lives have been forever changed by family discord. From moments like this and from listening to his family, especially his mother and father, Horton learned a great deal about the values by which to live. But there was something more in these stories, a kind of grace and dignity that was passed down by both his maternal and paternal ancestors. Horton Foote's heritage was rich with men and women whose show of courage in times of trouble influenced his own character; their spirit would haunt him for the rest of his life, and their stories would provide the foundation for his artistry.

> I believe very deeply in the human spirit, and I have a sense of awe about it because I don't know how people carry on. I look around and I say...what makes the difference in people? What is it? I've known people that the world has thrown everything at to discourage them, to kill them, to break their spirit. And yet something about them retains a dignity. They face life and they don't ask for quarters.... I've just seen

---

[12] Foote, *Genesis*, 23.

example after example of people enduring things I absolutely couldn't. I'm always measuring myself. Could I do that? Could I take that?[13]

At the center of Horton Foote's world were his maternal grandparents, especially his Grandmother Brooks. Foote described Mrs. Daisy Brooks, whom he called "Baboo," as being a "petite woman, always fashionably dressed, very feminine, fiercely aristocratic to her toenails," and a woman with "an enormous sense of pride."[14] Although she was not demonstrative in her affections, the young boy adored her; and since it was only a short distance to her house, he visited her every day. Horton relished the moments his grandmother spent recounting her early childhood in Oyster Creek, Texas, her courtship with her future husband, Tom Brooks, and the lives of her aristocratic ancestors. She made Horton feel special, and he grew up knowing she would respond to his every request. Horton admitted: "She offered an enormous sense of security. I always knew that if I ever needed anything, I could call on her. Time after time her generosity saved me,"[15]

Horton's feelings for his Grandfather Brooks were not quite so clear. They fluctuated between adoration and awe. Tom Brooks was a devoted father and grandfather, but he was also a man of great power who expected much from his children. He had risen from the poverty of his youth to become Wharton's most prestigious citizen, thus setting an example few could ever hope to match.

As a child, Horton was always loved and welcomed by his grandfather, whom he called Papa, and some of his most vivid childhood memories are of riding with him to check on his many cotton farms. In *Farewell*, Horton recalled that the roads at that time were dirt, gravel, or shell, and it was difficult to visit all the farms in one afternoon, or even one day, since visiting every farm meant getting out of the car and talking with the tenant farmers, inquiring about their health and that of their wives and children, and walking into each field to inspect the present state of the cotton crops. To get to the farms, they would pass tiny, dwindling towns, which had once bustled with the sounds of community life but had since been abandoned. Indelibly etched in the boy's mind was a vision of what remained of his grandfather's

---

[13] Samuel G. Freedman, "From the Heart of Texas," *New York Times Magazine*, February 9, 1980, p. 50.

[14] Horton Foote, interview by Marion Castleberry, 19 November 1988, Wharton, Texas.

[15] Ibid.

hometown of East Columbia—seven weathered plantation houses, one decaying store—where his grandfather had worked as a boy—and a small cluster of live oak trees that had once surrounded his ancestral home. The thought of this once stately house and the family who had lived here seized Horton's childish imagination. He would try to reconstruct the past, imagining what life must have been like when his grandfather's house stood magnificently on the banks of the Brazos River and visualizing the day his aunts, uncles, and cousins were primly dressed in their best clothes.[16]

Riding by these forgotten places, Horton would always question his grandfather. Why was this town abandoned? Why was it never more than a few stores and a handful of houses? Why did the people leave and go to another place? Mr. Brooks would try to soothe his grandson's curiosity, explaining how towns came to be and for what purpose, how changes left some of them abandoned, and how many were never meant to be more than a couple of stores that served the tenant farmers and the one or two families who owned the surrounding farmland. Then in the silence that always seemed to follow, they would contemplate what Wharton might have been like if circumstances had been different and what that might have meant to their family. In remembering the fertile landscape of towns like Columbus, Glen Flora, and Egypt, Horton would find settings for his plays that captured a sense of place and time that no longer existed, except in his mind's eye.

These kinds of experiences created a strong bond between grandfather and grandson, and left Horton with a rich understanding of small-town life in America. Sadly, the bond that formed between Horton and his grandfather was unexpectedly shattered when Mr. Brooks suffered a heart attack and died on 3 March 1925. His passing was the most devastating event in young Horton Foote's life, and it would have a profound and lasting effect upon him. "The event that always stuck with me," he admits, "the event I've been groping toward as a writer, was the day my grandfather died. Until then, life was magic. I never felt so secure in my life as sitting on the porch swing and knowing I was the grandson of one of the richest families in town and my grandfather was the most respected man in town."[17] Horton was only nine years old at the time, but for the rest of his life he could recall the incident in great detail:

---

[16] Foote, *Farewell*, 92–3.
[17] Freedman, 61.

In mid-March of my ninth year I came home from school, went all through the house looking for my mother, and when I couldn't find her went next door to a neighbor's who met me in her yard and said, 'I think you'd better go over to your grandmother's.' I went back through our silent house, into our back yard and slowly into my grandparent's back yard. Eliza, who cooked for my grandparents, and her sister Sarah were there. I went up to them as Eliza was saying, 'I knew someone in that house would die today when I saw a dove, a mourning dove, light on the roof of the house.' I stood looking at them until they noticed me, and Eliza said, 'Go in the house. Your mama is in there.' I started slowly toward the house when my mother appeared at the back door. She saw me then and came out to me. She was crying and she took me in her arms and held me and asked if I wanted to see my grandmother. I said I did, still not knowing what had happened, and she led me into the house, filled with people, men and women, dressed like it was Sunday all standing about and talking in low voices. Mother led me through the people to my grandparents' room and I saw my grandfather, his eyes closed, lying on a couch and my grandmother sitting beside him. My mother said, 'Little Horton's here, Mama,' and my grandmother turned to me, and I saw she was crying and she held out her arms to me and I went over to her and she began to sob and held me as I looked at my grandfather and I realized that he was dead. I didn't learn how he died until the day of the funeral, which I was not allowed to attend. I was kept at home with my baby brother, watched over by my father's mother and one of her sisters, my great aunt Lida. We could see the funeral procession from our porch and as we watched the slow movement of the hearse and the cars that followed, they told how my grandfather had been seized by a heart attack in town, collapsing on one of the main streets and dying before a doctor could reach him.[18]

Tom Brooks's death brought enormous grief and hardship to his family. Daisy Brooks, a remarkably resilient and faithful woman, mourned the loss of her husband for more than two years. Every afternoon she would visit his grave, and Horton would often go with her. He remembers that his grandmother, dressed always in black, carried flowers, and sometimes she would sit and cry for hours. By observing his grandmother's daily ritual, the boy learned that mourning was a vital part of the healing process and that grief was a subject relevant for all times: "When I was growing up, the dead were almost as alive as the living. People talked about them, remembered them,

---

[18] Foote, *Genesis*, 24-5.

reminisced...now everything is so anonymous."[19] For Horton Foote as a child there was no escaping or ignoring the unpleasant phenomenon of death; as a writer he would repeatedly explore its mysteries and challenges.

When Tom Brooks died, Laura Lee, the Brookes youngest daughter was married, living in Dallas, and expecting her first child. Foote remembers his aunt as gentle and shy by nature and very beautiful. Her husband, Oliver Ray, worked nights as a post office attendant and made very little money. Despite the fact Oliver was a tireless worker, with a wife and three children to support, he had to rely on financial help from Daisy Brooks. As a teenager, Horton would visit his Aunt Laura and Uncle Oliver once a year, and, on one occasion, he found on a table next to their bed a book called *How to Become an Executive*. His Uncle Oliver had been looking for a way out of his terribly frustrating night shift position at the post office. Unfortunately, Oliver Ray never managed to find another job; he stayed on at the post office until well after Daisy Brooks died and left Laura a share of her estate. He eventually retired, but soon after leaving Dallas, he became ill and died in Wharton with Laura and his youngest son by his side.[20] In later years, Oliver Ray's story would become Horton Foote's inspiration for the character Ludie Watts in *The Trip to Bountiful*, and his Aunt Laura, who lived well into her nineties, would be characterized with great affection in the play *Courtship*.

Horton's Aunt Rosa also experienced a series of hardships following her father's death. Rosa, the aunt with whom Horton was closest, was highly educated and ambitious, having graduated from the University of Texas and Columbia University with a master's degree. But soon after she married a handsome, good-humored fellow named Dick Johnston, he began to drink heavily. The couple's first child, a son, was born dead; their second, a girl, was named Daisy Brooks after her grandmother. Dick was never able to keep a job, and his drinking increased after he was forced to move his family in with his parents. For the sake of the baby, Rosa soon left her husband to live with her mother, who had left Wharton permanently and bought a house in Houston. Rosa eventually became a social worker, and, as Horton Foote recalled, "gave her life" to her brothers, "getting them out of scrape after scrape, never deserting

---

[19] Horton Foote, interview by Marion Castleberry, 18 November 1988, Wharton, Texas.

[20] Ibid.

them, no matter what they had done. She cared for Speed and Billy until the day she died."[21] Horton would later remember Rosa's love and sacrifice in a number of plays and screenplays: *Out of My House*, *The Death of the Old Man*, *Night Seasons*, and *Tender Mercies*, to name a few.

Daisy Brooks had one unremitting source of sorrow and shame in her life. "The one thing my grandmother could never understand," Horton once said, "was what went wrong with her sons."[22] The three Brooks boys (Tom, Speed, and Billy) had been reared in an atmosphere of respectability and had enjoyed the privileges of prestige and social position. Friends and relatives recall they were extremely bright and likeable, but none was blessed with their father's ambition. After Tom Brooks died, his three sons were plagued by one failure after another. As young men, the three brothers began to drink heavily, eventually developing into chronic alcoholics and hopeless gamblers.

Mr. Brooks tried to motivate his two older boys, Brother and Speed, by sending them to Allen Academy, a military school from which they barely graduated. Afterward, Brother enrolled at Texas A&M University, where his father had graduated with honors, but he did poorly in his studies while continuing to drink heavily. To make matters worse, Brother managed to get a young girl pregnant and rather than marry her he returned to Wharton where he took a job in a dry goods store. Afterwards, he married Mabel Horton, who had suffered through the accidental death of her first husband. After the birth of their child, Brother tried to be a devoted father. Miss Daisy even deeded Brother one of the family farms in hopes of encouraging him to behave responsibly, but in less than a year, he had mortgaged the land so heavily that the bank foreclosed on the property, and his mother had to pay off the debt to get the farm back. Following this failure, Brother went to work for a sulfur company in New Gulf, and one day eagerly announced he was going to run for the office of county clerk. Since his father had served many years as Wharton's county treasurer, Brother thought he had a good chance of winning, but when the votes were tallied, it was apparent he had lost by a landslide. As a result, he began to drink more and more, he and Mabel divorced, and he left Wharton, for a time

---

[21] Foote, *Farewell*, 151–56.

[22] Horton Foote, interview by Marion Castleberry, 19 November 1988, Wharton, Texas.

wandering around the world as a merchant seaman. He died at age fifty, a drunken derelict, picking fruit on an Arizona ranch.[23]

The younger brothers experienced much the same fate. Speed, Horton's favorite uncle, tried his hand at a cleaning and pressing business in Wharton, but his alcoholism and drug addiction soon led to the closing of his shop. He never worked again in his life, but he was later arrested for selling heroin in California and sent to San Quentin prison for ten years. His mother died when he was in prison. After being paroled, Speed returned to Houston and lived off the charity of his sister, Rosa, until she died.

Billy, the youngest of the Brooks boys, was only six when his brothers went to Allen Academy, and from all accounts he seemed destined to live a normal, small-town life. He was a popular young man, a good student, a gifted athlete, and a musician. Horton did not even suspect his Uncle Billy drank until he began attending town dances when he was thirteen. "But since most of the boys his age were drinking," Horton remembered, "it didn't seem strange to me, and if my grandmother knew about it she didn't seem concerned and always talked of his becoming a lawyer like his uncle Billy, for whom he had been named."[24] After Billy finished Jefferson Law School in Dallas, Miss Daisy obtained a position for him with a Wharton legal firm; but within two months, he disappointed everyone when he got drunk, quit his practice, and sold his books. Consequently, for the rest of his life, Billy survived on cash handouts given to him by his mother, who tried, unsuccessfully, to rescue her sons from their own destruction. Billy eventually died a lonely death in the Milby Hotel in Houston.[25]

Horton Foote would later explore the seeming futility of his uncle's lives in numerous plays and screenplays. He always believed that his uncles' misfortunes spoke to a larger, universal struggle that took place in Texas during the Great Depression. After World War I, a great demand for agricultural products, along with the discovery of mineral wealth, brought a much-needed economic boost to Wharton and Coastal Southeast Texas. The discovery of the world's largest sulfur deposit in Boling in 1923 and the flood of oil, which began in 1925, were providential to many Wharton residents. Impoverished families became

---

[23] Ibid.

[24] Foote, *Farewell*, 167

[25] Horton Foote, interview by Marion Castleberry, 19 November 1988, Wharton, Texas.

wealthy overnight, new towns like New Gulf and Spanish Camp sprang up, and new jobs were created, bringing hundreds of workers to the region. The city of Houston became the center of the chemical and petroleum industry in the nation, and many farmers and small-town merchants migrated to the city for more lucrative work. As a result, the physical and spiritual displacement caused by the uprooting of families and communities was devastating.

By 1930, the Great Depression had turned the confident optimism of the 1920s to confusion and bewilderment as the price of cotton fell to less than five cents per pound and oil dropped to ten cents a barrel. Oil was poured into earthen pits while its owners searched desperately for buyers, and farmers dumped their cotton along the roads to rot, because the sale price was less than the cost of ginning. Merchants who managed to stay in business were forced to sell on credit to neighboring planters and farmers while waiting for harvest time. And even though nature had been good to the region, the promise of bountiful crops could never be taken for granted, since Gulf hurricanes, drought, or floods often brought disaster.

The Wharton County Courthouse is filled with dismal records of merchants who overstocked their shelves and had their goods sold at auction to satisfy creditors. The tyrannical grip that cotton industry held on the town went unrelieved until the early 1940s when Wharton, growing more and more industrialized, began to lose its earlier identity and was transformed by the wealth that petroleum brought to the region. People whose identities were linked to their economic status saw their way of life disappear overnight. The Old Wharton, which was characterized by its Southern plantation aristocracy, gave way to the New Wharton, a community compliant with the manners and practices of middle-class America.

Horton Foote explained that in many ways his uncles were victims of these uncertain times. By the time they were teenagers, Tom Brooks no longer owned a store. He was a loan agent who bought and sold land that none of his family ever worked. Instead, farmers farmed all the land, and Horton's uncles, who had been raised in an aristocratic environment, "simply had no purpose or meaning in their lives. Unless you were a doctor, a lawyer, or a merchant," Horton recalled, "there was nothing for you to do in Wharton."

> Of course the doctors were all starving in those days and the lawyers weren't doing much better. There was simply no incentive. There was

nothing. The wealthier young men were given money, sent to college, and if they came back they merely took over the land. Maybe they would go out twice a week to see how the tenants were doing but other than that there was nothing for them to do. They thought of themselves as rich boys but they weren't. They were land rich but they still had to care for the land, pay off the mortgage, and they often had hard times when the crops failed. So, many of them became drunkards. Across the track there were women one could get for one or two dollars. The young boys had no sense of that either.[26]

In the final analysis, Horton admitted that there was no order to his uncle's lives. It had all been broken up, along with the plantations.

Horton and his younger brothers did not have to endure the same kinds of hardships his uncles and other young men of their generation had suffered. Horton remembers his own childhood as ordinary in the sense that he was serene and happy in a familial environment of absolute security. The one thing he seems to have missed during his childhood was sufficient time to spend with his younger brothers. When Horton left home at the age of sixteen to pursue an acting career, Tom, the middle brother, was only ten years old and John, the youngest, was eight. The differences in their ages meant they shared few common interests and experiences, but this fact seems not to have affected their love for one another. Horton contends they were extremely close, but while he enjoyed reading books and listening to his family's endless talk, his brothers found excitement in sports and country-western music. Since Horton felt quite comfortable as the center of his family's attention and intended to remain the favorite nephew and grandson, "a terrible sibling problem existed."[27] He would later recreate this kind of hidden competition in, for example, *Roots in a Parched Ground* and *Lily Dale*.

During his formative years Horton was exceptionally close to his mother, whom he describes as a woman of great dignity. She had a perceptive and deep-rooted social sense, and she could always make people of any social background feel at home. She dressed quietly, was soft-spoken, knew firsthand the perils of the world, yet never complained or burdened anyone with her fears or grief. She was honest with her children, and time after time she revealed through her actions that courage was one of life's most important virtues. Horton

---

[26] Ibid.

[27] Ibid.

characterized his mother when he commented on the type of women who populate his plays:

> I'm struck by these women who have very little in possessions but have great dignity, even though they've married young and often have to raise children alone. I write them from a sense of appreciation and admiration. They can be confident, though they've certainly been given more than their share of difficult problems to work out.[28]

Remembered as a loving but stern mother, Hallie taught her children the importance of fine manners, respect for elders, and devotion to family. She also passed along to Horton her love of music and enthusiasm for reading. Hallie was a talented musician who served as pianist and organist for the Methodist church and taught piano lessons to supplement the family income. Horton adored listening to his mother play, and with her guidance he learned to sing scores of religious hymns at a young age. While sitting on their porch at night, they also shared the sounds of country ballads and blues coming from the Mexican and black dance halls across town. Horton's father collected sheet music for popular songs, and many times Horton's mother would play the piano as the family sang tunes like "My Sweetheart's the Man in the Moon," "After the Ball," and "Hello, Central, Give Me Heaven." Eventually, this music and that of other popular and classical musicians, like the folk composer Charles Ives, would weave a tapestry of sound throughout Horton's dramatic canon, serving as a muse to the playwright, underscoring his poetic language, and functioning as metaphors in many of his plays.

Horton also enjoyed hearing his mother read aloud, and under her tutelage he became an avid reader by the age of six. The books he liked best and remembered most vividly from that time are Dickens's *David Copperfield*, Galsworthy's *The Forsyte Saga*, Arnold Bennett's *The Old Wives' Tale*, Maya de la Roche's *Jalna* books, Mark Twain's *Tom Sawyer* and *Huckleberry Finn* and Willa Cather's *Shadows on the Rock, Death Comes for the Archbishop*, and *My Antonia*. At age twelve Horton joined the Book-of-the-Month Club and Literary Guild and began to read poetry, specifically the collected works of Edwin Arlington Robinson, Dorothy Parker, Walt Whitman, and Edna St. Vincent Millay. Horton would often memorize and recite the poems with great pride to his friends at school,

---

[28] David Sterrit, "Let's Hear It for the Human Being," *The Saturday Evening Post* (October 1983): 37.

and even though a friend warned Horton's mother that Voltaire's *Candide* was unsuitable for a boy his age, Hallie never tried to stop him from reading that or any other book. She always supported her son in his reading, despite the fear of his Grandmother Cleveland that he would become a bookworm like his great-uncle James Roberdeau Foote, who according to her never worked a day in his life.[29]

From his mother, Horton inherited yet another Southern trait: a deeply ingrained religious faith, and, as a child, Horton became familiar with biblical stories. Hallie had grown up in a family of devout Methodists, and from her and their shared church experience, young Horton grew to respect and cherish the Bible as a "wonderful storytelling device that explains much about the family."[30] A deep faith in God became a natural part of his life, and he learned at an early age the moral and spiritual principles that were a dominant part of his character and writings. After Horton left home, he and his mother left the Methodist congregation to become followers of the Christian Science tradition. Until his death in 2009, Horton Foote maintained a deeply religious, but understated, practice of Christian Science, emphasizing self-reliance, discipline, and faith in the infinite goodness of God. For many years, a small Christian Science church, once used by Horton's mother and father, sat across the street from the house in which he was raised, reminding everyone of the importance of faith in the life of Horton Foote.

In his early years, Horton was not as close to his father as he was to his mother, because his father's clothing business kept him away from home as many as twelve hours each day, but Horton apparently never felt abandoned:

> Growing up without a father was a constant experience in my family. I think it was almost a fear for me and I always wondered what it would be like if I had lived through the hardships that my father experienced as a child. What would happen if I lost my father? I think that's what happens to a child. No, I never felt neglected. I admit that I wasn't as close to my father as I was my mother but I always felt very nurtured by him. I remember that during the Depression he would come home after a day's work, enter the house, see me and my brother in bed, and then get such a look of panic on his face. He would say that he felt like re-opening the

---

[29] Foote, *Farewell*, 140–41.
[30] Horton Foote, interview by Marion Castleberry, 12 March 1988, Wharton, Texas.

store just to make sure that we were taken care of. In that sense he was gone a great deal but I was with him, often.[31]

During his teenage years, Horton drew closer to his father and to the public world of Wharton. When he was eleven he began to work in his father's store after school, on Saturdays, and every day during the summer months. Business was usually slow. Long stretches of time passed when not a single customer entered the store, and on many days the business took in no more than $2.50.[32]

Albert Foote managed to survive as a shopkeeper through support of local blacks, with whom he had a strong connection. Because he had been partially raised by a black family, Foote befriended many poor blacks, most of whom worked as servants, sharecroppers, or at the cotton gins. On Saturdays, when almost everyone in Wharton County came into town to shop, as many as thirty-five black men, their wives, and girlfriends would stand in line outside the store till Foote could wait on them personally. He often kept his store open until ten or eleven o'clock at night outfitting them in shirts, hats, ties, and mail-order suits. Horton's father appears to have been a remarkably empathetic man, and because half of the blacks couldn't read or write, he would often serve as an amateur lawyer and broker for them. "They trusted him," Horton explained, "and he constantly received letters of appreciation and praise from them. My father was a great individualist, a man secure enough in himself to risk being known as a character."[33]

The bond between Horton and his father strengthened during this time as the boy began to realize the many demands of his father's job and the kindness he showed to other, less fortunate, people:

> I saw all kinds of people in my Daddy's store. I saw country people and lost people. I saw blacks who were unable to write their name or unable to pay more than $1.50 down for a suit. They just broke my heart. I have an enormous sense of that and I was always touched by them. I remember working in the store and old men would come in bored with nothing to do and my father would say to me, "don't leave me alone with them or I'll jump out of my skin." They'd stay most of the day and just sit and talk and talk and spit. Since business was anything but brisk I found myself listening. They took me into an entirely different world than I was used

---

[31] Horton Foote, interview by Marion Castleberry, 12 November 1988, Wharton, Texas.

[32] Ibid.

[33] Ibid.

to. They talked of weather, of the crops and the prospects of crops. They got into political arguments. Even on the busiest Saturdays I had time to listen as most of the black and white farmers wanted my father to wait on them. I stood by to wrap packages, or get change for my father listening to their country speech and voices and their stories again of weather and crops, of illnesses or hard times their friends were undergoing or their personal tragedies. There was laughter, too, teasing and joking. I learned to love these people, to look forward to Saturdays and to hear their voices and accents so different from my family's and to listen to their stories. I learned a lot about those kind of people.[34]

Horton's father never sheltered him from learning about the darker side of life, and, as a result, Horton carried into manhood a deep sense of the character, culture, and crises that shaped his hometown. He also formed a deep respect for his father and an understanding of the emotional ups and downs that were a part of life during the Great Depression. When writing, Horton often remembered this time and made a great effort to create a true sense of people trying to make their way in the world, people faced with what seemed like overwhelming financial obstacles.

Horton remembers that when the store closed on Saturday evenings, he and his father would go to a nearby restaurant, order a dozen fried oysters, and talk over the day's events: "We were closer then than we had ever been and I thought that was the grandest thing that ever happened to me, eating fried oysters with my father. We would always talk about the things that happened that day. He would sometimes be elated but more often he would be so depressed that he would cry."[35]

Even as a young child Horton sympathized deeply with his neighbors and relatives who were suffering from poverty and human injustice. One of his earliest and most revealing memories was of his Grandfather Brooks awakening him one night from a deep sleep, bundling him up, and taking him to see a parade of men riding on horseback down Richmond Road wearing white sheets and hoods and carrying torches. Years later, he found a white robe while looking through some of his grandfather's things that had been packed away and asked his grandmother about it. "I knew it was a KKK outfit," Horton said. "She took the robe from me and told me my grandfather had gone to a meeting once, but the meeting was all about hating Jews and Catholics,

---

[34] Ibid.
[35] Ibid.

which had nothing to do with the victory of the North or improving the South. He never went back."[36]

The first time Horton came face to face with the reality of historical slavery was as a teenager, taking a fourteen-mile hike to complete Boy Scout training:

> I stopped in a country store for a bottle of soda water and on the gallery [front porch] of the store was an elderly black man. As I drank my soda water we got to talking and he asked me my name, and when I told him he said he had been a slave on my great-great-grandfather's plantation. I have never forgotten the impact that made on me. Slavery up until then was merely an abstract statistic that I'd heard older people talk about. "Our family had one hundred sixty slaves, or a hundred twenty…" or whatever, but as I looked into that man's sorrowing face, I was shocked to realize that this abstraction spoken of so lightly ("we were good to them," "we never mistreated them") was a living, suffering human being.[37]

Years later, Horton had a similar reaction to a book given to him by his friends Joseph and Perry Anthony, containing two letters from Elizabeth Ramsey, a slave on his great-great-grandfather's plantation. Her letters were written to her daughter in Ohio, asking her for help buying freedom for herself and her son, John. According to the letters, Governor Horton agreed to grant Elizabeth freedom for $1,000, but he demanded $1,500 for John. In 1860, with the help of abolitionists, the daughter was able to raise nine hundred dollars and purchase her mother's freedom. Consequently, Elizabeth Ramsey was finally able to meet her grandchildren.

Horton was perplexed by these letters and tried to imagine what kind of man his great-great-grandfather actually was. "I don't judge him, really," Horton admitted, "but I also can't understand how a man—a deeply religious man from all accounts, who built a church with a balcony for his slaves and who was one of the founders of Baylor University—a Baptist college—could be so insensitive to other human beings that he was willing to buy and sell them. I tried to imagine…what it was like to live in that time, a white family, surrounded by and dependent on a hundred and seventy slaves. This wasn't the romantic idyll of the storybook legends, I'm sure of that. In any event, that way of

---

[36] John Guare, "My Trip to Bountiful," *Farewell: Remembering Horton Foote, 1916–2009*, ed. Marion Castleberry and Susan Christensen (Dallas TX: Southern Methodist University Press, 2011) 86–99.

[37] Foote, *Farewell*, 128–29.

life was all over five years after Elizabeth Ramsey wrote her second letter."[38] Horton's fascination with his grandfather would continue for the rest of his life, and he would explore the issue of slavery and human bondage in several of his plays, including *Convicts* and *The Last of the Thorntons.*

Although Horton was sensitive to the hardships of many people in Wharton, he was not blind to the pleasures of the new technological marvels around him. Automobiles jammed the streets, movies played in lavish theaters, and radios blared out musical rhythms. Horton learned to dance when he was a young teenager, and, even though his grandparents had condemned dancing as sinful, he often attended Friday night dances at the Norton Opera House, a large, cavernous building that had originally been used for Chautauqua productions, plays, and concerts. Some of his favorite dances were the foxtrot, the waltz, and a controversial variation of the two known as "belly rubbing," which involved "simply standing still and rhythmically rubbing your stomach against your partner's."[39]

Horton remembered that people of all ages attended the dances—the high school crowd, young married couples who had graduated from high school, and those in their early and mid-thirties who had been married for several years—and they all moved to the sound of professional orchestras playing popular tunes of the day like "Stardust," "Dream a Little Dream of Me," "Tiptoe Through the Tulips," and "Tiger Rag." Bootleg whiskey was readily available and Horton recalled, "cocktail parties for the young and older couples was the rage, so a good many of the couples would arrive at the dances drunk and during intermission would go out to the cars to continue drinking."[40] Arguments and fights often took place in the parking lot, along with infidelity, but chaperones—usually mothers of high school girls—were always there to protect their school-age daughters from any harm. The atmosphere of these dances, the inherent conflicts that the drinking and betrayal caused, would later become the subject of Horton Foote's first play, *Wharton Dance.*

Horton admitted that even though he loved dancing, movie going was his favorite childhood pastime, and he attended the Queen Theatre on Houston Street to watch his favorite stars whenever he could. The

---

[38] Ibid., 131.
[39] Ibid., 209.
[40] Foote, *Farewell,* 128–29.

boy's fascination with cinema and acting grew until, at age twelve, he awoke one morning and decided to be an actor. The feeling was akin to a religious calling:

> I remember taking walks with my parents when I was a very young boy, and we would pass the house of a Mr. Armstrong, a distinguished, white-haired gentleman, who would often be sitting on his porch; and as we would pass the house, after greeting Mr. Armstrong, my parents would always whisper, "That's Mr. Armstrong. He had a call in the cotton fields of Mississippi to go to Texas and preach." Now, Mr. Armstrong was a Baptist and we were at that time Methodists and Episcopalians, and so I imagined the call had come to Mr. Armstrong because he was of the Baptist faith, but my mother explained that she had heard such things happening to Methodists, too—and even to Presbyterians and Episcopalians, which at the time were the only religions represented in our little town of three thousand. I was full of questions about what "getting a call" meant, and my mother was rather evasive in her answers, so I sensed she didn't really know, and I often wanted to ask Mr. Armstrong what it was like, but never got the courage to do so. Anyways, as it turned out, some years later, when I was twelve, I got a call, but it wasn't to preach, it was to become an actor. Now, as far as I knew then, or know now, there had never been any actors in that town, and certainly not in my family.[41]

Horton recalled that he "just awakened one day with the sure knowledge that I wanted to be an actor; more, that I was going to be. Of that I hadn't the slightest doubt."[42]

Horton's only exposure to live theater had been in the third grade when he was cast as Puck in *A Midsummer Night's Dream,* and the time he saw the Dude Arthur Comedians, a traveling tent show that performed in town once a year. The tent was put up in a vacant lot owned by his great-uncle Albert, only a half block from Horton's house. He remembered three players particularly well—Dude Arthur, his wife Minnie, and Mickey Arthur, Dude's brother. "Mickey always played the juvenile roles," Horton recalled, "and before the show began and during intermission, when candy and popcorn were sold, he played the drums in the small orchestra that traveled with them. Mrs. Arthur played the ingénue roles until one year she put on a gray wig and began doing character parts. Dude Arthur played the comic characters, usually a red-

---

[41] Foote, *Genesis,* 27.
[42] Ibid.

haired rube. At the age of ten, eleven, and twelve, I thought this was the finest life there could be, traveling around the country with a tent show and performing. It must have been very simple and crude, but there was something about it that appealed to my young imagination."[43]

When Horton announced his plan to be an actor, his parents were amused at such a bold declaration from one so young. As the boy's determination grew, however, their amusement turned to concern. Both had serious reservations about their son entering a profession that offered such a limited chance of success. Horton and his father often clashed about his ambition, but in the end, neither parent refused their son his choice of vocations. In fact he was given every opportunity to pursue his interest in acting.

Around 1928, Horton's enthusiasm for the theater was bolstered by the creation of the Wharton Little Theatre (Horton saw every production put on by the group and performed in several of the shows) and the arrival of his cousin Nan Outlar, who understood his dream and supported his artistic endeavors.

> I think young Horton, who was then a high school student, considered me glamorous and sophisticated because I had been to New York and had actually seen plays on Broadway, and his burning desire was to become a Broadway star. We both had leanings toward the dramatic and theatrical and spent many an hour looking at movie magazines and discussing stars of the cinema. We had lots of other things we enjoyed doing together—like riding bicycles, drinking Cokes at Outlar Drugs, doing the Charleston and Black Bottom, participating in Wharton Little Theatre affairs, and making "Dagwood" sandwiches…. I certainly understood, admired and encouraged his desire to become an actor instead of the more prosaic plan his family probably envisioned for him— college and then returning to enter business with his father in a small haberdashery store on Milam St.[44]

Another person who inspired Horton was his high school speech and drama instructor Eppie Murphree. Miss Murphree, a young graduate of Texas Women's College, was well traveled and had seen many professional stage productions. She took Horton's ambition to be an actor very seriously and cast him in all the school productions, including *Square Crooks*, a popular comedy-drama that was chosen as the junior

---

[43] Ibid., 89.

[44] Nan Outlar, interview by Marion Castleberry, 16 November 1988, Wharton, Texas.

play. Miss Murphree remembers that Horton's performance in the play was one of his most masterful:

> When the curtain raised—it was the old roll-up kind with a heavy pole at the bottom—a young man was revealed asleep in bed, with his bare foot stuck out toward the audience. Since the stage was shallow, he had to ease his foot out after the curtain cleared the bed. Everything went as scheduled until the curtain almost reached the top. Then, wham! The rope slipped, the curtain fell, and the heavy pole hit the floor with a thunderous bang. Miraculously the bare foot jerked back just in time.[45]

More plays followed, and during his senior year Horton played the lead in the one-act play entered in the Texas State One-Act-Play contest. The play was about three college roommates, one of whom had a serious drug problem. Horton was cast as the addict, even though he knew nothing about drug addiction except for knowing a lady who was hooked on Paregoric. Nonetheless, Horton's performance must have been very convincing, especially in a scene where the young man confesses to his unsuspecting roommates that he is an addict, and then has a withdrawal episode in front of them. When the performance was over, the judges called Mrs. Murphree aside and asked: "Is that Foote boy afflicted or is that acting?" Murphree assured them it was acting, and they awarded Horton a medal for "Best Actor" of the tournament. But it was a medal he never received. When the judges called Miss Murphree onstage to ask about Horton's acting, she thought they were calling her up to announce the play had won first place. When she realized the play had *not* won, she was so disappointed she forgot all about the medal.[46] It was not until years later (2004) that Horton was finally awarded a "Best Actor" medal by the Texas State Drama Director, Luis Munoz, at Baylor University's inaugural Horton Foote American Playwrights Festival in Waco, Texas. Until his death, the medal hung proudly on his apartment wall, reminding him of one of the happiest times of his youth.

After graduating from high school in early summer of 1932, Horton pleaded with his parents to let him go to New York to pursue training as an actor. Since he was only sixteen years old, they argued he should attend college for at least two years, hoping the boy's madness would pass. Horton refused, so they compromised. His father told him if he would first work for a year, he could then attend California's famed

---

[45] Eppie Murphree, Speech to Wharton High School, 12 March 1988.

[46] Horton Foote, interview by Marion Castleberry, 19 November 1988, Wharton, Texas.

Pasadena Playhouse. Pasadena, they felt, would be a more wholesome atmosphere for a young man away from his family for the first time.[47]

That summer, Horton moved to Dallas to live with his Grandmother Brooks, who encouraged her grandson's endeavors and helped him enroll in the Woodrow School of Expression, where twice a week he studied drama and elocution. He also found a job as an usher at the Majestic Theatre, one of the city's largest movie houses, where he spent most of his time watching the current movies over and over. To Horton's dismay, Miss Woodward taught very little in the way of acting, but at a spring recital he did perform a scene from Chekhov's *Swan Song*, playing an old alcoholic actor who recalls his better days by reciting speeches from *King Lear, Hamlet,* and *Othello*. Horton's experience at the Woodward School was not a very productive one; it only encouraged him to pursue acting training at a more reputable school.

Horton returned to Wharton in May 1933, excited to leave for California and the Pasadena Playhouse. However, this was at the height of the Great Depression, and like so many Americans, Horton's parents were experiencing financial troubles. All around them were heart-breaking failures: banks were closing, people's savings were wiped out, and homes and farms were being foreclosed at a rapid pace. At the end of most weekdays, the cash register in Albert Foote's clothing store registered less than two dollars, and he was forced to renew a bank loan he had taken out years before to provide for the family. Horton admits that all he could think of was going to California to become an actor. He was not aware at the time of how his father sacrificed to find the money for his tuition. He recalled: "my father owned an old Colonial house which he had held on to for many years. All that he ever owned was that house. On the day he sold the house, he was asked to join a group of friends who were pooling their money to buy an oil well; but instead of investing in it, he sold it to pay my tuition. The oil pool was a successful one and made all of its participants wealthy; but if my father ever had regrets, he never burdened me with them."[48]

While the next six years were times of great personal and financial sacrifice for the family, they tolerated and even encouraged the young actor's desire to go to California. Horton's appreciation and love for his mother and father would later be revealed through his many characters,

---

[47] Foote, *Genesis*, 70.

[48] Horton Foote, interview by Marion Castleberry, 18 November 1988, Wharton, Texas.

who often make sacrifices to enable someone they love to fulfill their dreams.

Finally, in September 1933, Horton Foote said goodbye. His parents agreed that he and his mother would drive his grandmother's car to Houston, where he would catch a bus to California. His Aunt Lily, his father's sister, and his Grandmother Cleveland came to see him off, and Horton recalls that his departure was an emotional time for everyone, especially his mother, who kept her emotions under control until after he had boarded the bus. As the bus pulled out of the station, Horton turned to wave goodbye and saw his mother crying as she waved farewell.[49] Though he was only seventeen at the time, somehow he knew he was crossing a threshold that would take him away from his home forever. But his memories of Wharton, of the rich personal and regional past he had left behind, would inspire and sustain him as a person and as an artist for the rest of his life.

---

[49] Foote, *Genesis*, 31.

Part Two

An Actor Prepares

When I was growing up in Wharton, I had no idea of becoming a writer; I was determined to be an actor. And yet, now, looking back, I can see that in some subtle way, my talent, such as it is, was being nurtured for my future work.

—Horton Foote

3

Pasadena and Beyond
1933–35

The Pasadena Playhouse was an unlikely place for Horton Foote to pursue a career in the theater. Horton's parents had not chosen the school for its superior methods of teaching, but rather for their son's safety and protection. Founded by the young actor Gilmore Brown, the theater was an outgrowth of the enthusiasm for community theater that had swept across America during the 1920s. In 1925, Brown, along with his small company of artists, converted an old burlesque house into a theater and began putting on popular plays that appealed to the Pasadena community. Although Brown was not a great actor or director, he was a visionary, much like Margo Jones in Dallas and Nina Vance in Houston, and he had the ability to inspire people with his ideas about theater.

By 1928, Brown's theater company had become so successful that he organized the Pasadena Community Playhouse Association and, with money raised by the city of Pasadena, erected a handsome mission-style building with shops, a restaurant, a recital hall, a theater that seated more than seven hundred people, and a small theater-in-the-round space called the Play Box (the first of its kind in America). Brown also established the Pasadena Playhouse School of Theatre, which offered classes in acting, directing, and design.

By the time Horton Foote arrived there, the Playhouse was recognized as one of America's foremost community theaters (albeit in name only), praised for its professional productions of classical and contemporary works, and considered a stepping stone for actors to a film career in nearby Hollywood. The school featured a two-year curriculum and attracted aspiring actors from across the nation. The cost of studying at the school was five hundred dollars for the first year and two hundred fifty dollars for the second year—a lot of money for that time. The fee also included a room at a boardinghouse near the school.

One of the main reasons Horton's parents chose the Pasadena Playhouse was because Grandmother Brooks's sister, Mag, lived in Vista, only a short distance from Los Angeles. They felt that with Mag and her husband Walt nearby, Horton would have someone to turn to should he ever need help. Before boarding the bus in Houston and setting off for California, Horton had been assured by his mother he would stay with his Aunt Mag for the weekend then report to school the following Monday.

Unfortunately, things did not turn out exactly according to plans. Horton arrived at the Los Angeles bus station on an ordinary Saturday evening in September 1933, and just as his mother had promised, he was greeted by his Aunt Mag and Uncle Walt. After the usual hugs and handshakes, the couple took Horton to eat, then drove him around the city to see the sights. They rode down the Miracle Mile of Wilshire Boulevard, past the original Brown Derby, and past the Coconut Grove Ambassador Hotel with Aunt Mag ceaselessly quizzing Horton about their family in Texas. Horton was furiously talking away, giving her all the news from home, when she suddenly announced it was time to drive him to the YMCA in Pasadena. The young man was surprised and very disappointed, since he had fully expected to spend the weekend with them and visit some of the places he had always dreamed of seeing: Grauman's Chinese Theatre, the movie studios, and the houses of Hollywood movie stars. Later he learned the reason they did not take him in was because Walt was out of work, a result of his drinking, and the couple was living in a very modest tourist court. "I suspect they were at the moment ashamed for me to see them in such circumstances," Horton recalled, "not wanting me to tell my Texas family how they were forced to live."[1]

Horton spent the next few days alone, the first time in his life he had been alone, taking brief walks down Colorado Boulevard to look at the Playhouse and writing optimistic but painful letters to his parents telling them how much he loved Pasadena and how beautiful the scenery was in California. Although he tried to remain positive, in truth he was scared and lonely, and memories of his hometown left him melancholy. That Saturday night as he sat in his small room at the Y, Horton began to think of his father's store and "the black and white farmers who would be coming into the store, always cheerful on these Saturday nights, even when there was little money. It was also the time when cotton pickers and their families flooded the county and swelled the always-crowded Saturday night streets." But lonely or not, Horton knew somehow he

---

[1] Horton Foote, *Genesis of an American Playwright,* ed. Marion Castleberry (Waco TX: Baylor University Press, 2004) 32–3.

would "never fully go back to that life again."[2] He was moving further away from his home place and the secure world he had known as a child.

When Monday morning came, Horton paid his bill at the YMCA, ate breakfast, and walked to the Pasadena Playhouse. He arrived early at eight-thirty. The doors were locked and the large patio in front of the building was empty, except for a young man standing by himself smoking a cigarette. After greeting each other, the young man introduced himself as John Forsht, newly arrived by bus from Pennsylvania, then explained that his wallet had been stolen during the trip and he hadn't eaten in two days. Although he had very little money himself, Horton lent the young man a quarter to buy some breakfast. With this simple act of kindness, he began a long and cherished friendship.[3] Over the next several months, Horton would befriend many other people at the Playhouse, each of whom would have an impact on his life and his career: Charlotte Sturges, who taught Horton his first lessons about modern dance; Doc Grandby, who introduced him to the writings of Stark Young; Rosamond Pinchot, who led him to the great Russian teachers (Tamara Daykarhanova, Vera Soloviova, and Andrius Jilinsky); and Joseph Anthony, who would become one of Horton's most cherished friends and artistic allies.

After signing all the necessary registration forms for school, Horton was given the address of the boardinghouse where he was to live. His new residence was only a block from the school, a two-story yellow frame house on Oakland Avenue owned by a "nervous lady in her fifties" called "Boss."[4] Meals were provided as part of the tuition, and Horton was to share the floor with two elderly men and another student of the school, Charles Robinson from Honolulu, Hawaii. Although the boardinghouse was far from luxurious, it was a safe and comfortable place for Horton to sleep.

Classes took place five days a week, from nine to five, with an hour off for lunch. Horton recalled that the instructors impressed upon the students the importance of a practical education: "Training is not confined in theory. Students learn by doing! Assistant direction, costuming, stage managing, scene designing, even the actual construction and paint-

---

[2] Ibid., 33.
[3] Horton Foote, *Beginnings: A Memoir* (New York: Scribner Press, 2001) 27–8.
[4] Ibid., 30.

ing of settings and the work of stage crews."[5] While this philosophical statement meant nothing to Horton initially, he quickly discovered that acting was only a small part of what he was expected to learn.

He also took classes in fencing, diction, costume design, makeup, scene design, theater literature, and styles of acting. Two hours each day were set aside for play rehearsal, and the three directors hired by the Playhouse took turns directing the students in different plays. Horton studied diligently and worked hard, but even Gilmore Brown's weekly inspirational talks about what a rewarding life the theater could be if one had the proper dedication did not keep the young man from feeling discouraged with the training he was receiving. Since he had no talent for drawing, he accomplished little in either costume or stage design; even play rehearsals were often frustrating.

Within days after school began, Horton was cast in a Roman comedy along with John Forsht, John Pelletti, and Peter Engle. The play was directed by Tom Brown Henry, a talented but harsh taskmaster who, according to Horton, felt the best method of helping a young man to grow as an actor was to make insulting but witty remarks about his lack of talent and experience. His philosophy was simple and blunt:

> The theater is a tough place. To survive you have to be tough. Now I'm not going to help you by flattering you and telling you how good you are. You are here to learn, I believe. You won't learn by my flattering you, but by my telling you what you have to do to survive this lousy business. Now Gilmor Brown, who as you know is the artistic director of the playhouse, will be along one day and give you inspirational talks about how the theater is a temple and you must dedicate yourself unselfishly to it, and that's what he has done and that's worked for him, but I tell you you'll get kicked out of the temple if you don't know how to walk across the stage without looking like an automaton and talking so low you can't be heard.[6]

The cast was given six weeks of rehearsals after which, they would perform the play without props, scenery, or costumes. At that time, Horton had read very few plays, was not aware of Roman comedies, and knew nothing about how to perform his role, so his introduction to acting proved to be a miserable experience. Horton recalled that Henry put them on their feet the first day and watched as they stumbled about the stage, "not knowing how in the world to approach this material and

---

[5] Foote, *Genesis*, 33.
[6] Foote, *Beginnings*, 37.

afraid that we didn't understand a word of it."[7] To make matters worse, Henry told Horton that if he expected to become a successful actor, he would have to correct his Southern accent: "I soon realized that I came from a part of the world that was sort of looked down on by more sophisticated people."[8] Horton felt this sort of elitism was an attack on his identity, but despite the intimidating treatment, he faced all pretentiousness with his usual endearing smile and a passionate commitment to be the best actor he could.

Three days later after speech class, Miss Ong, the voice teacher, suggested Horton take private lessons to eradicate his Texas accent, and she offered the name of her own teacher, Blanche Townsend. Horton had very little money to spend, especially on private tutoring, but he used his lunch money to pay for two lessons a week. Voice classes began at eight o'clock in the morning, and Horton recalled that the first lessons consisted largely of breathing exercises. Each week Miss Townsend listened to him read dramatic monologues from *Hamlet* and *Romeo and Juliet* and demanded that he translate every word he read to phonetics. She appears to have been a very encouraging teacher, which was something Foote desperately needed at the time, but her training methods were antiquated. When Horton began to study the role of Hamlet, he asked Miss Townsend for help: "She would only hear me do 'Speak the speech, I pray you' and I had to say 'trippingly on the tongue' over and over. It almost ruined Shakespeare for me forever."[9]

Nonetheless, Horton memorized speeches and rehearsed Shakespearean monologues day and night hoping the vocal exercises would rid him of his Texas drawl. He had no idea what all of this had to do with acting, but his parents had taught him that if he worked hard everything would turn out fine. He kept reminding himself to be patient, but he was, in fact, frustrated and discouraged.

Although the speech lessons with Miss Townsend were frustrating and often of little value, they must have had some effect because shortly after Horton returned to Wharton the following summer, he discovered that his brother Tom was charging friends twenty-five cents to hear

---

[7] Foote, *Genesis*, 34.

[8] Horton Foote, interview by Marion Castleberry, 18 November 1988, Wharton, Texas.

[9] Foote, *Genesis*, 37.

Horton speak in "the most outrageous English accent you've ever heard in your life."[10]

Horton had a more positive experience when he performed the role of Sparrow in Ferenc Molnár's *Liliom*, directed by Byron Folger. "Rehearsals were a joy to me," Horton recalled, "I couldn't wait each day for rehearsals to begin." On the third day, Folger told Horton, "I think you're doing well with the part.... Just continue as you are and you'll be fine." That night Horton wrote the first really truthful letter home telling his parents how happy he was in school, how he enjoyed the role of Sparrow, and how much he admired the director.[11]

The only class Horton Foote seems to have truly enjoyed during his first semester was theater literature, partly due to his fascination with drama but also because the instructor took a special interest in him. Horton remembered Folger being passionate about plays as literature, knowledgeable about the stage conventions of the Greeks, the Elizabethans, Molière, the Noh plays, and the Chinese theater, and always willing to spend time with him during and after class to talk about novels, poetry, and drama. Horton also enjoyed Janet Scott's discussions of actors like Lynn Fontanne and Pauline Lord and playwrights like Eugene O'Neill.

But vastly more important than classes to Horton's development as a playwright were the stage productions he saw at the Pasadena Playhouse. Gilmore Brown encouraged the students to attend all the professional productions performed on the main stage. Horton tried to go every Friday and Saturday night, and after each show he and his friends would share their thoughts on the productions. One of the first plays he saw at the Playhouse was Oscar Wilde's *Salome*. Directed by Benjamin Zemach, founder of the Habimah Theatre, the production featured a young twenty-five-year-old actor by the name of Lee J. Cobb in the role of Herod. In *Beginnings*, Horton recalled that the scenery was stunning and quite beautiful, especially the great terrace of Herod's palace, and that the stage was lit very brightly to suggest moonlight. Horton recalled that when Lee J. Cobb finally made his entrance, he appeared to be a seasoned performer, not a twenty-five-year-old actor, and he literally took over the play, giving it a drive and passion that it had lacked until that moment. "How does he do it," the seventeen-year-

---

[10] Horton Foote, interview by Marion Castleberry, 19 November 1988, Wharton, Texas.

[11] Foote, *Beginnings*, 51.

old Horton kept asking himself. "How in the world does he do it? Will I ever be that good at twenty-five?"[12]

Over the next two years, Horton would learn a great deal about acting and theater from watching professional productions at the Playhouse. In addition to *Salome*, he saw numerous other productions, including Sidney Howard's *Alien Corn*; Lynn Riggs's *Road Side*, with Victor Jory; Molière's *Bourgeois Gentilhomme*, with Thomas Brown Henry; John Millington Synge's *The Playboy of the Western World*, with Douglas Montgomery; and George Bernard Shaw's *Saint Joan*, with Joseph Anthony as the Dauphin. Foote admitted that all the plays were performed with great originality, but none of the performances affected him like those of Eva Le Gallienne in three of Henrik Ibsen's works.

In the winter of 1933, Le Gallienne announced she would be bringing touring productions of *Hedda Gabler*, *A Doll's House*, and *The Master Builder* to the west coast. Horton had heard Le Gallienne's name mentioned often by his school friends but knew nothing about her and even less about the repertory company she had founded in New York City. For his eighteenth birthday, Horton asked Grandmother Brooks, who was in California visiting her two sisters at the time, to take him to see the great actress in *Hedda Gabler* at the Biltmore Theatre. Years later, Horton would point to this experience as crucial in his decision to focus on a realistic and poetic style of theater, as both an actor and writer.

Horton was mesmerized by Le Gallienne's performance as the ominous Hedda—sporting a bobbed hairdo, wearing a short skirt, and smoking a cigarette. "She was extraordinary," he recalled, "and the play made a deep and lasting impression on me."[13] Horton's grandmother sensed his excitement, and the next day she took him to see the matinee of *The Master Builder* with Le Gallienne as Hilda. Then, that evening they saw *A Doll's House*, with Le Galliene as Mrs. Linde. "She seemed so different to me in all these parts," Horton remembered, "and yet there was an essence that was always unmistakably hers. And the Ibsen plays moved me in a way no plays had before. Most plays, I realized after seeing these, were thin gruel of little substance."[14]

Horton's experience at the Biltmore Theatre, witnessing the moving scenes of people in distress, was his first encounter with realistic drama. Until that moment he had never considered that such theater could be

---

[12] Ibid., 77–8.
[13] Foote, *Genesis*, 37.
[14] Foote, *Beginnings*, 71.

created from stories of everyday life, but after seeing these productions, the future playwright would never stray far from the intensely felt realism of the modern theater. He became more determined than ever to become an actor, a dream that would eventually lead him to New York.

Eva Le Gallienne's influence did not end with her inspiring performances. Horton learned of her theatrical philosophy from her autobiography, *At 33*, which his grandmother bought for him, and he learned how she had founded the Civic Repertory Theatre in an abandoned theater on Fourteenth Street in New York. Le Gallienne had become famous for her exquisite performances in two Ferenc Molnár plays, *Liliom* and *The Swan*, and could have continued a successful career in commercial theater, but she felt an actor could only reach full potential by playing parts in great plays, both classic and modern. In Le Gallienne, Horton had found an artist to emulate, one who defied the commercialism of Broadway without sacrificing her standards of artistic excellence. Following Le Gallienne's model, Horton Foote would choose a similar career path, refusing to compromise his artistic vision or sense of truth for money, fame, or popular appeal.

When classes ended that first semester in spring of 1934, Horton packed his belongings and took a bus back to Wharton. He was excited about seeing his family again, but unsure of what he would find when he arrived home. In one of her many letters, Horton's mother had told him she and his father had moved into Grandmother Brooks's house while his grandmother was visiting her sisters in California. Like everyone else in Wharton, the Footes were having difficulty making ends meet, so they had rented out their house to earn some extra money. Even though Horton was accustomed to visiting his grandmother's house any time he wanted, it seemed odd to him for his parents and siblings to live there.[15]

Upon his return to Texas, Horton's cousin Nan met him at the bus station in Houston. And all the way back to Wharton, she talked about his uncles and how their behavior was killing his Grandmother Brooks. Nan was afraid that their extravagances and their drinking and gambling, were going to bankrupt their mother. Worse yet, his Uncle Brother, who was now a merchant seaman, had deserted his wife and child. His uncles Billy and Speed had moved to Houston to look for work, but after finding none, they had begun to drink themselves into oblivion.

---

[15] Ibid., 89.

Horton's grandmother had returned from California happy and contented, but a few weeks after returning to Wharton her health became increasingly unstable. She had lost weight, had constant asthma attacks, and was in bed now most of the time. To make matters worse, Nan informed Horton that his grandmother was intent on leaving Wharton after she regained her strength and moving to Houston to live with her daughter Rosa, who was out of work and having difficulty finding anyone to help with her baby.

When Nan and Horton arrived at the Brooks house, Horton's mother and his two brothers, Tom and John, were waiting on the porch to greet him. Horton remembered that his mother "seemed unchanged, and my brothers, grown taller, came down the porch stairs to take my suitcase."[16] When he entered his grandmother's bedroom, he could not believe his eyes. In California, she had been "energetic and outgoing and cheerful. She looked suddenly old and helpless in that enormous bed of hers," Horton recalled.[17]

After visiting with Mrs. Brooks for a short time, Nan drove Horton downtown to see his father, who was standing in front of his store when they arrived. When he saw Horton, he ran over to the car, greeted his son with a hug, and began to fill him in on everything that had been happening in Wharton. From their conversation, Horton learned that his father was suffering from the stress of having to care for Mrs. Brooks's business affairs, from worrying about the tenants renting his house, and from his anxiety over the wretched state of the cotton industry. While the cotton crop had been bountiful, there was no demand for it; and, consequently, it sat in warehouses, unsold, or in the fields, unpicked. The effect of the Depression on Wharton's economy was devastating, especially for storeowners like Albert Foote. Furthermore, Horton discovered that his grandmother had been forced to return from California after his uncles Billy and Speed had gotten drunk, started a fight, and ended up in jail. According to Horton's father, who was growing angry and resentful, their behavior was sending their mother "nearer the grave every day."[18]

Horton's father explained that when Mrs. Brooks went to California—in an effort to get away from her sons—he had uprooted the family so Hallie could care for her brothers. Apparently, Horton's uncles

---

[16] Ibid.
[17] Ibid.
[18] Ibid., 90.

had behaved themselves for a while, but the minute their mother returned Billy and Speed had gone on benders and Uncle Brother had run off to sea. After listening to his father's tirades, Horton became increasingly concerned and depressed, but fortunately a customer entering the store broke his father's dreary mood. Suddenly, his father, who had been worried about the recent lack of sales, brightened up and looked like a man on top of the world with no cares at all.[19]

On the third night of his visit home, Horton awoke with severe stomach pain. Dr. Toxie Davidson was called to the house, and he announced Horton was having an appendicitis attack; but, in the doctor's opinion, Horton did not appear to need surgery at that time. However, after applying the remedy of ice and rest, the pain did not subside and Horton lost consciousness. A few hours later, he was rushed to the Wharton Hospital for immediate surgery. Afterwards, Horton was in the hospital for ten days, during which time his mother and a former high school classmate, Ruby Davis, who told him he was very lucky to be alive, cared for him. His appendix had burst, and his mother, fearing he might die, had called the Methodist minister for prayer. When Horton questioned his mother about what Ruby had said, she began to cry and had to leave the room. That afternoon Horton's grandmother came to stay with him so that his mother, physically and emotionally exhausted by this time, could get some rest. Horton was tired as well, but had trouble falling asleep, so he asked his grandmother to sing a hymn, as she had when he was a child. As she sang his favorite hymn, *Blessed Assurance*, Horton finally went sound asleep.[20]

Horton awoke the next day to a procession of friends and family members—Aunt Lida, Aunt Loula, and cousin Nan had come to look in on him and share their stories of Uncle Billy Brooks, who had died from a ruptured appendix. On the tenth day, Dr. Davidson announced Horton could go home, and two days later the doctor told his mother to allow him to begin walking around the house and eating whatever he wanted. Horton soon regained his strength and began thinking about returning to Pasadena.

One July evening after supper, Horton, his mother, father, and grandmother were sitting on the front porch of their house when his father brought him a letter from the Pasadena Playhouse telling him of his new living arrangements. He would be living in one of two large

---

[19] Ibid., 92.
[20] Ibid., 104.

houses the school had rented for all its students. The letter also explained that John Forsht would be Horton's roommate. Horton immediately began to make plans for his return to school.[21]

Grandmother Brooks decided, and the family agreed, that Horton should ride the train to California this time, rather than the bus, since he was still recovering from surgery and the train would provide a more comfortable ride. On the day Horton left Wharton, his cousin Nan drove him to the train station in Houston with his mother accompanying them. There were no tearful goodbyes as the last time, only concern for his grandmother's health and uncertainty about her decision to leave Wharton.

As his family had hoped, Horton's train ride to California was a comfortable one; he could walk around when he needed, and there was plenty of food to be had in the diner. He had intended to sleep through part of the trip, but his mind kept wandering, thinking about Wharton and his grandmother, then about Pasadena and what to expect from the coming year. For the first time in his life, he began seriously to question his future. What if he couldn't get a job in the theater? Should he return to Pasadena for yet a third year? Could his parents afford the cost of that? Should he move to New York and try to break into professional acting? How could he get to New York with no money and no prospects for a job? Could he make a living with a job in the theater? Maybe he shouldn't go to New York after all. Such thoughts haunted him that night and in the weeks to come, but even though Horton was anxious about his future, he never allowed his fear to dismantle his dream of becoming an actor.[22]

When he finally arrived at the Playhouse from the train station, Horton was informed that he had been cast as Earnest in *The Importance of Being Earnest* under the direction of Janet Scott. The rest of the cast would consist of Peggy Carter as Cecily, Jody Schwartzberg as Lady Bracknell, and John Forsht as Algernon. John Forsht escorted him to his new room on the third floor of a run-down but comfortable house only three blocks from the school. John also introduced Foote to a new student, Doc Grandby, a recent graduate of Princeton University. Grandby was a likable man of sufficient means who, over the years, had collected a treasure trove of books and magazines that sparked Horton's interest. He would often go to Grandby's room to read his books, and it

---

[21] Ibid., 105.
[22] Ibid., 106–07.

was there he read his first copy of *Theatre Arts*, edited by Edith Isaacs, and where he was first introduced to *The New Republic* and the famous critic Stark Young, who would later become one of Horton Foote's strongest advocates and closest friends. One day Horton came across two books by Young, *The Flower in Drama* and *Glamour*, both of which would inform his understanding of the difference between American and the increasingly popular German styles of acting.

At the time, German theater was at the forefront of all artistic endeavors, and many of its leading actors, playwrights, and directors were immigrating to America as the Nazi regime brought more of German society under its repressive control. Most of the students at the Pasadena Playhouse—including Charlotte Sturges, Jody Schwartzberg, Doc Grandby, and John Forsht—were outspoken advocates of German theater and often discussed their favorite luminaries—Max Reinhardt, Alexander Moissi, and Mary Wigman. Horton had tried to enter into the conversations of his friends, but it was not until he read Stark Young's essay that he finally joined the chorus of students who extolled German theater and acting as the pinnacle of the profession. He certainly had no idea at the time he would one day be cast in a lavish Max Reinhardt production of *The Eternal Road*, a story combining biblical and pre-World War II Jewish history by Austrian playwright Franz Werfel, performed in 1937 at the Manhattan Opera House. During the fall of 1934, the Playhouse produced a dramatization of Dostoyevsky's *The Brothers Karamazov*, featuring two actors from Reinhardt's company. Horton and John Forsht attended the production and were highly impressed with the performances of Martin Koslick as Aliocha and Hans von Twardowski as Smerdyakov. In fact, Horton was so taken with the German actors that he saw two more performances and later recalled, "they seemed to be doing really very little but with such concentration and quiet authority that you really watched no one else."[23]

That spring, Horton watched the performance of another protégé of Reinhardt's, Rosamond Pinchot, who appeared in the play *John Brown's Body*. While the acting of Koslick and Von Twardowski had inspired him, Horton was mesmerized by the performance of the American-born Pinchot, and her beauty captivated him. Horton learned from Jody Schwartzberg that Pinchot was a New York socialite from a very rich family who had been discovered by Reinhardt on an ocean liner between Europe and the United States. She had been cast at the age of eighteen in

---

[23] Ibid., 119.

his production of *The Miracle,* and she had become an overnight sensation. She had come to Pasadena to get more acting experience, away from the demanding New York theater. After the performance, Horton was emboldened to go backstage and tell Pinchot how much he liked her in the play. He found her in her dressing room, alone, still in costume. To his surprise, Pinchot was pleased Horton had come backstage to see her. She was taller, as Horton later remembered, and much more beautiful than he had imagined. Rosamond and Horton chatted awhile on the Playhouse patio and began to open up to each other, Rosamond telling him about how she was discovered by Reinhardt, but admitting she was very insecure onstage. When Horton told her he wanted to go to New York to become an actor, she encouraged him. "That's what you should do," she insisted. "That's the only place to be if you want to be an actor."[24] Rosamond also told Horton about a Russian teacher, the legendary and controversial Maria Ouspenskaya, who had been with the Moscow Art Theatre and with whom she planned to study at the American Theatre Lab when she returned. After the play in Pasadena ended its run, Rosamond gave Horton her address and told him to contact her when he came to New York. Horton did not know it then, but the short time spent with Rosamond Pinchot was for him an introduction to a revolutionary approach to actor training and a new expansive vision of theater that would eventually become the cornerstone of his future work.

To Horton's delight, that second and final year at the Pasadena Playhouse turned out to be much more inspiring and enriching than the first. He became more confident of his talents and more determined than ever to learn as much as he could about the theater. He and his classmates were put in charge of the Recital Hall Theatre, a small space above the patio restaurant. As seniors, each student was cast in four plays and expected to build scenery and costumes, procure properties, and act as stagehands and stage managers for the shows. There was grumbling, of course, from some students who felt they had come to study acting, which meant they wanted to act all the time, not build scenery, stage manage, or work props. But Horton found his responsibilities to be both demanding and educational. He would go from rehearsing *The Importance of Being Earnest* to building and painting scenery—working all night some nights—to stage managing or assisting Miss Scott in her directing. Apparently Miss Scott took a liking to

---

[24] Ibid., 126.

Horton, and she urged him to learn all the technical skills he could. "She had gone to New York," she said, "to be an actress and one needed all the skills one could get to survive."[25]

After three weeks of rehearsal, *The Importance of Being Earnest* was performed before an audience that consisted of fellow students, a few friends, and relatives of the cast members. In *Beginnings*, Horton recalled that the performance was well received and Miss Scott was very pleased with his performance. For the first time, Horton got laughs on some of his lines. At first he was startled, but when he continued, he realized the audience was not laughing at him but at what he was doing with the character. It was an important lesson for a young actor to learn, and Miss Scott drove home the idea that various audiences always react differently. Some actors analyze what they do to get a laugh and then try to repeat the same action or inflection, she explained. But she warned Horton that when she'd tried that approach she felt self-conscious and her acting became flat and stilted. From Miss Scott, Horton learned to trust his instincts and to avoid catering to audience response, which was ever changing. Miss Scott also insisted Horton should always trust his emotions and inner sense of truth, a concept he would never forget.[26]

Shortly before the end of the term, Horton asked his diction teacher, Miss Townsend, if she thought he could make it as an actor in New York. "Anything is possible," she said. "It would depend, I think on your determination. I spoke with Louise last night and it occurred to me since you have become so proficient in phonetics that you should travel around Texas and write down phonetically the different dialects. It would be great training for your ear and in the end might be a way to make some money. There is a need for that kind of research."[27] Horton's heart sank, because he thought this was surely her way of telling him to reconsider his career as an actor and to stay away from New York. But as he began to walk away, Miss Townsend added, "What are you doing for the summer?" Horton admitted he had no plans other than returning to Texas to see his family. Miss Townsend then explained that she taught in a summer school connected with the Rice Players, a stock company on the island of Martha's Vineyard in Massachusetts. The owners of the theater had encouraged her to hire three young actors from Pasadena for the summer to study with her and to work with the students on scenes

---

[25] Foote, *Genesis*, 37.
[26] Foote, *Beginnings*, 116–17.
[27] Ibid., 127.

and plays. For their services, they would be given room and board, a few dollars a week for spending money, and the opportunity to perform bit roles in summer stock productions. Miss Townsend asked if Horton would like to work with her, and then announced she had already invited his best friend, John Forsht, who had agreed to come along. The third actor hired was Joseph Anthony, a graduate of the Pasadena Playhouse who was considered by many to be the most gifted actor the theater had produced. After being asked, Horton quickly answered with a resounding "Yes," and immediately sat down to write a letter to tell his parents about the offer. He explained in the note he would be able to visit them for only a short time during the summer months and asked his father if he would be able to help pay his train fare to Massachusetts. His father wrote back, telling him how very proud he was of him and that he would pay the train fare, but warning him that because of the Depression he would not be able to help him financially much longer.[28]

Horton invited John Forsht home with him at the end of the term. They rode the bus together from California to Texas, and Horton's parents made them both feel welcome. He showed John around town, and his relatives had them over for meals. The day they were to leave for Martha's Vineyard, Horton's father called him aside and said, "Here's fifty dollars. When this is gone, don't ask for more, because I won't give it to you." Horton took the money and thanked him, and he never asked him for another penny. "My father had a terror that I would turn out like my uncles and so he was very strict on me," Horton recalled. "At the time, I thought he was very stern for saying this; I just didn't appreciate all the sacrifices my father made for me. I think now if I had ever really needed anything, he would have helped, but I chose at the time to believe he would not, and so I never asked, even when I was hungry, and I went hungry many times in my first days in New York City. Anyway, I knew that John, whose father had died when he was an infant, had no one to give him even fifty dollars."[29]

When they arrived on Martha's Vineyard, Horton and John began taking classes from Miss Townsend, working on plays, and getting to know Joseph Anthony. Over the course of the summer, the three young men became close friends, and in time Anthony would become one of Foote's most cherished colleagues. In the summer of 1935, they were all struggling actors hoping to break into the professional theater.

---

[28] Ibid., 128–29.
[29] Foote, *Genesis*, 37.

Horton's Pasadena Playhouse experience had helped him land his first acting job with the Rice Players, but after two years of actor training in Pasadena, he was still confused about the style of acting for which he was best suited. He had grown to appreciate the works of Shakespeare and the Greeks but felt uncomfortable performing them. Ibsen and Chekhov were new to him, and very few American plays were being produced with regularity across the country. It was really not until the summer of 1935, while working at Martha's Vineyard, that Horton became aware of his potential as a Southern-born actor.

Horton stayed in Martha's Vineyard for almost two months, taking classes and working on scenes from *Candida* with a number of Miss Townsend's students. During this time, Miss Townsend announced she would direct Paul Green's play *The No 'Count Boy,* a Southern variation of John Millington Synge's *The Playboy of the Western World,* which tells the story of a young black boy who dreams of leaving his family and home to travel the world. There were no black actors in Martha's Vineyard at that time, and as Horton remembered, "In those days black actors and white actors simply did not work together, eat together in restaurants, or sit together in the audience."[30] Miss Townsend chose to produce the play with an all-white cast, in blackface, and selected Horton for the lead role, a part that the young man did not have to write out phonetically. He had been around provincial blacks all his life and was very knowledgeable about their customs, the way they spoke, and how they acted.

The No 'Count Boy was a huge success. As Horton remembered years later, "the theater was packed and I am sure not many of our audiences [made up of members of the stock company and people from town] had ever seen a play about blacks. I haven't read *The No 'Count Boy* in a long time and don't know what I'd think about it today, but then, for me and the audience, it was a welcome relief from the usual summer stock Broadway play with its hoked-up situations and unreal characters."[31]

Horton Foote's performance in *The No 'Count Boy* had little effect on his aspirations to become a Broadway actor; nevertheless, the experience created in him an awareness of the unique qualities of his own cultural background, the genuine American dialogue, and the regional subjects he remembered from his childhood. Horton had found an idiom he was

---

[30] Ibid., 37.
[31] Ibid., 38.

more comfortable with than Shakespeare, and later, he would draw on the Southern tradition for inspiration in writing his own plays.

By the end of the run of *The No 'Count Boy*, Horton knew he would not return to the Pasadena Playhouse. There was a brief moment of melancholy when he wondered if he would ever see his friends or the Playhouse again, but he quickly got over his feeling of sadness when he began to think about New York and starting a career in the professional theater. In the fall of 1935, with very little money in his pocket, Horton caught a boat from Martha's Vineyard to New York City in hopes of becoming a Broadway actor.

It would be forty years before Horton Foote returned to the Pasadena Playhouse, and by that time his life would have changed dramatically.

4

New York
1935–37

When Horton Foote and his friends John Forsht and Joe Anthony finally arrived in New York in 1935, Greenwich Village was the artistic center of America, a thriving community of small theaters, nightclubs, and crowded cafés where aspiring young artists lived and worked. At the time of their arrival, Horton had only twenty-seven dollars left of the fifty his father had given him during his last trip to Wharton, and John and Joe had only a few dollars they each had saved from their work with the Rice Players. So they pooled their money and rented a smaller furnished apartment over a dingy nightclub called the Welcome Inn on MacDougal Street. The Welcome Inn sat across from the renowned Provincetown Playhouse, famous for staging original works by playwrights Eugene O'Neill, Edna St. Vincent Millay, and Tennessee Williams and for introducing actors like Paul Robeson and Bette Davis. The apartment consisted of only three rooms and a tiny kitchen, but it was comfortable enough, and the young men felt it would suffice until they could afford to rent a better place.[1]

Joe, being a member of Actor's Equity, quickly landed a job with the Federal Theatre Project and was cast in a play with Estelle Winwood, a leading New York actress. Horton and John also found jobs working backstage as prop boys at the Provincetown Playhouse for a production of *The Provincetown Follies*, a musical review that had just gone into rehearsal. The work paid very little, but the money helped cover rent and offered the young men a glimmer of hope that they could find employment in the theater.

Horton discovered early on that the Depression had left New York economically ravaged and that the phenomenon of talking pictures, having decimated both vaudeville and winter stock companies, was beginning to make significant inroads into Broadway itself. Gone was the theater of the legendary manager-producers David Belasco, Charles Frohman, and Winthrop Ames, who had controlled all aspects of professional theater in New York since the 1890s. However, their

---

[1] Horton Foote, *Beginnings: A Memoir* (New York: Scribner Press, 2001) 14–141.

theaters—the Belasco, the Empire, the Lyceum, and the Little Theatre—were still in place, and the stories of their lives and their lavish productions were told again and again whenever actors gathered together.

Not surprisingly, one of the first things Horton did when he arrived in New York was make a pilgrimage to Eva Le Gallienne's Civic Repertory Theatre on Fourteenth Street. When he got there, he found it occupied by a left-wing political theater group called Theatre Union, which claimed to be part of "the new theater movement." This phrase meant very little to Horton at the time; he dreamed of becoming an acclaimed actor-manager, of having his own New York theater season and then touring the country, or of being like the idealistic Le Galliene and joining a repertory theater. To Horton, the "old theater" of the past was invincible, and he desperately wanted to be a part of it. However, as Horton would eventually discover, Broadway was changing, and opportunities for talented yet unproven actors were disappearing daily.

Once the *Provincetown Follies* opened, Horton and John began looking for acting jobs. They had been instructed by Joe and the other professional actors on Martha's Vineyard about the proper procedures to follow when looking for work, and as Foote admits, the phrase "making the rounds" quickly became as familiar to him as it was to the more experienced actors in the city:

> It meant arriving in the Broadway district around ten in the morning when the agents' and producers' offices were beginning to open, and going up and down Broadway and the side streets from 39th Street to 57th Street, and asking the receptionists of the agents and producers if any casting was being done that day. If the answer was yes, then came the next question: Is there a part for me? If the answer to that was no, you then went on to the next office; if the answer was yes or maybe, then you took a seat and waited, sometimes as long as five hours, for someone higher up to come out, look you over, and then you would find out if the receptionist's response had been the right one, or whether there would be a curt "not right." Sometimes there would be no comment at all, just a negative shake of the head. If you were lucky, they would say, "Come back and see Mr. So-and-So tomorrow," or luckier still, "Wait here and I'll give you a script to read."[2]

---

[2] Horton Foote, *Genesis of an American Playwright*, ed. Marion Castleberry (Waco TX: Baylor University Press, 2004) 39.

Horton arose faithfully every morning, put his nickel in the subway slot, and called on the offices of Broadway producers like Arthur Hopkins, Guthrie McClintic, Crosby Gaige, Oscar Serlin, Max Gordon, Herman Shumlin, the Theatre Guild, William Brady, and the Shubert brothers, who filled the theaters each season with new and exciting productions. He quickly learned how to ask the all-important question: "Anything today?" He also discovered that actors congregated during the day at the drugstore of the Astor Hotel and exchanged tips with each other about casting. He and John made a habit of going there twice a day, often having lunch and afternoon sodas and conversing with friends who gave advice and shared information about auditions.

One cold winter's day, while making the rounds, Horton landed his first acting job. He'd been walking the streets of Manhattan all day and was exhausted, but he'd promised to meet John Forsht at the Astor Hotel at three in the afternoon. With about a half-hour to kill, he decided to try one more office, the Jennie Jacobs Agency. As expected, Henry Weiss, the agent on duty, declared "No!" to the question, "Are you casting today?" But as Horton was walking out, Weiss stopped him and then informed the actor that he was sending him to Fox Studio on West Fifty-fifth Street to audition for a low-budget film.[3]

When an excited Horton arrived at Fox Studio, he was given a scene to look over for a few minutes, after which he was called in to read for a small role as a fourteenth-century scissors grinder in an industrial film created for advertising purposes. This kind of part was certainly not what Horton had hoped for, but it was three-days' work and the pay was fifty dollars a day. He read for the director, who told him he would make a decision about casting before seven that night and would call him.

Horton's room was on the first floor of the boarding house, and the phone for all the tenants was on the fifth floor. Seven o'clock came but no call. Seven-thirty came; still no call. Horton became very discouraged, thinking he'd failed to get the part. Suddenly, he heard the phone ring, and someone upstairs with an Italian accent yelled, "Footie! Footie!" An ecstatic Horton ran up the stairs, whooping with delight.[4]

The next day promptly at seven in the morning, he arrived at the Fox Studio for costume and makeup, as the director had requested, but Horton's scene was not shot until late in the afternoon. Apparently, he

---

[3] Foote, *Beginnings,* 149.
[4] Ibid.

wasn't too frustrated from the excessively long wait because in a letter to his parents, dated 19 December 1935, Horton explained that Fox Studio liked his work so much they wanted to film a close up of his exit and had called him back for another day of work:

> I got to see the picture in the projection room and it's quite good and it was certainly a funny sensation to see myself on the screen, and to hear myself speak. Modestly, I must admit I was pleased with the result. The one close up took about forty-five minutes. I had to remember everything I had done on my exit and duplicate it. For that forty-five minutes I got ten dollars. Everyone says at the studio I should get something worthwhile from it. You never know, however. My name is to be on the cast of characters list, so they'll at least know who I am.[5]

A few weeks later, Horton's cousin Nan Outlar wrote to tell him that Ed Roberts, an old beau of hers from Texas, was working in the New York office of Goldwyn Pictures and had asked that Horton come and see him about potential work. A couple of days after they met, Roberts called Horton to say that the studio was making some screen tests with the renowned comedian Milton Berle. They needed an actor to be in the tests, and Roberts asked Horton if he would like the work, which would pay a hundred dollars. Horton immediately accepted the offer and the next morning arrived at the studio promptly at seven. He was anxiously waiting in the makeup room when Milton Berle arrived with his mother, a proverbial stage mother who acknowledged Horton and ordered his makeup be applied immediately. After the makeup artist finished his task and left the room, Milton Berle walked up to Horton and explained there had been some confusion and the screen test would not be made, but since Horton was now in makeup, the studio would have to pay him. Horton left the studio that day confused and disappointed but very thankful for the hundred dollars.[6]

The earnings Horton made from his work on screen helped avert eviction and stave off hunger for a few weeks, but he had absolutely no luck finding another acting job for months afterwards, and the money Horton had made from his work quickly began to disappear.

In spite of his crippling budget, Horton found ingenious ways to attend the theater. Years later, he recalled that he always bought the second balcony seats, which cost fifty-five cents, but soon learned to look

---

[5] Horton Foote to Albert and Hallie Foote, 19 December 1935 (Horton Foote Papers).

[6] Foote, *Beginnings*, 150.

about the house at intermission for empty seats in more expensive sections. If the seats were still vacant after the curtain rose for the second act, he would claim one of them as his own. He also learned from his fellow actors that when he was totally broke to wait outside the theater until the first intermission, mingle with the audience out for a smoke or a breath of fresh air, and then walk nonchalantly in with them when the intermission was over, stand in the back until the lights were down and then scurry to an empty seat.[7]

The productions Horton remembered most vividly were Maxwell Anderson's *Winterset* with Burgess Meredith; *The Old Maid* with Judith Anderson and Helen Menken; Ibsen's *Ghosts* with the legendary Alla Nazimova; and Owen and Donald Davis's dramatization of Edith Wharton's novel *Ethan Frome* with Ramond Massey, Ruth Gordon, and Pauline Lord. Horton remembered that all of the shows were superbly acted, but he admits Pauline Lord's performance as Zenobia in *Ethan Frome* was the most moving he had ever seen, and it forever changed his outlook on the art of acting:

> I don't remember with what good fortune I was able to buy an orchestra seat for this play, but I do remember sitting there from the beginning, and that from that moment the fragile but overpowering figure of Miss Lord appeared on the stage, I was transformed; and it made me from then on dissatisfied with much of the acting in our theater. By what magic she accomplished what she did, I wasn't, and am still not, sure, but I felt that the life that day she brought to the stage, and the truth and beauty of it, made most other acting trivial and unimportant.[8]

Despite all the excitement of New York City, Horton became desperately discouraged during this time because he had set for himself the nearly impossible goal of becoming a Broadway actor by age twenty-two: "We do terrible things to ourselves. Imagine this twenty-year-old child worrying about being a Broadway star at twenty-two. But all around me, I'd see people who were forty and forty-five, who weren't Broadway stars and having a tough time, and that put the fear of God in me."[9]

The remainder of Horton's first year in New York was as rootless and displaced a time as he had ever experienced; but, Wharton, Texas, was

---

[7] Foote, *Genesis*, 40.

[8] Ibid.

[9] Horton Foote, interview by Marion Castleberry, 19 November 1998, Wharton, Texas.

never far from his mind. He wrote disingenuous letters to his parents, telling them how wonderful life was in New York. And his mother wrote back, often relating the events of a complete day in the life of his family and friends. Horton remembered that she wrote as if I had just left the day before, and in his lonely hours he would read her letters over and over.[10]

Horton often went hungry, and if it had not been for his job as a busboy at a New York restaurant, he would have had hardly anything to eat at all. On many occasions after the restaurant closed, he would collect the leftover food, take it to his apartment, and feed his starving friends. His mother's letters increased Horton's feelings of deprivation because she would describe in great detail the meals she prepared. Horton remembered: "I had to write and ask her to stop those descriptions, as I often had little money for food and the food available after reading her description seemed almost inedible."[11]

How Horton persevered during this difficult time, while others around him were abandoning their dreams and fleeing the theater for more lucrative professions, remains a great mystery. One explanation for Horton's resilience is that his enormous passion for the theater filled him with an unwavering sense of purpose and gave him the strength and courage to face several personal setbacks and disappointments. He also found inspiration in the love and support of his family, especially his parents, who wrote to him daily and often sent care packages with food and gifts they knew he liked. He also drew strength from his faith in an omnipotent, infinitely loving God as revealed in the writings of Mary Baker Eddy, founder of the Christian Science Church.

Horton's mother, Hallie, initially introduced her son to Christian Science when he was matriculating at the Pasadena Playhouse, at times mentioning in her letters the effect of Eddy's teachings upon her life, but Horton did not really take the religion seriously until after he arrived in New York. Horton recalled that during his early days in the city, after arriving from Pasadena, he was having a very hard time, struggling with all the disappointments, and needed help and guidance. One day, when he was with a friend who was not a Christian Scientist but who knew something about the religion, Horton recalled his friend saying, "You know, there is a phrase that if you get stuck, it might help you: 'Divine Love always has met and will always meet every human need'" (*Science*

---

[10] Ibid.

[11] Foote, *Genesis*, 41.

and Health 494). "Just use it as a kind of prayer," his friend said. "And I thought, 'Well I can use it.' And I did. That afternoon, I looked on the sidewalk, and there was a 10 dollar bill...I took it as a sign...And I thought, 'Well, if this is what it's about—I'm going to be a rich man!' But I soon learned that that wasn't what it was about, but I still became interested in Christian Science.... It's been a long, slow road, but I'm grateful for that moment, for that 10 dollar bill."[12]

This event marked the beginning of a spiritual journey for Horton Foote that continued for the rest of his life. Through the power of a simple prayer-idea from Mary Baker Eddy's book, *Science and Health with Key to the Scriptures*, Horton felt stirred to answer a call to learn more about Christian Science in much the same way he answered the call to become an actor. He began to spend time in a local Christian Science Reading Room, attending Class Instruction. As the years passed, he discovered that he needed to use Christian Science more and more, especially after he married and had children. The teachings of the Holy Bible and Mary Baker Eddy became irreplaceable guides in Horton's life:

> Christian Science has given me something to guide me as a human being...I don't like to think that I ever work to get an idea. My work mostly is trying to grow spiritually myself...Intelligent God-inspired forces bring each of us good opportunities—bring us into places of talent, productivity, and fruition...I attribute everything in my life to Principle, Mind. But...I don't want people to think that it's an easy thing...I'm being humbled all the time—like when someone says, "Horton, give it up." Just remember that things have a way of unfolding that you're always surprised about.[13]

Horton was always careful never to proselytize or force his beliefs on others, and he was adamant in interviews that he did not write from that point of view. But undeniably, the writings of Mary Baker Eddy and other Christian Scientists would influence his life and the ethos of his dramas, especially his views on the evils of materialism, the beauty and healing power of the female spirit, the need for forgiveness, and the infinite goodness and love of Mother-Father-God, who is both a nurturing mother and protective father. Mary Baker Eddy's teachings can also be seen in Horton's faith in the curative nature of prayer, his

---

[12] Jeffrey Hilder, "Everlasting Grace," *The Voice of an American Playwright*, ed. Gerald Wood and Marion Castleberry (Macon GA: Mercer University Press, 2012) 302.

[13] Ibid.,301–07.

belief in mankind as redeemable and courageously able to meet devastating change, and his understanding that "spiritual values beget spiritual values, and spiritual values lead you to hunger for more spiritual values."[14] Christian Science virtues that Horton expressed both as a man and playwright were kindness, compassion, generosity, and grace, as well as seeing others not as sinful but as fellow children of God.

When Christmas came that first year, Horton still had not found any other acting work. Nonetheless, he remained positive in his outlook and continued to write optimistic letters to his parents about the work he had acquired and about seeing his first snowfall. That first year in New York, John Forsht invited Horton to spend Christmas with him in Lock Haven, Connecticut, but, much to Horton's amazement, John explained that Horton couldn't stay with his family during the visit because there was not enough room at their house. Instead, Horton would have to stay with a family friend, a Professor Giese, who lived only a few miles away. On Christmas day it snowed, and Horton grew anxious to get back to New York to look for work. When he informed John he would be leaving after Christmas dinner, John said Mrs. Forsht had taken ill and had been rushed to the hospital. The family would not be having Christmas dinner at all, and he and Horton would have to eat at a restaurant.[15] From this experience, Horton discovered firsthand the enormity of the Depression and the tragic effects of poverty on families and young men and women throughout America.

That afternoon, Horton caught a bus back to New York, arriving in the city late at night. He awoke the next morning and dressed to make the rounds but quickly changed his mind when he realized the magnitude of the snowstorm outside. A package from his parents arrived that afternoon with a few gifts: a shirt, a pair of socks, a tie, a fruitcake, and a box of Christmas cookies. He spent the remainder of Christmas and New Year's holidays alone, listening to the music coming from the nightclub below his apartment. On New Year's Eve, a three-piece orchestra in the club played until four in the morning, and Horton stayed awake listening to an array of popular songs: "I'm in the Mood for Love," "Dream a Little Dream of Me," and "I'll Get By." He wrote a letter to his parents, thanking them for the gifts, telling them what a wonderful Christmas he'd spent with John Forsht and how confident he was that his career would take off in the coming year. Of course, the

---

[14] Ibid.

[15] Foote, *Beginnings*, 115.

truth was that he'd had a miserable Christmas and had absolutely no idea if he would ever become a successful actor.[16]

This was one of the lowest points in Horton's early career, and he considered giving up his dream of becoming an actor. But true to his nature, Horton persevered during this difficult time while others around him were leaving the theater for more profitable professions.

After months of setbacks, Horton Foote's life and career took a fortuitous turn one cold winter day in 1936. While walking down Broadway, he spotted an old friend from his Pasadena Playhouse days—actress and socialite Rosamond Pinchot. Horton hadn't seen Rosamond for two years and was thrilled to finally reconnect with her. Rosamond explained that she was studying acting with Tamara Daykarhanova, a distinguished protégée of the legendary Konstantin Stanislavski, at Daykarhanova's School for the Stage, and Rosamond needed an acting partner. "If you'd be interested," she said, "I'd pay your tuition and we could work on scenes together. I'm anxious to work on *Candida*. Would you be interested in working with me?"[17] Since job prospects were bleak, Horton jumped at the chance to learn more about his craft. Though unaware of it at the time, the training he was about to receive at the school and the friendships he would develop there over the next three years would be a crucial part of his early career and would have a long and lasting impact on his development as a writer.

All three acting teachers at the school—Tamara Daykarhanova, Vera Soloviova, and Andrius Jilinsky—were Russian immigrants who had fled to America to escape the cultural turmoil, taking place under the Stalin regime. Prior to teaching at the School for the Stage, Daykarhanova had worked as a teacher for Maria Ouspenskaya and Richard Boleslavsky, also colleagues of Stanislavski, at their New York acting school and theater. After Daykarhanova became head of the school, she invited Andrius Jilinsky and Vera Soloviova to join her at the school. Married to each other, Jilinsky and Soloviova had been members of the Moscow Art Theatre, where they worked closely with Stanislavski. When Michael Chekhov, the nephew of Anton Chekhov, decided to tour America in 1935, the couple joined him. When the company disbanded they remained in New York, joining Daykarhanova at the School for the Stage.

---

[16] Ibid.
[17] Ibid.,161.

Horton's initial encounter with Tamara Daykarhanova and her studio was rather serendipitous. He recalled Rosamond taking him to a small office to enroll in class and being interviewed by Frances Dietz. While in the process of answering a number of routine questions, he casually mentioned he'd studied at the Pasadena Playhouse. Dietz suddenly looked concerned and asked, "Does Madame know this?" Foote was confused by Dietz's reaction and became even more concerned when Madame Daykarhanova—a woman of about fifty-five with short dark hair, brown eyes, and pointed chin—entered the room and proclaimed: "You know we don't teach here like they do at Pasadena Playhouse. We are very strict here. Very, very strict.... You understand you will have to forget everything you learned at Pasadena school.... And you're willing to do this? " Without knowing what she was actually talking about Horton said, "Yes, ma'am."[18]

Horton's first encounter with Vera Soloviova took place in acting class. He remembered her as an attractive woman with "a round, lovely face and blue eyes," who always seemed to be smiling. In his personal memoir, *Lances Down*, published in 1932, Richard Boleslavsky wrote of Soloviova: "She was the only person I ever knew who could laugh softly and low, yet with all the vitality and vigor of an outburst. There was something of the child in her, or a singing bird. On the stage she was ecstatic and inspired, and her voice sounded like an organ."[19] Mary Hunter, a classmate of Horton's at the School for the Stage, wrote that, "no one who worked with [Soloviova] could ever forget the soft chuckle which preceded her comments on the scenes which she discussed with her students. It gave one a sense of warm personal delight and the feeling that you had done something well no matter how acutely she might point out your missteps."[20]

Horton said that on his first day of class, Soloviova entered the studio wearing a silk blouse, a tailored suit, and a captivating smile. Daykarhanova followed closely behind her and after a few minutes they asked, "Who has scene for today?" Several students raised their hands, and Madame Daykarhanova then announced the order in which the scenes would be presented. The actors she called on first began to rearrange some chairs and tables to establish a setting then prepared emotionally

---

[18] Ibid.,164.

[19] Andrius Jilinsky, *The Joy of Acting: A Primer for Actors* (New York: Peter Lang, 1990) 158.

[20] Ibid., 162.

for their scene. Horton later admitted: "I thought for a moment they were praying, but then suddenly they turned toward each other and took their places in the space they had created and began their scene."[21]

When the scene ended, Soloviova and Daykarhanova conversed in Russian for a few minutes and then offered specific criticism about the acting. Horton particularly remembered the specificity and insight of the critiques, and he heard, for the first time, the strange phrases the two teachers always used when criticizing their students' work: *actions, beats, wants, concentration, sense memory, through line, subtext, really listening, really seeing, colors, truthful, old-fashioned acting, acting clichés*. He would hear these phrases many times in the years to come as he worked with the two directors and honed his own acting skills under their tutelage.

After that first day, Horton left the Studio thoroughly confused but, nevertheless, sensing this was a place where he could learn something of value. Horton and Rosamond agreed to meet the next day to rehearse the scene they had chosen from *Candida,* but when he arrived at her apartment she informed him she had to go to Hollywood for a film shoot. Rosamond had intended to return the following week, but when Horton arrived at the studio on the day of performance, Madame Daykarhanova told him Rosamond had called from Hollywood to say that she would be unable to perform the scene. In fact, Rosamond did not return to New York at all that year, and Horton didn't see her again until they were in rehearsal for Max Reinhardt's *The Eternal Road* in 1937. However, as she had promised, Rosamond did pay for his tuition for the semester, allowing Horton to begin his all-important work with the Russian masters. Later he was given a scholarship of sorts. In exchange for helping out in the office and running the elevator when the regular operator was off-duty, his tuition was covered. A few weeks later, in scene study class, Daykarhanova suggested Horton sign up for technique classes with Andrius Jilinsky. Horton had no idea what "technique" was all about but Madame Daykarhanova explained he would be exposed to various acting exercises, sensory work, and concentration techniques designed to develop the actor's total acting instrument.

Intrigued, Horton immediately signed up for the class, joining other actors, like Joseph Anthony, Mary Virginia Palmer, and Mary Hunter, and he found early on that Andrius Jilinsky was the most talented and innovative teacher he had ever known or would ever know. In three years he learned more from Jilinsky about acting and the aesthetic of

---

[21] Foote, *Beginnings,* 166–67.

theater than he had ever imagined possible. Horton remembered Jilinsky as a tall, vigorous, handsome man with a graceful walk and a booming voice. Many years later Horton admitted, "I can hear him even now challenging, inspiring his students to a larger sense of theater and theater practice than their own undernourished, conventional American training had allowed. He loved teaching and he was patient and kind even to the least talented of his students. And he was generous with his knowledge to all of our young (and not so young) clamoring egos."[22]

Jilinsky was an early pioneer in what would become known as the "Stanislavski Method" of acting. His techniques, based on his studies with Konstantin Stanislavski, Yevgeny Vakhtangov, Richard Boleslavky, and Michael Chekhov, are commonplace today but in the 1930s they were considered new and revolutionary. Jilinsky's approach to acting was unconventional, deeply felt, psychologically detailed, and more impulsive and openly emotional than the English, German, and French styles prevalent at the time. He emphasized psychological truthfulness in the portrayal of characters, concentration on inner feelings, and a simple, true-to-life manner of moving and speaking, while drilling his students in concentration, relaxation, sensory recall, and improvisational exercises. A detailed description of his work can be found in his book, *The Joy of Acting*, which reveals his vision of the spiritual nature of theater, his commitment to truthfulness on stage, and his belief that the human heart is the primary impetus and guide to artistic creation. "I believe that the theatre must speak to human hearts," Jilinsky wrote, "Life is the sufferings of human beings, and art is about them. The actor who understands this will realize his responsibility. Every feeling he has goes into the soul of the people watching him act."[23] Jilinsky further explained that the creative element that guided his theater, which he called "living theatre," was inner truth: "If you want to create truth on the stage, you must be acquainted with your own truth, and the truth of your life. It is something that belongs not only to the tradition of acting, but to the moral content of the theatre."[24]

These new methods signaled the beginning of a revolt in American theater. "Those of us who became dedicated to this way of work," Horton explained, "felt we were in all ways turning our backs on the past. When I heard him say that all good actors know instinctively what

---

[22] Ibid.,170–71.
[23] Jilinsky, 6–7
[24] Ibid., 7–10.

he was trying to teach us, and that Pauline Lord, Laurette Taylor, and Walter Huston, whether they were aware of it or not, worked this way, I was willing to make any sacrifice to try and learn too. We believed," Horton added, "when we learned this way of working, our search would be over and a new world of theatre would be miraculously established."[25]

While Horton honed his acting talents under the Russian teachers' careful instruction, his training gave him a special confidence in the impact that good acting can have on drama. Jilinsky's passionate commitment as an artist, his conviction that there could be no higher calling than that of a life in the theater, his belief that theater should speak to the human heart, and the inspired nature of his teaching left an indelible mark on Horton's life and art.

The three years Horton spent at the Studio were relatively free of the kinds of frustrations he'd felt at the Pasadena Playhouse. In his New York studies he worked on a wide array of scenes from various genres with a diversity of partners, including *Ah, Wilderness!* with Betty Goddard, a friend of Arthur Hopkins and Pauline Lord, and *The No 'Count Boy* with Perry Wilson, the future wife of Joseph Anthony. Soloviova and Daykarhanova were quite taken with *The No 'Count Boy*, and they asked Horton and Perry to perform it at the final recital, an important event for the students, since many agents, directors, and producers came to evaluate the new crop of actors. After the well-attended recital, an agent from Warner Brothers told Horton the studio planned to produce plays in New York the following year and intimated there would be a role for him.[26]

During the summer of 1936, Horton worked as an usher and barker at a movie house on Forty-second Street, where he took tickets and marched in front of the marquee crying out the names of current movies. He even tried to work a second summer at Martha's Vineyard but found their method of acting so different from what he was learning at the School for the Stage that he longed to return to New York. After only a month in Martha's Vineyard, the excuse he needed came in the form of a phone call from Warner Brothers requesting he return to New York and begin rehearsals for *Swing Your Lady*. This opportunity would be Horton's first real taste of Broadway.

---

[25] Foote, *Genesis*, 42.
[26] Foote, *Beginnings*, 172–73.

When Horton got back to New York, he immediately went to the Warner Brothers office, only to discover that the play already had been in rehearsal for several weeks. He soon found out that in order for the studio to save money, actors cast in the smaller parts were called late in the rehearsal process. Since Horton's character appeared in only one scene, he wasn't called until the day his scene was to be rehearsed. He arrived at the theater not knowing any of the actors and with no knowledge of the play. The assistant stage manager, a man named Ben Edwards, greeted Horton, called him onto the stage, gave him a written copy of the scene, told him where to enter, and described the kind of energy he should bring to the stage. Edwards told him not to move around at all but to simply come on from down stage, go directly to his designated spot, give his speech, and then leave. He also told Horton to sit in the auditorium during the morning's run-through and watch as a stage manager read his part and the other parts that hadn't been previously rehearsed. According to Edwards, that afternoon the entire cast would participate in the run-through. That was all the instruction Horton was given; he didn't have time to memorize his lines or even rehearse before the run-through. Unfortunately, that afternoon when Horton was about to go onstage, he suddenly panicked, much as he had during his first weeks in Pasadena—he simply froze, unable to remember his lines or hear his cues:

> In those days, and I suppose still today, [the actors' union] Equity allows a management to rehearse an actor five days free. If at the end of that period they want you to continue, your contract goes into effect and you go on salary. At the end of the fourth day the stage manager called me aside and said, "You are going to be replaced." I was humiliated. Not only would I have to go back to the studio and tell them I had been fired from a job they wouldn't have wanted me to take in the first place, but I had the regrettable habit of writing extremely optimistic letters to my parents back in Wharton, so eager was I to reassure them that I was about to achieve success and financial security. Now I had to write them and tell them of my failure. It was a difficult letter to write, and I still feel the pain of it as I recall it here.[27]

Swing Your Lady opened ten days later, got terrible reviews, and closed after only two days. But Horton survived his humiliating experience with Warner Brothers, and, during the next two years, he was cast in more roles than ever before. He also performed in several more

---

[27] Foote, *Genesis*, 44.

scenes at the School for the Stage, including George Bernard Shaw's *Candida,* Lynn Riggs's *Cherokee Nights,* and Chekhov's *The Seagull.* He worked hard to develop his skills, and about a month after he lost the part in *Swing Your Lady,* he was cast as a supernumerary in Max Reinhardt's *The Eternal Road,* a dramatic spectacle about the wanderings of the Jewish people throughout history.

Reinhardt, an Austrian-born director who was famous for his eclectic approach to theater and his lavish productions at the Deutsches Theatre in Berlin, had immigrated to New York in the early 1930s to escape Nazi brutality. In 1937, he decided to produce *The Eternal Road* as a response to Adolph Hitler's persecution of the Jews in Europe and had asked Benjamin Zemach, the Jewish director and producer, to choreograph the production. Zemach had begun his search for actors for the show and in the fall began to seek out new talent at the School for the Stage. One day he walked up to Horton and offered him a role, informing him that good actors were needed to work with the dancers in the production. While none of the actors would have lines, they would be essential in establishing the reality of the various Old Testament scenes being dramatized in the show. The pay, Zemach announced, was twenty-five dollars a week. Horton accepted the offer and in mid-October began rehearsals for the show, which opened New Year's Day 1937.

Horton found the rehearsals for *The Eternal Road* quite enjoyable. He, along with the rest of the ensemble, was cast in more than one scene; sometimes he played an Egyptian, and at other times a Hebrew. In all, Horton was in eight scenes, the longest of which concerned the worship of the golden calf by the Israelites in defiance of God's edict against idolatry. "The scene," Horton recalled, "ended in an orgy, with the worshippers writhing in erotic ecstasy."[28]

Three weeks before opening, the ensemble joined the full company at the Manhattan Theatre, and Horton saw for the first time the huge barn of a theater in which the show was to be performed. He also got a look at the large, impressive set created by legendary designer Norman Bel Geddes, heard the haunting music by renowned German composer, Kurt Weill, and recognized from a distance the imposing figure of Max Reinhardt.

The Eternal Road opened as scheduled on New Year's Day, but it received mixed reviews and, much to Horton's dismay, closed four months later. One night that spring, after a performance, Horton met up

---

[28] Foote, *Beginnings,* 176.

with his friend, Rosamond Pinchot, now returned from Hollywood and cast as Bathsheba in the production. They had spoken briefly several times during rehearsals and had planned to work together again at the School for the Stage, but on this night, Rosamond's thoughts were not on scene work. Jed Harris, one of America's most revered directors and producers at the time, was waiting for her just outside the stage door, and after Rosamond briefly introduced the two men, she and Harris walked away into the darkness. Horton, who secretly loved and revered Rosamond, was very disappointed that he wasn't able to spend more time with her that evening. Sadly, he never saw Rosamond again.[29]

In January 1938, Horton was in the office at the School for the Stage when Frances Dietz came in holding a copy of the *New York Times* and looking very distraught. "I have something sad to tell you," she said. "Rosamond Pinchot is dead…Madame is very distressed. It is all so sad."[30] A front-page article announced Pinchot's death—she had committed suicide by carbon monoxide poisoning in the garage of her family's home in Old Brookville, New York. At the time of her death, Pinchot was only thirty-three years old and had been helping arrange the sound effects for Jed Harris's *Our Town* and trying out for work with touring companies. Rosamond's death was a tremendous shock to Horton, but to cope with his feelings of loss, he threw himself into his work with even more fervor.

The year before Pinchot's death, in the summer of 1937, Horton had been hired by the Maverick Theatre in Woodstock, New York, where he was cast in the role of Mio in Maxwell Anderson's *Winterset* and as Mister Mister in Marc Blitzstein's *The Cradle Will Rock*. Fortunately, the company Horton worked with was a very talented group who worked well together. In a letter to his father on Father's Day, he implied he was enjoying the experience a great deal:

> I've just finished pretty active work, for we're now in rehearsal of both the first and second plays. We open on the 23rd and run through [Monday]. *Cradle Will Rock* (2nd show) is done entirely to music. A pianist is playing all the time and there is no scenery. I have to sing a couple of solos—Thank God they're supposed to be funny. It's a pro-labor musical, and ran most of last winter in New York. I'm getting a rest the third week—or rather a semi-rest because we'll be working on the fourth show…. Our director is very nice, and I hear he likes me—which pleases

---

[29] Ibid., 178–79.
[30] Ibid., 179–80.

me very much because there's nothing so inharmonious as working against a director.[31]

After performing at the Maverick Theatre, Horton appeared in two plays by the One-Act Repertory Company: *The Coggerers* by the Irish playwright, Paul Vincent Carroll, in which Horton played Robert Emmet, and *The Red Velvet Goat* by Josephine Niggli, in which he played a sixteen-year-old Mexican boy. The shows opened at the Hudson Theatre with a cast of well-known Broadway actors, but reviews were less than favorable and the production closed after only five performances. Horton admitted that he was heartbroken, but he persevered and began to look for other work.

In 1939, Horton was cast in *Railroads on Parade*, a pageant spectacle created to celebrate the railroads of America at the New York World's Fair. Horton recalled that the show featured horses, wagons, trains, bicycles, cowboys, Indians, and Chinese peasants and that the production proved to be disappointing since the director had never directed before. Furthermore, Horton and the cast were asked to do three shows a day, and most of them were in eight scenes, which meant changing costumes twenty-four times. In the fall, *Railroads on Parade* closed for the season. The only really good thing to emerge from this experience was that Horton met Valerie Bettis, a talented dancer from Texas, who would later play an important role in his life and career.

That same year, Horton was hired by the Theatre Guild for a small part in Ernest Hemingway's *The Fifth Column*, directed by the legendary director of the Group Theatre, Lee Strasburg, and starring Franchot Tone, Lee J. Cobb, Lenore Ulric, and Katherine Locke. The production had a run-through on the stage of the Guild before leaving for New Haven then moving on to Philadelphia. During the run of the show, Lee Strasburg informed the cast that weaknesses in the script would require restaging and a number of rewrites. On Friday night of the second week, Strasburg asked the stage manager to tell Horton he would not be going on to Boston because they were cutting his scene from the play. *The Fifth Column* was not a critical success, and Horton returned to New York, disappointed but much wiser.

At this point, Horton's career as an actor was beginning to show evidence of an expected but unwelcomed pattern. Between acting engagements, he had to find part-time work, usually ushering in a movie

---

[31] Horton Foote to Albert Foote, Sr., 20 June 1937 (Horton Foote Papers).

house, and years later, he admitted that in many ways he expected that
to be the pattern of the rest of his life. What changed that expected
pattern was Horton's association with Mary Hunter and the American
Actors Company, a theater company created to escape the
commercialism of Broadway and promote artistry drawing on authentic
American voices. It was within this company, following an acting
improvisation by Horton, that legendary dancer and choreographer
Agnes De Mille would pose a life-changing question to Horton Foote:
"Did you ever think of writing a play?"[32]

---

[32] Foote, *Beginnings*, 198.

Part Three

Learning to Write

"These are my people, my stories and the plays I want to write, the only ones I know how to write."

—Horton Foote

5

The American Actors Company
1937–44

Mary Hunter, niece of novelist Mary Hunter Austin, founded the American Actors Company (also called the American Actors Theatre) in 1937. Hunter was a student at the School for the Stage when Horton enrolled there in 1936, and over the years they had become close friends, often encouraging each other's artistic endeavors. Hunter was well known in literary and theatrical circles, for example her close friends included Agnes De Mille, Lynn Riggs, Franchot Tone, June Walker, Lee Strasberg, and Katherine Dunham.

Both Horton and Hunter had grown dissatisfied with the commercialism of New York theaters. Hunter wanted to be a director, but since Broadway seldom hired women for such positions, she realized her chances for employment were quite limited. Furthermore, as Horton Foote explained, "We were all at Daykarhanova's being indoctrinated with the ideal of group acting. We were taught, and believed, that Broadway, with its dependence on stars, was ruinous to any real creativity. The Group Theatre was about to disband, but all of us at our studio felt that the group ideal was the correct one and that the failure of the Group Theatre had to do with Broadway economics as much as anything."[1]

That winter, with the encouragement of Andrius Jilinsky, Vera Soloviova, and Tamara Daykarhanova, Mary Hunter began rehearsing a group of actors from the School for the Stage in Clemence Dane's *Wild Decembers*, a play about the Brontës, the nineteenth-century literary family best known for producing such classics as *Jane Eyre* and *Wuthering Heights*. After two months of rehearsal, the play was performed at the Studio with Perry Wilson, Mary Virginia Palmer, and Frances Anderson as the imaginative Brontë sisters and John Forsht as their dissolute brother, Branwell. The production garnered a very positive and encouraging response from the Russians, and the following spring Hunter drew up plans for the creation of a permanent acting troupe, the American Actors

---

[1] Horton Foote, *Genesis of an American Playwright*, ed. Marion Castleberry (Waco TX: Baylor University Press, 2004) 45.

Company, using her friends and colleagues at the School for the Stage. The original members included John Forsht, Joe Anthony, Lonnie Hinkley, Perry Wilson, Betty Goddard, Frances Anderson, Mary Virginia Palmer, Mildred Dunnock, Helen Thompson, Jane Rose, Fanya Zelinskaya, Patricia Coates, Beulah Weil, Lucy Kroll, and of course, Horton Foote.[2]

Hunter's initial plan was to rehearse a play for three months during the summer, and, if the work proved worthy, perform it in New York in the fall. The company rented a house in Croton-on-Hudson that had been built for Raymond Duncan, dancer Isadora Duncan's brother, and featured a large studio space that was perfect for rehearsals and exercise classes. For some reason, which has never been explained, Hunter and the Russians did not select an American play for the company's first production, but rather Euripides's *The Trojan Women*, adapted by Edith Hamilton. The cast consisted of Mary Hunter as Hecuba, Perry Wilson as Cassandra, Frances Anderson as Andromache, Mary Virginia Palmer as Helen of Troy, Joe Anthony as the Captain, and Lonnie Hinkley as Menelaus. Horton and John Forsht were to play soldiers, and the rest of the women were to be the chorus.[3]

Horton remembered that the final run-through of the play at Croton was very moving and the company was convinced they would have great success in New York. However, critics savaged the New York production, staged on 24 January 1938 for its mediocre acting and directing. One reviewer was so bold as to say: "If Helen of Troy had resembled our Helen there would have been no Trojan War."[4] Horton was puzzled and frightened by the harshness of the attacks, and, as he later revealed, "I think now if Mary Hunter hadn't had financial resources (she played Marge in the popular radio series *Easy Aces*), and had not been as young and immature as most of us, it would have been the last of our company."[5] Fortunately, Hunter had an income and was very determined to continue the work she had begun with the ACC.

Mary Hunter realized, after the fact, that choosing *The Trojan Women* as the company's initial offering was a big mistake for such young actors. Then, since the group was named the American Actors Company, she decided from that time on they should produce solely American plays. In 1939, they established their first studio over a garage at 256 West

---

[2] Horton Foote, *Beginnings: A Memoir* (New York: Scribner Press, 2001) 184.
[3] Ibid., 185.
[4] Ibid.
[5] Ibid.

Sixty-ninth Street, built a small stage, installed platforms for seating which accommodated an audience of forty, and began rehearsing plays by established American writers whose works seemed to represent characteristic aspects of American life.

That same year, the ACC presented Lynn Riggs's *Sump'n Like Wings* and four short plays by E.P. Conkle and Paul Green. In 1940, they produced Green's *Shroud My Body Down*, and several other short plays, including Dorothy Thomas's *Duet*, John Martin's *Indiana Sketches*, and Conkle's *Madge* and *Minnie Field*, in which Horton, Joe Anthony, and John Forsht were cast. The troupe also began rehearsing *American Legend*, a folk venue that blended folklore, dance, and music, and featured group improvisations and the talents of choreographers Agnes De Mille, Katherine Dunham, and Jerome Robbins, with whom Horton became a close friend.

During rehearsals for *American Legend*, director Mary Hunter encouraged the actors to draw on their cultural heritage—especially the idioms and personalities of their diverse regions—and to pool their experiences to arrive at a meaning of "American." Hunter explained, "since the members of the company represented almost a regional survey of the U.S., the sources were rich and varied."[6] The cast was asked to mine their memories and evoke the characters they found there, improvising dialogues between them. They wrote scenes and monologues based on real situations, dramatizing but not fabricating. The goal was realism, not entertainment.

It was in these sessions—searching for authentic American voices and dramatic material—that Horton Foote began his return to Wharton, as actor and then as writer. Initially, he performed an improvisation based on his family's experiences during a Texas Gulf hurricane, a scene that instantly gained the approval of Agnes De Mille. After his performance, De Mille walked up to Horton and casually asked, "You seem to be in touch with some interesting theatrical material. Did you ever think of writing a play?" Of course, he had not, but as her suggestion took root, he began to write down his memories of Texas. "I got in touch with material that was...for lack of a better word, regional material," Horton recalled. "I really believe this material chose me more than I chose it...it is amazing to me how many of these themes keep repeating themselves, or attitudes, or approaches to character. I don't know if I ever

---

[6] Mary Hunter, Foreword, *Only the Heart* (New York: Dramatists Play Service, 1944) 5.

consciously worked on this, but I think I worked at whatever instincts I had matured, and I hope they got better and stronger."[7] Horton's imagination, which had never completely abandoned Wharton, was home again.

Horton called his first play *Wharton Dance,* and in the fall of 1940, the American Actors Company staged the piece along with one-acts by Paul Green and Thornton Wilder. Set in Wharton, Texas, on a Saturday night, the play depicts the tender relationships within a group of teenagers attending a community dance. While trying to protect the reputation of two friends, Bill and Lyda Belle, who defy their parents' wishes by dating each other, the youths are made privy to the secret conversations of their elders, whose lives have grown cold and lonely. As the orchestra plays popular music, like "Careless Love," the teenagers disregard their parents' wishes and experiment with alcohol and cigarettes, while dancing and scrutinizing everyone—both young and old—who enters the dance hall. Among the rich array of characters that appears are a woman whose husband has recently died, boys who drink whiskey and are sexually aggressive, a married Baptist Sunday school teacher who drinks and flirts, a judgmental old woman who characterizes the stringent religious lifestyle of the Methodist Epworth League, and a young man who confesses to his date that he is in love with another girl and secretly engaged to her. The drama intensifies as Jane, one of the teenagers at the dance, becomes frustrated over having to wait so long for Bill and Lyda Belle to arrive. When the couple finally shows up, however, the confusion and frustration of the night is relieved as the friends finally enter the dance hall, and Bill and Lyda Belle continue their secret rendezvous. As with many of Horton's plays, *Wharton Dance* contains a hint of the mysterious, as the teenagers climb the stairs to the dance hall, declaring, "What a night!" and begin to dance to the sounds of the blues music coming from the orchestra.[8] Nothing has really changed in Wharton, but the turbulence that lies beneath the calm exterior of the town has been exposed.

Horton admitted that *Wharton Dance* was largely reportage, even his use of real names, which he mistakenly thought honored his home place:

---

[7] Gary Edgerton, "A Visit to the Imaginary Landscape of Harrison, Texas: Sketching the Film Career of Horton Foote," *Literature/Film Quarterly* 12 (Winter 1989): 2–12.

[8] Horton Foote, *Wharton Dance,* (MS in Horton Foote Papers). Page references to *Wharton Dance* in the text refer to this manuscript.

"My memory of it is that it too was very improvisational in form, based on a real situation, and used the names of the boys and girls in what was known in high school as 'our crowd.'"[9] *Wharton Dance* is unquestionably the work of a beginning playwright, but already Horton was revealing his command of the simple, sparse language and languid atmosphere of a small Texas town, the dreams and frustrations of young people, and the tension between the innocence of youth and the fallen world of their parents. Over the next four years at the American Actors Company, Horton would continue to search for his own style and his unique personal voice within the regional tradition identified by Mary Hunter and Agnes De Mille.

Robert Coleman, a drama critic for the *New York Mirror,* came to see the production of *Wharton Dance* and wrote favorably of the evening, particularly of Horton's play and acting. Horton recalled: "Noel Coward acting in his own plays was the vogue then. Because of Coleman's review, I was interviewed by another reporter who wrote about my potential as a Texas Noel Coward. That was far from my mind, but I did want to act and I'm sure I thought that one way to get good parts was to write them for myself."[10] Suddenly, Horton found himself being hailed as a promising new playwright, even though he knew nothing about writing plays. He had not even admitted to himself that he wanted to be a writer, but when Mary Hunter requested that he write a three-act play, he accepted the challenge. Later, he revealed that he gradually began to feel a certain security about accomplishing the task before him, a security he had never felt as an actor.

In the winter of 1940, Horton boarded a bus in New York and headed for Wharton to write a new play. When he arrived in Texas, he discovered a number of changes in his hometown. For one, his Grandmother Brooks was living permanently in Houston, while renting out her house in Wharton, and Horton recalled, "it seemed strange not to be able to wander into her yard and house anytime day or night that I wanted."[11] Change had come, too, to his Grandmother Cleveland, who had recently been diagnosed with a terminal illness. The news of her declining health was unsettling to Horton, as was the realization that his uncles—Tom, Billy, and Speed—had become wastrels and hopeless derelicts. His brothers—John and Tom had also changed; they were no longer little

---

[9] Foote, *Genesis,* 46.
[10] Ibid.
[11] Ibid., 47.

boys, but young men, with the same questions about their futures he had faced six years earlier. Horton's brother Tom Brooks had enrolled in the University of Iowa to study acting, with hopes of joining his older brother in New York after graduation.

Responding to the familial changes that confronted him that winter, Horton wrote *Texas Town*, which the American Actors Company performed at the Humphrey-Weidman Theatre in New York on 29 April 1941.[12] Set in a small-town drugstore, *Texas Town* takes place during the Depression, on a day in which Pappy O'Daniel (the governor of Texas) is scheduled to make a campaign appearance in the town of Richmond. The play tells the story of two friends, Maner—proprietor of the local drug store—and Ray Case, both of whom are in love with an attractive girl named Carrie, who has been dating Maner. The stable, unadventurous Maner wants to stay put in his hometown, marry Carrie, and lead a conventional life. Carrie is torn between her mother's insistence she marry Maner, who will give her financial security and a respected position in town, and her deep feelings for Ray, her former boyfriend.

Ray, who has been victimized by a manipulative mother and mean-spirited brother, finds small-town life stifling and desperately wants to leave, hopefully with Carrie, to work with an oil crew. Ray, who is convinced that he will never find happiness if he stays in Richmond, confesses his feelings to his surrogate father Doc, a local physician with a fondness for whiskey. "I sit and listen to trains passing through the night," Ray says, and "I think about my Pa. We used to lie awake at night and listen. Sometimes he'd talk about the places he'd been—places he was gonna take me to. But he never did" (11).

With Doc's gentle coaxing, Ray finds the courage to break free from his mother's clutches and to turn his back on the town he despises. But before he can fully escape, his mother anticipates his flight and sets out to sabotage his plan. She sends the preacher to remind Ray of his responsibilities to the family. Then Tucker, Ray's brother, announces that their mother has driven off the oil man who intended to hire Ray. Fannie Belle, an unhappily married woman, eventually helps Carrie choose between going with Ray or staying in Richmond. "Don't ever do it," Fannie Belle says. "It isn't worth it. Die an old maid, but don't marry a man you don't love…and stay in a small town" (23). At that point, Carrie realizes the depth of her love for Ray and breaks off her engagement to

---

[12] Horton Foote, *Texas Town*, (MS in Foote Papers). All page references to *Texas Town* in the text cite this typescript.

Maner. After a rumor spreads around town that Ray was seen on the highway leaving town, Mrs. Case accuses the Doctor of poisoning Ray's mind against her and then pleads with Maner that her son must stay to reclaim the lost family land that was stolen from them.

Like Horton's own ancestors, the Case family had once been prominent in the town, and Ray's mother clings desperately to the fantasy that Ray can restore the family to its proper place in the community. In a scene anticipating one between Carrie Watts and her son Ludie in *The Trip to Bountiful*, Ray's mother remembers the large white house of her youth, with servants in the hallways, and its big front lawn covered with trees. Ray, however, sees only the charred foundation where the house once stood, the land gone to waste, and the weeds growing everywhere. Their conflict is age-old: one generation's need to hold on to the past versus the next generation's desire to break free.

When news comes that Ray has been killed in an automobile accident, Carrie and Maner are left to deal with their loss; they do so with courage and dignity. In the final scene, Carrie declares that Ray "was trying to show me freedom," which, if "right and true…can be found anywhere" (122), but in the final analysis there is no certainty that she and Maner can ever build a life together.

Horton Foote's accurate portrayal of a small town in *Texas Town* was acknowledged in several positive reviews. In his *New York Times* review of the play, Brooks Atkinson noted its authenticity:

> If *Texas Town* does not derive from Mr. Foote's personal experiences and observations, he is remarkably inventive. For none of the parts is stock theater, except perhaps the part he plays himself without much talent and with no originality. And it is impossible not to believe absolutely in the reality of his characters. The melancholy doctor who drinks in the back room, the hearty judge and his cronies, the bored wife who is looking for excitement, the chattering girls, the bumptious boys, the sharp edges of bad feeling that cut through the neighborhood leisure, the quick impulses of emotion, the sense of drifting without purpose or direction—these are truths of small town life that Mr. Foote has not invented…. Mr. Foote's quiet play is an able evocation of a part of life in America, and most of the acting is interesting and thoughtful.[13]

Atkinson also appreciated the fact a play so simply written could give a real and languid impression of a town changing in relation to the

---

[13] Brooks Atkinson, "American Actors Company Produces Horton Foote's 'Texas Town' on Sixteenth Street," *New York Times*, 30 April 1941.

world. *Texas Town* explored themes that would recur throughout Horton Foote's work for the next seventy years: a sense of the past, the inevitability of change, the universal longing for love and companionship, and the struggle to maintain one's dignity in the face of suffering and loss. The play's small-town setting, its array of simple but spiritually bankrupt people, and its characters' need for a sense of order and stability in their lives, are chief elements in all of Horton Foote's plays.

Besides prompting the attendance of Brooks Atkinson, Lee and Paula Strasberg, and Clifford Odets—who were impressed with the pro-duction—*Texas Town* also attracted the attention of Edward Choate, a representative of the Shubert brothers, dominant theatrical managers and producers in commercial theater during the first half of the twentieth century. Choate took an option on the play for a possible Broadway production. Horton was elated about signing the contract, even though Agnes De Mille warned him of the Shubert's devious practices. Later, when Choate began to give him a pep talk about the monetary rewards of Broadway theater and about how best to reach a vast audience, Horton realized that he had made a mistake in signing the contract. In order to meet Shubert standards, Choate explained, *Texas Town* would have to be greatly changed. The main change the Shuberts wanted was a different ending. In the original draft of *Texas Town*, Horton had Ray's character leave town, hitchhiking his way to Houston. At the end of the play, word comes from offstage that he has been killed in an automobile accident. Though Horton was satisfied with the original ending, he was not against trying a different one if it improved the play; so, over the next few weeks he penned two or three different drafts, also taking into account some other changes Choate suggested. Later Horton admitted that at the time he was "in awe of that world of commercial power and nodded my head as if I agreed with all he was saying. In my heart, I didn't, and when later I tried to execute a few changes I realized that was no road for me to travel as a writer."[14] As little as Horton understood then about writing, he instinctively knew he could never resort to formulas, nor could he fashion his work to the tastes of a producer, director, or audience. He was determined to write about what he knew best, with his own sense of truth, and in his own distinctive style.

---

[14] Foote, *Genesis*, 52.

After *Texas Town* closed, *American Legend* moved into the Humphrey-Weidman Studio Theatre for the final weeks of the season, and in the summer of 1941 the American Actors Company was invited to perform at the Montowese Playhouse in Branford, Connecticut. There, the group offered eight plays, including Lynn Riggs's *Green Grow the Lilacs*; James Thurber and Elliot Nugent's *The Male Animal*; and S.N. Behrman's *Brief Moment*.

After he performed the plays, Horton's desire to act left him as suddenly as it had appeared all those years before. "I had become obsessed now with writing and had begun working on a new play for the company," he admitted.[15]

In the fall of 1941, on the eve of America's involvement in World War II, Horton completed four one-act plays, *Night After Night, Celebration, The Girls*, and *Behold, A Cry*. Horton and Mary Hunter had agreed the plays would be the American Actors Company's next production, and they made plans to stage them shortly after the New Year. Since the production required four sets and a cast of eighteen, rehearsals would need to begin before Christmas; so Horton, Mary Hunter, Joseph Anthony, and Jane Rose (who was to serve as a fourth director) met in Mary's apartment on December 7 to discuss final casting and rehearsal schedules. They were sitting in the kitchen drinking coffee that morning when they heard on the radio that the Japanese had attacked the US naval base at Pearl Harbor. They all sat stunned and silent for a while, waiting for word from President Roosevelt, feeling certain the country would be involved in the war within a matter of hours. But they didn't let the threat of war deter them. After a lengthy discussion, they decided to continue with their production as planned, though the following day, as they had suspected, the US declared war against Japan. Nonetheless, Joseph Anthony began building the sets, and the company went into rehearsals a few days later. In January 1942, with US involvement in the war well underway, the American Actors Company presented Horton Foote's four plays at the Humphrey-Weidman Studio Theatre under the title *Out of My House*.[16]

In these plays, for the first time, Horton showed himself to be a dramatist of social protest in the vein of Clifford Odets. He also experimented with dramatic structure, overlapping events, and recurring characters, a

---

[15] Foote, *Beginnings*, 229.

[16] Horton Foote, *Out of My House*, (MS in Horton Foote Papers). Page references to *Out of My House* in the text cite this manuscript.

style, which anticipates *The Orphans' Home Cycle*. The initial play, *Night After Night* is concerned with the disintegration of a small Texas town as young people are forced to deal with cultural assimilation and a changing class system that threatens their lives and the peacefulness of their community. Set in Tell Miller's all-night restaurant during the 1930s, it opens with a glimpse of the characters, whose stories are revealed in more detail in the later one-acts. Among them are Minnie and Syd Bartell, a married couple who spend their nights drinking and blaming each other for their wasted lives; Ellen Belle Croy, an upper-class teenage snob who finds pleasure in insulting less fortunate people; Sonny and Babe Mavis, the children of a broken-down aristocratic family who have returned home from school to visit Red, their alcoholic sister, and Jack Weems, a sympathetic but confused middle-class youth who finds escape from the poverty, bitterness, and bigotry of his family and hometown in the local taverns.

The central character of *Night After Night* is Clara, a strong and compassionate young woman of German ancestry who is torn between returning home to her family, where she will spend her life as a field laborer, or continuing to work as a waitress at Tell Miller's restaurant, where she is forced to cope with insults and cultural prejudices. Tom Sloane, one of the young men in the bar, entices Clara to dance so the other youngsters can make fun of her, but Jack Weems, in a fit of anger, grabs a knife, starts at Tom, and must finally be restrained by Hog Jaw, a black man.

When Clara's brother Louie shows up to announce that her father wants her back home and reminds her the Bohemians are taking control of her hometown, acquiring more money and more land, Clara proclaims she will never go back to chopping cotton, feeding hogs, or hoeing corn: "I broke my back standing in the hot sun. Always behind in school. I never learned nothing because I couldn't start till after cotton was cut. I did it. Long as I could stand it...That's not enough...Working all year so's you can buy a tractor or a pig or a cow...That's not what I want" (10). More than anything else, Clara dreams that one of her truck driver customers will marry her and rescue her from her lonely existence. Whether her dream comes true or not is never answered. Jack Weems implores Clara to return to her people, articulating the play's central theme when he says: "Get out of this stinking hole. Leave these rotten bastards to their own death. You Bohunks are gonna finish us off, you're strong, make it quick. Help them to kill us. We're rotten and we're helping you by fighting amongst ourselves. We need you to finish it...make it quick" (18). The theme of the second play *Celebration* is introduced as Hog Jaw announces Emancipation Day for blacks in Texas, and he, Tell Miller, and Jack Weems speak of Red Mavis as "one wild white woman" (1). The final image of the play shows Clara peering out the window, waiting for her lover to rescue her, and attending to the customers who drink their lives away.

More images of moral and social decay appear in *Celebration*, the second play in *Out of My House*. After a year at college, Sonny and Babe Mavis have returned home to a party thrown by their older sister, Red. As the play opens, the siblings are drinking and reminiscing over Red's previous acts of violence, their shallow "celebration" contrasting with the jubilance of the freed slaves. The celebration soon turns tragic when Ellen Croy, a neighborhood snob, reveals that Red's mother, a shadowy figure whom her daughter describes as "a hideous coward" with "her face all hard from praying," (8) has ostracized Red from the family because of her drinking problem. The mother feels Red's image as a violent and dangerous woman does not speak well of her aristocratic heritage; but as Red understands it, her alcoholism is merely a symptom of the changes that threaten her family's existence: "Grandpa was an aristocrat. He was meant to rule. We were born different. But all around us, they had sprung to bind you. We're all that's left of the old. Grandpa told me that. But Mama, whispering her fears and her poisons, tried to make us forget it" (8). For years, Red has refused to listen to her mother's pleas to accept the family's fate, though she knows her Grandpa was himself a drunken outcast. Red has become hard, bitter, and spiteful; however, on this night, she will come to know the tragic consequence of her misplaced pride.

Red believes the family's future depends on Sonny's becoming a successful lawyer and reestablishing the family's aristocratic position in the community. Even though Sonny knows he will never accomplish Red's goal, he enjoys her liquor and the violent stories she tells about her encounters with common people.

Ellen Belle Croy and her boyfriend, Tom, soon arrive and begin to question the social status of the once proud Mavis family. The atmosphere turns violent when Ellen Belle declares that the town considers Sonny a joke and Red and Babe ugly freaks. Even though Red knows that her brother suffers from a heart condition that requires limiting his alcohol consumption, she becomes so enraged that she forces

Sonny to drink a bottle of whiskey to prove his manliness. Sadly, the final image of the play is that of Sonny slumped in his chair, dead from too much drinking.

In the next interlude, back at Miller's restaurant, Tell, Jack, and Hog Jaw discuss Sonny's funeral and mention that Sue Anthony is back in town because her brother Elmo has married Lillie Belle, a woman she strongly dislikes, without telling his family. This brief scene introduces the next play, *The Girls*, one of the funniest works in the Foote canon.

While the first two plays depict a number of changes in Texas society during Foote's childhood, along with the tragic effects of clinging to aristocratic family traditions, *The Girls* provides a humorous glimpse at familial relationships ruined by obsessive greed. It opens with Idella the maid preparing two spinster sisters, Nora and Sue Anthony, for a visit with their soon-to-be sister-in-law, Lillie Belle, and the controlling Aunt Lizzie. Most of the action involves keeping the high-strung Nora away from the gin and the sisters arguing that the family is wasting their lives waiting to inherit Lizzie's money—a theme echoed in *Expectant Relations* and *Dividing the Estate*. Although the two sisters actually detest their aunt, Nora and Sue have spent more than thirty years of their lives trying to ensure an inheritance from her. They feign love and loyalty while secretly hoping for Aunt Lizzie's death and are anxious over their aunt's attachment to Cousin Loula and the countrified ways of Lillie Belle. Nora and Sue's dreams come to naught when Lillie Belle and Loula, in a passion of religious fervor, tell the sisters they should confess their deceit and ask Aunt Lizzie's forgiveness. When they do, Aunt Lizzie, shocked and hurt by their confession, does not forgive them and vows never to speak to them again. Ironically, their disinheritance seems to free the women from the stress and pretense with which they have lived for many years. As the play concludes, Sue responds that this is their Emancipation Day and Nora starts drinking heavily, while Idella begins looking for a way the women can survive their newfound poverty. *The Girls* is not one of Foote's better works, but it does show his ability, early in his career, to create memorable characters with comic dialogue. Foote's fascination with the comedy of family inheritance, in which characters conspire to swindle rich relatives out of their estates, will become a permanent plot device in Foote's repertoire, reappearing in works such as *Expectant Relations* and *Dividing the Estate*.

In the fourth play, *Behold, a Cry*, Foote again explores the theme of family disintegration as it relates to the stresses of societal changes. Like

Texas Town, the play is based on family legend and centers on two brothers, loosely patterned after the playwright's uncles. The play opens with Mrs. Weems, her son Ford, and her father Robedaux discussing the social evils that have afflicted their town and left them destitute. (Mr. Robedaux had lost his business to Mr. Peters, a dishonest businessman who swindled Robedaux out of his shop.) Because Ford is tired of his grandfather's bitterness and constant harangues about society's failings, he asserts himself and proclaims his intention of securing a better life. His plan includes marrying his boss's daughter, moving to a nicer home, and extricating himself from his relationship with his alcoholic brother Jack. When Jack learns of Ford's plan, he is deeply hurt but agrees to leave the family rather than wreck their lives, as Ford had suggested his presence would do. However, Ford's anger explodes as he verbally assaults Jack's character and manhood. In response, Jack harshly condemns Ford as a hypocritical, arrogant bastard who cares for nothing or no one except himself. Mrs. Weems recognizes the truth of Jack's charges; however, she chooses to align herself with Ford. Jack is left grieving the loss of his family and questioning the value of his own life. In the end, he turns to Grandpa Robedaux for consolation and who offers him an impassioned speech, pleading for world harmony and brotherly love.

In the play's final scene, influenced by Clifford Odets's *Awake and Sing*, Foote depicts a grandfather who attacks economic oppression and indicts the capitalist system. Banished from the store he operated for fifty years by the heartless banker Peters, old man Robedaux rails against the unjust changes that have taken place in Texas. Ironically, people who came from all over the South to escape aristocratic domination have ended up bringing their own oppressive aristocracy with them. After a while, the newcomers, who were good men at first, are "afraid to think of other men, afraid to be kind" (20). Their greed has changed them, causing them to turn their one-time paradise into a living hell. Now, as Robedaux insists, they must wake up and "see things as they are" in order to right their wrongs and build a new utopia in Texas. The play ends with Jack, remembering those like himself who have lost faith in a better life, resolved to carry his grandfather's protest to Ted Miller's bar. Quietly approving, Robedaux says, "From my house it has begun and there's no stopping it" (21). Brooks Atkinson proclaimed this final scene the "best writing" of Foote's career, a "vibrant, glowing, and bitterly realistic" moment of theater.[17]

Even though *Out of My House* shows the playwright struggling with problems of plot development and dramatic structure, once again the plays mine Horton Foote's Wharton history for society's unfortunates, whom he treats with compassion and insight. These fully developed character types will later dominate Foote's dramatic landscape—youths who are physically and emotionally orphaned, young men who are haunted by feelings of futility and hopelessness, adults who are dislocated and forlorn, and women who are strong willed and heroic or victimized by their family and society. Emerging, too, is his talent for creating accurate and thought-provoking dialogue, for interpreting the darker aspects of family life, and for depicting the tragic consequences of alcoholism, death, racism, and greed. Taken together, the four plays return to themes Foote had always found in Wharton: a sense of place, the inevitability of change, and the resilience of the human spirit. Perhaps Mary Hunter best explains the real strength of *Out of My House* in a program note she wrote for the play:

> It does not seem that our kind of theatre should serve as the medium for intellectual analysis or strive to present economic schemes; but rather that it should fuse elements of flesh and blood experience and try through emotional transfer to open the audience's own understanding. The South has been called the nation's leading economic and cultural problem. This is a fact that we are in danger of forgetting under the fierce pressure of war. But we should be aware of it as a vital sector on that other front we must defend if democracy is to be worth the total war effort.[18]

Among the players cast for the production of *Out of My House* was Tom Brooks Foote, who had followed his older brother to New York in order to pursue an acting career. He and Horton were rooming together in a rented bedroom of the AAC's brownstone on Fifty-second Street, and through their shared experience, they had grown closer than they had ever been. In addition to being cast as Tom Sloane in *Out of My House*, Tom was studying acting with Andrius Jilinsky and had played the lead role in Lynn Riggs's *The Big Lake*. The young actor seemed destined for success. Then in the spring of 1942, the day before he was to sign a studio contract with Warner Brothers, Tom received a notice from his draft board to appear for a physical. He passed the exam and a

---

[17] Foote, *Beginnings*, 233.
[18] Hunter, 6–7.

month later left for training camp. Horton fully expected to be drafted as well, so he sold everything he owned and turned over the rough draft of a new play to a friend for safekeeping. Horton's mother sent a letter assuring him all would be well with both her sons, but her confidence would be short-lived.

Two weeks later, Horton and Joe Anthony received their draft notices and went for their physicals together. When the exam was over, Joe was accepted into the military, but Horton was rejected because of a hernia, which he'd known nothing about. This news was disappointing to Horton, since for a month he had been preparing himself to go wherever the US Army might send him. He had gotten letters from his brother and other friends describing the particulars of military service, and he had actually been looking forward to being drafted. The rejection left him feeling lost and totally disoriented.[19]

After leaving the induction center, Horton immediately called Mary Hunter, who counseled him to get back to writing as soon as possible. Mary gave Horton enough money to tide him over, and he quickly found a job as an elevator operator in a Park Avenue apartment, working from six in the evening until six in the morning. Since all the tenants were usually asleep by midnight, Horton wrote without interruption from twelve to six and by late summer of 1942, he had completed a new three-act play he called *Mamie Borden*. He submitted the play to Mary Hunter that fall.[20]

Hunter was very enthusiastic about producing the play and quickly cast it with Jeanne Tufts, Freeman Hammond, Constance Dowling, Jacqueline Andre, Richard Hart, and the Hollywood actress Hilda Vaughn. After Vaughn read the piece, she agreed to take on the part but wanted the title of the play changed because she felt that *Mamie Borden* would be confused with Lizzie Borden, the Massachusetts spinster who, in 1892, was tried and acquitted of killing her father and stepmother with an axe. Vaughn suggested the title, *Only the Heart,* a phrase from a Heinrich Heine poem. Horton thought Vaughn's suggestion was much too flowery and had nothing to do with the play, but since he could think of nothing better at the time and wanted her for the part, he finally agreed to her suggestion.

First produced at the Provincetown Playhouse in December 1942, *Only the Heart* is a realistic domestic drama that explores both specific

---

[19] Foote, *Beginnings,* 234–35.
[20] Ibid., 235.

concerns of the era in which it was written and the more universal theme of family destruction.[21] The action takes place in September 1921 in the small Gulf Coast town of Richmond, Texas, a prosperous community where the discontent of the war years has been replaced by a new order that values money and professional success. The action of the play centers on Mamie Borden, a charming and manipulative businesswoman whose obsessive drive for affluence and whose attempts to manipulate her family into positions of dependency lead to her own tragic downfall. Mamie is a type of woman generic to America's domestic life in the 1920s, and many of her more admirable qualities resemble those of the playwright's own Grandmother Brooks. Mary Hunter said her main concern in directing the role of Mamie Borden was to discover the real and essential qualities of the character and to emphasize those rather than focus on events. Mamie's most prolific character flaw is her deep need to control and manipulate others in such a way that they grow to depend on her, thus giving Mamie power and security rather than loving relationships. Responsible for the upbringing of her sisters after their mother's death and after their father's rejection of his role as familial guardian, Mamie admits she made many mistakes as a surrogate parent. For example, she forbade her sister India's marriage to Jack Turner, a kind but reckless young man, because Mamie felt his habits were not steady enough. India's rejection led to Jack becoming the town drunk. Mamie also ruins her own marriage by demanding her husband meet her unattainable standards for living, thus motivating him to take a Bohemian mistress. As a result, Mamie turns to work as a sedative to relieve her pain and adopts the philosophy that "as long as a person has work to do, you can get by…Get busy…then nothing can hurt you for long"(71). Mamie also manipulates her daughter Julia, forbidding her to attend college and persuading her to marry Albert Price, a young man whom Mamie feels she can control. Julia, caught between her desire to please her mother and her need to make a life for herself, relinquishes her feelings for Les Roberts, a young man she cares deeply about, and obeys her mother's wishes by marrying Albert. Although Mamie's authority over the family is now complete, problems begin to emerge. In time, Julia grows to love Albert, but she feels lonely and isolated because he is completely absorbed in his work as Mamie's business partner. In their obsession with finding oil on their land, Mamie and Albert fail to

---

[21] Horton Foote, *Only the Heart* (New York: Dramatists Play Service 1944). Page references in the text cite this publication.

notice how restless Julia is becoming or that she has taken to riding around town with Les, an act which arouses gossip all around Richmond.

The character of Julia, who owes much of her believability to the playwright's own mother, reveals Foote's sensitivity to the struggles of young women who are reared in a strict environment. When Julia faces the possible ruin of her marriage, she is forced to choose between her mother's desires and her own priorities. She chooses to save her marriage and confronts her mother with these haunting words: "Ever since I can remember I felt there was something wrong between us, about us. It frightened me. I felt strange and unnatural...Albert and I could never get along in this house, because every time he came near me, I could feel your fear. Your fear of anything warm and loving...That's why I'm leaving. I know now. That's what's driving me away" (70). Julia's announcement provokes Mamie to express her true feelings of hurt and loss. She angrily threatens to disinherit Julia and tries to persuade Albert to divorce her but Albert realizes the strength and truth behind Julia's pronouncement and follows his wife to Houston to begin a new life, free from Mamie's control. In the end, Mamie is left to face her secret fear—a bitter loneliness against which her only weapon, compulsive work, will surely fail.

Only the Heart is much better developed than the one-acts that comprise *Out of My House*. Family relationships remain the playwright's central focus, but in the later work, Horton takes pains to show us a more contained version of familial life. In *Only the Heart,* unlike the earlier plays, which show family members interacting with the community, the Borden family is cut off from the outside world and turned in upon itself. All the action takes place in the Borden home, and the family is small, with two parents, two children, and an aunt who, like Horton's black characters, serves as the source of family wisdom. Not only is the family isolated from the outside world, but isolation is also the key to their relationships with one another. They seldom genuinely communicate; rather, they are confused and reticent about expressing their true emotions. Mamie's inability to overcome her fearful past and her mistaken belief that survival depends on not letting people get close enough to hurt you is the real source of the family's failure. For her, the family is no longer a viable source of tenderness, love, and affection, but rather a battlefield where recurring quarrels are endlessly fought. Her tragedy is that she has become so conditioned by her past that she no longer knows how to be a nurturing sister, wife, or mother. Like her, all the Bordens are searching for love, trust, understanding, and security; but for each of them, fulfillment of such needs must come from outside the home.

In *Only the Heart* Horton Foote explored a situation that would later reappear in many of his plays—the flight of a courageous young woman to escape her filial bondage in order to retain her dignity, find personal identity, and achieve human potential. From the memory of his own mother and grandmother, Horton also proved his ability to create female characters that possess admirable virtues that make them believable and memorable: courage, endurance, and resolution. In the final analysis, Horton does not blame Mamie for her failure; after all, through no fault of her own she was forced to assume a man's duties and a man's role. Her inner sickness may well have been irreversible. What seems more appropriate is that Horton celebrates Julia's defiance and the spirit with which she strikes out on her own. As in real life, there is no guarantee at the play's end that Julia's life or the lives of any of these characters will improve, that Julia and Albert's marriage will survive the strains of a difficult beginning, or that Mamie can withstand the pain of losing her children, or, finally, expose her need to be loved. They must all face their fears and learn to cope with the indignities and heartaches of the human experience.

Only the Heart, Horton Foote's most mature work of the early 1940s, is a powerful indictment of parental manipulation and personal greed, but the themes central to the play are universal. The play considers not just one Wharton/Richmond family; it depicts the consequences of mankind's alienation in a materialistic post-war world. The tragedy of Mamie Borden is also the tragedy of many people following the war who, like her, believe, "there's gonna be more happy people in this country than was ever known before. Jobs for everyone...wages higher than was ever known before...Every paper you pick up says everyone's gonna be happy...Rich and happy" (32). Horton clearly demonstrates that affluence—when proclaimed as a virtue—leaves one disconnected, not only from family, but also from humanity as a whole. As Mary Hunter clarified, Horton Foote understood that life's greatest drama is the "deep fear of the give-and-take of love and the closeness of healthy personal relationships" aggravated by materialism and greed.[22] At this point in his career, Horton Foote's regional stories were becoming more

---

[22] Hunter, 7.

personal and were gaining universal resonance, a texture he would briefly abandon but return to in the 1950s.

Only the Heart was well received when it premiered at the Provincetown Playhouse. It garnered favorable reviews from several New York critics who applauded the production as an interesting and skillfully written treatment of the ancient theme of the dominating mother. The play also drew the attention of Luther Green, a major Broadway producer, who was taken by the play and wanted to stage it on Broadway with Pauline Lord in the role of Mamie. Green had brought the actress to see the play and wanted Horton to meet her. Horton was very excited about the possibility of working with Pauline Lord. Since arriving in New York, he had seen every play she had appeared in, and he was convinced she was America's greatest actress. For several days, Horton practiced what he would say to Miss Lord when he first met her, but things did not work out quite as he had planned. Foote remembered that Miss Lord spoke highly of his talent and his play but admitted that after much consideration she felt the part was just not right for her. Horton was devastated and wanted to find the words and wisdom to change her mind, but the more she explained her feelings the more he knew the actress was right.[23] Much to his dismay, Pauline Lord did not appear in *Only the Heart* or in any of his other plays. She died only a few years later at the age of sixty in Alamogordo, New Mexico, from complications following an automobile accident.

Despite its successful run at the Provincetown Playhouse, there were no producers willing to move *Only the Heart* to Broadway without a star to perform the role of Mamie. After Pauline Lord turned down the role, Luther Green's interest in the play waned and no one seemed to have any ideas about the right actress for the role. Then, almost a year later, Horton received a note asking him to lunch from a French producer, Jacques Therie, who called himself the George Kauffman of Paris. Therie told Horton he admired his work and wanted to stage *Only the Heart*, but he felt the play could be profitable on Broadway only if it were rewritten. He persuaded Horton to accompany him to Hollywood in the spring of 1944 to do rewrites on the play. From their earliest conversations, Horton felt that the changes Therie wanted were not going to be improvements, but the producer kept telling him that once he made the alterations to the script he would get the renowned actress Dorothy Gish to read the play. After several weeks, Horton finally produced a version that he and the

---

[23] Foote, *Genesis*, 55.

Frenchman agreed upon, though Horton was secretly displeased with the final result. Foote would later say, "Whatever raw power it originally had was diluted."[24] A short time later, Dorothy Gish read the play and after only a couple of days she called to say that she had no interest in playing the role of Mamie. Then, when Horton discovered that Therie could not raise the money for a Broadway production of *Only the Heart* as he had promised, the playwright returned to New York.

Arriving back in the city, Horton immediately showed the revised play to Mary Hunter and Helen Thompson, a former member of the Group Theatre and producer of *Only the Heart* for the Provincetown Playhouse, who suggested that he speak to Stella Adler about playing the role of Mamie. Unfortunately, like Pauline Lord, Adler said she liked the play but didn't feel the part was right for her. At this point, Horton had nearly given up hope that he would ever find the right actress to play the part of Mamie when, as fate would have it, Helen Thompson contacted him to say she had found all the backing needed for a Broadway production. She had raised about eighteen thousand dollars, which was more than sufficient to stage a play that had originally been mounted for less than three thousand dollars.[25]

The revised version of *Only the Heart* finally went into rehearsals in January 1944 with Mary Hunter as director and a cast that featured June Walker as Mamie. Walker, who had starred in *The Farmer Takes a Wife* with Henry Fonda and in *Green Grow the Lilacs* with Franchot Tone, was joined by Mildred Dunnock as her sister India, Eleanor Anton as Julia, Will Hare as Albert, and Maurice Wells as Mamie's husband, Mr. Borden.

Halfway through rehearsals, Horton received word that his brother Tom Brooks was missing in action over Germany. Since Tom's induction, Horton had corresponded regularly with his brother, keeping him abreast of the activities of his friends and sending him accounts of his theater experiences in New York. Tom answered by saying he had been assigned to a Flying Fortress as a radio-gunner and that he had traveled to Casablanca, Tunis, Sicily, and Naples. On December 9 he wrote this letter from a base in Italy:

---

[24] Horton Foote, interview with Marion Castleberry, 8 November 1988, Galveston, Texas.

[25] Foote, *Genesis*, 55.

Dear Horton,

I've written you twice since I left the states but both times the letters got water-soaked before I had a chance to mail them. Everything gets water-soaked here. But this time most of the fellows have gone to the movies so I can write and mail without interruption.

I suppose you will know before you get this that I'm stationed in Italy now. Except for the cold and rain it's really not too bad. I've had two missions toward my fifty required ones so far and tomorrow I go on the third. They are exciting of course but not as bad as I had anticipated from air, as I had heard. The Army thrives on rumors, mostly bad ones.

I won't go into detail about my days in Casablanca, Tunis, Sicily, and Naples but they have provided me with lots of conversational matter for long winter nights when I get back.

The field I'm on now is out in the sticks, away from a large town. We are the first new crew that has come into the squadron in some time. They have only recently come over from Africa and the supply department hasn't caught up with the outfit yet. What I'm getting at is that because of the lack of equipment we have learned to improvise.

When we got here the first thing tossed at us was an old battered up tent that we've since found leaks profusely. We put it up in a strong wind that made our first attempt at tent building all the more difficult. They told us that all the G.I. stoves were given out and on the first night we nearly froze to death. The next day we got a big oil drum, cut the bottom out, cut a door in the side and a hole for the pipe in the top. Then we went to the junk heap and procured a long pipe which I've fitted to the stone and stuck out the top of the tent. Until the third day we didn't realize that we needed a top on the tent but that night the rains came and drenched us while we slept. That night we also made a light out of a bottle full of fuel oil with a sock for a wick. We are pretty well settled now but we burn gasoline in the stove and every once in a while the darn thing gets so hot that we're always afraid it may blow up.

I have had several interruptions since I started and now I'd better get to bed because the call will come early tomorrow. If you'd like to send me a box of chocolates I certainly won't object and if you happen to see or hear from the Jilinskys give them my regards and send me their address. Also my best to Mary Jane and the others. And write me all the news. Be good.

Tom[26]

---

[26] Tom Brooks Foote to Horton Foote, 9 December 1943 (Horton Foote Papers).

In February, letters from Tom Brooks suddenly stopped, and Horton and his family began to worry about Tom's safety. On March 15 Horton's father wrote to him:

My darling boy:

> This morning I am sorry to say the first link in our little chain of five has been strained badly, but I will not yet say broken, for I have too much faith in God to give up that easy. We received a wire at 8:30 A.M. from the War department that Toots was missing in action since Feb. 23rd in a raid over Germany. I still hope he is a <u>prisoner</u>. If not, and he has passed on, of course the link in our little family chain of five has been broken, and we can only face the future with chins up, as we of course know he will meet whatever is beyond this life with clean hands, for I don't believe he did anything that hurt anyone here—
>
> It has been much harder on mother here this morning than myself. You know how friends in a small town are, and we have lots of them. They have been pouring in home all morning seeing her and offering sympathy. Son you would be proud of her if you were here and could see what a real sport she has shown through it all. To her and myself, Christian Science has never before been such a help as it is at this trying moment.
>
> I thank my all-knowing father many times for the blessing of you three boys, and your clean upright lives. You have all three been a pride and joy to me always, and I am also thankful I was bold enough to let each one of you take up your life work just as you wanted to—
>
> Mother and I so much enjoyed your last letter with clippings, and we have our fingers crossed and are praying for your opening success, which I know it will be, for dear boy you deserve it all—
>
> I know you are very busy at this time but am going to ask you to take a little time off and write mother at once, for she seems to get something out of your letters that nothing else can take the place of, and at this hour her heart is very heavy I assure you—
>
> I love you my darling boy with all my heart—
> Dad[27]

After reading his father's letter, Horton called home and said that he would return to Wharton immediately, but his parents insisted he stay in New York with his play, assuring him they were more than hopeful Tom was all right. Horton agreed, and sat down that night and wrote a letter to his brother. He enclosed the note in an announcement of the Broadway opening of *Only the Heart*:

---

[27] Albert Foote, Sr., to Horton Foote, 15 March 1944 (Horton Foote Papers).

Dear Brother:

As you see the big day is drawing near—My deepest wish is that you could be here to share it with me—

Well, we'll have many, many more to share together. Yours as well as mine—

Love, Horton—[28]

The letter was never mailed and weeks went by, and then months, with no word about Tom. The Foote family was left in limbo because military authorities couldn't verify his status.

Only the Heart finally received its Broadway premiere at the Bijou Theatre on West Forty-fifth Street on 4 April 1944 but the critics' reactions couldn't have been more disappointing. Reviews were extremely negative, with Lewis Nichols of the *New York Times* calling the play "talky, old fashioned, and dull" and Harold Barnes of the *New York Herald Tribune* calling it "a dreary domestic drama"[29] Even Horton's close friend Valerie Bettis, who attended the show on opening night, was not at all impressed with the production. Bettis suggested to Horton that he quit wasting his time with narrative drama: "Valerie was very much against what she considered the realistic theatre, and she wanted to see created a theatre that used more boldly the elements of dance, words, and music."[30] Of course, Horton had been interested in music and dance since his early days as a student at the Pasadena Playhouse, and by the time he met Valerie Bettis on the set of *Railroads on Parade,* he had become a strong proponent of modern dance. His enthusiasm grew while working with Agnes De Mille on *American Legend;* and later when rehearsing *Out of My House* at the Humphrey-Weidman Theatre, Horton got to know the legendary dancer Doris Humphrey, often seeking her out to discuss her thoughts on the theory and practice of dance. Horton's association with these great dancers and his interest in choreographic drama would eventually lead him into what was for him a period of radical experimentation with theatrical form.

Horton recalled that it was not until after the war ended in 1945 that he received news of his brother's fate. Lieutenant Eugene L. Senfield, co-

---

[28] Horton Foote to Tom Brooks Foote, 1 April 1944 (Horton Foote Papers).

[29] Lewis Nichols, "Review of *Only the Heart,*" *New York Times,* 5 April 1944; Howard Barnes, "Review of *Only the Heart,*" *New York Herald Tribune,* 5 April 1944.

[30] Foote, *Genesis,* 56.

pilot of a plane flying from Italy to Regensburg, Germany, later told how, during a mission, fifteen German Messerschmitt fighters shot down the B-17 carrying ten American soldiers. Only six soldiers, including Senfield, survived.[31] Unfortunately, the radio pilot, Tom Brooks Foote, did not. He was only twenty-three years old. Sergeant George T. Waters, another of the survivors, confirmed Tom Brooks's death, adding that Tom's body had been so disfigured by the crash that he had been buried in a military cemetery in Germany.[32]

The news of Tom's death was very hard on his parents. "My father put all of my brother's belongings in the attic," Horton recalled, "and then said to me that 'Someday when the pain and hurt are gone, you and your children can have them.' It must have been very rough for him. I don't think my mother ever got over it; she was never able to talk about it. I know it haunted her for the rest of her life. I will never forget sitting in the living room just after the war had ended and you could hear people celebrating the return of their boys. One woman, who had known my brother, came rushing into the house in tears. My mother became frantic and the woman said, 'Oh, Mrs. Foote say something to help me.' My mother broke down and began to cry. I believe that was the most insensitive thing anyone could have said to her at that time."[33]

Horton's own acceptance of his brother's death is reflected in instances in his writing where lives are meaningfully inspired by unexpected and undeserved losses. Many of the plays, from *Ludie Brooks* to *The Young Man from Atlanta* to *The Orphans' Home Cycle,* focus on grief's temptations and opportunities. As Reynolds Price suggests, Horton Foote's plays remind us "suffering (to the point of devastation) is the central human condition and our most unavoidable mystery. Yet we can survive it and sing in its face."[34]

---

[31] Morris J. Roy, *Behind Barbed Wire* (New York: Richard R. Smith 1946).

[32] Horton Foote, interview by Marion Castleberry, 18 November 1988, Wharton, Texas.

[33] Ibid.

[34] Reynolds Price, Introduction to *Courtship, Valentine's Day, 1918: Three Plays from the Orphans' Home Cycle by Horton Foote* (New York: Grove Press, 1986) xii.

6

Modern Dance
1944

During the 1930s and '40s, modern dance was everywhere in New York, and as Horton Foote admitted, "there were no playwrights being produced that could equal the seriousness of purpose and the storytelling talents" of these great artists.[1] Young dancers were constantly hiring a hall and giving solo concerts, often dancing to narrated poems. Horton became close friends with many of these dancers, including Merce Cunningham, Jerome Robbins, Erick Hawkins, Anthony Tudor, and Nona Sherman. Sherman, a member of the Humphrey-Weidman Company, was responsible initially for drawing Horton into the world of modern dance. Knowing Horton had been an actor, she asked him to join her in a performance of Carl Sandburg's poem, *The People, Yes*. Horton agreed, and after rehearsing the piece several times they presented it at the Ninety-second Street YMHA (Young Men's Hebrew Association), whose Sunday afternoon cultural programs were a springboard for aspiring artists in the 1930s and '40s.

Soon, Horton was caught up in the world of modern dance and avant-garde theater. After watching one of the performances of the Sandburg poem, a young black dancer, Pearl Primus, asked Horton to narrate Abel Meeropol's dark poem *Strange Fruit* for a dance she was choreographing. On the Sunday Primus gave her concert at the YMHA, Valerie Bettis, another modern dancer and choreographer, was in the audience with her future husband Bernardo Segall, a noted Brazilian pianist-composer. Afterwards, the Houston-born Bettis asked Horton to work with her on a John Malcolm Brinnin poem, *The Desperate Heart*, for which Segall had written a musical score, and Horton agreed. Rehearsals were held in Bettis's studio, and from day one, Horton found narrating the work exciting, challenging, and emotionally demanding. They performed the work at the Humphrey-Weidman Studio in 1944 in a concert sponsored by *The Dance Observer*, receiving a standing ovation at

---

[1] Horton Foote, *Genesis of an American Playwright*, ed. Marion Castleberry (Waco TX: Baylor University Press, 2004) 53.

the first performance. In fact, the trio performed the piece many times in dance recitals around the city over the next few years.

After the performance at the Humphrey-Weidman Theatre, Bettis told Horton of her desire to create a series of choreographic theater works, and she asked him if he had any plays that had not been produced. Fortunately, he had recently written a one-act drama called *Daisy Lee* (also called *Daisy Speed*), and they began work on it immediately, adding dance and music to enhance the story.[2]

The American Actors Company produced *Daisy Lee* in April 1944 with direction by Mary Hunter, choreography by Valerie Bettis, and music by Bernardo Segall.[3] The play opens with the sound of offstage voices asking if the central character, Daisy, is sad over the loss of her husband and the failure of their marriage. Daisy is seen standing on stage "twisted by suffering and pain" and "half bent in the silence" (1). In the following moments of the play, Daisy repeatedly moves to a piano, where she tries to play the tune she believes expresses her love for her husband, but she can't remember the song. A flashback reveals her mother warning Daisy not to marry a poor, shifty alcoholic. In another flashback, Daisy's sister says she killed herself in disappointment over her own marriage, a failed attempt to emulate Daisy's relationship with husband Charlie, a marriage her sister assumed to be happy. When the townspeople ask Daisy to publicly declare her unhappiness, rather than admit the truth she is transported to a purgatorial place and reunited with the dead Charlie. The reunion inspires Daisy's impromptu dance "to recall a happy life and her deep love for him," instead of her fear of emotional closeness, which she believes led to his death (7). At the piano she once more can't recall the song, but Charlie remembers it, humming the tune "coldly, insistently" and claiming he hated their life together, asserting Daisy knew of his loathing but just wouldn't admit it to herself (8). He also says her claim of happiness is a lie, as is her inability to remember the song. As the curtain falls, Charlie continues humming the tune, while Daisy mutters that she can't remember it.

Beginning with *Daisy Lee*, Horton's writing becomes more lyrical and abstract, and he paints a haunting portrait of old age, remorse, and loneliness. Once a wealthy and respected Southern belle, Daisy now lives in a hellish retreat of her own making, having been isolated for so long

---

[2] Horton Foote, *Beginnings: A Memoir* (New York: Scribner Press, 2001) 241–44.

[3] Horton Foote, *Daisy Lee*, (MS in Horton Foote Papers). Page references to *Daisy Lee* in the text cite this manuscript.

that she is incapable of connecting with other people. Her loneliness is unbearable, and in trying to stave off insanity, she has created a world of illusion in which to hide. In spite of her difficult life, Daisy shows amazing courage in refusing to accept madness as an option, but she cannot avoid the suffering and desolation her isolation brings. Lois Balcom, critic for *The Dance Observer*, noted that while *Daisy Lee* employed familiar themes, its use of offstage voices as a way of structuring character and plot was "original to the point of deserving the term 'daring.'"[4] The tale of Daisy Lee was so haunting to Horton, he would revisit her story years later in his play *In a Coffin in Egypt*.

Up to this point in his career, Horton's constant theme had been that of man's search for something beyond himself in which he could belong, such as home or family, and since many of his characters do not succeed in attaining a mystical union or an ideal state of belonging, they often succumb to loneliness. This ubiquitous sense of isolation and loneliness in American life, especially in Southern society, creates a rich tapestry in Foote's early experimental work. His plays explore the theme of loneliness from many diverse points of view: the loneliness of homelessness, the loneliness of personal failure, the loneliness caused by death or loss, the loneliness of failed love, the loneliness of family discord, and the loneliness caused by man's obsession with materialism and lack of faith in spiritual values.

Daisy Lee marked the first in a series of abstract, choreographic dramas dealing with the theme of loneliness that Horton would create with Valerie Bettis and Bernardo Segall. He would go on to create similar works with other musicians and choreographers including Martha Graham, the legendary teacher who at the time was revolutionizing the world of modern dance.

Later that spring the American Actors Company was approached by Sanford Meisner about co-producing a play he was directing at the Neighborhood Playhouse called *The Playboy of Newark*. Horton was elated when Mary Hunter asked him to serve as producer for the show. Aware of Sanford Meisner's illustrious career at the Group Theatre, Horton was excited to work with him. During this time, they became close friends, and Horton later gave Meisner a copy of his play *Miss Lou* to direct with his students.[5] Performed in 1944, *Miss Lou* is a one-act

---

[4] Louis Balcom, "Review of *Daisy Lee* by Horton Foote," *The Dance Observer* (15 February 1944): 20.

[5] Foote, *Beginnings*, 245.

drama that tells the story of a spinster, Lou Gordon, and her struggle to have a romantic relationship with Raymond Tuttle, a gentle and shy man, while her aging mother harshly criticizes her and her brother Peter harasses and aggravates her every time Raymond comes to call. The play was such a hit with Playhouse students that Meisner began to ask Horton to direct his advanced students in plays whenever Meisner got acting jobs and had to take a leave of absence. He also introduced Horton to Rita Morgenthau, dean of the school, who had first seen his work at the American Actors Company and knew of his interest in dance. Morgenthau often commissioned playwrights to create new works for students that incorporated all the disciplines of the school— music, dance, and acting. At Morgenthau's request, Horton wrote and directed three plays for the Neighborhood Playhouse in 1944—*The Flowering of the Drama, Goodbye to Richmond,* and *The Lonely.*

The more interesting of the three dance-plays is appropriately called *The Lonely,* which was choreographed by Martha Graham and scored by pianist Louis Horst.[6] Once again Horton's writing is abstract, but structurally the work is quite a radical departure from his previous writing, beginning with a pantomime on a stage divided into five areas. As Horton describes:

> Over each area is a light fixture suitable to the character of the place. At the back, to the left, are four women seated around a bridge table. To the far right are two women, grouped around the section of a bar. Behind the bar is the bartender. Standing under a street lamp, between the two groups, is a Prostitute. Down left is a tiny commode with a kerosene lamp on it. Seated behind the commode is a woman, wearing black cloth as a bridal veil. Down right is an area of light formed into a circle. A piano is playing a fast boogie tune in the distance. (1)

On this carefully designed stage the characters move ritualistically in and out of the light "with open and violent despair," accompanied by music (1). The dialogue focuses on Sam Mann, who has died, and whether he was happy when alive or, as his brother Tom believes, was haunted by a pervasive sense of loneliness. Conversely, his wife insists Sam was content. The women and bartender act as a chorus, describing the various actions and intentions of the townspeople, while Tom feels increasingly guilty for not loving his brother as he should, an internal conflict brought to life onstage as a choreographed, symbolic killing. The

---

[6] Horton Foote, *The Lonely,* (MS in Horton Foote Papers). Page references to *The Lonely* in the text cite this manuscript.

characters continue their mechanical movements, changing places as they play bridge and toss balls among themselves to pass the time.

At Sam's funeral, Tom continues to ask why so many people are lonely. The preacher, offering a stoical Christian response, insists, "Let us not mock God by asking for reasons. Accept. Let us accept. Joyfully, willingly" (13), but the people continue to amuse themselves with bridge, marked by the promiscuous changing of partners. Tom imagines he sees Sam, but the figure is merely an illusion, turning into the Preacher. And when a Young Girl approaches, saying she too is lonely, Tom tells her, "Don't be a fool" (19), as the players continue their games.

Like *Daisy Lee, The Lonely*, is an intriguing study of personal regret and devastating loneliness. Perhaps inspired by his grief over the death of his brother, Horton depicts the central character, Tom, as a victim of his own making, who is haunted and obsessed by feelings of guilt from not loving his deceased brother as he should. He seeks emotional solace from others, since he can no longer ask forgiveness of his brother; but, unfortunately, Tom finds no answer to his grief, believing that everyone has "a disease eating at our hearts," a foreboding sense of loneliness (6). Like a choric voice, the passage of lost and insensitive men and women moving rhythmically across the stage adds to the emotional effect of the play by its steady flow and intrinsic tension. And the continual effort by the townspeople to ignore their hopeless isolation by drinking, playing bridge, and tossing balls resonates with an absurdist perspective implying that trying to live a happy, morally upright life is a futile activity. Void of genuine religious feeling, the characters mechanically recite the Lord's Prayer—which in no way impedes their drinking binges and seductions. Finally, we are left with the haunting image of total isolation as the Woman Behind the Commode retreats into her house, pulls down the shades, and closes the shutters.

Rehearsals for *The Lonely* were a great time of learning for Horton Foote. "I have worked with many gifted, creative people," Horton admitted, "but none quite like Martha."[7] Graham brought the same kind of creative energy to rehearsals she brought to work on one of her major ballets. Horton recalled she was never overbearing, always interested in his ideas, and always inspiring everyone in the company to achieve his best work. "She made you feel as if you could take on the world," Horton said. "I've never been so charmed in my life. She acted as if it were a great privilege to work with me. With me! Imagine!" Since both

---

[7] Foote, *Genesis*, 56.

Horton and Martha Graham lived in Greenwich Village at the time (Horton in the Albert Hotel), they would often ride the bus together after rehearsals and discuss modern dance and how to transform American theater. "She would talk to me as if she had known me forever," he said.[8]

After Graham finished her work on *The Lonely*, Louis Horst came in to compose the music. Horst, also editor of *The Dance Observer*, became good friends with Horton, and aware of his growing interest in dance, Horst enlisted him to write for his magazine. Founded in 1933 by Horst and Ralph Taylor, *The Dance Observer* was designed to reflect the development and activities of modern dance in the United States. As Agnes De Mille explained, it was "devoted to modern dancing, because...there was not one literate voice to speak out for the new form."[9] Although Horton was always reticent to speak about this period in his career, humorously describing himself as writing "articles for *The Dance Observer*, denouncing current theater," and vowing "never to write another realistic play,"[10] he did publish a handful of commentaries from June 1943 to December 1946 covering such topics as the need for emotional truth in dance and theater, the development of new works, and commercialism in art.

In 1944, at the age of twenty-eight, Horton Foote wrote "The Long, Long Trek," a harsh criticism of the economic practices of Broadway at a time when he was experimenting with dramatic form and searching for a distinctly personal writing style that would convey the stories he wished to tell. He also wrote "Dance and the Playwright," in which he proclaimed that authenticity of emotion is essential in dance and theater and theorized that the most creative theater should have particulars that resonate with the universal. He asked writers to follow the best dancers away from "the dull naturalism" of the screen and "the tired, the true and the obvious" of the stage by imitating Martha Graham's *Letter to the World*, which integrated dance and theater. In Horton's mind, the goal was to use "rhythmic language" to escape "the restrictions of our realistic and naturalistic theatre."[11] In "Notes for the Future," Horton called for a theater with national or religious import, one that would

---

[8] Russell Freedman, *Martha Graham: A Dancer's Life* (New York: Houghton Mifflin, 1998) 125.

[9] Agnes DeMille, *Martha: The Life and Work of Martha Graham* (New York: Random House, 1991) 164.

[10] Foote, *Genesis*, 54.

[11] Horton Foote, "Dance and the Playwright," *The Dance Observer* 11.1 (January 1944): 7.

never seek "to escape the realities, the responsibilities, the understanding of life."[12] Underlying all his writing for *The Dance Observer* is a growing dissatisfaction with commercial theater and his pursuit of a unique approach to realism and truthfulness in American theater.

At the end of 1944, Horton wrote one more choreographic drama, *In My Beginning*, which was inspired by conversations with Bernardo Segall and Valerie Bettis. When Horton heard that the renowned French jazz composer, Darius Milhaud, was in New York, he called to ask if he would read the play. Milhaud read it, liked it, and agreed to write a score for the piece. They found a producer who took an option for a hundred dollars a month while he tried to raise money for a production, but unfortunately, the money didn't materialize and the play was never produced. Nevertheless, *In My Beginning* is one of the most intriguing works Horton penned during this phase of his career.[13] Subtitled "A Miracle Play With Music and Dance," the play divides the stage into three levels and features ritualized action, including an otherworldly offstage voice declaring that man is made in God's image, countered by a mulatto who sings the blues in "the manner of a small town whore" (1). A chorus of women describes the town's hysteria over reports of a healing by Mrs. Peters, a citizen of the town, which the Preacher assures is the work of the devil. Accompanied by music, a group of women lament their husbands' absence on pleasurable business trips, and Mrs. Ryan, daughter of Mrs. Peters, is bribed by a businessman to say her mother can't perform miracles. Mrs. Ryan's daughter, Sue, is harassed by the lecherous Ned and Pete while her father, who is having an affair with a mulatto woman, tries to protect her from harm. Mrs. Ryan encourages Sue to pursue George, who has reportedly become rich, and in one symbolic scene, Sue stabs her own father, declaring that his defense of her implies she will never be clean from guilt. Sue and George confess their self-hatred and fear, followed by Mrs. Peters's declaration that "God is love. And he that dwelleth in love dwelleth in God, and God in him...There is no fear in love" (2, 26), which inspires Sue to "cast out fear" and declare: "We alone can work the miracle. We alone can save ourselves" (2, 27–9). When Mrs. Peters suddenly disappears, followed by the rumor she ascended to Heaven, Ned Kelley, George's friend, is bribed by the Preacher and businessman to say Mrs. Peters left

---

[12] Horton Foote, "Notes for the Future," *The Dance Observer* 12.5 (May 1945): 56.

[13] Foote, *In My Beginning,* (MS in Horton Foote Papers). Page references to *In My Beginning* in the text refer to this manuscript.

with men in a car. Sue and George marry, open up an old saloon, and George assures her that "Love is strong. A growing thing. It starts from here; it goes, it returns, it is inclusive" (3, 11). With Sue and George expecting their second child, Mr. Ryan defends Sue by shooting Ned and Pete, and the chorus of women symbolically stabs their philandering husbands. Mrs. Ryan, who has become insane, tempts Sue to stab George while he sleeps, but Sue and George are finally united, separated from the others characters who declare the superiority of their Protestant homeland and the absence of miracles in twentieth-century life.

In My Beginning dramatizes the Christian assertion that forgiveness— the cancellation of one's destructive past—is not only an emotional necessity, but also a paramount virtue. Sue, who has been abused and neglected by her mother and seduced by Pete, seeks absolution from the guilt she feels, although that guilt is not totally of her making. She is able to cleanse herself of her sordid past only through the love and support of George, who offers her genuine and healthy intimacy, and because she comes to believe in the miracle of her own heart. Equally important, the play points to a central concern in all of Foote's work—the terrifying sense of spiritual isolation in America brought about by a loss of faith in God and the goodness of humanity. The play, which reveals a town caught in a moment of economic upheaval and social change (the fall of the decadent aristocracy and the rise of the materialistic middle class), confirms Mary Baker Eddy's thoughts that evil shows itself "in the materialism and sensualism of the age" and has a shaping effect on human values, leading to the sometimes unspoken assumption that having material possessions, comforts, and power is the only valid measure of fulfillment and meaning in human life[14] (Gottschalk 4). *In My Beginning* reminds us that men would be less lonely if they followed their own spiritual inclinations—the miracles of their heart—instead of the competitive and marketable aspects of the materialistic world.

While Horton's association with great artists like Valerie Bettis, Bernardo Segall, and Martha Graham inspired him to experiment with new forms of drama and approaches to theater, there were other, more pragmatic people in New York that counseled him to be practical, to stop writing about family life in small-town Texas, to avoid experimentation, and to turn his attention to writing successful Broadway works. One such person was the director-playwright Howard Lindsay, who wanted

---

[14] Stephen Gottschalk, *Rolling Away the Stone: Mary Baker Eddy's Challenge to Materialism* (Bloomington: Indiana University Press 2006) 4.

to push Horton into writing a more commercial type of play. Lindsay thought Horton had great promise as a writer, and he offered two words of wisdom to the young playwright: "The first was never to write a play about a character you wouldn't care to entertain in your own living room, and the second, that when he took a play out of town for tryout he never watched the actors when it was performed, but the audience to see when they got bored or restless."[15]Though Horton was disheartened by what Lindsay had to say, he did not take his advice. He knew he was destined to write about the place and the people he had not so much chosen, but who had chosen him as their spokesman. "There hasn't been a year that has passed that someone, somewhere, hasn't asked me to change the pattern of my writing," Horton remarked, "to find stories and people they think [are] what? More accessible to a larger public? More commercial? But no matter—I can't. Even if I wanted to, which I don't—I can't. These are my people and my stories, and the plays I want to write—really, the only ones I know how to write."[16]

Perhaps Horton knew well the feelings of another young Southern playwright, Tennessee Williams, who approached him that year about playing the role of Tom in a play he was writing entitled *The Gentleman Caller*. Horton had met Tennessee Williams when he brought his play *You Touched Me* to the American Actors Company, and he had seen him again in California when he was working with Jacques Therie. After Horton returned to New York, the two had kept in touch, and Williams had written to him to say he had a new play, which he felt had a great part for him. By this point in his career, Horton had lost all interest in acting, but he was very taken with the play Tennessee later renamed *The Glass Menagerie*. He was so taken that he asked Williams if he could do the "gentleman caller" scene from the play in a production at the Neighborhood Playhouse. Williams agreed, but as Horton recalled, two days before the scene was to be performed, one of his old friends from the Provincetown Playhouse who'd watched rehearsals met Tennessee and told him how pleased he was with the show. Even years later, Horton remembered his friend's reaction: "He said Tennessee had a stricken look on his face," and exclaimed, "'I've just sold the play to Eddie Dowling.'" When Horton heard that, he was afraid he would have to cancel the production, but Williams talked it over with his agent, Audrey Wood, who agreed to let the Neighborhood Playhouse

---

[15] Foote, *Genesis*, 57.
[16] Ibid., 59.

production go forward. So, as Horton remembered, "I directed, at least in part, the first production of the play that was soon to be known as *The Glass Menagerie*."[17]

Horton's work at the Neighborhood Playhouse was artistically rewarding, but it did not pay enough to support him—only about $75 dollars a month—so he was forced to find supplemental income elsewhere. He remembered reading that William Faulkner had once supported himself by working in a New York bookstore, so the playwright took a position as manager of the Pennsylvania Station branch of the Doubleday Book Shop, where he manned the night shift from five to eleven. The job proved beneficial to Horton in more ways than he had expected, providing him with steady employment, giving him time to continue writing plays, and allowing him to continue teaching at the Neighborhood Playhouse during the day. More importantly, while working at the Doubleday bookstore, Horton's life was changed forever when he met the lovely Lillian Vallish.

---

[17] Ibid., 56.

7

Lillian
1944–45

Horton had been working at the Doubleday bookstore for about a month when Lillian Vallish came in looking for a summer job. At the time she was a twenty-year-old honors student at Radcliffe majoring in English and had taken a semester off to work in New York. When she applied for a job as clerk, Horton was instantly taken by the lovely young woman and hired her for the night shift. As he later wrote in a letter to his parents, she was not only beautiful, she was also smart: "It was love at first sight"[1] That first evening, as he was getting ready to close the store, Horton asked Lillian if she would like to go for a walk. She politely refused, but Horton was persistent, and the following day he asked her again. This time she accepted. Their first date consisted of a stroll along the Hudson River. Later on they would go to an occasional movie or restaurant, but since neither of them had much money, they mostly just walked and talked about the poetry and novels they both enjoyed. Horton remembered that "she loved writing and books," and the two young people soon became inseparable.[2]

One warm summer afternoon, Horton's good friend Joseph Anthony, home on leave from the military, entered the store. Horton pointed to Lillian, standing behind the counter, and said, "Joe, that's the girl I'm going to marry."[3] Six weeks later Horton proposed and Lillian accepted, but she wanted to postpone their marriage until she graduated from college in the fall. Horton agreed they should wait until she got her degree. Then Lillian noted that her parents would not consent to the marriage because they "didn't approve of his profession or his prospects for making a proper living."[4]

---

[1] Horton Foote to Lillian Vallish, April 1944 (Horton Foote Papers).

[2] Horton Foote, *Genesis of an American Playwright*, ed. Marion Castleberry (Waco TX: Baylor University Press, 2004) 57.

[3] Wilborn Hampton, *Horton Foote: America's Storyteller* (New York: Simon & Schuster, 2009) 82.

[4] Foote, *Beginnings, 256.*

Toward the end of summer, Lillian took her fiancé home to Carmel, Pennsylvania, to meet her parents. Horton remembered it being an awkward visit. Lillian's father, Walter, seemed pleasant enough, but Mrs. Vallish took an instant dislike to him. She was so concerned about his ability to care for her daughter that "she looked up his name in Dun & Bradstreet, a publication that provided reliable credit information, and discovered that though Foote had produced a play on Broadway, he was basically penniless."[5]

Horton later learned that Barbara Vallish's attitude toward him stemmed from her great fear of financial failure. Although Walter, Lillian's father, who immigrated to the United States from Poland as a young man, had earned a college degree in his home country, the only work he could find in America was in a Pennsylvania coal mine. Walter's marriage to Barbara was an arranged one, and though she had very little formal education, she was the brighter and more ambitious of the two—and also much younger. To add to their financial difficulties, they had seven children—two boys and five girls—though the boys died in infancy, leaving the couple with only five daughters—Barbara, Polly, Dorothy, Rita, and Lillian.

Mrs. Vallish, determined to get Walter out of the coal mines, opened a small grocery store to serve the miners' families and persuaded her husband to leave the mines and help her in the store. As time went by, she began to realize there was not enough profit in groceries, so she took the family's savings from the grocery business and opened a furniture store. As the furniture enterprise prospered, she rented a four-story brick building in the middle of town. The family lived on the top floor, and the other three floors served as showrooms. The furniture business thrived, and the family became quite prosperous. As Mrs. Vallish continued to make money, she began to invest in stocks. One day she gave her husband a check for twenty-five thousand dollars to take to the bank to purchase shares of a particular stock, but the bank's president talked him into investing it all in a railroad instead. When the railroad went bust in the 1929 Wall Street crash, the Vallish family lost all their savings. By the time Horton and Lillian married, some fifteen years later, the loss of the money was still the source of a bitter dispute between the Vallishes, resulting in incessant quarreling and violent threats.[6]

---

[5] Hampton, *84*.

[6] Horton Foote, *Beginnings: A Memoir* (New York: Scribner Press, 2001) 261–63.

Over the years, Barbara Vallish became equally ambitious for her daughters, pushing them to attend college. Lillian's two older sisters eventually quit school and left home, but Rita, the sister to whom Lillian was closest, attended Radcliffe College in Cambridge, Massachusetts. When Lillian graduated from high school, she first went to the University of Pennsylvania to please her mother, but not liking it, she eventually transferred to Radcliffe where her sister had gone.[7]

Rita had since married George Mayberry, who had been an assistant professor at Harvard, and was by then book editor for *The New Republic* magazine. They had two children and lived in a large, old-fashioned apartment on East Seventy-sixth Street in New York, handsomely furnished by Mrs. Vallish. Soon after Lillian and Horton started dating, they began visiting the Mayberry's and were frequent guests at lavish dinners and parties. At George and Rita's, Horton met a host of publishers, critics, painters, and writers, including eminent abstract expressionist Robert Motherwell; Albert Erskine, later editor at Random House and formerly married to Katherine Anne Porter; Richard Watts, drama critic for the *New York Post*; Malcolm Cowley, renowned novelist and literary critic; Agnes Smedley, the famous war correspondent; Marianne Moore, acclaimed poet; and many other people of note. Horton remembered everyone voicing strong opinions about the young writers of the day, and their discussions were often passionate and spirited. But there was never any talk about modern dance. The only time Horton remembered dance being mentioned at all was when Albert Erskine said he despised Martha Graham and all modern dance, because he viewed it as ugly and much preferred ballet.[8]

By contrast, the conversation at Valerie Bettis and Bernardo Segall's downtown apartment almost always centered on music and dance, rarely on visual art or writing. Lillian joined Horton and his friends in their talks about theater and its future, while listening to the music of artists like Heitor Villa-Lobos, Gustav Mahler, and John Cage. It was at Valerie and Bernardo's that Horton first heard the music of Charles Ives, which would later provide inspiration for him during the writing of *The Orphans' Home Cycle*.[9]

Stimulated by discussions with Lillian and his friends, Horton began to take up reading once again after years of curtailing his favorite

---

[7] Ibid.
[8] Foote, *Beginnings*, 264–65.
[9] Ibid.

pastime for the more immediate concerns of acting, writing, and trying to make ends meet. He had always been a fan of William Faulkner, and he began to re-read his work, along with the poetry of T.S. Eliot, Ezra Pound, W.H. Auden, William Carlos Williams, Marianne Moore, and Wallace Stevens. He also read James Joyce, Evelyn Waugh, Flannery O'Connor, Eudora Welty, and Texas writer Katherine Anne Porter. He was particularly taken with a story by Porter that Lillian had given him to read—*Pale Horse, Pale Rider*, a tale of the 1918 influenza epidemic. Foote was intrigued by Porter's ability to transform memories of her past into a remarkably lyrical but realistic prose. He immediately recognized the similarities between himself and Porter and was influenced not only by her technique, but also by her use of Texas settings. Like Katherine Anne Porter, Horton Foote was drawn to the kind of poetic, true-to-life language and symbolic imagery of his native region, and he was interested, as was Porter, in depicting the mysterious realities of the human experience. In a 1965 interview, Katherine Anne Porter provided a manifesto that could likewise stand as an explanation of Horton Foote's purpose in writing:

> There seems to be a kind of order in the universe, in the movement of the stars and the turning of the earth and the changing of the seasons, and even in the cycle of human life. But human life itself is almost pure chaos...We don't really know what is going to happen to us, and we don't know why. The work of the artist—the only thing he's good for—is to take these handfuls of confusion and disparate things, things that seem to be irreconcilable, and put them together in a frame to give them some kind of shape and meaning.[10]

Horton credited Porter with helping him find a way to use the particulars of time and place without getting trapped in the quaintness of regionalism. "For good or bad," he remarked, "that is the path I have chosen to explore ever since."[11] Although there were marked differences between the two artists' works, Katherine Anne Porter continued to influence Horton Foote for the rest of his life, and in years to come he would cite her as a major influence on his writing.

When Lillian returned for her final year at Radcliffe in September 1944, she and Horton were resolute in their plans to marry after she graduated the following spring. It was the first time since their

---

[10] Barbara Thompson, "Katherine Anne Porter," *Writers at Work: The Paris Review Interviews*, 2nd series. (New York, 1963) 150–51, 161–62.

[11] Foote, *Genesis*, 156.

engagement they had been apart, and Horton missed her terribly. They wrote to each other frequently during the year, sharing their thoughts on the books they were reading, gossip about friends, shop talk from the bookstore, politics (it was a presidential election year and Horton was worried that Thomas Dewey might beat Franklin Roosevelt, who was running for a fourth term), and plans for their marriage. Horton often expressed his concerns over money and over Mrs. Vallish's attitude toward him. In one letter he urged Lillian to "get close to your mother and family again. We know that bitterness and resentment never accomplish anything."[12] Most of Horton's and Lillian's letters from this time speak of the genuine love and devotion each had for the other, but there were moments of uncertainty and doubt as well.

One such moment occurred in February 1945, when Lillian wrote to Horton asking that they postpone their marriage. She said she'd been under "terrific stress this term—emotional, mental and physical," and that she "would like to recuperate somewhat before assuming the many obligations that marriage carries with it."[13] She explained the delay would only mean waiting a few more months. Horton could hear Lillian's mother in almost every sentence he read and felt certain Lillian's lack of commitment stemmed from her mother's opposition to the marriage. On 12 February 1945, he replied calmly to her letter, refuting her arguments one by one:

> Dearest Lillian,
> Your letter came this morning and I don't understand two things—
> 1st—why we have to wait for so many months—2nd—why you say you'll spend most of the time with me, if the purpose of the postponement is to be with your mother.
> But with the above two I'm really just pulling hairs—really the thing is that it makes me afraid, not that you shouldn't spend some time with your mother, you should—but a reasonable, definite time. I have seen these things stretch out before where weeks become months, days— years. Now I've never spoken of the difference of our ages before— actually I don't think they make much difference as we are both mature and see and feel so much alike about things—but even with our likes I've been bucking around a long time without any center—you have become that center. I suppose you think well what is six months or three or four—Well, I ask you to please, please try to see that when you

---

[12] Horton Foote to Lillian Vallish, 23 November 1944 (Horton Foote Papers).
[13] Lillian Vallish to Horton Foote, 9 February 1945 (Horton Foote Papers).

have been counting on it like I have two weeks can become four months. I have never spoken emotionally about these things, because I knew with your school and my working here the best thing for both of us would be to take it and shut up but I've got to make you understand that it hasn't been very easy or pleasant and that I for one don't want it to continue unless it's absolutely necessary. I wish to God I could change all your Mother's objections to me but it seems I can't, and I can't help but feel futile about any future attempts. If I weren't so confident that our marriage would stand as a record—erase any objections—I might keep my mouth shut again but I do feel it, I feel it strongly. I feel we were building something good and strong this summer and I resent the weeks and months apart. I resent now having to meet you in bars, on busses, between appointments. I want to be alone with you, like this summer, to work together, to be idle together, to love and yes to quarrel and I don't want it four months from now. I want it as soon as possible.

Please try to see it my way. There are so many things to be decided—an apartment, thousands of little things I need to consult with you about. I'm again trying to make you happy dearest. I believe I can. I know you will bring me all the things my life has longed for so long. Let's not put it off one day longer than possible.

All my love,

Horton[14]

Throughout the spring, Horton and Lillian tried to answer the objections Lillian's mother kept making to their marriage. At one point, Lillian left Radcliffe and returned home to Pennsylvania for a few days to try to change her mother's mind and win her blessing. And Horton tried to overcome Mrs. Vallish's opposition to his choice of religion by taking instruction in the Roman Catholic Church. None of that, however, held any sway with Lillian's mother, and, in the end, Horton and Lillian, much like Horton's mother and father had done nearly thirty years earlier, decided to defy the wishes of Lillian's mother and elope.[15]

Horton and Lillian were married on 4 June 1945 at St. John Baptiste Church in New York. Lillian didn't even tell her mother about the wedding, and, subsequently, only Lillian's sister Rita and her husband George were there to represent the family. A few close friends also attended the ceremony. There was no honeymoon trip, and the newlyweds moved into the small apartment that Horton had been living

[14] Horton Foote to Lillian Vallish, 12 February 1945 (Horton Foote Papers).

[15] Foote, *Beginnings*, 256.

in at 148 West Tenth Street. After the wedding, Rita and George organized a reception for the newlyweds at their house in New Jersey and invited Mr. and Mrs. Vallish. At the reception, George's mother, Mrs. Mayberry, pulled Mrs. Vallish aside and scolded her for treating Horton so coldly. "Barbara, you've got to stop this," she said. "He is a nice boy."[16] The hard feelings between Horton and his mother-in-law continued for a while, but as years passed Horton and Barbara Vallish would become close.

When Horton married, he had only recently decided that writing was his true calling. Even though he had gained a reputation as a promising playwright, the commercial pressures and expectations of New York soon began to burden him. To ease the situation, Horton hired Lucy Kroll, a close friend and former member of the American Actors Company, who was at the time working for the Sam Jaffe Agency, to be his literary agent, to promote his writing, and to take care of all financial matters pertaining to his work. Kroll later formed her own company, the Lucy Kroll Agency, and Horton followed her, remaining with her throughout much of his career, until her death in 1997.

Horton gave Lucy Kroll two plays to send out to Broadway and Hollywood producers who had taken an interest in his work. The first of these plays was *People in the Show*, the most political play in Horton's entire canon.[17] Written in 1944, at the height of World War II, the work is based on the writer's experiences acting in *Railroads on Parade* at the New York World's Fair. During this time, anti-Jewish sentiment was high, and the snide remarks Horton heard from actors and others leveled against Jews—whether about moguls in Hollywood or fellow performers like Lee Strasburg and Sandy Meisner of the Group Theatre—pained the young actor. Their words were never intended to wound and certainly the intent wasn't to bring about the death of Jews, but now Nazis who were engaged in an act of genocide were using the same harsh bigoted remarks. *People in the Show* is Horton Foote's response to such prejudice. The story takes place during the run of a fictitious pageant, called "Century of Progress," at a World's Fair and features an array of characters unique to the writer's dramatic landscape—a drunken misfit actor, washed-up actresses living on memories of performances past, a married star having an affair with a younger man, a veteran actress

---

[16] Hampton, 96.

[17] Horton Foote, *People in the Show*, (MS in Horton Foote Papers). Page references to *People in the Show* in the text refer to this manuscript.

secretly in love with the husband of a fellow actress, and a self-absorbed playwright.

The play also addresses significant political and social issues of the time, such as the German invasion of France in 1940 and whether America should become involved in the war or stay neutral. The major concern for many of the characters in the play is whether the war will force the show to close and cause them to lose their paychecks. In the play, Horton also explores the issue of racial friction between blacks, as two actors, Stilwell—a Communist and civil rights activist—and Stetsie, a mild-mannered black man branded as an "Uncle Tom," voice their dislike for each other and argue about who best represents their race. Stilwell ends up being fired when she protests after not being served a cup of coffee in the theater's canteen.

The most significant issue running through the play is the anti-Semitism rampant in America before the war and the Fascist sentiments some Americans embraced during the conflict. The male lead in the play is a Jewish actor, Sam, who is having an affair with Irene, a Gentile. Most of the characters express overt anti-Semitic feelings throughout the course of the action, and the play ends with the death of the Jewish protagonist during a fight with Bob, a bigoted and misguided young actor who cannot tolerate the mixing of races. *People in the Show* is a bold and timely play, but it is not a great play for several reasons: some of the characters never rise above the role of stock figures, the dialogue is perplexing and sentimental at times, and occasionally the work seems disjointed, especially when the chorus of aging women—Doris, Bess, and Rita—banter on about the old theater of Frohman and David Belasco and the death of the new theater of the modern age. And even though the work rails against racial injustice, Horton did not show a strong talent for writing social criticism.

People in the Show aptly portrays the political and social discord that arose during World War II and culminated in violence, but the play implies a more pervasive theme, one that is spiritual and religious rather than political. Underlying the realistic action of the play is Horton Foote's assertion that all men are members of one family—not the biblical family of Adam in which brother kills brother—but the spiritual family that includes all mankind as sons and daughters of a common parent, Father-Mother-God. Influenced by Mary Baker Eddy, Horton envisioned the unity that an understanding of "God is Love" can bring to humanity. As Eddy wrote, "One infinite God, good, unites men and nations; constitutes the brotherhood of man; ends wars; fulfills the Scripture; 'Love thy neighbor as thyself' annihilates pagan and Christian idolatry, whatever is wrong in social, civil, criminal, political, and religious codes; equalizes the sexes, annuls the curse on man, and leaves nothing that can sin, suffer, be punished or destroyed."[18] Ultimately, *People in the Show* was a plea for universal brotherhood, urging everyone, all nations and races, to manifest God's peace in a world that was strained, tenuous, and wracked by war. Horton's sentiment of world harmony and his belief in the goodness of man is one he would embrace for the rest of his life.

Despite the boldness and timeliness of *People in the Show*, Broadway producers were unwilling to consider such a large cast show. Consequently, the play was not produced until 1948, when Vincent Donehue directed it in Washington, DC, with a cast that featured Eli Wallach and Jean Stapleton as the backstage lovers, Sam and Irene.

The second play Horton gave Lucy Kroll to send to Broadway producers was *Marcus Strachen*, the story of a young man of ambition who comes to a small Texas town in the 1890s with a small stake and an appetite for power.[19] Under the tutelage of his misguided aristocratic uncle, Colonel, who dreams of restoring the beauty and glory of the Southern way of life, Marcus quickly makes his way up the social ladder, marrying his boss's daughter, Eliza Robedaux, and multiplying his holdings many times through shrewd business decisions. As the play develops, Marcus is corrupted by his power and greed, becoming more and more hedonistic, drinking and gambling, and abusing his wife, all while keeping a mulatto mistress. After his mistress bears his child, Marcus defiantly admits his paternity to the entire community, an arrogant attempt to show his dominance. Instead, he is condemned by the church and banished by the preachers and self-righteous town leaders, leaving him with no place to go except to the local bar. Marcus is defiant, however, and refuses to leave his store and lands, declaring "I'm gonna stay here and not leave 'til I show you I'm bigger than all of you. I'm gonna take the mother of my nigger kid—and I'm gonna live with her—and she's gonna walk the streets of the town in dresses I buy—and take my kid with her—I'll get drunk and walk the streets...And I'll do

---

[18] Mary Baker Eddy, *Science and Health with Keys to the Scriptures* (Boston: Christian Science Publishing, 1934) 340.

[19] Horton Foote, *Marcus Strachen*, (MS in Horton Foote Papers). Page references to *Marcus Strachen* in the text refer to this manuscript.

anything that will make me master here" (2.3.39). At last Marcus is undermined by Tom Jordan, a businessman who is much tougher and smarter than he, and in a fit of rage Marcus shoots and kills Jordan rather than lose his store and land. In the end, with a lynch mob on his trail, Marcus leaves his wife and his mistress, and heads out with a much smaller stake than before to try his fortune elsewhere, haunted by a sense of loss and time misspent but having learned absolutely nothing and prepared to repeat the pattern. He will never know the peace and contentment his older brother Gordon has come to embrace. Gordon, who rejected his uncle Colonel's corrupting influence and chose a life of honesty, simplicity, and hard work, says:

> I'm beginning to see the possibility for a life free from the things that have bound us all, the greed for land, for power and the false appetites. I begin to see a man able to choose a world of right and independence, happy, strong in the choice. What I've found is for me. I think it's good. I think it can be heard and followed by all men and I think it is more insistent than the voice of evil and in the end must be heard and once heard followed and to deny is to perish…utterly…utterly. (3.3.26)

Like *Only the Heart*, *Marcus Strachen* is a powerful indictment of materialism and greed and contains a similar appeal for love and intimacy in a cynical world that favors money and power over healthy relationships. Told in a succession of small scenes, the play captures vividly the character and spirit of small town Texas following the Civil War, emphasizing the clash between middle-class values and the hedonistic tendencies of the fallen plantation aristocracy, the evils of alcoholism and gambling, and the effects of prejudice and racial injustice. Once again, Horton Foote affirms that a preoccupation with materialism has a negative effect on human happiness. An obsession with possessions, comforts, and power, Horton implies, leads to moral isolation and emotional devastation. Horton's thoughts seem to echo literary critic Stanley Hopper's assertion that "ours is the literature of the lost." We experience "the dark night of the soul…we are orphaned, alone, impotent."[20]

Lucy Kroll sent a copy of *Marcus Strachen* to John Gassner, president of the Theatre Guild, who then assigned his assistant, Molly Thatcher, to read and comment on the work. Thatcher found *Marcus Strachen* less

---

[20] Stanley Romaine Hopper, "The Problem of Moral Isolation in Contemporary Literature," *Spiritual Problems in Contemporary Literature* (New York: Harper & Brothers, 1952) 161.

than satisfying, and on 8 August 1945, she sent Horton a written response, complaining that the mood of the play was too grim and repressive without humor or real full-bloodedness. "It seems to me to lack attractiveness of whatever kind," she remarked, "but it is the work of a writer of both integrity and talent." Thatcher also lectured Horton, much like Howard Lindsay had done earlier, about taking "more account of audience reactions" and working harder to write plays that "will attract, will give pleasure. The pleasure can be of a deeply aesthetic kind—or it can be the pleasure of revelation—or simply of seeing a skill—or of the belly laugh—I don't care"[21]

Molly Thatcher's rejection of *Marcus Strachen* was indicative of the obstacles that Horton Foote and many other writers faced during the 1940s. Producers believed that after a decade of the Great Depression, followed by four years of war, audiences were not interested in serious drama. They wanted to be entertained. Consequently, producers began to book shows with greater entertainment value, mostly musicals and British comedies. By now, Horton was growing tired of the unreasonable demands of commercial theater and even though Mary Hunter finally mounted a production of *Marcus Strachen* at the American Actors Company, he was dissatisfied with where his career was headed. He later admitted, "There were just too many expectations and I wasn't being given a chance to fail."[22]

When the war ended in 1945, most of the members of the American Actors Company who had been in the service returned to New York City, but Mary Hunter was by then working for the American Theatre Wing, establishing acting, directing, and playwriting classes for returning veterans. Without her lead, the American Actors Company soon disbanded, leaving Horton without a place to perform his plays and without any hope the company would ever be revived. "It was a lonely feeling," he admitted.[23] Furthermore, Horton's friends who had served overseas returned home with news of a much different kind of avant-garde theater from that on Broadway. He remembered how—compared with the works of such French writers as Sartre, Camus, Ionesco, and Anouilh—"the New York theatre seemed grim and uninspired."[24]

---

[21] Molly Thatcher to Horton Foote, 8 August 1945 (Horton Foote Papers).
[22] Foote, *Genesis*, 57.
[23] Ibid.
[24] Ibid.

For a time, Horton tried to ignore the changes taking place in American theater by following Valerie Bettis's advice to concentrate entirely on works for a totally non-realistic, lyric theater, but as time passed he became more and more convinced that the pressures of Broadway were detrimental to any serious writing. Horton desperately needed a place to work that was free from commercial demands and expectations, a place where he could examine his previous work, safely experiment with dramatic form, and search for a distinctly personal writing style that would best convey his Wharton stories. As it turned out, Horton would not find a theater home in New York, but rather at the King-Smith School in Washington, DC. There he would find his true voice, and Lillian would prove her devotion to her husband and her ability to enhance and strengthen his career, as she would do for the next forty-seven years (until her death in 1992). And for his part, Horton would prove his mother-in-law's fears unfounded. Not only would he be a loving husband to Lillian throughout their marriage, but he would also turn out to be a very good provider.

8

Washington, DC
1945–50

The King-Smith School had once been an exclusive finishing school for girls from the South, but during the war it had fallen on hard times and had been transformed into a genteel boardinghouse for young women working in Washington, mostly in government jobs. At night, it offered classes in piano, painting, and literature for the residents, and, with the creation of the GI Bill, the school decided to institute a full-time curriculum with day and evening classes. Since music, dance, and theater were to be integral parts of the new curriculum, the school hired Bernardo Segall to teach piano and his wife, Valerie Bettis, to teach dance. Valerie in turn asked Horton and Lillian to join them in running the school and forming a new theater.

Uncertain how teaching responsibilities would impact his writing, Horton asked Vincent Donahue, a friend from the American Actors Company recently discharged from the army, to join them. Donahue agreed, and the Footes moved to Washington, DC, in the summer of 1945. Valerie and Bernardo were supposed to follow a short time later, but unfortunately that never happened because Valerie landed a role in a Broadway musical and was unable to meet her commitment to the school. After a few weeks the couple decided to remain in New York and consequently Horton, Lillian, and Donehue assumed leadership of the school and theater.[1]

Lillian, who had no training or experience in running a school or theater, became administrator for the King-Smith School and assisted Horton and Vincent in managing the theater company, King-Smith Productions. Under her guidance the school was very successful and soon acquired a healthy enrollment. And even though there was very little money for productions, over the next five years (1945–49), Lillian made sure that Horton was given ample time to write. From 1945–49, he penned three new plays—*Themes and Variations*, *The Return*, and *Homecoming*; directed works by Tennessee Williams, Henrik Ibsen, and

---

[1] Horton Foote, *Genesis of an American Playwright*, ed. Marion Castleberry (Waco TX: Baylor University Press, 2004) 267.

Garcia Lorca; and began writing one of the most important plays of his career, *The Chase*.

The first of Horton's plays to be produced by King-Smith Productions was *Themes and Variations*, scored by Robert Evett and choreographed by Angela Kennedy.[2] The play, an abstract-expressionistic piece, opens with Section I, called "The Country." As the curtain rises, a man acting as a chorus declares: "This is a joyous play. A celebration of the beauty and order of things. A hymn of praise for life. An untroubled play. A joyous play. A time for celebration" (1). The first section depicts a world of innocence in harmony with nature, where authority is caring and supportive and where the Preacher declares that he "will bless the Lord at all times" (5). As the play opens, two lovers—Henry Johnson and Anna Travers—are engaged, local children are baptized, and the Preacher assures a funeral congregation that God has "gone no place. Only our ignorance tells us he's gone. God says if we had the eyes to see, the ears to hear, we'd know there's not any separation" (9). As Section I closes, Henry sets out for the town where he intends to work and to learn law.

Section II, "The Town," opens with dialogue between "The Men" and "The Day Gossips," a chorus of women who want Henry to take notice of their young daughters. The gossips move ritualistically between a sewing circle, bridge, and dominoes. When Henry starts going to beer and poker parties, Anna encourages him not to waste his money but to save it for their marriage. Anna's words fall on deaf ears as "The Night Gossips" announce Henry's infidelities, pointing out that he has gotten drunk, lost his money, been late for work, and discontinued his study of law. It follows a pattern, they explain: "Boy from farm thinks he'll like town. Goes. Thinks he's found paradise, gets restless in Paradise, gets to thinking of other places" (42).

In Section III, called "The Dream of the City," Henry is tempted by a prostitute and falsely accused of stabbing a man by an Officer who beats him and leaves him for dead. He is enticed by gamblers and by women posing as Anna, but ultimately declares that he is "in love with a pure woman. I'm a God-fearing man" (49) and aligns himself with a Salvation Army couple, who convince him to write to his family for help.

The final Section of the play, "Poor Butterfly and Prodigal Son," opens with the Chorus denying the declarations of Section I, claiming

---

[2] Horton Foote, *Themes and Variations*, (MS in Horton Foote Papers). Page references to *Themes and Variations* in the text refer to this manuscript.

that this is "a tragic play." Now nature is out of balance. Sam, Henry's brother, tries to turn his parents against Henry, but the parents decide to pay off the mortgage on the home of Anna's family to do penance for "Henry's jilting Anna" (59). The Preacher assures Mr. Johnson that God will reward them for their action. Sam asks forgiveness from his parents for his words against his brother, and Henry returns as the Chorus declares that this is a play of joy and celebration "of the beauty and order of things. A hymn of praise for life" (71). Finally, Henry and Anna are reunited, and Henry proclaims, "I feel peace in my heart, Anna," and once again, as at the beginning, he misses a falling star, which she observes, as the Preacher enters and the people sing their hymn of praise (71–2).

The action of *Themes and Variations*, once again reflects Horton Foote's Christian beliefs, implying that man, represented as Everyman in the character of Henry, is destined to repeat this circular pattern of innocence, temptation, guilt, and redemption in a fallen world. Foote illustrates that the demands of living in modern society make difficult, almost impossible, that growth of the spirit which involves a sense of belonging to God and to nature. A major conflict in modern man, according to Horton, takes place between the biological impulses of his nature and the pressures and constraints of his social environment. But in the end, the writer affirms the transforming power of the female spirit to nurture and give life-saving affection to men who have lost their way. Anna stands by Henry throughout his many temptations and transgressions, ultimately offering him forgiveness for his wrongdoings.

Writing about the great mystery of human existence, Horton investigates the many sources that enable his characters to accept life courageously and to face death. One such source of courage is the intimacy between a man and a woman, as seen in the relationship between Anna and Henry in *Themes and Variations*. As Gerald Wood points out, "Whether or not the characters are defeated, the endless pursuit of personhood is completed by the return to the spirit of God. But while the language, images, and stories of Christianity surround Foote's characters with examples of loving community, the writer does not insist they follow his beliefs. Instead, religious experience is offered as a potential source of healing, but it always must be sought after by the individual and made real by the love of human beings for each other. Key to the health and happiness of his characters, whether religious or not, is a powerful intimacy that inspires courage and offers peace in the face of death."[3]

The Return, the second play Horton wrote at the King-Smith School, is much more realistic and formal than *Themes and Variations*, echoing the dramas of Henrik Ibsen, especially *Ghosts* and *Hedda Gabler*, which Horton had recently directed.[4] Written as a long one-act, *The Return* is a fascinating, psychological drama that explores the idea of guilt and personal responsibility. The play takes place in a room of a family home that has been refurbished to remove any evidence of a previous murder. As the story unfolds, we discover that one brother has killed his father in a fit of insanity, apparently caused by advanced syphilis, and the murderous brother is now in a sanitarium. Initially, Mother and Daughter agree to not mention the crime in an effort to sustain a sense of peace in their lives, hoping as well that the daughter's second marriage will succeed, the first one having lasted only a week. But when the second Brother returns, he challenges them to examine the events leading up to the murder and their own role in the killing of their father. He also announces that he has fathered an illegitimate child, made a failed marriage proposal to the mother of his daughter, and is making plans to gain custody and raise the child himself, since the mother refused his offer of marriage. Brother's insistence they discuss the past drives Sister mad, and in a moment of hysteria she imagines blood on the walls of their home. Finally, the mother accepts Brother's position but his sister cannot admit that she had anything to do with the murder. By refusing, the daughter aligns herself with death, claiming she is "not responsible," so she "too, can murder" (54). In a monologue that sums up the theme of the play, Brother proclaims: "each of us has his responsibility to the tragedy. If we have ignorance as our defense, let us see that as our guilt and seek wisdom…. A tragedy is completed only if the experience is wasted and we are lured into repeating it" (50). In the final analysis, Horton celebrates the individual's search for truth and asserts that the breaking of unhealthy cycles of violence and retribution is a pathway to forgiveness and personal freedom.

---

[3] Gerald C. Wood, "The Physical Hunger for the Spiritual: Southern Religious Experience in the Plays of Horton Foote," *The World is Our Home: Society and Culture in Contemporary Southern Writing*, ed. Jeffrey J. Folks and Nancy Summers Folks (Lexington: University of Kentucky Press, 2000) 249–50.

[4] Horton Foote, *The Return*, (MS in Horton Foote Papers). Page references in the text refer to this manuscript.

The final play Horton wrote and directed at King-Smith, *Homecoming*, is more abstract and minimalistic in style than either of his previous two works, using a chorus of gossiping men, establishing time and place by the simple repositioning of furniture and set pieces, and moving between the reality and inner consciousness of a doctor, Roy, who is essential to the health of his community, though lost in his private life.[5] Roy is deeply dependent on his mother for money and emotional stability. His wife, Marie, is desperate for his time and attention but quite annoying in her demands. The action of the play intensifies when Roy's old girlfriend, Connie, returns to town. Wanting to be in love as a way of filling his emptiness, Roy becomes obsessed with her. Connie accepts his advances, but she is too jaded from previous relationships with men to provide the support and love Roy needs. After Roy and Connie become lovers, she becomes as cold and demanding as his wife. When Roy's money runs out, he becomes frantic for ways to support Connie, finally even confessing his affair to his mother in hopes she will give him financial aid. But she refuses, and before the lovers can escape to their hideaway, Connie receives a promise of marriage from a previous lover who sends her money for passage to New Orleans. When Roy returns home and discovers she has left him, he kills himself.

Homecoming contains a number of memorable expressionistic images, such as Roy imagining a repentant Connie, who asks him to save her, to "Redeem me from my shame by loving me" (22), and the sudden appearance in the final act of an unidentified young girl who curtsies, speaks directly to the audience, and explains that Roy has hung himself. Her declaration casts a dream-like cloud over the rest of the play, especially when Roy speaks to Connie from the grave, declaring he committed suicide to make her feel guilty. Even bolder is a scene in which Roy climbs a ladder, imitating his obsession with tree climbing as a child, and moves back and forth between past and present time conversing with his mother and wife. This scene looks forward to Horton's one-act play *The Man Who Climbed the Pecan Trees*, in which a spiritually bankrupt and drunken Stanley tries to escape his ill-fated life by climbing trees on the courthouse square. Gerald Wood also points out that "in this late 1940s play, over fifty years before *The Carpetbagger's Children*, Horton Foote is already exploring a liminal dramatic space,

---

[5] Horton Foote, *Homecoming*, (MS in Horton Foote Papers). Page references to *Homecoming* in the text refer to this manuscript.

more indicative of Roy's consciousness than any objective or natural reality."[6]

By spring 1949, Horton Foote had run the course of his experimentation with music, dance, and theater, and having assured himself that he had learned his craft and knew his subject, he decided to return to New York. As he explains in *Beginnings*:

> as grateful as I was for the opportunity I had been given to have my own theater and to experiment as much as I pleased, I wanted to go back to my earlier way of writing. I felt I was a storyteller, and that I wanted to write plays simply and directly. And I thought of [Konstantin] Trepliov's speech in the last scene of *The Seagull:* "I'm coming more and more to the conclusion that it's a matter not of old forms and not of new forms, but that a man writes, not thinking at all of what form to choose, writes because it comes pouring out from his soul."[7]

By this time, Horton had been a playwright for nearly ten years. He had learned much about the theater from many varied and unexpected sources. From his Russian acting teachers, especially Andrius Jilinsky, he discovered that the primary goal of the theater artist is to be a seeker of truth, to "see what lies beneath the surface" in the lives of human beings, and to "speak to the human heart."[8] From great dancers, like Graham, Humphrey, Bettis, and De Mille, he discovered how to incorporate music and dance into his plays, and even though his future work would limit the role of these media for realistic ends, both music and dance would reappear often as central metaphors in his plays and screenplays. Horton had also been influenced by the directors he had known and worked with, especially Mary Hunter, who recognized his keen insight into the deep fear of the give-and-take of love and the closeness of healthy personal relationships, and made him aware that simply relying on a sense of place was not enough, if as a writer you weren't content with mere quaintness and parochialism.

During the 1940s, Horton found his place among the new realists of American theater, but unlike Southern writers such as Lynn Riggs and Paul Green, he was determined to rid himself of his regionalist ten-

---

[6] Gerald C. Wood, "Horton Foote at the American Actors Company, Dance Observer, and King Smith Productions: Nothing More Real than the Human Heart," *The Horton Foote Review* (2005): 73.

[7] Horton Foote, *Beginnings: A Memoir* (New York: Scribner Press, 2001) 278.

[8] Andrius Jilinsky, *The Joy of Acting: A Primer for Actors* (New York: Peter Lang, 1990) 3–10.

dencies. With the help of Katherine Anne Porter, he discovered the aim of truthfulness in art and found a way to use the particulars of time and place without being trapped in regionalism. In his essay, "The Artist as Myth-Maker," Horton expressed his belief that the writer should be a truth seeker, always willing "to risk the collision of myth and reality," an idea he found brilliantly expressed in Porter's *Noon Wine, The Old Mortality* and *Pale Horse, Pale Rider*. Even when creating fiction, Horton argued, the artist should use myths that are "truly rooted in a time and place" and not "degenerate into stereotype."[9] For Horton, myth should always be grounded in the real language, stories, and memories of ordinary, living people.

Horton's work would always be personal, but he did not have the autographical bent of Eugene O'Neill, nor did he possess Tennessee Williams's psychological angst. Horton was always more interested in dramatizing other people's lives than his own, and even though his voice was Southern, like Williams, he was not fond of depicting ludicrous or grotesque characters, choosing instead to write about ordinary individuals who showed unusual courage in the face of economic disaster or unexpected change. Neither was Horton prone to write political drama like Clifford Odets or moral lessons like Arthur Miller. His language of political protest sounded strained and rhetorical in *Out of My House* and *People in the Show*, even though the views he expressed were meaningful and heartfelt. Horton's writing would always rely upon the simple, sparse, and unadorned language of his native Wharton, Texas.

Writing and directing at the King-Smith School had clarified Horton's perspective on the theater and on life. The materials he had chosen, those he extracted from his close observation of life in Wharton, and those he would continue to write about were a sense of belonging, the search for home, the inevitability of change, and the resilience of the human spirit, but he was also intrigued by themes of loneliness and loss of faith in America. In *Wharton Dance, Texas Town, Out of My House*, and *Only the Heart*, Horton showed great insight into small-town mores, the problems of adolescents, the struggles of young women, the search for identity in a fallen world, and the effects of materialistic greed. Now, he believed that past injustices and violence do not exempt individuals from responsibility for their own lives, and he felt that guilt, when managed in a healthy way, could lead to personal freedom. But emotional freedom

---

[9] Foote, *Genesis*, 82.

can only be achieved when shared with loving companions, in imitation of a benevolent God, and never through fear or punishment. In Horton's dramatic landscape, courage and grace are possible when men and women seek the truth and follow the inclinations of their hearts.

In *The Chase*, the last play to be written at the King-Smith School, Horton returned to the storytelling style of *Only the Heart* and followed Katherine Anne Porter's advice in writing "real fiction," which transforms the details of history and locale into a higher order of art. His writing now exchanged abstractions of the past for particulars simultaneously real and mythic, creating a story that would resonate across all races and social strata.

The Chase is unquestionably the most mature and skillfully written play of Horton Foote's early career, revealing a major advancement in thought, language, and dramatic form.[10] The play is loosely based on an actual incident that took place in the playwright's hometown of Wharton on Christmas Day, 1945, and portrays friends and family members caught up in one of the most violent moments in Wharton County history. At the time, legendary sheriff Buckshot Lane was holding Pete Norris, an emotionally disturbed outlaw, in the Wharton County jail when Norris pulled a gun on Buckshot, shooting twice and slightly wounding the sheriff. Not wanting to kill his young prisoner, Buckshot lunged to disarm Norris, but before Buckshot could secure Norris's gun, the deputy sheriff intervened and killed the prisoner.

From this incident Horton created a play that examines the responsibility of a community in the making of a criminal and deals with the emotional conflicts of a Texas sheriff faced with the knowledge that killing to uphold the law can be as soul shattering as murder. In his 1952 essay, "Richmond U.S.A.," Horton elaborates on the drama's unseen background—the town of Richmond and its citizens—and the inherent conflicts of *The Chase*. He also clarifies his writing as a moral and social history of small-town America and defines his role of playwright as that of a social observer:

> My plays are generally placed in a small town in Texas. This town is not Wharton. It is a town of my imagination and combines characteristics of small towns I have known on the Texas Gulf Coast. I call my town Richmond. It is the county seat and has two cotton gins, an oil well and

---

[10] Horton Foote, *The Chase*, in *Horton Foote Collected Plays*, vol. 2 (New York: Smith and Kraus 1996) 61–112. All page references to *The Chase* in the text refer to this publication.

stores built around the courthouse square. Richmond is populated by people who trace their arrival to the Eighteen Thirties. Negro families who came with them as slaves, Mexicans who crept in as wetbacks during cotton-picking season, and Central Europeans who arrived in America in the early Nineteen Twenties.

The town is fed and sustained by its cotton farms, its grazing herds, its rice fields and its pecan groves. There are areas of flat, ugly prairie land; there are miles of bottom land dense with trees and foliage. Its people can grow crops three times a year. Its land is rich with oil and sulphur. Contrariwise, there are the hazards as well such as hurricanes in the fall before the cotton is picked, drought, too much rain during planting time, too frequent showers while the cotton is maturing. The people here spend a great deal of their time watching the skies—a year's work, a year's income can be wiped out in a day by a hurricane or too much rain. At one time the plantation system flourished; now the plantations have been broken up into small farms or ranches. "The White Man's Union" is defunct, and the Negro is beginning to vote and is slowly gaining admission to the universities. The segregation of the Mexicans is also breaking down. Of course, like most small Southern towns, Richmond is taking sides about all this. There are farmers, the oil crews, the cotton buyers, doctors, cooks and beauty parlor operators, the land owners, the bankers whose lives in some way are influenced by all these social changes. I have given them names. The white people are Mavises, Weems, Strachens, Robedauxs, Damons and Stewarts; the Negroes are Splendids, Lesters and Leroys....

I like to think of my plays as a moral and social history of Richmond. I try to choose for my characters problems, which are specific to their particular section and yet will have some meaning for the outer world. In my writing in the past, I have concentrated mainly on the problems of the upper and middle classes and the old land-holding aristocracy. Actually, aristocracy as it is known in the rest of the South is just a memory kept alive by the great aunts and the old men in Richmond. But, economically, such a way of life has hardly been feasible for twenty-five or thirty years. I saw the last of it go when I was a child. I heard it mourned and glorified and the passing of it finally accepted. The middle class now reigns supreme—their thinking, their tastes, and their culture. The prosperity of the region has made them flourish. Surrounding them, serving them are the poorer groups—the tenant farmers, the servants, the day laborers. These worlds seldom meet. They do meet in *The Chase*—brought together by the dehumanization of one man, Bubber Reeves, and a sheriff struggling to escape dehumanization. I have tried to make Richmond true to itself, true to the towns I have known. It has its tragedies and comedies, its rich and poor, its great virtues and its terrible injustices.[11]

At the moral center of this volatile world is Eldon Hawes, who has been sheriff of Richmond for almost fifteen years. He and his wife Ruby are expecting a child, and because they want to rear their son in a quieter, less dangerous atmosphere than that afforded a sheriff's family, Hawes has decided to purchase a farm and live a simpler life. His plans are interrupted by the escape from prison of Bubber Reeves, a local miscreant on the wrong side of the law most of his life and finally sent to prison for murder. Bubber has vowed revenge upon Hawes, who sent him away. The townspeople, cruel and abusive to Bubber as a boy, become hysterical at the news of his escape. Because many of them fear Bubber will come back to Richmond to avenge the wrongs they committed against him as a youngster, they pressure Hawes to capture Bubber, threatening to lynch him if the sheriff does not settle the matter. The town's cry for violence causes an ironic reversal of the classic Western plot. The sheriff, the only man in town who stands for law and order, must now protect the criminal rather than the townspeople.

The pervasive fear of the townspeople in *The Chase* aptly reflects the apprehension of Americans during the time Horton wrote the play. In the summer of 1949, Stalin's Soviet Union had exploded its first nuclear bomb. That fall, Communists seized power in China. In February 1950, Senator Joseph McCarthy of Wisconsin gave his first "Communists in the State Department" speech in West Virginia; and in June of the same year, the Korean War began as North Korea invaded South Korea. Even though such national concerns were evident in the play, Horton was more interested in uncovering seeds of violence and roots of individual courage in a small Texas town.

As in many of his plays, Horton Foote shows sympathy for all his characters, no matter how lawless and troubled. Bubber Reeves doesn't fit the preconceived idea of the depraved outlaw; instead, Horton depicts him as a young man who has been shaped by the corrupt society in which he has lived. The real criminals in the play are the townspeople who want to kill him. For example, when they were both children, a wealthy boy, Edwin Stewart, let Bubber take the blame for stealing money when he himself had robbed the cash register at the local drugstore, and when told about the robbery, Old Sunshine, the local

---

[11] Horton Foote, "Richmond USA," *New York Times*, 12 April 1952: C 1–3.

sheriff at the time, merely laughed, admitting that the law protects the upper class unfairly. Now Edwin is afraid Bubber will seek revenge for Edwin's deceitfulness and even goes so far as to threaten to keep Hawes from getting a bank loan he desperately needs to buy a farm if the sheriff won't place a deputy at his house.

Bubber's most ruthless enemy is Hawks Damon, a despicable town leader who calls for the escaped convict's life after Bubber robs his store. Damon commands the sheriff to hunt down and kill Bubber, declaring that the good people of the town will make sure he will never bother them again.

Bubber's mother, Mrs. Reeves, does everything she can to save her son, telling Sheriff Hawes that, as a boy, Bubber was told he was born wicked and when he did wrong, Old Sunshine would always advise her to whip the boy. Mrs. Reeves would beat Bubber and even dressed him like a girl to keep him home. Her misguided actions, along with those of the townspeople, led the boy to retaliate by breaking the law and com-mitting acts of violence, even murder. Now, Mrs. Reeves regrets her treatment of Bubber, and in hopes of saving him from the lynch mob, Mrs. Reeves tells Sheriff Hawes where to find her son. She hopes the sheriff can persuade Bubber to surrender before the townspeople find him.

When Hawes corners the fugitive by the river bottom, where he has been living with his girlfriend, Anna, and friend, Knub, Bubber brings about his own death by threatening the sheriff with a gun. Hawes, believing that Bubber intends to kill him, shoots in self-defense. Tragically, when Hawes examines Bubber's gun, he finds it empty. Sheriff Hawes has done the very thing he swore he would not do, and his action shatters him emotionally.

The play's final scene focuses on Hawes, whose failure to save Bubber still haunts him. Ruby finally awakens her husband to his role in Bubber's fate: "All I know is you did your best. You tried. That's all we can ask…. This chase didn't start tonight. It didn't end tonight. Don't run away Hawes. Keep on livin'. Keep on tryin'" (59). The play ends with Hawes's promise to speak to an uncontrollable twelve-year-old boy who has run away from home, and Hawes's acknowledgment that "all a man can do is try" (60). For Hawes, the chase continues.

Throughout the course of this final scene, Hawes undergoes a difficult transition, one that begins with guilt over his brutal past, moves to an almost paralyzing introspection, and ends with personal acceptance and the love and support of his wife, Ruby. Hawes bemoans having killed Bubber, and, like many of Foote's male characters, wants to rid himself of such violent actions, to find a sense of peace and absolution. In the end, Hawes does find courage in personal conviction and purity of motive. His fear and deep anger at human violence and brutality are rendered tolerable by the love of his wife and the realization that he might be able to spare another young boy from suffering the tragedy of Bubber Reeves.

In *The Chase*, Horton Foote created a powerful record of the horror and tragedy that result from prejudice, injustice, and mass hysteria. His concern for the moral and social decay of Richmond is clearly evident, as community malice, familial indifference, intolerance, and depravity threaten the lives of its people. In this small Texas community, fear and violence and the consequences are depicted credibly, but Horton did not lecture or preach. Rather, he allows us to observe human beings as they interact with one another without condemning or dictating what conclusions to draw. Horton portrays the conflict between classes and the fears that cause common people to rise up against law and order, but his major emphasis is directed at Eldon Hawes and his struggle to overcome the inescapable and unavoidable situation in which he finds himself. For what matters above all else is the final attitude the protagonist takes toward his humiliation, suffering, and personal failures.

Although *The Chase* stands as the finest achievement in Horton's early career, the play was not produced on Broadway for another two years. Initially Horton felt the story would resonate with New York producers, but after speaking with his good friend, director Harold Clurman, he was not so convinced. Clurman wrote to Horton to say he enjoyed reading the play but thought it needed work. Horton took Clurman's suggestions to heart and began revising *The Chase* at Lillian's family home in Pennsylvania in the summer of 1949. While he was working on the script, Lucy Kroll submitted it to a contest for new American plays, which carried a substantial cash prize. One of the judges was the renowned director and producer Herman Shumlin who, after reading the script, called Kroll to say he wanted to produce it on Broadway. Since it was against all rules of fair play for a judge to take an option on a competing script, Shumlin asked Horton and Lucy to withdraw *The Chase* from the contest. They granted his request, but in the end Shumlin never got around to producing the play and Horton was left without either the prize money or a Broadway production.

One of the more fascinating possibilities for staging the play came from an unlikely source. Horton had showed a copy of the script to Karl Malden, who was interested in playing the role of Sheriff Hawes. Malden gave it to his friend Mildred Dunnock, who in turn gave the play to her friend Patricia Neal. At the time, Neal was romantically involved with renowned actor Gary Cooper, and after reading the play Neal felt the role of Sheriff Hawes was a perfect part for him. Actress Celeste Holm heard about her friends' interest in *The Chase* and decided she would like to produce it with Cooper in the lead. Unfortunately, Holm was unable to raise the money for a production.

Horton had just about given up hope of ever seeing his play onstage when one day he got a call out of the blue from Gary Cooper, asking if he would meet with him. Cooper came to Horton's apartment and told him he liked the play very much and wanted to do it, but not as a stage production. Cooper asked to buy the film rights to *The Chase*, explaining that he suffered terribly from stage fright. The camera didn't bother him, but the thought of going onstage made him physically ill. Horton remembered him saying, "You know, I'm a very nervous man. I vomit after every take and would go crazy if I had to be on stage. I was on stage once at the Paramount Theatre in a personal appearance, and I had a breakdown. I can't do it." Since at the time Horton had no interest in adapting *The Chase* for the screen, he refused Cooper's request.

About six months later, Horton got a telegram from his lawyer, Arnold Weisberger, telling him that Gary Cooper had filmed *High Noon* and that he believed the character of Sheriff Kane was stolen from *The Chase*. Horton recalled thinking, "'Oh, marvelous. We can sue him and get a lot of scandal.' But when I went to see *High Noon*, I could honestly say it had nothing to do with my play. If this is what they think my play is about, I'm in deep trouble. It's about a sheriff, all right, but has nothing to do with my play, so I wouldn't sue."[12]

Meanwhile, two producers were competing to stage *The Chase*: Jean Dalrymple, who wanted to cast Franchot Tone in the role of Sheriff Hawes, and Jose Ferrer, who was something of a prodigy at the time and seemed the more likely of the two to get financial backing for a

---

[12] David Middleton, "Winning, Losing, and Compromising: The Screenwriter Contends for Personal Turf," *The Voice of an American Playwright*, ed. Gerald C. Wood and Marion Castleberry (Macon GA: Mercer University Press, 2012) 16.

Broadway production. Ferrer, who would also direct the play, wanted John Hodiak to play the lead. Horton preferred Tone for the role. Dalrymple had been the first to contact Horton about producing the work, but Lucy Kroll wanted to go with Ferrer. In a decision that Horton would later regret, he agreed to Lucy Kroll's request not to answer the phone when Dalrymple called with her offer. Consequently, Ferrer became producer by default. "Jose Ferrer was touching everything, and whatever he touched was working," Horton recalled.

> Remember he was the great actor-producer-director, and the first thing he did was ask for co-authorship, to which I said, "Oh, no, I'm not going to do that." This was the old practice in the days of strong producers. They would not get line credit, but they would get 40 percent of what you made. He insisted he was very good on script, and I said I was delighted to hear that. And he told me he was like a coach, that on *Stalag 17* he had come back between the acts and given the cast pep talks and it worked miracles. Anyway, he had a contract ready, and my agent was very eager. Ferrer said that I could stage the play and he would come in and get us really working.[13]

Horton signed the contract, and as it turned out he ended up directing the play himself.

Eventually *The Chase* was performed at the Playhouse Theatre on 15 April 1952 with a cast that featured John Hodiak in his Broadway debut as Sheriff Hawes, Kim Hunter as Ruby, Nan McFarland as Mrs. Reeves, Murray Hamilton as Bubber, Lonny Chapman as Knub, and Kim Stanley as Anna. The production also featured a young assistant stage manager by the name of Jason Robards, who also understudied John Hodiak. For the most part, Horton was pleased with the performances of the cast, especially the acting of Kim Stanley, who he believed was one of our great actresses. Horton, Lillian, and Kim became very close friends during rehearsals of *The Chase*, and afterwards Stanley would emerge from the production as one of the foremost interpreters of Horton Foote's work. They would go on to collaborate on another Broadway play, six live television dramas, and an acclaimed feature film.

While critics applauded the work of the actors in *The Chase*, they found the play itself lacking in craftsmanship. Richard Watts, Jr., of the *New York Post* said, "*The Chase* suffers from the tendency to repeat itself in the manner of an over-extended one-act play" and the powerful Brooks Atkinson of the *New York Times* stated: "Apart from some well-

---

[13] Ibid.

written small scenes, Mr. Foote's drama does not make much impression on the theatre."[14] What all of the critics failed to notice was what Horton Foote scholar Marian Burkhart recognized more than fifty years later, namely that *The Chase* is a commentary on the American myth of the individual who achieves justice single-handedly through violence and brutality. Burkhart argues that unlike the Western film *High Noon*, *The Chase* does not justify or glorify violence but instead depicts an ordinary man who does not want to kill the criminal but simply return him to prison. Burkhart asserts: "Perhaps one comes nearer to explaining [Horton Foote's] impact if one notes that for all its ordinariness, [his] world is neither calm nor orderly. What serenity exists—and serenity is, in a sense, his subject—exists against a background of endless violence"[15]

The Chase closed on 10 May 1953 after only thirty-one performances, and in the final analysis, Foote did not achieve the kind of Broadway success his contemporaries Tennessee Williams and Arthur Miller had enjoyed from their Broadway productions. Nevertheless, the decade of the 1940s was a very fruitful time for the playwright. He had seen his dream of being an actor give way to the truth that his talent really lay in writing, not in performing. He had written eighteen plays, many of them produced on Broadway and others in Off-Broadway theaters, and he had experimented with various theatrical forms. The 1950s would prove to be an even more extraordinary period of growth, as Horton Foote faced new challenges, explored a different kind of artistic medium, and became one of the true pioneers of the "Golden Age" of television.

---

[14] Richard Watts, Jr., "A Manhunt in a Texas Community," *New York Times*, 16 April 1952; Brooks Atkinson, "Review of Horton Foote's *The Chase*," *New York Times*, 16 April 1952.

[15] Marian Burkhart, "Horton Foote's Many Roads Home: An American Playwright and his Characters," *Commonweal* (26 February 1988): 111.

Part Four

Writing for the Screen

I don't write to honor the past. I write to investigate, to try to figure out what happened and why it happened, knowing I'll never really know. I think all the writers that I admire have this same desire, the desire to bring order out of chaos.

—Horton Foote

9

Making Peace with the Little Box
1949–54

Horton and Lillian returned to New York in the fall of 1949, only to discover that American theater was changing. Tennessee Williams and Arthur Miller were now considered America's leading playwrights thanks to highly successful Broadway productions of *The Glass Menagerie* (1945), *A Streetcar Named Desire* (1947), and *The Death of the Salesman* (1949). Both writers were receiving the sort of critical acclaim that Clifford Odets and Eugene O'Neill had received earlier and for which Foote longed. Elia Kazan now was considered America's greatest director because of his work with Williams and Miller, and many of the producers with whom Horton had worked when he first came to New York had either retired or passed away. Modern dance, as Horton remembered it, was also vanishing, and the dancers who continued to perform, like Martha Graham, found managing companies on a shoestring budget nearly impossible both on and off Broadway. The Theatre Guild and the Playwrights Company were still producing shows, but producers were finding escalating production costs ruinous to the American Theatre. All told, Broadway was undergoing a crippling economic decline. Unemployment among actors and directors was on the rise, and writers found themselves struggling to make a living in the legitimate theater. As Horton Foote noted, "playwrights had to look more and more to off-Broadway and regional theatres for productions."[1] While it was difficult to find financial backing for a production, the process of mounting a show on Broadway was the same. A producer selected a play, cast as many big name actors as possible, and then took it on the road to Boston, Philadelphia, or Baltimore for an out-of-town tour of at least four weeks. According to the critical response a show received, the play was revised, often recast, and sometimes a new director was hired. Nearly always, the playwright spent hours rewriting under the pressure of the impending New York opening.

---

[1] Horton Foote, *Genesis of an American Playwright*, ed. Marion Castleberry (Waco TX: Baylor University Press, 2004) 269.

After arriving in New York, Mary Hunter hired Horton to teach classes at the Theatre Wing, providing a bit of a relief from his financial concerns. But even though the teaching job was intellectually invigorating and gave him time to write, it did not pay enough to support his growing family. Lillian was now pregnant and expecting a child in the spring. In an effort to save money, Horton sold the car he and Lillian had bought in Washington and the couple stayed in a friend's apartment in Chelsea until they found one of their own in Greenwich Village. Horton also accepted a few commissioned writing jobs, including a ballet with words, entitled *Roustabout*, for the Musical Review, *Two's Company*, directed by his old friend Jerome Robbins and starring legendary actress Bette Davis (1952). He also had a couple of plays attracting some attention, but no producers were willing to take an option on any of his works. The money situation looked bleak, and the crisis became even more critical on 31 March 1950 when Lillian gave birth to a baby girl, Barbara Hallie, at the French Hospital in New York.

The Footes' financial situation took a fortuitous turn, however, when colleague Vincent Donehue helped Horton secure a job writing scripts for NBC's *The Gabby Hayes Show*, a weekly television series for children that featured the adventurous exploits of the Western character Gabby Hayes. The work consisted of formulaic writing, which Horton found less than satisfying, but it paid three hundred dollars a week, a substantial sum in those days. Horton stayed with *The Gabby Hayes Show* for only two seasons (October 1950 to December 1951), but his involvement with the program and the NBC television network helped set the stage for a more significant development in his career.

In 1951, Horton was commissioned to write a one-act play for NBC television's *Lamp Unto My Feet*, a religious-based television series seeking to enlarge its audience and alter the scope of its programming.[2] He had never written an original half-hour television drama, but he accepted the offer and drawing from memory and imagination, he penned one of his most overtly religious plays, *Ludie Brooks*. Inspired by an episode in the life of his grandfather, Tom Brooks, Ludie Brooks tells the story of an aging small-town preacher forced to cope with the death of his only daughter. Horton explained:

> My grandfather was very religious. He had attended church regularly and supported it generously with his money; but for some reason he had

---

[2] Horton Foote, *Ludie Brooks*, (MS in Horton Foote Papers). Page references to *Ludie Brooks* in the text refer to this manuscript.

never become a member. Mother said that when Daisy died, one of the neighbors came to him and asked, "Mr. Brooks, did it ever occur to you that the death of this child is God's judgment on you for not joining the church?" His face, my mother said, flushed. But he answered very simply, "No, Mrs. Davidson, it never did." Unless I asked about the two little girls [who had died in infancy] they were never mentioned, and there were no pictures of them anywhere. This puzzled me greatly.[3]

Other grieving family members in the story are Daisy, Ludie's wife; Maybelle, Martha's seven year-old daughter; and Mrs. Brooks, his mother, who recalls the time when her son "got the call" and switched from farming to preaching (2). Mrs. Brooks believes Ludie was a born farmer, but she accepts his choice of professions by admitting that while he is not the greatest preacher she has ever heard, he is "real sincere" (1).

As the teleplay opens, Martha has died and Ludie, after praying two days for her life to be spared, believes that God has forsaken him. To regain his sense of purpose, Ludie must first overcome his spiritual crises. The story reaches its climax when a neighbor, Mrs. May, intrudes on Ludie's privacy and asks him to pray for her son, who has been missing for weeks. Mrs. May asks Ludie to pray with her, and during the prayer she reveals the resolute nature of her Christian faith. Afterward, she tells Ludie he must trust in God regardless of the circumstances, saying without faith he could destroy himself with grief's inwardness: "Grief can cripple and destroy and consume us, just as much as drunkenness or sin, and…and how each of us meets our temptation is a matter of your heart and my heart" (22). In the end, Ludie renews his faith and finds the courage to return to the ministry and his calling to preach.

Ludie Brooks, which aired on NBC in February 1951, caught the attention of Fred Coe, a close friend of Vincent Donehue and the founding producer of NBC's *Philco-Goodyear Television Playhouse*, who recognized Horton's ability to write for the new medium. In 1952, Coe hired Horton to create nine original dramas for the *Television Playhouse*, thereby instigating one of the most productive and satisfying periods in Horton's career. Coe offered to pay the writer twelve hundred dollars for each show, and the network asked to retain in perpetuity all the rights to his plays. Lucy Kroll, however, insisted Horton retain his own dramatic copyright and all future rights to his play or he would not sign the contract. NBC agreed to Kroll's demands and on 27 April 1952 Horton Foote's *The Travelers*, which tells the story of Nadine Thornton and Sue

---

[3] Foote, *Genesis*, 26.

Stella Morrison and their efforts to find husbands during their two-week vacation in New York, aired on the *Philco-Goodyear Television Playhouse*. This production began a partnership between Horton and Fred Coe that lasted through 1956 and produced seventeen plays on live television, ten in 1953 alone.

Postwar America's enthusiastic embrace of television theater nurtured the partnership between Horton Foote and Fred Coe. Spectators by the millions chose to stay home and watch the black-and-white screen as creative artists from both Broadway and Hollywood began to migrate to the newer medium. Overnight, the number of Writers Guild of America members working in television grew from forty-five in February 1951 to one hundred ten by the end of that year. By 1952, the number had grown to such heights that Edward Barry Roberts, an NBC script editor, was prompted to comment, "The centers of production are swarming with would-be television writers... although paradoxically there aren't enough really good writers to supply the demand. Yet it is only through good writing that television will grow and fulfill its potential destiny.... We are all waiting...for the television artist playwright to appear."[4] The search for talented writers who could produce appropriate and imaginative television scripts resulted in the creation of a new form of drama—the teleplay.

Credit for the creation of original television drama must be given to Fred Coe. A graduate of Yale University's School of Drama, Coe had worked in television since 1945 when he became production manager of NBC in New York. By the time the network placed him in charge of the Sunday evening anthology series *Television Playhouse*, he had directed and produced so many successful productions for theater and television that he commanded respect and freedom. Consequently, when the *Philco-Goodyear Television Playhouse* premiered in October 1948, everyone at NBC supported Coe's mission to bring hit Broadway plays to America by way of television. But as Coe explained in his 1954 essay, "TV Drama's Declaration of Independence," this initial idea proved unworkable because theater dramatists did not create enough plays to cover television's demands. Originally, NBC took Broadway plays, trimmed them to an hour, and then cast a Broadway star in the lead role. However, within a couple of months it became obvious that this could not continue to work, because they would quickly run out of material.

---

[4] Edward Barry Roberts, "Writing for Television," *The Best Television Plays, 1950–1951*, ed. William Kaufman (New York: Hastings House, 1952) 300.

When Coe's original idea faltered, he tried converting classic dramas to television. Plays like Edmond Rostand's *Cyrano de Bergerac*, as well as works by Shakespeare, underwent major revisions before reaching the living-room screen. When these grew scarce, Coe tried short stories and novels, but this scheme also proved unsatisfactory because writers could not successfully cut a novel to fit within an hour format.

Eventually, Coe was forced to move away from published and produced works and to explore the use of original television dramas. As Coe explained, since writers were already researching topics, they decided they might as well write original scripts and documentaries to fit television's format, rather than purchase manuscripts written in other formats then spend time altering them to fit a one-hour time slot.[5]

Coe believed that television's hour-long program with its commercial announcements provided an excellent format in which to produce an original teleplay. The hour production corresponds to a three-act play, with the commercial breaks serving as curtains, allowing the writers to build to climaxes and the audiences to relax between peaks of dramatic tension. Fred Coe did not see television drama as a regressive step from the theater and, therefore, was able to assemble a creative and harmonious production team for the *Philco-Goodyear Television Playhouse*. Directors like Vincent Donehue, Delbert Mann, and Arthur Penn, and actors like Steve McQueen, Geraldine Page, Rip Torn, Julie Harris, Joanne Woodward, and Kim Stanley found a hospitable, creative environment at NBC. Fortunately, from the beginning, dramatic television and the Actors Studio—the premiere actor training school in America—sustained and nourished each other. Television budgets were very small at the time, and networks couldn't afford to pay established stars, so studio actors who would work for very little money, proved a godsend to the *Philco-Goodyear Television Playhouse*. Under Coe's guidance, the studio was able to create quality work within the preordained television structure. More importantly, writers Paddy Chayefsky, N. Richard Nash, Tad Mosel, Robert Alan Arthur, David Shaw, and Horton Foote (one of the few to achieve stature as a playwright before joining the staff) assumed a central position in television drama, gaining for writers the celebrity of stars.

The television writer was not only supported in his endeavors, but he was also considered the principal artistic source for the medium and

---

[5] Fred Coe, "TV-Drama's Declaration of Independence," *Theatre Arts* (June 1954): 29–32.

granted considerable control over the presentation of his material. Coe signed his writers to multi-show contracts, but more importantly he encouraged them to attend rehearsals and gave them an active role in casting. Horton Foote, like others, appreciated the respect Coe gave to writers. "We were the ones he featured very aggressively so that it became an hour for the writer," Horton said. "We were encouraged as writers not to find formulas that would please many people, but to...deeply please ourselves. So that was an enormous lesson for me and a great gift."[6]

Because of the control afforded them, playwrights were able to uncover the particular strengths of the medium and learn how to communicate their dramas effectively within the requirements of the electronic medium. Fred Coe pointed out that the writers knew "the physical problems of producing a 'live' show on TV," just as a professional Broadway playwright knew how many sets and characters were practical to use. They were "exposed to camera techniques, lighting problems...they came to the first script reading, and for the next ten days in which the show [was] wheeled and whacked into shape, the author [was] with his play."[7]

The flexibility of the television camera allowed directors to expand their simplified stage settings to include a realistic sense of movement and changing environment. And the camera followed actors around the studio and across different locales while keeping the characters and actions at an engaging distance. The effect of such kinetic eaves-dropping left the audience with a sense of having overheard part of another person's life. Television writer Paddy Chayefsky explained that, "the camera allows us a degree of intimacy that can never be achieved on stage.... In television, you can be literally and freely real. The scenes can be played as if the actors were unaware of their audience. The dialogue can sound as if it had been wiretapped."[8] Tad Mosel added that the medium encouraged the dramatist to "focus on one or two people or a situation in which the events were ordinary. Never before has there been a medium so suited to what I call the 'personal drama'—

---

[6] Gary Edgerton, "A Visit to the Imaginary Landscape of Harrison, Texas: Sketching the Film Career of Horton Foote," *Literature/Film Quarterly* 12 (Winter 1989): 5.

[7] Coe, 87.

[8] Ibid., 45.

that is, a play wherein the writer explores one simple happening, a day, or even an hour, and tries to suggest a complete life."[9]

Fred Coe believed that television's ability to bring intimate details of a performance to its audience, along with the practical constraints of staging live drama, made it a perfect medium for the character-based play. He was dedicated to presenting teleplays that probed human character and illuminated "the dark corners of the human heart."[10] It is not surprising, then, that when Fred Coe named his ten all-time favorite productions, he selected two works by Horton Foote, *The Trip to Bountiful* and *A Young Lady of Property*, because of their uniquely realistic depiction of human character and emotion.

Clearly, Horton Foote's triumph in television was the result of a perfect marriage of material and medium. The majority of television audiences consisted of the middle class, who responded to plays that spoke simply and compassionately about their lives, and Horton created effective and moving characters with which his audience could identify. Part of the audience's strong sense of recognition was due to the author's own identification with his material. Horton's teleplays were all inspired by stories he had heard as a youth, and his plots centered mainly on domestic situations, often depicting the plight of American women struggling to salvage some dignity and decency from a difficult world. Set in the imaginary Texas town of Harrison (a name he took from his grandfather Albert Harrison Foote), Horton's teleplays featured the very young and the very old who shared one of two common themes: an acceptance of life and a preparation of death.[11] The plays focused on the mythic patterns of going away and coming home, while simultaneously exploring the moral and social history of Wharton, Texas. It is little wonder that Fred Coe branded Horton Foote the "Chekhov of the Texas small-town."[12]

Another important dimension of Horton's work boded well for its success. From his beginnings as a writer, he had been attracted to the simplicity and economy of the one-act play form, which meant his plots were easily modified to fit the one-hour format. Horton later admitted that even though he was hired to write teleplays, his real interest

---

[9] Tad Mosel, *Other People's Houses* (New York: Simon & Schuster, 1956) ix.

[10] Coe, 70.

[11] Horton Foote, Introduction, in *Harrison, Texas: Eight Television Plays by Horton Foote* (New York: Harcourt Brace 1956) viii.

[12] Coe, 87

continued to be in the theater, so he used ideas that he had originally considered for the stage. "In those days," Horton remarked, "the theatre had little use or interest in the one-act play, so writing one seemed almost a futile exercise. Fred Coe, however, agreed with me that they were ideal for the limitations of live television."[13]

Horton also gained an appreciation of the mobility available from the television camera, but he believed that most cinematic techniques had already been absorbed into the craft of playwriting. "When I first began to write for the medium I found myself wanting to go every place, into set after set, for the sheer joy of moving around," Horton admitted. "I soon found that such freedom is meaningless unless you have a real need to change locale. Whether using one set or ten sets, there has to be a need in terms of your characters and your story or else the use of numerous locales simply clutters and confuses. When there is a need, however, how wonderful to be able to go directly to the place most effective for your action."[14]

At the start of Horton's television career, Fred Coe had told him that he would have to make peace with the little box, meaning its limitations. And make peace he did, discovering the key to mastering television was not the craftsman's knowledge of how to overcome shortcomings, but how to use the medium's greatest potential—intimacy. This was the word most often used to describe the nature of television drama, and Horton's success in great measure came from his understanding that the television camera could probe beneath the surface of external action for the more profound truths of intimate human relationships.

One of Horton's early teleplays, *The Old Beginning*, reveals much about the characters and themes the writer dramatized on television.[15] The play focuses on the archetypal father-son conflict, exploring the troubled relationship of H.T. Mavis, a wealthy real estate agent, and his son Tommy. Set in Mavis's general store in Harrison, Texas, during the 1950s, the play focuses on the problems that social change brings to families. Once a quiet and stable community, which served the cotton industry and its plantation society, Harrison is giving way to a new order of capitalism that few citizens can understand. H.T. Mavis, a

---

[13] Foote, *Genesis*, 220.

[14] Ibid.

[15] Horton Foote, *The Old Beginning*, in *A Young Lady of Property: Six Short Plays* (New York: Dramatists Play Service, 1955) 55–86. Page references to *The Old Beginning* in the text refer to this publication.

stubborn and temperamental man, represents a breed of businessman who values money and professional success above even the needs of his family. For years, Tommy has tried to please his father by learning the real estate business, but Mavis merely responds with aggression and hostility. When the play opens, Mavis has given his son a building to lease, which Tommy rents to a friend and local businessman. When Mavis discovers that Tommy has asked for only fifty dollars a month in rent, Mavis rents the same building to a stranger for three times the amount, then reprimands the boy for his lack of insight and business sense. Later in the play, comes the revelation that the man with whom Mavis has done business is a madman who travels the country falsely renting property from gullible businessmen. Mavis begs his son's forgiveness, but he is too late. Tommy recognizes his need for independence from his father, and as the play concludes, he leaves home to fulfill that need.

The conflict between father and son, explored in drama throughout history, was as timely a subject for Horton's audience as for audiences of the past. In *The Old Beginning*, Horton depicts a family torn apart by a father's obsessive drive for wealth. Like many of his generation, Mavis takes pride in his job and his materialistic success, but he has become so obsessed with work that he neglects his parental responsibility, sacrificing his son's need for a father to his own need for material achievement.

In the character of Tommy, Horton painted a vivid picture of a young man torn between loyalty and affection for his father and a desire to be his own man. The archetypal need to leave home, a pattern seen often in Horton's work, is the real subject of *The Old Beginning*, and in the end Tommy decides to abandon his former life to "feel free to do what I want" (40). His decision is not based on anger or frustration but on a clear commitment to his own needs, for his "own independence and self-respect" (40). Tommy's realization leaves him with an uncertain future, a common experience for many young people. As Foote's title implies, Tommy's leaving is an old beginning, one revisited each and every time innocence is lost in the pursuit of identity and self-fulfillment.

The Old Beginning, which aired 23 November 1952 on the *Philco-Goodyear Television Playhouse*, was praised by network executives for its authentic portrayal of a young man's quest for self-actualization, and the play garnered the attention of the Psychiatric Institute of America, which thought the teleplay should be shown to psychiatrists who were studying the father-son complex. But while the play dramatizes a recognized psychiatric dilemma, Lucy Kroll explained in a letter to Bette Davis, who was fascinated by Horton's television play: "Mr. Foote did not employ one technical or scientific word in his script and yet its truth and power met the test on such a high level."[16]

The Old Beginning revealed Horton's ability to create authentic adolescent characters for television. The second play he submitted to Fred Coe—*The Trip to Bountiful*—demonstrated his conviction that the plight of the elderly in American society was a subject equally worthy of contemplation by television audiences. *The Trip to Bountiful*, which would become Horton Foote's most beloved and enduring work, was initiated by a phone call from Fred Coe in February 1953. Horton recalled: "Coe had an advertising agency he had to respond to, so he'd ask writers to give him a general idea and he'd get clearance before they started on a project. Well, I was maybe superstitious, but I felt that if I told someone beforehand it would kill it for me. So I wrote *Bountiful* and then went to see Fred. I said I was working on a story about an old woman who wanted to get back to her hometown. He said, 'Fine, let's do it,' and the next day I gave him the play."[17]

On 1 March 1953 *The Trip to Bountiful* premiered on the *Philco-Goodyear Television Playhouse* with Lillian Gish as Mrs. Carrie Watts, John Beal as her son Ludie, Eileen Heckart as Jessie Mae, and Eva Marie Saint as Thelma.[18] The director was Vincent Donehue, who after years of working with Horton had learned how best to stage the writer's plays of subtle language and indirect action. *The Trip to Bountiful* was an overwhelming success, producing an avalanche of telephone calls to NBC. People were overcome by Lillian Gish's performance, Horton remembered. "People said, 'God bless you, Miss Gish,' and 'Thank God we've found you again,' and the chairman of CBS, William Paley, even called Lillian Gish to remark that 'television came of age tonight.'"[19]

---

[16] Lucy Kroll to Bette Davis, 11 April 1953 (Horton Foote Papers).

[17] Horton Foote, interview by Marion Castleberry, 19 November 1988, Wharton, Texas.

[18] Horton Foote, *The Trip to Bountiful*, in *Harrison, Texas*, 219–62. Page references to the television version of *The Trip to Bountiful* in the text refer to this publication unless otherwise noted.

[19] Horton Foote, interview by Marion Castleberry, 19 November 1988, Wharton, Texas.

The strength of Horton Foote's play and Lillian Gish's performance gained an afterlife for *The Trip to Bountiful* in an expanded version for Broadway that was produced by Fred Coe and the Theatre Guild and performed at Henry Miller's Theatre on 3 November 1953. Gene Lyons and Jo Van Fleet replaced John Beal and Eileen Heckart as Ludie and Jessie Mae, but the rest of the cast and the director remained from the television production. Once again, Lillian Gish was hailed for her performance of Carrie Watts, her final leading role on Broadway. "A moving honest performance, one of her all-time best," Robert Coleman of the *New York Daily Mirror* noted, and William Hawkins of the *New York World-Telegram and Sun* stated, "The penetrating sensitivity of her acting is a constant revelation. She has always been a genius in pantomime, and one of this play's exhilarating virtues is the quantity of moments when she clarifies an emotion, a relationship, or sometimes a whole life, without saying a word."[20] Brooks Atkinson, critic of the *New York Times*, remarked, "This is Miss Gish's masterpiece...she gives an inspired performance that is alive in every detail and conveys an unconquerable spirit."[21] Critics also praised the dramaturgy of the play and William Hawkins stated that Horton Foote had done the one thing necessary for a playwright: provide "disciplined material for expert actors" that completely captures an audience for an entire evening."[22] Fortunately, the original television broadcast has been preserved and is evidence of the simple beauty of Horton's teleplay, the range of Lillian Gish's talent, and the excitement of performing a live drama before a potential audience of millions.

The impulse behind the story of Carrie Watts was a legend in the Foote family of an aunt who, as a young girl, was not allowed to marry the man she loved because they were first cousins. Heartbroken, they each married other people, and years later, the woman returned as a widow to her hometown of Wharton, where each day the spurned man would pass her house and bow with affection. Horton recalls, "When I knew this woman, she seemed so unlikely to have had a past like that. She was living in rather humiliating circumstances at the time, but she

---

[20] Robert Coleman, "Review of *The Trip to Bountiful*," *New York Daily Mirror*, 4 November 1953; William Hawkins, "Review of *The Trip to Bountiful*," *New York World-Telegram and Sun*, 4 November 1953.

[21] Brooks Atkinson, "Lillian Gish Gives a Notable Performance in Foote's 'The Trip to Bountiful,'" *New York Times*, 4 November 1953.

[22] Hawkins, "Review of *The Trip to Bountiful*," 4 November 1953.

was doing it with a great deal of dignity."[23] Horton began trying to write the play from the beginning of Carrie's story, with her love for Ray John Murray being thwarted by her father because of a feud he had with Murray's father. However, the story became too unwieldy, especially in trying to include Ray John Murray's daily walk past Carrie's house, and Horton decided to focus the play on Carrie as an old woman longing to return home to Bountiful.

The Trip to Bountiful depicts the universal drama of going away and coming home, as Carrie Watts escapes from her veritable prison in Houston to revisit the town of her childhood in order to regain her sense of dignity after a lifetime of hardships and sacrifice. For twenty years she has lived with her son Ludie and Jessie Mae in their cramped apartment, and even though she is a loving and well-meaning woman, her children know, from experience, that living with her is not easy. They have a small income and no privacy and are ill equipped to deal with the memories, lost dreams, and sheer indomitable spirit of the old woman. Ludie and Jessie Mae are reluctantly approaching middle age, and after a year's illness, Ludie has only recently gotten a job in the city and Jessie Mae has begun to veil her discontentment and frustration by frequenting the beauty parlor, reading movie magazines, sipping Coke, and arguing with Mrs. Watts over the whereabouts of her monthly pension check. Horton explained that his Uncle Oliver Ray was his model for the character of Ludie Watts. "He was representative of that whole generation of country people who, after the Depression, migrated to the city," Horton admitted. "When I was about twelve I remember visiting him and seeing a book on his nightstand entitled *How to be an Executive*. Here was a man who had been taken out of the rural environment and put into an alien society to deal with things in which he had no training. I'm sure he felt helpless and alienated at times. But he was trying his best to adapt to his circumstances and provide for his family."[24] In the play, Ludie tries to maintain peace in the family, but he is inevitably caught between his affections for his mother and his wife, who continually have their petty clashes. Loving both women, he is unable to meet the needs of either woman. "Oh,

---

[23] Horton Foote, interview by Marion Castleberry, 19 November 1988, Wharton, Texas.

[24] Ibid.

Mama, I haven't made any kind of life for you, either one of you and I try so hard," Ludie proclaims.[25]

Mrs. Watts doesn't care for the family arrangement any more than her son or daughter-in-law. Life for her has become a claustrophobic and harsh existence of forced politeness, senseless battles, and demanded apologies. She is miserable in the city with its noisy radios, irate neighbors, and screeching automobiles, and she aches to see her beloved home place of Bountiful before she dies. Many times she has tried to slip away from Ludie and Jessie Mae in order to return to her rural home where she grew up, married, and buried two children. Now her heart is unreliable and her need has grown more urgent. As the play progresses, she manages to escape and catch a bus back home, aided by some kindly strangers: a young soldier's wife, an agent for the bus company, and a sheriff.

The play's emotional peak comes when Carrie is tracked down in a bus station where she is spending the night. She challenges the sheriff and the bus agent to help her reach her destination before Ludie and Jessie Mae arrive to take her back to Houston. On camera, Lillian Gish played this moment with great force and sincerity, her voice and body expressive of suffering and urgency. She confesses to having become, as her daughter-in-law has told her, a "quarrelsome, hateful old woman," and declares that all she needs to recover her serenity is a few minutes in Bountiful. Bursting with anger over all the years spent bickering with Jessie Mae, she rushes to the door, and when confronted by the sheriff, stumbles a moment from her heart condition. But Mrs. Watts, who has resigned herself to the death of her two children and the loss of the man she loved, will not be stopped. She is resolved to see her home one more time, and she cries out in anguish "Bountiful, Bountiful." Although the sheriff had ordered Mrs. Watts to remain at the bus station until her son arrives, he relents after hearing the heartbreaking story of her life and drives her the last few miles to Bountiful. When Mrs. Watts finally gets there, however, she finds it is not the place she remembered: the town has long since been abandoned and gone to waste, and her only friend Callie Davis has just died. The house in which she once lived is now desolate and run down. Carrie

---

[25] Horton Foote, *The Trip to Bountiful, Horton Foote Collected Plays*, vol. 2 (New York: Smith and Kraus 1996) 54. Page references to the stage version of *The Trip to Bountiful* in this text refer to this publication.

Watts is the last remaining witness to a place and time that has long ago vanished.

Mrs. Watts's journey to her sacred home is also replete with spiritual significance. From the beginning of the play, she finds courage in her faith in God, and she constantly sings hymns that remind her of the love and protection Jesus provides. At times she wonders if God is punishing her for marrying a man she didn't love, but she never asks why she lost her farm, the place where she sacrificed most of her life to create a home. In the bus station, when Thelma expresses her concern over her missing husband, a soldier stationed overseas, Mrs. Watts recites the Ninety-first Psalm, which expresses the very essence of her Christian faith. "He that dwelleth in the secret place of the most high abides under the shadow of the Almighty," Mrs. Watts proclaims. "I will say of the Lord he is my refuge and my fortress: My God; in him will I trust. Surely He shall deliver thee from the snare of the fowler and the noisome pestilence. He shall cover thee with His feathers and under his wing shalt thou trust: His truth shall be thy shield and buckler" (35). Through her faith, Mrs. Watts finds the courage and strength to confront her memories, respond to the healing rhythms of the land, and regain her dignity before returning to Houston, now more able to face the humiliations of life and to prepare for her death.

When *The Trip to Bountiful* was transferred to Broadway, Horton kept the focus of the play on Mrs. Watts, but he added some additional material to flesh out the characters of Jessie Mae and Ludie. For instance, in the television version, an impassioned Carrie Watts tears her social security check into pieces as the materialistic Jessie Mae calls her a "spiteful old thing" and Ludie cries. Horton substituted a more subdued scene in the stage version, in which Ludie demands that the two women stop arguing and Jessie Mae allows Mrs. Watts to keep the check and, with it, a bit of her dignity. The most important addition, however, came directly from Foote's memory of the death of his Grandfather Brooks. As they are about to leave Bountiful, Mrs. Watts asks Ludie if he remembers his grandfather:

> No, ma'am. Not too well. I was only ten when he died, Mama. I remember the day he died. I heard about it as I was coming home from school. Lee Weems told me. I thought he was joking and I called him a liar. I remember you takin' me into the front room there the day of the funeral to say good-bye to him. I remember the coffin and the people sitting in the room. Old man Joe Weems took me up on his knee and

told me that Grandpapa was his best friend and that his life was a real example for me to follow. I remember Grandmama sitting by the coffin crying and she made me promise that when I had a son of my own I'd name it after Grandpapa. I would have, too, I've never forgotten that promise. Well, I didn't have a son. Or a daughter.... Oh Mama. I lied to you. I do remember. I remember so much. This house. The life here. The night you woke me up and dressed me and took me for a walk when there was a full moon and I cried because I was afraid and you comforted me. Mama, I want to stop remembering.... It doesn't do any good to remember. (54)

For Ludie, the old home place holds painful memories, but, as he remembers his past, he is blessed with moral courage and empathy for his mother. As a result, by the end of the play, he's gained strength and improved his ability to reenter the urban struggle for a decent life. For Mrs. Watts, Bountiful is rich with family history and memories from which she can never fully escape. She is connected to the land—it defines her identity, holds the record of her personal struggles, and offers her strength against an unfair and troubled world. For her, the power of Bountiful exists not in the houses that were erected there, the farms that were carved into the earth, or even the people who once inhabited this small Texas community, but rather in the very soil and air of which it is composed: "Pretty soon it'll all be gone. Ten years...twenty...this house...me...you...But the river will be here. The fields. The woods. The smell of the Gulf. That's what I always took my strength from, Ludie. Not from houses, not from people. It's so quiet. It's so eternally quiet. I had forgotten the peace. The quiet. And it's given me strength once more, Ludie...I've found my dignity and my strength" (55).

For Carrie Watts, Bountiful represents a profound source of nourishment, a sacred place that will outlast time and preserve the memories of her life long after she has succumbed to death. When she speaks of the cycle of nature, she expresses an affirmation of life, an acceptance that Bountiful, as she knew it, now survives only in memory. Though the house is in shambles and the town is deserted, Bountiful lives up to its name, providing sustenance to Carrie Watts at the end of her life and enabling her to return to her less than bountiful life in Houston. Her final action is to kneel devoutly, scoop up a handful of earth, and let the sand run through her fingers. Having regained her dignity, this personal ritual signals she is ready to die, to return to dust herself. Her final words—"Goodbye, Bountiful,

Goodbye"—offer an elegiac farewell to the vanished world she has held so dear (60).

The Trip to Bountiful captures vividly and touchingly a number of universal truths about the human experience. The play pays tribute to the decency of ordinary people who barely scrape by but endure amid trying circumstances, and it focuses on such universal issues as coping with death and finding the courage to face adversity. It reminds us of the importance of family loyalty, of the need for compassion for the elderly, and of the necessity of squaring up memories with reality before completing life's journey. Most importantly, *The Trip to Bountiful* expresses the universal human need for a physical and emotional home.

The success of the original television and stage productions of *The Trip to Bountiful* garnered Horton Foote the sort of celebrity usually reserved for movie stars, and the work caught the attention of audiences from across the nation. Family and friends in Wharton were very proud of their native son, as evidenced by a letter from Albert Horton Foote, Horton's father. "Son, you don't know how proud I am of you. I always knew you would make it.... Oh how I have enjoyed going down the street, and having friends, strangers and all stop and tell me how wonderful your plays are, and damn it, you deserve every inch of it."[26]

With the income that Horton received from *The Trip to Bountiful*, he and Lillian were able to rent a bigger apartment. They found one in an elevator building on the Upper West Side, at Broadway and Eighty-ninth Street with a separate living room and dining room, two large bedrooms, one smaller room that could be used as a nursery, and a maid's quarters at the back. They had already moved in when their second child, Albert Horton Foote, III, was born 7 November 1952 in the same French Hospital where Barbara Hallie had been delivered.

Horton returned to television a month after *The Trip to Bountiful* aired with *A Young Lady of Property,* presented by the *Philco-Goodyear Television Playhouse* on 5 April 1953.[27] The play, written for actress Kim Stanley, concerned a motherless teenage girl, Wilma Thompson, caught between her yearning to escape small-town life and become a movie star and her desire to bring up a family in the empty house she inherited from her

---

[26] Albert Foote to Horton Foote, 27 March 1953 (Horton Foote Papers).

[27] Horton Foote, *A Young Lady of Property*, in *Harrison, Texas*, 1–40. All page references to *A Young Lady of Property* in the text refer to this publication.

deceased mother. Horton explained that the teleplay was inspired by an unforgettable childhood experience.

> When I was fourteen I read in the Houston papers about a Hollywood scout arriving in that city to look for acting talent. I talked my parents into letting me go to meet him, and my grandmother and one of her sons drove me in for an appointment. I don't know what I expected from all this, but there was little talk of a screen test when I had my interview, but only of lessons, including, as I remember, tap dancing. I had rather conventional ideas of what a Hollywood scout should look like and the young man I interviewed looked very unHollywood to me, looking like one of my uncles and talking as if he had never been out of Houston, Texas. What real use all of this was to me I was unaware of then, but the experience, given to a young girl eager to go to Hollywood, was used in *A Young Lady of Property*.[28]

Horton Foote's dramatic world is peopled with youngsters who have lost either a father or mother or both. Such is the case with Wilma Thompson, whose mother has recently died and whose father, a recovering gambler, is on the verge of marrying a woman his daughter rejects. Mr. Thompson, played by Jim Gregory, busy with his own problems and affairs, has left Wilma to her own devices and in the care of two other lonely people: Aunt Gert, played by Margaret Barker, and Wilma's confidante and black maid, Minna Boyd, played by Fredye Marshall. When the play opens, Wilma, overwhelmed by the loss of her mother and the jealously she feels about her father's new relationship with Sybil Leighton, has retreated into fantasies of Hollywood stardom and secretly plotted with her closest friend, Arabella Cookenboo, to secure a screen test from a Hollywood casting agent. Wilma believes she can be happy as a movie star, but as she discovers, dreams cannot substitute for real needs: "Maybe I was going to Hollywood out of pure lonesomeness...Daddy could have taken away my lonesomeness, but he didn't want to or couldn't" (18).

Wilma faces a crisis when she learns her father plans to sell the old family home without her knowledge. In a frantic effort to salvage the only link between herself and her dead mother, Wilma confronts her future stepmother and asks for help. To the child's surprise, Mrs. Leighton, in a beautiful performance by Vivian Nathan, empathizes with her and convinces Mr. Thompson not to sell the house. At last, Wilma realizes her real ambition is not to become a star at all, but to

---

[28] Foote, *Genesis*, 28.

stay in Harrison, bring up a family, and do something about the lonesome look of the family home. For the time being, she is content as a young woman of property, but whether she is able to fill the house with life again, we never know. Nevertheless, Wilma Thompson has taken her first step toward responsibility and adulthood.

No retelling of the story of *A Young Lady of Property* can give an adequate idea of the play's essence, for Horton Foote is an evocative stylist. In his intimate scenes centered on the Thompson family, he invests familiar domestic situations and ordinary folk, both white and black, with an appealing warmth. When the play premiered on television, the cast featured Joanne Woodward as Arabella Cookenboo and Kim Stanley as Wilma. Kim Stanley is compelling as Wilma, revealing a wide range of emotions from joy to sorrow and excitement to despair without any ostentation or histrionics. Fred Coe called it "one of the most distinguished performances in the history of television."[29] Coe also acknowledged that the structure of *A Young Lady of Property* was unique to the medium. Rather than showing Wilma's climactic confrontation with Mrs. Leighton, in which she regains her home and develops a much-needed relationship with her stepmother, Horton chose to have the young girl relate the incident through dialogue. As Coe explains:

> When Foote wrote this play, he omitted what is virtually a must scene in any work—that scene where the issues are resolved and the climax is drawn. We had many arguments about this. He wanted the girl to come before the camera and explain the situation, face to face with the audience. I wanted him to write the action instead of having a character talk about it. He won his point: We did it the way he wrote it. He was right. We broke all the rules, and everything turned out wonderfully. But it could never have happened except on television.[30]

Variety praised *A Young Lady of Property*, calling it one of the best shows produced by *Philco-Goodyear Television Playhouse* and a personal triumph for Kim Stanley, who gave a performance that was alternately amusing and moving. Lucy Kroll wrote to Horton that the renowned actress Bette Davis had been very impressed with the play and with Kim Stanley's performance and felt the playwright had "the quality of truth"

---

[29] Coe, 88.
[30] Ibid.

and could reveal the inner life of characters better than any other single writer of the day.[31]

During the next few weeks, Horton wrote *The Oil Well* and *Expectant Relations* for NBC, presenting variations on characters and themes that had appeared in his earlier stage plays. *The Oil Well*, which aired on the *Philco-Goodyear Television Playhouse* 17 May 1953, examines the degeneration of values and loss of intimacy that accompany an old man's desire for wealth.[32] Directed by Vincent Donehue, the teleplay features a central character named Will Thornton (played by E.G. Marshall), a man who dreams of becoming rich and fails but who cannot surrender his hope for a better life. Will, a simple cotton farmer, has lost pride and faith in his once noble profession. For more than twenty-eight years, he held on to the dream that some day oil would be discovered under his land, that he would no longer have to break his back farming, and that he could give his family anything they desired: a gas range, a television, a business, and a chauffeured car. However, Will's attempts to provide a more substantial life for his family have failed. He owes $10,000 from his first attempt to strike oil, and paying off the loan has drained his family of their resources and strength. As the action unfolds, Will is given the opportunity to get out of debt by leasing his farm to a reputable oil company or selling the land's mineral rights for $100,000 to H.T. Mavis who is trying to transform the rural Harrison landscape into a profitable resource. Will's wife, Loula (performed by Dorothy Gish), urges her husband to accept Mavis's offer, but Will chooses, instead, to hold out for more money. Of course, there is no oil, and when Mavis recants his offer, Will is finally forced to face the reality that life does not always turn out the way one hopes: "Why does this come to a man? He's led on to believe, to expect…and then everything is knocked out of his hands. His hopes are dashed. There is failure again…I can't go through it anymore…It's better not to expect, not to hope" (129).

Will does not realize his wife and children love him regardless of his failure in the business world, and, as he ultimately discovers, they hold the key to his future happiness and contentment. Will has withdrawn from his family and lost his closeness to the land, but his wife shares the same agrarian ideal as Carrie Watts in *The Trip to*

---

[31] Lucy Kroll to Horton Foote, 10 April 1953 (Horton Foote Papers).

[32] Horton Foote, *The Oil Well*, in *A Young Lady of Property: Six Short Plays*, 123–52. Page references to *The Oil Well* in this text refer to this publication.

Bountiful. Loula believes in the positive power of work and responds to the healing quality of the rural setting. Although she wants Will to have his oil well, they've been disappointed too many times before, and she knows that only the land and a crop in the ground can be counted on to feed them and keep a roof over their heads. As the play concludes, she offers her husband a way to cope with his feelings of personal failure: "Cry. Get it all out. It's better to let it come out, then you'll be tired and able to sleep, and in the morning you'll be rested and can get on with the work to be done here." When Will responds in despair that he "won't ever hope again," Loula concludes: "You think that now. But you won't stop hoping. You can't. And I wouldn't want you any other way. Not any other way in the world" (129). Ultimately there is a sense of continuity in *The Oil Well.* While the end of the play suggests that the Thornton family will face more hardships and sacrifices, at least they have accepted the life they have and can now move ahead together.

Expectant Relations also explores the disintegration of family relationships and loss of moral values that accompany an obsession with money.[33] The play, which aired on the *Philco-Goodyear Television Playhouse* on 21 June 1953, bears many resemblances to *The Girls,* a farcical comedy written by Horton Foote twelve years earlier. As in the earlier play, two selfish women prepare for the death of a rich relative they believe will leave them a large inheritance. Their hopes are ultimately dashed when they recognize that the relative has no intention of meeting their expectations. The action of *The Girls* revolves around two spinster sisters, Sue and Nora Anthony, and their strained relationship with a shrewish and rapacious aunt. *Expectant Relations* introduces us to two selfish cousins who engage in a competition for the money of their long-lived uncle. For twenty-five years the central character, Fannie Jackson, has been supporting her son and daughter-in-law with money her husband left the family. Now Fannie faces an economic crisis. Her savings are spent, and the Harrison bank is pressuring her to sell her house. Fannie has led a sheltered life and knows nothing about hard work or making important decisions. Each time she decides to sell the house, she receives a telegram from Uncle Samuel Edward telling her he will be coming to visit soon, and each time Fannie reads her uncle's letter she changes her mind about selling her house, hoping he

---

[33] Horton Foote, *Expectant Relations,* in *Harrison, Texas,* 115–52 Page references to *Expectant Relations* in this text refer to this publication.

will provide the money she needs. Cousin Lucy Dove, Fannie's vindictive and greedy counterpart, also expects a large reward and for years has been competing with Fannie for the favors of Uncle Samuel Edward. This delicate balance of family relationships overturns when both Fannie and Lucy Dove receive identical letters from their uncle inviting himself to their homes for supper on the same night. Predictably Uncle Samuel Edward never appears, forcing both women to acknowledge that the old man has been merely playing a cruel game with them. In the end, Fannie recognizes the absurdity of her actions, accepts her fate, and puts her house up for sale. Lucy Dove, on the other hand, refuses to face the truth and plots to have her uncle committed before he can remarry and leave his money to another woman.

An effective comedy, *Expectant Relations* achieves its humor from Horton's detailed depiction of the ludicrous behavior of two recognizable but unlikable characters. Viewers may laugh at the misdirected ambitions and petty faults of Fannie Jackson and Lucy Dove Murray, while admiring Uncle Samuel Edward's ability to frustrate and outwit them at the game of life; but serious overtones lie beneath the obvious humor of the play. These two women, once wealthy aristocrats who commanded the respect and love of their families and community, have become so obsessed with money and security that they have reduced themselves to mere scavengers. Their limited visions have turned them into unsympathetic and embittered old women who neither respect the feelings of others nor consider the value of human life. What prevents the play from being a cynical black comedy is the hope that Fannie will become enlightened from her experience.

Expectant Relations showed Horton's gift for comedy, but it failed to gain the kind of positive response from television viewers that his earlier teleplays had achieved, perhaps because the central characters of the play are less sympathetic and their conflict less familiar. Because of the audience's preference for Horton's somber mood plays, *Expectant Relations* was the only comedy the writer would submit to the *Philco-Goodyear Television Playhouse*.

Horton's next two plays, *The Death of the Old Man* and *The Tears of My Sister*, premiered on a new series called *First Person Playhouse* in July and August 1953, respectively. Directed by Arthur Penn, both were experiments in the use of the subjective camera, a technique whereby the television camera would itself be a character whose voice is heard but never seen by the audience. While this approach offered a new and unique perspective from which to view the action of TV drama, the beauty of the two plays lies in the dignity of Horton's characters and the accuracy of their language. In *The Death of the Old Man*, the camera is Will Thornton (performed by William Hanson), an old man who lies helpless on his deathbed unable to communicate with anyone around him, but who, nonetheless, relates his random thoughts and desperate concerns to the audience.[34] Throughout his life, Will has been a pillar of hope and strength to his family, serving as both father and mother to his own children as well as to those of his brother and cousin. Because he believed in the kindness of his family and of the world, his home was open to everyone. Instead of saving money or fretting about the future, Will invested his resources in living things and provided care and stability for those less fortunate; consequently, he has sacrificed his dreams and children's security for the comfort of his extended family. Now he is dying without owning his house or having any money left for his only daughter, Rosa (played by Mildred Natwick), who has cared for him all her adult life and sacrificed her own dreams for her family. His concern for Rosa's happiness and prosperity is the tender thread that keeps Will alive and drives the play to its ultimate conclusion.

One of Horton's unique gifts is his ability to portray women with great insight, understanding, and admiration. Through the character of Rosa Thornton, who is modeled after his Aunt Rosa Brooks, Horton revealed his compassion for those women who have been victimized by their families and by the harshness of life. When the play begins, Rosa is more than fifty years old, unmarried, and financially insecure. Having faced the death of her boyfriend in World War I and her mother's fatal illness, she has become withdrawn and dependent on her father. At one time she tried to make a life of her own in the business world, only to be verbally and emotionally abused by her boss. In an effort to ease her pain and growing sense of inadequacy, she slowly began to place the needs of her younger brothers before her own. Through her efforts, Tom and Jack were able to create happy and prosperous lives for themselves, but the affection Rosa gave her brothers and the sacrifices she made for them proved one-sided. Now, Tom and Jack have no room in their lives for a needy sister, and they

---

[34] Horton Foote, *The Death of the Old Man*, in *Harrison, Texas*, 95–114. Page references to *Death of the Old Man* in the text refer to this publication.

refuse to share their prosperity with her. Will Thornton's hope that his sons would remember Rosa's loyalty and return her love is dashed by a devastating fear that "kindness has gone from the world, generosity has vanished" (106).

The Death of the Old Man is one of Horton's darkest portraits of a world in transition. Gone are the innocent days of "the honeysuckle and the china berry and the figs an' the dew berry" (98). Gone, too, are the virtues of familial devotion, solidarity, and empathy. As Sealy, the black servant and silent guardian of the Thornton family, sadly admits: "The world changes.... Oh, yes, it changes.... Aeroplanes in the sky and so many wars I can't keep up with them, Mr. Will. It's everybody for himself, now, the women and the men, the brothers against the brothers" (102). In the dark world of this play, familial love has almost disappeared from the earth, but in one quick brush stroke, Horton Foote offers a thread of hope in the character of Cousin Lyd who unexpectedly arrives to be with Will when he dies. Because of her respect for the old man and her gratitude for his help years earlier, Cousin Lyd offers Rosa and Sealy a home in the country and a business from which they can squeeze out a modest living. Will Thornton is finally rewarded for a lifetime of generosity. Although the remainder of his daughter's life may be difficult and lonely, the old man can now die peacefully, free of worry and guilt, assured that Rosa will be provided for. Finally, we see Will's faith in his family reaffirmed— Rosa, Lyd, and Sealy recapture a sense of togetherness and gain the peace and contentment so important to Foote's characters.

While *The Death of the Old Man* combines a sense of loss with a wishful feeling of family harmony, *The Tears of My Sister* suggests the endless pain and sorrow of adolescent girls growing up in the broken world of their parents.[35] Horton Foote often centered his interest on the yearnings and fears of young women and the effect that economics and chaotic social conditions have on their hopes and aspirations for marriage. *The Tears of My Sister* is the second in a series of plays Horton wrote for dramatic television that depicts the effects of forbidden love on the lives of women. *The Tears of My Sister* is one of his darkest representations of this theme. The central character of the play, Cecelia Monroe, played by Kim Stanley and represented by the subjective camera, shares with the audience her frightened interpretation of the

---

[35] Horton Foote, *The Tears of My Sister*, in *Harrison, Texas*, 75–94. Page references to *The Tears of My Sister* in the text refer to this publication.

distressing circumstances surrounding the marriage of her eighteen-year-old sister and Cecelia's confusion over Bessie's unhappiness. Bessie (played by Lenka Peterson) is twenty years old, clearly of marriageable age by society's standards, and engaged to Stacey Davis, a man she does not love. Bessie's mother strongly supports her daughter's marriage to Stacey because he is rich and can offer her daughter a better life. Mrs. Monroe (played by Kathleen Squire) is broken from the recent death of her husband and by the frustrations of having to be both father and mother to her children. She believes that when Bessie is married, her life will become less burdensome. She and Cecelia can then sell the run-down boarding house they now operate in Harrison and return to Houston to begin a more productive life. Marriage has become little more than a shortcut to financial security for Mrs. Monroe, as it was for Mamie Borden in *Only The Heart*, and Bessie, like Julia in Foote's earlier play, is about to marry a man she cares nothing about because, as she admits, "My Mama and my sister need me and I have to think of my Mama and my sister" (92). Thus, the conflict between romantic love and practicality is played out, for Bessie is deeply devoted to another boy, Syd Davis, whom her mother rejects. Bessie considers running away with Syd, but her sense of family duty and loyalty prevent her from doing so; instead, she cries the nights away in an expression of loneliness and pain. Time and again Foote suggests that risk-taking and individual fulfillment are essential elements in marriage and among lovers, but Bessie possesses neither the understanding nor the courage to risk all for love. At the play's climax, Syd appears at Bessie's window and calls her name but the young girl can only echo the sentiments of her mother: "We have to be practical in this world, honey. We have to be practical" (92).

The Tears of My Sister, a remarkable study of young women at a crucial stage in their lives, reveals Horton Foote's keen understanding of the need for human companionship as well as the deceptive manner in which women often view their roles as wives and lovers. Perhaps the most telling example of this is Cecelia's recounting of her mother's belief that "men understand not a thing about the sorrows of women. She says it just scares them. She says all men want women to be regular doll babies all the time. Happy and good-natured with no troubles" (88). Mrs. Monroe's image of womanhood is not presented satirically but as a given, a harsh reality of a world where money is valued more than affection and women are idolized but seldom understood.

Ultimately, Mrs. Monroe emerges as a long-suffering woman of resolution and fortitude who wants the best for Bessie even though she unwittingly sacrifices her daughter's happiness. The play's tragic events are not precipitated by a flaw in her character but by a society that refuses to acknowledge human rights or the transcendent power of love.

Throughout his teleplays, Horton Foote depicted early twentieth-century society as disordered and rarely showed family relationships as harmonious. Instead, he created a host of defective parents and violated children who were the result of a sterile and destructive society. Horton consistently focused his attention on children of indifferent or self-serving parents, those corrupted by misplaced values, those exploited to assume parental responsibilities, and children who had been orphaned. These characters appear so frequently that they serve as a unifying motif in Horton's writing. With none of his fictive children did the writer identify more fully than with orphans. His interest in lonely and alienated children was, of course, the result of a strong identification with his father, who was himself abandoned at a young age. With the memory of his father's neglected childhood never to fade, Horton created a world populated by orphans, homeless victims of societal indifference and familial neglect.

Horton's depiction of home, however, was never confined to a specific place so much as it was reflective of a network of personal relationships. In his plays, home is not just a town or a house but rather a feeling, a sense of goodwill and happiness that is almost always connected to community, family, or faith. Horton's remark in a 1953 interview rings true for all his plays: "Every family, consciously or unconsciously, must have a spiritual and an emotional, as well as a physical home."[36] Horton understood that the individual's search for a sense of belonging is not merely a physical concern but an emotional quest that most often leads back to family.

Horton's teleplay, *John Turner Davis*, which aired on NBC's *Philco-Goodyear Television Playhouse* on 15 November 1953, focuses on this theme through the story of an abandoned twelve-year-old boy and his search for a sense of belonging.[37] The play, directed by Arthur Penn, is

---

[36] Fredrika D. Borchard, "Horton from Wharton," *Houston Chronicle Retrogravure Magazine* (4 October 1953): 7.

[37] Horton Foote, *John Turner Davis*, in *Harrison, Texas*, 41–74. Page references to *John Turner Davis* in the text refer to this publication.

set in 1933 during the height of the Great Depression. Times are extremely difficult in Harrison—many families have been devastated by economic collapse, and the hot Texas sun has destroyed any hope for a productive cotton crop. As the play opens, John Turner Davis, a child of migrant farmers, has been abandoned by his parents because of their inability to care for him. Left with his aunt and uncle, also migrants, John Turner has survived his loneliness and pain by working hard and by holding onto the hope that one day his parents will return. But they never come for the boy, and to make matters worse, the boy's aunt and uncle also desert him, because they, too, are unable to provide a home for him. John Turner is suddenly forced into the role of an orphan and cast adrift in a hostile world. However, his conflict is resolved with the help of Hazel and Thurman Whyte, a childless couple that takes pity on the boy and offers him a refuge of love and security. Initially, the boy refuses to accept the Whyte's kindness, insisting that his relatives will come back for him. Slowly, however, he comes to accept the fact that his family has indeed left him behind. Finally, as the much needed rain begins to fall upon the parched Harrison landscape, John Turner turns to the couple who have befriended him and expresses his hope for a better life: "Thank you. All my life I wanted to live in a house. I reckon I could get used to livin' in a house same as anyone" (73).

Perhaps Horton Foote was so successful a television writer because his characters and themes reflected a growing modern philosophy that was so much a part of the 1950s sensibility. The postwar family experienced great change primarily as the result of the distribution of affluence and the consumer culture that developed after World War II. The American economy was at an all-time high with almost one hundred percent employment; however, at the same time, Americans feared the possibility of nuclear disaster in a cold war. Horton Foote's adolescent characters hunger for deep and nourishing roots to sustain their lonely and unfulfilled lives, and they discover that these places are especially difficult to find in a postwar world crippled by trepidation, dislocation, isolation, and rampant materialism. Horton understood the devastating effects of this mindset on the children of that generation; and in a very real sense, his intimate domestic dramas held a mirror to the lives of television viewers and offered them a realistic glimpse of the unpleasant truths of the age.

Before *Television Playhouse* concluded its 1953 season, Horton had two other plays produced on NBC. The first of these, *The Rocking Chair*, offered a brief character sketch he wrote in 1948 while working at the King-Smith School in Washington, DC. Like much of his writing from this earlier period, *The Rocking Chair* is concerned with personal commitment to family and community. The action centers on Whyte Ewing, an aging doctor, who has decided to retire from public service after fifty-five years of caring for the people of Richmond, Texas. His retirement is an event for which his wife has long waited; for years, Loula has urged her husband to give up his practice and join her at home where they can live the remainder of their lives together in peace and quiet. The old man has finally promised to abide by her wishes, even though he is reluctant to forsake the many old and dispossessed people who need him and cannot afford the medical fees of younger, less personable doctors. As the play progresses, Ewing discovers he is an irreplaceable part of the community, for only he can provide the kind of personal care and attention his patients need. He also comes to realize he is friend as well as doctor to the people of Richmond, and his friendship is an important remedy for their pain and suffering. Ultimately, Ewing does not retire. He sacrifices his own dreams and those of his wife for the betterment of the town, and, by doing so, suggests that duty and devotion to other people are essential to human happiness.

Horton's final teleplay of the year, *The Midnight Caller* (which aired on *Philco-Goodyear Television Playhouse* on 13 December 1953) presented one of the most candid and disturbing portraits of love relationships gone awry that television audiences had ever seen.[38] In *The Midnight Caller*, Horton returned to many of the situations and characters he had explored earlier in *The Tears of My Sister*. Domineering parents bring about the crisis of the story, and the action revolves around a young woman, Helen Crews, who finds herself caught in love's emotional entanglements. The play opens in Mrs. Crawford's boarding house in Harrison, Texas, where Helen Crews has just moved with Alma Jean Jordan, Cutie Spencer, and Miss Rowena Douglas—three lonely women who become reluctant witnesses to the tragic effects of Helen's failed romance. Through their conversations, we learn that Helen once had been engaged to Harvey Weems but that her dream of marriage

---

[38] Horton Foote, *The Midnight Caller*, in *Harrison, Texas*, 153–86. All page references to *The Midnight Caller* in the text refer to this publication.

was shattered when Helen's mother, in an effort to control her daughter's life, forbade the young lovers from seeing each other. To make matters worse, Mrs. Weems, who also disapproved of her son's choice of mates, convinced Harvey to break off the engagement. For four years, the couple tried to sustain their relationship by disobeying their parents and meeting secretly. In time, however, they were unable to overcome the obstacles to their love, and Helen's feelings for the young man changed. On numerous occasions, she tried to end the relationship, but Harvey was unable to dismiss his love and passion for Helen. As a result, he turned to alcohol as a way of dealing with his loneliness. Now, every evening at midnight, he comes to Helen's window to call out her name and proclaim his undying love. The couple's unhealthy attachment and defiance of their parents has led to tragic effects: Harvey has become a hopeless drunk who, during the course of the play, tries to commit suicide, and Helen has been condemned by her family and community as a fallen woman. But unlike *The Tears of My Sister*, *The Midnight Caller* does not end in futility and despair. Helen faces her sorrow and accepts the truths that, with or without love, a person is ultimately responsible for his or her own happiness. By giving up her attempt to save Harvey from his self-imposed destruction, Helen can finally move on with her life and return the affections of another man, Ralph Johnston. As the play ends, she escapes the stifling world of Harrison and begins a new—and what promises to be a happier—life as Ralph's bride. But the joy that surrounds Helen's departure is shadowed by the melancholy loneliness left behind. We are reminded of Rowena, Cutie, and Alma Jean and their desperate search for peace and meaning in their lives, and we are brought back to the tragedy of Harvey Weems as he screams Helen's name from the jail cell where he waits to be taken to the asylum.

The Midnight Caller remains, to this day, one of Horton Foote's most realistic portraits of the limitations of love and the mysterious nature of human relationships, but it proved to be the most controversial play of the 1953 television season. Before it aired, Philco and Goodyear sponsors strongly objected to the play and wanted it censored because of its inference of pre-marital relations. Of course, there had been times during the "Golden Age" of television when the nagging worries of sponsors involved changing or picking at lines and sometimes the whole conception of a play had to be shifted. But for the most part Fred Coe shielded the dramatists from such commercial intrusion. In the case of *The Midnight Caller*, Coe and Horton did not pander to the demands of the sponsor; instead, they chose to present the play as the writer had originally conceived it. When the play aired on national television, a Philco distributor wrote to corporate headquarters saying several people told him that after seeing the show, they would no longer purchase Philco products. A woman wrote to the president of Philco complaining, "Not one person in the cast was a normal American. They were all neurotics for one reason or another. It is a shame with so many fine stories available such trash is forced on the public."[39] These letters all found their way to Fred Coe's desk, but he and Horton never openly discussed them, nor did they allow the incident to affect their goal of bringing quality theater to television. Despite such criticism, in April the *Philco-Goodyear Television Playhouse* won the prestigious Peabody Award and *Variety's* Management award, celebrating the pioneering efforts of Fred Coe and his team of dedicated writers.

During the 1954 season, NBC produced only two Horton Foote plays, *The Dancers* and *The Shadow of Will Greer*. The most impressive of these works was *The Dancers*, which aired on the *Philco-Goodyear Television Playhouse* on 7 March 1954.[40] Based on a story Horton's father had told him, the play centers on one of the writer's favorite themes: the adolescent's search for identity and companionship. Young Horace, a boy of sixteen, has journeyed to Harrison to visit his sister and brother-in-law, Inez and Herman Stanley. When he arrives, Horace discovers that Inez has been busy arranging a date for him to a dance with Emily Crews, the prettiest girl in town and the daughter of her closest friend. Horace, reluctant to go, claims that he does not know how to dance, but Inez, after a bit of coaching, persuades him to call on Emily even though she knows that the young girl is going steady with another boy. In the Crew's parlor, waiting for his date to appear, Horace discovers that Emily's mother disapproves of her daughter's boyfriend and is forcing her to go to the dance with him in an effort to drive a wedge between the couple. Humiliated, Horace flees the scene and takes refuge in the Harrison drugstore where he meets another teenager, Mary Catherine Davis, who also lacks confidence and is

---

[39] John Krampner, *The Man in the Shadows: Fred Coe and the Golden Age of Television* (New Brunswick NJ: Rutgers University Press, 1997) 73.

[40] Horton Foote, *The Dancers*, in *Harrison, Texas*, 187–218. Page references to *The Dancers* in the text refer to this publication.

crippled by feelings of inadequacy and unattractiveness. The two lonely youths are drawn to each other, and Horace invites Mary Catherine to go with him to the next dance. Ironically, at the moment the young man finds the courage to ask Mary Catherine for a date, his sister and Mrs. Crews arrange for him to escort Emily, who has decided to go with Horace this time because she regrets the way she treated him earlier. But Horace refuses to take Emily. He wants to take Mary Catherine, and nothing, not even the pleas of his sister, will prevent him from escorting his new sweetheart. As the two are about to leave for the dance, they admit to each other their anxieties over not being popular and not being good dancers. But secure in the knowledge that they respect and care for each other, they begin their first dance with more confidence and happiness than they have ever felt.

The Dancers treats the ordinary trials of young people with honesty, sensitivity, and compassion. As with so many of Horton's adolescent characters, Horace and Mary Catherine begin their road to shared happiness and self-discovery when they are able to trust each other and admit their common fears. That their story ends happily testifies to the playwright's belief that caring and intimacy breeds confidence, and that young people, if given the opportunity to find their own way in the world, will most often find the happiness and serenity they seek. Another equally significant aspect of the play demonstrates the healing power of intimacy and human contact. Dance has always played a significant role in Horton Foote's drama, and in *The Dancers*, the playwright not only employs the principles of dance but also the indelible image of the dance itself to give depth and meaning to his characters. As Gerald Wood explains: "In the dance a more physical and emotional side of human experience is released; intimacy becomes possible. But the movements of the dance are also governed by the rules of the form. Dance balances feeling with order, desire with tradition. In *The Dancers*, as in other plays by Foote, the dance is a precious, fleeting time when private desires and public needs, sensual spirits and fraternal affections are brought into harmony. It's as close as his characters get to a transcendent moment."[41]

While Horton was committed to writing for Fred Coe and the *Philco-Goodyear Television Playhouse*, he took a brief but important break from NBC in 1954. The reasons for his departure were both professional and

---

[41] Horton Foote, *Selected One-Act Plays of Horton Foote*, ed. Gerald C. Wood (Dallas TX: Southern Methodist University Press, 1989) 234.

personal. He had grown tired of the strenuous demands of television writing. He was weary of churning out a teleplay every month without sufficient time for thought and preparation: "I wrote ten plays between 1953 and 1954. I was exhausted. I just didn't have any more plays in me. You can't just crank them out. I had been storing them up over the years and, when they were gone, I wasn't going to just sit down and hack something out. Frankly, I don't think good writing could ever continue at that pace."[42]

Furthermore, Horton was unhappy with the intrusion and pressure being put on Fred Coe by commercial agencies. In an article for the June 1954 issue of *Theatre Arts*, Coe had concluded, "We are confident that the next five years of *Television Playhouse* will be just as restless, perplexing and magical as the first five."[43] Although written in the spirit of a manifesto, the article, "TV Drama's Declaration of Independence," would prove to be more of a eulogy. In August 1954, Coe was removed as the show's producer because an advertising executive was displeased by the number of shows with unhappy endings and complained that, "One week there'd be a story about a blind old lady in Texas, and the next week a story about a blind young lady in Texas."[44] Fred Coe's dismissal showed that sponsors and advertising agencies were asserting more and more control over the new media and its material, a fact that did not bode well for serious writers like Horton Foote. Without Coe's leadership, the positive ratings of the *Television Playhouse* dwindled and the writers began to withdraw.

There were darkening clouds on the horizon that didn't bode well for live dramatic anthologies, and those clouds would grow more ominous over time. Hollywood was quickly winning the tug-of-war that existed between the East Coast and the West Coast for the future of television. Television production had begun moving to Los Angeles as early as 1952 when CBS opened its mammoth Television City complex, described as "a complete motion picture studio designed especially for the electronic medium."[45] With the development of a new technology—videotape—the days of live television were numbered. Although Horton would go on to pen five more original dramas for television, including *The Roads to Home* (1955), *Flight* (1956), *A Member of the Family*

---

[42] Horton Foote, interview by Marion Castleberry, 18 March 1988, Wharton, Texas.
[43] Coe, 87.
[44] Krampner, *The Man in the Shadows*, 74.
[45] Ibid.

(1957), *The Night of the Storm* (1961), and *The Gambling Heart* (1964), he would never again replicate the productivity and enjoyment of the *Philco-Goodyear Television Playhouse* years. When asked about that time in his career, Horton responded with nostalgia: "I suppose you can't have the Depression or Roosevelt years again, and you can't have the old Philco Playhouse again. It was such a happy time that you have to shut it out of your heart."[46] Fellow *Television Playhouse* writer, Robert Alan Arthur shared Horton's sentiment when he wistfully wrote, "One of the reasons it was fun, probably the main reason, was because of Fred Coe. He was Big Daddy, Southern accent and all, and we were the family and while we were growing up we had ourselves a ball...We were a family in a certain time and place and then the time and place passed by, and we were no longer a family."[47]

Unquestionably, Horton Foote's own creative power of skillfully crafting dialogue and strong characters was best demonstrated and tested in the unique arena of live television, and his contributions helped bring about a great respect for television drama. During the "Golden Age of Television," Horton was recognized as one of the medium's greatest writers, and his work was considered among the very best of the era. Horton Foote's success on television would serve as a springboard for future Broadway productions and eventually earn him the reputation as one of America's foremost translators of Southern literature.

---

[46] Horton Foote, interview by Marion Castleberry, 18 March 2004, Waco, Texas.

[47] Krampner, *The Man in the Shadows*, 74.

10

Other Southern Voices
1954–61

As the future of live television anthologies dimmed, Horton Foote turned his attention once again to writing for the stage. In the spring of 1954, he began work on a new play, *The Traveling Lady*, which was scheduled to open at New York's Playhouse Theatre in October. Unfortunately, his writing was halted by the distressing news that his Grandmother Brooks had passed away. Her death on 29 April 1954 at age eighty left Horton and his family in a state of shock and grief. Horton, Lillian, and their two children traveled to Wharton to attend the funeral and celebrate the life of this gracious matriarch who had meant so much to them. Following the funeral service, the family returned to New York where, in the fall of 1954, Foote resumed his writing and completed the final draft of *The Traveling Lady*.

The Traveling Lady was written for actress Kim Stanley, who had emerged as the foremost interpreter of Horton's work. The play was inspired by an experience Horton and Lillian had one spring evening in 1952 while visiting family and friends in Wharton. Horton recalled that the couple decided to eat at a neighborhood drive-in restaurant where they met a carhop, a forty-year-old woman with a "gentle face," who was "worn tired" from trying to make a living for her family. This was the woman's "first day on the job," Horton added, and "she was embarrassed by her inefficiency in taking orders. The Footes were sympathetic to the woman's plight and for days afterward discussed what must have led her to this type of job. "How many people are there in our world with a lack of education, spiritual training and guidance, and a complete omission of family devotion? What moved this mature woman to become a carhop, having to compete with girls half her age? Had she been burdened by an unhappy marriage? Had death saddened her and forced her to seek employment and had her lack of training demanded her competing with obviously more attractive youngsters?"[1]

---

[1] Horton Foote, interview by Marion Castleberry, 18 March 2004, Waco, Texas.

The Traveling Lady, like many of Horton's teleplays, depicts a young woman's ability to cope with familial disappointment and life shattering change.[2] The action of the play centers on Georgette Thomas, a young mother, who arrives in the small Texas town of Harrison with her baby daughter, Margaret Rose, to await her husband Henry's release from the penitentiary. Searching for Judge Ewing, who rents houses, they find themselves at the house of Clara Breedlove and her brother Slim, a restless young widower who is grieving the death of his wife. Georgette reluctantly admits to the Judge that Henry is completing a prison term for stabbing a man during a drunken spree in her hometown of Lovelady. During the six years of his imprisonment, Georgette has worked and saved her earnings to help her husband get out of prison so that she and Margaret Rose, whom Henry has never seen, can join him. However, she discovers from Slim, a deputy sheriff, that Henry has been free for more than a month and has no intention of reuniting with his family. Surprisingly, since his release, Henry has been working as a yardman for Mrs. Tillman, a temperance advocate whose hobby is rehabilitating drunkards and wayward souls.

The lack of healthy parent/child relationships, a major theme in Horton Foote's canon, represents the central focus of *The Traveling Lady*. Orphaned as a child, Henry grew up in Harrison and gained the reputation of a miscreant. Like Bubber Reeves in *The Chase*, Henry was reared in an atmosphere of hostility and physical abuse. Kate Dawson, his guardian, often beat him in an effort to break his spirit and to keep him from following what she believed was a foolhardy dream to be a country western singer. To reinforce the theme, Horton aptly chooses the day of Kate Dawson's funeral as the backdrop for the action of the play.

Miss Clara Breedlove and Slim graciously offer to let Georgette and Margaret Rose stay at their home until Slim can contact Henry, but when Henry finally appears, he excuses himself by promising that he will find them a house to rent and return for his wife and daughter in an hour. He does not return; instead, he gets drunk, robs his employer, and attempts to skip town without being seen. But Henry's plan is thwarted by his decision to stop by the grave of Kate Dawson. Haunted by his memories of the old woman, Henry savagely mutilates her

---

[2] Horton Foote, *The Traveling Lady*, in *Horton Foote Collected Plays*, vol. 2 (New York: Smith and Kraus 1996) 113–72. All page references to *The Traveling Lady* in the text refer to this publication.

grave. He is soon captured and faced with returning to prison. Before he is carried away, however, he is granted a farewell meeting with his wife and daughter but sadly this meeting leads to tragic consequences. Believing he is unable to quit drinking—"just plain weak," and "not worth killing"—Henry begs his wife to forgive and forget him (159). In the final scene, Georgette allows Henry to meet his daughter, Margaret Rose, who asks him to sing *New San Antonio Rose*, a song Henry performed at a bar where he first met Georgette. Henry starts to sing the song but suddenly stops and makes a futile break for freedom; Slim and the sheriff block his escape. As Henry is led away in handcuffs, Georgette finally faces the reality that she cannot look to her husband for affection and support. Instead, reminiscent of Helen Crews in *The Midnight Caller*, she finds companionship with another man, Slim Murray, who has also faced the harsh realities of a failed marriage. After Slim declares his love for Georgette, the couple leaves Harrison for the Texas Valley, where Slim assures Georgette that jobs are plentiful and a better life is possible. In the final analysis, there is no assurance that Slim and Georgette will marry or live happily ever after, but in Horton's dramatic world, the ability to face hardships and loss and to move forward is seen as a virtue.

The Traveling Lady, the last of Horton Foote's plays to be produced on Broadway for forty years, premiered 27 October 1954 at The Playhouse Theatre in New York under the direction of Vincent Done-hue, with a notable cast that featured Jack Lord as Slim Murray, Lonny Chapman as Henry, and Kim Stanley as Georgette Thomas, a role which boosted the actress to Broadway stardom. Reviews were mixed, but Kim Stanley's notices were glowing. Brooks Atkinson of the *New York Times* wrote that Stanley's portrayal of Georgette, was "a stunning piece of acting"[3] and Walter Kerr of the *Herald-Tribune* added: "Toward the end of the evening she manages, in a few fumbling gestures and some broken sentences, to suggest three sorts of life all at once: the life of the child whose shoe she is buckling, the crude pleasure of her own remembered childhood, [and] the violent and wasted life of the man neither of them will ever see again."[4] Harold Clurman, in *The Nation*, compared Stanley's work to great actresses of the past: "Kim Stanley is

---

[3] Brooks Atkinson, "Theatre: Texas Drama," *New York Times*, 28 October 1954.

[4] Walter Kerr, "The Traveling Lady," *New York Herald Tribune*, 28 October 1954.

the youngest addition to that line of American actresses whose emblematic figures are Laurette Taylor and Pauline Lord."[5]

Soon after the reviews were in, members of the New Dramatists Playwrights Company—Maxwell Anderson, Elmer Rice, Robert Sherwood, Robert Anderson, Rogers Stevens, and John Wharton—voted for the first time in the group's sixteen-year history to promote an actor to star billing by placing their name above the title of the play after a production had already opened. "Kim deserved that pro-motion," Horton said in an interview with Jon Krampner: "She had enormous instincts and intuition [with] a wonderful sense of truth onstage and great emotional daring. She had a concentration onstage that was compelling. She could use stillness; she could use quiet. She could not say anything, and yet there was this compelling thing about her. She changed the whole style of acting in that period for young women."[6]

Despite its contribution to Kim Stanley's career, *The Traveling Lady* did not achieve popular or critical success and closed after only thirty-one performances on 20 November 1954. Perhaps the large stage of the Playhouse Theatre was not the most suitable vehicle for this particular piece, which seemed to call for the close-up of the camera to fully capture the emotions of the characters. Brooks Atkinson remarked that Horton Foote was not "a forceful playwright" and that he never made "a statement except in extremis." Atkinson further noted, however, that there were "genuine and very poignant scenes in the play" and that Horton Foote's impulses were "decent enough, but he lacks strength and goes to pieces in crisis." Nevertheless, the critic did recognize Horton's exceptional gifts: "In a theatre that is largely populated by decadent people who don't understand anything, it is a pleasure to watch Mr. Foote's characters behave like normal human beings.... If the whole performance is beautiful, it must be largely because Mr. Foote has written characters with enough flesh, blood, and heart to be actable."[7]

As Brooks Atkinson suggests, the characters of *The Traveling Lady* are at once humorous, complex, and true to life, and their struggle for happiness is universal. The humor in the play comes from the ludicrous interactions between Mrs. Mavis, an old woman on the verge

---

[5] Harold Clurman, "*The Traveling Lady* Review," *The Nation*, 11 November 1954.

[6] John Krampner, *Female Brando: The Legend of Kim Stanley* (New York: Back Stage Books 2006) 91.

[7] Atkinson, "Theatre: Texas Drama," 28 October 1954.

of senility, and her loving but frustrated daughter, Sitter. Mrs. Mavis continuously runs away from home and scandalizes her daughter with childish behavior. Although Sitter and Mrs. Mavis's relationship reveals a different kind of parent/child bond than that of Henry and Kate Dawson, it is nonetheless wrought with frustrations. Mrs. Mavis is nearly too much for Sitter to handle. When Sitter complains that she is worn out from looking after her mother, admitting that Mrs. Mavis is "fresh as a daisy," Sitter asks her how she can be so energetic and her mother replies: "From livin' right. I live right, honey. I eat my greens. I get my exercise and I eat cornbread every morning of my life" (57). William Hawkins, critic of the *New York World Telegram*, called the childish Mrs. Mavis the most interesting character in the play.[8]

Horton did not offer answers for Georgette or Slim, anymore than one finds answers in life, but he portrayed the suffering of these ordinary people with great depth. Georgette, who came from a broken home and was abandoned by her husband, and Slim, whose wife deserted him and subsequently died leaving him emotionally wounded and unsettled, all depict Horton's belief that there are no simple explanations for life's adversities or the deterioration of love. Yet, the affectionate relationship of the couple and their desire to have a stable family is redemptive. Horton reminds us that the healing power of intimate relationships and healthy connections to others most often brings peace and contentment to those faced with devastating loneliness.

Oddly, most critics did not comment on the psychological problems of Henry Thomas, which are the crux of the play, but nevertheless the character emerges as a tragic figure. Subjected to abuse and brutality as a child at the hands of a cruel and misguided old woman, Henry never experienced the love and warmth of a real family. Thus, as an adult, he repeats the same violent patterns he learned in his youth, a behavior resulting in his inability to connect with his family or accept intimacy from Georgette. Sadly, he remains rootless and self-destructive throughout the play. Stark Young called the moment Henry goes to the grave of his abusive guardian and ravages the flowers and earth as dark and hideous as anything in Strindberg. "Just how a dramatist, and not only in this instance, comes on an image, or such a motif, perhaps he himself does not know," Young suggests. "It might remind us of

---

[8] William Hawkins, "Review of *The Traveling Lady*," *New York World Telegram*, 28 October 1954.

what Coleridge, in one of those winged moments of his, said of science: 'All science begins in wonder and ends in wonder, and the interspace is filled with admiration.'"[9]

Loyal to the play that brought her stardom, Kim Stanley performed the role of Georgette Thomas twice more on live television: on *Studio One* on 22 April 1957, with Steven Hill as Henry Thomas and Robert Loggia as Slim Murray; and in London, on England's *Independent Television Authority's Armchair Theatre* on 27 July 1958. In a letter to Lucy Kroll on 11 March 1955, Stanley called *The Traveling Lady* "one of the greatest plays [she'd] ever worked in" and remarked that the play "deserved a better fate," referring to its short 1954 run on Broadway.[10]

At Stanley's behest, Horton condensed the play for CBS's *Studio One*, observing: "I feel the play has been improved...many of the [technical] problems in the Broadway play have been solved in the adaptation"[11] For her television performance Kim Stanley won the prestigious Sylvania Award. Produced by Fred Coe and directed by Robert Mulligan, the teleplay received high praise from television critics. Saul Levinson of the *New York World Telegram and Sun* praised both Stanley's performance and Horton's adaptation. "Last night *Studio One* presented the finest drama we have yet seen on television.... It spoke directly; it drew its characters most precisely; its language rang most clearly with the strong ability of poetry; it had something to say."[12]

Horton Foote's successes on the stage and on television—specifically *The Trip to Bountiful, A Young Lady of Property,* and *The Traveling Lady*—caught the attention of Hollywood producers. After *The Traveling Lady* closed in 1954, Warner Brothers lured Horton to California in order to adapt to the screen the work of another Southern writer, Clinton Seeley. Horton had resisted the call of Hollywood for several years because he felt the theater, not cinema, was his artistic home, and he did not relish the idea of tampering with recognized classics to fit the demands of another medium. However, he now had two children and a wife to support, and he found it impossible to turn down Warner Brothers's offer of fifteen thousand dollars for the job, a substantial amount of money for the late 1950s. For the most part, Horton found his time in

---

[9] Ibid.

[10] Kim Stanley to Lucy Kroll, 11 March 1955 (Horton Foote Papers).

[11] Horton Foote, interview by *New York Journal American*, 15 April 1957.

[12] Saul Levinson, "*Traveling Lady*: Rare TV Treat," *New York World-Telegram and Sun*, 23 April 1957.

Hollywood and his work on the movie, *Storm Fear*, pleasurable, largely because Cornell Wilde— the producer, director, and star of the film— treated him like a partner, inviting him to work with him daily to develop the movie and involving him in the final cuts. In return, Horton created a polished screenplay from Clinton Seeley's novel, the story of a bank robber who retreats to a mountain home where he is frightened by an imposing storm. Though the film was aptly produced, reviews for both the acting and direction were mixed and the movie eventually fell into obscurity.

Horton's brief apprenticeship in Hollywood convinced him that a dramatist who adapts another writer's fiction for the screen rarely receives any satisfaction for his labor. Adaptation requires taking on someone else's identity and submerging oneself in the work. Horton felt that while you don't have to feel the work is great literature, you do have to be sympathetic toward the material. However, with *Storm Fear* he was never able to connect emotionally or to identify with the novel completely. Through the experience he learned that an adapter can never entirely please the original author, nor can he satisfy the audience who has definite ideas and illusions about plot, characterization, background, and motivation. Worse yet, a writer must accept the fact that a motion picture is by its very nature a collaborative effort, and too often the words and even the story of a screenplay can be brutally altered or deleted by a director or producer. Horton noted in a conversation with his friend, John Guare: "I hate this term, 'writer for hire' which is the great Hollywood term. I think if you're just a writer, then you have no way of being part of the mechanism. And they let you know that they own the rights [to your work]. I think this is the most tragic thing about a screenwriter in that situation"[13] Although Horton was not pleased with his work on *Storm Fear*, he was very happy he convinced Cornell Wilde to cast actors Steven Hill and Lee Grant in the film, thereby liberating both actors from the Hollywood blacklist.

Following his brief but edifying stint in Hollywood, Horton returned to Wharton with his family for an extended visit. He had saved ten thousand dollars from his work with *Philco-Goodyear Television Playhouse* and Warner Brothers, and with part of his savings, he bought a burial plot in the Wharton cemetery next to those reserved for his parents and

---

[13] John Guare, "Conversation with Horton Foote," in *The Voice of an American Playwright*, ed. Gerald C. Wood and Marion Castleberry (Macon GA: Mercer University Press, 2012) 245.

grandparents. He used the remainder of his savings to live on and to support his writing.

In spring 1955, Lillian learned that she was pregnant with their third child. Walter Vallish Foote was born on 4 December 1955, and during that same year Horton Jr. turned three and Barbara Hallie celebrated her fifth birthday. As their family grew, Horton and Lillian began to reflect upon their future in New York and whether the city was the best place to raise their children. They wanted their kids to grow up in a small town, as they had done, rather than in a crowded city. So, in 1956, the couple started to explore potential homes outside New York. Eventually they settled on the small village of Nyack, New York, a rural community only thirty-two miles north of the city. Nestled along the Hudson River, Nyack was the birthplace of the famous artist Edward Hopper and had become home to several theater artists and writers, including Carson McCullers and actress Helen Hayes, with whom the Footes became close friends. After moving to Nyack, Horton and Lillian found themselves occupied with their active, growing family and their rapidly increasing collection of pets. They became involved with school and community activities and with remodeling the large rambling house they purchased. They also began attending a Christian Science Church in Nyack, frequenting Reading Rooms and taking their children regularly to Sunday school. During this time, Horton and Lillian became faithful members of the Christian Science Church. Lillian wrote to Horton, expressing how Christian Science had helped her through moments of loneliness and depression, frustration with the children, and financial concerns. "I, too, feel that I have gone a great big step further in Christian Science," she admitted. "It is a religion of great beauty and loveliness and I shall be eternally grateful to you, my darling, for bringing me to it. I don't know how I could get through many of these periods that I do occasionally encounter without it. Then I read an article or catch something in a church service and the fear lifts and I feel born again."[14]

While Lillian cared for the family, Horton continued to write for the home screen, even though the market for original teleplays was rapidly diminishing, first in the face of quiz shows and then from competition with filmed series, Westerns, private-eye melodramas, and situation comedies. In the spring of 1955, the *U.S. Steel Hour* aired *The Roads to Home*, Horton's bittersweet tale of the Jackson family's search for a home and their discovery that happiness does not reside in material

---

[14] Lillian Foote to Horton Foote, 18 January 1958 (Horton Foote Papers).

success but in nourishing connections to family and community. On 16 December 1956, ABC's *Omnibus Playhouse* premiered Horton's adaptation of Robert Hutchinson's short story *Drugstore Sunday Noon*, starring Helen Hayes, and on 25 March 1957, CBS's *Studio One* produced *A Member of the Family*, Horton's tale of family jealousy and failed dreams that featured renowned actor, Hume Cronyn.

The most personal of Horton's teleplays produced during this period was *Flight* with Kim Stanley, which aired on Fred Coe's new anthology series, *Playwrights '56*, on 28 February 1956. Reminiscent of *The Tears of My Sister* and *Courtship*, *Flight* dramatizes the real-life attempt of the playwright's mother to marry a man of whom her parents disapprove. In *Flight*, Horton speculated on what might have occurred if his mother had eloped with someone other than his father, and, not surprisingly, the outcome is rather bleak. The central character, Martha Anderson, must choose between leaving home to seek a new life with the man she loves or remaining with her proud and domineering family, who cannot fully understand her plight. She defies her parents' wishes and runs away from home; however, when she arrives in San Antonio to meet her fiancé, she learns that he has left town and abandoned her. The crisis of *Flight* is precipitated by parents who want to control their children, and, as in so many of Horton's works, choosing to break from such control is presented as a courageous necessity. Horton explained in his preface to the play:

> I chose the particular year of 1915 because it seemed that it was a time when many of the fixed and settled values in American life were changing or being re-examined and when the whole concept of family life and family responsibility was being altered. Many of my plays deal with the rootlessness of American life. My characters are often searching for a town or a home to belong to, or a parent, or a child—all parts of the family. A crisis occurs in [Martha's] life and [her parents] are prepared to shelter and protect her, to help in whatever way they can to repair the wrong or damage that has been done to her. She refuses them and chooses to go away to a city alone. Hers is an exodus, a flight that was unusual for a girl of her background and environment then. Today, for good or bad, it is constant.[15]

---

[15] Horton Foote, *Flight*, in *Television Plays for Writers: Eight Television Plays with Comment and Analysis by the Authors*, ed. Abraham Burak (Boston: The Writer 1957) 148.

Kim Stanley received glowing reviews for her performance as Martha Anderson, but the critical success of *Flight* could not prevent *Playwrights '56* from being cancelled a few months later. The anthology series fell victim to the growing popularity of *The $64,000 Question*, harbinger of a wave of quiz shows that helped bring live television drama to an end.

On 4 July 1956, *The Trip to Bountiful* opened for a brief run at the Arts Theatre Club in London, the first time a Horton Foote play had been performed outside the United States. Staged by the celebrated American director, Alan Schneider, the play starred the British actress Margaret Vines, who had once been called the most talented actress of her generation, in the role of Carrie Watts, John Glen, a veteran of Peter Brook's theater company and Stratford-upon-Avon, as Ludie, and the popular American actress, Mavis Villiers, as Jessie May. Although Schneider and Horton had high hopes for the production, it did not fare well with British audiences: "Bountiful was appreciated by my friends, but did not lead to bigger and better things," Schneider remarked. "The Sunday critics, Kenneth Tynan and Harold Hobson, each gave us a flattering paragraph; the dailies were merely polite. Straight American drama rarely succeeds in London."[16]

That same year, Horton also had eight teleplays produced on *Philco-Goodyear Television Theatre*, published by Harcourt Brace under the title *Harrison, Texas: Eight Television Plays* and he expanded his play *The Chase* into a novel of almost three hundred pages, fleshing out characters and exposing motivations behind their actions.[17] Published by Rinehart & Company Press, the novel closely follows the story of the play, focusing on Sheriff Eldon Hawes's failure to return escaped convict Bubber Reeves to prison. But the expanded narrative provides a fuller picture of the town of Harrison and introduces the reader to several new characters. In the novel, Horton depicts a town that is more volatile than that of the play. The Harrison, Texas, of the book is a place where young couples drink their lives away and spread vicious gossip about the marital infidelities of their elders. Equally disturbing is that the town's deputy sheriff actually considers lynching a black man being held in jail solely for the excitement and power it offers. In

---

[16] Alan Schneider, *Entrances: An American Director's Journey* (New York: Viking Penguin, 1986) 238–39.

[17] Horton Foote, *The Chase* (New York: Rinehart & Company, 1956). Page references in the text refer to this publication.

Harrison, parents manipulate and abuse their children, driving them to thoughts of suicide and acts of violence. The most interesting of the new characters is Miss Mattie, a spinster whose life has been dominated by her manipulative and mean-spirited mother. Since the death of her father, Miss Mattie has allowed her mother to control her life. Since Mattie was ten, she has been figuratively chained by her mother's side in a series of apartments and hotel rooms instead of a home. Mattie secretly dreams of "death and what it would be like when she or her mother died and she was finally alone.... And she felt the old bitterness rise again in her heart against her mother...and she thought: Die, Mama and leave me free" (136–7).

Mattie and her mother offer a striking counterpart to Bubber Reeves and his mother—another domineering parent who has tried to control her child's life. While Miss Mattie succumbs to her mother's abuse because "it made life so much easier if she didn't cross her," (3) Bubber has turned to crime and violence as a response to unhealthy family relationships. The underlying reason for Bubber's degeneration is clarified in the novel. His father is a weak, ineffectual man whose alcoholism and submissive nature has driven a wedge between father and son. To compensate for her husband's behavior, Mrs. Reeves has tried again and again to buy her son out of trouble, even going so far as attempting to pay for the secondhand car he stole rather than accepting his sentence to the state prison farm. Even though Bubber is a more compassionate character in the novel, he believes he is inherently evil and accepts the proclamation of his Sunday school teacher that his baby sister died as a punishment for his sins. His guilt has crippled him emotionally, and when his mother finally tells him that for his own good she can no longer support him, Bubber proclaims: "All right. Go. I'll hate you. I'll curse you until the day I die" (157). As he escapes into the night, it becomes clear that Mrs. Reeves cannot save Bubber, and she finally realizes the consequences of her misguided actions.

The novel follows the play closely with Mrs. Reeves soliciting the help of Sheriff Hawes in bringing her son to justice. But in the novel, after Bubber is killed, his parents bury him beside his baby sister. And in a scene at the graveyard (a sacred place of reconciliation and forgiveness in Foote's dramatic world), Mrs. Reeves blames herself for trying too hard to mold her son to her own image. "I always wanted a boy the town could be proud of," she admits, "I killed him trying to make him be someone they could be proud of" (238–9). The scene concludes with Mrs. Reeves and her husband vowing to remain in Harrison, near their dead children, and promising to tend their children's graves for the rest of their lives.

Hawes's character in the novel is similar to that of the play and his role as father figure to Bubber is equally significant, but in the expanded version he already has a child of his own and is better able to understand Mrs. Reeves's feelings of sadness and loss after he kills her son. Only thoughts of providing a home for his family and of being an attentive father to his baby boy give Hawes the strength and courage to quit his job as sheriff and move back to the cotton farm once owned by his father. At the end of the novel, Hawes looks forward to a happier life, and when another mother complains of trouble with her son, seeking the help of the authorities, Eldon Hawes has already resigned his position as sheriff. Rather than make amends for his failure by taking on another juvenile case, he leaves the problem to the new sheriff. In the end, he vows to become the kind of father his son needs by spending time with him and by building bonds of love and respect between them.

This change in the story's ending is significant and suggests that Horton's initial vision of *The Chase* was influenced by his own experiences as a father. In many of Horton's works, the male characters are tempted to reduce courage to willpower and physical action, much like Hawes when he continues the chase and assumes responsibility for protecting another young boy from suffering the same fate as Bubber Reeves. In the novel, however, Hawes undergoes a paralyzing introspection and tries to rid himself of the violent impulses that have plagued him by choosing to be less occupied with public responsibility and more attentive to his own security and that of his wife and son. He thinks back over the sixteen years he has held the job to locate the incident that has turned him from a man able to fall asleep as soon as his head hit the pillow to a man who spends most of his time thinking and brooding:

> He realized that it wasn't one incident or 10 or a hundred, but the accumulation of 15 years of looking into tired and hopeless faces, of punishing without hope of reformation, of being a symbol of fear and hatred to so many. And this last most of all he despised about his position, because Hawes had taken this office and tried to make good at it to please and be loved and at first the gratitude of his friends made up for the fears and the hate of the punished, but as time went on and he became taken for granted and his friends took his bravery and his

efficiency as a matter of course, he was left with only the fear and the hatred. (108–9)

In the end, Hawes chooses a life of quiet integrity back on the farm—a decision that suggests Horton's deepening understanding of the human condition and his growing awareness that all any one man can hope to accomplish in this world is to be a nurturing, loving father to his own children. To be a parent and moral guide to an entire town is too much to ask of one man.

The Chase received positive reviews from literary critics, especially W.J. Smith of *Commonweal* and Anthony Boucher of the *New York Herald Tribune*, who called it a powerful novel of character, "studying the moral and psychological problems of violence."[18] The most glowing evaluation of the novel, however, was by Horton's agent Lucy Kroll who wrote to him in a letter, "The work has vitality, economy, a drive, a humanity that is indeed exciting for me to experience. I could not put it down...how you gave so in essence the full depth of each and every person involved in this story, how your suspense drives not with plot or artifice but with the beating of the heart, the exterior and interior drive of each being, the subconscious, the unconscious, the mores, the culture, the climate of the town, its ancestry, its drives, its demanding and curbing influences."[19]

Apart from his faithful transposition of *The Chase*, Horton also began a series of adaptations for *Playhouse 90,* the final refuge for the "Golden Age of Television." *Playhouse 90* was conceived by CBS in 1956 as a prestige vehicle for the network and featured ninety-minute live dramas, although increasingly shows would be videotaped. In 1958, Fred Coe, along with John Houseman and Herbert Brodkin, were hired to produce the show that aired from Hollywood's Television City. Coe moved his base of operations to the West Coast and began to search for appropriate stories to tell. He immediately turned to the works of William Faulkner, a writer he greatly admired but had never produced. Faulkner had won the Nobel Prize in Literature in 1950, but his work was relatively unknown among the American reading public. Coe hoped to correct this oversight by televising Faulkner's stories. Coe knew only one other person who shared his respect for Faulkner—

---

[18] Anthony Boucher, "Review of *The Chase: A Novel,*" *New York Herald Tribune,* 6 February 1956.

[19] Lucy Kroll to Horton Foote, 12 April 1954 (Horton Foote Papers).

Horton Foote—and he immediately called the playwright to see if he was interested in adapting Falkner's novella, *Old Man*, for *Playhouse 90*.

Initially, Horton was reluctant to get involved with the project because Faulkner's work, a rambling tale about a prison-farm convict sent out in a rowboat to rescue a pregnant woman stranded during the Mississippi River flood of 1927, seemed almost impossible to adapt for live television. Anyone seeking to turn the story into a teleplay, Horton felt, had two main obstacles to overcome: how to convey the action and philosophical flavor of the work and how to realistically dramatize the story that takes place almost entirely on water. Coe had informed Horton that John Frankenheimer, one of television's most successful filmmakers, would be directing the show, and he had announced that he wanted the production to be performed live in sequence, the way television dramas had always been done. Even though Horton was uncertain about the feasibility of this approach, he was very taken by Faulkner's characters and story, and eventually decided that creating realistic scenery for the production was a technical concern, not a writer's problem. He recalled that while walking along the Hudson River and thinking over the dilemma, his instinct told him to "let the technical people handle it. If Fred Coe hasn't brought it up and John Frankenheimer...hasn't brought it up, don't worry about it. Write it like you have the Mississippi River and the flood and let them solve all the technical details."[20] Having arrived at his decision, Horton called Fred Coe, agreed to take on the project, and began translating Faulkner's river journey into an actable script.

Horton explained that by the time he started adapting *Old Man*, he had been an avid reader of Faulkner's works for nearly twenty years and considered himself in some measure, a student of his work.[21] Faulkner's world was certainly one with which Horton was very familiar. He had grown up on the Gulf Coast in a town where two rivers flooded constantly and he understood well the hardships that a flood brought to people. The characters of *Old Man*, which had first drawn the playwright to the story, were simple rural people who spoke a subtle language that Horton recognized instantly.

Horton's teleplay was faithful to Faulkner's novella, carefully adhering to the original plot and giving a sense of order to the

---

[20] Horton Foote, *Genesis of an American Playwright*, ed. Marion Castleberry (Waco TX: Baylor University Press, 2004) 158.

[21] Ibid., 157.

otherwise chaotic river journey. The script retained Faulkner's focus on a convict's rescue of a pregnant woman from the Mississippi flood and his safe, but unjust, return to prison, but Horton enriched the original by emphasizing the bond of love and respect that develops between the tall convict and the young woman. Horton was fascinated by the convict who, in spite of his chances to escape the flood, wanted only to get the woman to safety and return to serve out his sentence, and he was especially captivated by the character of the woman: "I never tired thinking of the woman," Horton admitted, "her passive acceptance of everything that happened was always a delight to me. She always found something in the journey to enjoy in spite of the cold and hunger, a painful childbirth, and infestation of snakes, and gunfire.... I wanted to establish a specific character for the woman. I made her a talker and gave her a detailed history."[22]

While Faulkner narrates the journey of the convict through internal monologues, giving limited attention to the other characters, Horton enlarged the woman's role, shifting the focus from the convict to his relationship with the pregnant woman. In Horton's version, the two characters create a surrogate family, which nurtures both of them during their horrific ordeal. The result of these changes is a more personal and humane story.[23]

Horton's adaptation helps to clarify and strengthen some of the obscure aspects of Faulkner's novella. Faulkner's convict reveals a desperate desire to escape from the world, first into the "birth canal" of the flooding river and finally back to the protective "womb" of the penitentiary, and he accepts ten more years of punishment for his attempted escape, since in prison he'll be "without no female companionship."[24] Horton's convict, on the other hand, cares deeply for the woman and anticipates a life with her and the child. He resents his capture and the additional confinement while the woman, eager to establish family ties, is willing to wait for the convict's release. In order to better emphasize the sense of companionship in the teleplay, Horton

---

[22] Ibid., 160.

[23] Rebecca Briley, "Southern Accents: Horton Foote's Adaptations of William Faulkner, Harper Lee, and Flannery O'Connor," in *Horton Foote: A Casebook*, ed. Gerald C. Wood (New York: Garland Press, 1998) 49–66. Rebecca Briley argues that the film is much more humane than the novel.

[24] William Faulkner, *Old Man*, in *Portable Faulkner*, ed. Malcolm Cowley (New York: Viking Press, 1974) 435–526. Page references to *Old Man* in the text refer to this work.

deleted much of Faulkner's obscene and derogatory language and inserted his own brand of gentle humor and sparse, straightforward language.

While Faulkner's *Old Man* is more humorous and psychologically complex, Horton's version develops more intimacy between characters and offers a more hopeful ending. Charles Watson points out that Horton's adaptation adds human appeal to the original work and is much easier to follow than the novella, but in order to create an actable script he was unable to capture the provocative quality of Faulkner's themes: the changing roles of male and female in modern industrial society and the convict's aversion to regimented life. "One does not get the feeling of a return to primitive existence," Watson explains. "The convict's complete inability in the story to function normally with women in complex society is not realized in the film"[25]

Although Horton was generally satisfied with the adaptation, he was disappointed in his inability to capture the savagery inherent in the visual aspects of the story—the flood, the snakes, the burning of the tree to make a paddle, the vastness of the flooded river. The realization of those elements was left to the creative artistry of John Frankenheimer and his production team.

After finishing the first draft of *Old Man* in Nyack, Horton sent it to Fred Coe and John Frankenheimer in Los Angeles. Both were equally thrilled with the script. After a few rewrites, Frankenheimer remarked to Horton that it was the best script he had ever worked with, and Coe responded by asking the playwright if he could fly to California to begin rehearsals. Two weeks later, Horton checked into the Montecito Hotel in Los Angeles, and that evening he attended a dinner party at John Frankenheimer's house where he learned that Sterling Hayden had been cast as the convict and Geraldine Page as the woman. He also discovered that Frankenheimer was still determined to shoot the performance in sequence, without the aid of videotape. To realize the director's vision, CBS had built two enormous water tanks in the studio to replicate the Mississippi River.

At the time, Frankenheimer's idea seemed workable but as rehearsals moved from an empty soundstage to the actual set, problems began to emerge. Once the tanks were filled with water, they proved to be so heavy that the foundation in the CBS studio cracked. CBS executive

---

[25] Charles Watson, *Horton Foote: A Literary Biography* (Austin: University of Texas Press, 2003) 147–48.

Charles Cappleman recalls: "We built the Mississippi River on Stage 43. Covering most of one soundstage was a tank just deep enough to float the rowboat Sterling and Page spend much of the show in. Technicians also rigged up the stage for the show's periodic rainstorm. A second stage was used for dry-land sequences."[26] "Everybody said that the show couldn't be done," John Frankenheimer adds. "The whole thing was just a nightmare. CBS thought the whole building was going to come down, and shored it up with big beams underneath"[27] Frankenheimer finally had to accept that he could not shoot the teleplay as originally planned but would need to use videotape and film the scenes out of sequence. Horton recalled, "I believe this was the first television show, for good or bad, that was successfully taped out of sequence; and because the show had quite an impact at the time it was done, it did much to end the era of live television."[28]

In spite of these unexpected complications, rehearsals for *Old Man* moved along satisfactorily. Horton was very impressed with rehearsals and the final production: "I am very happy and pleased with my working conditions. Everyone is extremely nice and helpful, and all seem deeply committed to the script." Horton was especially taken with the performance of Geraldine Page. "I can't wait to tell you about her," he wrote to Lillian. "She is not at all like she seems…she is very nice, and I like her."[29]

Even though Horton's work in Hollywood was rewarding, he missed his family terribly. He had not been away from Lillian for an extended time since they married, and the couple wrote to each other daily. Their letters contained a mixture of family news, day-to-day trivia, gossip from the workplace, and updates on rehearsals. They often wrote to each other about their children—usually in small stories about daily events or in brief statements of their feelings about each other and raising a family together. Their letters shed light on the ways in which Horton and Lillian provided emotional support for each other during the writer's long absences from home.

Horton not only received daily letters from Lillian, but he also wrote and received correspondence from his children. Even when the children

---

[26] John Krampner, *The Man in the Shadows: Fred Coe and the Golden Age of Television* (New Brunswick NJ: Rutgers University Press, 1997) 127.

[27] Ibid.

[28] Foote, *Genesis*, 167.

[29] Horton Foote to Lillian Foote, 24 October 1958 (Horton Foote Papers).

were very small, he often wrote separate letters to each of them and included all of their names above the address on the envelopes. Horton frequently commented in his letters that during his business trips he placed photographs of his wife and children in his hotel rooms and his temporary offices to keep him from becoming so lonely.

During the middle of Horton's stay in Hollywood, Lillian called with the news that she was again pregnant. Because Horton was frequently away on business trips, his mother suggested that Gladys, his parent's black cook, move to Nyack for a while to assist Lillian with housework and cooking. Gladys was an enormous help and source of companionship for Lillian. From the minute she arrived, Lillian's letters to Horton were filled with her impressions of Gladys's cooking and stories of Wharton. "I had Gladys roast us a turkey yesterday and it was so good," Lillian wrote. "The cornbread stuffing was the best I ever ate." Lillian also mentioned Gladys's cooking again, as well as her growing friendship with writer Carson McCullers: "I told Carson when you came back Gladys was going to cook a big pot of vegetable soup and corn bread and we would have her over to help eat it up."[30]

Back in Hollywood, work on the *Old Man* was coming to a close, and on 20 November 1958 the show was broadcast on *Playhouse 90*. It was an enormous triumph, deeply moving and visually stunning. *Variety Magazine* was ecstatic about the show and proclaimed: "The gifted Fred Coe-John Frankenheimer combo, aided by a brilliant Horton Foote adaptation, came up with a memorable 90 minutes of overwhelming drama." The review also praised the performances of Hayden and Page, and Walter Scott Herndon, the show's art director, for his "almost super realistic sets."[31] The production was later nominated for a prestigious Emmy Award for "Best Writing of a Single Dramatic Program." Horton did not win the award that year, but in 1997 he adapted the novella again for *Hallmark Hall of Fame* and won an Emmy on his second try.

The success of *Old Man* elevated Horton Foote's status in the entertainment industry. He garnered the reputation of a gifted adapter of Southern literature and was showered with offers from television and movie producers. He had enjoyed adapting Faulkner, and was open to other offers, but only if the material interested him enough to enter into

---

[30] Lillian Foote to Horton Foote, 27 October 1958 (Horton Foote Papers).

[31] "Tele Follow-up Comment: *Playhouse 90* review." Unsigned review in *Variety Magazine*, 15 October 1958, 34.

what he called the "painful process of entering someone else's creative world."[32]

In January 1959, Warner Brothers offered Horton a lucrative contract to adapt a screenplay based on Erskine Caldwell's Southern novel, *Claudelle Inglish*, which tells the story of a farm girl who tires of her dull life and transforms herself into the town trollop. Horton had had one previous experience with Warner Brothers, working on *Storm Fear*, and he had enjoyed collaborating with Cornell Wilde during the shooting of the movie. The writer expected the work on *Claudelle Inglish* to be much the same but he quickly learned otherwise:

> I arrived on the Warner Brothers' lot and punched the required time clock as I would on my arrival and departure each day, and I was led to a two-story building with a number of offices. Most of the offices were empty, except for the one assigned to me and the one occupied by Marion Hargrove, who was working on *Maverick*, a TV series.
>
> The first day, I remember my secretary telling me how it used to be when the offices were all filled with writers. She pointed out where Christopher Isherwood worked, and Faulkner, and she said that she hoped the offices would be full again one day with writers, working on screenplays for theatrical distribution. They never were.
>
> I worked for six weeks and saw no one the whole time except my secretary and Marion Hargrove. I had no idea who was to be the producer, the actors, or the director of the scripts I had written. My secretary, who was my information on all studio politics, inferred that the film might never have any of these, and she began to list the films written here on this lot that had never been produced at all.[33]

In late March, the studio finally accepted a draft of Horton's screenplay, and he returned home to Nyack. Over the next few weeks the writer heard that the studio had finally assigned the film to a producer who in turn had assigned his script to another writer, and then another writer, and then another. A year passed and one day his phone rang, Horton remembered. "It was yet another producer at Warner's, who said he had been assigned the film now and, after going over all the scripts, had decided mine was the best. He said that he had, based on mine, a final version, which he would like to send to me and that he would like to put me back on salary to do some final polishing. I thanked him and said I would be most happy to read this version, which I did; but after

---

[32] Foote, *Genesis*, 183.
[33] Ibid., 181–82.

reading it, I found it nothing to do with my original script."[34] Horton called the producer, politely thanked him for the offer, and then quickly declined the job. After hanging up the phone, he turned to Lillian and quipped, "Well that will be the end of my Hollywood career."[35] Of course, that was not the end of his career; on the contrary, it was only the beginning, but Horton knew that the days of the old studio system were numbered. The practice of hiring writers *en masse*, putting them in offices, and assigning projects for them to write without any contact with producers, directors, and actors would soon come to an end.

Claudelle Inglish, was ultimately released in 1961. Directed by Gordon Douglas and featuring a star-studded cast that included Diane McBain as Claudell, Arthur Kennedy as her father Clyde, Claude Akin as S.T. Crawford, and Chad Everette as Linn Varner, the film was attacked by critics who found the movie weighed down by a bad script, mediocre acting, and third-rate production values.

On 3 July 1959, Horton and Lillian celebrated the birth of their fourth child, a girl they named Daisy Brooks. At the time, Horton was working on a new play, *The Indian Fighters*, which tells the story of a young girl who leaves home to escape domineering parents. Horton hoped the play would garner the interest of Broadway producers. He believed that if the play were a hit he would not have to leave Lillian and the children again. In a letter to Lillian, he wrote: "I am glad you reread the *Indian Fighters* and that you liked it. I know that play has a very rich and wonderful destiny"[36] Unfortunately, *The Indian Fighters* went unnoticed, (the play was not produced for another forty years, not until 1997 under the title *The Day Emily Married*), and his time at home with Lillian, spending special moments with the children and enjoying the minutiae of daily life, would soon come to an end.

In the fall of 1959, Horton received a phone call from producer, Herbert Brodkin, who had been so inspired by the writer's adaptation of *Old Man* that he decided to film another Faulkner short story, *Tomorrow*, for *Playhouse 90*. Faulkner had originally written *Tomorrow* for the *Saturday Evening Post* magazine. The novella tells the story of a poor Mississippi cotton farmer, Jackson Fentry, who hangs a jury that would have otherwise acquitted a farmer of shooting and killing a young ruffian. The novella was later included in a collection of six mystery

---

[34] Ibid.

[35] Ibid.

[36] Horton Foote to Lillian Foote, 28 September 1959 (Horton Foote Papers).

stories under the title *Knight's Gambit*. All the stories in the collection were linked by a single protagonist—Gavin Stevens, a young lawyer who returns to Yoknapatawpha County to open a practice after matriculating from Harvard and Heidelberg. Unlike most mysteries, however, Faulkner's tales are not ordinary crime stories but psychological puzzles that Stevens solves with the aid of his young nephew, Chick Mallison. Faulkner's biographer Joseph Blotner called *Tomorrow* a detective story of character and fate, rather than of fact.[37]

Horton was once again reluctant to take on the adaptation of the Faulkner work, largely because he was unsure how to translate the novel's structurally complex narrative into cinematic terms. Faulkner's *Tomorrow* focuses on the details of Gavin Stevens's investigation of the mysterious motive behind Jackson Fentry's hanging of the jury. The story is told in the oral tradition, pieced together on front porches and from memory and hearsay. Gavin Stevens's nephew, Chick, now an adult, tells what he remembers as a boy of twelve about how his uncle Gavin Stevens lost his first case, one that he thought he would win. Stevens had defended Homer Bookwright, a citizen of Jefferson, Mississippi, who was charged with murdering Buck Thorpe, a drunken drifter who was about to run off with Bookwright's daughter. Because Thorpe had drawn a pistol on Bookwright at the time of the shooting, the evidence favored the defendant's acquittal. However, a lone juror, Jackson Fentry, insisted on voting for Bookwright's conviction and eventually forced the judge to declare a mistrial. Searching for an explanation to Fentry's actions, Gavin Stevens tours the countryside asking people who know the cotton farmer why they think he hung the jury. Piecing together the information he gathers, Stevens discovers the truth.

The answer goes back twenty years to the winter that Fentry left his father's farm to work as a watchman at Isham Quick's sawmill. There, on the day before Christmas, Fentry encountered a pregnant woman who was abandoned by her husband and family. Fentry takes the woman in and cares for her until her baby is born. When she dies after giving birth, Fentry assumes responsibility for the child and returns to his father's farm to raise him. Years later, the dead woman's family shows up at Fentry's door to claim their kin, and since the law sanctions their actions,

---

[37] Horton Foote, *Tomorrow & Tomorrow & Tomorrow,* ed. David G. Yellin and Mari Connors (Jackson: University of Mississippi Press 1985) 5 [hereafter cited as *Tomorrow & Tomorrow*].

Fentry cannot prevent them from taking the boy. The child grows up to be the rebellious Buck Thorpe. Fentry is on the jury and refuses to acquit Bookwright, the man who took the life of the young man who was once, for a tragically brief time, his son. As Stevens uncovers these facts, he understands why Jackson Fentry behaved as he did.

Stevens defends the farmer's actions by quoting from Shakespeare—"the lowly and invincible of the earth—to endure and then endure, tomorrow and tomorrow and tomorrow"—in order to explain to Chick the importance of Buck Thorpe to Fentry. It had been Fentry's dream that the child he called Jackson and Longstreet would grow up to perpetuate the Fentry name and to farm his ancestral land. By refusing to vote for Bookwright's acquittal, Fentry was proclaiming to the world that he would not free the man who killed the only child he would ever have. Stevens admires Fentry for continuing to endure without complaint, even though he has lost the son who would have given meaning to his life. Ultimately, *Tomorrow* takes on a mythic quality that reveals Faulkner's concern with "the lowly and invincible of the earth" who continue to hope for a better tomorrow in spite of the devastating hardships they are forced to suffer.[38]

After first reading *Tomorrow*, Horton was fascinated by the courage of Jackson Fentry, but as he began to think more about the work, he found himself especially intrigued by the character of the woman who gives birth to the baby boy. While deciding whether or not to accept the assignment, Horton found himself walking along the Hudson River, in Upper Nyack, thinking about how best to tackle the dramatization. He recalled: "the character of the woman became alive to me, even though Faulkner gives only a few paragraphs to her. He told me enough about her so that my imagination just began to work, and she became somebody I knew. I began somehow in the most obsessive, vivid kind of way to want to discover for myself, as a writer, what went on between Jackson Fentry and this 'black-complected' woman."[39]

That night, Horton began to dramatize the story of Jackson Fentry and the woman Faulkner never named. He worked on that element of the story throughout the night and finished it the next morning. Five days later, Horton finished a draft of *Tomorrow*. He retained the original spine of the Faulkner's story—the search for the reason Fentry can't vote Bookwright free—and he preserved the central theme of the

---

[38] Ibid., 3.
[39] Ibid., 15.

work—the hope that tomorrow symbolizes for the lowly and invincible of the earth. In Horton's version, however, the detective element at the core of Faulkner's story nearly vanishes while the love story between Fentry and the woman, who Foote named Sarah Eubanks, blossoms. The scenes between the two characters reveal the pride, tenderness, and compassion of Faulkner's original, but a significantly different story emerges because as Foote admitted, "the more completely I dramatized the relationship between Fentry and Sarah, the less room it left for the dramatizing of the other elements of the story."[40]

As in *Old Man*, Horton retained the essence of Faulkner's remarkable story but infused it with his own indelible voice. The character of Fentry remains true to Faulkner's creation, a man hardened both mentally and physically by the restrictions of his life. Sarah, who is estranged from her callous father and husband, is a courageous but vulnerable woman wounded by hardship and worn out by a world seldom run according to any rules of fair play. Sarah tells Fentry that she can never go back home to her papa who ordered her to leave his house because she married Eubanks, a ne'er-do-well. "My Papa has his pride; and I've got mine," she says.[41] Horton dramatized Fentry and Sarah's relationship from the time she arrives at the sawmill to the time of her death a few months later. We see Fentry's growing compassion for Sarah and his attempt to nurse her back to health. He does all he can for her, promising to build her the house she had always wanted and walking for miles to the store to buy her hard candy for Christmas (a scene that was later cut from the television version). When Sarah is about to give birth, Fentry fetches a midwife, and during the delivery it becomes clear that Sarah will not survive. Before Sarah dies, Fentry promises to raise her son as his own. Although the boy is the offspring of another man, Fentry's commitment to his son is fierce, illustrating Horton Foote's belief that true love, not blood, is the most powerful of all human bonds. As he promised Sarah, he cares for the boy until the woman's brothers come to take the boy away.

Horton fleshes out Faulkner's meager description of the relationship between Jackson and Longstreet and Fentry in perhaps the most telling scene in the play when Ed Pruitt asks Fentry what happened to the boy,

---

[40] Foote, *Genesis*, 185–95.

[41] Horton Foote, "*Tomorrow*: The Television Play," *Tomorrow & Tomorrow*, 69–70. All page references in the text refer to this publication, including the film version of the short story.

who by this time has been gone for several years. "What boy?" Fentry stoically answers (103). When viewed on the television screen, this moment becomes one of the most powerful and emotional in the play.

To lead up to these events, Horton decided to refocus the story, beginning the teleplay on the porch of the Pruitt's farmhouse with lawyer Douglas and his nephew Chick explaining to Ed Pruitt and his mother how Jackson Fentry hung his jury. The teleplay then reveals Fentry's story in flashback, with Ed Pruitt acting as narrator rather than Chick as in the short story. The drama ends back on the Pruitt's front porch with Douglas's reflection on why Fentry acted as he did in the courtroom. Robert Mulligan, who directed the production, liked the script but suggested Horton consider starting the teleplay with the trial rather than beginning it at the Pruitt house. Horton had initially wanted to open the play with the trial but he felt that the restricted playing time (seventy-two minutes) did not permit the addition of the courtroom scene and so he chose to begin the teleplay on the Pruitt's front porch.

Tomorrow starred Richard Boone as Fentry and Kim Stanley as Sarah, and was first broadcast on 7 March 1960. Critics hailed the teleplay, which aired live, as one of the best dramas ever produced for television. The day after the first showing, various TV critics noted in their reviews how effectively the adaptation demonstrated the tenderness, compassion, and patience of Fentry, especially in the scenes where the solitary farmer acts out flashes of tenderness and nobility toward Sarah and the boy. The *New York Times* called the performances of Richard Boone and Kim Stanley "warm, genuine, and poignant."[42] The show's success prompted CBS to rebroadcast the production the following year by means of a filmed transcription of the original transmission. Furthermore, Faulkner, who rarely voiced an opinion on adaptations of his works, said that he greatly admired Horton's version of *Tomorrow*. In fact, he wrote to Lucy Kroll, the writer's agent, giving permission for Horton to publish the teleplay and to share the copyright. Twelve years later, in 1972, Horton would write a movie version of the story starring Robert Duvall and Olga Bellin, which is considered by many to be the most faithful recreation of a Faulkner work.

With the success of *Tomorrow*, television producers were knocking daily at Horton's door with offers for him to adapt the work of other Southern writers. In April 1960, he flew back to California to begin rehearsals for *Playhouse 90*'s *The Shape of the River*, a play about the last

---

[42] Foote, *Tomorrow & Tomorrow*, 20.

fifteen years of Mark Twain's life, during which time the author experienced economic ruin and the deaths of his wife and two daughters. Horton had originally written *The Shape of the River* for Fred Coe and *Playwright's '56*, but the teleplay went unproduced when the anthology was suddenly cancelled by NBC. Coe was very impressed with the teleplay at the time, and after joining the CBS staff he called Horton: "Remember the play you wrote about Mark Twain? I want to do it for *Playhouse 90.*"[43] In writing the teleplay, Horton drew from every source he could get his hands on—personal letters, biographies, and Twain's autobiography. He also used Twain's 1935 collection, *Mark Twain's Notebook*, which includes his daughter Suzy's feverish outbursts after she becomes ill and her expressions of love for her father. From this raw material, Horton developed a work that is remarkably moving and poignant, replete with authentic Twain dialogue and true-to-life characters. Horton also used a generous amount of Twain's humor and wit to lighten the otherwise somber mood of the teleplay, and he captured with authenticity and clarity an aspect of Twain's personality that has intrigued biographers for years—the great sense of guilt the writer felt during the final years of his life. Horton recalled the intensity of his research: "I got everything I could possibly get hold of on Mark Twain. I was struck by the overwhelming tragedy he had to face. I don't know how he stood it all as well as he did, really.... I just remember being struck by the poignancy of those last years."[44] In the play's second act, Horton has Mark Twain exclaim:

> First I lose all our money in foolish and willful investments, and I have to tear my family apart and go on a lecture tour to pay off my debts. When it is over, Susy is dead, Jean has her illness which she will have the rest of her life, and Now Livy is stricken.... Oh, my God. Oh, my God. To have afflicted so those I love.[45]

In addition to writing the teleplay, Horton was also involved with rehearsals and in choosing the cast, which featured Franchot Tone as Twain, Leif Erickson as William Dean Howells, Katherine Bard as Livy, Nancy Rennick as Clara, Jane McArthur as Jean, and Shirley Knight as Suzy. *The Shape of the River*, which was videotaped live at CBS's

---

[43] Horton Foote, *Horton Foote's The Shape of the River: The Lost Teleplay about Mark Twain with History & Analysis*, ed. David Dawidziak (New York: Applause Theatre & Cinema Books, 2003) 8.

[44] Ibid., 17.

[45] Ibid., 87.

Television City, aired on 2 May 1960, only eleven days after the fiftieth anniversary of Mark Twain's death. Shirley Knight remembered, "We did it all in one shot...It was like doing a play, where you rehearse for several weeks and then you did it. I had done my share of live dramas by that time, so this didn't [faze] me. And we were very well prepared, thanks to Boris [Sagal], who was a very good director, and thanks to Horton, who suggested books we could read. The rehearsal period was a lot of fun because we all got along so well and we all wanted to do such a good job."[46] Horton was impressed with the actors, especially Franchot Tone who gave a stirring portrayal of Mark Twain. But despite Tone's outstanding performance, *The Shape of the River* did not appeal to television viewers and the show received poor ratings. Years later, Horton speculated that America was simply not ready to accept a dark, somber portrait of Mark Twain. "They didn't want to hear it," he said. "They still wanted to think of him as a humorist and a family author."[47] Shirley Knight added:

> Horton was very intent on showing another side of the man. I certainly didn't realize there were this many aspects to Twain before I did *The Shape of the River*. That was a time when we tended to mythicize great American figures like Benjamin Franklin and Mark Twain. And much of Mark Twain is the stuff that myths are made of. I seem to remember that he was born when Halley's Comet was in the sky and died when it had returned. That's the thing that wouldn't be out of place in a myth. And so is the epic fight back from bankruptcy. But the mythicizing we did before the sixties turned men like Franklin and Twain into jolly one-dimensional figures. Horton gave us someone who ended up being much more heroic because of the tragedy he faced. The wonderful thing about *The Shape of the River* was that you got the wonderful voices of both Mr. Twain and Mr. Foote. It was a remarkable time.[48]

Even though CBS did not deem *The Shape of the River* a success when it aired, the teleplay remains a remarkable portrait of one major Southern writer by another and one of the most compelling and humane works written about Mark Twain.

After *The Shape of the River*, Horton turned down several offers for adaptations. He hated being away from Lillian and the children, and he wanted to focus on his own work. Fortunately, in the summer of 1960,

---

[46] Ibid., 26.
[47] Ibid., 3.
[48] Ibid., 29.

CBS producer, David Susskind, called to ask if he would write an original teleplay for *DuPont Show of the Month*. The work, at least, would afford Horton the opportunity to stay in Nyack, and so he began to think of a story to tell.

Two years earlier a Hollywood film producer had approached Horton, asking him to think of an idea for a film, and he had written a story about his father. Horton recalled: "My father's father died when he was twelve, and his mother had to find ways to take care of him and his sister Lily Dale. For a time, she owned a boarding house in Wharton. My father had some pet chickens of which he was very fond. Once, when his mother had no money to feed her boarders, she—without asking my father—killed the chickens. When he found this out he became ill."[49]

Horton hurriedly submitted a very rough draft of a screenplay about his father, but the producers were not impressed and immediately rejected the script. Disappointed, the writer filed the draft away in his desk drawer and did not look at it again. But after his conversation with David Susskind, he took the draft out of his files and began to refashion the story of his father and the chickens. For Horton, the creative process was always a mystery, with his stories finding him in their own way and time. "I have a thing about putting drafts in a drawer," he admitted, "I'm a great believer in the 'refrigeration process.' Put it away and sometimes something happens to it; sometimes it sprouts, sometimes it diminishes. Often when you go back it's amazing how much of the work is done for you if you don't use your will too much.... You've got to let your creativity find its own kind of speed."[50]

Daniel Petrie, a young director who had recently made a splash on Broadway for directing *A Raisin in the Sun*, had been hired to direct the play, and when Horton finished rewrites, he invited the director to his house in Nyack to read the script. Petrie was very enthusiastic about the work and assumed that Susskind would share his enthusiasm. He was wrong. David Susskind did not like the story at all and was ready to reject the script, but fortunately there was another producer, Audrey Gellen, who was very excited about the teleplay. She convinced Susskind to defer to her judgment and to move forward with the scheduled spring production.

---

[49] Foote, *Genesis*, 114.

[50] David Middleton, "Winning, Losing, and Compromising: The Screenwriter Contends for Personal Turf," *The Voice of an American Playwright*, 5.

Gellen and Susskind put together a remarkable cast for the teleplay, which featured Julie Harris, Jo Van Fleet, Mildred Dunnock, E.G. Marshall, Fritz Weaver, Henderson Forsyth, and Marc Connolly, but before the show aired, a dispute arose over the title. Horton had initially named the play, *A Golden String*, a title taken from a William Blake poem: "I give you the end of a golden string/ Only wind it into a ball/ It will lead you in at Heaven's gate/ Built in Jerusalem's wall."[51] CBS advertisers agreed with Susskind that the title was too ambiguous for television and they insisted on finding a more suitable name. Horton came up with the title *Roots in a Parched Ground*, which he took from a William Carlos Williams poem: "Love itself a flower with roots in a parched ground."[52] Both Petrie and Gellen liked the name, but the advertising agency balked again, admitting that they were nervous about producing an original drama they feared was too depressing for the viewing public. Horton finally compromised and accepted their title, *The Night of the Storm*, which refers to the young boy in the story, who runs away from home during a storm. But even after the taping of the show was concluded, sponsors were still concerned about airing a show so melancholy. They wanted to cancel it, but Susskind finally convinced them to air the show on 21 March 1961.

The Night of the Storm, which was broadcast by CBS from New York, begins in 1890, after Julia Robedaux has moved back to her family's house with her children, Horace, Jr., and Beth Ruth. She has enlisted the help of her sister Callie in turning the old home place into a boarding house. Her husband, Paul Horace, Sr., is ravaged by alcoholism and awaits the day of his death at his mother's home. Paul Horace holds on to the hope that he will recover from his illness, mend his family, and guide his son in the study of law. This fragile dream is broken when he dies and Julia discovers that the boarding house is a losing proposition. Her only course of action is to move the family to Houston in search of more lucrative employment, but Horace, Jr., refuses to go and runs away during a violent storm. His mother believes he has drowned in a nearby river and gives him up for lost. Weeks later, Horace, Jr., reappears and discovers his family has moved to Houston without him. When Julia learns that her son is still alive, she returns to Harrison and, in a poignant scene, tells the boy she has remarried. Unfortunately, she cannot allow her son to go back with her

---

[51] Foote, *Genesis*, 116.

[52] Ibid.

because her new husband has refused to care for the boy. Twelve-year-old Horace is left alone with no more than his father's law books to comfort him. He also has the gentle guidance and concern of his father's best friend, Jim Howard, who offers to teach him law. As the play ends, Horace and Mr. Howard begin to study and to help each other cope with their pain.

Reviews for *The Night of the Storm* were mixed. *Variety* felt the script was overstated and weakly constructed, but the renowned critic Stark Young thought differently. He admired the play and phoned Horton, praising the production and urging him to rework the teleplay for the stage. Later, in 1962, Harcourt Brace published the script under the title of *Roots in a Parched Ground* and asked Stark Young to write a preface to the play. Young's words represent the most positive assessment of Horton's play. "When I read *Roots in a Parched Ground*," Young wrote:

> I am so touched by the purity of tone, the precision of writing—of beautiful love, devotion, and sweetness that its tragedies are scarcely horrors in themselves at all. The little boy, Horace, as the hero of the play, carries always the bitterness of pain, which overshadows every moment. He is the gentlest and sweetest child I have ever encountered in a story. And at the end of the play, when Horace is left alone, there is that tiny shadow of a mother, the movement of the dying father, so perfect in all that wonderment of his shone on and filled the boy's mind there among the shadows in the old empty house, the men and shadows of the day and his heart. We are talking about lovely things, about sweet people.[53]

Stark Young died shortly after writing the preface to *Roots in a Parched Ground,* and Horton did not return to the play for more than a decade. However, considering the extremely personal nature of the work, it is not surprising that it would become the initial story in Horton Foote's nine-play drama—*The Orphans' Home Cycle*.

After *The Night of the Storm*, Horton wrote one more original teleplay for the *DuPont Show of the Month—The Gambling Heart*, which aired on 23 February 1964. The play, featuring an all-star cast that included Ruth White, Sarah Marshall, John Cullum, Tom Bosley, Estelle Parsons, and Sudie Bond, tells the story of an aging mother, her two married daughters, and their husbands, one of whom is a compulsive gambler and turns ten thousand dollars into millions while the other husband is not so lucky. *The Gambling Heart* is important not

---

[53] Ibid., 117.

only because it contains characters and themes drawn from the playwright's own experiences, but also, because it was the last original Horton Foote play to be shown on television for nearly twenty years.

By 1961, Horton Foote had become one of the most sought after translators of Southern literature in the country, and movie studios were bombarding him with offers to undertake various film projects. Horton recalled, "I was very fortunate in the sense that because of *Philco-Goodyear* my identity as a writer was fairly established, so that consequently, Hollywood, being the copycat that it often is, any time there was a third-rate, or fourth-rate, or a fifth-rate Southern novel, they'd call me up and everyone thought I was a Southern specialist."[54] He refused to accept several offers, including James Agee's *A Death in the Family*, and when he did take on a project, the experience was not always positive. One assignment that really intrigued Horton was adapting Tennessee Williams's one-act play, *This Property is Condemned*, a Ray Stark presentation produced by John Houseman and directed by Sydney Pollack. Fred Coe, who was originally slated to serve as the film's producer, hired Horton to write the script. But when a company executive complained to Coe that Horton had created an art-house movie, which would not make a dime, Coe neither defended the writer, nor asked him to revise the script. He simply fired him. "Fred behaved very badly and almost ruined our friendship," Horton said later.[55]

As a result, he was less than enthusiastic when producer Alan Pakula and director Robert Mulligan called Horton with a proposal to adapt a novel by an unknown Southern writer. Robert Mulligan, who directed *Tomorrow* for CBS, and Alan Pakula, who knew Horton but had never worked with him, were both certain that the writer would immediately approve the project, but securing his consent was not as easy as they had first believed. Horton was weary of adaptation and concerned about his future as a dramatist: "I had previously adapted the two Faulkner stories (*Old Man* and *Tomorrow*), and here I was getting into the nature of adapting, which is very upsetting to me because I was losing my identity, you know."[56] Despite his reservations, at Mulligan's insistence

---

[54] Gary Edgerton, "A Visit to the Imaginary Landscape of Harrison, Texas: Sketching the Film Career of Horton Foote," *Literature/Film Quarterly* 12 (Winter 1989): 5.

[55] Krampner, *Man in the Shadows*, 145–46.

[56] Gerald C. Wood and Terry Barr, "'A Certain Kind of Writer': An Interview with Horton Foote," *The Voice of an American Playwright*, 40–56.

Horton agreed to read the book; however, when a copy arrived in the mail a few days later, he put it on a downstairs coffee table and forgot about it.

He might never have picked it up again if not for his wife, Lillian, who was greatly moved by the story and persuaded him to read the book. "She said, 'I know you're going to fuss and holler. But I really think you should at least read this and think about it,'" Horton recalled. "And, uh, I read it, and…it was…moving to me. I still didn't want to do it; she talked me into it."[57]

Little did Horton Foote know, but his participation in this particular project would change his life forever and propel his career to new, unexpected heights. The name of the unknown Southern writer—Harper Lee. The novel—*To Kill a Mockingbird*.

---

[57] Ibid.

11

Academy Award Winner
1961–68

When Harper Lee's *To Kill a Mockingbird*, a novel about growing up in Alabama during the Great Depression, was published in 1960, no one was prepared for the colossal response that the book received. Lee's story, which focuses on two children who encounter evil for the first time, remained on the *New York Times* bestseller list for nearly two years, eventually sold tens of millions of copies, and won the 1961 Pulitzer Prize for Literature. It is surprising, then, that no major movie studio purchased the rights to the book before it was published, a common practice in Hollywood. In fact, several studios rejected the book because they felt it lacked action, mystery, romance, and adventure. Consequently, producer Alan Pakula, and director Robert Mulligan, considered themselves fortunate when they were able to secure an option on the movie rights in 1961—virtually snatching it away from Warner Brothers and several other companies that had, by this time, shown interest in the novel.[1]

The team of Pakula and Mulligan had only one previous picture to their credit (a small budget film called *Fear Strikes Out*), so when they tried to attract financial backing for *To Kill a Mockingbird*, they were told they needed to have a major star in the cast. Pakula sent the novel to Gregory Peck, who he believed would be the ideal actor to play the role of Atticus, a father who helps his children overcome their fears and emerge more mature while undertaking the defense of a black man falsely accused of raping a white woman. Peck immediately felt a strong connection with the character. "I sensed it would be the role of my life," Peck said. "I called them at about eight o'clock in the morning and said, 'if you want me to play Atticus, when do I start? I'd love to play it.' I felt it was something I could identify with.... I felt I could climb into Atticus's shoes without any play-acting, that I could *be* him."[2] On the basis of the actor's acceptance of the role, Gregory Peck's film company,

---

[1] Jared Brown, *Alan J. Pakula* (New York: Back Stage Books, 2005) 41–42.
[2] John Griggs, *The Films of Gregory Peck* (Secaucus NJ: Citadel Press, 1984) 180.

Brentwood Productions, decided to finance the movie, and Universal Pictures agreed to distribute it.

Pakula and Mulligan's first choice to write the screenplay was Harper Lee herself, but she didn't feel she knew enough about dramatic form and was, at the time, working on another book in Monroeville, Alabama, where she was staying with her aging father. She was also reluctant to move to Hollywood, which would have been necessary had she accepted the job. She was, of course, very relieved when Pakula informed her that, after a good bit of coaxing, he had secured the services of fellow Southerner Horton Foote, whose work she greatly admired.

When Alan Pakula first approached him, Horton was reluctant to commit to the "back-breaking job," complaining that the novel "sprawls all over." [3] Pakula assured the playwright that Harper Lee had specifically requested him to adapt her book and suggested they meet and discuss the project. Horton agreed to speak with Lee at his home in Nyack, and from the moment they first met, the two writers became good friends. "I just fell in love with her. She liked me a lot, and we just had a good old time. We come from the same background, the same small towns…She's an extraordinary person. Anyway, and then she said, 'Now listen, you are going to write this, and I don't want to hear another word about this. I don't even want to think about it till it's done. You go ahead and don't worry about me at all.' So I never did." [4] "[Harper Lee] trusted that the book would not be emasculated in any way, or changed, that we would honor the book and be true to the book," Robert Mulligan said. [5]

Throughout the writing process, Horton worked closely with Alan Pakula, who had agreed to the writer's bold request to work on the screenplay in Nyack so he could be near Lillian and his children. Pakula drove from New York City to Nyack, a distance of more than thirty miles, almost every day. "Often we'd discuss what I had done that day, and he often gave me notes," Horton recalled. "He was wonderful to work with. He had great respect for the process of writing. And he never tried to tamper with your vision. He simply tried to help you free it." [6]

---

[3] George Terry Barr, "The Ordinary World of Horton Foote" (PhD diss., University of Tennessee, Knoxville, 1986) 149.

[4] Peter Roussel, "Profiles from Houston: Horton Foote," *The Voice of an American Playwright*, ed. Gerald C. Wood and Marion Castleberry (Macon GA: Mercer University Press, 2012) 164.

[5] Jared Brown, 43.

[6] Ibid.

Together Horton and Alan Pakula created a screenplay that remained remarkably true to the spirit and flavor of Harper Lee's story.

From the start, Horton felt at home in Lee's world. Her fictional town of Maycomb was not unlike Wharton, the small Southern town in which he had been born and reared. The characters, both educated and illiterate, resembled those of his own imaginative fiction; and the time of the novel, the Great Depression, was a period he had lived through and had written about for more than twenty years. Horton's understanding of this setting is evidenced in the first minute of the film as black-and-white images reveal a small Southern town on a typical summer afternoon in 1932, and the soft, Southern voice of an adult Scout Finch remembers what it was like to grow up in this "tired old" town. The novel is a "memory of a time that is gone, and yet we all want to hold on to it," Horton said. "It isn't that it's a perfect world—it's an imperfect world, but it's a world that we recognize." [7] Although told as remembrance, the story is not nostalgic. It is, rather, about seeing through other people's eyes until we can see for ourselves and about remembering to be grateful for the way we are taught by our elders early in life.

The real challenge in scripting *To Kill a Mockingbird* was not in recreating the atmosphere of the original work (for Horton had turned to the same setting in many of his plays) but in compressing the events of the novel, which encompassed two years, into a movie script of two-hours and in merging the two plots of the story into a continuous narrative without losing the thematic intent of the author. Harper Lee's novel offers a telling indictment of racial injustice as revealed through the story of Tom Robinson, a poor black laborer falsely accused of, and condemned for, raping a white girl, and a tale of the emergence of two youngsters, Scout and Jem Finch, from innocent childhood to maturity and social awareness. Both stories had to be told in a manner that would emphasize the contrast between the two plots and also express the larger theme of moral courage as embodied in the major protagonist, Atticus Finch.

Alan Pakula suggested to Horton that the film should maintain the point of view of the children, and to accomplish this the writer relied heavily upon a review of the novel by R.P. Blackmur, "Scout in the Wilderness," which compares *To Kill a Mockingbird* to *Huckleberry Finn*, and the character of Scout to Huck. This review, Horton admitted:

---

[7] Ibid., 44.

214

"strengthened my own feelings that we should discover the evil and hypocrisy in this small Southern pastoral town along with and through the eyes of the children."[8] To further illuminate the film's point of view—that of seeing an adult world through the eyes of children—Pakula hired composer Elmer Bernstein to write a musical score that would capture the spirit of youthful innocence, and he asked Stephen Frankfurt to create an opening title sequence that would evoke the mysterious world of childhood. Bernstein's haunting, evocative score combined with Frankfurt's image of a child opening a cigar box—full of crayons, marbles, a pocket watch, a knife, a harmonica, and a string of pearls—enhanced the mood of Horton's script and clearly established the film's point of view. Horton was also helped by Pakula's suggestion that he restructure the events of the novel (which ran over several years) to fit into a single year. "The two approaches, one subjective and one objective," Horton said, "helped me to find both a style and structure for the screenplay."[9] Horton's script, a model of compression, succeeds in one hundred and twenty-nine minutes of screen time, to fuse together the different components of Harper Lee's story.

The action of *To Kill a Mockingbird* takes place over two summers; and, like the novel, it moves along as leisurely as a Southern afternoon while interweaving the fantasy world of the children with the harsher realities of adult life. The screenplay revolves around Atticus Finch, a middle-aged lawyer and widower, and his two children: Jean Louise (Scout), his six-year-old daughter, and Jem, his eleven-year-old son. Atticus, a man of quiet but firm bearing, gently presides over his motherless children with tenderness and warmth and tries to teach them the value of human decency. Atticus is as close to an ideal father as one could imagine. He is thoughtful, sensitive, supportive, and a man of deep moral conviction. Terry Barr points out that "in many ways Lee's Atticus Finch is Horton Foote's kind of character: the head of a broken family; a relentless dreamer and believer in the basic honor and dignity of all living characters."[10] Atticus's philosophy and his devotion to racial justice are direct appeals to biblical values. His defense of Tom Robinson

---

[8] Horton Foote, Foreword to *Three Screenplays: To Kill a Mockingbird, Tender Mercies, and The Trip to Bountiful* (New York: Grove Press 1989) xii. All page references to *To Kill a Mockingbird* in the text refers to this publication.

[9] Ibid.

[10] Barr, 152–53.

is a clear illustration of what the parable means about caring for the least of our brothers.

The only apparently menacing figure in the children's world is Boo Radley, the grown-up son of the family living in the ramshackle house down the street. Boo is known to be crazy and has not been seen since his father supposedly locked him away years ago for stabbing him with a pair of scissors. Rumors of his frightening habits and appearance provide ample material upon which the imaginations of Scout, Jem, and their young friend Dill can take flight. Even though the children have never seen Boo, they visualize him as a monster. Jem describes him: "Well, judging from his tracks, he's about six-and-a-half feet tall. He eats raw squirrels and all the cats he can snatch. There's a long jagged scar that runs across his face. His teeth are yellow and rotten. His eyes are popped, and he drools most of the time" (12). The first half of Horton's screenplay is devoted to building the children's picture of Boo as they make timorous trips to the Radley house, run in terror from his stalking shadow, and find soap carvings in their likenesses hidden by the recluse in the hollow of a tree.

A more ambiguous, conflicting reality, however, is introduced into the lives of Scout and Jem when Atticus is asked to defend Tom Robinson, a young black man accused of raping a lonely and abused white woman, Mayella Ewell. As much as he might wish, Atticus cannot spare his children from the larger and more frightening world that lies beyond the sphere of their pleasant neighborhood; and when he agrees to take on the Robinson case, he exposes himself and his children to the prejudice and hostility of the community. Because the town is segregated and operates by separatist principles, the white townspeople—particularly Mayella's father, Bob Ewell—accuse Atticus of siding with "the nigger" against "his own kind" (41). At school, other children call Atticus slanderous names, taunting Scout and Jem; near the town dump they are brought face to face with the ugly world in which the Ewell's live; and at the courthouse, they watch as their father patiently withstands threats of violence. In one of the most powerful scenes of the film, the children follow Atticus as he stands guard outside the jail to which Tom has been moved during the trial. When a lynch mob suddenly gathers, Scout, innocent of the danger, disarms the crowd with her uninhibited chatter with one of the potential lynch men, Walter Cunningham, father of a boy she knows at school. Scout and Jem learn about their father's moral character in the face of conflict over Tom's trial, and their innocence is eroded as they witness the tyranny of social codes, the differences between human beings, and the value of courage and integrity.

Horton cleverly develops the Boo Radley plot alongside the action of the Tom Robinson trial. As Jem, Scout, and Dill sneak up to the Radley house one night, hoping to get a glimpse of Boo, a large shadow appears causing them to run away in terror. As Jem flees, his overalls become entangled in a fence. Later that night, Jem goes back to retrieve them but he discovers they have been gathered up and neatly folded where he left them. The mystery is further compounded when the children begin to find little gifts—two soap dolls, a broken watch and chain, and a knife— left in the knothole of an oak tree near the Radley house. The children's understanding of the world begins to alter while pondering the mystery of Boo, but it is at the courthouse that Scout and Jem are most affected as they observe justice and racism in conflict.

On the day of the trial, the children sneak into the courthouse's balcony where they sit with the black citizens of Maycomb. There, they witness the injustice of a white jury who convict Tom Robinson of rape, despite Atticus's skillful demonstration of his innocence. Though Atticus persuasively shows that Tom had no sexual relationship with Mayella and is guilty of nothing but kindness, Tom condemns himself when he answers a question from the prosecutor by saying: "I felt right sorry for her" (65). The white jury, who consider Tom's remark to be the very height of insolence, finds the black man guilty. As Atticus leaves the courtroom in defeat, the black people in the upper gallery, along with Scout and Jem, stand in his honor. Minutes later, we discover that Tom was shot to death as he tried to escape from custody.

The two plots of the story come together late in the film as the bigoted and brutal Bob Ewell takes revenge upon Atticus by attacking Scout and Jem as they walk home through the woods at night following a Halloween party. Jem is knocked unconscious, and Scout manages to struggle out of her bizarre ham costume that has obscured her vision just in time to see Bob Ewell lying dead next to her and a shadowy figure running from the scene, carrying her injured brother. At home, Scout is embraced by her father and then led to her room where Jem lies in bed. As she relates her story to the sheriff, Atticus points to a mysterious man standing behind the door and acknowledges him as the one who carried Jem to safety. When Scout looks up, she finds herself face to face with the dreaded Boo Radley, who has been lovingly watching over the children all along. As the two look at each other in a moment of innocent respect,

Scout realizes that the phantom of her childhood fears has saved her from the menace of the real world. Then Atticus graciously introduces his daughter to Mr. Arthur Radley, humbly bestowing on the recluse the dignity of his real name, and Scout takes the hand of her new friend to walk him home. Standing on the Radley porch, Scout pauses to view the world from Boo's perspective and remembers that Atticus had once told her: "you never really knew a man until you stood in his shoes and walked around in them" (80). Horton reminds the audience of the heart of the story, the relationship between Atticus and his children, by giving Scout the final lines: "I was to think of these days many times; of Jem, and Dill, and Boo Radley, and Tom Robinson...and Atticus. He would be in Jem's room all night. And he would be there when Jem waked up in the morning" (80).

While Horton's screenplay of *To Kill a Mockingbird* remains faithful to Harper Lee's vision, his adaptation is not without compromise. By necessity, the writer was forced to eliminate several of the characters from the novel and to shift the focus of the original from the larger community of Maycomb to the Finch family in particular. He also omitted historical background on the town and the Finch family while emphasizing Atticus as the ideal father and depicting his honorable dealings with his impoverished neighbors, the Cunninghams, Calpurnia, and Mrs. Dubose. Horton also modified Lee's coarser language in the trial scene, while at the same time interpolating into the script dialogue taken directly from the novel, as in the scene where Atticus remembers the time his father gave him a gun and warned him not to shoot mockingbirds: "I remember when my daddy gave me that gun. He told me that I should never point it at anything in the house. And that he'd rather I'd just shoot tin cans in the backyard, but he said that sooner or later he supposed the temptation to go after birds would be too much, and that I could shoot all the blue jays I wanted, if I could hit them, but to remember it is a sin to kill a mockingbird." When Jem questions his father, Atticus responds: "Well, I reckon because mockingbirds don't do anything but make music for us to enjoy. They don't eat people's gardens, don't nest in the corncribs, they don't do one thing but just sing their hearts out for us" (33).

If fidelity was the guiding principle of Horton Foote's work on *To Kill a Mockingbird*, the film also contains many passages of dialogue which are highly characteristic of the playwright's own fiction. Horton admitted that childhood memories of intentional eavesdropping played an important part in the adaptation. Examples are evident in one scene where the children, listening through the bedroom window, overhear a crucial conversation between their father and the sheriff, and in another where the camera pauses on Atticus listening from the front porch to his children talking in bed about the mother they barely remember.

The screenplay also mirrors some of Horton's thematic concerns and preoccupations. The focus on family life in a small, Southern town, the central ideas of courage and dignity in the face of human injustice, and the emphasis on motherless children coming to terms with life's ambiguities are themes he had often explored. Above all else, Horton's screenplay of *To Kill a Mockingbird* exemplifies the principles of eloquent silence and understatement that are so much a part of his writing style. Harper Lee best explained Horton's achievement as a screenwriter when she stated:

> Horton Foote's screenplay is a work of such quiet and unobtrusive excellence that many people have commented on the fact that the film's dialogue was lifted chapter and verse from the novel. This is simply not so. Scenes humorous, scenes tender, scenes terrifying, each with a definite purpose and value, blended so delicately with the original, created the illusion that these were Harper Lee's words. If the integrity of a film adaptation is measured by the degree to which the novelist's intent is preserved, Mr. Foote's screenplay should be studied as a classic.[11]

In addition to creating an extraordinary screenplay, Horton played a major role in casting the film. An exhaustive search was undertaken to fill the pivotal roles of the children. Robert Mulligan insisted on casting "kids who are kids, not actors" and he was determined to cast Southern children, since he wanted young actors who possessed authentic accents. [12] With this in mind, Alan Pakula hired Alice "Boaty" Boatwright, an exuberant Southern woman who worked in the publicity department at Universal, to conduct auditions throughout the South. In cities like Winston-Salem and Raleigh, North Carolina, Dallas, New Orleans, and Atlanta, Boatwright interviewed more than five hundred children vying for the roles of Scout and Jem, but none of them seemed suitable for the roles. Boatwright remembered that all the little girls who auditioned for the role of Scout looked "like Shirley Temple," and she

---

[11] Harper Lee, "A Word:" Introduction to *To Kill a Mockingbird* (New York: Brentwood 1964) v.

[12] Jared Brown, 45.

was looking for a tomboy.[13] Three weeks into her search, Boatwright became frustrated and was about to give up when a young girl from Birmingham, Alabama, named Mary Badham, unexpectedly walked through the door. Mary, the daughter of a retired Army general, had never acted before, and at first she was unsure about trying out for the role. But the moment she opened her mouth Boatwright knew she had found her Scout. "She was just adorable," Boatwright recalls. "She was wearing jeans and a little striped T-shirt. She had a very short gamine haircut. I said, 'Mary, you're just so cute. How old are you?' And she said 'Nine," sounding very Southern. I said, 'Well, you look younger and she said, 'Well, if you drank as much buttermilk and smoked as many corn silks as I do, then you might be smaller too.'"[14] That was all Boatwright needed to hear and she immediately called Pakula. "I've found the child," she exclaimed. "There's a little girl here that I cannot wait for you to see."[15] A few days later Boatwright found thirteen-year-old Phillip Alford, who she realized was perfect for the role of Jem. Ironically, the two children had grown up in the same Birmingham neighborhood and knew each other. After Boatwright recommended Badham and Alford, the children flew to New York for screen tests. Rather than have the children read or perform scenes for their audition, Robert Mulligan placed each child before a camera and simply asked them questions. He was looking for truthful behavior and natural responses, and as he later remembered, "they looked like they could be brother and sister. They both had a quality I was looking for. They were bright. They were alive. They both seemed to have active imaginations."[16] Mulligan cast Mary Badham and Phillip Alford in December 1961. Soon after, he cast nine-year-old, John Megna, who had appeared on Broadway in *All The Way Home*, as Scout and Jem's friend Dill, a character who was based on Truman Capote, Harper Lee's childhood friend. Pakula recalled that Megna was "a very unaffected kid and he was not a movie kid."[17]

When casting the older actors, Mulligan and Pakula wanted to retain the sense of discovery so prevalent in the novel and, except for Gregory Peck, they chose to cast Broadway actors who were unknown to motion

---

[13] Mary McDonagh Murphy, *Scout, Atticus & Boo* (New York: HarperCollins, 2010) 54.

[14] Ibid.

[15] Jared Brown, 46.

[16] Ibid., 47.

[17] Ibid.

picture audiences. Horton recommended several of the actors ultimately selected, notably Crahan Denton as Mr. Cunningham, Frank Overton as Sheriff Heck Tate, Brock Peters as Tom Robinson, Ruth White as Mrs. Dubose, Estelle Evans as Calpurnia, Collin Wilcox as Mayella Ewell, Paul Fix as Judge Taylor, and James Anderson as Bob Ewell. Horton convinced Kim Stanley, who was by that time a major movie star, to read the voiceover narrations of the adult Scout. Stanley's voice was essential to the success of the film, establishing both the tone and the story's point of view. According to Mulligan her voice "was so important in pulling you in and [establishing] the sense of the South, and the sensibility."[18]

Horton also recommended a young, unknown actor, Robert Duvall, for the crucial role of Boo Radley, the silent recluse who saves the lives of Scout and Jem. Some months earlier, Horton, his wife Lillian, Kim Stanley, and Robert Mulligan had seen a production of *The Midnight Caller* directed by Sanford Meisner at the Neighborhood Playhouse in New York. They were all impressed with the production but were literally bowled over by the performance of young Robert Duvall, who played the anguished alcoholic Harvey Weems. Horton understood how essential it was to find the right actor for the part of Boo, and one evening he mentioned to Lillian in a phone call from California that he and Mulligan weren't able to find an actor for the role. Lillian remembered *The Midnight Caller* and suggested that they consider Duvall. Horton took his wife's advice and recommended the young actor to Mulligan, who remembered the performance as well and immediately signed Robert Duvall to his screen debut as Boo Radley.

Although Boo does not appear on screen until the final scenes, his presence is pivotal to the plot and the atmosphere of the movie. It is in his rescue of Scout and Jem where the two threads of the story come together, as the specter of the children's fantasies saves them from the adult world. Not only must he save them, but he must also represent the antithesis of the evil that nearly destroys them— and he must do this without saying a single word. The choice of Robert Duvall as Boo proved to be a stroke of genius, as his portrayal of the mysterious and shy recluse is one of the most impressive performances in the history of cinema. The recognition that flows between Scout and Boo is one of those magical moments very few movies ever achieve. The beatific expression and glow on Duvall's face at the conclusion of *To Kill a Mockingbird* made quite an impression on moviegoers at the time; and

---

[18] Ibid., 48.

even today, those who have seen the movie remember Boo Radley in the scene. *To Kill a Mockingbird* marked the beginning of a friendship between Robert Duvall and Horton Foote that would last for more than fifty years (until Horton's death in 2009), during which time they would work together on four more films—*Tomorrow, The Chase, Convicts,* and *Tender Mercies.*

Unfortunately, not everything went as smoothly as the casting or the filming of *To Kill a Mockingbird.* While Horton was in California assisting Mulligan with casting, he found himself at the center of a dispute over the set. Pakula and Mulligan were determined to film the movie in black and white and to reproduce a bygone era so completely that the audience would be reminded of their childhood. A great deal of consideration was given to filming *To Kill a Mockingbird* in the South, and Pakula, Mulligan, and production designers Alexander Golitzen and Henry Bumstead searched the region to find locations that would be suitable for a film that takes place during the Great Depression. Initially, the production team considered using Harper Lee's hometown of Monroeville, "hoping that it could double for Maycomb," but the town had changed radically since the 1930s. "The Monroeville of 1961," Mulligan remembered, "was replete with television antennas, neon signs, new storefronts," and no longer had the feel of a small town.[19] With this in mind, the decision was made to film the picture in Hollywood on the back lot of Universal studios and Golitzen and Bumstead went about designing a set they felt captured the world of Harper Lee's novel. There was one problem, however. For the Finch house, they had designed a huge structure with pillars that looked like an antebellum mansion from *Gone with the Wind* and which was completely inappropriate for the Finch house. Work on the set had already begun when Horton finally saw the drawings. He recalled the designers phoning him "out of great pride" and inviting him to come to their office to see the sketch of the house. He walked in and proclaimed, "My God Almighty! This is wrong, this isn't her house...it's a cottage, it's simple, and I began to describe it."[20]

After Horton's reaction, Bumstead dismantled a number of houses found in a small town in the San Fernando Valley scheduled for demolition and then rebuilt them on the Universal Studios back lot. The town was quite similar to the one in the novel, with a bungalow for the

[19] Jared Brown, 48–49.
[20] Roussel, 165–66.

Finch home and a courthouse that was almost an exact replica of the one in Monroeville. Built at a cost of $225,000, the set consisted of more than thirty buildings and was one of the largest and most realistic ever built in Hollywood. At the end of the day, Golitzen and Bumstead were so successful in creating Maycomb that for years after the release of the film people would approach Robert Mulligan with comments like "I know exactly where you shot that" or "It's my uncle's town." When Harper Lee visited the set, she was actually stunned that it looked so much like her own Southern town.[21]

Production of *To Kill a Mockingbird* got underway in February 1962 and from the beginning things worked beautifully. By all accounts, the shooting of the film was one of those rare occasions where everyone on the set worked well together. Gregory Peck felt that much of the credit for the collaborative atmosphere during the shooting was due to director Mulligan's sense of delicacy in working with the children, aided by the family feeling that seemed to gather around the production, and the crew that made the children seem natural on the screen. "It was altogether a marvelous experience to work with them," Peck said.[22]

While filming *To Kill a Mockingbird* was an exhilarating time for the actors, Universal studios was less than confident about the success of the movie and they treated it as a low-budget film rather than the cinematic masterpiece that it was to become. To begin with, they refused to pay for Horton to be on the set for the duration of the filming, and Pakula could not convince studio executives that the writer's presence was necessary. After the movie was finished, Universal executives were concerned about the reception of the movie and threatened to make cuts in the final print. Luckily, Gregory Peck had insisted in his contract with Universal that Pakula and Mulligan would have control over the final cut of the film and consequently the movie remained intact. Horton explained, "Universal did not like the picture very much, and if they had got their hands on it, God knows what they would have done, but they couldn't."[23]

Even though Universal could not make any changes to the movie, studio executives who were concerned about reactions to the racial elements of the story arranged for the film to be shown in Washington, DC, to members of Congress and the Supreme Court before they would

[21] Jared Brown, 49.
[22] Griggs, 181.
[23] Edgerton, 6.

issue the final print. Finally, Universal wanted to market *To Kill a Mockingbird* as an art film, releasing it only in small theaters in large cities.[24] Once again, Gregory Peck insisted the premiere be held at Radio City Music Hall in New York and exhibited in first-run commercial theaters. Studio executives did not really get behind the movie until after it had won several Oscar nominations and had become one of the most profitable movies ever made by Universal.

When *To Kill a Mockingbird* was finally released on 14 February 1963, it drew exceptional critical and popular praise. The release of the movie was well timed because that year saw Southern racial problems explode into headlines with sit-ins, freedom rides, and mass demonstrations. Many critics saw To *Kill a Mockingbird* as a moral exposition of the plight of blacks in America, but it is now evident that the film's qualities are far more enduring than was first realized. As *New York Herald Tribune's* Judith Crist suggested, *To Kill a Mockingbird* is not only a moving indictment of racial injustice but also a timeless story of childhood dreams and fears. "The story may seem slightly sentimental," Crist stated, "but its stature and lasting substance stem from the beautifully observed relationship between father and children and from the youngsters' perceptions of the enduring human values in the world around them."[25] For Alan Pakula, Robert Mulligan, and Horton, the most important words of praise were from Harper Lee, who was simply thrilled with their work. "I can only say that I am a happy author," Lee remarked. "They have made my story into a beautiful and moving motion picture. I am very proud and very grateful."[26]

Although *To Kill a Mockingbird* was not actually released until February 1963, it qualified for Academy Award consideration in 1962 because it had been shown in Los Angeles before the end of that year. It received nominations in categories for Best Picture, Best Actor, Best Direction, Best Supporting Actress, Best Art Direction, Best Cinematography, Best Musical Score, and Best Screenplay. When the awards were presented, Alexander Golitzen and Henry Bumstead were honored for their art direction; Gregory Peck was awarded the Oscar for Best Actor; and Horton Foote carried home the Academy Award for Best Screenplay.

---

[24] Jared Brown, 54.

[25] Griggs, 182.

[26] Ibid.

Horton was invited to Los Angeles for the ceremony, but since he had not been there for the filming, he decided to stay in Nyack. He was very happy to be selected as a nominee but he had little hope of winning the Oscar. He expected Robert Bolt and Michael Wilson to receive the award for their adaptation of *Lawrence of Arabia*, so he decided to watch the awards at home with his family. The presenter of the award was Bette Davis, who had long admired Horton's work, and when she opened the envelope and shouted out "Horton Foote for *To Kill a Mockingbird*" the writer was literally bowled over. "I hadn't really dressed that day," Horton recalled. "I had been writing all day and I stayed in my pajamas. We were sitting in my son's room, who had the only television in the house, and my oldest son had gotten disgusted and said, 'Well, *Lawrence of Arabia* is getting everything.' He went to bed and went to sleep. Then when Bette Davis announced that I had won the award, the phone started ringing. You would have thought that I was the president of the United States. People I hadn't heard from in years called me."[27] Within minutes, his front doorbell rang, and his Nyack neighbors descended on the house to congratulate him. The next day Horton received more than fifty congratulatory telegrams as well as several letters from colleagues, most notably playwright Tad Mosel and director John Frankenheimer.

The success of *To Kill a Mockingbird* thrust Horton Foote into the Hollywood spotlight, stimulated interest in his own works as potential movies, and established his reputation as a screenwriter for the remainder of the decade. And in October 1963, Horton teamed up again with producer, Alan Pakula, and director, Robert Mulligan, to film his play, *The Traveling Lady*—the story of Georgette Thomas's courageous attempt to save her marriage to her rebellious husband—which had been produced on Broadway a decade earlier. Originally the film was called *Highway*, but after numerous discussions with production executives the title of the film was changed to *Baby, the Rain Must Fall*, following the rise to number twelve on the *Billboard* charts of an Elmer Bernstein song written for the film and recorded by folksinger Glenn Yarbrough. Produced by Columbia Pictures and shot on location in Horton's hometown of Wharton and nearby Columbus, Texas, *Baby, the Rain Must Fall* did not meet with the same kind of enthusiastic reaction as *To Kill a Mockingbird*. But the film nevertheless revealed that Horton's play could

---

[27] Marion Castleberry, "Reflections on the American Theatre: A Conversation with Horton Foote," *The Voice of an American Playwright*, 283.

be as emotionally effective on the big screen as it had been earlier on television and on the stage.

Alan Pakula worked closely with Horton to shape the screenplay of *Baby, the Rain Must Fall* just as he had for *To Kill a Mockingbird.* "The character of Georgette was very attractive to Alan," Horton recalled. "He had great compassion for her and he was very sympathetic to her plight."[28] The primary focus of both the play and screenplay, like much of Horton's work, is on the relationship between parents and children, highlighting the hardship of broken families and the misery caused by parental abuse and neglect. The unbreakable cycle resulting from misguided methods of child rearing is a dominant theme in both versions.

In addition to opening up the action of the story, Horton made several subtle but significant changes in characterization, and he enlarged the story by shifting the major focus of the work. We learn more about Georgette's troubled past, about the death of her mother, about her relationship to her negligent father, and about her estrangement from Henry but the most significant change in the screen adaptation is the fuller picture we get of Henry Thomas. Henry's sincere efforts to be a good husband and father, his quest to become a country-western star, and his attempts to overcome the ill effects of his upbringing are at the heart of the screenplay.

Baby, the Rain Must Fall opens as Georgette and her daughter, Margaret Rose, arrive in Columbus, Texas, where they look forward to a surprise reunion with Henry, who Georgette believes will soon be released from prison. From Slim, the quiet-spoken deputy sheriff, Georgette learns that her husband has been in town for some time, having been paroled to Miss Kate Dawson, the Puritanical spinster who had raised the orphaned Henry since he was a ten-year-old. As the screenplay makes clear, Miss Kate and Henry have never gotten along; in her early attempts to control the boy, she systematically beat him to quell his outbursts of defiance, until the neighbors finally complained and stepped in to stop the abuse. Now, Miss Kate, ailing but still indomitable in spirit, refuses to talk to Henry in person, but she does send him iron-worded messages demanding that he remain steadily employed or she will have him returned to prison. The film explores the troubled relationship of Miss Kate and Henry more fully than the play and this

---

[28] Jared Brown, 66.

closer look allows the audience to feel more sympathy for the young man.

Henry's dreams and ambitions are also significantly altered in the film. While the play suggests that he has aspirations of forming a musical band, the screenplay clarifies the depth of Henry's love for music. Becoming a country-western singer has always been his dream, and his only true happiness comes from strumming his guitar and singing at local roadhouses. But Miss Kate has ruthlessly fought to stifle his dream, and during the film she warns Henry that she will turn him over to the sheriff as a parole violator unless he renounces his ambitions and enrolls in night school. Throughout the film, Henry dwells in constant fear that the old woman will carry out her threat.

Georgette is the only one who supports Henry's dreams. Determined to build a family life and find happiness for herself and Margaret Rose, she works as a waitress to help earn their keep so her husband can save his money for a trip to Nashville or California, where he can sell his songs. Henry promises Georgette that, one day, he will be famous like Elvis, and for a brief time he responds to Georgette's love and sacrifice. He genuinely tries to be a dutiful husband and father, but the emotional burdens in his life ultimately explode in a violent and savage fight with a loudmouthed roadhouse patron. Word spreads quickly about Henry's latest trouble, and he is left terrified that Miss Kate will take action. He utters vague promises that he will give up his music, but he is unable to carry through with the old woman's demands. One evening, after building up the courage to confront Miss Kate, he becomes so terrified that he cannot ascend the stairs to her bedroom. Her very presence, even behind a closed door, paralyzes him; and all that he is able to do, as he runs out of the house, is scream out that he will not quit his musical band.

Miss Kate's menacing influence over Henry becomes even clearer in the film when she summons him to her house on the night of her death. As the malevolent old woman sleeps, Henry quietly sits remembering his childhood and the time, after being abandoned by his parents, when he was discovered alone and crying by Judge Ewing and placed in the care of Miss Kate. Suddenly, Miss Kate awakens; and after seeing Henry sitting patiently by her side, she utters a final bitter bequest: "You're no good, Henry, never have been. You're not worth killing." Miss Kate dies with only a curse for her adopted son. As the scene slowly dissolves, the audience is left with an indelible image of the years of loneliness and pain that the young man suffered as a child. The scene makes clear that the neglect and abuse Henry received as a child at the hand of Miss Kate will ultimately prevent him from fulfilling his responsibilities to Georgette and Margaret Rose. In Horton Foote's dramatic world, the lack of childhood intimacy often causes loneliness, paralysis, and dislocation in adulthood.

At the funeral the following day, Judge Ewing informs Henry that Miss Kate has left him only a few mementos, that her house is to be sold to satisfy debts, and that she has bequeathed her silver to her neighbor, Miss Tillman. Henry is seemingly unconcerned with material possessions for he believes that with the old woman out of the way he can continue to pursue his dream of becoming a singer and not go to school as he had promised. However, even in death, Kate Dawson continues to torment Henry as Judge Ewing explains that her last wish was for him to study for a profession and that the sheriff send him back to prison if he continued his music.

Angered by the news, Henry breaks into Miss Kate's house to steal whatever valuables the old woman has left behind. He finds nothing except a few pieces of silverware and a lone belt strapped to a nail on the pantry door, the symbol of his abused childhood. As his emotions reach a fury, he runs out of the house into the cemetery, where he begins to savagely mutilate Miss Kate's grave. The cinematic montage of Henry tearing through Miss Kate's abandoned house and stabbing the old woman's freshly dug grave with the very shovel he had used only hours earlier to plant a tree with his little girl, powerfully expresses a past that will not die and the violence that often erupts from unhealthy parental attachments and lack of intimacy. Any hope for Henry to have a new life with his family withers away the moment he rails against Miss Kate. Georgette watches as Slim tries to restrain her maddened husband, but his actions come too late for Henry, who is destined to return to prison for breaking his parole. In the film, as in the play, Henry tries to escape from the sheriff after a last meeting with Margaret Rose, but his actions are not so much an attempt to flee from the burdens of family life as they are an effort to escape from the memory of Kate Dawson and the hostility of the small Texas town that would not give him a chance to go straight.

At this point in the film, the focus of the action returns to Georgette, whose attempts to save her marriage and protect her husband from the destructive influence of Miss Kate have failed. Though she has experienced an emotional nightmare, Georgette manages to survive her heartache and continue her search for personal fulfillment. With the aid of Slim, she and Margaret Rose leave for the Texas valley, where nice towns, good people, and plenty of opportunities for employment offer hope of a better life.

In the play, Slim announces his love for Georgette, suggesting that the couple will one day build a stable and happy life together. The resolution of the screenplay, however, is less optimistic than the original play. As Slim drives past the house where Georgette, Henry, and Margaret Rose briefly shared their hopes and aspirations, the camera zooms in on the tiny chinaberry tree planted by Henry and Margaret Rose, as though to emphasize the pain, agony, and broken dreams this family has had to endure. Finally, the camera pauses at a fork in the road, giving Georgette one final glimpse of Henry before he is escorted back to prison, and we are suddenly reminded of the mysterious nature of human suffering and of the remarkable courage with which this woman carries on with her life. This final image also offers a brief hope of reunion between Georgette and Henry while at the same time underscoring the ambiguity of life itself, as suggested in the title song: "Baby, the rain must fall/ Baby, the wind must blow/ Wherever my heart leads me/ Baby I must go."

As he had done in *To Kill a Mockingbird*, Horton injected a good bit of social commentary into the screenplay of *Baby, the Rain Must Fall*. He accentuated the small-minded pettiness and hatred that can occasionally corrupt a small town and, in doing so, portrayed Henry as a victim of societal neglect. Besides the problems caused by Miss Kate's misguided methods of child-rearing, the lack of a father figure in Henry's life has crippled the young man emotionally and stunted his development as an adult. Ultimately, Henry emerges as a more sympathetic and compassionate character than he was in the stage and television plays. In the earlier versions, Henry fails because of his own shortcomings, specifically his alcoholism, but in the film, his demise is brought about by the neglect and cruelty of the people who inhabit his hometown.

Baby, the Rain Must Fall has never received the praise it deserves. Since the time of its release in January 1965, critics have argued that Horton weakened his original story by moving the focus of the story from Georgette and Slim to Georgette and her husband, Henry. But clearly, the most powerful aspect of the screenplay is the deepening of the relationship between the two characters and the addition of the Kate

Dawson character. The film is also more successful than the play in showing the anguish of the Thomas family, the reasons for Henry's downfall, and the compromises that Georgette must make in order to survive her loss. Furthermore, Ernest Laszlo's stunning black-and-white cinematography captured the beauty and isolation of a small Texas town, and the movement of the camera allowed for the addition of situations and locales that place Henry and Georgette in a larger social context. What we see of their daily lives makes their need for love and affection all the more apparent.

Baby, the Rain Must Fall is an ambitious and affecting film. As with all of Horton's work, the dominant tone of the movie is touching and poignant. Lee Remick's performance as Georgette Thomas reveals the talent of a great, underrated actress who portrayed the very essence of Horton's tender and courageous Texas woman struggling to save her marriage and make a life for herself and her daughter. Her bond with the four-year-old Kimberly Block, who played Margaret Rose, appears authentic and convincing. When the film was released, Bosley Crowther of the *New York Times* praised the relationship between mother and daughter and praised Kimberly Block's ability to portray Margaret Rose with naturalness and authenticity. Steve McQueen's portrait of Henry Thomas, the unconnected drifter, whose dreams of stardom do not mesh with the responsibility of caring for his neglected family, is arguably one of the best performances of his career. No doubt the actor's own troubled background informed his performance, and his vulnerability and natural aggressiveness was well suited for the role of the abused man pursuing his dream to be a musician while railing against an unjust world that will not give him a break.

Filming *Baby, the Rain Must Fall* was a happy and unforgettable experience for Horton. Since the movie was shot primarily in his hometown of Wharton, the writer took a personal interest in the movie. For instance, he helped Robert Mulligan scout for shooting locations around Wharton and assisted him in casting extras for the film, which included several of his friends and family members. Horton's mother and father performed non-speaking roles in the movie, as did his cousin Nan Outlar, who, after viewing the movie's Texas premiere in Wharton on 4 February 1965 at the Rio Theatre, wrote Horton to complain jokingly that she had gotten only a "bare glimpse of my glamorous self as I followed the pall bearers and casket down the steps at the old house on Resident St." However, she "LOVED the picture" and had to admit that cutting her scene out of the movie "didn't really hurt the picture."[29]

By all accounts, shooting *Baby, the Rain Must Fall* was similar to *Mockingbird*, in that everyone on the set worked well together. But the production was not without incident. On 22 November 1963, while filming on location in Columbus, Texas, news came on a local police car radio that President John F. Kennedy had been shot in Dallas. The entire cast and crew were stunned and gathered around the radio to hear that Kennedy had died en route to Parkland Hospital. Photographer William Claxton remembered that, "a pall was cast over the entire group. Lunch break was called, but very few of us could eat. Steve [McQueen] took the news of the assassination of President Kennedy very hard."[30] As feelings of fear and grief descended upon the company, Alan Pakula decided to suspend shooting, leave Texas, and head back to Hollywood, where the set was recreated on a Columbia sound stage and the film was completed several months later. Looking back, it is likely that the death of President Kennedy influenced the film in a profound way. The sadness and emptiness of a shattered dream and uncertain future must have certainly affected the actors and filmmakers alike, translating to the dark, melancholy mood that permeates the picture. Ultimately, however, *Baby, the Rain Must Fall* remains one of Horton's most impressive dramatizations and an unsung treasure of American cinema.

The next screen adaptation of a Horton Foote work illustrates how quickly expectations about a motion picture can be dashed by conceptual confusions and creative problems. In 1965, legendary Hollywood producer Sam Spiegel—who spearheaded such landmark films as *On the Waterfront*, *The Bridge on the River Kwai*, and *Lawrence of Arabia*—informed Horton that he intended to translate *The Chase* into a feature film. *The Chase* had first come to Spiegel's attention in 1952, following its brief run on Broadway, but it was not until four years later (1958), after he read Horton's novel, that Spiegel showed real interest and acquired the film rights to the book and play. "[Horton] had made changes in both plot and character," Spiegel explained, "and I began to see motion-picture possibilities, although with a somewhat different emphasis."[31] In order to bring *The Chase* to the screen, Spiegel hired the Oscar-winning

---

[29] Nan Outlar to Horton Foote, 7 January 1965 (Horton Foote Papers).

[30] Marshall Terrill, *The Life and Legend of a Hollywood Icon* (New York: Triumph Books, 2010) 211.

[31] Jeff Brown, "The Making of a Movie," *Holiday* (5 February 1966): 87–88.

scenarist Michael Wilson. Spiegel wanted Wilson to turn Horton's intimate drama into a script of epic proportions that depicted all the social strata of a small Southern town and focused on the harsh realities of greed, bigotry, and brutality that lay beneath the façade of morality in American life. In broad terms, Spiegel hoped the socially conscious film would uncover the hypocritical moral values and corrupt power struggle that accompanied the nation's ongoing battle between the affluent and the poor. The catalyst of the clash would be the sudden arrival of an escaped convict, which stirs up a lynch mob mentality in a small town.

Unfortunately, none of Michael Wilson's several adaptations met with the producer's approval, so in 1963, Spiegel hired the renowned playwright, Lillian Hellman, to write the screenplay. Hellman, who had enjoyed great success on Broadway with a series of acclaimed dramas—*The Children's Hour* (1934), *The Little Foxes* (1939), and *Watch on the Rhine* (1941)—was an open sympathizer with left-wing political groups in the 1930s. In 1952, she had appeared before the House of Un-American Activities Committee, and, after skirting around the issue of naming names, had been blacklisted from Hollywood. Throughout her exile, the Hollywood community spurned Hellman, but she remained decidedly socialist in her politics. After agreeing to adapt *The Chase*, her first screenplay since being blacklisted, it became apparent that Hellman intended to use the film as a personal soapbox. Hellman, who was offered $125,000 for her work on the screenplay, wrote to Spiegel and expressed her desire to turn Horton's play and novel into a "major" cinematic *tour de force*. "You said that you wanted the picture to be 'large.' So do I, but I always have trouble with the word large," she said.[32]

Spiegel and Hellman, like the rest of the world, were still in shock over the assassination of President Kennedy, and both of them envisioned *The Chase* as a statement on the senseless violence that led to the assassination of the president and the mysterious murder of Lee Harvey Oswald.[33] Hellman agreed with Spiegel that the film should concern itself with a society that was not too distant from frontier life. "Such a society would carry with it violence, because it must contain many displaced people who find that frontier no longer exists," she wrote. "Texas, unlike most of the South, is rich and powerful, and often shows a

---

[32] James Robert Parish, *Fiasco: A History of Hollywood's Iconic Flops* (Hoboken NJ: John Wiley & Sons, 2006) 46.

[33] Jeff Brown, 87–88.

kind of anger that its convictions do not govern the rest of America. I would think this is one of the reasons for the spitting at Adlai Stevenson and possibly one of the reasons of the handling—not the killing itself—of the Kennedy murder. It also accounts for Mr. Ruby."[34] According to Spiegel biographer Natasha Fraser-Cavassoni "there were even those in the cast of *The Chase* who were told it was the story of Lee Harvey Oswald."[35] (269).

Hellman's screenplay accentuated everything that Horton had restrained in his play and novel. She used Horton's original story, which tells of Sheriff Edwin Hawes courageous but futile attempt to return Bubber Reeves to prison, as a departure, turned drama into melodrama, and touched upon nearly every social disease troubling America during the decade of the 1960s, including greed, injustice, adultery, alcoholism, apathy, and even religious fanaticism. Also, contrary to Horton's small town of Richmond, Hellman's Tarl, Texas, is an extremely cynical and class-conscious world, resembling a feudal state with millionaire Val Rogers as lord and ruler. Rogers owns the oil fields in which the citizens work, the housing developments where they live, the bank in which they keep their money, and the local college where their children attend school. Rogers is shown respect by the citizens of Tarl, not because he is a worthy man but because he has money and power. He wants to believe that everyone loves him, but his relationship with his son proves otherwise. In establishing Jake as a proper heir to the family fortune, Rogers has forced the young man into a stifling and destructive mold, which includes a loveless marriage to a young socialite, who neither respects her husband nor finds him physically attractive. Jake and his wife appear together in public to please Rogers, but both must go outside their marriage to find companionship. Jake is in love with the wife of the escaped fugitive, Bubber Reeves, but their relationship is far from idyllic. Jake and Anna's weekly meetings at a local motel, played out in a volatile combination of passionate desire and sexual frustration, merely illustrate the extent to which they are separated by money and social differences.

The protagonist of the film, Sheriff Calder (Hellman's cinematic equivalent to the heroic Edwin Hawes), is an honest man committed to justice, but in the movie, his privileged position with Val Rogers, who has adopted him as a kind of surrogate son and appointed him sheriff,

---

[34] Ibid.

[35] Natasha Fraser-Cavassoni, *Sam Speigel* (New York: Simon & Schuster, 2003) 268.

leads the townspeople to conclude that he is merely a patsy. Rogers believes he owns the sheriff, but, during the course of the film, he learns otherwise when Calder refuses to bow to his power. After discovering that Jake and Anna are lovers, Rogers tries to get Calder to tell him where Bubber is hiding out so he can prevent the fugitive from killing his son. Calder, who tries to conceal Bubber's whereabouts in order to protect him, refuses to answer Roger's request. Subsequently, with Rogers on the offensive against Reeves, the town erupts into mass hysteria and explodes into a riot of beatings, gunshots, fires, and explosions. Three vigilantes savagely beat Calder, Bubber is discovered holed up in an automobile junkyard, and Jake is mortally wounded while trying to help Reeves escape. Calder rescues Bubber from the mob and returns him to town, but, as they ascend the steps of the county courthouse, a gunman—an obvious reference to the shooting of Lee Harvey Oswald in Dallas a few years earlier—kills Bubber. Calder, reduced to the level of the rest of the townspeople, brutally beats the assassin. Of course, there can be no positive ending to such an uncompromising screenplay, and as the film reaches its logical conclusion, Calder and his wife Ruby pack up and move to their farm in an effort to escape the violence and corruption of the town.

In preparing the screenplay, Spiegel and Hellman gave a great deal of consideration when shaping the role of Sheriff Calder to the fact that Marlon Brando had long been slated to appear in the film. Spiegel had first approached Brando in 1956, suggesting that he play the role of Jake, the town's wealthy young man, to Marilyn Monroe's Anna. But seven years later, Brando was too old to play the ingénue part and was consequently hired for $750,000 to play the role of Sheriff Calder. Spiegel sank another small fortune into the supporting cast, which included Angie Dickinson as Calder's wife Ruby, Jane Fonda as Anna, E.G. Marshall as Val Rogers, the British actor James Fox as Jake, and a relatively unknown young actor Robert Redford as Bubber Reeves. To round out the ensemble, Spiegel cast an array of emerging personalities such as Robert Duvall, Diana Hyland, Robert Bradford, and Paul Williams as well as an assortment of veteran actors, including Martha Hyer, Janice Rule, Henry Hull, Bruce Cabot, and Miriam Hopkins.

To guide the cast, Spiegel wanted to hire a talented director who would give the picture prestige in the eyes of the Hollywood community. He showed the screenplay to several renowned directors— Elia Kazan, David Lean, Joseph Mankiewicz, William Wyler, and Fred

Zimmerman—but all of them rejected the project after reading the script. Spiegel then turned to director Arthur Penn, who was a personal friend of Lillian Hellman and Horton, with whom he had worked during the *Philco-Goodyear* television days. Having recently been nominated for an Oscar for his brilliant direction of *The Miracle Worker* (1962), Penn had been acclaimed by the European cinema community and was considered by many in Hollywood as an eminent new moviemaker. In addition, Penn was a political liberal and shared the progressive philosophy of Spiegel and Hellman.

Penn was initially enthusiastic about working with Spiegel, but as he became more involved with the project, he realized that *The Chase* was in trouble and that the producer was not to be trusted. Before relocating from New York to Hollywood for the shoot, Penn spent a good deal of time with Lillian Hellman trying to fine-tune the screenplay, unaware that the script was undergoing another metamorphosis in California. Dissatisfied with Hellman's work, Spiegel had secretly hired the English scenarist, Ivan Moffat, to rewrite the script without informing either Hellman or Penn. Moffat, who had been nominated for an Oscar for his work on *Giant* (1956), was working on *The Heroes of Telemark*, a film starring Kirk Douglas, when he received an urgent call from Spiegel's office. Far more accustomed to writing melodramatic star vehicles than socially conscious films, Moffat found his work with Spiegel intolerable, remarking that the producer kept a tight rein on his writers: "He was crablike and all-controlling. Sam would hold on to everything."[36] Despite countless rewrites, Moffat was unable to please Spiegel, who felt that Moffat's writing lacked originality and depth. So, in a final attempt to salvage the script, the producer turned to Horton, who tried, unsuccessfully, to edit the overblown screenplay and to recapture some semblance of his original story and voice that had been lost in translation.

Horton's work came to naught once the twenty-two week shooting began in May 1965. "Sam Spiegel asked me to come on the set the first day of shooting to check everything for authenticity," Horton recalled.

> The set that day was in a drugstore and it seemed adequate, until I saw an Indian squaw sitting there. I went running back to Sam's office and asked, "What is an Indian squaw doing in a drugstore in Harrison?" He had no idea and immediately called the scenic designer, who said she was there because he had seen a picture in a book with an Indian squaw in a Texas drugstore. That drugstore turned out to be in faraway West Texas.

---

[36] Ibid., 272.

However, in the meantime, the scene had been shot, squaw and all, and to redo it would cost fifty thousand dollars. So to this day, the squaw sits in the drugstore.[37]

Horton's frustrations were also shared by Arthur Penn, who found *The Chase* to be a burdensome film to make. "It required a certain amount of baby-sitting," Penn confessed. "Miriam Hopkins, who played Bubber's mother, needed a great deal of care. Now I have nothing but compassion for a former movie legend playing an old lady, but it takes up time."[38] A cameraman who did not share his artistic vision also weighed down Penn. Spiegel, who believed he was above consulting with the director on the all-important position of cinematographer, hired Robert Surtees, a Hollywood veteran and winner of three Academy Awards. Unfortunately, Surtees became ill early in the filming process and had to be replaced. Then, without consulting Penn, Sam Spiegel hired another veteran, Joseph LaShelle, who was highly respected but who did not understand or agree with the director's method of working. "It should be a close relationship, but I found him to be difficult and slow," Penn said. "For the night scenes, he would be lighting until midnight. And, in *The Chase*, we had a lot of night scenes."[39]

Things went from bad to worse as filming dragged on, with Spiegel and studio executives trying to salvage the movie and to control the large production costs, which eventually rose to more than five and a half million dollars at a time when the average Hollywood feature film cost just over one million. By the time the filming concluded, there was no longer any rapport between Arthur Penn and Sam Spiegel, and Penn returned to New York to direct a Broadway play, *Wait until Dark*. Since Spiegel had shown a complete lack of interest in the actual shooting of the movie, Penn believed he would be left on his own to edit the film. To his consternation, however, Spiegel gave the director a choice: did he want to edit the movie in Los Angeles or London? Since Penn was in the midst of rehearsals in New York, Spiegel knew that the director would find neither suggested location feasible, so he shipped the footage to England where he and veteran editor, Gene Milford, edited *The Chase* without Penn's participation. When Arthur Penn was finally able to fly to London, he found "eight reels of pretty well-finished film." Penn admitted: "It was nothing that I would conspicuously differ with, but it

---

[37] Horton Foote, interview by Marion Castleberry, 20 March 2004, Waco, Texas.
[38] Fraser-Cavassoni, 273.
[39] Ibid.

lacked my sense of rhythm. I'm not saying that the film would have necessarily been better if I had edited it, but I just knew the rhythm that was in my gut and it was not on that screen. The tempos were not right and I pride myself on the tempo and on the accumulating velocity that is part of the volume."[40]

Ultimately, the immense talents of all the artists involved with *The Chase* could not keep the movie from becoming a cinematic failure. An ambitious producer bent on controlling all aspects of filmmaking, a director determined to elevate the film to an art form by expressing his own point of view within the work, and a screenwriter attempting to prove her artistic marketability after a fifteen-year political exile from Hollywood made a contradictory collaborative team. Their artistic differences resulted in a movie that, according to critic Bosley Crowther, was a conventionally opulent melodrama that had been overproduced by Sam Spiegel, over plotted to the point of incoherence by Lillian Hellman, and over directed by Arthur Penn: "Everything is intentionally overheated, the emotional content, the pictorial style, the directing, the acting, the fist-fighting, the burning of the junkyard at the end—everything. The only thing that is not overheated—at least I don't think it will be—is the audience's reaction. This is a picture to leave you cold. That's because it is so obvious and so outrageously clumsy an attempt to blend a weak but conceivably dramatic theme of civil rights with a whole mess of small-town misbehaviors of the sort that you get in *Peyton Place*. And it has an ending that was not in Mr. Foote's play but was evidently inspired by a very tragic occurrence in Texas in 1963. More bad taste."[41]

In spite of its unfavorable reception, *The Chase* proved to be an important learning experience for Horton Foote. He saw first-hand how tricky it is to make a good movie and how producers, directors, and actors can be crippled without a coherent and actable script. More importantly, as Horton admitted, he learned that "if you sell your work to a Hollywood studio, they own it. That's why I never would do it again. That's the last time I did it."[42]

True to his word, Horton never again sold his work to a Hollywood studio, but in order to support his growing family he agreed in 1966 to join renowned producer-director, Otto Preminger, in bringing K.G.

---

[40] Ibid.

[41] Bosley Crowther, "Review of *The Chase*," *New York Times*, 19 March 1966.

[42] Al Reinert, "Tender Foote," *Texas Monthly* (July 1991): 135.

Glidden's novel *Hurry Sundown* to the screen. The novel's timely story of racial prejudice and the debilitating effects of poverty in Texas no doubt interested Horton, but he initially rejected the offer because he was afraid of "getting into the nature of adapting" and did not want to "lose his identity."[43] However, Preminger was determined to have Horton on his team, and he enticed the writer with a lucrative financial package that the writer could not resist. Horton tried to please Preminger, who he admired greatly, but his efforts to moderate the novel's melodramatic structure and stilted language did not suit Preminger's purposes, and, before shooting began, the two began to argue about the script's style and approach. Horton tried to make the best of the material, though not a single word of his was used in the final shooting script; and while he is credited as co-writer with Thomas Ryan, he maintains that he had nothing to do with the film's final construction.

Horton's experiences with *The Chase* and *Hurry Sundown* convinced him that Hollywood was not for him, and he steered clear of feature films until 1972, when he returned as an independent filmmaker. "I knew that this wasn't working for me," the writer said. "This ten million dollars and what are the distributors going to think, and can we get this star and that star. It was just driving me nuts. So I left. I never lived out there [Hollywood] but I just never did take any more jobs."[44]

Horton was at a crossroads in his career and needed to reevaluate his personal and artistic goals. He was still receiving offers from Hollywood and was more than able to make a living from this venue if he chose to do so. On the other hand, the mainstream motion picture industry was no longer a satisfying outlet for his kind of storytelling. To make matters worse, original television drama was a thing of the past and Broadway was no longer interested in Horton's kind of traditional family stories. During those times of political and social unrest, realistic dramas were ignored by Broadway, which became the staging area for a new generation of artists whose ideas and writings reflected the social revolution that beset 1960s America. Younger writers like Edward Albee, Leroi Jones, and Sam Shepard dominated the New York stage with plays that revealed a country plagued by political turmoil, racial injustice,

---

[43] Gerald C. Wood and Terry Barr, "'A Certain Kind of Writer': An Interview with Horton Foote," *The Voice of an American Playwright*, 228.

[44] Gary Edgerton, "A Visit to the Imaginary Landscape of Harrison, Texas: Sketching the Film Career of Horton Foote," *Literature/Film Quarterly* 12 (Winter 1989): 7.

sexual revolution, the mushrooming hippie movement, and the war in Vietnam. Horton suddenly found his work no longer commercial for stage, screen, or television.

Confused by such artistic rebellion and frustrated with the practices of Hollywood, Horton also recognized the negative effects of America's moral and social volatility on his own family. He and Lillian had become disenchanted with Nyack's upper-middle-class competitiveness, especially in the schools, and they were concerned with the drug culture that was making huge inroads in the town. Several of Nyack's young people were turning to drugs and mischief, and he and Lillian wanted to protect their children from this unsafe environment. So, with the setbacks in his career fresh on his mind and the immediate needs of his family weighing heavily on him, Horton moved his family from Nyack to the New Hampshire woods where they withdrew from the public eye. "I just thought I should sort of hold still for a while," Horton recalled. "I was rather displaced. I've never liked Hollywood...and I thought the Broadway that I knew was collapsing all around, and off-Broadway was going in for a kind of—what I call "cartoon theater," where everything is so exaggerated you're almost hit over the head with it. They'd also discovered nudity and a certain kind of language that, as Katherine Anne Porter says, is 'tired old words.' I was interested in the new developments, but I didn't feel a part of them. So for a number of reasons my wife and I decided to relocate."[45]

The move to New Hampshire would bring colossal change, immense grief, and immeasurable happiness to Horton Foote and his family. And during this time, Horton would redefine himself as an artist, establish his artistic independence, and create more original dramas than at any other time in his career. He would write many of the works for which he would later receive great acclaim—masterpieces such as *Tender Mercies* and *The Orphans' Home*—and he would validate his place as one of America's foremost writers.

---

[45] Lauren Porter, "An Interview with Horton Foote," *The Voice of an American Playwright*, 111.

Part Five

Grief and Perseverance

"How can human beings stand all that comes to them? How can they?"

—Horace Robedaux, *1918*

12

New Hampshire
1966–74

Horton Foote's life changed considerably when he moved his family
from Nyack, New York, to the relative "backwoods" of New Boston, New Hampshire, on 5 May 1966. He and Lillian had been looking
for an authentic eighteenth-century home for several years, answering
countless newspaper ads for houses in New York, Massachusetts, and
Maine. The couple would often go on weekend excursions to investigate
the ads, but time and again they were disappointed to discover that the
houses were not authentic eighteenth-century dwellings or, worse yet,
that they had been renovated by the owners. So when Lillian showed
Horton an ad in *Yankee Magazine* publicizing an untouched eighteenth-
century saltbox in New Boston, New Hampshire, Horton had good
reason to be apprehensive. But as his daughter Daisy remembers, "after
a bit of cajoling and because my father really did believe that the house
was out there somewhere, he agreed to drive the five hours north. And I
went with them. That day my parents found their home...It was a
glorious house complete with numerous fireplaces including the wide
deep fireplace in the keeping room, wide textured floorboards, and an
attic that would become my father's study."[1]

Horton paid nineteen thousand dollars for the house and surrounding fifty acres, which was located at the end of a long dirt lane called
Bedford Road. The home was very secluded, with the nearest neighbor a
mile away, and often friends and business acquaintances driving up
from New York or from nearby Boston would find themselves lost and
have to call Horton for directions. For director Robert Mulligan, as for
many others, the journey to the Foote home was an unforgettable
experience. "Every time I think of the Footes, I place you all in your
house in the woods and I can remember clearly the look and feel of those
rooms full of old wood and warmth. The one image which remains
etched forever is the cold day Alan [Pakula] and I drove up from Boston
and found ourselves bouncing along that narrow, frozen dirt road

[1] Daisy Foote, "Horton Foote, a collector remembered," *The Antiques Magazine* (5
March 2009): 8.

wondering if we'd ever see you—and then seeing you, Horton, standing on a rise in the middle of the road, waving and smiling at us."[2]

After moving to New Boston, the family began restoring their home and furnishing it with antiques brought up from Nyack and purchased from New Boston area stores. A decade earlier, when they bought their first house, Horton and Lillian had been frustrated to learn the furnishings they liked were too expensive for their budget. One day they stopped at an antique shop and, after looking around, discovered that the storeowner was charging less for her furniture and accessories than the major furniture stores in which they had shopped for new items. As a result, they purchased a few pieces—a small rug, some chairs, a cupboard, and two small chests—and returned to the store the next week, and then the next, searching for unique pieces of furniture or art. Soon, without realizing it, they had become avid antique collectors.

During these early days in New Hampshire, when none of Horton's works were being produced, collecting and selling antiques became not only an enjoyable pastime for Horton and Lillian but also an important means of income for the family. Lillian became a successful broker and astute assessor of eighteenth-century furniture and art, and during Horton's periods of insecurity and doubt, she supported her husband and family, both financially and emotionally. It was during this period that Horton began to question his future as a writer. "Lillian was selling real estate," Horton remembered, "and we both loved antiques and sometimes I'd say, 'Maybe I'll open an antique shop.' She'd always say, 'Stick to the writing.' She never doubted it. We'd get in the car and I'd say, 'Lillian, I can't stand the theatre, the state it's in. I can't stand Hollywood. I have no talent as a novelist. I love poetry but it's not my form. I'm stuck with plays, and what am I doing? What's going to happen? And she kept me going.' She never lost faith, and that's a rare thing."[3] With Lillian steadfastly by his side, Horton Foote doggedly continued to pursue his vocation, with no guarantee that the plays he was writing at the time would ever be produced.

Horton admitted that he felt lost during this time since he neither approved of what was happening in the theater nor understood the disorder crippling America: "The drugs, the racial tensions. I didn't want my children mixed up in all of that. They wouldn't understand [the

---

[2] Robert Mulligan to Horton Foote, 30 July 1972 (Horton Foote Papers).

[3] Russell Freedman, *Martha Graham: A Dancer's Life* (New York: Houghton Mifflin, 1998) 50.

racial problem] because they had gone to school with black children all their lives. I didn't know what the hell was going on."[4] He was also confused by other events, such as the war in Southeast Asia, the shocking assassinations of national leaders, the destruction of the environment, and the restlessness and rebellion of the nation's youth. Like other Americans, Horton watched as the country suffered violence, racism, and economic upheaval. But perhaps even more distressing to him was the realization that his own private world was changing as well. During the 1960s and '70s, Horton was forced to watch his children grow up in a turbulent world, to cope with the death of his parents, and to stand helplessly by as his hometown of Wharton was enveloped by sprawling urban expansion and technological advancement. Almost overnight, Wharton evolved from an insular community of thirty-five hundred people to a suburb of nearby Houston with a population of nearly ten thousand inhabitants. The cotton fields in which Horton had roamed as a child were replaced by tract houses, motels, and apartment buildings, and the downtown area, where his father had owned a clothing store for more than fifty years, was neglected for the convenience of nearby shopping centers. Richmond Road, which for decades had been a quiet and serene street shaded by oak and sycamore trees, was converted into a dismal stretch of asphalt flanked by a car wash and a series of fast-food restaurants.

Writers have often cited America's break with tradition as one of the most disturbing legacies of these two decades in America's history. Sociologist Hazel Hertzburg concluded that this generation of Americans judged little in man's past as worthy of saving and thereby created a society "characterized by a sense of estrangement," and historian John Gardner warned against the evil effects of technology and the destruction of the environment when he stated that people would get "richer and richer in filthier communities until we reach a final state of affluent misery."[5]

Horton was very sensitive to the moral and social changes taking place, and his writing from this period reflects his concern about the breakdown of traditional contracts and values in America. His unease would cause him to explore more deeply the theme of courage in the face

---

[4] George Terry Barr, "The Ordinary World of Horton Foote" (PhD diss., University of Tennessee, Knoxville, 1986) 164.

[5] William Leuchtenberg, *The Unfinished Century* (Boston: Little, Brown & Company 1973) 857–58.

of devastating change, and his characters would search for peace and contentment in a world drastically altered by industrialism, war, and changing socio-economic conditions. By his own admission, Horton had always written to discover a sense of order and meaning out of what sometimes seemed like total confusion. He had often used the fictional town Harrison to explore the problems of contemporary America and render them meaningful on his own terms. He was not a political playwright in any sense, but he never lost sight of the horrific political and social realities of the Texas he knew, where the memory of slavery and Reconstruction was still fresh. During the 1970s, he would often return to Harrison to grapple with the nature of change and to explore the roots of courage. And yet, the works that would grow out of his self-imposed exile would be something entirely new. His plays would reveal a high level of artistry and output that would surprise even the playwright himself. Among Horton's creations would emerge comedies such as *Blind Date* and *Dividing the Estate*, and darker, more complex dramas such as *The Roads to Home, In a Coffin in Egypt, The Man Who Climbed the Pecan Trees, The One-Armed Man, Night Seasons, Land of the Astronauts, The Prisoner's Song, Pilgrims,* and *The Habitation of Dragons.* He would enter the world of independent filmmaking with his adaptation of *Tomorrow,* pen his first original screenplay, *Tender Mercies* (a cinematic *tour de force* that would win him a second Oscar), and compose his personal masterpiece, *The Orphans' Home Cycle,* a nine-play saga based on the lives of his mother and father. By the 1980s, these works, along with a dozen others, would begin to appear in theaters and movie houses across the country, garnering Horton great acclaim and establishing him, in the words of critic Brooke Allen, as "the greatest American playwright of the last century."[6]

Although none of Horton's plays were being produced in New York, he was still being contacted by Hollywood producers and could have made a respectable living as an adapter of Southern literature. On the other hand, the mainstream motion picture industry was no longer a gratifying outlet for the kinds of stories Horton wanted to tell. He had always hated the idea of becoming a "writer for hire," but he had to accept a few commissioned assignments to put bread on the table. During this time, he wrote unproduced screen adaptations for *Ordeal by Hunger* by George R. Stewart (1966), the story of the Richard Donner

---

[6] Brooke Allen, "Horton Foote's Staying Power," *The New Criterion* [London] (5 September 2012): 2.

Party and their tragic journey to California; *Fool's Parade* (1969), David Grubb's Western novel about three ex-convicts trying to go straight; and *April Morning* (1972), Howard Fast's novel about the Revolutionary War.

In 1967 Horton teamed up again with Alan Pakula, Robert Mulligan, and Gregory Peck on *The Stalking Moon*, a Western novel by Theodore V. Olsen that tells the story of a white woman who, after living with the Apaches, tries to escape with her mixed-race son. Horton found the movie too formulaic for his tastes and disagreed with the content, specifically the ending of the screenplay and the progress of the film. After spending a couple of weeks in California making daily rewrites on the script, he withdrew from the project, leaving Alvin Sargent to receive credit for the screenplay. Although Alan Pakula offered to give Horton screen credit as co-author, he refused. When asked why Pakula and Mulligan didn't use his script, Horton responded, "They didn't like it. And I didn't agree with the changes they wanted to make so I just said 'God bless you and go ahead.'"[7] While Horton's dismissal from the film did not ultimately affect his friendship with Pakula, the two were careful not to discuss the subject. "It was a difficult thing for me and I'm sure for Alan. We were close friends, and it's very difficult to reject a friend's work," Horton admitted.[8]

During this time, Horton also wrote the book for a stage musical of Margaret Mitchell's epic novel *Gone with the Wind* (1968), financed by British theater producer, Harold Fielding, directed and choreographed by Joe Layton, and composed by Harold Rome. The musical opened at the Theatre Royal, Drury Lane, in London on 3 May 1972 with a cast that featured June Ritchie, Harvey Presnell, Patricia Michael, and Robert Swann. Horton was excited about the project and thrilled when he met Princess Anne following the opening night performance, but it did not take long for him to realize that the multi-million dollar production was not going to yield anything near what Fielding had promised. By January 1973, the producer wrote to Lucy Kroll, admitting that the production was in financial trouble (losing nearly £6,000 a week) and he expected "the directors of Drury Lane to give notice."[9] After a limited run in London, a revised version of the production was mounted at the Dorothy Chandler Pavilion in Los Angeles by the city's Civic Light Opera Association, with Lesley Ann Warren and Pernell Roberts in the

---

[7] Jared Brown, *Alan J. Pakula* (New York: Back Stage Books, 2005) 75.

[8] Ibid.

[9] Harold Fielding to Lucy Kroll, 2 January 1973 (Horton Foote Papers).

lead roles. But after an unfavorable reception from critics and audiences alike, the musical fell into obscurity, and Horton was left discouraged and confused once again.

Horton's unwillingness to compromise artistic integrity for commercial success eventually propelled him into the world of independent filmmaking. In 1968, despite his disappointing experiences with *Hurry Sundown* and *The Stalking Moon*, the writer decided to take a big risk and enter the world of independent filmmaking with *Tomorrow*, which he had adapted for *Playhouse 90* a decade earlier. Soon after finishing his stint with *The Stalking Moon*, Horton received a phone call from director Herbert Berghof, who ran a small off-Broadway theater in Greenwich Village, the HB Studio Theatre, with his wife, renowned actress Uta Hagen. Berghof was a Viennese-born director with a passion for American plays and a sincere desire to foster new voices in American theater. He had just read *Tomorrow* and wanted to transform Horton's teleplay into a stage production that would feature Olga Bellin as Sarah Eubanks and Robert Duvall as Jackson Fentry. His production, because of his agreement with Actors' Equity, could have only ten performances, but his staging of *Tomorrow* would become a landmark moment for everyone involved. Even though Horton did not know Berghof very well at the time, he respected the director's talents and agreed to let him produce the play.

Tomorrow was presented at the HB Playwrights Foundation on Bank Street on 15 April 1968.[10] Horton and his family caught the train from New Hampshire to New York to see the final dress rehearsal. The stage version did not depart a great deal from the teleplay, with one exception—the lawyer, Thornton Douglas, rather than Ed Pruitt, served as narrator of the play so that he could address the audience directly as if they were the jury. The real difference between the television and the stage play was Robert Duvall's portrayal of Jackson Fentry, which Horton found very moving. Duvall brought an authenticity and depth to the character that went far beyond what Richard Boone had done earlier in the television version. Olga Bellin also impressed Horton in the role of Sarah, the woman whom Fentry loves in adversity and loses in death.

---

[10] Horton Foote, "*Tomorrow*: The Film," in *Tomorrow & Tomorrow & Tomorrow*, ed. David G. Yellin and Mari Connors (Jackson: University of Mississippi Press 1985) [hereafter cited as *Tomorrow & Tomorrow*]. All page references in text refer to this screenplay.

Producers Paul Roebling and Gilbert Pearlman were equally impressed with the performances of Duvall and Bellin, and two weeks later they phoned Horton to ask if they could make a theatrical film of *Tomorrow*. They wanted him to supply the script and Duvall and Bellin to revive their roles of Fentry and Sarah. Roebling and Pearlman hoped to make an independent film of the highest quality, and they set the production's budget at a little over $400,000, not a large sum for a feature film by today's standards but about three times the amount spent on the television program. Furthermore, the producers planned to shoot the picture in black and white on location in Tupelo, Mississippi, William Faulkner's homeland, to make it as authentic as possible. Paul Roebling, who was married to Olga Bellin and wanted to promote his wife's career, was very intent on expanding the character of Sarah, and demanded that Horton write some new material that would keep the memory of Sarah alive in the second half of the film. Horton tried to appease Roebling, but most of the new material he wrote was cut in the rehearsals before the filming began.[11]

Roebling and Pearlman made one more demand that affected the film in a significant way. They did not want Berghof to direct the movie. They felt that while he was a very talented artist, Berghof had no cinematic experience and was an unpredictable director, lacking the communication skills needed to guide a low-budget film. Paul Roebling suggested Joe Anthony, Horton's old friend from the American Actors Company, as the film's director because he trusted Anthony's directing abilities and felt he possessed an affinity for simple people and simple circumstances that the film needed. Horton was torn between the two directors. He couldn't argue with the choice of Anthony as director—after all they had been close friends and colleagues for forty years—but he also felt a sense of loyalty to Berghof, who had rediscovered the teleplay in the first place. Horton clearly did not want to choose between the two, but when Robert Duvall, who had become personally involved with the project, agreed with Roebling and Pearlman, Horton finally had to admit that Joseph Anthony was the best choice. Eventually, Gilbert Pearlman informed Berghof of their decision in a letter, explaining that financing for the movie could not be obtained without a firm guarantee that they would hire a director with previous screen credits. Berghof was understandably hurt by the letter, but he and Horton remained close friends through it all.

---

[11] Horton Foote, "The Visual Takes Over," in *Tomorrow & Tomorrow*, 163–66.

Horton, nevertheless, was excited about the prospect of filming *Tomorrow* and began work on the screenplay with a sense of renewed optimism. Since the running time of the movie was expected to be about half an hour longer than the television drama, he expanded the original story beyond the earlier scripts. He put the trial scene into the film version and decided to have Douglas, who acted as narrator for the stage production, narrate the film as the character had done in the stage production. This enabled the playwright to cut the episodes with the Pruitts, Papa Fentry, and Chick Mallison and to restore scenes that had been dropped from the television play because of time limitations. The movie opens with a brief sequence that depicts the shooting of Buck Thorpe by Homer Bookwright; then, while the credits roll by, we witness Douglas's final appeal to the jury and Fentry's refusal to acquit the defendant. Douglas declares that he intends to discover Fentry's motives for hanging the jury. Fentry's story is then told through an extended flashback, in the manner of the television version of *Tomorrow*. From this point on, the screenplay, like the teleplay, focuses upon the bond of affection that develops between Fentry and Sarah and upon Fentry's heroic endurance of the loss of his adopted son.

Nearly all the key scenes from the original script appear in the movie. One noteworthy episode, which was cut from the television show, occurs when Fentry gives Sarah a sack of candy as a Christmas present, and she suddenly begins to weep. A woman of great pride, Sarah explains that she never used to cry. Even when her father banished her from his house for marrying a man of whom he disapproved, she did not cry, but faced up to her situation as best she could. Lately, however, she weeps at the slightest provocation, because as she admits, "I'm just tired and nervous. Somebody will come up to me and say 'Good morning' or 'Good evening,' and I'll cry" (140). Joseph Anthony notes that this scene illustrates Horton's talent for using revelatory dialogue to illuminate a character's personality. "That whole scene," says Anthony, tells us more "about Sarah, her past, and who she is, and the kind of person she is, than anything she could have told about herself"[12]

As an example of Horton Foote's ability to employ the camera effectively to convey the deeper feelings of a character, Anthony notes a scene where Fentry addresses Sarah's dead body, vowing to care for her child. Fentry, seated above Sarah's body, is seen only from the shoulders

---

[12] Joseph Anthony, "Directing: To Reveal the Behavior of People," in *Tomorrow & Tomorrow*, 177–81.

up; that is, we see his essence. "I don't know why we met when we did," he says, "or why I found you when you were all wore out, and I couldn't save you no matter how bad I wanted to. I don't know what they done to you to make you turn so on them. But I don't care. I promised you I'd raise him and I will. Like he was my own" (147). Then Fentry slowly rises, spreads the blanket over Sarah's body, moves to the baby's crib, and promises: "I will be your Momma and your Papa. You'll never want or do without while I have a breath of life in my bones" (147–8).

By articulating the actions and silences of the deeply private Fentry, Horton enhanced the mood, tone, and theme of Faulkner's prose. The wonder of the scene is that Robert Duvall shows almost no surface emotion, yet somehow manages to project the loneliness, torment, and tenderness of a man who bends to misfortune as a tree bends to the wind. Had Horton given the character more to say, had the character explained his thoughts in these lines, or had the actor fallen into hysterics, the moment would have been diminished. Fentry's affection for Sarah displays itself only for a few moments after her death. This restrained style, which suggests meanings and emotions beyond the literal actions and words of the text, exemplifies a characteristic strength of Horton Foote's writing.

Although most of the action between Fentry and Sarah is confined to a one-room cabin, Horton created several new scenes for the movie that take advantage of the visual and physical freedom provided by the camera. He placed the characters outside the cabin as much as possible; dramatizing the moment Fentry shares his dream with Sarah of building a house, Sarah's burial, and Fentry's difficult trip home with the baby and a goat. Beyond this, he used the material surroundings of Faulkner's Mississippi homeland to evoke the emotional reality of the characters. For example, Sarah and Fentry, after they have been together about a month, are sitting in the cabin on a cold, rainy night when she begins to talk about floods, about Jesus walking on water, and concludes her monologue with the statement: "They say God is gonna destroy the world next time by fire" (129). Then she goes to the window, peers out, and the scene dissolves to a warm spring day and Sarah seated in a chair watching Fentry wash clothes in an iron pot. She is in good spirits, and she ponders whether her baby will be a boy or a girl. Though Fentry and Sarah's relationship has become trusting, Sarah's tone reveals a foreboding that she cannot conceal, no matter how warming the sun or how comforting Fentry's attentions. By showing the characters' lives in both their physical and emotional settings, Foote reveals their need for companionship, further emphasizing Fentry's loss.

Additional sequences, such as Fentry's trip home with the baby and Sarah's burial, enhance the film in much the same way, as does the montage of scenes that depict the five years from Jackson and Longstreet's birth to the time when his uncles come to take him. These scenes show Fentry picking cotton with the baby strapped to his back, tenderly lifting the boy in and out of his wagon, and playfully catching a fish for their supper. He cares for the child with a love that fulfills all the passion he was unable to express to Sarah. This montage is remarkably moving, especially when one considers that Duvall created it entirely from improvisation.

In casting the role of Jackson and Longstreet, Joseph Anthony, at the suggestion of Horton and Duvall, chose a local boy from Possum Trot, Mississippi, named Johnny Mask, who was, at age seven, small enough to play a four-year-old. Johnny had absolutely no acting skills, and Duvall spent hours building a rapport with him. When the cameras began to roll, however, Johnny became nervous and he was unable to speak his lines with any sense of truth. Ultimately, Duvall found a way around the boy's awkwardness by letting Johnny speak spontaneously, then improvising the scene as it was filmed. Horton no doubt had this series of images in mind when he remarked that, "in film, the visual, sometimes in subtle ways, really takes over. The visual has an emotional impact that you can't get in the theatre, and you can get it better on film than on live television."[13]

Near its conclusion, the film returns to the courtroom where it began. A close-up of Fentry in the jury room some twenty years later, as he utters his final rejection of Bookwright's acquittal, serves as a reminder of the love shared by him and Sarah, and we recognize the nobility of this man who has endured the most painful suffering. Finally, as Fentry rides away on his mule, Thornton Douglas explains the farmer's reason for hanging the jury and expresses the story's central theme: man will not only endure but he will also prevail.

Director Joseph Anthony points to Faulkner's theme as the primary reason for the lasting appeal of *Tomorrow*: "To me, the universality of its theme is the meat of it, the power of it. The specific quality about the South is only color to me. The accents, the cotton fields, the wind, and the sawmill give it an authentic flavor. But if it were only a local portrait,

---

[13] Foote, "The Visual Takes Over," 164.

it would not be as significant a piece of literature. The film is a reminder for humankind everywhere about primitive, basic needs and the wonderful quality of human beings who can endure under degradation and still remain magnificent and unique."[14]

Throughout the filming of *Tomorrow*, Horton felt wanted and appreciated. Producers sought after his opinions, and he was welcome on the set and in the editing room during the entire process. He worked closely with Joseph Anthony, scouting out shooting locations around Tupelo, and was instrumental in securing the courthouse in Jacinto, Mississippi, where the courtroom scenes were eventually shot. The Corinth Historical Society, who objected to the filmmakers entering their sacred building, controlled the courtroom, and they were concerned that *Tomorrow* would make a mockery of Faulkner's South in the manner that other films had done, by emphasizing sex and violence. Horton assured them that their film had nothing to do with any contemporary political issues or social ills and was more about the capacity of love in the most unexpected places. He sent a copy of the screenplay for the committee to read, but, even after discovering that the script contained no lynchings or rapes, they were still wary of granting Horton and Anthony access to the courthouse. Luckily, while reading a book on the Battle of Corinth, Horton discovered that Colonel Rogers, who was killed in the Battle of Corinth and revered as a hero in Jacinto, was the grandfather of two sister spinsters, Miss Sally and Miss Lottie, who lived across the street from his grandparents in Wharton. Once the ladies of the Historical Society heard this, they welcomed the friend of Colonel Roger's granddaughters and gave Horton and Anthony permission to use the courthouse.[15]

While serving as a location scout, Horton immersed himself in the local life of Tupelo. He enjoyed driving around the countryside with Joseph Anthony and looking at old houses and farms. It reminded him of being a boy and traveling the dirt roads around Wharton with his grandfather to visit the farms he owned. Horton fell in love with the poor people of Mississippi, and wrote Lillian to say that he felt like he was home in Texas, mainly because there were so many farmers around Tupelo that were still producing cotton. "The people are very proud of

---

[14] Anthony, 180.

[15] Horton Foote, *Genesis of an American Playwright*, ed. Marion Castleberry (Waco TX: Baylor University Press, 2004) 84.

their heritage," he wrote. "They are individualists and especially independent."[16]

Besides enjoying the camaraderie that existed between the cast and crew of *Tomorrow* and the community of Tupelo, Horton learned a great deal about low budget filmmaking:

> I learned that film really should be like theatre, in the sense that in theatre, the writer is, of course very dominant to be quite frank. I mean we are sought after. We are at the rehearsals. If we don't like something, we speak our minds. We help with the casting. It is always a collaborative effort, and I am not one who believes in antagonism with the director— that it's the writer against the producer—I really think that it should be an enormous cooperation with everybody to achieve a final work of art.[17]

As gratifying as *Tomorrow* was for Horton, there were some disappointments. The writer discovered that an independent production doesn't always guarantee artistic autonomy for the writer; the power still lies in the hands of the editor. The editing process for *Tomorrow* proved to be slow and tedious. After shooting in Mississippi for six and a half weeks, there was more than four hours of rough footage to be edited, and Joseph Anthony worked for eighteen weeks with editor Reva Schlesinger to pare the material down to a manageable hour and a half. Paul Roebling explained: "Whole chunks had to simply come out of the film and that left us still with four hours. We got it down to two hours and we still knew it was too long. We always felt that as good as the film was what was going on was too fragile to hold an audience's attention for that length of time."[18]

Unfortunately, some of the most powerful moments in Horton's screenplay were left on the editing room floor. There were several scenes about Sarah's background that were cut, along with a sequence with Fentry coming back from Sarah's grave and revisiting the site where he was going to build their house. The most moving of the scenes cut was one in which Fentry encounters the adult Buck Thorpe. Horton admitted he was never able to satisfactorily dramatize on film what happened when Fentry decided to see for himself the evolution of the man who had once been his son. In all three versions "we attempted this meeting

---

[16] Horton Foote to Lillian Foote," 6 February 1970 (Horton Foote Papers).

[17] Gary Edgerton, "A Visit to the Imaginary Landscape of Harrison, Texas: Sketching the Film Career of Horton Foote," *Literature/Film Quarterly* 12 (Winter 1989): 7.

[18] Reba Schlesinger, "Editing a Loved One," in *Tomorrow & Tomorrow*, 181–84.

of Fentry and Buck," he explained. "I think it was most effective in the theatre. There was something immediate and quite wonderful about the meeting of the two in the scene that occurred in the play version. In the screen version, the scene was shot but eventually cut."[19]

Joseph Anthony's decision to leave out the scene angered Robert Duvall, who felt that this was his best work and believed the scene was crucial to the story. "I didn't see the final print of *Tomorrow* before it was shown," Duvall recalls. "In fact, I didn't see the film until a year or so after I finished working on it. It turned out to be a good film, even a great film, but it was inferior to what it should have been. I have to say I was stunned when I saw it. They had cut out the scenes I did with the boy after he grew up. In my opinion, the audience had to see Fentry see the boy grow up, and then Fentry's decision not to acquit the man who killed the boy would have more meaning, make more sense."[20]

Reva Schlesinger admitted that the ending of the film was created in the cutting room as an alternative to the original scene:

> Joe Anthony had shot material for an ending with Fentry and the grown-up boy, Buck. We used local people for a lot of the parts, like the preacher, who turned out to be simply marvelous. But the boy he chose for Buck just didn't have it; it came out so poor in comparison with the quality of everything else, we couldn't use it. So we had to go with another ending. But I didn't do it myself. We all sat down and faced the problem together. There was no money the way there usually is in Hollywood. We couldn't say, 'Well, we'll just go out and shoot what we need. Would it be great if we had this or that?' We had to go with what we had, and so cooperatively we tried things, talked about things, and finally agreed on what we could do and we went ahead with it.[21]

While the editing was a source of frustration for Horton and Duvall, the film's lack of box office appeal was even more troubling. Despite favorable notices from critics like Rex Reed, who wrote that *Tomorrow* "stands majestically among the best American art films," the movie did not receive a positive response from audiences.[22] When it opened in 1972, *New York Times* critic Vincent Canby denounced the film for not supplying a cinematic equivalent to the distancing device provided by

---

[19] Foote, *Genesis*, 175.

[20] Robert Duvall, "You Must Draw From Within Yourself," in *Tomorrow & Tomorrow*, 172–75.

[21] Schlesinger, 185.

[22] Foote, *Tomorrow & Tomorrow*, 23.

Faulkner via the multiple narrators of the story, and he criticized the slow pace of the movie.[23] Largely because of Canby's review, *Tomorrow* was a flop at the box office and did not receive the kind of distribution it deserved, much to the dismay of Roebling and Pearlman, who could not raise enough money to market the film properly. After a few scattered play dates around the country, *Tomorrow* sank into obscurity for more than ten years. Fortunately, after Horton and Duvall both won Oscars for *Tender Mercies* in 1983 the film resurfaced in a second release in major cities across the country. Sheila Benson, film critic for the *Los Angeles Times*, boosted the film's resurgence when she reviewed *Tender Mercies* and mentioned the earlier *Tomorrow*. "Never has a performance been so fiercely championed and so little seen by the movie going public," Benson stated. And she called Duvall's portrayals of Mac Sledge, the down and out country singer, and Jackson Fentry, the Mississippi dirt farmer, works of "great simplicity, dignity, and insight."[24] The film found an even wider audience in 1984, when it was telecast for the first time on PBS.

Without question, *Tomorrow* is a powerful film that is fundamentally true to its source yet heightens the integrity of the original work and strengthens its dynamics by the rearrangement of some incidents, the cutting of others, and the development of characters—Sarah Eubanks in particular. The film pares down the plot to the essentials, while it keeps and enhances the detail and atmosphere of the short story's locations simply by photographing them. The film also does something else; it places life on the screen, and life becomes automatically fascinating for having been framed. Thus, by attracting our interest in the protagonist, Jackson Fentry, it confers a tragic importance on a lowly cotton farmer to whom we wouldn't normally give a second thought in real life. Although Horton Foote did not necessarily set out to create a tragic character, the fact of Fentry's love and heroic endurance is undeniable. *Tomorrow* moves us because it evokes universal truths about the human condition and, in so doing, brings beauty, harmony, meaning, and hope to the lowly and invincible of the earth. Because the makers of the film had the courage not to ignore Faulkner but to tap into his literary power and tragic vision, *Tomorrow* is rightly considered the best screen adaptation of a Faulkner work ever made.

---

[23] Ibid., 22.

[24] Sheila Benson, "Robert Duvall's Vein of Troubled Loneliness," *Los Angeles Times*, 6 March 1983, 21.

Although *Tomorrow* was a rewarding experience for Horton, after three months in Mississippi he sorely missed his family and wanted to return home to New Hampshire. He felt bad that his work had taken him away from home so much during the children's formative years, and he knew that Lillian needed his assistance in caring for the children and in the day-to-day operations of their home.

During their early years in New Hampshire, Horton and Lillian often discussed in their letters to each other a number of domestic concerns—the cost of renovating their home, their dwindling budget, and above all their worries about rearing their four children in the troubled decade of the seventies. When the family relocated to New Hampshire in 1966, the Footes' youngest daughter Daisy was five years old, Walter was eleven, Horton Jr. was fourteen, and Barbara Hallie, the eldest daughter, was sixteen and entering her junior year in high school. From the beginning, Barbara Hallie made it clear that she was not pleased with her father's decision to uproot the family and leave suburban Nyack for the woods of New Boston. She felt displaced in her new environment. "Moving was fine for them. It was hell for me," she recalls. "I had to leave my senior year in Nyack, New York, and say goodbye to my friends and become a stranger. Everybody else in the family liked New Hampshire."[25] In a moment of frustration, Barbara Hallie screamed at her father, "I just want you to know that you've ruined my entire life." Shaken by his daughter's outburst, Foote pleaded, "Please give me a chance," and then tried to assure her that everything would work out fine. Barbara Hallie remembers that this was the first time she had ever seen her father cry.[26] Early on, Barbara Hallie acted out against her mother and father by letting her schoolwork slide, but after a few months, she began to flourish in school and to feel secure in her new surroundings. She immersed herself in the small-town culture, made a score of new friends, and emerged as a happy, confident young woman.

Barbara Hallie graduated from Goffstown High School in the spring of 1968, and left home to attend college at the University of New Hampshire, where she met Jeff MacCleave, whom she later married in July 1972. After their wedding, Barbara Hallie and Jeff moved to Boston, where she took a job in a public relations firm. Even though the job was a lucrative one, she wasn't happy with the work, and she began to feel out

---

[25] Hallie Foote, interview by Marion Castleberry, 10 October 2002, New York.
[26] Rebecca Luttrell Briley, *You Can Go Home Again* (New York: American University Studies 1993) 139.

of place and restless at the firm. Following a period of personal reflection, she realized that her real passion was for acting, and while she had previously rejected the notion of a theatrical career—perhaps as an act of silent rebellion against her parents—she nonetheless sought out her father's help in pursuing a career in the theater. Horton felt that his daughter needed to study the craft of acting with a reputable teacher. He had heard great things from Dan Petrie and Lucy Kroll about an instructor named Peggy Feury, who ran the Loft Studio in Los Angeles with her husband Bill Traylor, and he suggested that Barbara Hallie get in touch with her. Echoing his own father's words from forty years earlier, Horton told his daughter that if she really wanted to attend acting school in California, he would pay her tuition. After speaking with Peggy Feury, Barbara Hallie was even more certain that her decision to become an actress was the right one, and she began making plans to move to Los Angeles. Even though Jeff was not enthusiastic about his wife's aspirations, he agreed to accompany her.

The couple arrived in California during the summer of 1974. From the beginning, Barbara Hallie found her studies with Peggy Feury exhilarating. She took acting classes four days a week, and she was able to earn her Screen Actors Guild card after landing a couple of small roles in two low-budget films. Horton wrote to Joseph Anthony that Barbara Hallie was very happy there, but, unfortunately, within the year her marriage to Jeff started to come apart. The couple's breakup was fueled by Jeff's lack of support for his wife and exacerbated by their financial problems. To make ends meet, Barbara Hallie worked as a temporary employee for several businesses: a Beverly Hills clothing store, a typing agency, and an insurance company. She approached each job with a sense of gratitude, believing that all the hard work would pay off one day, but Jeff seemed unable to settle into the fast-paced world of California or to find a job that gratified him. He tried working at a meat company, a Harley-Davidson dealership, and even considered opening up his own motorcycle repair shop, but none of these jobs lasted more than a few weeks. Horton and Lillian were concerned about Jeff's inability to find work, and throughout the ordeal they sent money to support their daughter and son-in-law. Horton confided to Joseph Anthony that Barbara Hallie and Jeff were:

> ...having a mixed experience—partly satisfying and partly not.... The difficult part is that Jeff is having trouble finding a job he likes, or a job of any kind really—and although he has the promise of two they are still

promises and their savings are evaporating rapidly, as savings have a way of doing. Barbara Hallie has lined up a waitress job four nights a week in a restaurant she found out about from a student at school, so I'm sure they will find a way to manage. But I think the greatest hurdle is that Jeff is extremely disappointed in California. I don't know what he expected but not smog, dampness, and not much sunshine. I think young people build up such a fantasy about the place.[27]

Jeff took classes at UCLA in an effort to better his situation, but after only a couple of semesters he quit his classes and announced to Barbara Hallie that he was going to start a construction business. At this point, divorce seemed inevitable, especially after Jeff began to avoid Barbara Hallie and hang out with a group of undesirable and dangerous motorcycle bikers. By the end of the year, Barbara Hallie and Jeff had dissolved their relationship, and in the spring of 1975, they applied for a divorce.

Throughout the ordeal, Horton and Lillian remained encouraging and sensitive to their daughter's feelings. They recognized Barbara Hallie's artistic talent and trusted that she would make her way in her chosen profession. "We are blessed in that child," Horton said of Barbara Hallie, "as we are in all of our children, mainly I think because for some reason we have made them feel they are the most important thing to us, as I guess they really are. I think we instinctively think of them, even before we think of ourselves, and I'm sure they know that."[28]

Through it all, Horton and Lillian supported their daughter. Barbara Hallie continued to excel in her studies with Peggy Feury, and Horton would sometimes attend her classes when he was in California on business. In her letters to her parents, Barbara Hallie always expressed her love and appreciation for their help and encouragement, and many times she spoke of her reverence for her father's writing. Horton's trust in his daughter would eventually pay huge dividends as Barbara Hallie would emerge as a respected actress of American theater and the preeminent interpreter of her father's work. In 1994, Barbara Hallie married Devon Abner, a young actor from California. Each of them has had rewarding acting careers while also promoting Horton Foote's legacy.

Barbara Hallie's younger brother, Horton Jr., who was in the ninth grade when his family moved to New Boston, also found the adjustment

---

[27] Horton Foote to Joseph Anthony, 30 September 1974 (Horton Foote Papers).

[28] Horton Foote to Lillian Foote, 27 February 1970 (Horton Foote Papers).

from suburban Nyack to small-town New Hampshire very challenging. For one thing, he was not a great student, and he chose to act out against his parents by playing the rebel in school. Horton and Lillian were very concerned when his grades began to plummet shortly after moving to New Hampshire. Horton was in California working on *The Stalking Moon* when one day he received a letter from Lillian, who was terribly upset about Horton Jr.'s poor showing in school. At Lillian's request, Horton wrote his son, in part to inspire him and in part to request that Horton Jr. mail his English homework to California so that he could examine his work. His letter must have motivated the boy to some extent because a few weeks later, Horton wrote to say that he was generally pleased by Horton Jr.'s improvement in grades and conduct but that a D in math was simply not good enough. Although Horton and Lillian tried to motivate their son to become a better student, the truth was that Horton Jr. would never be a great scholar. And even though he loved playing baseball and soccer, he was not a gifted athlete like his younger brother Walter.

Horton tried to appease his displaced children, especially Horton Jr. and Walter, by showing an interest in sports. His letters to the children are brimming with thoughts on basketball and soccer and questions about the children's competitions. Horton Jr. remembers that "even though as a child [my father] was more interested in movie stars than baseball scores, he and my mom went to almost all of my brother Walter's basketball games and my soccer matches. When Daisy began jumping horses, she soon had a horse, and my mother and I would travel to all of her events. If my brother and I would invite him to watch a Red Sox or a Celtic game with us, he would always decline saying, 'I can't. I just get too nervous.' Actually he would rather have been reading poetry or taking a ride with my mother, but he didn't want us to think that."[29]

Horton Jr.'s schoolwork was average at best, but he managed to enroll at Plymouth College after graduating from Goffstown High School. Apparently, he carried his rebelliousness with him to college, and after two months of not attending classes or applying himself to his studies, he dropped out. Since this was the height of the Vietnam War, one type of deferment from the war was based upon a young man being enrolled in a college or university, and Horton Jr. suddenly found that he

---

[29] Horton Foote, Jr., "Memorial Essay," *Farewell: Remembering Horton Foote, 1916–2009*, ed. Marion Castleberry and Susan Christensen (Dallas TX: Southern Methodist University Press, 2011) 3-4.

was eligible for the draft. Horton and Lillian were concerned their son would be sent to the battlefields of Southeast Asia, especially after his notice arrived with an extremely low draft number. In an attempt to keep him from being sent to Vietnam, Lillian and Horton advised Horton Jr. to enlist in the Army rather than wait to be drafted. The Army recruiter promised that if he would sign up for three years, instead of the usual two, he would be sent to Germany or France. In the spring of 1972, Lillian wrote to her husband that Horton Jr. had "passed the physical in A-1 condition" and would leave for training at "Fort Dix on April 26 or 28."[30]

Horton was away from home filming *Tomorrow* when Horton Jr. left for boot camp on the morning of April 26, but Lillian wrote to him that afternoon, describing their son's departure. "It was difficult to watch him walk up those steps and through that door," Lillian said, "I felt a part of my life had passed by, but I do feel it can be a positive experience for him. Evidently, the sergeant had put him in charge of his unit for the trip and I think that made him feel good. And he's a friendly, warm fellow and he'll get along fine."[31] Horton responded by saying:

> Your letter about Horton's leaving arrived as I left the hotel to meet Alan Pakula for breakfast. I began to read it as he came driving up in a taxi and I took one look at him after just having read your description of having said farewell to Horton, and I started to bawl like a baby. Fortunately we were already in a taxi and he is such a sympathetic fellow, he began to cry too. It was quite a scene. I was glad really to have been with him at that time, and I am glad that Horton's leaving was so harmonious. He's a wonderful lad and I know he's on his way to a marvelous life.[32]

Following boot camp, Horton Jr. was sent to Germany as promised, where he spent three years as a military policeman. Following his tour of duty in Germany, he joined Barbara Hallie in California, where he studied acting for a time with Bill Traylor at the Loft Studio. After moving back to New York in the 1980s, Horton Jr. began to supplement his income as an actor with the profits he made as the owner of a popular restaurant, Tavern on Jane, in Manhattan. He continues to prosper as an actor and businessman.

The youngest of the Foote children, Walter and Daisy, took their family's move to New Hampshire much easier than their older siblings.

---

[30] Lillian Foote to Horton Foote, 2 April 1972 (Horton Foote Papers).
[31] Lillian Foote to Horton Foote, 26 April 1972 (Horton Foote Papers).
[32] Horton Foote to Lillian Foote, 30 April 1972 (Horton Foote Papers).

Walter was eleven years old when the family relocated, but he was tall for his age and had a real passion for athletics. Horton and Lillian supported Walter's dream of becoming a basketball player. "I too once had a calling," Walter remembers:

> In 5th grade, at the age of ten, my friends and I organized our own basketball team. The school was poor and could not afford uniforms. Dad came to the rescue, buying us all tank top t-shirts, gym shorts, and red numbers that we each ironed onto our jersey. We only played two games that season, but that was all it took to get me hooked. My Dad nourished my dream in any way he could. He could not teach me how to shoot or dribble, but he would build a court for me to practice on. He would send me to basketball camp to learn from those who could teach me well. While my Dad read Pound, Eliot, O'Conner, and Cather, I studied Red Auerbach, Sam Jones, Satch Sanders, and Don Nelson. I tried to perfect a jump shot, within a stone's throw away from where my father wrote *The Orphans' Home Cycle*.[33]

Walter's enthusiasm for basketball grew over the years, and he honed his skills in high school and at summer camps. After graduation he accepted an athletic scholarship to nearby Springfield College. Although Walter excelled at school, both as a student and an athlete, he questioned his future and wondered whether he should pursue basketball as a profession. As a freshman in college, Walter wrote to his father expressing his insecurities about Springfield, and Horton responded with a letter that speaks volumes about the way in which he taught his children important spiritual values:

> Whatever you finally decide about Springfield, you know that we are with you, because we know it will be a good and correct decision. It seemed right at the time to go there, but we won't let false pride or human will keep us there. But remember the doubt about being in your right place will in some measure assail every freshman.... Mom and I can always help when you are as honest as you were in your letter. And never feel you haven't done enough, or are not a good enough [Christian Scientist]. You have a full, busy day. You are very active in many ways. God is supporting you in all your activities. You don't have to sit around and think about the sun in order to get the benefit of the sunshine, its light, heat, beauty. No, you just have to open the blinds and let it in. The sunshine takes you over and to get rid of darkness, you don't have to chase it away. All you have to do is turn on the light switch and the

---

[33] Walter Foote, Speech delivered at the Horton Foote Memorial, 11 May 2009.

darkness vanishes. So it is with our lives. Don't struggle with the problem—turn on the light switch (the right idea) that dispels the problem.[34]

Soon after Horton wrote this letter, a knee injury ended Walter's basketball career, and he transferred to the University of Texas, where he received his Bachelor of Arts degree in history. Later, he received his Juris Doctor degree from the University of Pennsylvania Law School and joined a corporate real estate firm in New York. Even though Walter chose a more business-oriented career path than his brother and sisters, he always surrounded himself with creative people, and later, he would complete an intensive Film Workshop at New York University, where he wrote, directed, and produced two films, *Atonement* and *The Tavern*. In 1984, Walter married Lin Tien, who gave birth to two children: Tyler Clinton, born 1 May 1993 and Lillian, born 8 June 1995. Walter and Lin's marriage ended in divorce in 2001, and in 2003 Walter married Diana Buglewicz, a young actress from Williamsburg, Colorado. Together Walter, Diane, Tyler, and Lillian built a happy life in Scarsdale, New York. Tyler currently attends Princeton University on a baseball scholarship and Lillian is following in her grandfather's footsteps, studying creative writing at Yale University.

Daisy, the youngest child, was a bright-eyed five-year old when her family moved to New Hampshire. Initially, small-town life seemed strange to Daisy, but New Hampshire eventually worked its way into her heart. While Walter spent much of his time on the basketball court, Daisy's passion followed a different path. Shortly after the move, Daisy was outside playing when a woman rode by on a horse. She stopped, introduced herself, and announced that she was going to be teaching horseback riding. Daisy begged her parents to let her take lessons, and they quickly obliged. They bought her a pony, and once she proved that she could care for the animal, her father bought her a registered quarter horse. Horton and Lillian took her to equestrian events, where she competed with other young riders. Although the addition of a horse to the family meant boarding costs, Horton never complained or questioned the purchase; instead, he supported Daisy's endeavors in every way he could. Daisy recalls their relationship as special:

As a child I can remember riding my horse up our dirt road and seeing my father driving from the opposite direction, our dog Clarence sitting

---

[34] Horton Foote to Walter Foote, 27 September 1974 (Horton Foote Papers).

shotgun. My father's hands would be going a mile a minute, his lips moving. I knew he couldn't see me, so I'd pull my horse over to the side and pray he didn't meet any other drivers on the way. I'd often tease him later: "Who were you talking to Daddy? Did you and Clarence have a nice conversation?" He'd laugh and say, "I was working on a play, honey, and I got so much done."[35]

While Daisy loved horseback riding, she also inherited her father's fascination with storytelling and love of theater. Always an attractive and affable girl, she was cast as the lead in several high school plays. Her mother, in a letter to legendary actress Lillian Gish, wrote, "Daisy is bit by the acting bug. She says she doesn't want to go away to college but go to a theatre school—Horton and I'll just bide our time and see what develops"[36]

As a child, Daisy never had a clear idea of what her father did for a living. She knew he was a writer, but she didn't know what that meant except that he was away from home a lot working on a film or a play. Barbara Hallie remembers that "people in town thought Dad was a crazy rich New Yorker who'd stay up all night writing and then walk out on our dirt road wearing his pajamas, figuring out his plays. People thought he must be an alcoholic. My sister Daisy would say, 'Daddy, put on some clothes.'"[37] Daisy's most vivid memory of her father at work was after he finished the third play of The Orphans' Home Cycle—Convicts. "It was winter," Daisy recalls, "a snowstorm was raging outside our remote farmhouse. And that night my mother and I sat by a woodstove as Dad read his play to us. That night I started to understand and admire what my father did. He was no longer just a dad but also a playwright with this amazing gift for telling a story."[38]

Following graduation from Goffstown High School, Daisy decided to follow her father's lead and become a writer. Her parents felt that a basic knowledge of American literature and history would benefit her writing, so they enrolled her at Dickinson College in Pennsylvania, where she pursued a liberal arts degree in American studies. She entered school a serious-minded student, determined to improve her writing and learn as much as she could, but apparently by her sophomore year her studies

---

[35] Daisy Foote, "Memorial Essay," Farewell: Remembering Horton Foote, 5–6.

[36] Lillian Foote to Lillian Gish, August 1972 (Horton Foote Papers).

[37] John Guare, "My Trip to Bountiful," Farewell: Remembering Horton Foote, 100.

[38] Daisy Foote, "The Pleasure and Pain of Doing Like Dad," New York Times, 23 August 2012.

started to slide when she pledged the Delta Nu sorority and began to date a series of young men, none of who were especially interested in academics. Daisy turned out to be the child who concerned her parents the most. "By her junior year," Wilborn Hampton explains, "Daisy had become such a party girl that, along with some classmates, she decided to stay at school and hang out when the nuclear accident at nearby Three Mile Island was forcing thousands to evacuate their homes. Horton was so concerned that he telephoned the father of Barbara Hallie's former roommate, CBS News anchor Walter Cronkite to ask just how serious the threat of a nuclear meltdown was. Advised there was a real possibility of a disaster that could devastate much of Pennsylvania, Horton finally laid down the law with his daughter. He called Daisy and in no uncertain terms told her: "Young lady, you get in a car and get home this very day!"[39] She immediately returned to New Hampshire.

By her senior year, Daisy had become even more rebellious. Without warning, she wrote her mother to say that she was engaged to one of her professors, medievalist Tom Reed, and that after graduation they were to be married. Horton was stunned and Lillian was so upset she burst into tears. As they had planned, Daisy and Tom married after she graduated from Dickinson College, but almost as quickly as it began, the marriage started to break apart largely because of Reed's lack of encouragement for his wife, who was struggling to find her voice as a writer. By the spring of 1984, Daisy and Tom decided to divorce. Later, in 1997, Daisy married Tim Guinee, a talented young actor from Houston, and together they have built successful careers in the entertainment industry, Daisy as a playwright and Tim as an actor and filmmaker.

Throughout Daisy's struggles, Horton and Lillian remained encouraging and supportive. Horton believed strongly in his daughter's talent and encouraged her to keep writing. He read all of her work, and when she finally wrote her first produced play, *The Villa Capri*, Daisy sent it to her father for his response before allowing anyone else to read it. "Over the next 15 years he would be the first to read a new play of mine," Daisy later said, "He'd call and ask, 'Do you have the time to talk?' He would ask a series of questions. These questions would help me to see that some part of the play wasn't as clear or as strong as it could be. Yes, there were arguments, but he always won. He just had a

[39] Wilborn Hampton, *Horton Foote: America's Storyteller* (New York: Simon & Schuster, 2009) 208–09. My discussion of the Foote children's early lives has been greatly aided by Wilborn Hampton's biography, *Horton Foote: American's Storyteller*.

nose for what was phony, what wouldn't hold…. Who I am as a writer is completely tied to him, Horton Foote, my dad."[40]

Clearly Horton Foote was an exceptional father: kind, gracious, and loving. When he was home, he attended all of his children's activities and supported their dreams in every way he could. Because of his children, Horton became active in the local school, dutifully attended town meetings, and graciously taught Sunday school at the Christian Science church in nearby Manchester, New Hampshire. When he was away on business, he wrote to his children every day with words of encouragement and instruction. He certainly wasn't a perfect father, but his children always felt blessed to have had him as a parent. Horton Jr. expressed it best when he wrote: "Lord knows, as a family we have had our moments. Some good, some not so good and he himself was not perfect. He had a temper, he could be stubborn, he was obsessed about his writing, and an awful swimmer, and I can still hear him call my mother—"Hon, will you come here a second"—when he needed her to fix something around the house. Nonetheless, as a father, and a husband, on a scale of one to ten, I would have to objectively give him a 9.9."[41]

Indeed, an undeniable fact about Horton Foote was that he dearly loved his children and worshipped his wife, Lillian. Horton and Lillian's daily example of a respectful, devoted commitment to each other and their family life gave their children a deep sense of security, self-esteem, and well-being that cast a glow over the Foote children. Lillian's words to her husband best expresses the special relationship they shared: "I realized once more how deeply I do love you. You have been always so good to me, so understanding and appreciative—I only have a keener awareness of that as the years go by. My life with you has been a full and satisfying one—I believe our children are an expression of the trust and love we've shared together these years.[42]

Raising four children certainly contained moments of frustration and doubt for Horton and Lillian, but a more pressing concern for Horton Foote was the failing health of his father, who was suffering from what appeared to be severe dementia caused by what doctors diagnosed as blood clots damaging his brain. On the set of *Tomorrow*, Horton had received letters from his brother John, informing him of his father's lapses in memory and the irrational behavior that was having a dele-

---

[40] Daisy Foote, "The Pleasure and Pain of Doing Like Dad," 23 August 2012.
[41] Horton Foote, Jr., "Untitled Essay," *Farewell: Remembering Horton Foote*, 4.
[42] Lillian Foote to Horton Foote, 15 February 1978 (Horton Foote Papers).

terious effect on his mother. John was driving to Wharton from Houston every weekend, as much to comfort his mother as to care for his father. "Truthfully, I can't see any improvement in Dad," John Speed wrote. "Last Sunday he got mixed up several times with both mother and me." He added that his mother was "starved for someone to talk to."[43] Horton hired a male nurse, Elrese Kendricks, to sit with his father and to give his mother a much-needed break, but she refused to leave her husband's side. As the weeks passed, Albert Horton's condition worsened, and he began to wander from home and get lost for hours. He became more and more disoriented and, over time, was unable to carry on a sensible conversation. "He is completely incompetent of leading a normal life," Horton's cousin Nan wrote.[44]

Horton decided the best thing to do was move his parents to New Hampshire, where he and Lillian could care for them. So, that winter he traveled to Wharton to accompany his mother and father on their two-thousand-mile trip to New Boston. The flight from Houston to New Hampshire was without incident, but as soon as they arrived at Horton's house, his father began acting irrationally, running up and down the stairs like an angry child, screaming that he wanted to go home. The episode broke Horton's heart, and he later admitted that it was the worst night of his life, seeing his father, with whom he had been so close his entire life, behaving as though he were a total stranger. The event also made a lasting impression on the Foote children, who couldn't understand why their grandfather didn't recognize them or why he felt like a prisoner in their home. "It might as well have been Siberia for our Grandfather," Walter recalls, "His sole mission during his stay there was to somehow find a way to get back home. 'Son, when's the next train to Wharton? I've got to get on that train.' He would offer us money, cigars, and whatever other currency was available to him if he could just get on that train to Wharton."[45]

In an attempt to restore some sense of normalcy to the home, Horton had an apartment built for his parents above the garage, but Pap-Pap, as the children called their grandfather, continued to find a way to escape his imagined prison every chance he got. Walter remembers that many mornings when he and Horton Jr. would come down for breakfast, they would find their grandfather dressed and standing at their front door—

[43] John Speed Foote to Horton Foote, October 1972 (Horton Foote Papers).

[44] Nan Outlar to Horton Foote, 7 November 1972 (Horton Foote Papers).

[45] Walter Foote, "Speech."

eager to open his store in Wharton. During his entire stay in New Hampshire, Albert Horton seldom recognized anyone except his wife, Hallie, and as time passed, he began to have difficulty even remembering her. As his condition worsened, Horton's mother decided to take Albert Horton back home to Wharton. Initially, Horton rejected the idea, but at his mother's bidding he reluctantly agreed to let them return. He knew deep down there was nothing he could do to help his father's condition or to lighten his mother's burden. The following spring Horton flew to Wharton to visit his father, and although Albert Horton didn't recognize his son, he looked up from his bed, smiled, and said, "You have a nice face."[46] This was the last time Horton communicated with his father, who died 23 March 1973 and was buried in the town cemetery a few days later.

Following her husband's death, Horton's mother became severely depressed. In an effort to lighten his mother's grief, Horton arranged for her to take a trip to California to visit relatives, and while in Los Angeles she saw a production of his musical *Gone With the Wind*. But the trip did not seem to help her mood, and when she returned to Wharton, she became very despondent and seemed to lose her will to live. Horton later recalled how his father's memory loss and subsequent death caused great strife for his mother during her last two years of life.

> That was hard because my father had always been so responsive to my mother, always. My mother had such strength but after my father died she experienced an enormous sense of loss. They had always been so close. Our cook Catherine Davis, a black woman who had been with my family many years, told me later that my mother would often say to her, "I don't know what I'm going to do. He comes to me all the time and says you have to come on. I just can't make it without you." Just before her death she picked out her dress to be buried in and I have always felt that she willed her death.[47]

Hoping that he might rekindle his mother's passion for life, Horton had Lillian fly to Wharton and bring her back to New Hampshire. But less than a year after his father died, Horton's mother passed away on 19 February 1974. Heartbroken, Horton took her body back to Wharton for the funeral and buried her next to his father.

Horton was devastated by the loss of his parents. Within a year he had lost the two strongest connections to his past. After the death of his

---

[46] Hampton, 172.

[47] Horton Foote, interview by Marion Castleberry, 18 March 1988, Wharton, Texas.

mother, Horton stayed in Wharton for a couple of weeks sorting through personal papers and making decisions about what to do with his parents' belongings. The house in which he was raised was now empty, and Horton began to think about the life of his parents, who had lived in the home for fifty-nine years. Working through his grief and trying to understand his parents' legacy, Horton was compelled to write *The Orphans' Home Cycle*, his remarkable nine-play masterpiece that dramatizes the lives of his mother and father and the town that surrounded them during the early years of the twentieth century.

13

The Orphans' Home Cycle: 1974–77

When Horton Foote returned to New Hampshire, he discovered that New England was experiencing a harsh winter and a severe fuel shortage. He and his family kept warm by using their fireplaces and wood stoves, and, as Horton recalled, "Because I have never been a fan of snow, I stayed in the house a great deal, going through letters and photographs I had brought back from Texas and thinking of my mother and father"[1] Horton spent several weeks peering over old family photographs and reading personal letters his mother and father had written each other. There were photographs of his Grandfather and Grandmother Brooks, his brothers, and his extended family, including many aunts and uncles, some of whom he had never met. The letters Horton's parents had written were equally meaningful. They characterized some of the most private and significant moments in the couple's lives: their courtship and elopement, the birth of their children, the hardship they endured during the Depression, and the pain they felt over the death of their son, Tom Brooks. The letters also contained intimate expressions of their love for each other and the heartache Horton's father felt his entire life from having been abandoned by his mother after his father's death. Horton's parents had lived through times of great adversity, yet they had faced their hardships with dignity, courage, and without protest or complaint. They had set an example that would forever inform Horton's life and writing.

Reading his parents' letters over and over, Horton started making notes for what would become a series of plays based on the lives of his mother and father in Gulf Coast Texas during the early years of the twentieth century. He began writing the story of his family in the winter of 1974, and less than three years later he had completed drafts of nine plays—*Roots in a Parched Ground, Convicts, Lily Dale, Courtship, The Widow Claire, Valentine's Day, 1918, Cousins,* and *The Death of Papa.* "I wrote the cycle plays without knowing whether they'd ever be staged, Horton

---

[1] Horton Foote, *Genesis of an American Playwright*, ed. Marion Castleberry (Waco TX: Baylor University Press, 2004) 117.

recalled: "I just became obsessed with them."[2] Horton called his cycle *The Orphans' Home*, a title taken from a phrase in Marianne Moore's poem "In Distrust of Merits," because, as he explained, the metaphor seemed very apt for this young man, one who is, in a sense, looking for a home and for roots, one who always felt like an orphan and who always felt abandoned by his mother: "The world's an orphans' home/ Shall we never have peace without sorrow?/ without pleas of the dying for help that won't come/ O quiet form upon the dust, I cannot look but must."[3]

Each of the plays in the cycle is self-contained, but together they form a larger saga that tells the story of Horace Robedaux from age twelve when his father dies and he is abandoned by his mother, and continuing until he becomes a husband and a father himself at age twenty-seven. The cycle ends with *The Death of Papa*, a play in which Horace's nine-year-old son Horace Robedaux, Jr., (the playwright's fictional counterpart) experiences the death of his grandfather, an event that forever changes the destiny of his family.

The Orphans' Home Cycle is not only a vivid portrait of a young man's search for a family and home but also an evocative and imaginative record of a time and place that has largely vanished from the American consciousness. Set in the Texas Gulf Coast town of Harrison, the plays form a moral and social history, covering the years 1902 to 1928, a period that saw the decline of the cotton plantation aristocracy after the Civil War, the emergence of a mercantile and oil-based economy, the transition from rural to urban life, and the tragedies of World War I and the Spanish influenza epidemic of 1918. As in Faulkner's Yoknapatawpha saga, Horton's cycle extends beyond the story of the Robedaux family and Harrison, Texas, to the entire South, and, finally, to all America. Horton acknowledged that the cycle depicts a time of far-reaching social and economic change:

> The aftermath of Reconstruction and its passions have brought about a white man's union to prevent blacks from voting in local and state elections. But in spite of political and social acts to hold onto the past, a way of life was over; and the practical, the pragmatic were scrambling to form a new economic order. Black men and women were alive who knew the agony of slavery, and white men and women were alive who owned

---

[2] Horton Foote, interview by Marion Castleberry, 18 March 1988, Wharton, Texas.
[3] Marianne Moore, "In Distrust of Merits," *The Complete Works of Marianne Moore* (New York: MacMillan-Viking Press, 1956) 173–74.

them.... And so with the 1918 influenza epidemic, which causes such havoc in the play *1918*.[4]

While writing the plays, Horton listened continually to the musical recordings of modernist composer Charles Ives, whose compositions of Americana music he had purchased on a trip to New York. The playwright had always been inspired by music and dance, but in *The Orphans' Home Cycle*, he achieved an almost seamless synthesis of music, dance, and language. Horton later testified to how profoundly he was influenced by Ives's work. "I would listen over and over to the music," he explained in an interview with Crystal Brian. "I got to know the symphonies, the songs, the sonatas, the concertos, the piano pieces—all of it intimately."[5]

In her groundbreaking book, *Orphans' Home: The Voice and Vision of Horton Foote*, Laurin Porter describes the parallels between Ives's use of "found music," blending fragments of hymns, spirituals, folk songs, and popular tunes to create his own musical pieces, with Horton Foote's blending of various stories and voices as well as popular melodies, chain gang songs, old Negro spirituals, and country tunes to construct his plays.[6] Horton uses "found" materials throughout the nine plays as characters sing hymns, the sound of dance music drifts from one room to another, and characters listen to a Mexican band from across town or to the church pianist practicing next door. Horton explained that in writing *1918*, the first of the cycle plays to be written, he tried to pull off an "Ivesian experiment":

> I wanted several times during the play to have a collection of sounds— music being played in a room where a scene was being played, simultaneous music coming from the house next door, and music playing down the street....
>
> In the other plays, I used music much more conventionally to help define the period of the plays and to create certain moods. In *Roots in a Parched Ground*, I used songs of the day to establish the life of the Thornton family. In *Convicts*, I used the songs "Ain't No Cane on the Brazos," "Rock Island Line," and "Golden Slippers." The first two are

---

[4] Horton Foote, Introduction to *The Orphans' Home Cycle* (New York: Grove Press, 1989) 2.

[5] Crystal Brian, "Be Quite and Listen: The Orphans' Home Cycle and the Music of Charles Ives," in *Horton Foote: A Casebook*, ed. Gerald C. Wood (New York: Garland Press, 1998) 91.

[6] Laurin Porter, *Orphans' Home: The Voice and Vision of Horton Foote* (Baton Rouge: Louisiana State University Press, 2003).

heard offstage and are sung by the convicts as they work. "Golden Slippers" is sung by a convict at the burial of Soll, the owner of the plantation who has forbidden any hymns to be sung at his funeral. The great folk singer Leadbelly told me many years ago that he sang "Rock Island Line" while he was working on a Texas prison farm. In *Lily Dale*, I used the song "Lily Dale" not only atmospherically, but also to advance the plot. In *The Widow Claire*, the song "Waltz Me Around Again, Willie" is used as part of the story.... In *Courtship*, Elizabeth and Laura Vaughn are forbidden by their father to dance or to go to dances, although we learn in the course of the play that they have both learned to dance from girlfriends. Additionally, throughout most of the play, the girls can hear dance music in the distance and imaginary dancers waltz in and out. In *Valentine's Day*, Elizabeth and Horace sing to each other and the spinster boarder can be heard practicing a song, which she is about to sing at a local public event. In the last plays, *Cousins* and *The Death of Papa*, music disappears, although in *Cousins* an older Lily Dale is involved with composing and finding a publisher for her songs.[7]

Each of the cycle's nine plays has its own distinct mood and style, with its own musical sensibility, but when performed together as a whole they form a complete symphony revolving around multiple variations on a central theme—the search for family and home. "The pattern as I see it," Horton admitted, "is the search of the dispossessed Horace, the homeless, seeking and finding a home. For me, the writer, I think the task is the old reoccurring one I always seem to set myself—to find a sense of order in disorder, a shape to chaos."[8] Horton's use of "found music" ties the story to a specific time and place while at the same time infusing the work with universal resonance, inviting the audience to make its own connection to family and home through its associations with familiar sounds and melodies. In writing *The Orphans' Home Cycle*, Horton was true to his own sense of home:

> I remember, as a boy, sitting on my porch at night, or on the gallery, and down in the flats I could hear black music, or once in a while in the distance you could hear a little Mexican band, or I could hear a child practicing, or Sunday nights you could hear a choir in the distance. So it was part of it, part of life. All you know now is that inevitable radio or

---

[7] Foote, *Genesis*, 129–30.
[8] Ibid., 120.

television, but it's not only the music, it's also the sounds. And, particularly, in small towns, I think you're very conscious of it.[9]

In reference to the unique structure and language of the cycle that "is pruned and shaped but not visibly transformed," Reynolds Price proclaims that Horton Foote is "unquestionably the supreme musician among our great American playwrights. More even than with Tennessee Williams, Foote's method (and his dilemma) is that of the composer. His words are black notes on a white page—all abstract signals to the minds of actor and audience, signs in which all participants in the effort...must make their own musical entity."[10]

In addition to employing a musical construction, Horton avoided most of the established literary conventions employed by most contemporary dramatists: stage directions with a precise description of setting and personae, complicated plot lines, well-prepared climaxes, withheld information and the building of suspense, and heightened language. Laurin Porter explains that Horton "recasts dramatic form to achieve his ends in unique ways. Both in his structuring of the cycle as a whole and within individual plays, he employs devices that are more commonly associated with the novel than drama: recurring motifs, character doubling and tripling, parallel and inverted episodes, even the pairing of entire plays. In this interplay of character and image, of play against play, he breaks new ground, bending drama, that, most restrictive of genres, in new and striking ways."[11] Eschewing traditional dramatic form, Horton Foote, much like Chekhov, spreads out his canvas for our contemplation, not seeking to win over our sympathies for individual characters but instead showing us a spectacle of the human condition as he envisions it. He allows his audience to explore with him the good, the bad, the sinner, and the divine in all of us without condemnation or sentimentality.

Through its unique structure, *The Orphans' Home Cycle* tells a moving and poignant story that gains momentum and complexity as it unfolds. Horton depicts three generations of three families (those of Horace's mother, his father, and his wife Elizabeth), and he tells the stories of other citizens of Harrison, whose lives converge and collide with Horace's. Throughout the cycle, the Robedauxs, Thorntons, and Vaughns are faced with death, betrayal, dislocation, sibling rivalries, elopements,

---

[9] Brian, 91.

[10] Reynolds Price, Introduction to *The Orphans' Home Cycle*, 6.

[11] Porter, *Voice and Vision*, 18.

estrangements, reconciliations, and all the other minutiae of family life specific to coastal southeast Texas during the early years of the twentieth century. The plays are filled with quiet exchanges between people who desperately want to understand their plights but who are constantly confronted with loss and suffering over which they have no control. Horton's principal thematic concern in the cycle is with the courage to face inevitable change, a subject not confined by place or time but bursting with universal significance. These plays are about "change," Horton explained, "unexpected, unasked for, unwanted, but to be faced and dealt with or else we sink into despair or a hopeless longing for a life that is gone."[12]

The process of change in *The Orphans' Home* actually begins with the cycle's first play, *Roots in A Parched Ground*, as Horace Robedaux, the fictive re-incarnation of Horton Foote's father, must face the separation of his parents and the death of his father. *Roots in a Parched Ground,* is a reshaping of Horton's teleplay *The Night of the Storm,* which was first broadcast by CBS on the *DuPont Show of the Month* on 21 March 1961. The teleplay, set in 1890 in the town of Harrison, opens to reveal the boarding house that Horace's mother, Julia, operates to support her family. When Horace discovers that Julia, who is estranged from her alcoholic husband, is planning to move to Houston to find work, Horace runs away from home, confiding in his sister, "I'm going to hide out until Daddy gets well and then I'm going to live with him. I'll work in the store and I'll read law and when I get grown, we'll practice law together."[13] When Horace cannot be found during the night of the storm, his mother moves to Houston, leaving her son to make his own way in the world. That evening, Horace's father dies, and soon after his mother marries an insensitive man who refuses to accept the boy into his family. Horace, abandoned and orphaned, longs to be reunited with his family, but he is finally left to face his ominous future alone. As the play ends, Horace is left with nothing but his father's books and the gentle guidance of his father's best friend, Jim Howard, who has promised to teach him law.

Horton extensively revised the original story of *Roots in a Parched Ground* because it did not fit into the cycle as it was unfolding. "I had made the mother of Horace in the first version of the play a much more sentimental woman than I now believed her to be," Horton explained,

---

[12] Foote, Introduction to *The Orphans' Home Cycle*, 2.
[13] Foote, *Roots in a Parched Ground* (New York: Dramatists Play Service 1962) 30.

"so there was nothing to do but completely rewrite the play."[14] In *The Night of the Storm,* Horace's mother, Julia, is clearly more sympathetic than her counterpart, Corella, in the final version. Unlike Julia, who is caught between her sincere love for Horace and her need to support herself and her daughter, Corella is emotionally distant and completely insensitive to her son's needs. For example, when Horace asks Corella if he can come live with her and her new husband in Houston, she seems oblivious to his fears of being abandoned. "I kind of want to go to Houston and live with you, Mama," Horace says. Corella responds with, "What, son? I didn't hear you. I was listening to Lily Dale" (91).[15] The conversation stops as her attention turns to her daughter banging out a song on the piano. Although not stated directly, Corella's, "I didn't hear you," reveals the dearth of motherly feelings she has for Horace and the callous manner in which she treats him. Throughout the play, Corella's heartlessness and lack of nurturing brings into sharp focus Horace's deep feelings of rejection and isolation.

In reshaping the story, Horton also altered the time of the play from 1890 to 1902, a date more closely linked to the actual date of his grandfather Albert Harrison Foote's death. When *Roots in a Parched Ground* opens, Horace is twelve and his sister, whose name has been changed to Lily Dale, is ten. They have been living with their maternal grandparents, the Thorntons, because their mother, having separated from their father, is already living in Houston and planning to marry Pete Davenport. Their father, Paul Horace, once a respected lawyer, lies dying from alcoholism in the Robedaux house nearby. An ineffectual man, Paul Horace has allowed his mother and siblings to move into his house even though there is not enough room or money to support them.

One of the most intriguing themes in *Roots in a Parched Ground* is the decline of the antebellum aristocracy, suggested in the moral and economic decay of the Robedaux and Thornton families. Both families persist throughout the cycle, so we learn about their origins, their misfortunes, and their crises over three decades. To begin with, the Thornton's most illustrious ancestor was the governor of Texas. John Howard, Paul Horace's law partner, explains that the governor's "plantation ran from here to the coast" (28), but descendants of Mr. Thornton, the governor's son, believe that they were cheated out of their

---

[14] Foote, *Genesis,* 118.

[15] Horton Foote, *Roots in a Parched Ground,* in *The Orphans' Home Cycle,* 19–98. All page references to *Roots in a Parched Ground* in the text refer to this publication.

lands and aristocratic inheritance. They have long ago left the plantation and moved to town where they live simply and prudently. Virgie Thornton, one of five Thornton daughters, bemoans the hardships her family suffered after the war and demeans her sister Corella, who now makes men's shirts in Houston and plans to marry a common working man. But even while family members lament their change of fortune, they are not inclined to display a sense of doom, or to dwell upon the past. However, they put a very low premium on education and are insensitive to Horace's desire to become a lawyer, like his father. The family is afraid that Horace will become ineffectual like his Uncle Terrence Robedaux, who reads Greek and Latin all day and does not work. When Horace asks his grandfather for help with schoolwork, Mr. Thornton remarks, "I can't son. I know nothing about all that. You'll have to do that on your own" (63). Mrs. Thornton believes that the trouble with the Robedaux family is "too much education" (22). Mrs. Robedaux, on the other hand, is incensed that the Thorntons do not see to it that young Horace goes to school. "Corella doesn't care. None of them went to school. Mr. Thornton doesn't have any education to speak of, and certainly none of his children have. Why should they worry or concern themselves about Horace?" (12). Nonetheless, the Thorntons are a fascinating family because they accept life readily, question little, and celebrate freely and enthusiastically.

Horton differentiates between the two families through the use of music. The Thorntons are repeatedly associated with music, singing, and dancing, while in the Robedaux house the silence of death pervades the atmosphere. When the play opens, the family is singing "Meet Me Tonight in Dreamland," which enrages the Robedauxs next door as Paul Horace lingers on his deathbed. Mrs. Robedaux sends word by young Horace to tell his mother's family to "cut out the noise" (27), even though Paul Horace finds the music soothing and has sent word through Horace for the family to sing "all they want" (32).

Unlike the Thorntons, the Robedaux family does not have an agricultural origin, but they once owned a fleet of ships in Galveston and sold cotton for the Confederacy. Mrs. Robedaux, the proudest aristocrat in the play, tells how the Robedauxs were all lawyers, doctors, and scholars who after the war were left bankrupt and forced to live as commoners. Now the family is destitute with little hope for a prosperous future. Paul Horace and his brother Terrence have classical libraries and read Latin and Greek, but both have become dissipated, lost their family's money and position, and are almost completely ineffectual in any practical sense of the word. The family has not only experienced financial and social ruin but also suffers from moral decay. A good amount of animosity and hostility exists between the Thorntons and the Robedauxs, and, since Paul Horace and Corella separated, the families quarrel constantly. Grandmother Robedaux considers the Thorntons's love of dancing frivolous, and the Thorntons condemn the Robedauxs for their misplaced obsession with reading and learning. Corella cannot stand to be in the presence of her mother-in-law and blames her for her problems with Paul Horace.

Since their parents' estrangement, Horace and his sister, Lily Dale—victims of the bitter separation between their mother and father—have been torn between the bookish Robedauxs and the carefree Thorntons. Horace loves and respects his father, but Lily Dale's opinion of Paul Horace has been shaped by the Thornton's criticism, and she has sided with her mother in the separation. According to Mrs. Robedaux, Lily Dale is entirely her mother's child, "clearly a Thornton, silly, flighty, vain, self-centered" (27). Having never developed a relationship with her father, Lily Dale doesn't want to see her dying father and excuses herself from attending his funeral, convinced that if her parents are divorced then he is no longer her father. Divorce, jealousy, and prideful bickering are slowly destroying the families, and their venomous attacks against each other have as much to do with their downfall as their poverty, their drinking, and their lethargy. On this parched ground, Horace Robedaux must plant his roots.

In *Roots in a Parched Ground*, and throughout the cycle, Horton stresses the need for constructive father/son relationships. He creates additional moments in the play that highlight Paul Horace's desire to be a good father, even though it is clear that his alcoholism has caused him to neglect his children. Paul Horace is soft-hearted, gentle, and kind—traits that at times have endeared him to Horace and Lily Dale but more often have caused confusion and disappointment. For instance, Paul Horace promises he will take Corella and the children on a cruise when he recovers from his illness. Horace clings to this dream, though it leaves the boy heartbroken when his father dies. Paul Horace is especially concerned about his son's education, and although he is terminally ill he obtains the promise of his best friend, John Howard, to support Horace in studying law. After his father passes away, Horace is more determined than ever to emulate his father, to get an education, and to become a lawyer. He tells his fishing buddies, Lloyd and Thurman, that he is going to reform, to give up tobacco, go back to school, and read law with John Howard. But in the realistic world of Horton Foote, such aspirations are not always realized. Unlike in *The Night of the Storm* where John Howard's presence following the death of Paul Horace offers a glimmer of hope to Horace, in *Roots in a Parched Ground*, the boy's dream is completely dashed when John Howard suddenly dies.

The death of John Howard leaves Horace confused and disillusioned. He is also disappointed by the townspeople of Harrison who fail to take responsibility for his welfare. Aunt Gladys assures Horace that he has not only a mother but also "a grandmother, aunts, and an uncle to take care of you" (69). George Tyler announces, "We all will look out for him," Uncle Terrence Robedaux declares, "I'll help him as long as I'm here," and Mr. George Tyler echoes, "We'll all help you, son" (73). Ultimately, however, none of them live up to their promises as changing circumstances, poverty, and Horace's feelings of self-doubt leave the boy discouraged and rootless.

Despite their reassurances, Horace cannot depend on his friends in Harrison to meet his emotional needs, nor can he trust his mother and new stepfather for help. Pete Davenport, who should have accepted the role of father to Horace, doesn't want to raise the boy. He believes Horace should quit school and go to work, since that is what he had to do when he was a twelve-year-old boy. The fact that Davenport worships Lily Dale and has chosen to raise her as his own daughter underscores his harsh treatment of Horace. In one of the most painful scenes in the play, Horace anticipates meeting Pete for the first time, returning to Houston with his mother and sister, and enrolling in law school as he promised his father. When Pete rejects Horace, saying "Lawyers are a dime a dozen," and Corella, deferring to her husband, tells her son they don't have room for him in Houston, Horace withdraws emotionally from his mother and stepfather. Later, aware of his inability to keep his promise to his father, he tells his friends simply, "I'm on my own" (94). Horace is left to his own resources, and his innocence lost, but in spite of his painful experiences, he does not give in to despair or fall victim to grief. Horace is determined not to repeat the failures of his family or those of John Howard, whose two children died in a fire ten years earlier, leaving his marriage broken, his wife a recluse, and his life in shambles. Instead, Horton Foote celebrates Horace's ability to endure the misfortunes that threaten his life and the courage with which he faces his tenuous future. Respecting the past and the spirit of his father, Horace is determined to place a tombstone on his father's grave, and when the play ends he has begun to earn money for the monument by selling fish he catches in the river and by picking up empty whisky bottles in the backstreets and alleys of Harrison. Rejected, he tells Mr. George Tyler, "I'm giving up law. I'm going to be a merchant" (97). For the first time, he cries, and as he begins to walk toward town, the singing at the Thornton house begins again. Horace is left to grow up in transient fashion with extended relatives who cannot provide the love he so desperately needs. The play closes with the image of a young boy isolated and alone, bereft of father and mother, an orphan whose only home must be the one he can create for himself. Horace is, as Marjorie Smelstor suggests, "a twentieth century Adam who accepts the ambiguity of knowing that he must create his own sense of place, his own state of mind, his own connection among self and other and environment."[16]

While *Roots in a Parched Ground* illustrates the hardships caused by social and moral decay, the cycle's second play, *Convicts,* depicts the chaos and evil effects of slavery and violence in Texas during the aftermath of Reconstruction. Set in 1904, in Floyd's Lane, Texas, the story begins after young Horace, now thirteen years old, has been separated from his family for almost two years. During that time, he has worked for his Uncle Albert Thornton in a store on the Gautier sugar-cane plantation, which is farmed by black convicts from a nearby prison. Horton Foote explained that, "the life of the plantation in *Convicts* and the fact of this particular plantation being worked by convicts are imagined. What is not imagined is the fact that convicts worked on plantations. I saw them often as a boy working in cotton fields in my county. I did not imagine the fact that my father, as a boy, went to work in a plantation store, the only white child on the plantation, and lived with a black couple.... What I imagined, too, was the relationship between the owner of the plantation and young Horace. What I did not imagine was Horace's obsessive desire to earn the money for a tombstone to put on his father's unmarked grave. He was not able to accomplish this feat until 1918."[17]

---

[16] Marjorie Smeltzor, "The World's an Orphans' Home: Horton Foote's Social and Moral History," *Southern Quarterly* 29.2 (Winter 1991): 14.

[17] Foote, *Genesis,* 123.

When *Convicts* opens, Horace is essentially cut off from society and left to fend for himself in a place where violence and brutality seethes below the surface of everyday life.[18] During his stay on the plantation, the boy has tried to earn enough money to buy a headstone for his father's grave, but the plantation owner Soll Gautier, an embittered racist and greedy old man, refuses to pay the boy what he is owed. It is Christmas Eve, and Horace has been abandoned by his Uncle Albert Thornton, who has returned to Harrison to gamble, leaving his nephew to spend the holiday on the convict farm. In the span of this day, the boy witnesses the killing of one black convict by another, a half-white convict worked to death in the fields, and the murder of a black convict by a county sheriff who earns his income in proportion to the number of prisoners he leases to old Soll.

Horace, surrounded by agony and brutality on every side, must also contend with the drunken madness of Soll, who, fearing that the prisoners are plotting to kill him, repeatedly fires his rifle at imaginary murderers. Even though Soll refuses to pay Horace the money he owes him in back wages, he repeatedly promises to buy "the biggest goddamned tombstone in Texas" for his father's grave, with "angels on it and two Confederate veterans" (135). But Soll, a broken and emotionally bankrupt man, reneges on his assurances to Horace in the same way he does on all his promises. He even lies about buying an ostentatious monument for his own father's grave. But because Horace is sensitive to Soll's past—the death of his mother in childbirth—and empathizes with the old man's hidden fears and vulnerability, the boy agrees to sit with him while he dies. Watching Soll's demise teaches the young boy a great deal about the mysteries of death, which have haunted him since his father's passing, as well as the realities of life in a separatist society. Horace learns that racism and violence were a major part of the world of his ancestors, and even though he was not present at his own father's death, by observing Soll's passing, he is able to forgive his own father for his transgressions against him.

Horace's sensitivity to others is evident throughout the play, and his first appearance dispels the idea that he feels any self-pity. When we first see him, Horace is talking with a convict, a murderer named Leroy, who has been chained to a tree. Even though the boy is aware of the horrors of slavery, he does not make judgments based on race or consider

---

[18] Horton Foote, *Convicts*, in *The Orphans' Home Cycle*, 99–166. Page references to *Convicts* in the text refer to this publication.

himself segregated from the less fortunate. He shares his tobacco with Leroy, and he is the only person who takes time to ask Leroy his name. Horace is also genuinely concerned about the man Leroy killed, and, afterward, when the sheriff kills Leroy, Horace voices his concern that his grave, as well as that of the man he killed, be marked with a proper tombstone. Horace treats everyone he meets with the same kind of respect and caring, especially the black couple, Ben and Martha Johnson, who were born and raised as slaves on the Gautier plantation and who act as surrogate parents to Horace. Ben is very protective of Horace and shows a deep affection for the boy; Martha also feels protective of Horace and defends him against Soll's demands. When Soll reneges on his promise to pay Horace all the back wages he is owed, she defends the boy saying, "I'm disgusted. This poor boy is out here working to get a tombstone for his daddy's grave. And he's been here six months and you ain't paid him nothing yet" (118). Martha also tries to address Horace's spiritual concerns as best she can. The youngster worries about what will happen in heaven when his sister, who "calls her stepfather 'Daddy'...comes face to face with her real daddy." Martha, who clearly has no answer for such mysteries, simply replies, "Read the Bible. All that is in the Bible someplace" (126). Horace can only hope that she is correct, but his confusion over such heavenly matters quickly turns to concern for Martha when she admits that she "don't know who [her] daddy is" (126). In the play, young Horace is subjected to an assortment of violent and fearful acts, but he survives his ordeal with the help of Ben and Martha, whose love and tenderness foster in the boy a lifelong affection for black people, who as Horton Foote explains: "were otherwise invisible to Southern whites in those years."[19]

In *Convicts*, Horton painted a vivid and disturbing picture of a dying world, a dark vision of the Southern plantation society collapsing under the burden of human injustice. All the characters are isolated from each other and entrapped by a past they neither cherish nor comprehend. But, as Horace discovers, none is more lonely and disturbed than Soll Gautier. While Horton often treats Soll as a comic, almost farcical, character, he also reveals him to be a tragic figure, morally and spiritually impoverished and emotionally disconnected from the world around him. As Laurin Porter suggests, Soll Gautier "represents the moral bankruptcy that results when one race is given total power over

---

[19] Horton Foote, interview by Marion Castleberry, 19 November 1988, Wharton, Texas.

another. Soll also represents the antithesis of positive Southern values, particularly those of family, religion, and civilized living."[20] A once celebrated Civil War hero, Soll hates his greedy brother Tyre and feels contempt for his drunken niece and her husband, Asa and Billy Vaughn, who have been waiting for him to die for years so that they could inherit his property. He resents the blacks who labor in his fields, and his years of prejudice toward them have brought the old man nothing but bitterness and pain. Soll's distrust has driven him insane, as evidenced by his fear that a convict named Tucker is lurking in his bedroom closet and waiting to kill him in his sleep. The only people Soll feels comfortable around are Horace, because he is white, Ben, who serves as overseer of the plantation, and Ben's wife Martha, who cooks for the old man. But even their acts of kindness cannot keep Soll from suffering a terrifying and degrading death.

Soll's demise is viewed through the prism of Horace's innocence, as the young boy keeps his promise to "sit by his side with a gun after he died, until he was buried," (145) even though he is drawn into the old man's story against his will. The contrast between the steadfastness of young Horace and the faithlessness of old Soll establishes the play's central paradox. Laurin Porter points out that these two strands of action, Horace's determination to secure a tombstone for his father and his vigil at Mr. Soll's deathbed, link *Convicts* with *Roots in a Parched Ground*. "The vigil, in particular, provides an ironic counterpoint to the death of Paul Horace in the earlier play," Porter explains.

> If Horace's father is a flawed, ultimately weak man, he is at least kind, gentle, and concerned about his son. If he has a failing, it is that he cannot stand up to his mother—hardly a criminal offense. His death is experienced as a tragedy, at least to Horace and his own mother and siblings, and the deathbed vigil is portrayed with gravity. The death of Mr. Soll, on the other hand, can be regarded as almost a parody of its *Roots* counterpart, and Soll himself, unlike the distinguished if disappointing Paul Horace, representative of the very attitudes that led to the South's demise.[21]

As Soll nears death, with his wooden casket nearby, he asks Horace to read from an 1865 newspaper article about Texas being denied reentry into the union, and then grasps the boy's hand in a viselike grip. When

---

[20] Porter, *Voice and Vision*, 138.
[21] Ibid., 136.

Soll finally dies, Ben releases Horace's hand, a symbol of the passing of a once glamorous and proud, albeit inhumane, way of life.

In the play's final scene, Horton reminds us of the inevitability of change, death, decay, and the futility of trying to impede the passing of life by marking it with any real permanence. As Ben covers Soll's grave, he speaks words that echo those of Carrie Watts in *The Trip to Bountiful*. "Six months from now you won't know where anybody's buried out here," Ben says, "not my people, not the convicts, not Mr. Soll. The trees and the weeds, and the cane, will take everything. Cane land, they called it once; cane land it will be again." As the curtain falls, the convict Jackson sings "Golden Slippers," and Ben concludes, "The house will go, the store will go, the graves will go—those with tombstones and those without" (166). By play's end, Horace understands that death is permanent and takes away any promise for a hopeful future, whether that means making amends for one's transgressions or taking a new direction in life. Nonetheless, he refuses to relinquish his dream to place a tombstone on his father's unmarked grave. The gravestone remains a powerful symbol, a tangible reality of Horace's promise to his father and of the love they could never share.

Horace's story continues in *Lily Dale* when he travels to Houston to visit his mother and sister, Lily Dale, with whom he has lost touch since his father's death.[22] Horton Foote explains that the play was inspired by his thinking about the "anger and rage" his father felt whenever the name of his stepfather was spoken.

> The idea of the play came to me after recalling what happened to my father when he earned enough money to take a six-week business course in Houston. His mother had promised to give him breakfast every morning. One morning when he arrived for breakfast, she met him at the door visibly nervous. She said in a loud voice, "Thank you for bringing me the milk and eggs," and she quickly shut the door. Before the door shut, he saw his stepfather back in the house and he realized his mother was giving him breakfast without his stepfather's knowledge or approval. For some reason, he was home that day and she was in terror he would discover what she was doing. I decided not to use that situation but to invent one similar in emotional complexity, one that could happen to a younger, more vulnerable Horace. I also knew the stepfather doted on my

---

[22] Horton Foote, *Lily Dale*, in *The Orphans' Home Cycle*, 167–242. Page references to *Lily Dale* in the text refer to this publication.

father's sister, Lily Dale, and gave her a great deal of affection. I wanted to include that in the play.[23]

When the play begins, Horace, now twenty years old, is employed as a clerk in a mercantile store in Glen Flora, a three-hour walk from Harrison. He has not heard from his mother and sister for more than a year, so when Corella sends word in a letter that she would like to see him, Horace eagerly accepts, ever hopeful of renewing his relationship with his family and of possibly finding more lucrative work on the railroad with his stepfather. But Horace's reunion with his mother and sister evolves into an emotional nightmare that eventually leaves him an orphan in spirit if not in name.

In Houston, Horace discovers that the only reason he can spend time with his mother and sister is that his irascible stepfather, Pete Davenport, is away in Atlanta visiting relatives. But when Pete returns from his trip earlier than expected, he quickly orders Horace to leave. Pete clearly does not want Horace in Houston, and when Lily Dale points out that her mother gave her brother two dollars to visit them and two more to return to Harrison, Pete chastises the boy: "You're a grown man. Aren't you ashamed to take money from your mama? When I was your age, I had been supporting my mother and my brothers and sisters for eight years. Nobody ever gave me anything and I never asked for anything. What kind of man are you gonna make, taking money from a woman at your age?" (191–2). Pete's harsh words wound Horace deeply, and the young man eventually falls prey to a mysterious fever, an emotional breakdown that forces him to remain in Houston several weeks under the care of his mother. While recovering from his illness, Horace has hallucinations and bouts of hysteria. After he awakens, Lily Dale informs her brother: "You thought Mr. Davenport had a butcher knife and was trying to kill you. You kept screaming. 'He's trying to slit my throat. Don't let him slit my throat.' Mrs. Westheimer heard you all the way upstairs and thought we were being murdered and made Mr. Westheimer go for the police" (201–2).

After his fever subsides, Horace has one last chance to restore his troubled relationship with Lily Dale, but he discovers that her memories of the past and her feelings for their late father are as resentful as his are forgiving. Horace understands the importance of coming to terms with his heritage, no matter how troubling, but Lily Dale refuses to face her

---

[23] Foote, *Genesis*, 123.

past. "I want to forget everything that happened back then, everything," she screams. And she fantasizes about "happy times, pleasant things," and not about "drunkards and dying and not having enough to eat" (231). Lily Dale describes a recurring dream she has about Horace dying. In the dream, her mother wants to bury her son in the family plot in Houston, but Lily Dale strongly disapproves: "No we won't. I'll not have him buried with you and Mr. Davenport and me. I want him buried with his father where he belongs" (229–30).

Lily Dale's insecurity and selfishness drives Horace further away from her. She refuses to allow her brother to be part of the family circle she enjoys, even though he has never asked her for anything. In Horton Foote's world, characters who fail to make peace with their pasts are ultimately disconnected from the world around them, devoid of healthy attachments to others, and fearful of the process of life and death. Without an emotional home, Lily Dale has no true identity, and her narcissism has paralyzed her. She dreams of herself as a famous pianist and believes that happiness resides in material possessions, in new homes and expensive clothing, which have been promised to her by her future husband, the optimistic Will Kidder. Denying any connection to her paternal family Lily Dale has become in the words of the song for which she was named, a poor, lost Lily Dale.

Lily Dale's behavior, coupled with her mother's refusal to stand up to her husband, further isolates Horace from his family, and he eventually leaves Houston emotionally wounded and confused. He returns to Harrison, "where he belongs," having realized that he can no longer connect with his mother and sister, nor can he recapture the neglected years he has spent without a family. Yet, somehow, after confronting the demons of his past, Horace is able to rise above his pain and to face the uncertainties of the future with a sense of dignity and courage. In the final scene of the play, Horton Foote illustrates the spiritual implication of Horace's horrific experience. On the train ride back to Harrison, Horace encounters Mrs. Coons, a fervent Baptist woman whom he had first met on his ride into Houston. During their initial meeting, Mrs. Coons warned Horace that he should be concerned about "the wrath of my God," and suggested that he get a Bible and inquire about his baptism. But Horton Foote's God is not the angry one the old woman worships, and baptism is clearly not Horace's problem. As Gerald Wood points out, "Like Flannery O'Connor, Foote uses this obnoxious evangelical to remind Horace of the love and grace which is his religious heritage."[24] During their second meeting, Mrs. Coons, the steadfast wife of an alcoholic, ministers to Horace after finally recognizing the depth and seriousness of the young man's pain and confusion. With no earthly father to turn to, Horace seeks the help of his heavenly Father to give him understanding and to heal his shattered family. He asks Mrs. Coons to pray for them: "Pray for us, Mrs. Coons, pray for us" (242). With growing sincerity, the woman offers up a heartfelt prayer for each member of the family, a prayer that exemplifies the playwright's belief in a merciful and loving God: "Father, I've been asked to remember in my prayers this young man, and his dear mother, Corella, and his dear sister, Lily Dale. Father of mercy, Father of goodness, Father of forgiveness..." (242).

It is remarkable that after all the pain he has suffered at the hands of his mother and sister Horace still cares enough to pray for them. He is an extraordinarily compassionate young man, whose forgiving nature reflects the attitude of respect and awe the playwright had for his real father. More than revealing Horace's admirable traits, however, Mrs. Coon's prayer serves as a kind of rebirth for the young man, an important moment of recognition that frees him from guilt and provides the strength for him to move ahead with his life. At this moment, Horace acknowledges that in order to be part of a family, he must create that family himself through God's mercy and grace.

As a Southerner, Horton Foote writes within the Judeo-Christian tradition, whose central myth is the "fall from grace." While Horton, like fellow Southerners William Faulkner, Katherine Anne Porter, and Flannery O'Connor, is interested in the loss of innocence, he is not, as Gerald Wood points out, obsessed with the impotence, failure, and ignorance resulting from the loss of Eden. Horton's concern is not so much on the loss of grace but on its recovery, not on leaving home, though that is important, but on finding new ways to return home.

> In Foote's essentially mental theatre, the exit from Paradise is both natural and necessary for the development of authentic experience. Unlike his fellow Southern mythic realists, he is focused on ways of returning to Edens never imagined by the innocent mind. More like William Blake, Foote imagines these other, *psychological*, Edens, just outside the disoriented present. Foote's home is an ever-changing and never fully realized state of mind, not a place or time in history. The distinctive story

---

[24] Gerald C. Wood, *Horton Foote and the Theatre of Intimacy* (Baton Rouge: Louisiana State University Press 1999) 75.

for Foote, his version of the Southern fall from grace, is the rite of going away and coming home, the eternal need for both roots and wings.[25]

Thus, in *The Orphans' Home Cycle*, home is not just a town or a house but rather a feeling, a sense of peace and contentment that is connected to community, family, and faith. Horton's belief that every family, consciously or unconsciously, must have a spiritual and an emotional as well as a physical home, rings true in the play. The writer understood that Horace's search for a sense of belonging is not merely an individual concern but a universal quest for all mankind.

As much as *Lily Dale* is about rejection and paralysis, the next play in the cycle, *The Widow Claire*, is about acceptance and transition.[26] When Horace returns to Harrison, he leads for a time a somewhat reckless lifestyle, drinking, smoking, and gambling. When we next see Horace, it is 1912, and the young man is preparing for a date with the attractive widow, Claire Ratliff. During the course of the play, Horace comes face to face with the complexities of romance and sexuality and the mysteriousness of human companionship. Horton Foote pointed out that:

> the story of *The Widow Claire*, the last of the cycle plays to be written, is largely imaginary. What I did not imagine is the relationship my father had with a widow and her two children before he began "calling" (as they used to say) on my mother. The widow was older than he was and why their romance discontinued I have never known. I used to see her in later years walking by my father's store, a handsome but matronly woman. If my father happened to be in the front of the store, she would usually stop and talk to him. I was often nearby, and the conversation was always most pleasant in a general kind of way. "It's a nice day, isn't it? Need rain, don't we?" they would say. She had had a tragic life; Lewis Higgins tells of killing her son in the play *Cousins*. While watching them talk, exchanging their rather impersonal remarks, I could not imagine them ever being young and interested in each other.[27]

The Widow Claire follows the story of Claire Ratliff and her children and their relationship with Horace and another suitor, Val Stanton. Interspersed with scenes at Claire's house in Harrison are scenes at a boarding house where Horace rooms with his poker buddies—Archie

---

[25] Ibid., 62.

[26] Horton Foote, *The Widow Claire*, in *The Orphans' Home Cycle*, 243–318. Page references to *The Widow Claire* in the text refer to this publication.

[27] Foote, *Genesis*, 124.

Graham, Felix Barclay, Spence Howard, and Ed Cordray—characters based on actual friends of Horton Foote's father, some of whom the writer knew personally and some who had died before he was born. "None of them ever amounted to much," Horton recalled. "They had little ambition, gambled and drank in excess, and in some ways were victims of a very difficult time of social adjustment for young, white males. My father often talked about them and how their lives ended, speaking sometimes with fondness and sometimes with sadness. My mother often told me that it was in some ways a miracle that my father had escaped the fate of his friends."[28]

When the play opens, it is quickly apparent that Horace's affection for Claire will eventually lead to disappointment as his friends tease him about her reputation for dating several men at one time and warn him about her two boisterous children, Buddy and Molly. Horace, unmoved by their jokes, genuinely cares for Claire, but during the course of the evening, he finds that their warnings and premonitions are true. Claire Ratliff, struggling to pick up the pieces of her life after the unexpected death of her husband the year before, describes for Horace her feelings of desperation as a twenty-eight-year-old woman with two children to rear. "I thought I was so in love with my husband when I married him that I didn't worry if he was rich or not," Claire remarks. "He didn't leave me destitute, you know. He left me this house and two rent houses. Sissy nags me all the time to marry again, find someone who is fond of children. But not me. I'm twenty-eight, and I've been married twelve of those twenty-eight-years—a mother for ten of them" (270). Claire dreams of a life free from parental responsibilities, but her situation, like that of Corella in *Roots in a Parched Ground*, demands that she marry a man who will dominate her completely in exchange for taking care of her children.

Claire is drawn to Horace because of his thoughtfulness and honesty and because he is kind to her children. Horace has learned from his own deprivation that a father figure is absolutely essential in a child's life, and, unlike most of Claire's other suitors, the young man sympathizes with Buddy and Molly's lack of paternal love and guidance. Buddy even speculates that his father's clothes would fit Horace and voices his desire for Horace to be his father. But Horace, who has no job and very little money, knows that he cannot throw himself into such an arrangement at this time. By night's end, the young man is as defeated in his attempts at

---

[28] Ibid.

courtship as he was in *Lily Dale* when he tried to rescue his mother and sister from their bewildering family life.

Time after time, Claire's ten-year-old son Buddy turns up at Horace's boarding house, even after Horace has retired for the evening, pestering him and calling him back to his mother's place for one reason or another. Horace remains unruffled by the boy's requests, even though he and Claire are barely able to kiss or talk without the children clamoring to be sung to or told a story. Nor does he wince when the widow asks him which of two men, Val or Ned, she should choose to marry. Horace's trips grow more frustrating, however, and he is finally drawn into a fistfight with the aggressive Val Stanton. Although Claire stands helplessly by as Horace is attacked by the stronger suitor, the incident awakens her to the decision she must make by morning. The next day, Horace stops by Claire's house, where he learns that the widow has decided to marry Ned, an elderly but wealthy salesman from Galveston. Of all the other men Claire has dated, her children most like "Uncle Ned" because he treats them with respect and fatherly affection. Unlike Horace's mother, who chose her own comfort and that of her daughter's over the needs of her son, Claire sacrifices her freedom and personal longings to marry a man who cares for her children and offers them a promising future. Although Horace is disappointed by the news, he understands that Claire's decision is the best for her children, and he reconciles himself to yet another defeat as he waves goodbye to the widow. As Claire waves farewell to Horace—the young man who might have given her the love she hoped for had circumstances been different—we are left with the haunting portrait of a time and place where life seemed simpler but was, in fact, filled with the same kind of disappointment and compromise as our present age.

Horace finds no relief from his loneliness in *The Widow Claire*, but his life changes for the better when in *Courtship* he finally meets Elizabeth Vaughn, the beautiful and serene daughter of the wealthy Harrison businessman, Henry Vaughn.[29] *Courtship* tells the story of the couple's budding romance and of Elizabeth's courage to follow her instincts and marry the man she loves, despite his lower social standing and her family's adamant disapproval. "*Courtship* was based on facts that I brooded over a great deal in my young life," Horton explained. "I was told early on, I forget now by whom, that my maternal grandparents had

---

[29] Horton Foote, *Courtship*, in *The Orphans' Home Cycle*, 319–64. Page references to *Courtship* in the text refer to this publication.

objected strenuously to the marriage of my mother and father and that my parents had to slip around finally to see each other because my father was not allowed to come to my mother's house. My maternal grandfather, for some unexplained reason, wanted none of his girls to get married. I know also, from my mother, that she had almost defied her father earlier and run away with another suitor (he managed the local picture show). I dramatized that in an earlier play called *Flight*. However, my mother lost her nerve at the last minute and did not leave. This suitor left town, and she began to see my father and they fell in love."[30]

Set in 1915, on a warm summer's evening, *Courtship* is a mosaic of conversations between Elizabeth, daughter of the aristocratic Henry Vaughn, and her younger sister Laura that occur on the front veranda of their family's Victorian house. Through the girls' intermittent stories, we learn of their fears of growing up, their frustrations with the repressive Victorian environment in which they live, and their eagerness to break free from the restraints imposed upon them by their straitlaced parents. The Vaughns are substantial, God-fearing people who expect their children to accept the standards by which they themselves have lived, even though those standards are often unreasonable and unfair. When the play opens, Elizabeth's father, Henry Vaughn, has forbidden his daughter from attending the community dance with Horace because he cannot tolerate dancing and does not approve of Horace as a suitable companion. Henry Vaughn seems at first to be a domestic tyrant and monster of possessiveness. However, as the evening wears on, we come to understand his parental anxieties when Elizabeth and Laura respond to the horrifying stories of elders who were victimized by the same sins against which they have been warned. When they discuss Elizabeth's heartbreaking engagement to Syd Joplin and recount the tragic plight of young Sybil Thomas, who on this day marries Leo Theil, a man she does not love, and then dies from complications surrounding the birth of her premature baby, we become aware of the plight of young women during the early years of the twentieth century.

Horton's characters are all storytellers of one kind or another with a constant need to tell and listen to stories. The stories told throughout *The Orphans' Home Cycle* become an evolving oral history, and the act of listening connects both characters and audience with their own memory and sense of home and family. But as Horton makes clear "no memory is

---

[30] Foote, *Genesis*, 125.

really faithful, it has too far to go, too many changing landscapes of the human mind and heart, to bear any sort of really trustworthy witness."[31] Throughout the cycle, Horton's characters are constantly seeking the truth but must finally accept that reality is ever changing. In *Courtship*, Horton uses stories of heartbreak and unhappy marriages, told throughout the play, to help audiences understand what a complex and serious thing it was during the early twentieth century for a young woman to make a decision about marriage. "Marriage then was so final," Horton pointed out, "and women were so dependent upon their husbands. It was not an easy choice to defy your parents and marry someone of whom they did not approve,"[32] as Laura, Elizabeth's sister, understands:

> Laura: Everything bad that happens to a girl I begin to worry it will happen to me. All night I've been worrying. Part of the time I've been worrying that I'd end up an old maid like Aunt Sarah, and part of the time I worry that I'll fall in love with someone like Syd and defy Papa and run off with him and then realize I made a mistake and part of the time I worry… (*Pause*) that what happened to Sybil Thomas will happen to me and… (*Pause*) Could what happened to Sybil Thomas ever happen to you? I don't mean the dying part. I know we all have to die. I mean the other part…having a baby before she was married. Do you think she loved Leo? Do you think he loved her? Do you think it was the only time she did? You know… (*Pause*) Old common Anna Landry said in the girl's room at school that she did it whenever she wanted to and nothing ever happened to her. And if it did she would get rid of it. How do women do that?
> Elizabeth: Do what?
> Laura: Not have children if they don't want them?
> Elizabeth: I don't know.
> Laura: I guess we'll never know. I don't trust Anna Landry, and I don't know who else to ask. Can you imagine the expression on Mama's face, or Aunt Lucy's, or Mrs. Cookenboo's if I asked them something like that? (*Pause*) Anyway, even if I knew, I would be afraid to do something like that before I got married for fear God would strike me dead. (*Pause*) Aunt Sarah said that Sybil's baby dying was God's punishment of her sin. Aunt Lucy said if God punished sinners that way there would be a lot of dead babies. (358)

---

[31] Horton Foote, telephone interview by Marion Castleberry, 20 March 2004.

[32] Foote, *Genesis*, 125.

But the message of *Courtship* is not about the deleterious effects of family oppression, the evils of divorce or alcoholism, or even about the harsh reality of death. *Courtship* is a love story as seen through the eyes of a young woman, Elizabeth Vaughn, who, within a climate of mystery, heartbreak, and confusion, courageously announces her determination to break free from the social restraints that have been bequeathed her in order to marry the orphaned salesman, Horace Robedaux. Breaking away from her mother and father's manipulation, Elizabeth chooses to elope with Horace, thereby becoming an orphan and joining Horace in his quest to create his own family and home. Horton celebrates Elizabeth's courage to choose and to follow through with her decision to marry the man she loves. When she announces to Laura that she is marrying Horace, fully aware that her mother and father might not forgive her, she takes her first steps toward independence and self-realization, two important objectives for all of Horton Foote's women.

The fifth play in the cycle, *Valentine's Day*, set on Christmas Eve, 1917, begins almost a year after Elizabeth and Horace's elopement and marriage.[33] Horton explained that the play is based on fact:

> My mother and father did elope, and her parents would not speak to her, until after she became pregnant. The first half of the play ends with the reconciliation of Elizabeth and her parents. Horace and Elizabeth have a room in a boarding house, and I often heard my parents' stories about the other roomers: a spinster who worked in a millinery store, the owner of the boarding house and her son, who was a compulsive gambler and often drunk. There was also Bessie who lived in the neighborhood and visited my mother every day. She insisted on calling my mother Mary, though it was not her name. Bessie was not so much retarded, as she is sometimes played, as she was eccentric. We meet, too, Elizabeth's brother for the first time. He is a composite of my own Uncles and of many brothers I knew and observed growing up. One of the models for this brother really went to Texas A&M for a brief period, but flunked out. His father had gone to A&M earlier, had put himself through college, and had made fine grades. Brother...is like so many men I have known in the South, and all over America, who had successful fathers and yet felt themselves to be utter failures.[34]

---

[33] Horton Foote, *Valentine's Day*, in *The Orphans' Home Cycle*, 365–416. Page references to *Valentine's Day* in the text refer to this publication.

[34] Foote, *Genesis*, 126-127.

In *Valentine's Day*, Horace and Elizabeth are expecting their first child. They have taken up residence in the parlor of Mrs. Pate's boarding house where they carry out their daily routines and interact with an odd assortment of people, all of who have been emotionally damaged by family tragedies. Chief among them are: Miss Ruth, a lonely spinster who longs for a loving relationship like Horace and Elizabeth's; Bobby Pate, a troubled man who has allowed a failed marriage and runaway wife to turn him into the town drunk; and Mr. George Tyler, a dignified old Southern gentleman, whose increasing insanity cannot help but touch the lives of everyone around him. Despite the occasional intrusion of friends and neighbors, Horace and Elizabeth's marriage is secure; and for the first time in his life, Horace is happy and content:

> I am no orphan, but I think of myself as an orphan, belonging to no one but you…I intend to have everything I didn't have before. A house, some land, a yard, and in that yard I will plant growing things, fruitful things, and I will have a garden and chickens. (*Pause*) And I believe I might now have these things, because you married me. I said to myself before our marriage, "She'll never marry you, no matter how much she says she loves you, because her father will stop it. He's a powerful man and he will prevail as he does in all ways." But he didn't stop us; you did marry me, and I tell you I've begun to know happiness for the first time in my life. I adore you. I worship you…and I thank you for marrying me. (395–6)

Horace's dreams are clearly within reach when Mr. Vaughn, in a spirit of reconciliation, announces that he is prepared to deed the couple a parcel of land and build them a new house next to his own. Horace accepts Mr. Vaughn's gracious offer, with the stipulation that the deed be made out in the name of Elizabeth, but he proudly rejects his father-in-law's attempt to finance his opening of a haberdashery. The family does not resolve all of its differences by the end of the play, but the healing process has begun, and together they happily anticipate the birth of a new baby into the family.

Elizabeth is one of Horton's strongest and most admirable female characters. Patterned after the playwright's mother and wife, Lillian, she is seemingly always resourceful and compassionate, but she often reveals moments of doubt and uncertainty. Throughout the play, Elizabeth confides her inner feelings to Bessie Stillman, a simple but caring girl who loves guinea pigs and serves as Elizabeth's confidante. When Bessie innocently asks Elizabeth if she and Horace will love each other on their twenty-fifth wedding anniversary as much as they do today, Elizabeth responds emotionally: "I don't want to get old, Bessie, and I don't want Horace to get old. I want everything to stay as it is. When I'm seventy-two Mama and Papa will be dead unless they live to be a hundred. I don't want anybody I love to die, Bessie, ever, not Horace, not Mama, not Papa. Not Brother, not my sisters, not my baby I'm going to have" (410). In spite of Elizabeth's heartfelt admission, Foote understands that life persists and that there is no escape from the harsh realities of death. Beneath the pleasantries and discreet reconciliations in *Valentine's Day* lies a psychic turbulence that threatens the family's future happiness. Elizabeth's ne'er-do-well younger brother succumbs to alcoholism and gambling, and Mr. George Tyler is driven to madness and suicide by his failures as a husband and father and by the haunting ghost of Horace's Aunt Mary, whose love he betrayed some thirty years before.

Horton explained that the character of George Tyler was based on a man he remembered from his childhood: "When I was growing up, I heard of a man who never left his house and was confined to his bedroom in the second floor, except when he had fits, as they were called, and he would try to run away. He was, of course, insane, but his family would never send him away. Once, he tried to kill himself; consequently, he was forbidden to eat with a fork or knife. I never met this man but he was as real to me as if I had known him. I also heard that, as a younger man, he had been in love with one of my father's aunts. Everyone assumed the two would marry, but a cousin came to visit from Louisville, Kentucky, and she took him away from my father's aunt, and they married instead. In the play...he appears intermittently in the early part of the play at Horace and Elizabeth's room in the boarding house, with an unexpected Christmas present for Horace. He appears later, too, after he has run away from his home."[35]

Because George Tyler's son, Steve, looks out for him with devotion, the old man has escaped confinement in an institution, even after threatening to kill his wife with a butcher knife. As the story unfolds, his confusion and desperation escalate until he runs away from his son and hides out at the river. Fleeing from the sheriff and his deputies, Mr. George finds his way back to the boarding house, where he discusses with Horace the death of his father, Paul Horace, and seeks his forgiveness for failing to live up to the promise he made to his friend.

---

[35] Ibid.

George: Where is Mrs. Pate? I'd like to say hello to her.

Horace: She's not home. She's off with Mr. Bobby in Galveston. He's taking the Keeley Cure.

George: Is he drinking again?

Horace: Yes Sir.

George: Isn't that too bad. Your daddy drank, son.

Horace: Yes Sir.

George: It killed him.

Horace: Yes Sir.

George: He was a close friend of mine, you know.

Horace: Yes Sir.

George: I went to him, I said, "I've come to you as a friend. We all have troubles. Get hold of yourself for the sake of your baby son and little daughter…get hold of yourself." But my talking didn't do a bit of good. It never does, you know. I was just wasting my breath. He broke your mother's heart. How is your mother?

Horace: She's well.

George: Your father sent for me before he died. Did I ever tell you this?

Horace: No Sir.

George: He said: "George, I'm going to die. Promise me you'll look after my children. Promise me you'll never let them go hungry." (*Pause*) I didn't keep my promise. And I'm sorry; I didn't keep my promise about a lot of things. (*Pause*) You say Mary's dead?

Horace: Yes Sir.

George: They won't let me die. I want to die and they've been chasing me all through the river bottoms. They give me no peace. First they want to kill me…my own wife tried to poison me and then when I want to take my own life they do all in their power to stop me. I've had a difficult life, you know, since I betrayed Mary. I've had no happiness. I've been punished unmercifully for what I've done. (*Pause*) But I'm tired. Tired of running the river bottoms. Tired. (*Pause*) (Miss Ruth sings: "Lorena") Do you know the way to my home?

Horace: Yes Sir.

George: Will you take me there? I'm very confused. I tried to get there twice, but I'm confused.

Horace: Yes Sir. (401–2)

Horace does take Mr. George to his son, Steve, but the old man breaks free once again and runs across the courthouse square, finally committing suicide by stabbing himself.

Tragedy seems to be around every corner in Harrison, but in the final analysis, *Valentine's Day* is a Christmas story, a tale about forgiveness and reconciliation. Like George Tyler, all the characters in the play are orphaned in one way or another and they all seek peace, contentment, and nurturing family relationships: Bessie seeks in Elizabeth the sister she does not have; Miss Ruth, the "songbird of the South," longs for the drunken Bobby Pate to return the love she has given him; Mr. Vaughn seeks reconciliation with Elizabeth and asks for God's forgiveness for the disappointment and hostility he feels toward Brother; Horace wants Elizabeth to forgive him for his jealousy of her father's prestige; and the Baptist preacher prays for reconciliation between all parents and children. Ultimately, the characters must come to realize that forgiveness is attainable through love and understanding, as Elizabeth tells Bobby Pate when he asks about her reconciliation with her father: "Everybody has forgiven everybody now" (413). By the end of the play, Horace and Elizabeth have created a home for themselves and their dispossessed neighbors, a haven of hope and serenity. As Mr. Vaughn finally recognizes: "There's peace in this room and contentment. That's why I like to come here, I think. I said to Mrs. Vaughn. 'They don't have much but they're contented. You feel that.' I hope you find contentment in your new home. I'd buy that for you if I could, but of course, you know things like that can't be bought" (413). Throughout *Valentine's Day* Horace and Elizabeth show their resourcefulness and strength of character as they cope with all the tragedy and sadness that surrounds them, but at the end of the day we sense their contentment will soon be tested in a more acute and profound way.

Change is the one certainty in Horton Foote's dramatic world. All his characters are consistently forced to cope with the knowledge that time and circumstances are continuously eroding their traditions, their family bonds, and their social identities. In the seventh play of the cycle, *1918*, Horace and Elizabeth must contend with the effects of a worldwide influenza epidemic and the death of their only child.[36] Foote remarked that *1918* is about imagined death and real death: "The imagined death is the fantasy that I'm sure many young men were having during World War I, of what would happen if they went overseas—about how they might die. But the real death that came in silently was the horrendous flu

---

[36] Horton Foote, *1918*, in *The Orphans' Home Cycle*, 417–78. Page references to *1918* in the text refer to this publication.

epidemic."[37]More than in any other play in the cycle, *1918* explores the depths of human loss and grief as reflected in Horace's simple but profound question: "How can human beings stand all that comes to them? How can they?" (443). Horton explained, that *1918*, the seventh in the cycle, is almost totally imagined:

> My mother and father never had a child who died, but what I did not imagine was the flu of that year. I heard often how the terror of the Spanish influenza, as it was officially called, came into our hometown. In truth, it killed more people worldwide than World War I. No one knew where it came from or how it stopped. One day it was there taking lives, and the next day it was gone. Whenever my mother and father talked about the flu (they both had it) they would end up calling out the names, like a litany, of the young men they knew who had been killed by it. I can hear them now calling out, "T. Abell, John Barclay, Marshall Elmore"—on and on the list would go. What I did not imagine, too, was the offer my grandfather made to my father; that if he wanted to join the Army, he would take care of his wife and new baby. In the play, I have the flu keep him from facing that decision; how it really happened I do not know. It was at this time too, my father got the money to put a tombstone on his father's unmarked grave. The real tombstone he placed there is a simple one. It has the name of his father, the date of his birth and death, and at the very bottom of the inscription "Erected by his son." In *1918*, the death of the baby girl is imagined; actually the baby would have been me. I survived the flu in real life, but I delayed my birth in the play for dramatic purposes until the end of *1918*.[38]

1918 opens on an autumn day as the citizens of Harrison are doing their patriotic best to protect the home front from the war that is raging in Europe. The women of the community spend their days at the Red Cross rolling bandages, the men drill in the town brigade every afternoon, and all participate in parades and patriotic songs with an optimistic attitude that the conflict will soon be over. Even though Harrison has escaped the horrors of war, many of its young men, both black and white, have not been so fortunate, and families are now starting to face the loss of their sons as casualties of war and to cope with the deadly flu virus that threatens the entire community. While the town is preparing for the unexpected, Horace, Elizabeth, and their baby daughter have settled into the new home built for them by Mr. Vaughn.

---

[37] Horton Foote, interview by Marion Castleberry, 19 November 1988, Wharton, Texas.

[38] Foote, *Genesis*, 129.

At first glance, Horace and Elizabeth's fortune seems full of promise as their dry cleaning business is prosperous, their marriage is happy and secure, and nine-month-old Jenny has brought a new sense of joy and purpose to their family. Horace has also paid to have a tombstone placed on his father's grave, even though he is not exactly sure where it should be placed. Not knowing which grave is his father's, he questions everyone until he satisfies himself with its location and then has an expensive marker placed on the site. At last his promise has been realized, and Horace feels at peace and finally reconciled to his father's memory.

Although the Robedaux family seems contented, their life is far less serene than it appears. Brother Vaughn has just flunked out of Texas A&M University and has become a major worry to his family. While many of Harrison's native sons have gone off to fight overseas, Brother spends his days sitting in movie houses, watching glorified images of war heroes on the silent screen, and gambling away his father's money. Having gotten a young girl pregnant and piled up heavy gambling debts while away at school, Brother is afraid to tell his father the truth about his situation. He turns to Elizabeth, who loans him money from her savings to pay for the young girl's abortion. Brother wants to enlist in the army in spite of his father's objection, and by the end of the play, the relationship between father and son has been irreversibly damaged.

Unlike Brother Vaughn, Horace has helped the war effort as much as he could by committing his entire savings of four thousand dollars in the latest Liberty Bond drive. He has not felt free to enlist in the military because of his responsibility to Elizabeth and the baby, but, to squelch any suspicion that he is afraid to fight, he announces to his friends that if it weren't for his family he would immediately sign up for duty. Mr. Vaughn overhears Horace's remark and offers to care for Elizabeth and Jenny while he is away in Europe. Horace is shocked by his father-in-law's generosity, but before he can tell Mr. Vaughn the truth, that he doesn't really want to go overseas, both men fall prey to the influenza virus. Weeks later, when Horace awakens from his delirious nightmare, he discovers that his wife and daughter also contracted the flu. While Elizabeth survived the sickness, baby Jenny had died the week before. Elizabeth tries to comfort Horace, but the baby's death brings a grief to the couple that nothing can allay, not even the welcome announcement that an armistice has been declared.

As in many of Horton's plays, death and grief reverberate throughout *1918*, but ultimately the play is a tribute to courage and human endurance. Despite Elizabeth and Horace's tragic loss, in time they are drawn back into the world of Harrison by their friends, their family, and the birth of their second child. The courageous Elizabeth is not, however, without her misgivings, as the loss of Jenny to influenza has left her afraid and emotionally paralyzed. She confides to Bessie, "I wake up in the night afraid, now. Afraid... (*Pause*) I tell you now I don't want this baby if anything is going to happen to it afterwards. I don't want it at all. I couldn't stand going through again what I went through when I lost Jenny" (466). Later, she admits that she feels confused by her inability to fully submit to the will of God. Elizabeth fears that God took her baby because she named the child after her dead sister:

> It bothered me so I had to go talk to the preacher and he said that was just superstition.... That had nothing to do with it. That God wouldn't take a baby for something foolish like that. "Then why did God take my baby?" I asked him. He couldn't answer that. He said there was bound to be a reason, but he didn't know it. Bessie, I have to tell you this. I have to tell somebody this... Remember how I used to always talk to you before the other baby came? You know how happy I was about having that baby. And now Bessie, I'm ashamed but I'm not happy about having this baby. I don't want this baby. I want my other baby back. I want Jenny back. I don't want this baby at all. (Pause) And I'm afraid of ever saying that and thinking that. Afraid that I'll be punished for not submitting to God's will in all this. That's what our minister, Mr. Myers, told us we must do...that I must ask God for the understanding to see His will that Jenny died. Do you believe that, Bessie? Do you believe it was His will that Jenny died? (469)

There is, of course, no answer to Elizabeth's question; but fortunately in *1918*, love is stronger than fear, and the young mother's doubts are finally transformed into a faith that offers peace even in the face of death. At the end of the play, Elizabeth and Horace find comfort in each other and look forward to a more peaceful time where, in the words of Mr. Vaughn, there is: "no sickness, no killings, and no war" (477).

The conclusion of *1918*, as Gerald Wood suggests, represents Horton's radical faith in "an endlessly loving God—as imagined by Mary Baker Eddy—who calls his children home. In the words of the hymn sung at the end of the play, 'Oh, the peace of God be near us/ Fill within our hearts Thy home/ With Thy bright appearing cheer us/ In Thy blessed freedom come.' A benevolent God of love, peace, and order leads the characters beyond themselves. Personal grief is transformed into a call for intimacy, and the God of judgment is reborn as the God of mystery, offering the path and the personal understanding of the Christian stories as imagined by Horton Foote in *1918*."[39] *1918* is, finally, a celebration of family and community in an innocent, optimistic period in American life. It is a dramatic eulogy to an earlier age when a man could transcend loss, endure war and disease, and rise above his station in life by the kind of support system derived from personal relationships—even if those relationships involved considerable pressures and conflicts.

The final two plays of the cycle, *Cousins* and *The Death of Papa*, take up Horace and Elizabeth's story at a time when their main concerns are centered on their aging parents and the inevitability of their deaths. *Cousins* focuses on the Thornton family and the near-death experience of Corella, Horace's mother, and is set within a comic context. *The Death of Papa*, which begins with the death of Henry Vaughn, is treated as a tragedy for both the family and the town of Harrison.

Cousins, the eighth play in the cycle, opens in Horace's clothing store in 1925, during one of the most economically depressed periods in Harrison's history.[40] The town has not prospered since the end of World War I when the demand for cotton declined, and now the heavy summer rains have taken away what little hope farmers and merchants have for a productive harvest. Horton explained that *Cousins* is the most difficult play in the cycle for non-Southerners to understand:

> Even for Southerners, I would think now "Times are a-changing." Still in my day, it was this cousin and that cousin and he's your first cousin once removed or your fourth cousin on my daddy's side and on and on and on. In between all the cousins and talk about cousins, one, I hope, senses the hard realities of the life of my characters. In this play Horace and his store have fallen on hard times. Indeed the whole county is suffering from what we call today a recession. In those days, as I remember, it was just referred to as hard times or bad times, in contrast to the good times that World War I provided. There are bad cousins and good cousins in the play. There are brutal cousins and sensitive ones; there are prosperous cousins and poor cousins. During the play, there is another opportunity for Horace to find some kind of union with his mother and sister in Houston. The attempt fails, as it does in their one last meeting in his store

---

[39] Wood, *Horton Foote and the Theatre of Intimacy*, 83.

[40] Horton Foote, *Cousins*, in *The Orphans' Home Cycle*, 479–564. Page references to *Cousins* in the text refer to this publication.

in Harrison. At the end of the play, he is together with his wife, to whom we sense he has become even closer.[41]

In *Cousins*, Horace's fortunes have been greatly affected by the recession, and he has had to borrow heavily from the bank to keep his store open. But even though he is worried about the town's failing economy, he has managed to keep his business afloat by catering to black laborers. This practice has infuriated many people in Harrison, including his own relatives who refuse to "go in his store because of all the colored trade" (487). During the play, Horace must not only contend with the racial biases of his extended family members—most notably his garrulous Cousin Gordon, who works as a clerk in Horace's haberdashery, and Cousin Lewis, a drunkard who continuously recounts his killing of Cousin Jamie—but he must also deal with his sister Lily Dale's selfish behavior and his mother's failing health.

Early in the play, Horace learns that Corella desperately needs an operation. Her illness is the result of physical and emotional exhaustion brought on by her unceasing worry over Lily Dale, who has selfishly allowed her mother to care for her entire family while she practiced piano. As Lily Dale's husband Will Kidder explains to Horace, "between Lily Dale and your mama, they know every doctor in Houston, and as you know, your mama wasn't at all satisfied with her last two operations and Lily Dale has had two herself, not counting the Caesarean for the baby" (505). Lily Dale also has severe headaches and she, Will, and her mother have sought the advice of fortunetellers. The characters' obsessive drive for money and material possessions has alienated them from each other and set them on a fruitless journey for physical, external security and happiness. Even worse, Lily Dale secretly blames her mother's poor condition on Horace's Cousin Minnie Robedaux, who confronted Corella in the ladies' room at Foleys and admonished her for abandoning Horace as a child and for treating him so callously as a man. Throughout his family's bickering and condemnation, however, Horace somehow maintains his dignity and integrity.

Everyone in *Cousins* must face his or her own demons, even the selfish and narcissistic Lily Dale, who learns that life does not always work out as planned. Her fantasy of becoming a famous musician is foiled when a thief, masquerading as a music publisher, disappears with her two-thousand-dollar investment. For the first time in her life, Lily

---

[41] Foote, *Genesis*, 133.

Dale must cope with the kind of personal humiliation and disappointment that her brother has been subjected to for years. Lily Dale lives for the future and has bitter memories of her paternal family, but Horace has embraced his past and learned to extend his love into the entire community of Harrison. He shows compassion and empathy to everyone in town, both black and white, and as the curtain falls on *Cousins*, Horace resumes his life and reenters his workday world with a deeper understanding of what it means to be part of a family and community. Cousin Minnie, realizing the futility of holding onto her bitterness toward Horace's mother, Corella, reminds her cousin of the ephemeral nature of family relationships and the importance of having a spiritual and emotional home: "Dead. So many are dead. So many of the cousins. Of course, there are new cousins, their children, and their children's children, but I've lost track of most of them. A family is a remarkable thing, isn't it? You belong. And then you don't. It passes you by. Unless you start a family of your own" (557).

Cousin Minnie's speech sets the stage for the final play in the cycle, *The Death of Papa*, which dramatizes the death of Horton Foote's maternal grandfather and the enormous repercussions the patriarch's passing had on his family.[42] Reflecting upon the importance of this event in his own life, Horton remarked: "My grandfather, who seemed impervious to all mortal ends, died when I was nine, and the reverberations and changes from that death continued for many years. It was soon after that I was to see a quiet, serene street (in front of my grandparents' house) begin its slow but steady descent into a metaphor for all the ugly, trashy highways that scar a great deal of small-town America."[43]

The tragedy of *The Death of Papa* is filtered through the eyes of young Horace Jr., the playwright's fictional counterpart, who is ten years old when the play begins. Horace Jr. is an inquisitive boy with an insatiable appetite for his family's stories, even though his grandmother warns him about repeating everything he hears. Horace Jr. loves to read books as well, a fact that disturbs his grandmother Davenport, who thinks too much education is a curse. At one point, Corella reprimands Horace Sr. for allowing his son to read too much: "I can name you boy after boy that were overeducated like Terrence Robedaux and weren't worth killing" (641). Horace's impassioned defense of his son not only establishes

---

[42] Horton Foote, *The Death of Papa*, in *The Orphans' Home Cycle*, 565–645. Page references to *The Death of Papa* in the text refer to this publication.

[43] Foote, Introduction to *The Orphans' Home Cycle*, 1–2.

Horace as a loving father, but it is also the closest he will ever come to expressing his true feelings about the pain his mother caused him. "And I can name you boy after boy whose family had no interest at all in them or what they learned. Who no one cared if they went to school or if they didn't. What they had to bear, what they had...I could tell you heart-breaking stories...about those boys" (641). Determined not to make the same mistake with his son, Horace assures Horace Jr., "I'm going to stand by you in any way I can and I'm going to see you get an education if you want one. I don't want you ever to have to scratch around the way I have" (620).

Horace also understands the importance for his son to be deeply rooted in his family heritage. Like his father, Horace Jr. attempts to remember all the stories he hears about his ancestors, and he tries to treat everyone he encounters, both black and white, with compassion and understanding. When the young boy questions Gertrude, the family's black housekeeper, about why she goes to school, she replies: "To help our race" (579). Later, when he asks his mother what he can do to "help my race, too," Elizabeth replies, "Start by being a good man; that will help all the races" (608). By the end of the play, Horace Jr. emerges as a sensitive, emotionally secure young man, a character that Samuel Freedman described as "quite clearly, a writer in the making" (Freedman, xii). Concerning his place in the drama, Horton Foote explained:

> Consciously, I have only used myself in my writing twice: once in my play *Wharton Dance*, which as I remember was too autobiographical for comfort and second in *The Death of Papa*, in which I was the age of Horace Jr. when my grandfather died. I remember walking home from school and coming into my house and being aware that it was empty. This was very unusual for me, because never before had I come into my house without my mother and my two brothers always being there. On this day, however, they were not and so I went across the street to play with a friend. His mother soon came out, looking very solemn, and said she thought I had better go to my grandfather's house. Our backyard faced my grandparents', and I remember running through our frontyard into our backyard, and there in my grandparents' backyard I could see their cook Eliza, their chauffeur, her brother, Walter, and Eliza and Walter's sister Sara, who lived and worked next door. I slowed down and tried walking casually into the yard. I remember them talking about seeing a dove alight on the house that morning and that that surely meant someone in the house would die before the day was out. Then they

noticed me, and told me I should go into the house and see my mother. I went up the back stairs and met my mother standing in the back hall. Still there was no mention of my grandfather, but she asked if I would like to see my grandmother. I said, "Yes," and she led me through the back hall into the front hall past the living room. I saw a crowd of people dressing in their Sunday best in the living room and my mother took me to my grandmother's room and led me inside. I saw my grandmother leaning over my grandfather's body crying, and I realized he was the one who had died.[44]

Horton dramatized the day of his grandfather's death exactly as he remembered it, and in doing so revealed the devastating impact of the patriarch's passing on his family. Elizabeth is overwhelmed with sorrow as she runs to embrace Horace Jr., crying, "Son! What are we going to do? What are any of us going to do? (570). Mrs. Vaughn is stricken with grief, having lost her companion and the friend she thought would shelter her from life's harsh realities. "Oh, my God!" she exclaims. "Henry tended to everything ever since we were married. I feel so helpless! So very helpless!" (588).

After his burial, Mrs. Vaughn erects an impressive tombstone in the family plot and takes daily trips to the cemetery to mourn over her husband's grave. She often takes her grandson, Horace Jr. with her and in the process teaches him about the mysteries of death and of the importance of remembering and grieving over those who have died.

While Elizabeth and Mrs. Vaughn find constructive ways to mourn their loss, Brother is emotionally devastated by his father's death and paralyzed by his inability to live up to his father's image. Mrs. Vaughn wants to believe in her son, so she puts Brother in charge of his father's modest fortune, hoping the young man will rise to the occasion. The challenge proves too much, however, and he is unable to control his excessive drinking or to hold onto the land and money his father left to support the family. He finally has to confess, "I worshiped my father," and acknowledge that his failure stems from knowing "I can never in any way live up to him. Not in any way be worthy of him" (616). Brother's fall from grace is viewed through the prism of Horace's life. After losing his father at age twelve, Horace was forced to dig in his heels and support himself. "When I got into trouble," Horace admits, "there was no one I could turn to to help me out...there was a time I felt very bitter about it. I felt no one cared about me at all" (634–5). Although

---

[44] Foote, *Genesis*, 133–34.

orphaned as a child, Horace emerges, in *The Death of Papa*, as the very essence of a strong and loving father, the only man who can live up to the standard set by Mr. Vaughn. Ultimately, Horace Robedaux becomes a man fully connected to his home. "I used to feel sorry for you when you would come and call on Elizabeth," the now rootless Brother admits to Horace. "I'd hear Papa and Mama talking and they said you were practically an orphan and had no home. Now you have a home and I don't." (645). Horace has overcome humiliation, sorrow, and death, in order to build for himself and his family an orphans' home, a sacred place of stability and renewal that will help them weather future hardships. Marian Burkhart, in her article "Horton Foote's Many Roads Home," speaks for everyone who sits in awe of Horace Robedaux's remarkable journey from rootlessness to love and personal fulfillment. "How did Horace, who suffered more and received less than any other of the *Cycle's* principal characters find his way to compassion, to joy, to generosity?" Burkhart asks.

> Why is he scrupulously honest when in his need as a child he was cheated and cheated again? To these questions there is no answer. He just is, as Elizabeth just knew and just chose. Their goodness, their wisdom, remains a mystery. We can answer, of course, the grace of God, but if we have any understanding at all of what those words mean, we ought to realize that they merely restate the mystery theologically. We ought to realize, too, the magnitude of Horton Foote's achievement. In choosing to praise such gentle heroes, to give them the fame that is their due, Foote has assessed American character, American myth, and the American ambience more accurately than just about any other figure in the American theatre.[45]

The Orphans' Home Cycle was born from Horton Foote's desire to understand his own identity and his own place in the history of his family. He began writing the plays under the most personal of circumstances, the death of his mother and father, whose passing inspired him to write his most ambitious and definitive examination of change, loss, and courage. He began with a moral and social history of Wharton, Texas, in the first two decades of the twentieth century, and ultimately created a vivid portrait of life in small-town America that is virtually unequalled in American literature. *The Orphans' Home Cycle* is Horton Foote's acknowledged masterpiece, the most impressive and

---

[45] Marian Burkhart, "Horton Foote's Many Roads Home: An American Playwright and his Characters," *Commonweal* (26 February 1988): 114–15.

skillfully written work in his entire canon, and ranks among the very best of Eugene O'Neil, Thornton Wilder, Tennessee Williams, Arthur Miller, or August Wilson. Horton is the only writer ever to complete a nine-play cycle based on a single family in a specific time and place. In these plays, Horton traced the life and death of his own family and all the people who came into contact with them in the small town of Harrison, Texas, while reminding us of the importance of family, community, and religious faith in our turbulent and chaotic world. Recording the inexorable movement and change of life itself, he wove a subtle and intricate commentary on the importance of family to personal responsibility and contentment by dramatizing the interplay of relationships as families experience birth and death, joys and misfortunes, happiness and heartbreak. Horton's compassionate depiction of small-town family relationships in *The Orphans' Home Cycle* is his greatest contribution to American drama.

While depicting the effects of a changing moral and social order on families, Horton Foote, also, with even greater emphasis, celebrates the regenerative power of individual courage and resilience. His characters are filled with an extraordinarily vigorous life, humor, irony, and beauty, best illustrated by Horace Robedaux and Elizabeth Vaughn, who are driven by a need to connect with something beyond themselves—a family, a community, or God—and compelled to transcend their unfulfilled lives in order to find peace, love, and contentment. Horton's characters are all orphans searching for a home, for a sense of meaning and order in an ocean of circumstances.

The historical significance of *The Orphans' Home Cycle* is best explained by novelist Harper Lee, who wrote in a letter to Horton: "You are recording an American society that is disappearing before our eyes. In your cycle of plays we see its mores, its values, its deep schisms and deficiencies—a way of life that will be history when our grandchildren are grown. But with your steady gaze and wisdom they will have something priceless: the truth of what made them who they are."[46] In time, *The Orphans' Home Cycle* would bring Horton great honor and acclaim, but he would not see the plays performed together for more than thirty years. Trying to locate the financial backing for a production of *The Orphans' Home Cycle*, Horton was inspired to enter a new phase in his career as an independent filmmaker, and to begin work on his most

---

[46] Harper Lee to Horton Foote, 12 March 1997 (Horton Foote Papers).

celebrated and admired screenplay, the Academy Award-winning *Tender Mercies*.

Part Six

A Second Act

[Horton Foote] has a specific voice, a specific style, and he has never abandoned it, even though it cost him. He has never cut his talent to the fashion of the time. And because he wrote his plays, whether they were going to be produced or not, he got what most American writers don't get—a second act.

—Alan Pakula

14

Independent Filmmaker
1978–90

By the spring of 1976, Horton Foote had completed drafts of eight plays in *The Orphans' Home Cycle: Roots in a Parched Ground, Convicts, Lily Dale, Courtship, Valentine's Day, 1918, Cousins,* and *The Death of Papa*—and he desperately wanted to see them performed together onstage. At the time, however, American theater was going through major changes, and Horton knew there weren't any commercial theaters financially or artistically capable of producing such a substantial work. While he had been living in New Hampshire, the experimental dramas that had dominated the New York theater scene during the late sixties and early seventies were no longer in fashion, and new plays were seldom produced on Broadway. "The New York commercial theatre was a dismal scene," Horton said. "Many of the lovely theatres were being torn down. These included the Empire, the Hudson, the Forrest, the Playhouse (where my plays *The Traveling Lady* and *The Chase* had been produced, as well as Tennessee Williams's *The Glass Menagerie*), the Maxine Elliot, the Morosco, the Bijou, and the Helen Hayes."[1] While Broadway was being transformed, both financially and artistically, young writers like Sam Shepard, Romulus Linney, John Guare, Lanford Wilson, and David Mamet emerged as harbingers of a new generation of writers who were energizing the Off-Broadway and Off-Off-Broadway theater scenes. Their works were being performed tastefully but inexpensively in regional and small theaters throughout the country as well as in coffeehouses, storefronts, basements, and churches. Shows with smaller casts were now the fashion, and any space that could accommodate actors and an audience was a potential playhouse.

Realizing the transitory state of New York theater, Horton turned to public television, which seemed to be the only venue with the money and resources to produce the cycle as he had envisioned it. The main outlet for original drama was PBS's *American Short Story* series, supported by the National Endowment for the Humanities, so Horton

---

[1] Horton Foote, *Genesis of an American Playwright*, ed. Marion Castleberry (Waco TX: Baylor University Press, 2004) 230.

sent the eight plays to his friend Robert Geller, the show's executive producer. After reading them, Geller informed Horton he really liked the plays but felt there should be a ninth work written to complete the cycle. Horton agreed and wrote *The Widow Claire*, chronologically the fourth play in the cycle. With *The Orphans' Home Cycle* now complete, Geller set out to convince executives at PBS to produce the entire cycle on the *American Short Story Series*. But even after Horton agreed to adapt Flannery O'Connor's *The Displaced Person* (1977) for the series, the money for *The Orphans' Home Cycle* was not forthcoming.

Disappointed but undaunted, Horton continued to search for a television studio that would be willing to produce all nine cycle plays. He sent four of the plays—*Roots in a Parched Ground, Convicts, Lily Dale,* and *The Widow Claire*—to Phil Capice, executive producer of Lorimar Productions, a subsidiary of Warner Brothers, asking him to consider filming *The Orphans' Home Cycle*. Sadly, nothing came of Horton's submission to Lorimar. He then sent a letter to his cousin Peter Masterson, a well-known New York actor and director, asking for his help in getting the cycle plays produced at the Actors Studio in New York. "I am enclosing the first five plays," Horton wrote.

> When I first finished them I gave them to Bob Geller, as it seemed easiest to get them first performed on PBS. However, they wanted to put them on file and early budgets called for five million dollars, which was discouraging. In the meantime, I have begun to feel they should be done first in the theatre. But I really haven't known where to turn. I thought perhaps the Actors Studio might be a proper beginning. Anyway, as you know, Bob Duvall has read and wants to do *Convicts*. He's going to do it with Herbert Berghoff. No one else has seen the other plays except for Bob Geller and an Executive Producer of Channel 13, and my close personal friends, Stewart Millar and Joseph Anthony. Stewart was anxious to direct them for Geller and Joe, although he says he has retired, [and] has intimated he would un-retire to do them. However, if any of them appeal to you (except *Convicts*) and you would like to do them at the Studio, I would be most interested in exploring it with you.[2]

Masterson was unable to find the financial backing to produce any of the plays at the Actors Studio, and Horton was left once again without a theater in which to perform his work. Ever resilient, Horton decided then and there to take matters into his own hands by becoming director and producer of the plays himself. He felt that *Courtship, Valentine's Day,*

---

[2] Horton Foote to Peter Masterson, 17 November 1977 (Horton Foote Papers).

and *1918* would be the most likely of the nine plays to receive successful stage productions, but he recognized early on that he had to find a suitable cast for the shows. He was especially concerned about finding someone to play the role of Elizabeth Vaughn. Over the years, he had worked with many wonderful actresses—Kim Stanley, Geraldine Page, Eva Marie Saint, Julie Harris, and Joanne Woodward, to name only a few—but by now they were all past the age of performing the role. Horton simply couldn't think of anyone capable of embodying the spirit and courage of the young wife and mother. However, miraculously, he found the perfect actress for the role when his daughter Barbara Hallie, who was studying acting with Peggy Feury, invited him to Los Angeles to see her perform the role of Wilma Thompson in a production of *A Young Lady of Property* at the Loft Theatre. Horton was so moved by his daughter's performance that he immediately called his wife, Lillian, in New Hampshire to tell her: "I have found my Elizabeth."[3]

At the time, Horton had not heard any of *The Orphans' Home Cycle* plays read aloud, so he asked Barbara Hallie to gather a group of her fellow acting students to read *1918*, the only play of the cycle he had brought with him from New Hampshire. The reading took place in Barbara Hallie's tiny apartment in Los Angeles, and Horton found the actors' work so encouraging that when he returned to New Hampshire, he called his friend Herbert Berghof in New York to ask if he could direct *Courtship, Valentine's Day*, and *1918* at his HB Studio Theatre on Bank Street.

Berghof had recently produced two of Horton's plays at the HB Studio Theatre: *A Young Lady of Property* with Lindsay Crouse (1976) and a staged reading of *Night Seasons* (1977), the story of Laura Lee Weems and her futile attempts to break free from the emotional paralysis that has tragically defined her life and left her without a physical or emotional home. Berghof saw the opportunity to perform *The Orphans' Home Cycle* plays as a major boon for his theater, and he enthusiastically agreed to produce them. Horton decided to direct the plays out of sequence, "to stress the fact that they were each complete to themselves," beginning the series with *Courtship* in 1978, followed by *1918* in 1979, and *Valentine's Day* in 1980.[4]

The HB Studio Theatre was a small, ninety-nine-seat, Off-Broadway house, which had a contract with Actors Equity that limited the run of its

---

[3] Foote, *Genesis*, 118.
[4] Ibid.

productions to ten performances. No one was paid at the HB—not actors, directors, or playwrights—and theater critics were not invited to review the productions, a tradition giving Horton freedom to work on his plays without interference. Herbert Berghof's support during this time was very significant to Horton's career, helping to renew the playwright's passion for the theater and to spark a revival of interest in his plays. "I worked closely with Herbert for a number of years at the Playwrights Foundation," he explained. "Herbert directed four of my plays there and produced a number of others. He gave me a theatre home and rekindled my faith in theatre."[5]

In spring 1978, Horton began rehearsals for *Courtship* in the sitting room of his Greenwich Village apartment, which he and Lillian had sublet in order to be close to the HB Studio Theatre. Horton worked with the main cast (consisting of Barbara Hallie as Elizabeth, Gypsy DeYoung as Laura, Carolyn Coates as Mrs. Vaughn, and Richard Cotrell as Mr. Vaughn) for about three weeks, after which time the remainder of the ensemble joined them in rehearsals. Horton's old friend Valerie Bettis also came in to choreograph the dance sequences in the play. This proved to be an enjoyable time for Horton, who was happy to be working in the theater again and thrilled to be directing such a talented cast.

Courtship opened on 5 July 1978, a date that biographer Wilborn Hampton points to as "the start of Foote's second career."[6] The show, as Horton remembered, was scheduled to begin on July 4 but because of the excessive heat wave crippling New York City, the opening of the play was postponed until the next night. "The theatre was not air conditioned," Horton recalled, "but the night was pleasant enough and the performance went well."[7] *Courtship* turned out to be a great success and audience response was enthusiastic.

After the triumph of *Courtship*, Horton was encouraged to direct *1918* the next season. As thrilled as he was to be working on *The Orphans' Home Cycle*, however, Horton was nearly broke, and in order to continue working on the plays, he needed to find a way to support the productions. His agent, Lucy Kroll, suggested that he consider writing a screenplay. At first, Horton thought she meant doing another

---

[5] Ibid., 12.

[6] Wilborn Hampton, *Horton Foote: America's Storyteller* (New York: Simon & Schuster, 2009) 219.

[7] Foote, *Genesis*, 119.

adaptation, and he explained that he was so consumed with his own plays that he didn't want to adapt anyone else's work. Kroll explained that she meant for him to write an original screenplay, something he had never done before, and she asked him to call her when he had an idea of what he wanted to write. With a compelling story, Kroll felt sure Horton could get a cash advance from a Hollywood studio, and she offered to arrange a meeting with a producer in Hollywood so he could pitch his idea. Horton had never liked the notion of pitching a story. He had been accustomed to showing a written draft of a screenplay to prospective producers and was horrified by the thought of verbally describing or pitching an idea. "Lucy, I can't do that," Horton remarked. "Well," Kroll said, "for God's sake, try it." Since the financial pressures were so great, Horton finally agreed, "All right, I'll try," he said.[8]

Although pitching a work was unfamiliar territory for Horton, things went surprisingly well in Los Angeles. Lucy Kroll got in touch with Alice "Boaty" Boatwright, whom the writer had first met during the filming of *To Kill a Mockingbird.* Boatwright, who liked Horton's story a great deal, then scheduled a meeting between the playwright and Gareth Wigan, a producer at Twentieth Century Fox. The playwright recalled that when he entered Wigan's office he "was so embarrassed that I wanted the earth to swallow me up. I mumbled a few sentences and to my surprise he made some kind of sense out of my mumblings. He called my agent to come to the West Coast the next week to draw up the contract for my services."[9]

The story that Horton told the producer centered on the struggles that his nephew, Tom Foote (his brother, John's, son), and his country western band (the George Strait Band) was having breaking into country-western music. The story revealed the hardships the young man's occupation brought to his family:

> And so basically I told a very straightforward story about these five young men from very disparate backgrounds, all having to do part-time jobs to keep themselves going. And they're trying to get ahead, and they have tribulations, like going to a place where another band already had been hired and they don't get paid. And I also had one scene where they were in pick-up trucks at night, and they would pass one of these big buses with a band, a country and western band, that arrived. I really just

---

[8] Ibid., 173.
[9] Ibid.

described kind of the atmosphere of their lives. And I said that it would end up…with finding a way to succeed.[10]

After Horton pitched the story, the producer admitted he found the idea intriguing but believed that somewhere in the screenplay there should be an older man who could serve as a contrast to the younger boys. "Then he had me go and look at *Breaking Away*, which was a popular film at the time, to, as he said, 'show you how Fox can handle this treatment.' And I liked that part. And so he said, 'O.K., you have your agent come out.' That's all there was to it."[11] A few days later, Lucy Kroll flew to California to finalize the contract, but the morning she arrived in Beverly Hills, she read in *Hollywood Reporter* that the producer with whom Horton had spoken, had been fired the day before by Twentieth Century Fox, along with several other executives, including Alan Ladd, Jr., one of America's most successful film producers and former president of Fox. Following the studio shakeup, Hollywood was no longer interested in filming Horton's screenplay. The news was very disappointing, but because the writer had by this time become so deeply involved in the story, he decided to finish the screenplay without the support of a studio or an advance. As Horton began to jot down ideas for the screenplay, he thought more and more about the older man, suggested to him by the producer, and slowly the character of Mac Sledge began to take shape:

> I began to think about this man and who he could be to fit into this world of country music…and I decided to make him a once-famous performer. When you work on material of your own, you go into an uncharted world. Everything has to be found—story, character, style. At that time, I had never known any famous country-western singers; but I had known famous actors and actresses whose careers had been ruined because of drunkenness and some who'd overcome alcoholism. I also knew about fame and loss of fame, ambition and loss of ambition. All my life, I had known non-singing Mac Sledges—pained, bewildered, inarticulate— good men really, at least with a desire to be good, whose lives were in a shambles, totally out of control.[12]

Horton's decision to shift the focus of the story from a country-western band to an older man not only helped focus the screenplay, but

---

[10] Horton Foote, telephone interview with Gerald C. Wood, 15 March 1988.
[11] Ibid.
[12] Horton Foote, Foreword to *Three Screenplays: To Kill a Mockingbird, Tender Mercies, and The Trip to Bountiful* (New York: Grove Press 1989) vii.

it also provided an opportunity for the writer to create one of his most memorable characters, Mac Sledge, an alcoholic country-western singer struggling to regain a sense of order in his life with the help of a loving and steadfast woman, Rosa Lee, and her fatherless son, Sonny. Relying on his history with actors and his knowledge of alcoholism, Horton completed an early draft of the story he called "The Singer and the Song" which Gerald Wood describes as "a coastal southeast Texas story equally attentive to Mac and the band," a screenplay much different from the final shooting script.[13] "Mac enters before the boys in the band," Wood explains. "Early in the treatment his story is integrated with theirs. Rosa Lee is there, though she and Mac are not linked romantically until Mac's problems with Dixie are well developed. Foote had not as yet focused on the Mac/Rosa Lee/Sonny triad."[14]

After finishing the initial draft, Horton read the story to Robert Duvall. "My daughter [Hallie] was friendly with Bob [Duvall] and the girl he was going with at the time," Horton recalled, "and she said 'Do you know Bob can sing?' I said, 'No, I didn't know that." So I said, 'Well, I think I have something that would interest Bob.' I invited Bob and Gail and my daughter down. I think poor Bob thought I was going to give him a screenplay to read, but I made him sit down and I read it to him. And he liked it. It would have ended our friendship I guess, if he hadn't."[15] Inspired by the basic values of dignity and courage and the theme of redemption inherent in the screenplay, Duvall immediately announced he wanted to play the role of Mac Sledge.

Since there was no Hollywood studio interested in the screenplay, Horton and Duvall agreed to produce the movie themselves as independent filmmakers. Independent filmmaking was not as prevalent then as it is today, and the two had no real knowledge of raising money on their own. At first, they tried to carry out a conventional search—contacting major studios and cable networks—without success. To make matters worse, Horton was busy directing *1918* at the HB Studio Theatre, and Duvall was working on his film *Angelo, My Love*, which he was financing himself. Their commitments left precious little time to look for

---

[13] Gerald C. Wood, *Horton Foote and the Theatre of Intimacy* (Baton Rouge: Louisiana State University Press 1999) 88.

[14] Ibid.

[15] Ronald Davis, "Roots in Parched Ground: An Interview with Horton Foote," *The Voice of an American Playwright*, ed. Gerald C. Wood and Marion Castleberry (Macon GA: Mercer University Press, 2012) 75–6.

money. When they couldn't arrange their own financing, the two artists turned to Philip and Mary Ann Hobel, successful documentary film-makers looking to enter the world of feature films.

Horton and Philip Hobel first met in the spring of 1979 at the HB Studio Theatre, following a sold out performance of *1918*. The production, which featured most of the same cast as *Courtship*, was a huge hit, and Hobel was so moved by the performance that he found Horton backstage and expressed his desire to bring *1918* to the screen. Although Horton was sincerely touched by Hobel's offer, he explained that he was too involved with *Tender Mercies* to think of producing another film at that time. Hobel then asked to read *Tender Mercies*. He liked the script a great deal and announced that he would like to produce the film.[16]

As documentary filmmakers, Philip and Mary Ann Hobel had considerable experience in raising money and they seemed quite optimistic about getting the movie made. But their optimism soon turned to disappointment when studio after studio refused to support the film. Country-western music was not very popular at the time, and Hollywood executives did not think a story about a struggling country-western singer was a marketable commodity. Consequently, *Tender Mercies* did not go into production for another two years.

Not only did Horton and Duvall have difficulty finding financial support for *Tender Mercies*, they also had trouble finding someone to direct the film. Horton's early choice for director was Barbara Loden, a respected film actress and director who had written and produced the independent film *Wanda* in 1970, but Loden was diagnosed with cancer and had to withdraw from consideration. Besides Barbara Loden, all the other American directors Horton considered—Arthur Penn, Robert Mulligan, Dan Petrie, and Delbert Mann—turned down the project. Horton and Duvall were disheartened, but Philip Hobel remained surprisingly optimistic, reassuring both artists—and perhaps himself—that they would find a reputable director and eventually get the film made.

Throughout all the anxiety and confusion over *Tender Mercies*, Horton continued to find encouragement working in television and theater. He took on a few projects during this time to support himself and Lillian and to pay for his children's college expenses. One of his most notable projects was an adaption of William Faulkner's *Barn Burning* for *American Short Story Series* that aired on 17 March 1980. Directed by Peter

---

[16] Foote, *Genesis*, 174.

Werner and starring Tommy Lee Jones, Horton created an actable screenplay from Faulkner's short story about the barn burner, Abner Snopes, and his son Sarty, whose desperate pride in his father is threatened when he can no longer justify Snope's lawlessness. "With *Barn Burning*," Horton explained "I knew the people in the story like the back of my hand. I had seen their prototypes in my father's store and the streets of my town when I was a boy."

> I was able to flesh out some minor characters and invent additional scenes that I felt were necessary in the screenplay, and all went well until I reached the end of the story. Then, Faulkner, in the last two paragraphs, compresses time in a way a dramatist never can, so that the whole experience became inner and subjective. The first of the two paragraphs starts, 'At midnight he sat on the crest of a hill.' The second paragraph continues, 'He knew it was almost dawn, the night almost over. He could tell that from the whippoorwills.' In those two paragraphs, between midnight and near dawn, the boy is alone with his thoughts, his guilt, his continuing inner defense of his father, his emotions, and finally his wordless decision to go on alone. I worked and worked on these last two paragraphs. What I finally came up with was acceptable, in my opinion, but in no way did I match the original ending."[17]

Although Horton was dissatisfied with his treatment of Faulkner's original ending, the writer's resolution, in which Snopes drives off in a wagon silhouetted against the burning barn while his son runs in the opposite direction, is a striking image that expresses Sarty's inner conflict and his choice of societal responsibility over his commitment to his father.

Horton also directed *Valentine's Day* at the HB Studio Theatre in 1980, with a noteworthy cast: Hallie Foote as Elizabeth, Granger Hines as Horace, James Broderick as Mr. Vaughn, Rochelle Oliver as Mrs. Vaughn, Irma Levesque as Bessie, and Matthew Broderick in his professional stage debut as Brother. The production was well received, proving once again that a play from *The Orphans' Home Cycle* could attract and entertain New York audiences.

During the time Horton was working at HB Theatre, the status of *Tender Mercies* remained uncertain. At one point, things looked so bleak that even the usually optimistic Philip Hobel became frustrated and disheartened. Then one day in 1980, John Cohn, a producer at EMI films, a British film and television production company, called Horton out of

---

[17] Ibid., 183.

the blue and said that he had read the screenplay of *Tender Mercies*. Cohn told the writer that he had been given a stack of screenplays to read, and in looking through them he saw the name Horton Foote. Cohn had long admired the writer's work and felt confident that EMI would be willing to finance the film, based on the reputations of Horton Foote and Robert Duvall.

The movie was promised a budget of four and a half million dollars, but even after financial backing was secured it took a year before the cameras actually started rolling. First, a suitable director had to be found. After a good deal of discussion, EMI, together with Robert Duvall and Philip Hobel, asked Horton for permission to send a copy of *Tender Mercies* to Bruce Beresford, an Australian filmmaker who had received critical acclaim for his movie *Breaker Morant*. Even though Horton liked the film very much, he was unsure about Beresford as a director and wondered if sending a script to someone so rooted in Australian culture might not be a waste of time. In spite of Horton's objection, Duvall and the producers decided to send the script to Beresford anyway and the director responded almost immediately, asking if he could meet with Horton to see if the two could work together harmoniously. Beresford, who was at his home in Sydney at the time, remembers that *Tender Mercies*, "this gentle story of a down and out Country and Western singer and his relationship with a Vietnam War widow and her young son captivated me from the first page. I found the dialogue particularly impressive. It was simple, straightforward, never seemed to strive for effect, and was devoid of the one-line gags so characteristic of film scriptwriters. I found it almost unbearably moving and was quite sure it was written with a precise ear for the cadences and phrases of the Texans among whom the story was set. Immediately thinking that the script could be with other directors and without even getting to the end of the story, I phoned the producers in New York (Philip and Mary Ann Hobel) and told them I would direct the film."[18]

Beresford then flew to America to meet Horton Foote. The two artists liked each other immediately, and that week they flew to Dallas to introduce the director to North Texas, more specifically to tour the town of Waxahachie, a small farming community thirty miles south of Dallas where Arthur Penn's *Bonnie and Clyde* and Robert Benton's *Places in the*

---

[18] Bruce Beresford," Memorial Essay," *Farewell: Remembering Horton Foote, 1916–2009*, ed. Marion Castleberry and Susan Christensen (Dallas TX: Southern Methodist University Press, 2011) 22–4.

Heart had been filmed. Soon after touring Texas, Beresford was hired after receiving final approval from Robert Duvall, who had a clause in his contract giving the actor final say over the choice of director.

Once Beresford was brought onboard, several pressing issues had to be confronted immediately, the most critical of which was finding a suitable shooting location for the film. Horton was determined to make the movie in Texas, and the Hobels, for a number of pragmatic reasons (mostly money) were resolved to shoot the film in the Deep South: Georgia, Florida, Louisiana, or Arkansas. Robert Duvall, who would later be listed in the credits as a co-producer, supported Horton, as did director Bruce Beresford, who found the land and the people of north central Texas similar to his native Australia and ideal for his vision of the film. Horton remembered that the director kept saying over and over, "It's just like Australia."[19] The filmmakers eventually decided upon the Texas location because as Philip Hobel explained, "We wanted the authentic look and sounds of Texas and now feel that the landscape and people are integral to the success of it. In a play you have a clear stage, but in film you have to be true to the place. This is something Robert Duvall sensed and needed as an actor. But the film also transcended its location: there's something mythic about it."[20]

Even after the Texas location had been agreed upon, there was disagreement between Horton Foote and Bruce Beresford over the exact look of the landscape to be used in the film. Horton had imagined the setting to be like the rich farmland and woods surrounding his hometown of Wharton, but Beresford, less interested in specific locations than the writer, envisioned a limitless sky and barren terrain that would establish the pervasive sense of loneliness and isolation that defines the emotional landscape of the characters. What the filmmakers finally agreed upon was significantly different from Horton's usual coastal southeast Texas setting, but as art designer Jeannine Oppewall noted, the location offered a perfect place for the story to unfold:

> The producer and director had been scouting locations in Texas for some time before they had hired me, as is frequently the case, and they had seen a place outside Dallas that they thought might be a potentially good location for the motel set. So soon after I arrived, the local location manager and scout, Dannette Goss, took me to have a look at it, to see what I thought about its workablility. The location consisted of an old

---

[19] Foote, *Genesis*, 187.

[20] Robert Duvall, telephone interview with Gerald C. Wood, 17 September 1990.

tumbled down tenant farmer's shack on a two-lane road between Palmer and Waxahachie, in the middle of an utterly flat cotton field. There were no other human structures in sight. It was exactly the kind of place that would make one begin to understand why people like Mac and Rosa Lee would get together—in part because there is simply very little else for one's eye to settle on. The landscape itself was strong and suggested a kind of interior loneliness and demanded of its inhabitants a quiet resignation and self-sufficiency.[21]

On this relatively barren site, Beresford had a gas station and motel set built that was so realistic drivers actually pulled into the station asking to fill up their gas tanks. Jeannine Oppewall later gave the motel the name *Mariposa*, a Spanish word for butterfly, which symbolized the spiritual resurrection that Mac Sledge would experience there. Placed against a vast and empty sky, the setting would become for Mac a place of refuge and resurrection while for Rosa Lee and Sonny the *Mariposa* motel was home, a shelter against a violent and ambiguous world.

After settling on the Texas location, Horton and Beresford returned to New York to begin selecting the movie's cast and crew. They chose a top-notch crew featuring Russell Boyd as cinematographer and William Anderson as editor, both of whom had worked with the Beresford on his earlier films. They also selected Elizabeth McBride as costume designer, and Jeannine Oppewall as art director. The filmmakers, as well as the Texas crews who assisted them, were totally committed to the project, worked together beautifully, and were well equipped to create one of the most stunning films in American cinema.

Horton and Beresford also chose an ensemble of actors that featured Betty Buckley as Dixie, Mac's embittered ex-wife; Ellen Barkin as Sue Ann, Mac and Dixie's daughter; and Wilford Brimley as Harry, Dixie's agent. Allan Hubbard, who played Sonny, and Tess Harper, who played Rosa Lee, were both cast in Dallas. Nine-year-old Allan Hubbard was chosen from among several children whom Beresford auditioned for the part because of his simple, rural manner and his ability to relate to the character's yearning for a father. When he was cast, filmmakers were unaware that Hubbard's own father had died at an early age, just as Sonny's had in the film. So it is not surprising that Hubbard and Duvall cultivated a trusting father/son relationship during the shooting of the movie that is captured beautifully onscreen, especially in the improvised scenes where Mac teaches Sonny how to play the guitar. Hubbard also

---

[21] Jeannine Oppewall, telephone interview with Gerald C. Wood, 2 October 1990.

developed a genuine love and respect for Horton Foote and a deep connection to the writer's work during the making of *Tender Mercies*. "I was from a small Texas town [Paris, Texas], and a culturally un-savvy family," Hubbard recalled. "We knew nothing of filmmakers, screen-writers, or their ilk. So when I first met Horton Foote on the set of *Tender Mercies* in the fall of 1981, he was introduced to me explanatorily as the man who wrote the movie.... I would later learn this writer, this man with an unforgettable literary name, was highly influential and uniquely talented with his own voice and a subtle approach to his craft that was unrivaled. I would also discover he, among all others, best captured in words the very day-to-day existence I lived and breathed as a small town Texan.... What I was to say made sense, as if it were written for me."[22]

Tess Harper was performing on stage in Dallas when she attended a casting call for a minor role in the film. Beresford was so taken with the actress's ordinary yet poised demeanor that he immediately cast Harper in her feature film debut as Rosa Lee. Beresford's choice proved to be the right one; when filming ended, Robert Duvall, who seldom praises fellow actors, gave Harper a blue cowgirl shirt as a gift with a card that read, "You really were Rosa Lee."[23] Harper later admitted that she felt a deep kinship to the character of Rosa Lee: "My little key to the character was I was raised in a fundamentalist background, and even though I'd been away from it for some time, recognized the better parts of funda-mentalism in Rosa Lee—Christian grace."[24] Harper also told Gerald Wood that she interpreted the character as "a kind of plains Madonna" who is "trying to empathize and understand what the people around her are going through" without verbalizing it. She added, "there is real love and respect [between Rosa Lee and Mac]...but it's not your passionate, typical movie love story. It's much deeper than that. She needs him, too; she needs a father for her son and she needs the companionship."

Tender Mercies was an equally important project for Robert Duvall, who established his reputation as one of America's greatest actors with his Oscar-winning portrayal of Mac Sledge. Not only did Duvall give a magnificent performance, but he also wrote two of the songs featured in the film. As he often does in creating a role, he used improvisation and creative imitation to develop the character of Mac Sledge, driving more than six hundred miles of roads in East Texas, searching for just the right

---

[22] Alan Hubbard, "Untitled Essay," *Farewell*: *Remembering Horton Foote*, 128–30.
[23] Tess Harper, telephone interview by Gerald C. Wood, 24 April 1991.
[24] Ibid.

accents, watching how people moved and held their bodies, and talking to farmers and musicians. Most helpful to Duvall were the audiotapes of a man from Pittsburg, Texas, whose speech the actor found most fitting for the character of Mac. He also joined a small country-western band from Italy, Texas, and performed with them every free weekend he had during the shooting of the film. "Man, I wanted my character to be real," he said. "But I love it, too. I love talking to those people. You know, that's what all my acting is really about. Dignity. Trying to find the dignity in man. Because the average workingman has dignity that the Hollywood establishment has overlooked."[25] Indeed, it is this sense of dignity that Duvall captures in his portrayal of Mac Sledge.

The actual shooting of *Tender Mercies* began 2 November and ended on 23 December 1981. For the most part, the cast and crew got along well during the filming, but with such a tight schedule and the filmmakers working long hours, tension was extremely high on the set. Beresford and Duvall began to disagree over several issues, not the least of which was how scenes should be set up, the use of close-ups, which Duvall felt at times were inappropriate, and the pacing of the movie. Beresford was a meticulous director who planned every scene, every single moment, with painstaking care while Duvall preferred a more improvisational, spontaneous approach to filmmaking. The actor felt restricted by Beresford's directorial method and the director was infuriated by Duvall's independent spirit and habit of speaking directly to other actors on the set, advising them about character interpretation and line delivery. The tension between the two artists came to a head one day when Beresford became so infuriated with Duvall on the phone that he walked off the set and flew back to New York. Beresford was ready to quit the film until Horton Foote accepted the role of peacemaker and convinced Duvall to speak with the director. Duvall flew to New York, met with Beresford, and after ironing out their disagreements the two returned to work on the film. The actor and director never completely resolved all their differences, but they learned to respect each other and to work together for the betterment of the film. In the end, Beresford was left with the realization of Duvall's cinematic talent: "Things did get better as we went along. I have great admiration for him as an actor. He had Mac Sledge down perfectly."[26]

---

[25] Judith Slawson, *Robert Duvall: Hollywood Maverick* (New York: St. Martin's Press, 1985) 160.

[26] Ibid.

There were not only concessions made between Beresford and Duvall, but there were also compromises made between director and screenwriter. Beresford felt that the shooting script was too diffuse, and even though he respected Horton's characters and language, he believed the story would benefit from more economy in place, plot, characters, and theme. The process of shooting helped to focus the story on Mac Sledge, his search for a family, his relationship with Rosa Lee and Sonny, and his final acceptance of life. As Gerald Wood points out, "collaboration actually helped Horton Foote return to his instincts as a writer. Robert Duvall, Brad Wilson (Duvall's assistant), and EMI added a musical score that, except for the final song, gave appropriate highlights and nuances to the script. The grandparents (though initially included in the shooting) were dropped, as was a sexual relationship between Dixie's agent, Harry, Sue Ann's career and interest in the band, and Menefee (Sue Ann's boyfriend), except for the brief shot of him in a car. As the Hobels (the producers), Beresford, and Anderson pushed economy, Dixie became a less complex, more negative character, and Rosa Lee's confusion was minimized, as was her interest in singing." The shooting script for *Tender Mercies* became "another Foote study in the transformative power of intimacy and responsibility."[27]

Tender Mercies is Horton Foote's most definitive cinematic work, and Mac Sledge is one of the writer's most memorable characters.[28] Much like Henry Thomas in *Baby, the Rain Must Fall*, Mac Sledge is a man whose life and career in country music have been ravaged by personal disappointments and alcoholism. We are never actually shown the incidents leading to Mac's failure, or those that have caused him to drift hopelessly from one town to another in search of a panacea for his pain, but brief flashes of dialogue and a few brief scenes between Mac and his ex-wife, Dixie Scott, provide a glimpse of his troubled past.

Mac begins his rocky road to country-western stardom at a young age, roaming from town to town, playing in any roadhouse or honky-tonk bar that would hire him. His marriage at seventeen quickly ends in divorce when his wife, unable to cope with the demands and pressures of her husband's lifestyle, runs off with another man. Heartbroken, Mac begins to write songs about his experiences, and by the time he meets his second wife, Dixie, he has cut a number of records and made a name for

---

[27] Wood, *Horton Foote and the Theatre of Intimacy*, 89.

[28] Horton Foote, *Tender Mercies*, in *Three Screenplay*, 81–148. Page references to *Tender Mercies* in the text refer to this publication.

himself on the music circuit. For a while, Mac and Dixie share a cordial relationship, but when Dixie refuses to keep her promise to give up her singing career and then begins making hits of Mac's songs, the marriage is doomed. Dixie's career flourishes while Mac's popularity plummets. Eventually, Mac turns to the bottle to escape his feelings of inadequacy, and his treatment of Dixie grows violent and abusive. At one point, he even attempts to kill his ambitious wife. Finally, Dixie, no longer able to tolerate the pain of their relationship asks for a divorce. When the film begins, Dixie's celebrity is at its height. Although she knows her career has been firmly built on the music and lyrics of her ex-husband, she has never forgiven Mac for his failure as a father and husband. For years, Dixie has successfully kept Mac away from his daughter, Sue Ann, by refusing to let her read the letters he has written to her and by prohibiting him from making contact with the girl. Dixie's anger pervades the film; in one scene she ferociously drives Mac away from her dressing room before he can even get a glimpse of Sue Ann, and in another she refuses to look at a song he has written for her to record. Now, after years of trying to drown his sorrow and regret in alcohol, Mac awakens in a run-down Texas motel abandoned and penniless. As the musical refrain of "It hurts so much to face reality" plays in the background, it is quickly apparent that Mac Sledge has hit rock bottom and now stands at the sharp edge of death. But unlike Henry Thomas, whose life is destroyed by his own misgivings and excesses, Mac, much like Horace Robedaux, is a survivor who finds the courage to hold onto his convictions and dignity and to build a promising new life with Rosa Lee, a young widow whose husband was killed in Vietnam, and her ten-year-old son, Sonny.

The film opens with a fight between Mac and a shadowy, unknown figure in a dark motel room. Reminiscent of the biblical image of Jacob wrestling with God, the scene quickly establishes the wretchedness of Mac's soul and the violence that haunts his life. Two days later, Mac emerges from his drunken stupor to face the bright Texas sun hovering over the Mariposa motel and gas station, which appears on screen as a fragile refuge in a barren wilderness. Mac admits that he can't pay the bill, so the owner of the motel, Rosa Lee, gives him work picking up trash and pumping gas. She offers Mac a room, meals, and two dollars an hour with the stipulation he doesn't drink on the premises. More importantly, Rosa Lee offers Mac a quiet strength, simple faith, and straightforward acceptance of life that enables him to overcome his failing voice, ruined career, and lost family. After paying off his debt, Mac quietly indicates he would like to stay on and, soon, Mac and Rosa Lee's love for each other and subsequent marriage bring about the emotional and spiritual rehabilitation of the disillusioned singer. As with Horace and Elizabeth Robedaux, marriage is a healing influence for Mac and Rosa Lee, alleviating the anguish and loneliness that have plagued both their pasts.

In keeping with Horton's reserved writing style, there is nothing sensational about Mac's transformation or about his marriage to Rosa Lee, no miraculous conversion, over-heated proposal, or fancy wedding ceremony. In fact, the wedding that does happen occurs off stage, and Mac's proposal is so reserved that, on the surface, it appears uneventful. Mac Sledge, much like Jackson Fentry, is a taciturn man who finds it difficult to express his feelings. When Mac proposes to Rosa Lee, the two are working together in the wind-blown garden behind the motel. Mac tells Rosa Lee he has given up drinking and admits he has deep feelings for her. He wonders aloud if she would "think about marrying" him, and she replies simply, "Yeah, I will" (97). There are no histrionics in the couple's exchange; Mac and Rosa Lee simply look into each other's eyes and then resume their gardening, seemingly aware that amid the hard conditions of their lives caution is the most sensible way to handle such matters of the heart. Later, when a country-western band appears at the Mariposa to meet Mac, he introduces Rosa Lee as his wife, indicating the couple has been married off screen in a modest ceremony. Although we do not see any of the other crucial events in the life of the family, such as Mac's actual conversion to Christianity or the death of Sue Ann, Mac Sledge eventually finds peace and contentment in a simple life with Rosa Lee and Sonny and rediscovers the joys of writing and singing music. He ultimately moves from death to life, from despair to a man redeemed, expressed most beautifully in the lyrics of his song *If You'll Hold the Ladder*: "Baby, you're the only dream I've/ Ever had that's come true/ There's so much more to reach for/ Thanks to you/ All I've heard is me till now/ But I see what we've got/ And if you'll just hold the ladder/ Baby, I'll climb to the top" (135).[29]

Not only does Mac gain strength from Rosa Lee's unconditional love and support but he also learns about the power of Christian faith that has sustained her through a troubled life. The title for *Tender Mercies*,

---

[29] Roy M. Anker, *Catching Light: Looking for God in the Movies* (Grand Rapids MI: Eerdmans Publishing, 2004) 124–43.

Foote's most overtly religious film, was taken from a verse in the Book of Psalms 145:9 (KJV), where King David praises God for bestowing his tender mercies upon him. Christian scholar Robert Jewett has noted that Horton Foote's reference to God's tender mercies is also reminiscent of the Apostle Paul's letter to the Romans, in which he appeals to Christians through the mercies of God to live their lives in service to a world full of people like Mac Sledge, his egocentric and addicted former wife, Dixie, and his doomed daughter, Sue Ann (KJV Romans 12:1). "But what is of particular interest," Jewett points out, "is that such tender mercies are largely invisible. Both for Paul and for Foote's story, faith is required because the mercies of God are elusive, intangible, and off camera."[30]

In its understated manner, *Tender Mercies* demonstrates the kind of spiritual promise that defines this simple passage: "The Lord is good to all: and his tender mercies are over all of his works" (KJV 145:9). The key to Mac's transformation is the undeserved love of Rosa Lee and the grace of her God, whose tender mercies are regenerative. Rosa Lee trusts in the goodness and mercy of her heavenly father, and her faith has been a source of strength that has seen her through the death of her first husband, her fears of rearing her child alone, and her struggles with Mac's alcoholism. She expects little from life and her daily prayers offer simple expressions of gratitude for the peace and contentment that fills her soul. "All she asks for are certain moments of gentleness or respite," Horton Foote explains. "She has a sense of appreciation for what she has; it's nothing to do with grandness or largeness, but just thanks for a nice day or some such thing. Mac must learn to evaluate and appreciate this quality in her."[31] Rosa Lee does not preach or condemn, her words are always comforting; but, in spite of her assurances, there is a psychic turbulence that boils beneath Mac's placid demeanor, and when Dixie refuses to look at a song he has written for her to sing, he curses: "I don't give a Goddamn about any of this no more so what in hell is wrong with me?" (112). Rosa Lee tries to console her husband—"It's bound to be hard on you.... I love you. When I thank the Lord for his tender mercies, you and Sonny head the list"—but when she asks him to sing the song Dixie rejected, Mac's voice falters and he storms out of the house, jumps into his pickup, and drives to a nearby bar (112). With his soul screaming out,

---

[30] Robert Jewett, "The Mysterious God of *Tender Mercies*," *Saint Paul at the Movies* (Louisville KY: Westminster/John Knox Press, 1993) 55.

[31] David Sterritt, "Horton Foote: Filmmaking Radical with a Tender Touch," *Christian Science Monitor* (15 May 1986): 38.

he yields to temptation but then realizes that alcohol is not what he is thirsting for and pours the whiskey on the ground. The next morning he returns home to Rosa Lee who, after spending an anxious night waiting for his return, has been reciting Psalm 25: "Show me thy way, O Lord; teach me thy paths. Lead me to thy truth, and teach me; for thou are the God of my salvation; on thee do I wait all the day" (KJV). This prayer embodies the themes of love and fidelity that stood firmly at the center of Horton Foote's life and work. In many ways, the story of Mac Sledge is the story of the playwright himself, who repeatedly survived the ups and downs of his career with the help of his wife Lillian. His daughter Hallie admitted:

> There's a kind of woman my father always writes—gentle but very strong. Often, they seem dependent on the man, but they exhibit this strength. These women survive and they do it with dignity. Rosa Lee in *Tender Mercies* is sort of fearless. She could allay the fears in Mac. And that's how my mother is. She believes so completely in my father and his talent. It's almost like she had a plan for him. She's the rock, she's the rock.[32]

Mac Sledge's spiritual transformation, like most of the other major events in the film, occurs offstage. We see him soon after his conversion at the local Baptist church, where Rosa Lee sings in the choir and where Mac is able to belt out the hymn *Jesus Saves* with powerful feeling, a sign of his acceptance of Christ. When Mac is ready, he is baptized along with Sonny, and Rosa Lee is finally able to witness both her husband and her son embrace the Christian faith that has sustained her. The film then cuts to a few days later and a small dance hall, the Plowboy's Club, where the new country band is performing with Mac as their featured singer. The consequence of Mac's faith in God appears to be a renewed sense of peace and happiness with his family and band, but in Horton Foote's world, as in life, contentment is fleeting and violence is ever present. Though Mac has accepted Rosa Lee's religion, he does not comprehend the deeper meaning of his newfound faith until he is faced with the death of Sue Ann.

In addition to expressing themes of love and faith, *Tender Mercies* emphasizes the father/child relationship so prevalent in Horton Foote's dramatic canon. One of the most moving scenes in the film occurs when

---

[32] Freedman, Samuel G. "From the Heart of Texas," *New York Times Magazine* (9 February 1986): 50.

Sue Ann, Mac's daughter, comes to see her father after many years of separation. Mac admits that he had written his daughter letters over the years, but she had never received them. Dixie had kept them all from her daughter in an effort to sever the relationship between father and child. Sue Ann confides: "I told my mama I was coming. She said she'd have me arrested if I did" (127). During their conversation, Sue Ann asks about Mac's harsh treatment of her mother, about his alcoholism, and about his memories of their family. Mac answers her questions as honestly as he can, while carefully praising Dixie as a good mother, but when Sue Ann asks him to repeat the words of a song she vaguely remembers him singing to her when she was a child, he suddenly becomes reticent. Not wanting to come between the girl and her mother and too overcome with emotion to think clearly, Mac says that he does not recall the song, and watches helplessly as his daughter walks out of the house and out of his life. As she drives away, Mac walks to the window and begins to sing the song, *On the Wings of a Dove*, his voice expressing both love and anguish: "When Jesus went down to the waters that day/ He was baptized in the usual way/ When it was done/ God blessed his soul/ He sent him his love/ On the wings of a dove/ On the wings of a snow white dove/ He sends his pure, sweet love/ Signs from above/ On the wings of a dove/ On the wings of a dove (129).

Mac and Sue Ann have finally made contact, but for Sue Ann this moment with her father has come too late. Robert Jewett believes that this scene, in which Mac refuses to acknowledge having sung the song to Sue Ann, "is a denial of a decent and tenderly caring aspect of Sledge's relationship to his daughter years ago. His singing had conveyed a sense of divine care that the child had needed and now yearns for again, far more than the fancy cars and big allowances that her mother was providing. Mac Sledge had conveyed God's tender mercy to his daughter without fully understanding it himself, and now he turns his back on it. Only when his daughter drives off does he return to the living room humming the song he knows full well."[33] Mac's decision not to sing the song is a failure he can never change or amend. A few days later, Sue Ann is killed in a car wreck while eloping with Menefee, a member of her mother's band. The news of her death is almost unbearable to Mac, testing his faith beyond measure. In his despair, Mac questions his trust in a God that could take the life of his only child:

---

[33] Jewett, 62.

I was almost killed once in a car accident. I was drunk and ran off the side of the road and I turned over four times. They took me for dead, but I lived. And I prayed last night to know why I lived and she died, but I got no answer to my prayers. I still don't know why she died and I lived. I don't know the answer to nothing. Not a blessed thing. I don't know why I wandered out to this part of Texas drunk and you took me in and pitied me and helped me to straighten out and married me. Why, why did this happen? Is there a reason that happened? And Sonny's daddy died in the war. (*Pause.*) My daughter killed in an automobile accident. Why? You see, I don't trust happiness. I never did, I never will. (144–5)

Mac Sledge cannot trust happiness because it is too tenuous and inexplicable. In Horton Foote's world, as in real life, faith does not protect one against death, and, in the end, there are no assurances that life will be free from adversity. For Horton, life is a divine mystery and brutality is an ever-present reality. Ultimately, Mac must accept the fact that all he can do is to respond in faith to the tender mercies that God has bestowed upon him. Rosa Lee has no answers for her husband's questions either, but she offers him a reason to live, as well as a way to deal with his sorrow. Every night before she goes to bed, she thanks God for all his tender mercies, most importantly her husband, her child, and their life together. Her family is what truly matters to Rosa Lee, for it is the most precious of God's gifts. In the end, Mac survives his loss by drawing strength from this same wellspring of faith and hope.

The final scene of the film depicts the beginning of the healing process for Mac and Sonny, two orphans who have slowly moved toward friendship and the familial wholeness for which they have yearned. Although Mac has lost the chance to reconcile with his daughter, he now has a second chance to be a true parent to Sonny. Likewise, Sonny, who has longed for fatherly companionship, finds a friend and father in Mac Sledge, who has been completely transformed by love. As the film concludes, a new future is emerging between stepfather and son in the midst of the great mysteries of life and death. As Mac and Sonny toss a football back and forth, Rosa Lee peers through the screen door with a look of contentment, and the melody of a country-western song is heard: "You're the good things I threw away/ Coming back to me every day" (148). When the action fades away, we are left with the image of a family moving through the cycle of life empowered with a new sense of courage and dignity.

Tender Mercies proved to be a great learning experience for Horton Foote. He discovered a good deal about the business of filmmaking, about budgeting, and about the day-to-day problems that go along with making an independent film. He was on the set every day, and innocently thought that once a film was edited then everyone could go home and just wait for the opening. As he explained, "For a film financed by a studio, the period after it is edited is a whole new ballgame. The agents, the studio heads, the press agents, the distributors, and the theater owners are all full of advice—'I don't like it; it's too long, too slow, how can we sell it'—it goes on and on. Philip Hobel...was able to listen to everyone, to those who liked the film and those who didn't, and to keep pressing for an opening date."[34]However, Hobel came dangerously close to not getting what the filmmakers wanted most, a successful opening. Universal Pictures, who had agreed to distribute the film for EMI, decided it would not open the film in America; instead, to fulfill its contract with HBO they would open it only in Europe. No one knows why, but EMI eventually changed their minds, opening the movie on 4 March 1983, in only three theaters—one in New York, one in Los Angeles, and one in Chicago—and that was where *Tender Mercies* played for its entire run. The film was released during the time of year when distributors usually get rid of all of those movies they don't think are worth releasing in the prime times of Christmas and the midsummer months, and as a result executives at Universal Studios spent very little on the movie's promotion. When Willie Nelson offered to help publicize the film, one of the more candid of the marketing executives at Universal said, "We know how to sell *The Best Little Whorehouse in Texas* but how do you market *Tender Mercies*?"[35] It is not surprising then that *Tender Mercies* fared poorly at the box office, and following its all too brief run, Universal sold the film's rights to cable TV, which meant it would not receive any more distribution. When *Tender Mercies* unexpectedly received five Academy Award nominations a year later, Universal hoped to redistribute the movie, but the cable companies began to televise the film a week before the Oscars, thwarting any attempts at re-release. With such poor distribution, it is remarkable that *Tender Mercies* received nominations for Best Picture, Best Actor, Best Director, Best Original Screenplay, and Best Original Song, which was written and performed by Robert Duvall. Ultimately, *Tender Mercies* won two awards—Duvall won for Best Actor and Horton Foote won for Best Original Screenplay.

---

[34] Foote, *Genesis*, 175.
[35] Ibid.

The film also received the Writers Guild Award for best picture and was the American entry in the 1983 Cannes Film Festival.

In the final analysis, *Tender Mercies* is a remarkable film, a work so well made it is hard to believe it marked the first time Horton Foote had written directly for the screen. The movie's unique achievement, besides the excellent performances given by Robert Duvall, Tess Harper, Betty Buckley, Wilford Brimley, Ellen Barkin, and Allan Hubbard, must be attributed to Horton's moving story and literate script, which represents the screenwriter's fullest expression of the complexities of human relationships and the need for sustaining connections to family, community, and God. The movie reveals Horton's perceptive understanding of the ephemeral nature of success, his compassion for people beset with personal problems and professional disappointment, and his unwavering belief in the promise of hope and reconciliation. In *Tender Mercies*, Horton Foote transformed ordinary experiences into a work of poetic transcendence.

What really distinguishes *Tender Mercies* from other movies is the purity of its vision. Through all the compromises and difficulties of making the film, Horton's original story and themes were never abandoned. "The excitement of *Tender Mercies*," critic David Sterritt wrote, "lies below the surface. It's not the quick change of fast action, the flashy performances or the eye-zapping cuts. Rather, it's something much more rare—the thrill of watching characters grow, personalities deepen, relationships ripen and mature. It's the pleasure of rediscovering the dramatic richness of decency, honesty, compassion, and a few other qualities that have become rare visitors to the silver screen. It feels good to have them back again."[36]

Tender Mercies renewed Horton's faith in the collaborative nature of cinema, restored his reputation as one of America's master dramatists, and catapulted the writer into the most active period of his professional life at age sixty-seven. More importantly, the critical success of *Tender Mercies* allowed Horton to exercise considerable control over his future film projects. Horton admitted that while he was filming *Tender Mercies* he fell in love with the process of moviemaking. "I loved being on the set every day and going to watch the dailies at night," the writer admitted. "However, I didn't want to spend another two or three years getting a project financed. My wife and I had a long talk about how to proceed. We'd been so impressed with the Texas crews and Dallas as a film center

---

[36] Sterritt, 36.

that we began to wonder if it wouldn't be possible to do a film outside the studio system."[37] By this time, Horton Foote had grown tired of the kind of studio interference that had plagued his earlier movies, and he knew that if he was to continue to express himself through cinema, he had to gain greater control over all facets of his work: "I just feel you have to be in charge. And I felt that even on *Tender Mercies* I hadn't been in charge as much as I wanted to be. Bruce Beresford and I got along very well. But there were certain decisions I thought I would have made differently—at least wanted a chance to do differently."[38] Horton's determination to gain such authority in a medium that customarily belonged to the director and producer would do much to invigorate independent filmmaking in America during the 1980s.

More determined than ever to film *The Orphans' Home Cycle*, Horton along with his wife Lillian formed their own production company for the purpose of translating the cycle plays to the screen independently. The first of the works to be filmed was *1918*, and the filmmakers' first task was to find a suitable director for *1918*, someone who understood Horton's vision and had a technical knowledge of filmmaking. At about this time, Jerry Calaway, the lead cameraman for *Tender Mercies*, suggested that they take a look at the work of Dallas filmmaker, Ken Harrison, a local Dallas director who had received critical acclaim for his three short films, *Mr. Horse, Last of the Caddoes*, and *Hannah and the Dog Ghost*. A few days later in a room at the Brookshire Hotel in Waxahachie, they met Harrison and reviewed his work. They liked what they saw, hired the director immediately, and told him that they wanted to make a film in Dallas, using Texas crews and Texas financing. With that, Horton and Lillian entered the unpredictable world of independent filmmaking even though they had never raised money before or been faced with the myriad of problems in starting such a project. With the assistance of producers Lewis Allen and Peter Newman of Cinecom International in New York and Ross Milloy of Guadalupe Entertainment Company in Austin, they raised a modest budget of $1.8 million and hoped to begin filming *1918* in Waxahachie by the fall of 1983.[39]

From start to finish, *1918* was a labor of love, and appropriately, the project became a Foote family enterprise. Foote, who served as co-

---

[37] Foote, *Genesis*, 175.

[38] Gerald C. Wood and Terry Barr, "'A Certain Kind of Writer': An Interview with Horton Foote," *The Voice of an American Playwright*, 228.

[39] Foote, *Genesis*, 175–76.

director, and Lillian, as producer, spent several months in Texas searching for a good location to shoot the film. With the help of a local banker and entrepreneur, L.T. Felty, who was instrumental in turning Waxahachie into a national film center, Horton and Lillian selected a Victorian house as their primary location and then decorated it with furniture from their own home in Wharton. The Foote children also became deeply involved with the film. Daisy worked as a production assistant, Horton Jr. served as casting director and was cast in a supporting role in the film, and Barbara Hallie performed the role of Elizabeth, which she had originated at the HB Theatre. The remainder of the cast members were all part of Horton Foote's extended theatrical family. William Converse-Roberts was chosen to play Horace; Michael Higgins was brought in to play the role of Mr. Vaughn, Elizabeth's father; Rochelle Oliver was recast as Mrs. Vaughn, a role she had originated at the HB Studio Theatre; and Matthew Broderick reprised the role of Brother, a part he had played earlier in the stage production of *Valentine's Day*.

Once the cast was selected, Horton rented a rehearsal space in New York, where he worked with the actors before they moved to Texas for the filming. On the first day of rehearsals, he received a call from producers Peter Newman and Lewis Allen asking him to come to their office to discuss a serious matter. Horton remembered: "I went there immediately after rehearsal, and they were very sober-faced indeed. They asked if I would be willing to postpone the film until spring and they gave very concrete reasons why it seemed necessary to do so. [The reasons were largely financial.] I trusted them both and accepted their decision to postpone. I then had the unhappy task of returning to the actors and technicians to explain what had happened.... I don't know if the actors believed that the film would ever be made."[40]

Since Horton and Lillian had already taken a lease out on a house in Waxahachie, they decided to return to Texas and wait out the winter in anticipation of the start of production. As it turned out, the postponement was an unexpected blessing. "The winter of 1983–1984 was one of the most severe on record in Texas," Horton recalled, "with icy cold weather (the temperatures approaching zero on many days) and snow that stayed on the ground for weeks. Because *1918*, like all my

---

[40] Ibid.

films, was done on location and not in a studio, we would have been wiped out on the lean budget we had to maintain."[41]

Spring did finally arrive and filming began in March 1984. Fortunately, Horton had kept most of the Texas crew who had worked on *Tender Mercies,* and once the cold weather subsided they were anxious to get started. Horton hired his cousin Van Broughton Ramsey as costumer, Nancy Baker as editor, and Czech-born George Tirl as cinematographer. Tirl, who had studied at the Swedish Film Institute with Ingmar Bergman, drew inspiration from Horton's collection of nineteenth-century paintings to create a unique style for the film, and he used natural outdoor lighting to capture the mood and look of the movie. For the sound of the film, Horton insisted upon found music, and rather than using artificial sources, a soundtrack featuring period wartime music and popular tunes was created. Horton explained that filmmakers tried "to create a montage of sound. This was a period when band music was played in town, people sang in choirs, and folks played the piano at home."[42]

True to the spirit and tone of Horton's original stage play, *1918* is a detailed and beautiful film that recreates the writer's vision of bereavement, grief, and family survival in a small Texas town experiencing the effects of both World War I and the worldwide influenza epidemic that broke out during the final year of that war. Director Ken Harrison successfully opened up the stage play with street scenes and exteriors but kept the focus on Horton's original story, the hardships and sustaining love of Horace and Elizabeth Robedaux. Ken Harrison, taking Horton's advice, illuminated the subtle variations in character actions and mood and focused on the emotional lives of the characters. The outstanding performances of the cast, especially Hallie Foote, who is stunning as Elizabeth Robedaux, and William Converse-Roberts, who plays Horace with fervor and believability, captures the hope and despair of a bygone era with a profound and remarkable honesty. While *1918* lacks the intensity and depth of *Tender Mercies*, the film has a quiet manner and warm sensibility that make it a worthy successor to the earlier movie. When the film was released later that year (1984), it received mostly positive reviews and fared remarkably well at the box office, especially for a film that was shot on such a small budget. While

---

[41] Ibid., 177.

[42] Horton Foote, interview by Marion Castleberry, 19 November 1988, Wharton, Texas.

Horton was satisfied with his initial foray into independent filmmaking, his next movie project, *The Trip to Bountiful*, would receive wider distribution and eventually win the hearts of America.

While editing *1918*, Horton got a phone call from his cousin, Peter Masterson, who as creative advisor for the Sundance Film Institute was searching for a script to use in his first attempt at film directing. Masterson, best known for writing and directing *The Best Little Whorehouse in Texas*, had thought about filming *The Trip to Bountiful* for some time, but the idea did not solidify until after a conversation at the Sundance Institute with his friend Robert Redford, who suggested that for his filmmaking debut he should choose a work which was both economically feasible and personally meaningful to him. Remembering an Off-Broadway production of *The Trip to Bountiful* he had seen in 1962 at the Greenwich Mews Theatre in New York, Masterson immediately called Horton, requesting the rights to the play. Over the years, Horton had received numerous offers to adapt the play, but a movie never materialized because the playwright could not agree with producers or directors on the casting of its protagonist, Carrie Watts. For more than thirty years, Horton refused to allow the play to be filmed with any number of popular stars whom Hollywood producers proposed, hoping that Lillian Gish would eventually reprise her original television role in a movie. By this time, however, Gish was ninety-two-years-old and much too frail for location shooting in Texas. After a good deal of discussion, Horton and Masterson realized that they shared a common vision, and Horton consented to write the screenplay when he discovered that the director agreed with his choice of Geraldine Page as Carrie Watts. Horton had worked with Page previously on the *Playhouse 90* production of *Old Man* and had enjoyed her performance. "I thought that Geraldine would have an understanding of this particular kind of woman better than any of her contemporaries," Horton stated. "She has a sense of place. Carrie Watts is a woman who's been through a great deal; there's a spiritual quality about her that keeps her going. She has a manifest strength from all sorts of unexpected sources. She's a survivor—and I think Geraldine grasps that."[43] Masterson and Horton were certainly right about Geraldine Page, for the power and poignancy of the film can be attributed to the actress's performance, as well as that of her

---

[43] Myra Forsberg, "Hallie Foote Relives Her Family's Past," *New York Times*, 13 April 1986, sect. 2, 21–2.

supporting cast: John Heard as Ludie, Carlin Glynn as Jessie Mae, Rebecca De Mornay as Thelma, and Richard Radford as the sheriff.

After casting, the next step in bringing *The Trip to Bountiful* to the screen was to find financing for the production. Masterson suggested that Sterling Van Wagenen, a close friend and co-founder of the Sundance Film Institute, be hired as producer. With his guidance, the film-makers raised a modest budget of $2 million and put together an impressive production team, consisting of Fred Murphy as cinematographer, J.A.C. Redford as composer and music designer, Philip Lamb as art director, Gary Jones as costume designer, and Jay Freund as editor. Horton was involved with all aspects of the production, including casting, editing, and rehearsals.

Even though Horton was working on the film *On Valentine's Day* at the same time, driving back and forth between locations, he was on the set of *Trip to Bountiful* as much as possible. He and Masterson worked together closely and were in continuous communication about the film: "We'd talk about it. I'd give my ideas. It was a very sharing time. [Pete] is very thorough and thinks out quite logically what he wants to do. Usually people I work with are people I've worked with before, I know about, or we share an aesthetic in common.... This was a very constructive time on the whole for everybody. We had disagreements, minor ones. They cropped up from time to time, but they were quickly resolved."[44]

The Trip to Bountiful unfolds on the screen much like it did on television and on the stage. The movie, like the earlier versions, offers a touching portrait of Carrie Watts, who longs to run away from her Houston apartment, where she lives with her son and his nagging wife, in order to return to her home of Bountiful, fifty miles away. Carrie, wanting only to embrace the memories of her past and to regain her dignity before she dies, plans and schemes until she has an opportunity to escape. Then, with an unconquerable will, she begins her lonely and treacherous journey back to the place of her birth. Along the way, she is aided by Thelma, the sympathetic young wife of a World War II soldier, and by a kindly sheriff from the town whom her son and daughter-in-law have put on her trail and who allows Mrs. Watts to complete the final stage of her journey. Upon arrival in Bountiful, the old woman

---

[44] Horton Foote, *Horton Foote's Three Trips to Bountiful*, ed. Barbara Moore and David G. Yellin (Dallas TX: Southern Methodist University Press, 1993) 123. All page references to the screenplay of *The Trip to Bountiful* refer to this publication.

learns that the friends of her youth have all died or scattered, and her childhood house is no longer the spacious mansion of her memories but, instead, a crumbling wreck. Though Carrie is allowed only a few minutes to revisit Bountiful that is time enough to confront her memories and plunge her hands into the earth of her birthplace.

In adapting the play to the screen, Horton made only minor changes to his original script. He created a few scenes to take advantage of the mobility of the camera and to give his story a greater sense of reality: "The scenes that I wrote fresh were when [Mrs. Watts] was waiting, having to change buses, when she talks to the black lady and they discuss Corpus Christi and what that means; then her walking to get the bus; her going to the railroad station and seeing Jessie Mae and Ludie, and we can go with her and see how she hides, which we couldn't do in any other medium..." (204). In neither the play nor the television version could Mrs. Watts's trip be fully dramatized, and that was a task Horton set for himself in writing the screenplay. "I hoped to do this without turning it into a travelogue and diluting the power of the scenes that had served so well dramatically in the earlier versions," Horton explained. "In my screenplay, Mrs. Watts takes a local bus from her apartment to the railroad station, then walks from the railroad station to the bus station, gets on a bus to Harrison, and finally is driven by car to her home in Bountiful. It wasn't much of a trip at all, really, and I hoped all this could be shown without sentimentality. Pete Masterson's direction and choice of location [the countryside around Waxahachie and Venus, Texas] and Geraldine Page's performance all supported and strengthened my vision of that part of the trip."[45]

Among the other creative elements which contributed to the film were the beautiful settings of Neil Spisak, the colorful photography of Fred Murphy, inspired by Edward Hopper paintings, and the musical score by composer J.A.C. Redford, which utilized guitars, hammer dulcimers, harmonica, accordion, and even a tin whistle to capture the spirit of Carrie Watts's journey. Redford occasionally used strings behind the other instruments and, noting Horton's injunction that he remember the hymns, he expanded the old Christian song *Softly and Tenderly* into a pervasive theme. Like the screenplay, the music is calling Carrie Watts home, not just to the place of her birth, but also to the roots of her existence. Her spiritual journey is set in motion during the opening scene, one of the most haunting and memorable in the history of

---

[45] Foote, Foreword to *Three Screenplays*, vii.

American cinema. As the credits roll, we are transported to a field of bluebonnets where a little boy runs in slow motion, followed closely by his mother. In the background we hear a woman's voice sing the opening verse of the hymn: "Softly and tenderly Jesus is calling/ Calling for you and for me/ See, on the portals he's waiting and watching/ Watching for you and for me/ Come home, come home/ Ye who are weary, come home/ Earnestly, tenderly, Jesus is calling/ Calling, O sinner, come home" (195–6). The haunting refrain of the old Christian song and the essence of Horton's screenplay are consonant elements, calling everyone to reconcile with their family and God. In the final moment of the movie, Ludie and Jessie Mae appear to take Carrie Watts back to Houston, and she quietly consents to return, secure in the knowledge that the remainder of her life will be enriched as a result of her final contact with Bountiful.

As elsewhere in his fiction, Horton suggests in *The Trip to Bountiful* that if suffering breaks some people, others like Mrs. Watts can be ennobled by it. On film, Carrie Watts becomes a universal symbol for lost hopes and dreams, for regrets and missed chances, for courage and integrity, and for the great mysteries of life and death. Geraldine Page gives an once-in-a-lifetime performance, capturing with honesty the heartbreaking grandeur of Carrie Watts, who prevails with dignity and strength amid trying circumstances.

When *The Trip to Bountiful* was released by Island Pictures in December 1985, the film received universal acclaim, garnering rave reviews from critics like Rex Reed: "One of those rarefied, indelible films about the human heart we never seem to get on the screen these days," and Vincent Canby who praised both the film and its star: "As Mrs. Watts, Geraldine Page has never been in better form, nor in more film control of the complex, delicate, mechanism that makes her one of our finest actresses.... *The Trip to Bountiful* works perfectly as a small, richly detailed film."[46] The film went on to receive an Academy Award for Geraldine Page and a nomination for Foote for screenwriting. When actor F. Murray Abraham announced at the Academy Awards that Page had won the Oscar (her first win in eight nominations) she thanked everyone involved with the film and then ended the evening by saying: "It's all your fault, Horton!"[47] Since that time, *The Trip to Bountiful* has

---

[46] Rex Reed, "Review of *The Trip to Bountiful*," *New York Post*, 20 December 1985; Vincent Canby, "Review of *The Trip to Bountiful*," *New York Times*, 20 December 1985.

[47] Al Reinert, "Tender Foote," *Texas Monthly* (July 1991): 110.

become a significant part of popular culture and one of Horton Foote's most admired and beloved works.

During the making of *The Trip to Bountiful*, Horton was also filming *On Valentine's Day*, which tells the story of his parents' elopement, initial year of marriage, and the birth of their first child. Like *1918*, *On Valentine's Day* was a family affair with Lillian and the Foote children reprising their contributions on and off camera. The crew and cast of *On Valentine's Day* was largely the same as *1918*, except for the addition of Steven Hill as the suicidal Mr. George Tyler. "When I was writing the screenplay," Horton stated, "the challenge was to use the great variety of scenes that the film can afford without overwhelming the thrust of the story, which is the growth of the young couple."[48] Horton was able to maintain a balance between the interior world of the Robedaux house and the exterior world of Harrison by filming outdoor scenes that focus on the evolving insanity of Mr. George Tyler from the moment he runs away from home and hides at the river to when he commits suicide on the courthouse square. Steven Hill's performance as Mr. George Tyler is especially convincing and offers an emotional contrast to the more contented and secure Horace and Elizabeth. Produced by Lillian Foote and Calvin Skaggs of Lumiere Productions, *On Valentine's Day* was hailed as a thoughtful and literate film that proudly rejected current movie fashions, emphasized character and action, and celebrated the power of the spoken word at a time when most films stressed flashy, fast-paced action and aggressive editing. Vincent Canby best summed up the effect of *On Valentine's Day* when he stated: "In this era of breathtaking pacing, of jump cuts, of soundtrack music that rivets the ears as the mind slumbers, there is something revolutionary about a movie in which one has to pay attention to the dialogue and coordinate it with the images, which may or may not contradict what's being said. Equally revolutionary is the way in which the film celebrates—without sentimentality—a kind of family life that now seems as remote as the Ice Age."[49] David Sterritt added: "If anyone has a chance of reclaiming the word 'auteur' for authors—after years of seeing it used as a synonym for movie directors—it's certainly this soft spoken Southerner, who's never afraid to reject the Hollywood rule book in favor of his own insights and

---

[48] Foote, *Genesis*, 187.

[49] Vincent Canby, "Valentine's Day from Horton Foote," *New York Times*, 11 April 1986.

instincts."[50] *On Valentine's Day* was a huge success for Horton Foote, and the film was selected in 1986 as the official American entry for the Venice Film Festival, the Toronto Film Festival, and the US Film Festival.

As quickly as Horton finished editing *On Valentine's Day*, he began work on *Courtship*, which recounts Horace and Elizabeth's romance and their decision to marry against the wishes of Mr. Henry Vaughn. While Horton had filmed both *1918* and *On Valentine's Day* on modest budgets of $1 million, financing for *Courtship* proved elusive and for a time it appeared that the film would not get made. Fortunately, Lindsay Law, executive producer for PBS's *American Playhouse* series, came to the rescue with the necessary financial backing and, as Horton recalled, was almost completely responsible for financing *Courtship*. Law's plan was to air all three films, *1918*, *On Valentine's Day*, and *Courtship*, together as a five part mini-series, under the title *Story of a Marriage*, on *PBS* during the Spring of 1987.

For *Courtship*, however, Horton and Lillian made some major changes in the production team. During the filming of *On Valentine's Day*, a disagreement had arisen between Horton and Ken Harrison. Although Harrison is listed as director on both *1918* and *On Valentine's Day*, his primary responsibility was to set up the scenes to be shot once the actors were on location. Horton actually rehearsed the actors and directed the performances.[51] Since Horton was already working with the actors, he hired Howard Cummings, an art and production designer for *American Playhouse*, to serve as director of *Courtship*, and he also moved locations from Waxahachie, Texas, to Brookhaven, Mississippi. The Foote family reprised their earlier contributions: Horton coached the actors and shaped their performances, Lillian served as producer, Barbara Hallie performed the role of Elizabeth, Horton Jr. portrayed the character of Steve Tyler, and Daisy got in front of the camera for the first time, playing the cameo role of Allie, one of Elizabeth's close friends. The rest of the cast remained the same except for Amanda Plummer, who gave a stirring performance as Laura Vaughn, Elizabeth's younger sister. In *Courtship*, as in his earlier films, Horton Foote created a work of deceptive simplicity which used the minutiae of everyday life to evoke the deeper meanings and mysteries that face us all—questions of love and marriage, life and death.

---

[50] David Sterritt, "Horton Foote: Filmmaking Radical with a Tender Touch," *Christian Science Monitor* (15 May 1986): 1, 36.

[51] Hampton, 214.

When *Story of a Marriage*, debuted on 6 April 1987, television critic Don Merrill proclaimed that Horton's work "is the kind of thoughtfully written, capably performed drama old-timers are thinking of when they wax nostalgic about the Golden Age of television." Merrill also pointed out that one of the highlights of the series was an early moment from *Courtship* when Elizabeth and Horace reveal their love for each other on the veranda of her home while her father fumes inside the house. "It is a credible, touching love scene during which the two engage in awkward conversation that makes us understand how deeply they care for one another. It is remarkable writing, beautifully acted—a description which applies to their performance not just in that scene but throughout the series."[52]

After filming *Courtship*, Horton wrote *Emma*, an unproduced film adaptation of Flaubert's *Madame Bovary*, for Roland Joffe and the BBC and adapted Bette Bao Lord's best-selling novel *Spring Moon* (1988) for his good friend Alan Pakula. *Spring Moon*, which follows the story of the character Spring Moon, a spirited young woman whose life spanned the tumultuous years of the 1890s, when China was on the brink of war with Japan, to the days of Mao Tse-tung and the cultural revolution of 1966. Pakula hoped the film would be his most successful motion picture. He had planned to shoot the movie in the Suzhou province of China with an all-Chinese cast, but unfortunately the project was never completed. Soon after Pakula cast the film, the brutal suppression in Tiananmen Square occurred, and Bette Bao Lord expressed her preference that *Spring Moon* not be made, which put an end to the proposed film.[53]

The Widow Claire was the next cycle play that Horton wanted to film, but after signing contracts, hiring a crew, and renting a house in Waxahachie, the project fell through when prospective producers backed out, leaving Horton and Lillian to break their contracts with the technical unions in Texas. Horton lost a great deal of money from *The Widow Claire* debacle, but he was, nevertheless, eager to accept MGM's offer to film *Convicts*, the last of *The Orphans' Home Cycle* plays to be filmed during the 1980s. Directed by Peter Masterson and starring Robert Duvall as Soll Gautier, Lucas Haas as Horace, James Earl Jones as Ben, Carlin Glynn as Asa, Mel Winkler as Jackson, and Starletta DuPois as Martha, the film was shot in 1989 but not released until 1991. Like the play, the film tells the story of thirteen-year-old Horace Robedaux who goes to work on Soll

---

[52] Don Merrill, "Review: Story of a Marriage," *TV Guide*, 4 April 1987.
[53] Jared Brown, 289.

Gautier's convict farm to earn enough money to buy a headstone for his father's grave. Shot outside New Orleans on an old abandoned farm adjacent to the Mississippi River, Peter Masterson successfully opened up the original play with sweeping shots of plantation buildings, convict shacks, a weed-choked graveyard, a wide expanse of cane fields, and realistic scenes of violence against the convicts, all of which contribute to our understanding of the confusion and moral decay of Foote's characters. Isolated in some degree from each other, the characters are all trapped in a past they neither cherish nor comprehend. None are more lonely and secluded than Soll Gautier, once a Civil War hero who has become a senile, drunken, and bitter old man. Robert Duvall gives an inspired performance as old Soll, and Lucas Haas is compelling as the young Horace. Together, Duvall and Haas, along with the rest of the ensemble, create a remarkably realistic, richly detailed commentary on human fragility, the harshness of slavery, and the mysteries of life and death. When *Convicts* was finally released in 1991 by the Sterling Van Wagenen Entertainment Company, it received mostly mixed reviews. *Variety Magazine* intimated that while Robert Duvall added another memorable character to his reputation, *Convicts* was a static, un-cinematic play. Other actors noted by the critic were James Earl Jones, who gave "a quite understated" portrayal of Ben Johnson, and Carlin Glynn as the dissolute Asa Vaughn. The reviewer argued that the picture of this "decadent society" would not please Southerners but was vividly realized "in microcosm," and noted "a powerfully modern, almost militant turn" portrayed by Calvin Levels, who plays Leroy, the convict in chains.[54] Biographer Wilborn Hampton believes that *Convicts* made a better movie than a stage play. In opening up the story for the camera, Foote was able to take the audience to an old-time sugarcane plantation at the turn of the twentieth century and show the life of black convicts who were assigned to work the fields. The setting gave the film a sense of reality and authenticity that could not be achieved on a stage.[55]

Horton Foote's commitment to independent filmmaking during the 1980s not only inspired other filmmakers, but his authentic, character-based movies also served as viable alternatives to the cinematic flash and fast-paced action of many Hollywood films. During his work on *Tender Mercies, The Trip to Bountiful,* and *The Orphans' Home Cycle,* Horton developed a unique approach to moviemaking that other screenwriters

---

[54] *Variety Magazine,* "Review of *Convicts*," 2 December 1991.

[55] Hampton, 217.

and independent filmmakers would eventually embrace. With his first attempt at independent filmmaking, *Tender Mercies*, Horton came to understand the true essence of collaboration, and once he and Lillian established their own production company, intent on bring *The Orphans' Home Cycle* to the screen Horton developed an extremely personal approach to filmmaking. He worked only with directors he trusted, and he often insisted on rehearsing the actors himself and coaching them throughout the shooting process. Such collaboration helped to ensure a more authentic recreation of the style and period of his screenplays.

Horton also developed a kind of personal philosophy about filmmaking that would guide his future work. He believed that most movies were far too focused on image, location, and fast-paced action and not enough on the emotional landscape of characters. Many screenwriters, he believed, wrote specifically for Hollywood stars and audience appeal rather than remaining faithful to their own sense of truth. Horton' s alternative to this kind of writer was what he called the "composer," the writer who avoided overwrought action, manufactured images, and artificial sound for the beauty of the human voice, dramatic silences, and subtle musical scores.

Finally, Horton feared that the control of distribution by studio producers would become just as monopolistic as the control of production. Following *Tender Mercies*, he began to assert himself more and more into the process of editing and distribution to ensure that his cinematic vision and sense of place remained pure and vibrant. The control that Horton Foote garnered in his films provided an opportunity for him to tell his stories in his own unique way, free from the frustrations of Hollywood, and while he admitted that independent filmmaking was a lonely row to hoe, it was ultimately, "the only way to go if you want to have your work done correctly."[56] Gary Edgerton best expresses Horton's unique contribution to independent film when he wrote:

> The most intriguing and remarkable member of the [independent filmmaking] renaissance is Horton Foote. Where all the other American independents working today are part of the so-called "film culture" generation that first came of age during the 1960s and 1970s, Horton Foote has been a celebrated writer of stage plays, teleplays, a novel (*The Chase*), and screenplays for nearly five decades. In contrast, his contemporaries are either a vital part of the Hollywood establishment, or

---

[56] Horton Foote, interview by Marion Castleberry, 20 March 2004, Waco, Texas.

are no longer making motion pictures. The independent nature of Foote's films is, therefore, unique when considering his age and generational perspective; his work also exhibits a richness and integrity that is a vivid indication of how much can be achieved when a talented film artist is attuned to his instincts and can focus his intentions and resolve...Foote writes, produces, directs, and edits feature films that are out of the step with the American mainstream; his motion pictures are gentler in pace, subtler in effect, and designed to disclose those moments of insight and poetry which lie hidden within the ordinary lives of his characters.[57]

Although Horton Foote hoped to film the rest of *The Orphans' Home Cycle*, following *Convicts* he took a much-needed break from independent filmmaking, turning his attention once again to the stage, where his work was experiencing a remarkable and unexpected renaissance.

---

[57] Gary Edgerton, "A Visit to the Imaginary Landscape of Harrison, Texas: Sketching the Film Career of Horton Foote," *Literature/Film Quarterly* 12 (Winter 1989): 3–12.

15

Themes and Variations
Stage Plays of the 1980s

By the 1980s, Horton Foote had created more drama than in any time since the early fifties when he was a writer of television scripts for NBC. In 1978, he returned to the stage to direct three plays from his *Orphans' Home Cycle* at the HB Playwrights Foundation in New York; in 1983, he released his film *Tender Mercies;* and in 1985, he debuted his movie adaptation of *The Trip to Bountiful.* The success of these works sparked a renewal of interest in Foote's drama, and professional theaters such as the Loft Theatre, the Ensemble Studio Theatre, the Manhattan Punch Line Theatre, and the Actors Theatre of Lousiville, Kentucky, began presenting productions of his new one-act plays as well as his full-length pieces. In 1985 alone, the playwright had four plays running concurrently in New York, and the next year (1986), Horton Foote, at age seventy, was called "Dramatist of the Hour" by *Dallas Times-Herald* arts critic Don Hulbert.

During the years when few of his plays were being staged, Horton penned more than twenty new works. In addition to *The Orphans' Home Cycle* and *Tender Mercies,* he wrote no fewer than five full-length dramas: *Night Seasons, The Old Friends, The Habitation of Dragons, Dividing the Estate,* and *Talking Pictures.* He also wrote a series of one-act plays: *A Coffin in Egypt, Arrival and Departure, The Man Who Climbed the Pecan Trees, Blind Date, The One-Armed Man, The Roads to Home, The Road to the Graveyard, The Prisoner's Song,* and *The Land of the Astronauts.* These plays, like those he created during the "Golden Age" of live television drama, reveal continuity in style and theme and offer variations on plots, characters, and motifs which had surfaced years earlier. In these plays, Horton explored such subjects as the erosion of traditional values, the quest for emotional and spiritual fulfillment, the break up of the family, and the repressive forces within the small Southern community of Harrison, Texas. Gerald Wood points out that many of the "earlier plays tend to be...more affirmative than the later ones" and "the conflicts in the dramas of the fifties tend to be more clearly defined for both characters and audience than...in his later work."[1] Characters cannot always cope with adversity in these later works, and they often seem troubled by a pervasive sense of emotional dislocation and a profound loss of identity and meaning. The pervasive rootlessness and sense of hopelessness in these plays also point to Horton's belief that at the heart of modern society lies a destructive moral and spiritual wasteland that must be faced and dealt with courageously. Horton Foote's emphasis on the spiritual in these works is one of his unique contributions to American theater.

Horton's one-act play, *A Coffin in* Egypt, vividly expresses this evolving dramatic vision and focus on the spiritual.[2] The play was originally directed by Herbert Berghoff and performed by Sandy Dennis at the HB Studio Theatre in New York in 1980 and later performed by Glynis Johns in 1998 at the Sag Harbor Theatre under the title, *In a Coffin in Egypt*. Clearly patterned after Kathrine Anne Porter's short story "The Jilting of Granny Weatherall," Rebecca Briley, Horton Foote scholar, suggests in writing the play Horton was not only "paying tribute to the author he considers his greatest influence...he is inviting the audience to make this connections between his character [Myrtle Bledsoe] and Porter's."[3] The play centers around ninety-year-old Myrtle Bledsoe, who, having reached the end of her life, is trying to make peace with her past and accept the inevitability of her death. In an evocative monologue, Myrtle expresses her innermost fears to her unconcerned nursemaid, Jessie Lydell, as the two women sit together in the drawing room of Myrtle's Victorian mansion located near the small farming community of Egypt, Texas.

When *A Coffin in Egypt* begins, Myrtle's mind is flooded with happy thoughts about the days she spent as a young bride, her exciting trips to Europe and New York, and the grand lifestyle she enjoyed as the wife of a Southern aristocrat. She proudly recalls her youthful beauty and intelligence, her talent as an actress, her two children, and the people who helped to shape her character. At first glance, Myrtle appears to have lived a life of Southern propriety, but as she continues to ramble

---

[1] Gerald C. Wood, Introduction to *Selected One-Act Play of Horton Foote,* ed. Gerald C. Wood (Dallas TX: Southern Methodist University Press, 1989) xv.

[2] Horton Foote, *A Coffin in Egypt,* in *Getting Frankie Married—and Afterwards and Other Plays* (Lyme NH: Smith and Kraus, 1998) 1–76. Page references to *A Coffin in Egypt* in the text refer to this publication.

[3] Rebecca Luttrell Briley, *You Can Go Home Again* (New York: American University Studies 1993) 184.

from one fragmented memory to another, a psychic turbulence emerges from beneath her calm and restrained voice. While Myrtle enjoyed great wealth and position, she also suffered misery and shame at the hands of her faithless husband, Hunter. She speaks bitterly about her loveless marriage and recalls her many unrequited chances for happiness with the man she really loved, Captain Lawson, and her neglected opportunities to pursue a career as an actress. Lacking the courage to follow her instincts, Myrtle ignored her needs for intimacy for more than seventy years and remained with Hunter until his death. Now, as her life draws to an end, Myrtle recognizes that she has cheated herself. She yearns to return to an earlier time when, as an innocent nineteen-year-old bride, she first set eyes upon the lush cotton fields and prairies of Egypt. "If I could have one day to live over before I die," she admits, "I'd choose one of those lovely clear spring days, we used to have out here when I came here first as a bride and I'd get my horse and ride across the prairie at sunrise to the East and ride all day on and on" (41). Myrtle laments a life that can never be restored. The world for which she yearns no longer exists, and the old woman has become a tragic victim of time, trapped by her own limitations and eccentricities. "I used to tell Hunter that when I died I wanted to be cremated and have my ashes taken to one of the beautiful places I'd known as a young woman," she recalls, "but now, I don't care. Who is there left to take my ashes anywhere? Anyway, they have a place for my body between Hunter's grave and my two girls and that's where I'll end in a coffin in Egypt" (56). Reminiscent of *The Trip to Bountiful*, *A Coffin in Egypt* expresses the need for every person to have a spiritual and emotional home and the importance of squaring up memories with reality before completing life's journey. But unlike Carrie Watts, Myrtle Bledsoe does not discover a sense of dignity in the final stage of her life; instead, having reached the end of her road, she finds nothing but despair and hopeless resignation. With no past to which she can belong and no future to which she can look forward, Myrtle exists from day to day by withdrawing into a world of illusion. There is much to admire in the character of Myrtle Bledsoe, such as her intelligence, her charm, and her devotion to family, but her story finally implies that those who ignore their better judgements and forsake their dreams often end their days bitter and rueful.

That same year at the HB Theatre (1980), Horton directed his one-act *Arrival and Departure*,[4] a companion piece to his play *The Road to the Graveyard*. The play introduces the Hall family as they await the arrival of a new family member in 1902. While their mother, Lilly, gives birth to a baby boy, the Hall children pass their time naming books of the Bible, playing kick-the-can, and talking about topics most often reserved for adults: what it means to be a woman, what their futures might hold, where they will be buried in the Harrison graveyard, and why their Aunt Reenie sings sad songs. Through their discussions, we discover that Reenie is married to Ned, an ineffectual alcoholic, who cannot hold down a job or support a family. Reenie hopes that Ned will arrive by train, rescue her from her loneliness, and take her back to their home in Galveston. He never does, and at the end of the play, the young woman finds herself forsaken and bereft of love and intimacy. As she sings the haunting tune of "Red Wing," she yearns for what she will never have— an emotional and physical home—and she must learn to cope with her immense loneliness. *Arrival and Departure* offers up another victim to loss and futility as Horton Foote illustrates a haunting portrait of innocent children exposed to the lonely and unfulfilled lives of their elders.

The Man Who Climbed the Pecan Trees was first staged in 1981 by William Trayler at the Loft Theatre in Los Angeles and featured Peggy Feury as Mrs. Campbell and Horton Foote, Jr., as Stanley.[5] It was later produced in 1988 by Curt Dempster at the Ensemble Studio Theatre in 1988. The play, like *A Coffin in Egypt*, depicts the pain of loneliness and the horror of emotional displacement. However, rather than revealing the effects of change upon the elderly, the play, focuses on the extent to which young people are often haunted by personal misfortune and social pressures. Horton explained that *The Man Who Climbed the Pecan Trees* was inspired by the experiences of his own family, and that the seeds of the play went back to 1930, five years after the death of his Grandfather Brooks. "See that pecan tree up yonder," Horton told Samuel Freedman. "When my grandfather gave his land to the city, there was a pecan tree bigger than that on it. There was a gentleman's understanding they'd never cut the tree down. Well, part of me says I don't understand not

---

[4] Horton Foote, *Arrival and Departure*, (MS in Horton Foote Papers). Page references to *Arrival and Departure* in the text refer to this manuscript.

[5] Horton Foote, *The Man Who Climbed the Pecan Trees*, in *Selected One-Act Plays*, 265–90. Page references to *The Man Who Climbed the Pecan Trees* in the text refer to this publication.

honoring things ancient, things like trees, families. And part of me says that I don't believe in the aristocracy."[6] Both of these impulses come together in *The Man Who Climbed the Pecan Trees*, which is set in Harrison during the years of the Great Depression.

Modeled after Horton's Grandmother Brooks, Mrs. Campbell, an aging widow, has resigned herself to the formidable task of caring for her three grown sons, who have become a source of disappointment and concern to her. While Mrs. Campbell's husband was alive, she dreamed of keeping the family together by building houses for the children next to her own, but following his death and the loss of the family's fortune, her expectations have collapsed. The old woman clings pathetically to the hope that her sons will be successful and happy, but without their father's stabilizing presence, the boys succumb to stressful social pressures. As the play opens, one of her sons, Brother, has become an endless source of guilt and shame after losing seventy-five thousand dollars to a fraudulent insurance agent, who had once been a trusted family friend. Her second son, Davis, has been crippled by an ugly and painful divorce. Both Brother and Davis have led turbulent lives, but their younger brother Stanley (to whom the title of the play refers) has allowed his loveless marriage to Bertie Dee Graham to destroy his life, turning him into a hopeless alcoholic. Stanley and Bertie Dee, once a seemingly perfect couple, married when they were eighteen out of a sense of duty to their fathers and an arrangement of marriage made when the children were only nine. Mrs. Campbell recalls that their wedding was "a happy day for all of us," but Stanley remembers the event as fraught with problems: "We were married in the Baptist Church to please Bertie Dee's father. The church was packed. She was crying like her heart would break… We went to Galveston on our honeymoon and she met another couple on their honeymoon and she danced every dance with him…holding him real close the way she liked to dance with everybody but me…I have been cheated. Married at eighteen and cheated" (286–7). Now, Stanley's resentment and his repeated complaints that he has been "cheated" out of his youth have ruined his relationship with Bertie Dee as well as his reputation in Harrison. After taking all the abuse she can from her husband, Bertie Dee locks him out of the house and forbids him to see their son. For Stanley, the breakup of his family results in the loss of his sanity.

---

[6] Samuel G. Freedman, "From the Heart of Texas," *New York Times Magazine* (9 February 1986): 61–2.

When the curtain closes, Stanley has retreated from reality into a world of infantile illusions where each evening he gets drunk and climbs the pecan trees in the courthouse square, "trying to get to heaven" (286). Stanley clings to his mother in fear that he will "fall out of the trees one night" and kill himself. "When I was a boy I climbed the water tower once," he cries, "I could see everything for miles. The river, the courthouse, the gin, the pumping plant, the houses in town, the farms...Help me, Mama...or someday I'm gonna fall and kill myself. (He sings:) 'In the gloaming,' Oh, my darlin'...Am I falling now, Mama?" (289). While *The Man Who Climbed The Pecan Trees* is a realistic depiction of a broken family it is also a symbolic portrait of the loss of spiritual values in modern society, and in the final analysis, the play reflects the defeat, disillusionment, and terror of people who are victims of great social and personal changes over which they have no control. *The New York Times* critic Walter Goodman, reviewing the Ensemble Studio Theatre production of *The Man Who Climbed the Pecan Trees*, wrote: "This slice of Texas Gothic is notable mainly for the character of Mrs. Campbell, which Mr. Foote has written with a sad sort of humor and which Lois Smith plays as a woman who has known so much pain and loss that to admit even to herself how bad things are would destroy her whole world. 'The main thing is that none of us get discouraged,' she says to her thoroughly discouraged household. Her strength is fragile, but it is all that holds the family together. 'Don't look back,' she says, even as she seeks comfort in the old photograph album and reminisces about how Stanley was always crazy about climbing trees."[7] Following the play's successful run at the Ensemble Studio Theatre, *The Man Who Climbed the Pecan Trees* was selected for inclusion in *Best One-Act Plays* and *The Best American Short Plays* (1990).

The second of the plays to debut at Peggy Feury's Loft Theatre in 1981 was *Blind Date*, which was later produced by the Ensemble Studio Theatre in New York (1986).[8] Unlike *The Man Who Climbed the Pecan Trees*, *Blind Date* is a comedy of manners, which shares a number of similarities with Horton's earlier play, *The Dancers* (1954). Here again, two teenagers are thrown together against their wills by a domineering elder who wants to control their lives. The play takes place in 1928, in the

---

[7] Walter Goodman, "Review/Theatre: Marathon of One-Acts," *New York Times*, 14 July 1988.

[8] Horton Foote, *Blind Date*, in *Selected One-Act Plays*, 363–90. Page references to *Blind Date* in the text refer to this publication.

living room of Robert and Dolores Henry. Dolores, once an admired high school beauty queen who wants her niece to be more like her, has finally been able to arrange a date for the ill-mannered, Sarah Nancy, with Felix Robertson, a "sensitive boy" from a "lovely family" (369). Dolores knows that Sarah Nancy is a blunt and sarcastic child who has never had a successful relationship with a boy, but she desperately wants to improve her niece's reputation with men and to tame her irascible disposition. Dolores tries to teach Sarah Nancy the proper way to conduct herself on a date and attempts to refashion the girl in her own image. She even goes so far as to create a ridiculous list of topics for her to talk about with her new beau. But when Felix, a would-be mortician, finally arrives at the Henry home, Sarah Nancy makes it abundantly clear that she has no intention of assuming her aunt's flirtatious manner. Instead of being nice to her suitor she treats him like an old shoe and admits that she considers him a boring stupid lout. Sarah Nancy's attitude delights her uncle Robert, who believes it is much better to be "honest than gracious," as much as it distresses her aunt Dolores, who retires for the evening with a sick headache (387). Felix also retreats from the playing field, but he soon returns to apologize to Dolores for his inconsiderate behavior. When they are finally left alone, Felix and Sarah Nancy admit to one another that they are not very good conversationalists but that they do like each other. When the play ends, they have established a common bond of honesty between them as they contentedly and wordlessly pore over a stack of Dolores's old high school yearbooks.

In *Blind Date*, Horton celebrates the capacity of human beings to stand up to the indignities of the human experience and reminds us that young people, if given the opportunity to find their own way in the world, will usually discover the peace and contentment they seek. *New York Times* critic Frank Rich, reviewing the Ensemble Studio Theatre production of *Blind Date*, called the play "a gem of a vignette," adding to the impression that Horton "seems to rejuvenate himself with every passing year."[9] *Blind Date*, which continues to be one of Horton's most popular and produced one-acts, was selected as an entry in *The Best Short Plays* of 1988.

---

[9] Frank Rich, "Review of *Blind Date*," *New York Times* 5 May 1986.

In 1982, Herbert Berghoff produced Horton's haunting full-length play, *The Old Friends*, a sequel to his earlier work, *Only the Heart*.[10] *The Old Friends* tells the story of Sybil Borden who, following her husband's death, returns to Harrison to be near her family: Mamie Borden, Mamie's daughter Julia and her son-in-law Albert Price, and old friend, Gertrude Ratliff. After spending most of her life on the road with her husband Hugo, an oil speculator, Sybil, desperately wants to return to her hometown to build a new life for herself, but when she arrives she discovers that Harrison has changed from the caring community she once knew. Greed has replaced compassion, and affection has been exchanged for control and domination. Equally troubling, Gertrude, Mamie, Julia, and Albert are not the same people Sybil grew to know and love as a child. Instead, they have become selfish and malicious social creatures, corrupted by greed, materialism, alcoholism, and infidelity. Gertrude, whose husband has just died, tries to drown her loneliness in drink and to control the lives of everyone around her. Mamie, who for years has manipulated the lives of her daughter and son-in-law, now longs to escape the prison she has created and to move in with Sybil, who she knows will treat her with respect. Julia, who is trapped in a loveless marriage to Albert, flirts and seduces younger men to avoid facing the reality that she is growing older and is no longer attractive to her husband.

When the play begins, Sybil's plan to build a new home in Harrison appears gloomy but she eventually finds love and companionship in the person of Howard Ratliff, a generous and kind man who has secretly loved her for years. While Sybil and Howard's family and friends spend their days paralyzed by alcoholism and greed, Sybil and Howard rekindle their love for each other and secretly slip away to marry, Gertrude tries to manipulate Howard, her brother-in-law, with promises of land and wealth. As the play concludes, Howard and Sybil begin to put their lives and new house in order, recognizing the importance of their love and commitment to one another in the midst of this cynical and cruel world. As Sybil explains to Howard, creating a home is not unlike seeking an identity: "I try to put this house together like I try to put my life together and it keeps being torn apart" (60). Howard and Sybil's future together is ambiguous and uncertain, but in the end there is hope that they can overcome the emotional and spiritual confusion

---

[10] Horton Foote, *The Old Friends*, (MS in Horton Foote Papers). Page references to *The Old Friends* in the text refer to this manuscript.

that besets their old friends in Harrison and can build a loving and peaceful life. While Horton has not abandoned his former view that a healthy family can overcome most of life's hardships and temptations, he seems more aware that fewer families in our present age enjoy such secure and loving relationships. The bitterness and confusion of the characters in *The Old Friends* make Horton's vision of the family as a caring and nurturing agent of God all the more poignant and urgent. *The Old Friends* is an intriguing and emotionally moving play that illustrates the need for familial intimacy in a confused world.

On 25 March 1982, the Manhattan Punch Line Theatre in New York produced *The Roads to Home*, Horton's trilogy of one-act plays consisting of *A Nightingale*, *The Dearest of Friends*, and *Spring Dance*.[11] Directed by Calvin Skaggs with a cast that included Hallie Foote, Carol Fox, and Rochelle Oliver, Horton's trilogy dramatizes the pain of not belonging, of having no personal attachment to a person or place. Set in the 1920s, *The Roads to Home* centers around three women, Mabel Votaugh, Vonnie Hayhurst, and Annie Gayle Long, all refugees of small towns, who are trying to get back home. "They don't do that consciously," Horton explains, "but they constantly find ways to refer to or think about the place they came from. They spend their time trying to reconstruct their past lives. It's a variation on a theme."[12]

The first of the three one-acts, *A Nightingale*, centers around Annie Gayle Long, a young Houston housewife and mother of two, who has lost her hold on reality after the birth of her second child. Lately, Annie has begun dressing in her summer clothes, riding the streetcars of Houston at all hours of the day or night, and turning up without warning at the home of Mabel Votaugh, a childhood acquaintance from Harrison, where she seeks attention from Mabel and her friend Vonnie. The women nod politely and pretend nothing is wrong despite Annie's constant displays of erratic behavior. For no apparent reason, she begins to sing *My Old Kentucky Home* and to form her hand into a miniature pistol, whispering "pow, pow, pow" as though she were shooting the top off a flower. Annie's eccentricities make her friends uncomfortable, but Mabel and Vonnie seem more concerned with the young woman's haunting memories of old scandals and personal tragedies in Harrison. Mabel remembers Harrison as a wonderful community, but Annie

---

[11] Horton Foote, *The Roads to Home*, in *Selected One-Act Plays*, 291–362. Page references to *The Roads to Home* in the text refer to this publication.

[12] Horton Foote, interview by Marion Castleberry, 20 March 2004, Waco, Texas.

remembers it as a brutal and unforgiving place where she first encountered the horrors of human injustice and cruelty. Annie's parents moved to Harrison from Rhode Island when she was a child; but as she recalls, her mother "never did care" for the town (300). She hated the excessive rain, the poor medical care, the saloons, and the ostracism her family received from neighbors. Annie's father made a good deal of money in Harrison, eventually becoming president of the town bank, but his wealth could not protect his family from an array of tragedies and misfortunes.

The Gayles lost four children to sickness shortly after moving to Texas, and sometime later, Mr. Sledge, Mr. Gayle's best friend, gunned him down on the main street of Harrison. Annie Gayle never forgot the incident or the sounds of Miss Rosa Daughtey praying over the body of her dead father. She tried to carry on with her life by attending college, by marrying Mr. Long, and by raising two children. Yet no matter how hard she tried, she could not escape her past. Now, trapped in a world of grief and despair, all she asks from anyone is "tenderness and mercy" (312). Annie Gayle's recounting of her father's murder has become a plea for help, a cry for spiritual understanding. She insists that if she had known how to pray, her father would not have died: "I went to him lying on the pavement. Miss Rosa Daughtey came up to me and she said to pray like you've never prayed before. 'I don't know how to pray'" (302).

Annie begs Mabel and Vonnie to teach her how to pray, but her friends do not know how to empathize with her anguish and pain. Rather than minister to her real needs, they attempt to teach Annie "The Lord's Prayer," and then pity her for not knowing the prayer. Gerald Wood explains that although "there is genuine hunger in the play for a system of beliefs and values that would give direction and meaning to the characters' lives...for many, like Vonnie and Mabel, easy literalism and the public display of religion are more important than a genuine sense of compassion" (292).

When Mr. Long finally appears to escort his wife home, it is clear that nobody can prevent Annie from retreating farther away from reality. Mr. Long feels incapable of giving his wife the kind of care she desperately needs. Afraid that he will lose his job, or perhaps his own sanity because of his wife's condition, he decides to admit Annie to the state mental institution in Austin where she will at least receive some attention. When the play ends, Annie, confused and bewildered, cannot understand her husband's decision, or the extent to which her life is about to change.

A Nightingale shows the broken life of Annie Gayle Long to be part of the general breakdown of the human community in both Harrison and Houston. *The Dearest of Friends*, on the other hand, assumes a narrower focus, exploring the intimate world of Eddie and Vonnie Votaugh and their futile attempts to attend to their failing marriage. The play opens a few months after Annie has been committed to the asylum in Austin. Vonnie has just learned that her husband Eddie is having an affair with another woman, Rachel Gibson, whom he met on a recent train ride to Harrison. Eddie believes that he really loves Rachel, and he has asked his wife for a divorce. Vonnie refuses, and, outraged by Eddie's infidelity, she runs next door to her dearest friend Mabel for consolation. Vonnie worries that her lack of religious commitment is the root of her lonely life and empty marriage. She was, as she confesses, "born a Baptist" and expects to "die one" but she can't help wondering what her life would be like if "[they'd] stayed home and gone to church" (329). While Horton Foote's work often seems to point an accusing finger at American society for its lack of Christian charity, he does not hesitate to condemn the hypocrisy of those people who substitute superficial religiosity for true spirituality.

When Vonnie finally confesses her situation to Mabel, her friend seems more concerned with the petty details of Vonnie's trip to Harrison than with her feelings of rejection and humiliation. When Eddie finally enters the scene to speak to her, Vonnie is utterly confused by his response. Eddie, burdened by the guilt of his infidelity, tries to understand his passion for Rachel Gibson: "I'm very confused," he cries. "I've tried to live right all my life, to be good and do the right thing" (343). Although Vonnie does not fully understand her husband's bewilderment, deep down she knows that she can do nothing to heal their relationship, except pray. The play concludes with Vonnie's announcement that "if prayer does any good, he'll get over it. I pray night and day that he does.... And God usually answers prayers. So I'm just going to keep on praying and I know He won't let me down this time" (343). Finally, there is no assurance that Vonnie's prayer will be answered, no certainty that Eddie will stand by his wife, and no guarantee that their marriage can be salvaged. The only surety at the end of *The Dearest of Friends* is the pain and regret of two people who have allowed their love to die and, more importantly, Vonnie Votaugh's decision to trade her artificial religiosity for sincere and heartfelt prayer.

In *Spring Dance*, Horton concludes the tragic saga of Annie Gayle Long. Set in 1928 in the state mental institution in Austin where Annie has been confined for four years, the play opens with the asylum's annual spring dance. Annie could easily be the belle of the ball, but she is having difficulty remembering her past. She cannot, as she says, keep everything "straight and clear" (354). She remembers she is married, or she was once, and her husband would be understandably upset if she were to dance with another man. She politely declines the invitations of her young suitors, Green Hamilton and Dave Doshon, and takes refuge in her memories of "chinaberry blossoms" and better times gone by (347). The reality of Annie's situation is that Mr. Long has long ago divorced her and placed her children in the care of her mother, Mrs. Gayle. Annie's family has totally abandoned her, and nobody has visited or written to her in more than a year. When the play ends, she knows that she will never see her children again and that she will spend the remainder of her life in the asylum; but rather than dwell upon such thoughts, she, like Myrtle Bledsoe, retreats into her own private fantasy world where grief and loneliness can no longer touch her.

In *Spring Dance*, Annie Gayle Long's disturbing journey has ironically led her to a new home. As she sits with the other patients in the asylum, Annie's conversations reveal that she is no further down the road to recovery than she was in *The Nightingale*, but at least she is in a place where she feels safe from the violence and spiritual isolation of the outside world. The same cannot be said of Mabel Votaugh and Vonnie Hayhurst. Even though they have not been confined to an asylum, their homes have become little more than domestic prisons where they must battle daily against the maddening forces of boredom and emotional neglect. Held captive by their loneliness and lack of intimacy, Mabel and Vonnie have become two lost souls searching for "tenderness and mercy" in a world they neither cherish nor fully understand.

In *The Roads to Home*, Horton Foote again expresses his belief that a sense of belonging is essential to human happiness and personal fulfillment. To Horton, a home is much more than a mere building or something you own. It is a state of mind that connects us with others, holds the key to our identities, and offers an emotional refuge in times of trouble and distress. Like all his works, *The Roads to Home* shows Horton Foote's deep sympathy for society's unfortunates. The plays dramatize the longings and frustrations of those people who find themselves confined to a strange and alien environment in which they have little or no control. Characters search for spiritual connections and emotional contentment but they most often find a world bereft of friendship, charity, and human compassion. A sense of loneliness pervades these plays, and insensitivity and greed deny happiness to those who are different in faith and temperament. "I try to look at the past with an objective eye," Horton has said. "No time is really wonderful, so I'm not nostalgic about the past. You know, life does defeat a lot of people, and you've got to face that reality. I have great compassion for those who can't survive life. My heart has been broken many times by people I loved who couldn't find a way."[13]

In 1983, Horton returned to television, writing a commissioned teleplay, *Keeping On*, for Barbara Kopple and PBS's *American Playhouse*. The movie, which aired on 8 February 1983, was the only fiction film directed by award-winning documentary moviemaker Barbara Kopple. Like her earlier documentaries, *Harlan County, USA* and *The American Dream*, *Keeping On* is a fictitious story about a group of textile workers and the struggles they encounter in a small Southern town when they attempt to unionize. Dick Anthony Williams portrays a minister who encourages the activities of a labor unionist played by the renowned actor, James Broderick. The minister's support of the workers' cause polarizes the community, and politicians and industry executives in the community ultimately ostracize the cleric. *Keeping On* is an evocative and moving portrait of social and economic politics in small-town America, echoing the same concerns of the 1979 Emmy award-winning film, *Norma Rae*, which starred the popular actress Sally Field.

In 1984, the Actors Theatre of Louisville produced a revival of *Courtship*, and the following year, on 15 May 1985, the Ensemble Studio Theatre in New York, under the direction of Artistic Director Curt Dempster, presented *The Road to the Graveyard*, a production, which helped to reestablish Horton's reputation as one of America's greatest dramatists.[14] *The Road to the Graveyard* captures the anguish and pain of an ordinary family facing the disintegration of their way of life during the Great Depression. Horton has stated that he originally wrote *The Road to the Graveyard* in 1955, and one can see similarities between this

---

[13] Ibid.

[14] Horton Foote, *The Road to the Graveyard*, in *Selected One-Act Plays*, 429–60. Page references to *The Road to the Graveyard* in the text refer to this publication.

play and many of the writer's earlier pieces, such as *Only the Heart, The Tears of My Sister, The Death of the Old Man,* and *The Midnight Caller.* Once again, the playwright depicts a family in transition, caught at the brink of its collapse. The play's characters are searching for a sense of identity, trying to escape the indignity of a repressive family environment. *The Road to the Graveyard* opens in the Victorian home of the Hall family in 1939, shortly before the onset of World War II. Here, India Hall, a fifty-year-old spinster, who we first meet as a young girl in *Arrival and Departure,* cares for her aging parents and prays that her middle-aged brother Sonny will seize the opportunity to open his own movie theater, an act that would provide a future for both of them. But Sonny, fearing to strike out on his own, is torn between a sense of family duty and his desire to marry Bertie Dee Landry, a woman who has been deemed unsuitable by his parents because of her Cajun ancestry. For years, Sonny has been unable to choose between his own dreams and those of his family, and India has been trapped by her unceasing devotion to others.

India Hall has always placed the needs of her family above her own. Brought up to care for others, she never married or learned a trade because she was too busy helping pay for the education of her older brother Thurman and cooking for her aging, senile parents. Her lifelong friend and fellow spinster, Lyda Darst, who share the grimness of India's plight, asks: "What is wrong with you all? Why didn't you drive us out of the house and make us learn something to support ourselves by? Who's gonna take care of us when they're gone? Nobody" (438). Consequently, both Lyda and India are now living lonely and unfulfilled lives with no hope for a proper future. When the curtain falls, nothing has changed in the Hall household. Mr. and Mrs. Hall are locked within a world of confusing senility, Sonny continues to work as a lowly usher at the local movie theater (and to suffer from sick headaches and upset stomachs), and India remains imprisoned in her own home where each day she watches the hearse go by on its way to the graveyard and mourns her unrequited chances for happiness. The absurdity of the world Horton created in *The Road to the Graveyard* is most evident in the play's final haunting scene in which Mr. and Mrs. Hall are seated on the veranda, aimlessly staring into space, as their children snatch imaginary rabbits from the air for their senile mother.

The Road to the Graveyard portrays a family struggling with its dreams and the bitter reality of poverty and cultural decay during the Great

Depression. *New York Times* critic Frank Rich best describes the mood created by the play. "The only peace in this play," Rich remarks, "is indeed the discordant peace of the graveyard. A family is dying, and so is a social order soon to be upended by World War Two. In roughly a half-hour, [Foote] surveys the tragic ruins of a household—even as he looks back, with more anger than nostalgia, at a world whose idyllic glow belies all manner of unacknowledged neuroses and sexual and economic injustices." Rich goes on to call *The Road to the Graveyard*, "among the finest distillations of [Foote's] concerns" and concludes that the Faulknerian *Graveyard* created a "magnetic field of anxiety almost suffocating in its intensity."[15]

In July 1985, Herbert Berghof produced three more Horton Foote one-acts—*Blind Date, The Prisoner's Song,* and *The One-Armed Man*—at the HB Playwrights Foundation under the title "Harrison, Texas." While *Blind Date* is a humorous portrait of adolescent companionship, *The Prisoner's Song* and *The One-Armed Man* focus on an array of small-town adults trying to survive in a world that has been transformed by materialism and greed. The central characters in *The Prisoner's Song,* John and Mae Murray, are a young couple searching for a place to put down roots and begin a new life.[16] The play opens in 1927, and John has been out of work for some time, but clearly he is an energetic and thoughtful man who loves his wife and sincerely wants to be a successful businessman. His wife Mae, ever hopeful that their future together will be much brighter, explains that John has overcome a number of personal tragedies and proudly announces that her husband, a recovering alcoholic, has not had a drink in eight months. She is unaware of the full extent to which John has been emotionally handicapped by his previous failures. John is driven to achieve financial success by Mae's father, who does not trust his son-in-law to provide for his daughter and who believes that John will one day succumb to alcoholism. Although John has stopped drinking, he yearns for the day when his father-in-law will apologize to him and admit that he "was wrong about you. You're a fine man" (398). Now, after having moved aimlessly from one job to another, John has only fifteen dollars left in his savings with which to buy groceries and pay the rent. Yet, he insists that Mae not "worry [her] pretty head about

---

[15] Frank Rich, "Stage: In Marathon '85, 'Road to the Graveyard,'" *New York Times*, 27 May 1985.

[16] Horton Foote, *The Prisoner's Song*, in *Selected One-Act Plays*, 391–414. Page references to *The Prisoner's Song* in the text refer to this publication.

such matters" (395) since one day he will be a "millionaire" with his "own oil wells" (398). John's fantasy conceals his deeper fears that his father-in-law's words might actually be prophetic and that he will never be able to find work in Harrison.

As outsiders, the Murrays are unaware of the evil effects that oil has had upon the community of Harrison. In Mae's hometown of Livingston, people are still "waiting there every year to see what the cotton crop is going to do" but here they "sit up nights thinking of ways to spend [their] money in order to outdo each other" (396). Mrs. Estill, the Murray's landlady, explains that Harrison has been corrupted by greed. "When oil was discovered, and the people working for the oil companies moved in, everyone went a little crazy" (400). To make matters worse, the town has lost the spirit of friendship and solidarity it once possessed. Southerners despise Yankees, neighbors manipulate other neighbors, and the wealthy take advantage of the poor. The only person in town to show concern for John and Mae's dilemma is Luther Wright, an aristocratic friend of Mae's father.

Luther Wright has never recovered from the death of his only daughter, Mary Martha. During the play Luther convinces John and Mae to accompany him to the cemetery. Ever hopeful that Luther will return their kindness by offering John a job, they try to comfort the old man. Mae even sings "The Prisoner's Song" over his daughter's grave while being stung by red ants because as Mr. Wright explains, the song "was Mary Martha's favorite" (407). But Luther, like Ludie Brooks, can do nothing to bring his daughter back from the grave. He can only question whether or not her death is God's punishment for his indifference to religion. Paralyzed by his loss, Mr. Wright is unable to move beyond the suffering and grief to sympathize with others in need. While John and Mae serve as Luther's kind and thoughtful companions, their generosity goes unrewarded as Mr. Wright allows his selfish sorrow to dominate their relationship. When the curtain falls, he remains trapped in his self-imposed world of grief and despair, and John and Mae Murray are left questioning their future in Harrison.

The Prisoner's Song, one of Horton Foote's most impressive one-act plays, shows Harrison evolving from a traditional, orderly community to a chaotic and artificial place where the Christian values and customs of the past are no longer practiced or revered. The play suggests that neither money nor power can substitute for true peace and contentment, a theme Horton has frequently explored in his works.

The One-Armed Man, the third one-act to be produced by Herbert Berghof under the title "Harrison Texas," is Horton Foote's darkest and most pessimistic tale of community disintegration, human injustice, and spiritual isolation.[17] Set in Harrison in the 1920s, the play depicts a society in selfish pursuit of money and material success. The plot centers on a twenty-one-year-old laborer, Ned McHenry, who was fired from his job at a local cotton gin after tragically losing his left arm in a mechanical accident. Ned's handicap has prevented him from finding other work in town, and for months, he has been living in abject poverty. When the story begins, he has returned to the cotton gin to request that his former employer, C.W. Rowe, give him back his job so that he might regain his dignity and get on with his life. Rowe, fully aware of McHenry's predicament, is too concerned with the declining prices of cotton and with his dreams of "oil wells" to show any compassion for the young man (419). McHenry, having been driven to madness and rage, lashes out against his former boss. He pulls a gun on Rowe and then forces him to repeat the "Lord's Prayer" again and again while demanding that he "give [him] back his arm" (424). Rowe, realizing that McHenry has lost all touch with reality, begs for mercy and then gives several lame reasons why he cannot hire a one-armed man. But at the very moment he thinks McHenry might spare his life, the young man kills him and then turns the gun on Rowe's assistant, Pinkey Anderson, who has suddenly appeared to inspect the situation. When the curtain falls, we are left with the haunting image of Pinky trying desperately to say the words of the prayer he doesn't really know: "How in the hell does it go? My God, how does it go? You killed him…I'm gonna pray. I'll think of something. Our Father…which art in heaven. Our Father. Hallowed be thy name. Our Father" (428). The conclusion of the play is left to the imagination, but clearly Horton wants the audience to perceive McHenry, Rowe, and Pinkey as victims of a society where people have been so dehumanized that harmony and serenity are impossible to achieve and the value of human life has been reduced to nothing.

Like *The Prisoner's Song*, *The One-Armed Man* reveals Horton Foote's compassion for individuals and families wrecked by economic upheaval and human injustice. Both plays show a new day of technological progress emerging in Harrison, but in *The One-Armed Man*, Horton focuses on the spiritual poverty and deprivation associated with this

---

[17] Horton Foote, *The One-Armed Man*, in *Selected One-Act Plays*, 415–28. Page references to *The One-Armed Man* in the text refer to this publication.

new social order. Gerald Wood agrees, calling *The One-Armed Man* "more religious, even visionary, than...political."[18] The play ends with the haunting image of three men who, bereft of authentic spiritual connections, have been destroyed by the evils of social change. But while social inequities abound in Harrison, Horton expands his vision to emphasize the breakdown of the human community and the universal dismay of spiritual isolation. When viewed through the prism of our current age, with its realities of war and mass murders, *The One-Armed Man* is a powerful plea for human compassion and understanding in a world threatened by violence and a lack of empathy.

In 1986, two of Horton Foote's plays from *The Orphans' Home Cycle—Lily Dale* and *The Widow Claire*—were presented on Broadway. The first of the plays to be staged that fall was *Lily Dale*, which dramatizes Horace Robedaux's nightmarish journey to Houston and his encounter with Corella and Lily Dale, his insensitive mother, and his narcissistic sister, an encounter which leaves him emotionally and spiritually transformed. The play, performed at the Samuel Beckett Theatre on Theatre Row, was directed by William Alderson and starred Don Bloomfield as Horace, Julie Heberlein as Corella, and the popular actress Molly Ringwald as Lily Dale.

The production received mixed reviews. Clive Barnes of the *New York Post* recognized Horton Foote as a master craftsman and remarked that the distinctiveness of the play was "the manner in which its atmosphere, texture, and construction are merged into one dramatic artifact—an artifact almost pictorial in its effect."[19] Allan Wallach of *New York Newsday* also expressed his respect for Horton's work, noting that he would like to see all nine installments of *The Orphans' Home Cycle* on successive nights and concluding that *Lily Dale* offered "a generous sampling of the penetrating insights into character and the sepia-toned nostalgia we've come to associate with Foote."[20] Frank Rich of *The New York Times* agreed with both Barnes and Wallach but found the acting to be lacking, with the exception of Don Bloomfield as Horace, whose talent he compared to that of Robert Duvall and Geraldine Page. Rich concluded that the play was a "modern, psychologically subterranean drama" that in the character of Horace conveys "the spirit that ennobles

---

[18] Wood, *Selected One-Act Plays*, 410.
[19] Clive Barnes, "Review of *Lily Dale*," *New York Post*, 21 November 1986.
[20] Allan Wallach, "Review of *Lily Dale*," *New York Newsday*, 21 November 1986.

Mr. Foote's characters—a blind, unshakeable faith that nothing, not even death, can derail the pilgrim who must go home again."[21]

During the run of the play at the Samuel Beckett Theatre, Molly Ringwald was replaced by Mary Stuart Masterson (the daughter of Peter Masterson and Carlin Glynn), whose stirring performance gave rise to a televised version of the play that aired on *Showtime* on 9 June 1996. In a letter to Horton, Lucy Kroll praised the change from Ringwald to Masterson, stating that Masterson "is a lovely actress who brought the play into balance.... Mary Stuart's discipline, training, and character as an artist are reflected in her Lily Dale. It makes Horace's journey to find his family and his realization that he is an orphan and must make his life on his own, come across with greater emotional impact."[22]

Shortly after *Lily Dale* closed at the Samuel Beckett Theatre, *The Widow Claire* opened at the Circle in the Square Theatre in New York on 17 December 1986. Directed by noted stage and screen director, Michael Lindsay-Hogg, and featuring Hallie Foote as Claire and Matthew Broderick as Horace, the production received favorable reviews. Frank Rich wrote an appreciative assessment of *The Widow Claire*, calling Matthew Broderick's performance "impressive," Hallie Foote's portrayal of Claire Ratliff "perfect," and Horton's play "the work of an artist who knows just what he wants to do and how he wants to do it." In *The Widow Claire*, Rich concluded, "Mr. Foote is a chronicler of the quotidian. His Texans often survive and sometimes prosper, though not until they've cracked open just enough for attentive onlookers to discover the hard compromises, devastating losses, and unshakeable faith in familial love that have forged their spirit."[23]

Clive Barnes of the *New York Post* also praised the performances of Broderick and Hallie Foote and the direction of Lindsay-Hogg, but suggested that the play would work better on the big screen. "Whole scenes appear to be visualized for the camera's eye," Barnes wrote, "and watching the play, one can almost sense where the picture would be tightened for a close-up, one can guess at the Harrison street scenes integral to the story, one can see that special video-emotional build-up of brief cumulative impressions which screams silently for the images of a

---

[21] Frank Rich, "Review of *Lily Dale*," *New York Times*, 21 November 1986.
[22] Lucy Kroll to Horton Foote, 9 February 1981 (Horton Foote Papers).
[23] Frank Rich, "Texas Survivors," *New York Times*, 18 December 1986.

screen rather than a stage."[24] Following the Circle in the Square production of *The Widow Claire*, the play was included in *The Best Plays of 1986–87*, but regrettably, the work was never filmed.

The last of Horton's one-act plays to debut during the 1980s was *The Land of the Astronauts*, originally directed by Curt Dempster at the Ensemble Studio Theatre in May 1988.[25] The play, set in the spring of 1983, is Foote's most contemporary portrayal of Harrison and focuses on the loss of intimacy within families, the celebrity worship of the 1980s, and the trivialization of the basic spiritual and emotional experiences essential to human happiness. In *The Land of the Astronauts*, the familiar landscape of Harrison and nearby Houston have changed into figurative tinsel towns where dreams of the luminous future can tempt a man and deceive him into believing that wealth and happiness are just beyond his outstretched fingers. The story begins in the office of Harrison's sheriff, where Lorena Massey is searching for her husband Phil, who had left home several months before to look for work in Houston. Phil had promised his wife and his daughter, Mabel Sue, that as soon as he found a job in the city, he would send for them, but Lorena has not seen or heard from him for more than a week. Lorena now fears that something terrible has happened to her husband.

Lorena's situation—that of a young mother abandoned by a wandering husband—is similar to Georgette Thomas's in *The Traveling Lady*. Soon after their marriage, the Massey's had moved to Harrison, Phil had begun working in his brother's restaurant as a waiter, and Lorena had taken a job as an attendant at the Colonial Inn. For a time, the family lived comfortably, but Phil soon grew tired of working as a waiter. He had always dreamed of becoming an astronaut; consequently, he enrolled in college where he hoped to receive the kind of education that would enable him to get a job with NASA. In reality, Phil knew that space travel was "foolish," but he hoped that someday he would get the chance to "go up into space and leave this earth and all its troubles and frustrations behind" (493). Searching for a better life, he has now moved to Houston where he hopes to find a more rewarding and lucrative job. However, in reality, Phil is unable to find work, and for weeks he has been wandering the streets of Houston in a state of utter confusion,

---

[24] Clive Barnes, "Foote's 'Widow' a small slice of Texas life," *New York Post*, 18 December 1986.

[25] Horton Foote, *The Land of the Astronauts*, in *Selected One-Act Plays*, 461–507. Page references to *The Land of the Astronauts* in the text refer to this publication.

hopelessly searching for the Space Center, and proclaiming to the world that he is an "astronaut that [has] lost his way" (487). Phil's admission is clearly a socio-political commentary by Horton Foote who understood that all of us, both the ordinary waiter and the astronaut, are continuously searching for a better life than our world can offer. And as Horton reveals, the Murrays are not the only family in *The Land of the Astronauts* who are experiencing the pain and frustrations of economic upheaval and emotional dislocation. The Taylors, who own and manage the Colonial Inn, join them in their misfortunes. Like the Murrays, the Taylors live in economic uncertainty, where day after day they must work without hope for a better future. While they do not admit their longings openly, unlike Phil, everyone in Harrison yearns for the kind of paradise that Phil Massey seeks. As his daughter, Mabel Sue's teacher admits, the place that Phil envisions sounds "like heaven to her" (483).

When the play concludes, Lorena finds Phil in Houston still searching for his astronaut paradise. After reuniting, they talk honestly to each other about their lives and their future as a family. Phil finally admits his fears to Lorena: "I'm tired and discouraged and I can't pretend any longer. I work in a restaurant and I go to school at night. Day after day, year after year. And nothing happens. I go to Houston to look for work and nothing happens and I want something to happen. Is that too much to ask? I want something for once to happen to me. I am tired of reading about things happening to other men. I want something to happen to me. Why can't I go up into space and leave this earth and all its troubles and frustrations behind?" (497). Lorena, who embodies Horton Foote's deepest convictions, reminds her husband that even if he could leave the earth, "you would have to come back down sometimes, or you would die" (497). Although Phil remains heartbroken and discouraged, he finally accepts Lorena's advice to "swallow [his] pride," and "come on home," returning to his job as a waiter (497). Sadly, Phil will never realize his dream of becoming an astronaut, but by facing his circumstances realistically, he equips himself to deal with the rest of his life. *The Land of the Astronauts* portrays the obsessive longing of ordinary people to escape the pressures and responsibilities of the present world for an imagined land of peace and personal gratification. Ultimately, however, the play confirms that life's obstacles and great sorrows are inevitable and must be confronted head on with courage and dignity.

During the waning years of the 1980s, two of Horton's full-length plays were produced: *The Habitation of Dragons* (first performed in 1988 at the Pittsburg Public Theatre and later filmed for Turner Network Television's *Screenworks* in 1992), and *Dividing the Estate* (first produced in 1989 at the McCarter Theatre in Princeton, New Jersey, and later directed by the Gerald Freedman for the Great Lakes Theatre Festival in Cleveland, Ohio on 11 October 1990).[26] Each of these plays continued Horton's depiction of the lives of small-town Texas families and resumed with greater intensity his exploration of moral and social themes he had introduced in his earlier one-acts.

Horton's most ambitious work during the decade was *The Habitation of Dragons*, which opened on 28 September 1988 and ran through 8 October 1988 at the Pittsburg Public Theatre under the direction of the playwright. The production featured a cast that included Horton Foote, Jr., as George Tolliver, Marco St. John as Leonard Tolliver, Matt Mulhern as Wally Smith, and Hallie Foote as Margaret Tolliver. The play tells the story of a Texas family devastated by a series of horrific tragedies during the Great Depression. Originally written during the 1950s and later revised in 1964, *The Habitation of Dragons* is a sequel to Horton's earlier play *The Summer of the Hot Five* (1955), which tells of two brothers, George and Leonard Payne, who are divided in temperament and ambition. Set in 1935, *The Habitation of Dragons* also centers around two brothers, George and Leonard Tolliver, in conflict over George's desire to sell his share of the family farm to finance a run for county attorney. Leonard has become a noted lawyer, and his younger brother George has given him the opportunity for success by waiting to go to law school until his older brother finished his degree and set up practice in Harrison. Even though Leonard has, according to Mrs. Toller, "worked and schemed and planned every day of his life that things might be easier" for the family, he has used George as a pawn in the pursuit of his own ambitious ends and then deserted his brother when the time came for him to return his generosity. Over the years, George's sacrifice and Leonard's blind ambition have created a wedge between the brothers. Their estrangement has been reinforced by Leonard's support of Billy Carter, his brother-in-law, in the race for county attorney and by his rigid, despotic control of the family estate following the death of his father.

---

[26] Horton Foote, *The Habitation of Dragons*, in *Horton Foote: Four New Plays, 1988–1993* (Newbury VT: Smith and Kraus, 1993) 1–62. All page references to *The Habitation of Dragons* refer to this publication.

The central action of *The Habitation of Dragons* is precipitated by the past sins of an absent father. Leonard and George's father, Mr. Tolliver, died years earlier in what the family has chosen to call a "hunting accident" (13) but during the course of the play, we learn from the lonely and penniless Uncle Virgil that the patriarch's death was not an accident at all. His mysterious death was in fact a senseless suicide, which marked the beginning of the ruination of the family's image. Although George does not remember his father very well, Leonard carries with him powerful memories, as related by his mother who remembers that her son and "his father were inseparable" (13) and that when Leonard, who was fourteen, heard that his father was accidently killed he "grieved so he took sick, and…has never gone hunting or fishing again" (14). During the course of the play, Leonard reveals that for years he had lied about his father's death. He informs the family that he had found Mr. Tolliver's suicide note. "That's why I took sick," he explains, "and I couldn't tell anybody what I'd found…I was so ashamed of him and what he'd done that I couldn't stand to hear him even talked about" (39). Burdened with shame and grief over his father's selfish act, Leonard has become obsessed with fulfilling the role of substitute father and counselor for his family.

While Leonard has controlled the family fortune with a tight fist, George has become stifled with anger and rage against his older brother, finding it difficult to hit back or stand up for himself. "I don't discuss my plans with you because it occurs to me that everything I want to do on my own you immediately oppose them," George explains. "I know in advance what your reaction will be. It has been precisely the same in anything I wanted to do that didn't sacrifice my life to building up your career, your law practice, your ego, and I might add, your bank account. Anyway, I'm going to run for County Attorney and if I lose, I'll continue to practice law" (7). Although bitter when Billy Clanton, Leonard's brother-in-law, wins the election of County Attorney, George, as promised, manages to build a respectable law practice without his brother's support. But George has been immensely hurt by his brother, and during the course of the play, he must lay aside his anger and forgive Leonard for his transgressions against him.

What makes *The Habitation of Dragons* an intriguing drama are the motivations of the major characters, who somehow find the courage to face tremendous adversity and to carry on with their lives. More complex than many of Horton's creations, the characters' backgrounds and familial relationships require close scrutiny. Leonard, who is determined that his two sons, Horace and Leonard Jr., will not have to experience the same kind of burden he faced growing up, has become a self-centered workaholic, ignoring the emotional needs of his wife and children. His commitment to maintaining his father's image and his family's financial security has driven him to neglect the very thing he wants more than anything in the world—the love of his wife and sons. While Horace and Leonard Jr. are clearly devoted to their father, they prefer spending time with Wally Smith, Leonard's business partner, who "loves to ride and fish and hunt" and gives the boys the kind of fatherly attention and affection they seek. Not only has Leonard's children turned to Wally for attention but Leonard's wife, Margaret, is having an affair with him. Margaret admits that she is "in love with Wally" and would "like a divorce" (30).

When Leonard learns of his wife's infidelity, he confronts Margaret, but before he can fully respond to her betrayal a fire siren is heard, signaling that someone has been lost in the river. George breaks the news to Leonard and Margaret that their two boys have accidentally drowned while swimming with Wally. Leonard and Margaret are devastated by the tragic turn of events, which grows even more upsetting when the enraged Billy Clanton, in defense of his sister's honor, murders Wally and is arrested in the Tolliver's front yard. From the darkness of this horrific event, the characters in *The Habitation of Dragons* must find meaning and acceptance for their unbearable loss and grief.

An obsession with punishment and the desire to be punished for one's sins resurfaces again and again throughout the play. All of the characters in *The Habitation of Dragons* seem to view God as a merciless arbiter of their lives, and they cannot forgive themselves unless some punishment cleanses them from their self-destructive guilt. Margaret is convinced that she is to blame for her children's death, that she is being punished by God for her infidelity: "Their death is my punishment. I am responsible for the death of my babies. I want to die" (32). Leonard, unwilling to admit his own role in the tragedy, also holds Margaret responsible for the boys' death, proclaiming: "Her whorish will is to blame.... It's for her sins my boys were killed. Their death is her punishment," (31). Unable to forgive herself and paralyzed by her grief, Margaret suffers an emotional breakdown and is admitted to a psychiatric hospital in Galveston. There, Margaret relives the death of her sons night after night in a vivid and horrific dream in which Horace and Leonard Jr. call out to their mother from the river but she is unable to reach her sons before they drown.

Leonard could help Margaret bare her grief, but he is so emotionally unstable that he cannot forgive Margaret for her infidelity or accept his own responsibility in the death of his children. Leonard's ultimate journey to absolution must begin with repentance for his own "dragons," which have ruled his life since his father's suicide. He must seek forgiveness for his own offenses before he can reach out to Margaret and begin the healing process.

Leonard's mother, Lenora, sums up the view shared by the entire Tolliver family, when she asks, "What's happening to us? The death of two little boys, Wally's death. Have we committed some terrible sin? Are we being punished?" (48). Horton Foote provides no answers to Lenora's piercing questions but he does offer a way for the characters to deal with such overwhelming grief. Just as often as the characters utter the word "punishment," the word "forgiveness" is also spoken. Although Mrs. Tolliver feels that the death of her husband and grandchildren are God's punishment for their sins, Horton's real interest is with redemption, not retribution. His God is not the wrathful one the Tolliver family worships, and during the course of the play Leonard discovers, in much the same way as Horace in *Lily Dale*, that his Heavenly Father is not one of revenge but one of goodness and mercy. "*The Habitation of Dragon*, a title taken from the Book of Isaiah 34:16, is about forgiveness," Horton explained. "It is about how difficult it is to forgive others and oneself."[27]

While forgiveness does not answer all the questions posed by *The Habitation of Dragons*, it is the path that Leonard ultimately follows. Over the course of the play, Leonard's life comes unraveled, and he discovers that the axioms he has built his life upon are false and meaningless. No matter how powerful or wealthy Leonard may become, he cannot avoid the fact that change is an inevitable part of life. "My God, how a man's life can change in a day, a week, an hour, a second," he declares. "I wanted to stand up and scream out to everybody, have compassion, have humility. Your lives, the fabric, the pattern, the bone, the essence can be destroyed overnight. Can be torn so to pieces that they can never be put together again." (43)

With the death of his children, Leonard's financial fortune melts away into legal aid for Billy Clanton and medical care for his wife, Margaret, and eventually, he has nothing left of his worldly treasure but

---

[27] Horton Foote, interview by Marion Castleberry, 20 March 2004, Waco, Texas.

the family farm. George, having sold his portion of the farm to his brother at the beginning of the play, approaches Leonard about buying back the land. Having now replaced Leonard as head of the Tolliver family, George has built a reputable law firm, assumed the position of county attorney (following Billy Clanton's arrest), and begun to prosper financially. Recognizing his brother's need for money, George approaches Leonard with a fair offer to buy back his share of the farm. But Leonard, who plans to escape the trials of Harrison for distant Canada, assures George that he needs to sell the land for $500 an acre—a sum he knows his brother cannot afford. George points out that he sold his half of the farm for much less, but Leonard, refusing to cooperate or acknowledge his brother's point of view, explodes into a jealous rage: "Don't you have enough now? You have a wife. A law practice. You're expecting a child. You're County Attorney. You have exactly what you want. Are you so greedy? What else do you want from me? This house? This land?" (56–7).

As George starts to walk away, Leonard recognizes his folly, swallows his pride, and ultimately slays his inner dragon. "George, I'm sorry," Leonard cries out. "I didn't mean that. I'm glad for whatever you have…. Take the land for exactly what I paid you for it…. Please forgive me, Brother. I'm half crazy; I don't know what I'm doing or saying" (57). For the first time, Leonard asks for forgiveness, taking his first step toward understanding and acceptance.

Soon after confronting George, Leonard begins the reconciliation process with Margaret. Heartbroken by the loss of his children, Leonard has tried to put Margaret out of his mind, continuously refusing to accept her pleas of forgiveness, but he ultimately realizes that running away from his problems cannot solve them. The two are finally reconciled when Leonard prevents Margaret from shooting herself and then sits with her afterward until she drops off to sleep. When Margaret awakens from another terrifying dream, Leonard comforts her, recalling the days when as teenagers they envisioned a much happier life: "I wanted so to please you in all things. Sitting here now, watching over you, looking at you asleep and sorrowing, I wanted again so to please you" (59). Leonard recognizes his need for forgiveness and realizes that there are more ways to violate one's marriage than committing adultery. Neglecting one's wife and ignoring her emotional needs are just as damaging as infidelity. Leonard slowly pieces his life back together by forgiving himself, Margaret, and his father for their failures. With understanding and reconciliation comes Leonard's realization that he can stay in Harrison, rebuild his relationship with George, and work things out with Margaret, who needs his love and support more than ever.

In the final analysis, it is the befuddled Uncle Virgil who best describes the healing balm of forgiveness that cleanses Leonard from his overwhelming anguish and grief. Like the rest of the Tollivers, Uncle Virgil is tormented by his past. Having refused to lend Leonard's father money when he desperately needed it, Virgil believes that he is to blame for his brother's suicide. In the play's final scene, the old man tells Leonard of a dream that haunted him as a young boy. In Virgil's dream he was in a room alone except for a preacher, who kept repeating "Forgiveness." Virgil kept crying and the preacher continued to repeat "Forgiveness."

> Virgil: And I woke up to tell my Mama and Papa about the dream, and, of course, they weren't there. No one was there, and I was alone. Who was there to forgive? Forgiveness. That's all he said. But what was there to forgive, except myself, or ask forgiveness of? Nobody.... Except myself.... I broke my brother's heart, and he died. By his own hand, he died. Did you break your brother's heart?
> Leonard: Yes sir.
> Virgil: And did he die?
> Leonard: No, sir. He is alive, and his heart has mended very well.
> Virgil: Are you alive?
> Leonard: Yes, sir, and my heart is broken.
> Virgil: Who broke it?
> Leonard: I did....
> Virgil: Do you think it will mend?
> Leonard: I hope. In time. (*Virgil leans his head back on the chair. He closes his eyes. Leonard is watching Margaret as the lights fade*). (61)

Virgil's words assure Leonard that no matter how desperate circumstances may seem, there is always hope, for from "chaos and darkness, reeds and rushes...life can continue" (Isaiah 35:7). Leonard recognizes that love and intimacy make forgiveness possible and that reconciliation with others always begins with the forgiveness of one's self. While tragedy and sorrow have visited the Tolliver family, at the end of the play there is a profound sense of hope and optimism.

The Habitation of Dragons holds a special place in Horton Foote's canon. The play is one of playwright's most penetrating depictions of the ability of individuals to endure appalling personal tragedies. In an interview printed in the program of the Pittsburg production, Horton stated:

> I am in awe of how Leonard Tolliver has taken what has happened to him. I'm not sure that I could respond that way. There is a point, as the play begins to find its own accumulative life, where something takes over. And you look at it and say, "Well yes, I wrote this, and that is exactly how it went, but where did it all come from?" I have four children and I can't imagine anything worse than losing them. Especially, as in *Habitation*, when it is senseless tragedy. That I think is the hardest thing to make peace with. I'm in awe of the last part of the play. I think it is daring, very bold; and as far as modern literature is concerned, there are not many that would end this way; most of them would end with some punitive thing. I believe it; I don't know if I can accept any credit for it; I just woke up and there it was.[28]

When *The Habitation of Dragons* was first performed in Pittsburg, George Anderson, arts critic for the *Pittsburg Post Gassette*, wrote a provocative review of the play in which he assessed the work as "a genuinely American tragedy" that presents "a disintegrating family against the backdrop of a crumbling society." Sequences in the play arise, Anderson notes "to extraordinary emotional power" and even while the plot sounds like "daytime drama," in Foote's measured prose it is never "maudlin or mundane." Anderson concluded that *The Habitation of Dragons* is clearly an attempt at a "major American play" that would make "an exceptionally strong film since Texans seem to demand the landscape the stage cannot afford them."[29]

Although *The Habitation of Dragons* has never received a production by a major commerical theater in New York, it did prove to be a viable vehicle for the television screen. On 8 September 1992, the play was presented as the second installment of the TNT *Screenworks* series, a marquee program created for Ted Turner's cable network by Steven Spielberg's Amblin Entertainment and Michael Brandman Productions.

---

[28] Bob Zeller, "An American Playwright: World Premiere: *The Habitation of Dragons* by Horton Foote," *Playbill* of Pittsburg Public Theatre, 29 September 1988, 24–5.

[29] George Anderson, "Ambitious Dragons Opens PPT Season," *Pittsburg Post Gazette*, 29 September 1988.

Spielberg and Brandman's purpose for the series was to design a showcase that would bring America's most distinguished playwrights, directors, and actors back to television. Besides Horton Foote, other writers featured in the series included David Mamet, Keith Reddin, and Lee Blessing. Horton was extremely pleased when he discovered that he would be involved in all facets of making the film. He helped with the casting, the editing, and the direction. More importantly, he served as the movie's location scout and was instrumental in making sure that *The Habitation of Dragons* was shot in Texas and not in a Hollywood studio. The authenticity of the Texas setting became an important factor in enhancing the film's credibility. Performed by an impressive cast that included Jean Stapleton, Frederic Forrest, Pat Hingle, Maureen O'Sullivan, Roberts Blossom, Brad Davis, and Hallie Foote, *The Habitation of Dragons* proved to be even more effective on television than it had been in the theater. Tony Scott, television critic for Variety, noted that Pat Hingle and Jean Stapleton gave memorable interpretations, while Hallie Foote's performance as Margaret was "a stunning and definitive study." Scott always stated that Brad Davis's performance of George, his final role before his death on 5 August 1992, was "a tight, well-thought-out-portrayal."[30]

The last Horton Foote play to be produced during the 1980s, *Dividing The Estate* (1989), is a sharply written comedy of manners, thematically linked to the the writer's earlier works, *The Girls* and *Expectant Relations*, in its comic treatment of familial inheritance and greed.[31] The work focuses on the Gordon family, a once proud and prosperous Southern clan facing financial ruin. Set in 1987, the play is one of Horton's most contemporary works and takes place against the background of a major American stock market collapse and mounting government taxation, as farming and oil industries are in decline and banks and financial institutions are folding in ever-larger numbers than during the Great Depression.

Dividing the Estate depicts the struggles among three generations of Gordon children as they gather in Harrison to convince their beningnly domineering matriarch, Stella, to divide their family inheritance. The children, driven by self-interest and the threat of financial collapse, argue

---

[30] Tony Scott, "Review of *The Habitation of Dragons*," *Variety Magazine*, 7 September 1992.

[31] Horton Foote, *Dividing the Estate*, in *Horton Foote: Four New Plays*, 115–74. Page references to *Dividing the Estate* in the text refer to this publication.

for their fair share of the family estate in hopes that the money from the sale of five thousand acres of farm land will save them from economic ruin and provide them with a fresh start in life. None of Stella's children, who are all over fifty-years-old, has ever held down a regular job; instead, they have lived off a montly allowance from the family estate. As the play unfolds, family members bicker over how the property should be partitioned and who should assume control of the estate.

Despite her advanced age and erratic memory, Stella Gordon still rules the stately old family home, with its cotton fields long unplanted and its surrounding residences torn down to make room for strip malls and fast-food joints. For years, Stella has refused to give in to such change or to relinquish control of the family estate. She has continuously forbidden her children from dividing their inheritance, holding onto the belief that the land can one day be as productive as it once was. "Don't talk to me about difficult times," Stella proclaims. "We got through the depression, when people were abandoning their land, selling it all over this county, but my father held on to our land, scraped together the money to plant cotton and every year, pay our taxes and keep body and soul together. Just look at what is surrounding us. Fruit markets and fast food restaurants. That's what happens when you sell your land" (125). Stella's misguided pragmatism is not shared by everyone, of course, especially not by her ninety-two-year-old black servant Doug. Patterned after Chekhov's ancient servant Firs in *The Cherry Orchard*, Doug has become too feeble to carry out his duties and too proud to relinquish his position to the young generation of black houskeepers. Doug understands that times have changed, and when Stella commands him to "put in a garden...get some pigs, and some chickens and cows," he admits "I'm an old man. I can't do that anymore.... You can't find people to do work like that no more" (121). While Stella and Doug live on the precarious line between past and present, Stella's children live fully in the present, barely surviving in an economy that sits on the edge of total collapse. Stella harbors no illusions regarding her children: "I know what you're all up to," she declares. "Plotting behind my back. The minute I'm dead you'll sell this house, divide the land and it will all be gone. Well, you'll never do it while I'm alive" (125). When both Stella and Doug die unexpectedly, the children are left to make the all important decision of whether or not to divide the estate. Much to their chagrin they discover that no matter how hard they try, splitting up their inheritance may not be the wisest thing to do.

Stella has entrusted the running of the house to her dutiful daughter Lucille and the management of the estate to Son, Lucille's level-headed, forty-year-old son. Son, the most rational of the Gordon offspring, draws a salary for managing the family farms and distributing the allowances. He arbitrates, as best he can, the selfish interests of his alcoholic uncle Lewis and his sharp-tongued aunt Mary Jo who lives in Houston with her husband Bob, a real estate broker, and their narcissistic daughters, Sissie and Emily. When the play begins, Son is hoping the family will give him a raise so he can afford to marry Lucy, an affable and socially conscious schoolteacher. Lewis, the alcoholic uncle, can't hold down a job because of his gambling and drinking habits, is in need of ten thousand dollars in cash because he is being blackmailed by the hostile father of Irene Ratliff , the immature nineteen-year-old girl he has been dating. Son recognizes that the family is extended beyond its means and stands on the brink of financial ruin. Consequently, he tries to prevent his uncle from borrowing the money, but Lewis demands that the estate be divided because he is "tired of having pittances doled out to [him] by [his] nephew every month" (123). Because of the critical financial problems in which the family finds itself, Son advises keeping the estate intact and slowly paying off debts. He also makes the radical and unfavorable suggestion that the entire family find jobs and move into the ancestral home in Harrison to conserve much-needed income. Unlike his elders, Son has come to terms with the unethical manner in which his family has acquired its wealth. His great-grandfather was a Yankee carpetbagger, who accumulated a vast estate during Reconstruction, and his grandfather Gordon, who managed the farm profitably, led a promiscuous sexual life, fathering white and black children "all up and down the county" (131). After his grandfather's death, Son's father, Charlie (who has just died when the play begins) supervised the estate, but, as Lucille explains, he "dropped over dead in the heat of summer. He slaved every day for this family—not his family even, but mine, and what thanks did he get for it…. An early death is all he ever got. All they did was to take advantage of your father's good nature" (145).

The catalyst for most of the humor in *Dividing the Estate* is Mary Jo, Stella's socialite daughter from Houston, who has already borrowed heavily from the estate but desperately needs more money to pay for her daughter's lavish second marriage. But paying for Sissie's wedding is the least of Mary Jo and Bob's worries; more important is the fact that they have lost their house in Houston, and his real estate business has taken a nosedive. Houston is "dying on the vine" (137), and Mary Jo confesses: "Bob is too proud to tell you this, but I'm not. He's at his wit's end. He has not sold any real estate in the city of Houston for four months. He has not earned a red cent in four months" (141). Mary Jo has dreams of selling an oil lease to solve all her finacial problems but her idea of a quick fix—dividing the estate—is a foolish fantasy. The Gordon family learns that the land is of no value on the current real estate market, and the only way they can protect their inheritance against huge government taxes and court costs is to hold on to the property and to reclaim Harrison as their home. But even holding onto what they have does not answer all the Gordons' concerns, for, as Bob acknowledges, it is no longer "profitable to grow cotton" in Harrison, as the "chemical plants are poisoning the environment" on the Gulf Coast, and "Mexicans are coming in droves from Mexico"(122).

The Gordons are faced with the hardships of social and economic change, and by play's end, the forces that have divided the characters for years serve to tie them together. When Lucy suggests that the family could all move in together and Son proposes that they could all get jobs "until the bank loan is paid off," Mary Jo retorts, "I'm not good at this communal living. I'm not Vietnamese and I'm not Korean" (170), and then quips, "I've never worked a day in my life...Maybe we could get a job at Whataburger with brother's girlfriend" 172). Little does she know that her humorous boasting may soon come to pass. Right on cue, the girlfirend, Irene, arrives with Lewis, who enters the discussion. Irene comes from Harrison's lower class, for whom Mary Jo can barely conceal her disdain, but ironically, it is she who points out Mary Jo's selfish folly. When Mary Jo declares that she will pray on bended knees every night for oil to be discovered on the land so that the family can finally divide the estate, Irene remarks:

> Irene: Oh. My Mama told me that her Mama told her that her granddaddy struck oil out on his farm a long time ago. He couldn't read or write and he went crazy with all the money from oil, and had a lot of kids, twelve, I think. And he went down and bought them all cars—big expensive cars, Reos and Packards and Buicks—and they moved into town here from the country and parked all the cars out under the Chinaberry trees and everybody in town used to ride by their house. To see all them new cars parked in the yard, and one day a man from the Valley came to town and knew my great-granddaddy couldn't read or write and he took advantage of him and sold him some land...
>
> Mary Jo: On bended knees. On bended knees.

Lucille: What happened to the land?

Irene: Well, Mama says when her granddaddy went out to the Valley to look at the land he bought, it was all under water and worthless. And all that was left to show for all of his oil money was them cars he bought his kids. She said people in town used to ride by all the time to see all those cars sitting under the Chinaberry trees.

Lucille: Under the Chinaberry trees. My.

Lewis: You remember Irene's grandfather. He ended up as the town night watchman. John Moon.

Lucille: Oh, yes.

Lewis: We had this joke—John Moon only comes out at night.

Mary Jo: I'm praying every night on bended knees.... Praying every night for my deliverance on bended knees. Praying for an oil lease.

Irene: Yes, Ma'am.

Lucille: John Moon. Yes, I remember him.

Irene: All I say is, if you strike oil watch out for crooks from the Valley. They will see your land under water every time. Every time.

Lucille: John Moon. My I hadn't thought about him for the longest kind of time.

Mary Jo: I'm praying...I'm praying.... (*Curtain*) (173)

Mary Jo's refusal to face the reality that death and taxes are permanent fixtures in contemporary America or to embrace her family's dire economic situation produces the play's most humorous scene. On a more serious level, the exchange suggests that the solidarity of the Gordon family is the only thing keeping it from suffering the pain and humiliation other families have experienced in Houston and Harrison. Only by putting aside their differences and pulling together can they save their family and build a life for their descendants. In the final analysis, *Dividing the Estate* is a cautionary tale about the evils of materialism and the need for genuine and lasting values in a changing world.

The decade of the 1980s was a remarkably rewarding time for Horton Foote. From 1980 to 1990, more than twenty of his works were performed on stages and screens throughout America and Europe. In 1983, Horton, at age sixty-seven, was awarded his second Academy Award for the original screenplay, *Tender Mercies*, and he followed this accomplishment with *The Trip to Bountiful*, a motion picture in which Geraldine Page became the third actress to win an Oscar in a Foote screenplay. These works, along with the performance of *The Road to the Graveyard* at the Ensemble Studio Theatre (1985) and productions of several *Orphans'*

Home Cycle plays, catapulted Horton into one of the most active periods of his career. In 1988, he was elected to the Fellowship of Southern Writers, and in 1989 he received the prestigious Lifetime Achievement Award at the annual William Inge Festival in Independence, Kansas. By the end of the decade, Horton Foote had assured his place as one of the most compelling voices in American Theatre. He had entered the second act of his illustrious career.

Part Seven

The Final Homecoming

Death, if I don't think of you, you'll vanish.

—Horace Robedaux in *1918*

16

The Signature Years
1990–2000

The decade of the 1990s saw the tempo of Horton Foote's life and career quicken with a steady succession of screenplays and award-winning dramas. Following the release of his film *Convicts* in 1990, Horton tried his hand at acting (after almost fifty years), providing the voice of Jefferson Davis for Ken Burns's critically acclaimed PBS documentary, *The Civil War* (1990). In 1990, the Asolo Theatre of Sarasota, Florida, premiered Horton's play, *Talking Pictures,* a bittersweet tale about a woman who plays piano for silent movies and whose life is changed by the advent of the talkies. That same year, *The Trip to Bountiful* was produced by four regional theater companies, the A.D. Players of Houston, the Zachary Scott Theatre of Austin, the Actor's Theatre of Louisville, and the New Harmony Theatre of Indiana. In spring 1991, the Great Lakes Theatre Festival of Cleveland, Ohio, celebrated Horton's contributions to American theater with a stirring production of *Dividing the Estate,* staged by renowned director Gerald Freedman. The American Conservatory Theatre of San Francisco also presented "A Great Day with Horton Foote," honoring Horton's illustrious career with staged readings of *Convicts* and *Courtship* and an acclaimed production of *1918,* directed by Sabin Epstein.

In summer 1991, the distinguished actor Gary Sinise approached Horton about writing a screen adaptation of John Steinbeck's 1937 novel *Of Mice and Men,* the tragic tale of two displaced migrant ranch workers, George Milton and Lennie Small, struggling to keep their dreams of home alive during the Great Depression. Sinise, cofounder and artistic director of Chicago's Steppenwolf Theatre Company, had long admired *Of Mice and Men,* and in 1961 he performed the role of George opposite his friend John Malkovich's Lennie. Thirty years later (1990), Sinise secured the film rights to the novel and stage play from Steinbeck's widow, Elaine, and approached Horton Foote about adapting the story to the screen. At first, Horton was reluctant to take the offer, fearing that the story was much too familiar for American audiences to accept yet another version. "I had seen many productions of the play, and I almost didn't want to do it," Horton admitted, "because I felt it was just too set in our minds. But Gary Sinise was so passionate about it that I really felt I had to reinvestigate it."[1] While re-reading the novel, Horton was struck by the timeliness and relevance of the story, particularly how it reflected the rootlessness and migratory conditions so prevalent in contemporary America.

Horton's film adaptation is remarkably faithful to both the letter and spirit of Steinbeck's original work, brilliantly capturing the mood and rhythm of the novelist's fictive world. While Horton left intact the tragic tale of George (Gary Sinise), the intellectually keen ranch hand, and Lennie (John Malcovich), the field hand with the strength of a giant and the mind of a child, film critic Vincent Canby noted that the screenwriter enriched the original story by illuminating a pervasive theme in the novel that had never previously seemed significant:

> Horton Foote's *Of Mice and Men* is a mournful, distantly heard lament for the loss of American innocence. This has always been in the Steinbeck novella, but it is the dominant mood of the film, which is gorgeous in the idealized way of beauty remembered. The wheat fields are golden, the skies blinding blue. There is stylized perfection about the seediness of the run-down Tyler ranch, where George and Lennie find work at the beginning of the film. The hired hands work all day in 90-degree heat, and though they mop their brows, they don't seem to sweat. This *Of Mice and Men* doesn't mean to be either realistic or melodramatic, that is, in the manner of the Lewis Milestone's far darker 1940 adaptation.[2]

While *Of Mice and Men* received positive reviews from critics, the movie did not fare well at the box office and grossed only around five million dollars, a sum that barely covered production costs. Fortunately, in 1993 MGM made the film available on VHS, and in 2003 it was released on DVD. Since that time, the movie has aired frequently on television and garnered an impressive following of admirers who favor Horton Foote and Gary Sinise's 1992 *Of Mice and Men* over Milestone's classic 1939 film, which had been championed by movie historians for nearly sixty years.

---

[1] Buzz McLaughlin, "Conversation with Horton Foote," in *The Voice of an American Playwright*, ed. Gerald C. Wood and Marion Castleberry (Macon GA: Mercer University Press, 2012) 160.

[2] Vincent Canby, "New Facets Highlighted in a Classic," *New York Times*, 2 October 1992.

Although this was an artistically rewarding time for Horton, it was also a time of misfortune and immense grief. In August 1992, Horton's beloved wife, Lillian, passed away after a brief illness. Although there was never an official diagnosis given for Lillian's death, biographer Wilborn Hampton believes that cancer seemed almost certain.[3] Lillian had first taken ill in the fall of 1991, while she and Horton were residing at their Wharton home. Lillian, a strong and vibrant woman, began to suffer from unexplicable pain and acute weight loss. After only a few weeks, her health had worsened to such an extent that she and Horton decided to return to New York to seek guidance from a Christian Science practitioner. After receiving a less than an encouraging report, Lillian entered a Christian Science hospice in Princeton, New Jersey, where she lingered until her death on 5 August 1992. Lillian was 69 years old.

Lillian's death was a devastating blow to Horton, who, for forty-seven years, had depended on her unwavering love and devotion. She had not only been a loving and steadfast wife, but she had also been her husband's most supportive and practical colleague. Over the years she had produced several of her husband's works, and she had been the inspiration for virtually every play and screenplay he had ever written. She had given Horton four children and had kept his dreams alive during the dark moments of his life and career. Lillian had been Horton's protector and comforter, and now he was forced to face the world without her.

Following her death, Lillian's body was cremated and a small service was held in Horton's New York apartment on Horatio Street for family members and close friends. A few days later, her ashes were flown to Texas where they were interred in the Wharton County cemetery alongside the graves of Horton's ancestors. It was a very sad time for the writer, and for months after the service at least one or more of his children was always with him. Often during the night, they would hear him pacing in his room, weeping and calling out for Lillian. At one point, Horton told Michael Wilson, a young director from the Alley Theatre in Houston who had become a close friend to the family, "I don't know if I'll ever be able to write again. I wrote everything for Lillian."[4]

Until his own death in 2009, Horton felt an unquenchable sense of longing for Lillian, who he felt was his soul mate and the only woman he

---

[3] Wilborn Hampton, *Horton Foote: America's Storyteller* (New York: Simon & Schuster, 2009) 223.

[4] Michael Wilson, interview by Marion Castleberry, 14 May 2013, New York.

would ever love. "I had a friend in New Hampshire," Horton explained, "whose husband passed on and she said, 'I'm like the swans, I only mate once.' I thought that was kind of sweet. I still think of what Lillian would say about things. I'll talk to her and say, 'I'm learning this—aren't you pleased with me?'...If you find your real mate and if you've had a happy marriage, I think you'd better say, 'Thanks a lot and that's it.'"[5]

Lillian's was not the only death Horton had to confront during the decade. On 6 October 1990 his good friend Herbert Berghof had unexpectedly died from a heart attack. Less than three years later, Joseph Anthony passed away at the age of eighty in a nursing home in Hyannis, Massachusetts, followed a mere nine months later by his longtime friend and mentor Agnes De Mille, who was struck down by a stroke in her Greenwich Village apartment. Shortly thereafter Horton's brother John Speed succumbed to Alzheimer's Disease and died on 13 February 1995. Other friends and colleagues of Horton's also passed away during this time, including Lucy Kroll, the playwright's devoted literary agent, director Mary Hunter Wolf, who nourished the writer's early work as artistic leader of the American Actors Company, actress Kim Stanley, who embodied Horton's characters better than any other actress of her generation, and filmmaker Alan Pakula, who had been one of Horton's closest friends since they had first worked together on *To Kill a Mockingbird*.

Horton was deeply affected by the deaths of so many of his loved ones, and the result of this loss can be seen in the elegiac, lugubrious vision that appears in his later works. He was especially bewildered by the senseless death of Alan Pakula on 19 November 1998, the result of a horrific car accident in which a metal pipe smashed through Pakula's car on the Long Island Expressway, striking him in the head and killing him instantly. In a letter to Pakula's widow, Hannah, Horton expressed his deepest sorrow over the loss of his friend by quoting absurdist playwright Samuel Beckett: "I know your sorrow and I know that for the likes of us there is no ease for the heart to be had from words or reason and that in the very assurance of our sorrow's fading there is more sorrow. So I offer you only my deeply affectionate and compassionate thoughts and wish for you only that the strange thing may never fail you, whatever it is, that gives us strength to live on and on with our

---

[5] Sheila Benson, "Horton Foote," *The Voice of an American Playwright*, 204–05.

wounds."[6] The quote calls attention to the profound sense of sadness and isolation Horton himself felt during this time.

Somehow through all the disappointment and grief, Horton Foote persevered, like so many of his characters who face the pain of overwhelming tragedy, learn to accept life on its own terms, and move forward. In the end, it was the theater that renewed and sustained Horton Foote during this dark period of his life.

Soon after Lillian's burial, Horton returned to work. In late August he began rehearsals for *The Roads to Home*, a trilogy of thematically connected one-act plays first performed by the Manhattan Punch Line Theatre in 1982. The play, which tells the story of three women living in Houston who long to return to the small towns of their youth, opened for a month's run at Lamb's Theatre of New York on 28 September 1992. Directed by Horton Foote and starring Hallie Foote and Jean Stapleton, *The Roads to Home* was a big success, receiving mostly positive reviews from critics. David Richards of the *New York Times* commented: "Our loud violent times are not particularly hospitable to retiring creatures like these…. Admittedly, his roads to home are little byways—not even paved, I suspect, and doubtless no wider than a Model T. But they lead someplace humane and caring, where heartbreak doesn't have to be desperate and noisy to merit our concern."[7] Frank Rich, arts critic of the *New York Times*, also praised the production. "Any list of America's living literary wonders must include Horton Foote," Rich wrote. "And here Mr. Foote is now, in a small playhouse in the shadows of the Broadway behemoths, directing his own script, meticulously tending to a vision that has deepened but not wavered throughout his long career. *The Roads to Home*, a trilogy of related one-act plays first seen briefly Off-Off Broadway a decade ago, is modest Foote but *echt* Foote. The setting is Texas. The time is long ago (the 1920s). The lives on display are unexceptional, undramatic. And just when the audience is set to relax into an elegiac reverie that might resemble nostalgia, the playwright finds a way to make his characters' inner turmoil so ferociously vivid it leaps beyond their specific time and place to become our own."[8] Rich called Hallie Foote's portrayal of Annie Gayle Long "the central and

---

[6] Horton Foote to Hannah Pakula, 1 March 1999 (Horton Foote Papers).

[7] David Richards, "Review of *The Roads to Home*," *New York Times*, 29 September 1992.

[8] Frank Rich, "1920s Lives that Leap into the Present," *New York Times*, 18 September 1992.

transporting performance" in the plays. He was especially moved by the third one-act, *Spring Dance*, in which Annie, while hospitalized in an asylum in Austin, dreams of her childhood and the dances she attended as a youth.

As quickly as Rich's review hit the newsstands, directors and producers lined up to see the show. One of them was a young director named James Houghton, a graduate of the Meadows School of the Arts at Southern Methodist University, who had been introduced to Horton's work while matriculating as a student in Texas. Houghton knew Horton Foote primarily through his movies, *To Kill a Mockingbird* , *Tender Mercies*, and *The Trip to Bountiful*, and through two stage productions— *1918* and *Valentine's Day*—he had seen as a student in Dallas. Houghton remembers being impressed by the power and authenticity of Horton's work, and he was especially moved by the "gentle storm" that existed in the plays.[9] By the time Houghton saw *The Roads to Home*, he had opened his own theater in New York— the Signature Theatre Company—that was dedicated to producing an entire season of plays from the literary canon of a single playwright. The Signature's first season (1991–92) had been devoted to Romulus Linney, a close friend of Horton's, and the playwright had attended the opening of Linney's masterpiece *The Sorrows of Frederick*. During intermission, Horton and Houghton had discussed the possibility of the Signature producing a season of four of his plays but the writer was too preoccupied with other matters to take on a project of such magnitude at the time, and he wasn't sure he was ready for such scrutiny. "I was out of New York the next season [1992–93]," Horton recalled, "when they did Lee Blessing's plays but I was again in the city for the Edward Albee plays given in their third season [1993–94]. I was able to see most of these, and I was again very impressed by the theatre's work. So when Jim Houghton approached me once again, I decided to take the plunge."[10]

Horton agreed to devote the 1994–95 theatrical season to the Signature, with one stipulation: that the majority of the four plays produced by the theater be new works or at least plays that had not been performed in New York. The Signature decided to open the season with *Talking Pictures* (September 1994), a play that had been staged twice before—once at the Asolo Theatre in Florida (1990) and once at Stages

---

[9] Hampton, 228.

[10] Horton Foote, Introduction to *The Young Man from Atlanta* (New York: Dutton Press, 1995) ix.

Repertory Theatre in Houston (1990)—but had never been performed in New York. The second play to be staged was *Night Seasons* (October 1994), which was originally produced by HB Studio Theatre in 1982 and had recently been performed by the American Stage Company in 1993. Both new pieces, *The Young Man from Atlanta* (January 1995) and *Laura Dennis* (March 1995), were chosen as the final two plays of the season.

By committing an entire year to the Signature Theatre, Horton Foote was making a bold attempt to re-establish himself in the national theatrical center of New York, much like he had done in the 1950s with *The Trip to Bountiful* and *The Traveling Lady*. And because of the Signature's format of presenting sequential productions, designed to encourage an intimate and immersive exploration of the playwright's theatrical vision, critics and audiences alike were urged to assess Horton's total dramatic output, evaluate his unique storytelling ability, and examine his major themes and ideas. Leading up to the opening of each show, there were articles written about Horton and interviews with the playwright and his daughter Barbara Hallie, who starred in three of the four productions. Together with the performances, the large amount of press about the playwright and his work created a renewed interest in Horton's writing and introduced him, at age seventy-eight, to a new generation of admiring artists and theatergoers.

The year Horton spent with the Signature Theatre at the Kampo Cultural Center proved to be one of the most satisfying and creative periods of the writer's career. Before rehearsals began, Edward Albee, whose work had been showcased in Signature's third season, sent Foote a brief note saying:

> Dear Horton: You will probably have a frightening experience with the Signature Company this coming season. You will discover you are working with eager, dedicated, talented, resourceful, gentle, and thoughtful people whose main concern will be making you happy. This will be frightening. Even more, they will succeed in making you happy. This will be even more frightening. Don't fret about it; just go with it. Have a wonderful season.[11]

Albee's words turned out to be amazingly prophetic. Horton later remarked, "It was a wonderful experience and satisfying on every count. I don't know how many playwrights get that opportunity. You know I've worked with actors nearly all my life now, and usually actors find a

---

[11] Ibid., xii.

way to complain, often quite rightly. At the Signature we had not always the best conditions, everyone had to kind of make do—but the theatre somehow managed to create a good feeling that permeated the whole experience."[12] Not only was Horton supported in his writing but he was also encouraged to be present at all casting sessions, to go to rehearsals, and to attend as many performances as he could. The Signature offered a very collaborative working environment, and whatever the theater company lacked in material resources, it made up for in energy, effort, and commitment to artistic excellence.

The Signature series began auspiciously with *Talking Pictures*,[13] Horton's bittersweet tale of Myra Tolliver, a piano player at a small-town movie theater during the era of silent films, whose life is changed by the advent of the talkies. The play was directed by Carol Goodheart, a talented actress/director who had worked with Horton on *The Orphans' Home* films, and starred Barbara Hallie Foote as Myra Tolliver, Seth Jones as Willis, and Eddie Kaye Thomas as Myra's son, Pete.

Horton explained that the inspiration behind *Talking Pictures* came from thinking about the day when talking pictures were first introduced in Wharton, and about the mysterious disappearance of the lady who had played piano for the silent films. "She and her son lived across the street from me and I never knew what happened to her," he recalled. "She just appeared one day and then, when talkies came, she disappeared. I knew that piano-playing lady and her son, and many years later I wrote a play based on my memory of her."[14]

Set in the summer of 1929, *Talking Pictures* is a richly textured work that skillfully balances comedy, drama, and music to reveal the traumatic effects of societal change on the ordinary men and women of Harrison. Horton employs the most theatrical image of the era—the infant talkies—to comment on the resilience of the human spirit juxtaposed with the loss of spiritual values and integrity in a world being transformed by affluency and technological expansion. The older, agrarian customs of Harrison are giving way to a new industrial order, which features the speed of the automobile, the convenience of the telephone, and the appealing sights and sounds of motion pictures.

---

[12] Jim O'Quinn, "Eye of the Beholder," in *The Voice of an American Playwright*, 186.

[13] Horton Foote, *Talking Pictures*, in *Horton Foote: Four New Plays, 1988–1993* (Newbury VT: Smith and Kraus, 1993) 175–224. All page references to *Talking Pictures* in the text refer to this publication.

[14] Horton Foote, interview by Marion Castleberry, 10 May 2002, New York.

Foote sets the events of the play only a few months before the stock market crash that triggered the Great Depression, a fact that makes the characters' search for stability in this encroaching modern world all the more poignant. Horton's characters experience personal traumas as severe and disturbing as those of their fictive counterparts on the movie screen.

In *Talking Pictures,* Horton examines the effect that this societal upheaval has on the traditional family, as husbands, wives, parents, and children struggle to make sense of their new identities. When the play opens, Myra Tolliver, a young divorcee and single mother, is preparing for the inevitable—the day the local movie theater goes talkie and she loses her job as pianist. Myra barely survives by moving from town to town, making only enough money to support herself and her fourteen-year-old son, Pete. Now, they hope to put down roots in Harrison, even though the town's sole movie theater, the Queen, is in jeopardy of being converted to a talking picture house.

Myra is not the only character facing inexorable change. During the course of the play, Mr. Jackson, Myra's landlord, is bumped from his engineer's position in Harrison, to one stationed in nearby Cuero, and then bumped back again. Mrs. Jackson realizes the mutability of this practice and questions her husband about the serious possibility that buses will soon take the place of trains altogether: "What'll happen to the trains if everybody starts riding the bus?...one day we could wake up and find there are no trains at all" (198). Mrs. Jackson doesn't yet know how prophetic her words will become; in only a few years her greatest fear will be realized. By play's end, the Jacksons will stay in Harrison, which means Myra and Pete can remain in their one room apartment above the Jacksons' garage.

Myra supplements her income by giving private piano lessons to the Jacksons' daughters, sixteen-year-old Katie Belle and her younger sister Vesta, both of whom are experiencing the pains of growing up. Sixteen-year-old Katie Belle, a central catalyst in the play, is searching for her place in the world as she moves beyond her family, explores the boundaries of her community, and questions her inherited religious beliefs. Her questions and discoveries, usually comic in nature, invite the audience to contemplate and assess the ideals of family and faith in a more rigid and innocent era. Katie Belle's religious beliefs have been informed by her preacher, Brother Meyers, who has warned her against the sin of watching motion pictures. Although Mrs. Jackson tells her daughter that Brother Meyers is "a good man, but extreme in his views," Katie Belle is intrigued by the preacher's didacticism and narrow interpretation of the divine. Katie Belle is especially sensitive to others, and she is very concerned about the state of Myra's soul: "Do you think people that attend motion picture shows are going to Hell?...Brother Meyers says if they go on weekdays they are liable to go and if they go on Sundays they are bound to. I certainly don't think Myra is going to Hell, do you?" (186).

While Katie Belle is intrigued by Brother Meyers's sermons, she has begun to question his authority and understanding of the Bible. She is drawn by the example of her family and Myra to trust her inner voice, a voice that tells her to dig deeper, to seek the truth. Her world is no longer as black and white as Brother Meyers has led her to believe.

While teaching the Jackson girls to play the piano, Myra entertains them by recounting movie plots and discussing the troubled lives of movie stars. The girls are especially fond of Al Jolson's movie, *The Singing Fool*, which Katie Belle often recounts with great fervor:

> I remember there was this man and he was a famous singer and he was married. Right? And they had a little boy and he loved his little boy very much, but then he and his wife separated and one night when he was to sing his little boy got sick and died. But he had to go on stage and sing anyway, even though his heart was breaking.... Miss Myra said everybody in the picture show was crying. (181–2).

Both Katie Belle and Vesta are fascinated by the humanity of this story and the remarkable perseverance of the singer who attempts to lift himself from the depths of paralyzing despair. Myra also connects with the movie, finding within the film's music a sorrow deeper than her own and a much-needed assurance that she is not alone in the world. As she sings the central song of the movie, we are made aware of the loneliness and heartbreak Myra has already suffered: "Friends may forsake us/ Let them all forsake us/ I still have you, Sonny Boy./ You came from heaven/ and I know your worth./ You made a heaven for me right here on earth./ But the angels they got lonely/ And they took you because they were lonely/ Now I'm lonely too, Sonny Boy" (182).

The lyrics of the song become all the more poignant and painful when Pete, who is himself lonely and discontented, announces to his mother that he wishes to move to Houston to live with his father, Gerard Anderson. While Myra has worked hard to provide for her son, Gerard knows nothing about bringing up the boy. An ineffectual and insensitive man, Gerard believes in the supremacy of money and material possessions. Pete's decision to live with his father breaks Myra's heart, but she will not prevent him from moving for fear that one day he would hate her for her decision. Ironically, when Gerard shows up in Harrison announcing that he is married again and postponing Pete's move, the young boy realizes that things are not going to work out as he had hoped. He discovers the truth about his father—that his second wife Jackie Kate has filed for divorce and kicked him out of their house. Before play's end, Pete must come to accept his father's shortcomings and make peace with his mother. Though he does eventually decide to remain with Myra, he struggles for a time with his own sense of loneliness before finally accepting the fact that his mother plans to marry Willis, a bricklayer, who was abandoned by his wife, Gladys, five years earlier. Willis is devoted to Myra but he cannot ask for her hand in marriage because he is still legally married to Gladys. Willis is hopeful that with his steady work and raise in pay he can finally save enough money to pay for a divorce and marry Myra. Though fond of Willis, Myra is not deeply in love with him. She knows, however, that he will be a good provider and a loving companion, and, much like Claire Ratcliff in *The Widow Claire*, Myra chooses fidelity over romantic love and accepts his proposal. Clearly, Myra is happy that Pete will stay with her and for the chance he has to provide for both of them since the talkies have finally come to Harrison.

As Horton often does, he introduces plot complications and resolutions through character and story with humor. Myra and Willis's wedding plan is interupted when Gladys, Willis's ex-wife, unexpectedly shows up in Harrison, hoping to escape her abusive boyfriend, Ashenback, and to win back Willis's favor. After several comic episodes between Gladys and Ashenback, Willis finally gets his divorce when Gladys and Gerard fall head over heels in love with each other and leave for Mexico, where they can purchase a quick, cheap marriage license. The couple's extreme romance reveals just how superficial their love really is and just how trivial relationships can become in an escapist society, dominated by greed and materialism.

Other characters involved in their own life journeys and discoveries are the Jackson girls, who continue to practice piano while Estaquio Trevino, a young Mexican preacher boy their own age, tests their ideas about religion. Estaquio's father, a Mexican Baptist preacher, has arrived in Harrison to establish a Spanish-speaking church, a dream that is never realized in the play. Estaquio visits the Jackson home often during the course of the play. He revels in his zealous faith, spouts prayers by rote, recites the book of *Genesis*, sings the hymn "Rock of Ages" in Spanish, and proclaims that Jesus was a Baptist, much to the delight and fascination of Mrs. Jackson, a devout Methodist. At first, Estaquio's sermonizing appears overbearing, but by the end of the play it is clear that his zealousness is a result of a troubled family life:

> The devil got hold of my Mama, you know.... My Papa prayed and prayed but he won out. She ran off and left Papa and me. She hated Church. Hated the Bible. Hated hymns. Hated Jesus.... We saw her on the street one day in Mexico City, but when we went up to her she said she didn't even know who we were. (196)

Sadly, what once drove Estaquio's mother to leave her family is what now protects her son from bitterness and heart-rending grief. Through it all, Estaquio's faith sustains him, and by continuously recalling "The Lord is my Shepherd" and "Rock of Ages," the young boy holds out hope that his family will one day be reunited. Mrs. Jackson's final request for Estaquio to sing "Blessed Assurance" not only emphasizes the young man's need for compassion and stability but also underscores Mrs. Jackson's own need for peace and order in the face of chaos and inexorable change. In the play's final scene, however, Estaquio is no more assured of his future than when he first arrived at the Jackson house. His father, unable to establish a Mexican Baptist church in Harrison, announces that both father and son will have to return to Mexico. Estaquio's departure leaves Katie Belle and Vesta with dreams of someday running away to that exotic land and reestablishing their relationship with Estaquio. "I bet I get to Mexico one day," Katie Belle declares.

In the play's final scene all is well in Harrison, as Katie Belle sings "Rock of Ages" in Spanish and Myra and Willis sit on the front porch "lost in their own thoughts," having received Pete's blessing for their upcoming marriage. They have faced their difficulties and heartbreaks with dignity and now look forward to the future with a renewed sense of identity and courage. In the final analysis, *Talking Pictures*, is a tale about acceptance and transition, a story about the resilience of the human spirit and the need for genuine and lasting values in a cynical and unpredictable world.

The Signature Theatre production of *Talking Pictures* was a promising beginning for Horton Foote's presentation of four plays. The production received positive reviews from critics, who found the show entertaining and insightful. David Richards of the *New York Times* wrote that despite its "dusty provincialism," the play offered a unique perspective on "broken homes, heartbreak, [and] looming unemployment."[15] Vincent Canby was impressed with Horton's characters, who profess Christian beliefs yet who are threatened "by the tempation to surrender to despair. They can't go on, they won't go on, they go on—sometimes raffishly, like Gladys, sometimes in quiet triumph, like Myra Tolliver."[16] The most informative critique of the Signature production was written by Susan Underwood in her essay "Texture in Horton Foote's *Talking Pictures*":

> Carol Goodheart's fall 1994 production of *Talking Pictures* finely balanced the serious implications of even the most humorous moments. Played with pathos, the script maintains the integrity of its dramatic undertones and the serious universal themes. Thus, Foote's comic moment is made poignant by the force of its own sobering resonance, and the 'texture' of the play is strengthened by the blending of the dark moment with the light. Standing seemingly quite apart from the structure, plot, and significant serious themes, the comic moment actually suggests the most serious motivations of the play, probing the deeper lives of the characters and suggesting their capacity for discovering stability by creating human connections.[17]

The second Horton Foote play produced during Signature's 1994–95 season was *Night Seasons*, which had been staged the previous year by the American Stage Company of Teaneck, New Jersey.[18] Both the American State Company production and the Signature Theatre production were directed by Horton, and both starred Hallie Foote and Jean Stapleton.

Originally penned in the 1970s, *Night Seasons* was, as Horton recalled, inspired by a childhood experience—a visit to the home of his 93-year-old great-aunt:

---

[15] David Richards, "Review of *Talking Pictures*," *New York Times*, 27 September 1994.

[16] Vincent Canby, "Review of *Talking Pictures*: 'For Horton Foote the Pictures Speak Volumes,'" *New York Times*, 2 October 1994.

[17] Gerald C. Wood, ed. *Horton Foote: A Casebook* (New York: Garland Press, 1998) 154.

[18] Foote, *Night Seasons*, in *Horton Foote: Four New Plays*, 63–114. All page references to *Night Seasons* in the text refer to this publication.

We went on her birthday, and my mother said to her, "Happy birthday and many more," and she answered, "Don't wish me that, Honey." And that literally was the seed for this play. The Laura Lee that I based the play on did have a stroke and die. She was dead a number of years by the time my mother and I visited my great-aunt. And there was a son. They were a banking family. He was notorious for his moods and their fights [he and his wife]. Of course, lots of things changed, but that was the genesis.... There was a cousin whom the family financially helped, and there was a cousin who sang. Whether they sang trios together, I have no idea. And there were two suitors...that I've always heard about that she was supposed to marry. She became very bitter toward the family.[19]

From these fragments of memory, Horton created a dark and disturbing tale about Laura Lee Weems, a woman who spent an entire lifetime searching for a sense of home and trying to escape the control of her domineering mother, Josie. The story of the Weems family is told through the use of flashbacks, covering the lives of its members from 1917 to 1963 as they go about their lives and struggle to find their places in society. The play is framed by the occasion of Josie's ninety-third birthday, a time which should be full of joy and celebration but which becomes a day of sorrow, regret, and painful memories. Josie, who once sought absolute control over her family, has ended up a confused old woman who can no longer even remember which of her children is alive and which is dead. To her lone birthday guest, her niece Dolly, Josie admits that what really haunts her thoughts and dreams is her daughter, Laura Lee, who was never happy because her family spoiled any chance she had for independence and autonomy, especially where money was concerned. Laura Lee blames all her troubles on her mother, who she believes interfered in her life, ignoring her need for individuation and sabotaging her relationships with men. Laura Lee had two chances at marriage ripped from her—one by the elitism of her mother toward her fiancé Mr. Chestnut and the other through Laura Lee's inability to make up her mind about marrying Mr. Barsoty, another suitor with a golden singing voice but no economic prospects.

Mr. Chestnut, a baker, is devoted to Laura Lee and hopes to marry her, but Josie believes that his profession is financially undesirable and beneath her daughter's social standing. Josie, who will not validate Laura Lee's emotional decisions, convinces her husband to offer Chestnut a position at the family's bank, thus requiring the young man

---

[19] Porter, "Unpublished Interview," *The Voice of an American Playwright*, 223–37.

to move to Houston in order to receive training for his new position. Mr. Weems attempts to meet the demands of his wife and the needs of his daughter, so he agrees to give Chestnut the job, but he also puts away money for Laura Lee to do with as she wishes, knowing that her mother is trying to run her life. But even her father's good intentions undermine Laura Lee's decision to marry Chestnut. When Mr. Weems mentions to his daughter that her fiancé might be a "fortune hunter," Laura Lee is left confused and afraid (74). When Chestnut asks her to join him in Houston, Laura Lee refuses to go because she is scared they cannot live on the money he earns. She is also emotionally paralyzed by the thought that she might wind up in a loveless marriage like her brother Thurman, who can't leave his embittered wife Delia because she has threatened to expose his adultery and undermine his reputation as a banker. Ironically, years later when we hear about Chestnut, he has become a wealthy businessman with a lovely wife and four children.

While Josie has not always had her daughter's "best interest at heart," Laura Lee is not merely an innocent victim of parental neglect and emotional abuse (85). She is ultimately the one who is unable to act or to seize her own destiny. She rejects Barsoty's marriage proposal, just as she did Mr. Chestnut's, and, by doing so, foregoes any opportunity for independence and autonomy and passes up a chance at marriage. All Laura Lee really wants is love, but without the courage to leave home Laura Lee can never achieve the freedom essential for companionship and contentment.

In *Night Seasons*, Horton uses music to illuminate Laura Lee's failed attempts at love by intercutting the action of the play with lines from the ballad "Sweet Alice Ben Bolt" and other popular tunes of the era. When the trio of Laura Lee, her cousin Rosa, and Barsoty sing together from behind a backlit scrim, the audience is reminded of Laura Lee's troubled past and the horrifying result of her inability to courageously follow her heart. Sadly, Laura Lee never marries, and for the rest of her life she harbors the deep loss of the two men she loved.

Without an identity of her own, Laura Lee lives out her final years emotionally paralyzed, playing bridge by day and attending picture shows at night to cope with her unrelenting sleeplessness. By age sixty, Laura Lee lives with her mother in a cramped apartment, bitterly agreeing to reside there until she can find a house for herself. However, everywhere she turns, she is at odds with her family, for whom money always comes first. Even though Laura Lee's father has put away a substantial savings of forty-five thousand dollars for his daughter, she ultimately has no control over her finances. Laura Lee wants to buy a small cottage owned by Mrs. Reeves, but her brother, Thurman, ignores her wishes and sells the house to one of his customers. "Do you know what [Thurman] did to you today?" Delia tells Laura Lee. "He told Mrs. Reeves that you wouldn't pay her price for the house, that it was too much, and then he told one of his bank customers who is buying to rent property that he thought he could get it for a thousand dollars less than she asked you, and he went over to see her and she sold him the house" (97).

After the death of Mr. Weems, Thurman continues his campaign to inhibit Laura Lee's independence by scaring her with the story of "Miss Nanie Stanfield," who "tried to live by herself and then a man started peeking in her window and she had to give up and go live at the hotel" (107). Once more, Laura Lee agrees to live with her mother, who she despises, and Thurman again delays the search, this time taking a year to complete a title search and then waiting until the war is concluded. At age sixty-three, Laura Lee dies, never having realized her dream to have a home of her own.

In his seminal essay, "Boundaries, the Female Will, and Individuation in *Night Seasons*," Gerald Wood rightly argues that *Night Seasons* is an exploration of "failed intentions and autonomy in women, a dark variation of [Foote's] study of intimacy as the heart of courage."[20] Certainly Horton Foote's dramatic landscape is filled with characters, both men and women, who fail to connect lovingly with their surroundings or with others, but *Night Seasons* represents the writer's fullest, most mature vision of this theme. Most often, in Horton's imaginative world the most significant and sought after character is the loving and nurturing parent, and it is through identification with this figure that a child's sense of self can be fully realized. But such a relationship relies on clear emotional boundaries between the child and the parent. Without these boundaries, as is the case of Laura Lee, the bond between parent and child is experienced as emotional paralysis and loss of self. Gerald Wood explains that Laura Lee "chooses to follow her mother's return to an endless repetition of the past," thereby "siding with death over life."

---

[20] Gerald C. Wood, "Boundaries, the Female Will, and Individuation in *Night Seasons*," in *Horton Foote: A Casebook*, 171.

According to the writer, every child is naturally drawn toward a profound sense of intimate attachment, which then encourages him or her to move beyond that bond toward other loving connections. Such benign intimacy, also recognized in a wholly loving father/mother God, nurtures individuation, which is the goal of all Foote characters. *Night Seasons* is a dark play because Laura Lee, unable to find the boundaries between herself and others, primarily her mother, cannot find within herself the power to choose her own life. Unable to follow the archetypal movement from roots to wings and back again, Laura lives without the light of freedom or the transcendent movement of the seasons. She is lost in unredeemed time.[21]

As *Night Seasons* concludes, the meddling Josie has outlived her daughter, and at age ninety-three she has been told by her son, Thurman, that she should live only three more years in order to escape estate taxes. Josie finally recognizes her life has been empty and foolish, marked by greed and manipulation. She admits to her niece that she "just don't want to think about anything anymore" but then asks: "Who do you think Laura Lee loved the most? Barsoty or Mr. Chestnut?" (113). Josie's final words, an expression of her guilt and regret, invoke images of the lovely girl who was Laura Lee Weems and the memories of a "long ago, forgotten music" that defined her lonely life. As the curtain fades, the haunting tune of "Sweet Alice Ben Bolt" is heard as Josie proclaims: "Living is to be my punishment" (113). Finally, the audience is reminded of the quietly destructive effects of a life without love, dominated by materialism and exploitation.

The Signature Theatre's production of *Night Seasons* was well received by audiences and critics alike. Ben Brantley wrote an appreciative review of the play for the *New York Times*, calling the play "a lucid anatomy of a subject that has always obsessed the author: the elusiveness of home,"[22] and Marian Burkhart of *Commonweal* commented on the experimental structure of the work. "The more realistic past is revealed through flashbacks, some clearly Josie's memories," Burkhart noted, and then concluded by praising Hallie Foote's performance and her ability to be both a collaborator and a star.[23]

---

[21] Ibid., 171–72.

[22] Ben Brantley, "Review of *Night Seasons*: 'Night Seasons,' Father and Daughter on the Idea of Home," *New York Times*, 7 November 1994.

[23] Marian Burkhart, "Two Footes Forward/Horton and Hallie: Signature Events," *Commonweal*, 13 January 1995.

The third play Horton chose for the Signature season was *The Young Man from Atlanta*, a play he had written four years earlier.[24] In 1992, with the support of Michael Wilson, the young Associate Artistic Director of the Alley Theatre, Horton had arranged a reading of the play in Houston, hoping that the Alley Theatre would produce the work. Michael Wilson recalls that, "it was a very sad time, because Lillian had suddenly died right before the reading, and Horton was afraid that he could never write again because he used to always write for her."[25] The reading, which featured Carlin Glynn and Richard Bradford, went very well; but unfortunately, the Alley passed on producing the play, a decision that confused Horton and infuriated Wilson. Two years later, both Horton and Wilson were vindicated when the Signature Theatre presented *The Young Man from Atlanta* and the play went on to win several prestigious awards, including the Pulitzer Prize.

According to Horton Foote, *The Young Man from Atlanta* was inspired by an actual event in the lives of his aunt and uncle, Lily Dale and Will Coffee, and their only son, William, who as a young man committed suicide:

> The play is based on a true story. I had an uncle...who was the first [person] in my family to become a Republican, which horrified them. He was what you would call a go-getter. Everything was about the American Dream and they had a son, who was my age, maybe a little younger, who was very bright and had none of his father's ambitions. The father was an athlete. The boy was not an athlete. He didn't want anything to do with it, but he had a wonderful mathematical mind. And he attended piloting school.... When the Second World War broke out, he volunteered and went into the Air Corps. I don't think he flew, but he was an operator or something, and he lived through the war, and then he came back home. He couldn't swim and one day...he went down to the beach, walked into the water, and he never came out. He drowned. He was involved, my father told me, with a young man. And my father and the friends of his family thought this young man was out to blackmail them; not overtly but in other ways. So that was the basis of the story. I tried to fathom, to understand, to think like them. Another thing was that the father had a very tragic end in the sense that he lost his job. Suddenly gone were all his dreams of power and pride, not just for himself, but for the whole

---

[24] Foote, *The Young Man from Atlanta*. All page references to *The Young Man from Atlanta* in the text refer to this publication.

[25] Michael Wilson, interview by Marion Castleberry, 14 May 2013, New York.

capitalist system in Houston which had tried to become the hub of the world. He got fired because they wanted a young man.[26]

From these familial events, Horton constructed a moving and effective social and family drama that celebrates the courage and resilience of an ageing couple to overcome devastating loss and withstand the dissolution and destruction of the foundations upon which they have built their lives. Previously, Horton had fictionalized his aunt and uncle as Lily Dale and Will Kidder, who appear in three of the nine plays in *The Orphans' Home Cycle*: *Roots in a Parched Ground*, *Lily Dale*, and *Cousins*. We first meet Lily Dale when she is ten and follow her through different phases of her life until we see her at age sixty in *The Young Man from Atlanta*. When we first meet Will in *Lily Dale*, he is in his twenties; he is approaching middle age in *Cousins*; and he is sixty-four in *The Young Man from Atlanta*. When Horton finished writing *Cousins* in the late 1970s, he had no intentions of ever revisiting the characters, but as he admits, a few years later he began thinking about them again, "cut off from their beginning roots, trying to make a life in the ever-growing Houston; and soon after I began working on the play."[27]

Set in 1950, in postwar Houston, *The Young Man from Atlanta* opens with Will and Lily Dale Kidder dealing with the mysterious events surrounding the death of their only son, Bill. Even though Will had hoped Bill, a celebrated World War II hero, would join him in the wholesale grocery business, he had instead moved to Atlanta to take a job as a traveling salesman. One day, while on a business trip, Bill stopped at a lake in Florida and, not knowing how to swim, walked into the water and drowned. "Why, in the middle of the day in a lake in Florida out in deep, deep water if you can't swim," Will asks, convinced that his son has committed suicide but unable to share his thoughts with his wife, Lily Dale, who has persuaded herself that Bill's death was accidental. After their son's death, Will and Lily Dale were contacted by Bill's former roommate, Randy Carter, a young man from Atlanta, who is never seen but is nonetheless the catalyst of the play's action. Will wants nothing to do with Randy, but the young man preys on Lily Dale's grief, assuring her that Bill had lived in the faith that she herself professes and convincing her to give him thousands of dollars from her savings. Throughout the play, there is an unspoken assumption that Bill

---

[26] Marion Castleberry, "Reflections on the American Theatre: A Conversation with Horton Foote," *The Voice of an American Playwright*, 269–70.

[27] Foote, Introduction to *The Young Man from Atlanta*, x–xi.

was a homosexual, and that Randy, the young man from Atlanta, was a predator who had something to do with Bill's suicide.

Will Kidder is one of Horton Foote's most intriguing characters. "The Will Kidders of this world," Horton explained, "I've known all my life, North and South—optimistic, confident that their world is the best of all possible worlds, admiring business success above all other things."[28] When we first meet Will at the offices of the Sunshine Southern Wholesale Grocery, he is the very model of a successful Texas businessman as he shows his protégé, Tom Jackson, the blueprints of a new house he has built for himself and Lily Dale. The house is a monument to Will's success and belief that a competitive, optimistic go-getter like himself can achieve "the best of everything...the biggest and best" (2–3), and that the biggest house in Houston can somehow insulate him from the death of his son. "The new house will help us get away from a lot of memories," Will says, and "to celebrate the new house I'm buying my wife a new car" (11). Assured that he works "for the best wholesale produce company" (3), Will lives under the illusion that his success will continue forever on its upward spiral; but when Ted Cleveland informs him that he is being fired from the company, for which he has worked the better part of his life, Will's faith in hard work, loyalty, and fair play comes crashing down around him.

Will finds himself confronting unprecedented financial problems. When Cleveland offers him a monetary settlement from the company, Will stubbornly refuses to accept the offer, believing that he can borrow enough money to start his own company. As the play progresses, Will is forced to let go of his misplaced pride and to face the reality that his job, the center of his life, is no longer his and that the commercial world he once called home no longer welcomes his kind of optimism and competitiveness. Before his son's death, Will believed confidently in the rewards promised by the American dream; but now, after years of plenty, his security has been taken away from him, and when the bank turns down his request for a loan, he is unprepared to deal with the crisis. Horton's dramatization of Will Kidder exposes the unyielding desire of the American male to sacrifice self-reflection and self-knowledge to the competition of the external world. Horton Foote portrays Will as a man without an emotional home.

At the time of Will's firing, he and Lily Dale have already moved into their new house and are supporting Lily Dale's widower stepfather, Pete

---

[28] Ibid.

Davenport. Facing the financial hardships in front of him, Will confronts Lily Dale and asks her to loan him enough money from her savings to start his business. Lily Dale tries to evade the request, pointing out that they have access to the money Will had given Bill over the years. But Will reveals there is nothing left of the money he had given his son and he has no idea how the cash was spent. Will has discovered that his son gave Randy a sum of a hundred thousand dollars and fears that Bill was misled and cheated of his money. The pain of this discovery is intensified when Will finds out that Lily Dale has not only been in communication with Randy, which he had forbidden her to do, but that she handed over fifty thousand dollars of her savings to the young man, who claimed he needed the money to pay for his mother's operation and to care for his sister's three small children. The strain of having been fired from his job and the revelation that Lily Dale has been in secret contact with Randy, even given him large amounts of money, causes Will to suffer a heart attack. Suddenly, the couple is forced to face a tenuous future with a set of beliefs incapable of supporting them in their new circumstances.

Lily Dale is unquestionably one of Horton Foote's most complex and fascinating female characters. In his introduction to *The Young Man from Atlanta*, Horton admitted that he had always had "ambivalent feelings" toward the character of Lily Dale. "In the earlier plays, even as a child," Horton said, "she seemed to me vain and selfish and not very admirable, but when I came to her again in this play I wanted to make her more complex, give her more humanity and vulnerability, always keeping in mind her many faults."[29] As Horton depicts her, Lily Dale is indeed more sensitive and aware than earlier versions of the character, but she is also vulnerable to Randy's maneuverings. When we first meet her she has chosen to deny the truth surrounding her son's relationship to Randy Carter or to accept the facts about Bill's suicide. Instead of dealing honestly with her loss, Lily Dale has abandoned any activity that reminds her of her son, including playing and composing music, and she has taken refuge in a superficial religion that leaves her open to Randy's machinations. "Every time I feel blue over missing Bill," Lily Dale explains, "I call his friend and I ask him to tell me again about Bill and his prayers and he does so so sweetly" (30). Even though Carson, Pete's great-nephew who coincidentally once lived in the same boarding house as Bill and Randy, assures Lily Dale that Randy is not to be trusted and

---

[29] Ibid.

that most of what he has told her about Bill is untrue, she will not deny her motherly feelings for the young man nor believe that he had anything to do with her son's death.

A noteworthy aspect of *The Young Man from Atlanta* is the relationship that develops between Lily Dale and her maid, Clara. Clara, a black woman who has not enjoyed the benefits of prosperity with which Lily Dale has been blessed, shows a spiritual understanding and strength her employer seems to lack. So, too, does Etta Doris, the Kidders' former cook, who has long had religion as a staple in her life, supporting her through adversity and hardship. These black women, as they do so often in Foote's work, embrace a personal theology that closely reflects the writer's own vision of a loving God, a comforting Mother/Father/God "who is going to take care of you" (52). When Lily Dale describes Bill's death to Clara, saying that everything is "just awful," and that she feels "so betrayed, so hurt, so humiliated" (50–51) the maid asks her "where is your Christian faith" and then expresses a profound, yet simple truth that Lily Dale must ultimately acknowledge: "Everything changes. The Lord giveth and he taketh away.... We're here today and gone tomorrow. Blessed be the name of the Lord" (84). As Clara understands, life is a mystery, a journey of endless change, "unexpected, unasked for, unwanted, but to be faced and dealt with, or else we sink into despair or a hopeless longing for a life that is gone."[30] Although the suspense surrounding Bill's death is the central catalyst of the play's action, the primary theme of the play is neither suicide nor homosexuality but rather how Will and Lily Dale deal with the ambiguities surrounding their son's death and how they confront the adversity and suffering that has befallen them.

A major concern in *The Young Man from Atlanta*, as in many of Horton's plays, is the absence of a caring and nurturing father figure, seen in Will's inability to connect lovingly with his son. In the play's final scene, Will recognizes that his life has been a delusion. His single-minded pursuit of the American dream has left his wife not only childish but also lonely, and, worse yet, it has denied him the love of his son. Will confesses that he never felt close to Bill, and professes that his indifference was born of vanity and conceit:

I tried to be a good father, but I just think now I only wanted him to be like me. I never tried to understand what he was like. I never tried to find

---

[30] Horton Foote, Introduction to *Four Plays from The Orphans' Home Cycle* (New York: Grove Press) xii.

out what he would want to do, what he would want to talk about. Life goes so fast, Lily Dale. My God. It goes so fast. It seems like yesterday he was a baby, and I was holding him in my arms, and before I turned around good he was off to school, and I thought, when he comes back he'll come into the business and I'll be close to him. I was never close to him, Lily Dale. How was your day? Fine, son, how was yours? And then he was gone. I want my son back, Lily Dale. I want him back. (105)

Will's confusion deepens as the play comes to a close. Lilly Dale apologizes for deceiving Will and admits that the reason she befriended Randy was because without Bill she became lonesome and needed the reassurance that her son had become religious before his death. Lily Dale tries one last time to persuade Will to speak to Randy, but he refuses because, as he admits, "there are things I'd have to ask him and I don't want to know the answers" (108–9). As he considers the reasons why his son gave money to his roommate, Will suddenly stops himself and proclaims, "Whatever the reasons, I don't want to know. There was a Bill I knew and a Bill you knew and that's the only Bill I care to know about" (109). Ironically, having spent the entire play trying to get Lily Dale to face the truth about Randy Carter and their son's suicide, Will chooses to accept the confusion surrounding Bill's death and to embrace his own uncertain future.

As the play concludes, Will and Lily Dale are reconciled to their fate. Horton Foote explains that, "they don't know the truth about their son. That kind of truth evades them. They have, I think a kind of innocence. They have no perspective. They wouldn't know how to evaluate it. They only know that there are things about their son they didn't know about, and didn't understand. And Will—who probably does know more than Lily Dale knows—doesn't want to know more."[31]

Finally, Will wants only to retain his memory of his son and to return to the thing he knows best: work. He decides to swallow his pride and accept the lesser job his former boss has offered him. Lily Dale, on the other hand, will resume teaching music while continuing to cling to Randy Carter, who for her is the "sweet boy" who loved Bill and comforted her in her loneliness (110). Even though Will recognizes that life is elusive and indeterminate, he assures Lily Dale that "Everything is going to be all right" (110). While their life will never be the same, Will and Lily Dale finally face their grief and misfortune with courage and dignity. Will has gained insight and strength by admitting to his

---

[31] O'Quinn, 188.

delusions about the American dream and by confessing his failures as a husband and father. Lily Dale has recognized her own fantasies, especially those that played a role in Bill's death, and she has found a way to deal with her vanity and disappointment. Rejecting the fact that her son was homosexual and that his roommate Randy Carter had something to do with his death, Lily Dale comes up with her own reasons for Bill's demise, creating a necessary fiction with which she can live. Will and Lily Dale's choice not to uncover all the facts surrounding Bill's suicide gives them a sense of freedom to move ahead and make tolerable lives for themselves. More importantly, by acknowledging their son's death as an inexplicable mystery, they are able to confront the false hopes and dreams that have separated them for so many years. As Gerald Wood points out: "Such intimacy and courage in the face of death—their son's and their own—is inspired by their acceptance that finally everything, and everybody, is sacrificed to God's mysterious order."[32] By dramatizing this tragic event in his family's history, Horton Foote created two of his most memorable characters, Will and Lily Dale Kidder, while reminding us that the human spirit is capable of overcoming unexpected adversity and misfortune in any era, no matter the time, the place, or the circumstance.

The Signature Theatre's production of *The Young Man from Atlanta* was directed by Peter Masterson and starred Masterson's wife Carlin Glynn and Ralph Waite, well known for his work on the television series *The Waltons*. The play, which opened at the Kampo Theater Center on 27 January 1995, was an instant hit, even though it ran for only twenty-six performances. Vincent Canby, critic at the *New York Times*, said the play was "one of Mr. Foote's most serious and scathing works…a work that will haunt you long after the performance."[33] Frank Rich, enamored with the play's craftsmanship, pointed out Horton's accurate portrayal of the "psychic fissures just below the surface of middle-class American life,"[34] and Clive Barnes of the *New York Post* wrote: "This is that rare thing, a living play about living—and it brings luster to Broadway."[35]

---

[32] Gerald C. Wood, "The Nature of Mystery in *The Young Man from Atlanta*," in *Horton Foote: A Casebook*, 187.

[33] Vincent Canby, "Review of *The Young Man from Atlanta*: Nameless Menace In Latest By Foote," *New York Times*, 30 January 1995.

[34] Frank Rich, "Review of *The Young Man from Atlanta*," *New York Times*, 23 April 1995.

[35] Clive Barnes, "Review of *The Young Man from Atlanta*: Foote's Great Step Forward," *New York Post*, 30 March 1995.

The Young Man from Atlanta was clearly the most acclaimed production of the 1994–95 Signature Theatre season. Its success would eventually catapult the play to Broadway, the first of Horton's works to be performed on the Great White Way since *The Traveling Lady* debuted at the Players Club in 1954.

The final play of the Signature season was another new play, *Laura Dennis*, which opened on 10 March 1995.[36] A long, one-act melodrama, *Laura Dennis* is about a young woman's search for home and her quest to understand the sordid truth about her family. The title character of the play is a teenage girl in Depression-era Harrison poised in that trembling moment when life can go in any direction. One second she is thinking of what she will wear to a dance; the next, a murder leads to a shattering revelation that changes her life forever. Based on actual events that happened to the descendants of Colonel Isaac Dennis, who according to family legend stole the property and inheritance of Albert Clinton Horton's descendants, the play is set in Harrison, Texas, in 1938. The Dennis family has fallen on extremely hard times, even though they still own a good deal of land from which they can profit from an oil lease. When Laura was an infant her father, Roscoe Dennis, killed his cousin, Harold Dennis, for having an affair with Laura's mother, Cynthia. Soon after the murder, Roscoe died, and Cynthia, in order to escape the consequences of the event, abandoned baby Laura and moved to South Dakota to give birth to her and Harold's son, Harvey. When the play opens, sixteen years have passed since these events, and now Harvey lives with an adoptive family, the Griswolds, and Lena Abernathy, a seamstress, provides a residence for Laura. The cost of Laura's upkeep is paid by her uncle Edward Dennis, a wealthy man who wants little to do with Laura's life. Such is the legacy of the Dennis's many infidelities.

Laura, like so many of Horton Foote's characters, is essentially orphaned, but she longs to reconnect with her mother, who now lives in South Dakota with her new family. Laura writes to her mother often, hoping that when her mother recognizes how grown up and mature she is she will want Laura to visit, or better yet, come and live with her. A high school senior, Laura is beginning to discover her burgeoning sexuality and to wonder about her future. A sweet and polite girl, Laura is both confused and excited by the disreputable stories she hears about

---

[36] Horton Foote, *Laura Dennis*, in *Horton Foote: Getting Frankie Married—and Afterwards and Other Plays* (Lyme NH: Smith and Kraus, 1998) 139–80. All page references to *Laura Dennis* in the text refer to this publication.

her family's past, about her mother's infidelities and her father's jealousies. In the course of the play, Laura meets a distant cousin, Velma Dennis, a pitiful drunk who is upset because her mother, Ethel, is marrying Seymour Man, a young cowboy, who in any other circumstance might have married her rather than her mother and rescued her from loneliness and isolation. When Ethel sees Velma drinking out of a whiskey bottle and tries to take it from her, Velma cries out to Ethel, in front of Seymour: "Go to hell. Go to hell. You know that old husband of yours was always saying you were sleeping with Laura's daddy, my cousin" (76). Velma becomes so frantic over the thought of her mother marrying Seymour that she threatens suicide and has to be sedated.

Velma's actions disgust Laura, but the young girl knows that her cousin remembers the history of her family better than anyone else in Harrison and she is desperate to uncover the truth. Velma's antics, however, are the least of Laura's concerns as parallel lives and familial stories start to reappear and converge in her world.

We soon discover that Harvey Griswold is also involved with Verna Kate, who accuses him of fathering her baby. Verna Kate admits that her pregnancy and her fear of being scrutinized by the citizens of Harrison are the reasons she has moved to Atlanta. But Harvey denies that he is the father, revealing any number of other boys, who could have impregnated the girl, but Verna Kate's father, Mr. Nelson, doesn't believe Harvey and threatens to kill him. Harvey's parents attempt to protect him, barring him from leaving the house but they cannot ensure his ultimate safety.

Harvey is attracted to Laura and wants to take her to the school dance. But he is forbidden to date Laura, not because of past offenses, but because Harvey is Laura's half-brother, a fact that has been kept secret by his adoptive parents and by everyone else in Harrison. Shaken by all the turmoil surrounding him, Harvey disobeys his parents and decides to take a walk downtown to think through his situation. Passing by the very movie theater in which his father was gunned down years earlier, Harvey is shot and killed by Verna Kate's father.

Laura hears the news of Harvey's death and her connection to him at the same time she receives a letter from her mother saying that she wants nothing to do with her. "Do you realize if my mother walked into this yard right now, I wouldn't know her," Laura admits. "She would have to say, 'Laura Dennis, I'm your mother,' before I'd know who she was. (A pause.) I went to school with my brother for I don't know how many years and I didn't know who he was and he didn't know who I was" (176). Laura is devastated by her mother's rejection and by having lost a brother she never really knew. But finally, she recognizes that the only way to escape the disturbing familial cycle of infidelity and murder that has plagued her life is to leave Harrison, and never look back. She decides to take her share of an oil lease her uncle has sold, seven thousand dollars, and use it to pay tuition to a college in New Orleans. Unlike her cousin, Velma, who left Harrison years before only to return to a life of drunkenness, failed dreams, and loneliness, Laura will create for herself a loving family and community that never really existed for her in Harrison. In *Laura Dennis*, Horton Foote once again examines the nature of family, the power of story, and the eternal search for home, concluding that while some people, such as Laura Weems are destroyed by familial manipulation, rejection, and loss, others, like Laura Dennis, find within themselves the courage to accept their fate and create their own sense of home.

Directed by Jim Houghton with Missy Yager performing the title role of Laura, Hallie Foote portraying Laura's alcoholic cousin, Velma, and Peter Sarsgaard performing the role of Harvey Griswold, *Laura Dennis* did not receive the kind of positive response from critics that *The Young Man from Atlanta* had garnered, largely because of its melodramatic trappings. Ben Brantley, chief drama critic at the *New York Times*, found the play interesting but one of Horton Foote's lesser works and Clive Barnes, writing in the *New York Post*, noted that Laura lives in a town of "quiet violence," where people mostly survive. He concluded that the play had "no real moral, except to say life is difficult at best, hell at worst, and survival is only a temporary blessing."[37] When compared to *The Young Man from Atlanta*, which had preceded it, the production of *Laura Dennis* seemed pale and uninspired.

As the 1994–95 Signature season came to a close, there was a great deal of discussion about transferring *The Young Man from Atlanta* to Broadway, but the move was postponed, much to the dismay of the cast and playwright. There was also an offer from CBS to make a television movie of the play that never materialized because network producers wanted Horton to rewrite the ending of the play, to create a scene in which the young man from Atlanta would appear onstage. Horton was thrilled by the network's offer to film the work but he was determined not to rewrite the play. He explained that it was imperative for the

---

[37] Clive Barnes, "Review of *Laura Dennis*," *New York Post*, 14 March 1995.

young man to remain unseen so that the hostility he raises in Will and the hope he represents to Lily Dale continue to be the final image left in the audience's imagination. Needless to say, a movie version of the play was never made.

Shortly after the run of *The Young Man from Atlanta*, Horton was notified that his work had been awarded the 1995 Pulitzer Prize for Drama, the first and only time the playwright would receive such an honor. On the night of the Pulitzer awards ceremony, Jim Houghton hired a limousine to drive him and the playwright uptown to Columbia University where the event was held. It was a great achievement for Horton, and Houghton remembers that while riding home in the limousine, his wife turned to a distracted Horton and asked him how he was feeling about his achievement. "He turned with his soft, welling, gentle eyes and said, "I miss my wife, Lillian. I wish she were here. We all quietly spent the ride home thinking of their forty-eight years together and the weight of loss and love on that night of celebration as the Manhattan skyline passed before our eyes."[38]

The Pulitzer Prize spawned several other awards for Horton Foote, including the Lucille Lortel Award (1995), the Academy Award in Literature from the American Academy of Arts and Letters (1995), the RCA Crystal Heart Career Achievement Award from the Heartland Film Festival (1995), the Outer Critics Circle Special Achievement Award (1995), and induction into the Theatre Hall of Fame (1996). He was elected into the American Academy of Arts and Letters (1998), and awarded the Gold Medal for Drama from the American Academy of Arts and Letters (1998), the first time a writer had received such honors in the same year.

The Pulitzer also inspired an influential essay by Frank Rich, arts critic of the *New York Times* who happened to be a member of the Pulitzer Prize committee. Rich used the occasion of Horton's crowning achievement to praise the writer's lifetime of work in the theater and to criticize the current economics of Broadway.

> Fifty-four years ago this week a young man from Texas named Horton Foote made his playwriting debut in New York with a drama called *Texas Town*. Brooks Atkinson, the critic of *The Times*, declared it a "feat of magic."

---

[38] James Houghton, Introduction to *Horton Foote: Getting Frankie Married—and Afterwards and Other Plays*, viii.

Last week and some 50 plays later, Mr. Foote, now 79, won the Pulitzer Prize for Drama for *The Young Man from Atlanta*. In the intervening half century he has passed through Broadway during its Golden Age...and won two Oscars in Hollywood. But incredibly, Mr. Foote is now in some ways back where he started in the theater. Not only is he still writing about the same Texans but his Pulitzer-winning play, just like *Texas Town*, was staged on a shoestring in a tiny Off-Off-Broadway playhouse.

Though the play received good reviews, no producer moved it to a larger home off Broadway, let alone on, for an extended run—so financially risky has it become to mount a serious drama requiring nine actors in the commercial theater. Even now, post-Pulitzer, *The Young Man from Atlanta* is not assured a future New York production. If Mr. Foote's plays have much to tell audiences about the psychic fissures lying just beneath the surface of middle-class American life in this century, what does it also say about America that playwrights of his stature must now fight to be heard.

If *The Young Man from Atlanta* could be seen now, what a catharsis it would offer audiences whose lives or hearts have been touched by the horrors of Oklahoma City. Set in the cocky Houston of 1950, it tells of a couple whose bedrock belief in America and in God takes them just so far when their only son, a World War II hero, inexplicably kills himself.

Months after seeing this play, I can still hear Mr. Waite's gruff voice swell unexpectedly on the line "I just want my son back," keeping company with the rest of us who have known inconsolable grief. Great artists like Horton Foote give us this, and more. Why do we give them so little in return?[39]

Soon after Rich's column appeared in the *New York Times*, Horton was approached by David Richenthal, a wealthy New York lawyer and award-winning producer, about moving *The Young Man from Atlanta* to Broadway. After securing rights to the play, Richenthal immediately called for the production to be restaged with some minor changes made to the script. He planned to open the show on Broadway after tryouts at the Alley Theatre in Houston, the Huntington Theatre in Boston, and the Goodman Theatre in Chicago. Since Horton was desperate to return to Broadway after forty years, he was willing to do whatever necessary to ensure the play received its just rewards. He was thrilled to learn that Peter Masterson would again direct the Broadway-bound production

---

[39] Horton Foote, *Genesis of an American Playwright*, ed. Marion Castleberry (Waco TX: Baylor University Press, 2004) 151.

and that the original cast would remain intact, with Ralph Waite and Carlin Glynn repeating their performances as Will and Lily Dale Kidder. Everyone was collaborative and optimistic as the ensemble performed for appreciative audiences and critics in Horton's home state of Texas. However, problems began to surface when the production moved to Boston. For some reason, which is not completely clear, Richenthal became dissatisfied with the way the performances were going at the Huntington Theatre. Biographer Wilborn Hampton blamed the situation on Peter Masterson, who he claimed "was sometimes absent from rehearsals." "Foote tried to talk to his cousin and caution him that Richenthal might fire him," Hampton explains, but "Masterson…took little notice of the advice."[40]

For her part, Carlin Glynn wanted to explore a different, more humorous, side of the character of Lily Dale, but Masterson remembers, "Horton didn't agree with Carlin's interpretation and he told her so."[41] Artistic differences continued to develop between company members until in one bold act the producer fired Masterson, Glynn, Waite, and all but one member of the original cast. Richenthal defended his position by arguing that such a major production needed bigger names, more star power, than had appeared in the Signature performance. Soon after, the producer hired Robert Falls of the Goodman Theatre in Chicago as director, signed Rip Torn to play Will Kidder, and brought in Shirley Knight to replace Carlin Glynn as Lily Dale.

Needless to say, the original cast was shocked by David Richenthal's hasty decision, and Masterson and Glynn were devastated by what they felt was an obvious betrayal. They couldn't believe that Horton did not stand up for them against the producer, "especially," Masterson admitted, "after all the years of hard work and sacrifices we made to ensure Horton's work was done well."[42] Horton was equally confused by the situation. He was emotionally torn between his desire to see *The Young Man from Atlanta* on Broadway and his loyalties toward his family, who had been an important part of his life and career for more than fifty years. But ultimately, there was very little he could do to change the state of affairs, except to pull the play from future productions. Believing in the power of this work and desperately

---

[40] Hampton, 236.

[41] Carlin Glynn and Peter Masterson, interview by Marion Castleberry, 3 October 2012, Hudson, New York.

[42] Ibid.

wanting the play to reach a wider audience, Horton chose to abide by the producer's wishes and to support the new director and cast. Sadly, the firing of Masterson and Glynn created a rift between the couple and Horton that never entirely healed, and although their relationship was eventually restored to some degree of amiability after the filming of *Lily Dale* in 1997, they never worked together again.

The new version of *The Young Man from Atlanta* opened at the Goodman Theater in Chicago on 20 January 1997 and ran through March 1 of that year. Critical response to the play was mixed, ranging from admiration to confusion. Cindy Bandle, theater critic for the *Chicago Tribune*, remarked that the production was "a marvel of keenly observed and precisely expressed detail, which "carrie…a tremendous emotional force," even while "it is unabashedly, unself-consciously and very honestly an old-fashioned play." [43] Generally, critics praised Shirley Knight's performance but found Rip Torn's interpretation of Will Kidder less convincing. Richard Christiansen of the *Chicago Tribune* wrote that Torn brought too much of his television situation comedy to the role while Knight, "unperturbed by such baggage is perfect in every nuance, right down to her neatly polished fingernails." He added, "This is Lily Dale's play and Knight makes it a memorable one."[44]

After playing at the Goodman for two months, the production opened on Broadway at the Longacre Theatre on 27 March 1997. There was widespread commentary by reviewers in newspapers, television, and radio shows that brought much-needed attention to Horton Foote's work. The production also received praise for its humanity and honest treatment of contemporary American life. Ben Brantley wrote a complimentary review, commending the actors for conveying "an honest sense of the characters' pain and anxiety," and concluding:

> The splendid Ms. Knight, who doesn't waste a single fluttery gesture, brings an Ibsenesque weight to a woman frozen in the role of petulant, spoiled child bride. She's what Nora might have become if she had squelched her doubts and stayed on in her doll's house. And Torn has an imposing quality of emotional largeness that brings mythic dimensions to this small-scale drama without bursting its seams. His face, at times the very image of gruffly smiling, good old boy virility, can dissolve,

---

[43] Cindy Bandle, "Review of *The Young Man from Atlanta*," *Chicago Tribune*, 27 January 1997.

[44] Richard Christensen, "Review of *The Young Man from Atlanta*," *Chicago Tribune*, 29 January 1997.

instantly and harrowingly, into something like the mask of tragedy made flesh. One is also always aware that Will's hearty friendliness and assurance are the flip side of a volcanic, despairing anger.[45]

In spite of all the praise, some critics who saw the original Signature production found Rip Torn's performance lacking the depth and compassion that Ralph Waite had brought to the role. The most scathing assessment of Torn's interpretation came in a letter to Horton from Marian Burkhart, freelance critic for *Commonweal*. Burkhart thought Torn's performance was the most disappointing aspect of the production:

> I wrote you before that Brantley had missed the nuances of Will's refusal to "know" Bill's homosexuality. Well, he missed it because Torn missed it. I still can see Ralph Waite making that speech and making the fullness of its meaning and of his acceptance of his son and that son's sacrifice. I can see him as well tell Lily Dale that they will be "all right" with his belated understanding that the "best and the Biggest" are not available and wouldn't be worth the cost he has been too willing to pay if they were. That again, Torn missed entirely. In Waite's performance the opening scene introduced Will's tunnel vision gradually and with dignity. Torn simply shouted the phrase every time so that once could not even see him as limited indeed, but not a buffoon. I think Torn's central error was to play the part as larger than life. Will is not. It is his life-like size that makes his plight so moving and meaningful. In any event, I hope both Torn and the production gather whatever honors they're nominated for so that the play runs long enough so that maybe Waite can come back and do it right.[46]

Horton was thrilled when *The Young Man from Atlanta* was later nominated for three Tony awards, including a nomination for Best Play. But his excitement quickly faded when Alfred Uhry's *The Last Night of Ballyhoo* was chosen to receive the Tony and producers of *The Young Man from Atlanta* abruptly closed the show. Once again, Horton came face to face with the realities of commerce over art; apparently, producers cared more about making money than they did about ensuring the play reached a wider audience.

While the run of *The Young Man from Atlanta* did not end as expected, Horton had nonetheless reached a pinnacle in his theatrical career. Not

---

[45] Ben Brantley, "Review of *The Young Man from Atlanta*," *New York Times*, 28 March 1997.

[46] Marian Burkhart, letter to Horton Foote, 5 April 1997.

only had he created from his family history one of his most authentic and enduring expressions of human loss and perseverance, but at age eighty-one he had also been recognized as one of America's foremost writers. Having received the Pulitzer Prize and a Tony nomination for *The Young Man from Atlanta*, Horton Foote had once again established himself as a major voice in American theater.

During the run of *The Young Man from Atlanta*, Horton worked on two movies for television. The first of these was *Lily Dale*, the final play of *The Orphans' Home Cycle* to be captured on screen. Directed by Peter Masterson and starring Tim Guinee as Horace, Sam Shepard as Pete, Stockard Channing as Corella, and Mary Stuart Masterson as Lily Dale, the movie aired on *Showtime* on 9 June 1996. Horton's bittersweet tale of Horace Robedaux's nightmarish attempt to reconnect with his estranged mother and sister, Lily Dale, was performed with directness and sensitivity, but the movie did not receive the kind of positive reviews the screenwriter had expected. *TV Guide* remarked that, "Foote's usual strength is characterization, but this adaptation fails there as well. Sam Shepard is stolid at best, Masterson merely dislikable (and uninterestingly so). As a mother and son unable to resume a relationship that was taken away from them, Stockard and Tim Guinee are appealing and able; the script's failure to tell us more about them is the chief failing."[47] Even though most critics found *Lily Dale* wanting, Variety critic Tony Scott lauded the film as "an engrossing video play" and "serious engaging television." [48]in 1997 the film received the Dallas/Fort Worth Film Critics Association Lone Star Award for Best Teleplay.

The second screenplay Horton wrote was *Alone*, which aired on *Showtime* in December 1997. Directed by Michael Lindsay-Hogg, who had previously directed *The Widow Claire* at the Circle in the Square Theatre, the original made for television film featured the star-studded cast of James Earl Jones, Shelley Duvall, Frederick Forest, Piper Laura, Chris Cooper, Ed Begley, Jr., and Hume Cronyn, who Horton had first worked with on CBS's 1957 production of *A Member of the Family*. According to Horton, *Alone* was born of the sorrow and loneliness he felt following the death of Lillian. Grief is clearly at the heart of the film, which examines the life of farmer and recent widower, John Webb (Hume Cronyn), and explores how the fabric of an entire family can unravel with the loss of a single member. As the film opens, Webb has

---

[47] *TV Guide*, "Review of *Lily Dale*," 10 June 1996.
[48] Tony Scott, "Review of Lady Dale," *Variety Magazine*, 9 June 1996.

been depressed since the death of Bessie, his wife of more than thirty years, and he must now muster the strength to harvest his crops without the help of his daughters Jaclyn (Joanna Miles) and Grace Ann (Roxanne Hart), who have left home to build lives for themselves in Houston. Webb has just learned that his overseer and best friend Grey (James Earl Jones) has given into his children's pressure to move to Houston. Isolated on his farm, Webb is confronted with severe loneliness until he is visited by his nephews, Carl (Frederic Forrest) and Gus Jr. (Chris Cooper), who bring an offer from a large oil company to drill on his land. Carl and Gus have inherited fifty percent of the mineral rights to Webb's land from their father, and they have been promised big money if they can convince their uncle to sell his share of entitlements.

At the same time, Webb's financially penurious daughter, Jaclyn, moves back home to Harrison with her husband Paul (David Selby), who is unemployed. Webb gives his son-in-law a job, but Paul is unsuited to farm life, and Jaclyn and her family soon return to Houston. Gus Jr. and Carl also leave when Webb's land fails to produce the amount of oil they had anticipated. Facing loneliness and isolation, Webb welcomes the return of his kindly friend Grey, who could not abide living with his daughter and her family in Houston. With Grey's help, and that of his former housekeeper Lois (Starletta DuPois), John Webb is finally able to accept the devastating loss of his wife and to find a way to cope with his loneliness. As the film concludes, he is able to share with his friends both cheerful and painful memories of Bessie and to find courage and comfort in the religion he shares with his black friends.

Under the direction of Michael Lindsay-Hogg, the impressive cast of *Alone* gave moving performances that reflect the inescapable solitude of the elderly and portray with intensity and authenticity the conflicts that arise between ordinary people as some try to strike it rich while others turn their thoughts to memories, hard work, and friendship.

Although *Alone* features several brilliant performances, Hume Cronyn, specifically, captures the hardship and heartbreak of John Webb, a lowly farmer whose life is thrown into turmoil by the death of his wife and the inability of his well-intentioned daughters to fit him into their lives. When, at the film's conclusion, Webb sings his favorite hymn, "Blessed Assurance," Cronyn breaks the heart of the audience and reminds us of the remarkable transcendence of the human spirit. *Alone* was released on DVD in 1998, but in spite of the stirring performances of the cast, the movie has remained an overlooked masterpiece. It has never received the critical or popular attention it deserves.

In spring 1997, Horton was commissioned by Universal Studios to adapt Laura Ingalls Wilder's novel *Little House on the Prairie*, the tale of the life struggles of the Ingalls family on a small farm in Walnut Grove, Minnesota, during the 1870s. Horton created a remarkably actable screenplay from Wilder's story, which had originally aired as a successful television show with renowned actor Michael Landon for nine seasons, but unfortunately the feature film never materialized.

While working on the adaptation of *Little House on the Prairie*, the Playmakers Repertory Company, a small, regional theater in Chapel Hill, North Carolina, presented the world premiere of *The Death of Papa*, the final play in Horton's *The Orphans' Home Cycle*. The production, which opened on 8 February 1997, was a huge success, one of the most rewarding productions in the history of Playmakers Repertory. The excellent cast, which included Nicholas Shaw, Ray Dooley, Hallie Foote, Matthew Broderick, Ellen Burstyn, Ray Virta, and Polly Holliday, gave stirring performances, and director Michael Wilson revealed his deep understanding of Foote's oeuvre and his ability to hold the production together even after Matthew Broderick, an avid squash player, injured his knee and was forced to open the run of the show on crutches. The friendship and trust that developed between Horton and Wilson during rehearsals for *The Death of Papa* proved to be the most important professional relationship Foote would have during the final decade of his life. The two men first met in 1987 during a speaking engagement in Winston-Salem, North Carolina. Wilson recalls:

> During my senior year at the University of North Carolina at Chapel Hill, I took a modern drama class that changed my life. Our professor, Dr. Milly Barranger, had just been to New York to see Horton Foote's new play *The Widow Claire*, starring his daughter, Hallie, and Matthew Broderick. My teacher had so much passion for the delicate beauty of that play, and it really resonated with me. So that week, when my sister invited me to her house for a movie night, I told her I'd like to watch *The Trip to Bountiful*. From the moment my sister put the tape in the VCR, I was transfixed. Here I was, at the beginning of my adult life—graduation was approaching, and I had so much fear and anxiety churning inside me—and I was incredibly moved by the story of Carrie Watts, a woman at the end of her life, trying to get home to Bountiful, Texas. I didn't want my sister to see, but I was crying. I thought it was the most beautiful, truthful...heartbreaking, triumphant, *real* human story I had ever seen.

Then, a serendipitous thing happened: I was visiting my family in my hometown of Winston-Salem, and Horton Foote happened to be there for a speaking engagement. I was about to head off to study playwriting at Harvard's summer drama program, but I was still unsure about whether I wanted to pursue a career in film or theatre. After hearing Horton speak, I went up and asked him for advice. "I don't give advice," he said, "but I will tell you I've had my greatest satisfaction from my work in theatre." So that's exactly what I decided to do.[49]

After spending a couple of years working as a house manager at the American Repertory Theater in Cambridge, Massachusetts, Wilson took a job as artistic associate of the Alley Theater in Houston. As fate would have it, during Wilson's second year on the job, the Alley gave a retrospective on Horton Foote's contributions to American theater. Horton, Lillian, and their children all came to Houston for the celebration, along with Robert Duvall, Jean Stapleton, Harper Lee, and a parade of other artists that had appeared in Horton's works over the years. During this time, Wilson began to develop a close friendship with Horton and Lillian, who often invited him to dinner at their home in Wharton. Wilson remembers that, "after dinner, we'd sit in the front parlor, and Horton would tell me about his life in the theater, how he started out as an actor, his training at the Pasadena Playhouse, his work with the American Actors Company, and his experimental work with Martha Graham and Jerome Robbins. Horton taught me so many lessons, but most of all, he taught me a deep respect for actors. Thanks to him, I've cultivated a vast curiosity and patience for actors while they're building their performances."[50]

Wilson's relationship with Horton deepened over time, so much so that the young director became almost an adopted member of the Foote family. When Wilson was hired as the Artistic Director of the Hartford Stage Company in 1998, the first thing he decided to do was to make Hartford Stage the artistic home of Horton Foote, and the first play he directed there was *The Death of Papa*, which starred Jean Stapleton, Dana Ivey, Andrew McCarthy, Frankie Muniz, Devon Abner, and Hallie Foote. The play was performed to great acclaim, with audiences and critics applauding Horton's craftsmanship and requesting to see more of his poignant, heartfelt dramas. During the next decade Wilson and

---

[49] Frank Rizzo, "Michael Wilson Knows What He Likes," *American Theatre* (May/June 2009): 24.

[50] Michael Wilson, interview by Marion Castleberry, 14 May 2013, New York.

Horton would honor that request by producing more than a dozen shows, including the fiftieth-anniversary production of *The Trip to Bountiful* and the world premiere of *The Orphans' Home Cycle*.

In 1997, Horton's adaptation of *Old Man* for CBS's *Hallmark Hall of Fame* earned him a Christopher Award and an Emmy for Outstanding Writing for a Miniseries or Special, thirty-seven years after his initial adaptation of the short story had garnered a similar nomination. Foote also had two more new plays produced by regional theaters in New York and Alabama. In 1998, the Bay Street Theatre in Sag Harbor, New York, presented an acclaimed production of *A Coffin in Egypt*, directed by Leonard Foglia and performed by the well-known actress, Glynis Johns. That same year, the Alabama Shakespeare Festival of Montgomery, Alabama, presented the world premiere of *Vernon Early*, Horton's poignant tale of a country doctor whose spirit has been eroded by the pressures of his job and the lingering depression he shares with his wife over the loss of their adopted child. A reworking of Horton Foote's earlier play, *The Rocking Chair*, *Vernon Early* is set in Harrison in the fall of 1950, and, as in the original work, most of Harrison's citizens are sick at heart, wounded by issues of aging, isolation, love, alcoholism, and racial inequality. But through all the bleakness of life there remains a small flicker of hope reflected in the spirit of the sad, long-suffering doctor, Vernon Early. The production, directed by Charles Towers and starring Jill Tanner and Philip Pleasants was hailed by critics for its excellent performances and for the beauty and lasting power of Horton Foote's play.

Although the 1990s were very productive years for Horton Foote, they also included moments of immense sorrow and loss. The death of Lillian in 1992 was a devastating blow to Horton, an event which forever changed his life and from which he never fully recovered. Yet, in spite of the misfortune and grief, Horton, like so many of his characters, managed to persevere. With the coming of the new millennium, he began to reflect on his sixty-year career. The result of his thinking about the past and reflecting upon his hometown of Wharton, and the many influences (both personal and literary) his family had on life, was the 1999 book, *Farewell: A Memoir of a Texas Childhood*, the first of two autobiographical accounts of the people and events that had given shape and substance to his art. He also began work on several new plays, including *The Last of the Thorntons*, *The Carpetbaggers Children*, *The Day Emily Married*, *Getting Frankie Married—and Afterwards*, and *The Actor*, all of which would receive impressive productions and reach a broad, more culturally diverse, audience. The success of these works during the next decade would establish Horton Foote as America's greatest storyteller and most beloved dramatist.

17

The National Medal of Arts
2000–09

The 2000s continued to be productive and creative years for Horton. It was a decade in which, with a growing and appreciative audience, the playwright continued to receive acclaim for his many artistic achievements. Entering his sixtieth year as a writer, Horton was honored with the Last Frontier Award from the Edward Albee Theatre Conference in Alaska, the New York State Governor's Arts Award, the Texas Medal of Arts Award, and the PEN/Laura Pels Foundation Award for Drama to a Master American Dramatist. Horton cherished each award, but his proudest moment came on 20 December 2000, when he received the National Medal of Arts from President William Jefferson Clinton.

A lifelong Democrat, Horton and his family had long admired Bill Clinton, so much so that when Horton's first grandchild was born in 1993 and his son Walter named him Tyler Clinton Horton in honor of his great-great-grandfather, Albert Clinton Horton, Horton boasted: "I hope they call him Clinton. I do love my President."[1] Horton and Bill Clinton had first met in 1999 when James Houghton and Frank Rich (with the help of Sidney Blumenthal) secretly arranged for Horton and his daughter Daisy to meet with the president in the Oval Office of the White House. Their meeting had been everything Horton had dreamed of, as the president was warm, friendly, and remarkably attentive. He showered Horton and Daisy with kindness and with the kind of respect usually reserved for dignitaries and political leaders. Later on 12 October 1999, Horton wrote to President Clinton saying:

> Dear President Clinton:
> I want to thank you again for seeing me and my daughter, Daisy, in the Oval Office last week. It meant so much to both of us. It's no doubt in my mind that you are a very great President, and I'm equally sure that history will recognize this and give you full credit for all you've done. You've blessed our country in so many ways.

---

[1] Sheila Benson to President William Jefferson Clinton, 30 April 2000.

All Good Wishes,
Horton [2]

When Horton returned to the White House on 20 December 2000 to receive his National Medal of Arts award, Clinton greeted him like an old friend, with great reverence and appreciation. Conferring the National Medal of Arts upon Horton, Clinton praised the writer's contributions to the arts and enumerated Horton's many honors, including two Academy Awards, an Emmy, a Pulitzer Prize, and his induction into both the Theatre Hall of Fame and the American Academy of Arts and Letters. Before placing the medal around Horton's neck, Clinton remarked:

> Believe it or not, the great writer Horton Foote got his education at Wharton—but not the Business School. He grew up in the small town of Wharton, Texas. His work is rooted in the tales, the troubles, the heartbreak, and the hopes of all he heard and saw there. As a young man, he left Wharton to become an actor and soon discovered the easiest way to get good roles was to write the plays yourself. He has not stopped since. Among other things, he did a magnificent job of adapting Harper Lee's classic *To Kill a Mockingbird* for the silver screen and of writing his wonderful *The Trip to Bountiful* and so many other tales of family, community, and the triumph of the human spirit.... Today, we honor him for his lifetime of artistic achievement and excellence.[3]

For the rest of his life, Horton cherished this moment and his friendship with Bill Clinton. He considered the National Medal of Arts the most meaningful honor he ever received. "When they put that recognition in my program," Horton later revealed, "I insist that they say Bill Clinton was the one that gave it to me."[4]

Horton could easily have rested on his laurels after receiving the nation's most prestigious award, but instead, he used the event as a springboard for his career. He continued to travel the country, lecturing and appearing at numerous colleges and universities who presented him with honorary degrees and held festivals to celebrate his many

---

[2] Horton Foote to President William Jefferson Clinton, 12 October 1999 (Horton Foote Papers).

[3] Horton Foote, *Genesis of an American Playwright*, ed. Marion Castleberry (Waco TX: Baylor University Press, 2004) 1.

[4] Marion Castleberry, "Reflections on the American Theatre: A Conversation with Horton Foote," *The Voice of an American Playwright*, ed. Gerald C. Wood and Marion Castleberry (Macon GA: Mercer University Press, 2012) 283.

contributions to film and theater. Among these were Baylor University, Southern Methodist University, Brigham Young University, Dickinson College, the University of Hartford, Drew University, the University of the South, and the American Film Institute. These tributes, along with the appearance of several new books devoted to his life and work, further established Horton as one of America's most talented and revered dramatists. Chief among these works were Gerald C. Wood's *Horton Foote and The Theatre of Intimacy* (1999), Laurin Porter's *Orphans' Home: The Voice and Vision of Horton Foote* (2003), and Horton's memoir *Beginnings* (2001), in which the writer recounts his early years in Pasadena and New York as an actor and writer. With the arrival of the new millennium, Horton was clearly riding a wave of popularity, national recognition, and professional activity.

In addition to the honors, Horton continued to work in the theater, writing and directing new plays. In spring 2000, he directed the world debut of his daughter Daisy's play, *When They Speak of Rita*, at New York's Primary Stages, and on 21 November 2000, the Signature Theatre presented the world premiere of Horton's *The Last of the Thorntons* as part of its tenth-anniversary celebration of the theater's founding. Directed by James Houghton and starring Hallie Foote and Estelle Parsons, *The Last of the Thorntons* was one of the most affective portraits of homelessness and old age ever staged by the Signature.[5]

The genesis of the play, like so much of Horton's drama, is rooted in an episode in the writer's own life. "One summer, when I was visiting my friends Joe and Perry Anthony in Cape Cod, Joe, who knew that my great-great-grandfather had been a slave owner, gave me a book of slave letters [from Elizabeth Ramsey, a slave on the Horton plantation]. Then when I was rehearsing *Young Man from Atlanta* in Houston…the woman playing the part of the maid gave me the same book. These things all came together somehow when I was writing the play."[6]

After reading the letters, Horton began to reflect upon his family's legacy as slaveholders, trying to understand how his great-great-grand-father, Albert Clinton Horton, a deeply religious man, could be so insensitive to other human beings that he could buy and sell them. What finally emerged from Horton's meditation on the subject of slavery is *The Last of the Thorntons*, a play that focuses on the disintegration of a once

---

[5] Horton Foote, *The Last of the Thorntons* (Woodstock NY: Overlook Press, 2000). Page references to *The Last of the Thorntons* in the text refer to this publication.

[6] Porter, "Unpublished Interview," 234.

proud and affluent slave-owning family—the Thorntons (closely based on Horton's ancestors, the Horton's)— and the hardships that the family's past transgressions bring to the last surviving member of the clan.

Set in Harrison, Texas, in 1970, *The Last of the Thorntons* tells the haunting tale of Alberta Thornton, an early victim of dementia, who at age sixty is confronting the end of her life. When the play opens, Alberta has suffered an emotional breakdown and has been confined to a Harrison nursing home where, along with other townspeople such as Lewis Bowen and Annie Gayle Long, she spends her days dreaming of the past and fearing that she will be forgotten. Each of the nursing home residents lives on memories, often delusional ones, trying to come to terms with the harsh changes that life has dealt them. They endlessly repeat stories from the past as a way of dealing with a present that is passing them by.

Images of loss and displacement dominate the play, from the first sound of a piano playing to the last poignant recollections of a lost life. The first noticeable dislocation in the play is the characters' confused sense of place. The nursing facility in which they live was once Harrison's hospital. Once a place where children were born, the facility has a violent history and the characters often speak of Toddy Hodges who killed his cousin Huston and then dumped his bloody body on the hospital's front gallery. "No one is born here now," Clarabelle, the African-American nurse, explains, "They just bring the old here now to be taken care of until they die" (19). Most of the characters in the play do not want to be in the nursing facility, and they speak often about returning home. Unfortunately, as Lewis admits, there is no home left for their return. Home for these characters has become merely a state of existence and survival.

Although the character of Alberta is depicted with great humor and compassion, she is clearly one of Horton's most woeful and heart-breaking creations. Throughout the play as she struggles to let go of un-realized dreams and a lost way of life, she shares a moving lifetime of memories, including both pride and misgivings about her family's legacy. We discover that Alberta, the youngest of three sisters, never married because her father was obsessed with the need to continue the family name after his death. "Of course if you marry after I die there will be no one left with the name Thornton, "Alberta's father tells her. "Promise me you'll never marry" (49). With no family left to care for her and no home to go to (the family plantation fortune having dwindled to a tiny duplex in Houston that is to be sold by her unscrupulous nephew), Alberta is forced to face a life that promises more heartbreak than joy.

The play examines the incessant legacy of contrition associated with racism and human slavery, a subject that had haunted the playwright for years. Alberta's great-grandfather was acting governor of Texas during the Mexican-American war, and he once owned a plantation with 170 slaves. Alberta is obsessed with guilt over her family's having owned slaves, and she recalls having once read a book of letters written by former slaves, two of which were composed by Elizabeth Ramsey who had once been enslaved on the Thornton plantation.

> And this slave was writing to her daughter who was freed and living in Ohio, and her daughter wanted to buy her from Colonel Thornton and her mother was writing to tell her that Colonel Thornton wouldn't sell her unless her daughter could pay him a thousand dollars or find a woman her age to replace her, and she said in the letter she had a son that her daughter wanted to buy too and she wrote that Colonel Thornton wanted fifteen hundred dollars for him or else a boy fifteen years old to replace him. Then there was a letter written a year later from Elizabeth Ramsey to her daughter and she said Colonel Thornton would take eight hundred dollars for her now, and she felt that was a fair price because she didn't think she was worth a thousand dollars, but he wouldn't sell her son now for any price as he was training him to be one of his overseers on one of his plantations. (50)

Such injustices haunt Alberta, and she apologizes to every black person she meets, even though Clarabelle, an African-American nurse employed by the nursing home, sees Alberta's need for forgiveness to be absurd: "I said to her, you are talking to the wrong woman. I never been nobody's slave" (17).

Beyond Alberta's need for absolution, she imagines being pursued by slaves on her great-grandfather's plantation. She was brought to the nursing home after an episode in which she hallucinated that a group of slaves was descending on her home in vengeance over her ancestors' enslavement of the black race. Alberta believes "there was a curse on my family for owning slaves" (49). After coming to her senses, Alberta decides the slaves who appeared in her hallucination were actually hippies, a more immediate target of her fear and anxiety.

When Alberta is not trapped in a fantasy world, she spends her days talking to Fannie Mae Gossett, who works at the drugstore and delivers medicine to the residents at the nursing home. Fannie Mae, like Alberta, never married, but she finds comfort in connecting with others and takes time to visit with her elderly friends. Fannie Mae is a kind of walking oral history of Harrison, and she relates to Alberta better than any of the other characters in the play. She enjoys listening to Alberta sing old songs, and she remembers Alberta's love of movies and movie stars, especially Rudolph Valentino in *The Sheik*. Fannie Mae listens patiently to Alberta's confused and rambling recollections about her childhood dream of going to Hollywood to be an actress and then attentively admires Alberta's autographed photographs of Rudolph Valentino and Barbara La Marr. Fannie Mae is especially impressed by the fact that Barbara La Marr had written on the back of Alberta's photo, "Lest ye forget" (87).

When asked about this moment in the play, Horton noted, "Alberta has been robbed in many different ways. In some ways she's a variation of Wilma Thompson in *A Young Lady of Property*.... The real-life model for Alberta really did dream of going to Hollywood. She showed me two pictures she had of Rudolph Valentino and Barbara La Marr. On the back of her photograph, La Marr had written, 'Lest ye forget.'"[7] This scene, as dramatized in *The Last of the Thorntons*, is one of the most touching moments in the play. It is an evocative image of a lost and forgotten world, a time and place that has vanished from the American consciousness.

As Alberta and Fannie Mae continue to share their thoughts, Horton reveals how fragile memory can be and how it can affect people very differently. Alberta's life is a mass of muddled memories from the past, while Fannie Mae, a much older survivor, owns her own home and remembers the past with fondness and great enthusiasm. According to Horton, "there are only two kinds of memory, really, in the play. Fannie Mae...lives by memory. The past is more real to her than the present. It doesn't bother her at all; that's just how she lives. She's like a reporter. She provides all the fact, fills in the details for everybody, [and] gives them the history. Alberta's memory is very subjective. Sometimes it's a release for her [that is, recalling a memory from the past], but usually it's very painful."[8]

The play ends as it begins, with the nursing home residents seated in their customary places in the institutional waiting room. Only Alberta,

---

[7] Ibid., 235.
[8] Ibid.

who has always feared being left alone, remains standing, isolated and frozen in time. Her broken memories are her only companions. In the play's final moment, "The Sheik of Araby," one of Hollywood's most romantic love songs, plays in the background as Alberta recalls the major events in her troubled past and comes to accept, however painful or disconcerting, her place in this confused and uncertain world:

> We were known as the Thornton girls. And we always stuck together, like Willa said. They can't ever separate us. They've tried. When my mama died, our aunts, good women they were too, separated us. My aunt Reenie took Mabel, my aunt Loula took Willa Marie, and aunt Gert took me, but then Willa got divorced, and Mabel became a widow and got divorced and we all came together and...(pause). If only I hadn't gotten nervous, but I heard what I thought were slaves and they turned out to be hippies, and Willa and Mabel were dead then, and I'm the last of the Thorntons. (*She is quiet now*). (90)

Ben Brantley, theater critic for the *New York Times*, best describes Alberta's fate in his *New York Times* review of the Signature Theatre's production of *The Last of the Thorntons*:

> In the plays of Horton Foote, the road to home is ultimately a road to nowhere. His chronicles of the fictional town of Harrison, Texas are pervaded with a sense of rootlessness that hardly accords with the American ideal of small-town solidity. We are all orphans, Mr. Foote keeps suggesting in his polite, laconic way. It is an existential given. The years have tempered neither the basic bleakness of this perspective nor the eloquence with which it is rendered by Mr. Foote, who is a singular artistic mix of ruthlessness and sentimentality. *The Last of the Thorntons* is, in its own way, as unrelenting an assessment of the human condition as *Waiting for Godot*. *Thorntons* looks at life from the brink of its end and finds it much as it always was, only more so. Existence as a process of loss and dispossession has reached its wintry climax here. Yet against the waiting darkness Mr. Foote's characters continue to glow in vibrant, soulful detail.[9]

Following the Signature Theatre's acclaimed production of *The Last of the Thorntons*, Horton continued to write, reflecting upon the changes that had taken place in America over the past century. He was specifically interested in how the Civil War, the most traumatic event in the nation's history, had affected everything in his hometown of

---

[9] Ben Brantley, "Wry Smiles Temper the Anguish of Old Age," *New York Times*, 4 December 2000.

Wharton. The result of his thinking about the past was the drama *The Carpetbagger's Children*, Horton's most complex and elegiac work.[10]

At first glance, *The Carpetbagger's Children* appears to be a typical Horton Foote play, with its depiction of a declining Texas family, the Thompsons, who are forced to adjust to the loss of a land-based economy and the traditional morality that accompanied their agrarian way of life. As in other Foote plays, the landscape of Harrison is seen in all its abundance and brutality, transformed first by the breakup of the plantation system, then the cotton gin, and finally by urban sprawl. *The Carpetbagger's Children* also focuses on a number of recognizable themes: parental manipulation, sibling rivalry, powerful avarice, family violence, and emotional paralysis. The need for courage in the face of disappointment, deceit and death is stressed once again. But as much as *The Carpetbagger's Children* resembles other Foote works, the play is unique and innovative.

The Carpetbagger's Children was originally composed to pay homage to Anton Chekhov's *The Three Sisters*, a work Horton had admired since first reading it sixty years earlier. Horton hoped to create a fitting tribute to the Russian master who shared the writer's interest in the decline of aristocratic societies, created intriguing female characters, and preferred to write about the great mysteries and ambiguities of life. However, while writing the play, the playwright discovered that Chekhov's realism did not suit the needs of his play, and so he decided to employ a non-traditional approach to storytelling. Disregarding the fundamental principle of dramatic composition—that drama is communicated through action—Horton wrote a memory play in which most of the action is imparted through a series of interrelated monologues told by three sisters—Cornelia, Grace Anne, and Sissy—and three brief dramatic episodes, in which the characters enter into past or imagined conversations and assume the character of others in the family and community. Cornelia, the matriarch, examines a ledger book, Grace Anne, the family outcast, attends to her sewing, and Sissie, the youngest sibling, studies sheet music, as the old women share their collective memories of their family's history in Harrison, to which their father, Joseph Thompson, a Union soldier, returned after the Civil War as a carpetbagger. The sisters recall the death of their beloved sister Beth, of Grace Anne's elopement

---

[10] Horton Foote, *The Carpetbagger's Children* and *The Actor* (Woodstock NY: Overlook Press, 2003). All page references to *The Carpetbagger's Children* and *The Actor* in the text refer to this publication.

with Jackson Le Grand, of Brother's repeated failures in business, and of Cornelia's failed relationship with Leon Davis. While each of the three sisters tells her side of the family saga, including the mental breakdown of their mother and the loves and losses each sister endured, a recurring tune, "The Clanging Bells of Time," which was their mother's favorite song continues to creep into their narrations. Horton, as he so often does, employs music to reinforce both theme and action, and by play's end, this combination of music and narrative creates a complex network of interrelated stories and episodes that comprise not only the collective history of the Thompson family but also that of Harrison, Texas, from 1870 to the present.

The Thompson family's relationship with the town of Harrison is the central concern in the play as the sisters have inherited twenty thousand acres of land that their father amassed after the Civil War. The land not only symbolizes a powerful legacy to his family but it also represents the root of the children's identity and confusion. The sisters disagree about how their father rose to power and how he originally obtained his property. Cornelia, the dutiful daughter who was forced to assume her father's business interests after the many failures of her brother and the death of her older sister, Beth, supports the official family story that her father had come to Texas with the Union Army, liked what he saw, and then returned after the war to live there. One of only a handful of Republicans in the town, he was appointed county treasurer and tax collector and was able to buy up property when landowners failed to pay their taxes. Although Cornelia accepts her father's version of the past, she is aware that others in town do not agree with her sense of the truth, including her sister, Grace Anne, who recalls that her "so-called friends" believed her father "was sent here as part of the Reconstruction when the Yankees took over the county and the courthouse, and he got himself appointed county treasurer and tax collector, and when…people couldn't pay their taxes, he grabbed land right and left and held onto it" (17). The sisters' memories about their father's rise to power do not coincide, but the one thing the sisters all agree on is that their father made them promise to never sell or divide a piece of the land he had acquired.

The sisters are also united in situating the death of their sister, Beth, as the beginning of the family's decline. Cornelia begins the play by recalling how Beth, who was everyone's favorite, loved to dance. When she suddenly became sick after visiting her cousins in St. Louis and physicians could find no cure for her illness her father brought her back to Harrison on a train. Colonel Hawkins, a Southern patriot who Mr. Thompson had befriended after saving Hawkins from economic ruin, arranged for some of the men in town to meet the train and escort Beth home in a wagon. Cornelia remembers that the men covered the streets with straw so Beth would have a smooth ride home and that "the street in front of our house was covered with straw every day the whole time she was sick, so that the wagons and the horses passing the house went by as silently as humanly possible" (14). Three weeks later Beth died, leaving the family broken and emotionally devastated. Then, shortly after Beth's funeral, Mr. Thompson called Cornelia into his room and appointed her overseer of his business interests, a decision that would ultimately entrap Cornelia in the demanding and all-consuming role of family provider and matriarch.

As the play progresses, Cornelia's heart hardens when she is forced to make difficult decisions that affect other people's lives. During a time when cotton-picking machines are replacing farmhands and farmers are being forced to sell their land, Cornelia must change her method of farming in order to save the family plantation from ruin. Her decision to dismiss the tenant farmers and remove them from the land haunted Cornelia for the rest of her life: "It almost killed me the day I had to go out and tell the tenants I had to change how I was farming or I'd lose everything. I don't know whether they believed me or not. Old Jake Tillman and his wife had been on their place nearly forty years and his daddy ten years before him, anyway they cried and I cried when I told them. Some of the others just didn't look at me while I was talking to them. Just stared down at their feet and I couldn't even see their faces" (39).

Cornelia is also burdened by her father's decision to disinherit Grace Anne for eloping with Jackson Le Grand, an ineffectual man who the family believes married Grace Anne for her money. Grace Anne recalls, "Mama and Papa never wanted us to marry, you know.... They thought everybody was after our land and our money. Well I defied them and eloped with Jackson Le Grand and when Papa heard what I'd done, he and Brother were after us to stop us, but...by the time Brother and Papa found out where we were it was too late to stop us. He sent word to where we were honeymooning not to bother ever to come home again with or without my husband, and I never did while Papa was alive" (17).

After her father dies, Grace Anne and Jackson demand their share of the family inheritance, forcing Cornelia to choose between her pledge to keep the family farm intact and her devotion to her strong-headed, rebellious sister. Cornelia offers Grace Anne a settlement of seven hundred fifty acres of land and twelve thousand dollars, with which Grace Anne buys a house for her family. Unfortunately, Jackson is no farmer and within ten years he has lost all the land. After learning that the bank has taken over the property, Cornelia buys back the land, restoring the estate Joseph Thompson had bequeathed his children. The incident creates a rift between the two sisters, and Grace Anne never completely forgives Cornelia, as evidenced in a scene following the death of their father. Cornelia explains to Grace Anne that she was to share in whatever the estate made after certain expenses were deducted, but deep down Grace Anne questions her sister's true intentions:

> Grace Anne: What expenses?
> Cornelia: Well, I was to get a salary as I had for some time.
> Grace Anne: (*Speaking from the chair.*) For what?
> Cornelia: I was going to manage the Estate and Papa specified in his will that I was going to be paid for that.
> Grace Anne: (*Getting up from her chair.*) How much?
> Cornelia: Two hundred dollars a month.
> Grace Anne: Mercy, that's a fortune. Why that's more than Jackson Le Grand makes at the cotton gin keeping their books.
> Cornelia: (*Turning away from Grace Anne.*) Well, I almost answered her back, but I said to myself, Cornelia, consider the source, she has always been jealous hearted. (19)

When Grace Anne enters the conversation, it is almost as if, for just a few seconds, the past is being relived, as if it were taking place in the present moment. However, the confrontation between the sisters never actually occurs because it never took place in the past. Since the past is the only thing that holds meaning for the characters, it is evident that any chance at reconciliation between the sisters vanished years ago. Cornelia and Grace Anne's troubled relationship becomes even more perplexing when Cornelia later announces that Grace Anne is dead.

While Grace Anne was a fighter, Sissie, by her own admonition, was a recluse, a frightened songbird with a lovely voice but a hollow spirit. "I always liked being the baby," she recalls, "I liked being told what to do and what not to do, what to think and what not to think" (19). Sissie never questioned the actions of others and she always put on a happy face no matter the situation. However, because she was afraid to break ties with her family, Sissie, like Laura Weems, could never bring herself to join her husband, Ralph Goodman, in Houston. Instead, she lived with her Mama in the family house, and Ralph, who could not afford to leave his job in the city, visited her in the country "every other weekend" (22). Somehow, through it all Sissie is able to remain happy by singing songs she remembered from Sunday school: "Brighten the Corner Where You Are" and "Jesus Loves Me," among others.

As Sissie describes her unhappy marriage, she reaches back even further to another story embedded in the family's collective conscious-ness, that of Leon Davis's betrayal of Cornelia. As Sissie remembers, "I was sitting on the gallery with Mama when Leon Davis who had been married to my cousin Lenora and had shot and killed her father he said in self-defense and had been acquitted, appeared one day" (30). Mrs. Thompson, who was showing signs of increasing senility, invited Leon to dinner and he quickly established a close relationship with Cornelia who was smitten with Leon's knowledge of business and mathematical figures. Leon and Brother also developed a friendship, and Leon convinced both Brother and Cornelia to invest large sums of money in a fictitious insurance company. Brother, who believed Leon actually loved Cornelia, asked Leon to be best man at his wedding but on the day of the ceremony Leon failed to show up. He betrayed Cornelia and ran off with the fifteen thousand dollars she had invested in his business. With Brother serving as his own best man, the wedding ceremony finally took place but no one heard another word from Leon until one day Cornelia showed Brother a clipping about his death in San Diego, California. "Who sent that to you? Brother asked. She handed him the envelope and he saw there was no name and no return address on it, and there was nothing inside the envelope but the newspaper clipping" (37).

Sadly, Cornelia could not alter the past, nor could she escape the burdens of time. Soon after Brother's wedding, Sissie died in her sleep, leaving Cornelia as the sole caretaker of her failing mother, who became more confused, talking about Beth, Papa, and Sissie as if they were still alive and claiming their father was a general in the Union army who had received many medals. Cornelia recalls that she hired two black ladies to help with her mother, who insisted that her father brought Quakers to teach the slaves to read and write, which caused the Ku Klux Klan to threaten to burn down their house. Cornelia doesn't believe the story ever took place and then adds that she found her father's military discharge papers that proved that he was a private, not a general. When Cornelia showed her mother her father's army uniform, which she had retrieved from the attic, Mama spit on her and ordered her out of the room.

In the plays final monologue, Cornelia tells the audience that the family home, the oldest in Harrison, is being listed in the National Register of Historical Places by the United States Department of the Interior and that a plaque is to be placed on the house which reads: "The Joseph Thompson house built in 1870 by Joseph Thompson, a Soldier in the Union Army" (41). Mama, of course, insists that the Historical Society has it wrong and that Papa was a general in the Confederate Army, wounded at the Battle of Shiloh. History, it seems, has become as mutable and unclear as life itself. Ironically, now that the house has been officially recognized as part of Harrison's history there is no one left in the family who cares. Mama is lost in a world of senility, and Papa, Beth, and Sissie are all dead. Grace Anne, Brother, and his wife will attend the ceremony but they are no longer interested in helping Cornelia with the old plantation, which is no longer being farmed.

The play ends with Mrs. Thompson calling out to Cornelia, who admits that she knows what the old woman wants but realizes there is no sense in telling her the truth—that Sissie is dead—because she won't believe her. "The only way to shut her up," Cornelia concludes, "is to go in the next room and pretend I'm Sissie and sing for her, pitiful voice that I have" (41).

Before the curtain falls, the play transcends realism altogether as Cornelia clutches her father's uniform and begins to sing "The Clanging Bells of Time," accompanied by Grace Anne and Sissie. Finally, the sisters, both living and dead, are united by the memory of their shared stories and their mother's favorite song: "O, the clanging bells of time/ Night and day they never cease/ We are wearied with their chime/ For they do not bring us peace/ And we hush our breath to hear/ And we strain our eyes to see/ If the shores are drawing near/ Eternity! Eternity!" (41).

The Carpetbagger's Children is a theatrically courageous work that illustrates Horton's talent for crafting beautiful and moving drama outside the confines of traditional realism. The play demonstrates, through its innovative dramatic structure, both the challenges and limitations of memory and the power of the past to define one's identity and one's place in the universe. It is not only a mournful evocation of the inevitability of loss and the end that awaits all humanity, but it is also a powerful reminder that opportunities for making amends and restoring relationships quickly disappear. Gerald Wood explains that in *The Carpetbagger's Children*, as in much of his recent work, "Foote is less assured than in his earlier plays about identity as the final stage of individual lives. Less confident that healthy families and responsible communities can be established in the world of time, his later writing has become benedictory and elegiac."[11]

After writing *The Carpetbagger's Children*, Horton sent the script to director, Michael Wilson, who had by this time become artistic director of the Hartford Stage Company. Wilson wanted to perform the play in Connecticut, but since the play had been originally commissioned by the Alley Theatre, Horton was required to work out a deal with artistic director Greg Boyd whereby Wilson would rehearse the play for two weeks in Hartford before premiering the production in Houston, transferring it to the Guthrie in Minneapolis, and finally restaging it at the Hartford Stage Company. As planned, *The Carpetbagger's Children* began preview performances at the Alley in the spring of 2001 with Roberta Maxwell in the role of Cornelia, Jean Stapleton as Grace Anne, and Hallie Foote performing the part of Sissie. There was a great sense of excitement and anticipation as the production went into previews but only two days after the show opened disaster struck. Tropical Storm Allison hit the Texas Gulf Coast, flooding the downtown arts district of Houston, including the Alley Theatre. Water completely swamped the theater and destroyed all the set pieces, furniture, and costumes for *The Carpetbagger's Children*. After five days, the floodwaters receded, but the Alley Theatre was so damaged that Horton and Wilson were forced to cancel performances there and move the production to higher ground. Wilson arranged to transfer the play to Houston's Stages Repertory Theatre, a much smaller space but one that Horton knew well since *Talking Pictures* had been performed there in the 1980s.

The Carpetbagger's Children opened at Stages Repertory to enthusiastic audiences but with the aftermath of the storm, very few drama critics attended the show. In fact, only one New York critic, John Lahr of *The New Yorker*, flew down and reviewed the production; however, Lahr's

---

[11] Gerald C. Wood, "Variations on the Monologue: Brian Friel's *The Faith Healer* and Horton Foote's *The Carpetbagger's Children*," *The Horton Foote Review*, vol. 2 (2009): 37, 38.

review, "Texas Bittersweet: Horton Foote's homage to *The Three Sisters*," made up for the overall lack of critical attention, and set the stage for the play's eventual transfer to New York's Lincoln Center. In his review, Lahr called the play "theatrically daring," noting that Horton's writing is like "bittersweet music—a rhapsody of ambivalence," and concluding that "by all conventional standards of stagecraft *The Carpetbagger's Children* should not work. But, thanks both to the actresses' charisma and to the fine filigree of Foote's storytelling, it does."[12]

After playing at the Alley, *The Carpetbagger's Children* took a month-long detour to the Guthrie Theatre in Minneapolis before arriving back at Hartford Stage Company, where it ran for another month. Audience reception continued to be encouraging, and Horton and Wilson were hopeful that the play would garner the attention of a Broadway producer willing to move the production to New York. But everything changed on September 11 when the World Trade Center was attacked. The nation was caught off-guard by the sudden and horrific act of violence, leaving New York emotionally devastated and the Broadway theater community frozen in grief. Horton, who happened to be in Hartford on the day of the attack, described his impressions of New York two weeks after the attack:

Riding down the West Side Highway last night, on my return to New York, it was reassuring and comforting to see old familiar landmarks unchanged, and I realized once again how I love this wonderful city. My first introduction to another reality was passing a building in the heart of the city, doors opened wide, all lit up and on the walls were pictures of the missing. Hundreds it seemed to me. Then all around suddenly were state police cars and our driver had to leave the highway at the Javits Center and detour. Policemen now everywhere. When Hallie and I reached our apartment again everything seemed life as usual. The doorman welcomed us home and no mention of what had been happening. Our apartment was of course unchanged, but we decided to walk over to Horton's restaurant on Jane Street. He was away attending a funeral on Long Island. The wife of one of his bartenders, married only three months, had been killed in the bombing. On our way over we passed on Jane an apartment with a memorial sign pasted on one of its windows with the names of three best friends or maybe family. The day of the bombing we had awaited all day by the phone for news of my son,

---

[12] John Lahr, "Texas Bittersweet: Horton Foote's homage to 'The Three Sisters,'" *The New Yorker*, 10 September 2001.

Walter's wife [Lin Chin]. We knew she was at work on the 50th floor of one of the buildings. She did survive we learned late in the afternoon.[13]

Within this climate of fear and uncertainty Broadway showed a lack of confidence in producing new, unproven works. Consequently, *The Carpetbagger's Children* remained relatively obscure until André Bishop, artistic director of the Lincoln Center Theatre and good friend of Michael Wilson's, read John Lahr's review of the play and decided to drive from New York to Hartford to see a matinee of the play.

As it turned out, Bishop loved the show, and after returning to New York, he immediately began plans to move the play to the Lincoln Center. After a good deal of negotiating and reshuffling of performance schedules, Bishop secured the Lincoln Center's Mitzi Newhouse Theatre for *The Carpetbagger's Children*, which opened on 25 March 2002 to great acclaim. The production was a rewarding experience for everyone concerned, and audiences responded so positively to the play that performances were extended through 30 June 2002. Critical response was equally encouraging. Ben Brantley of the *New York Times* said "few dramatists today can replicate this kind of storytelling with the gentle mastery that Mr. Foote provides," adding that the play is "both sentimental and ruthless, toting up the losses in one generation's life with warm compassion and a cold awareness that to live is ultimately to lose."[14] Wilborn Hampton, also writing for the *New York Times*, noted that, "Mr. Foote has returned to his familiar fictional Texas town of Harrison to narrate, through the three sisters 'reminiscences, nothing less than a social and economic history of 20th century America. If the story of the Thompsons represents the dissolution of the American family, it also finds the hope of reconciliation that only time can offer; if it rues the changes that a machine that picks cotton can bring to a way of life, it also discovers the new opportunities that only time can extend."[15]

Not only did *The Carpetbagger's Children* receive popular and critical acclaim but the play was also honored with the American Theatre Critics New Play Award in 2002. That same year, Horton's teleplay *The Rocking Chair* (initially penned for television in 1952) was adapted to the stage by Jack Sbarbori, artistic director of the Quotidian Theatre in Bethesda,

---

[13] Horton Foote to John Guare, 24 September 2001 (Horton Foote Papers).

[14] Ben Brantley, "Theatre Review: a Fractious Family's Decline, with Vintage Mustiness," *New York Times*, 26 March 2002.

[15] Wilborn Hampton, "Three Actors Are One Another's Other Audience," *New York Times*, 5 July 2013.

Maryland. The Ensemble Studio Theatre in New York also presented Horton's one-act *The Prisoner's Song* under the direction of noted actor, Harris Yulin, and the South Coast Repertory Theatre of San Diego, California, presented the world premiere of *Getting Frankie Married—and Afterwards*. Directed by Martin Benson and produced by Jean and Tim Weiss, *Getting Frankie Married—and Afterwards* examines what happens when a son repeats a father's sexual transgressions.[16] In a style ranging from farce to tragedy, the play tells the tale of Fred and Frankie, a traditional couple who have been dating for more than twenty years. Even though Frankie longs to be married, Fred has never asked for her hand until today. As the story unfolds, we discover that Fred's imperious mother, Mrs. Willis, may be dying and she would like to see her son married before she goes. Everybody in town whispers that Frankie is already Fred's common-law wife and that a wedding seems foolish. They also gossip when Carlton Gleason comes back to town, because Carlton is reputed to be Fred's father's son by another woman. Fred's father married his mother hastily to avoid marrying Carlton's mother. Now history is about to repeat itself. Just as Fred proposes to Frankie, the young and lovely Helen Vaught slaps him with a breach of promise lawsuit, claiming that she quit her job after Fred proposed to her. As if this isn't trouble enough, when both women, Frankie and Helen, turn up pregnant, Fred finds he has spawned two families, just like his father before him. He is eventually forced to face up to his transgressions and to find a way to placate the two women he loves. Fred gives up his family inheritance in order to support his children, but in the final analysis he cannot change the past nor escape the stifling control of his domineering mother. As the curtain falls, Fred is alone, sobbing uncontrollably, as Mrs. Willis calls out to him and Helen says bitterly, "Fred, don't cry. It ought to make you happy that your mother is speaking" (288).

Although the plot of *Getting Frankie Married—and Afterwards* resembles that of a soap opera, Horton, like no other writer, is able to locate the humanity in the lives of his characters. Fred, who maintains his futility and incompetence throughout the play, exudes an amazing sense of dignity and kindness, and he is remarkably forthright in his

---

[16] Horton Foote, *Getting Frankie Married—and Afterwards* in *Horton Foote: Getting Frankie Married—and Afterwards and Other Plays* (Lyme NH: Smith and Kraus, 1998) 225–88. Page references to *Getting Frankie Married—and Afterwards* in the text refer to this publication.

dealings with Frankie, who radiates with dignity and solemnity. Even the irascible old Mrs. Willis is vulnerable in her fear of sickness and death. Although *Getting Frankie Married—and Afterwards* is not one of Horton's better-crafted works, it does reveal the writer's ability to depict, with remarkable accuracy, both the comedy and tragedy in ordinary life and to capture the essence of a specific time and place with poignancy and emotional authenticity.

After *Getting Frankie Married—and Afterwards* closed, Horton finished his most autobiographical play, *The Actor*. He was commissioned to write the play by the Tony Award-winning Young Conservatory program of San Francisco's American Conservatory Theatre. The Conservatory stages four productions yearly, serves as the nation's leading producer of new works written specifically for young actors, and participates in international exchange programs with other theater companies in Europe. In 2000, when Horton was first approached about writing a play, the Young Conservatory had aligned itself with the National Theatre in London, who had a similar program. "The National goes out into the provinces and works with selected theatres," Horton explained. "The [commissioned] plays are submitted to these theatres, and the theatres then choose the ones they want to perform. Anyway, the National Theatre representatives flew over, saw *The Last of the Thorntons*, and commissioned me to write a one-act play for them. I wrote *The Actor*."[17] The production of *The Actor* chosen by the National Theatre, from among the several different theaters involved, debuted in the Cottesloe Theatre on 10 July 2002 and was restaged the following year by the American Conservatory Theatre in San Francisco.

As well as being autobiographical, *The Actor* echoes the structure of *The Carpetbagger's Children* as the central character of the play, fifteen-year-old Horace Robedaux, Jr., addresses the audience directly in monologues and through brief scenes played out between his family and friends in Harrison. Set in the middle of the Great Depression, the play tells of young Horace Jr.'s call to be an actor, his desire to attend acting school, and his parents' gracious acceptance of their son's seemingly quixotic vocation. Although Horace Jr.'s parents want their son to receive a college education and find a stable job, they eventually support his dream. The senior Horace, a struggling businessman, makes it possible for his son to attend acting school when he sells a house he had

---

[17] Castleberry, "Reflections on the American Theatre," 276.

been renting for income and gives Horace Jr. the money he could have invested in a lucrative oil investment.

In writing *The Actor*, Horton created a poignant love poem to his family and located the source of his remarkably courageous and resilient career, a career that lasted seventy years. As young Horace Jr. prepares to leave his family to study acting at the Pasadena Playhouse, he echoes the playwright's devotion to his own parents as he speaks directly to the audience and remembers:

> Daddy gave me my bus ticket and told me to be careful of pickpockets, and I said I would. He gave me a twenty dollar bill then, which he said I should save in case of an emergency of some kind came up. I thanked him and mother began crying then and said they were going to miss me. I said I would miss them too. Daddy said they were both very proud of me and felt I would have a wonderful success, but to always remember that if things didn't work out in California or any other place, I could always come back to my home and be welcomed and there would be a place for me to work in his store. I thanked him for telling me that. I never did go back during their lifetime except on visits, though, many a time when I was lonely and discouraged I wanted to. But then I remembered my call and kept on going somehow. (92)

After presenting the world premiere of *The Carpetbagger's Children* in 2001, the Alley Theatre and Hartford Stage teamed up again in 2003 to co-produce the fiftieth-anniversary revival of *The Trip to Bountiful*, Horton's tale of Carrie Watts's courageous journey back to her old home place. Directed by Michael Wilson, the production featured Hallie Foote as Jessie Mae and Devon Abner, as Ludie Watts. Jean Stapleton had originally planned to perform the title role of Carrie Watts but she had to withdraw due to illness. Consequently, Dee Maaske, who had performed the role at the Oregon Shakespeare Festival the year before, was hired to replace Stapleton.

The fiftieth-anniversary production played to great acclaim in both Hartford and Houston, performing to sold-out houses and garnering the praise of critics who found the play as poignant and moving as it had been five decades earlier. Everett Evans of the *Houston Chronicle* wrote, "Foote's sympathy for ordinary, even *failed* people—not just gallant Carrie but also ineffectual Ludie and superficial Jessie Mae—is extraordinary. What Horton understands most profoundly…is human limitations." Evans praised Michael Wilson's direction of the play, noting that "he exploits the interpersonal dynamics: the unspoken family tensions, the prickly humor of Carrie and Jessie Mae's wrangling, Carrie's poignant encounters with strangers she meets on her journey." The critic also admired Dee Maaske's portrayal of Carrie Watts, pointing out that the actress skillfully captured the character's "slyness, her sadness, her resignation and ultimate reclamation of her dignity," and concluded that Hallie Foote's performance was a "superlative characterization of the maddening, bossy, trivial, and self-centered Jessie Mae."[18]

In 2004, Primary Stages, an Off-Broadway theater founded in 1984 to assist playwrights in the process of developing new plays, mounted another of Horton's previously unproduced works, *The Day Emily Married*. Originally written in the late 1940s, *The Day Emily Married* (originally called *The Indian Fighters*) went through a number of revisions before receiving its world premiere at Silver Springs Stage in Silver Springs Maryland in 1997. Horton had refused to produce the work for nearly forty years because several of the people on whom the characters were based were still alive, including his Aunt Lida Horton, the prototype of the play's central character, Lyd Davis. Horton explained that *The Day Emily Married* was inspired by his thinking about his colorful and gregarious aunt and the ramifications of her influence on his family and hometown of Wharton:

> She...figures in a lot of my plays. It just may be as references because my father whom I write about in *The Orphans' Home Cycle* was abandoned essentially by his mother, and she became a kind of mother-figure to him. I never explicitly state that [in *The Orphans' Home Cycle* plays], but you can tell whenever he talks about her in the plays it's with great warmth. And I was fascinated with her as a child because she was a kind of repository of all the tales about her family. And she was a great exaggerator and fascinating. For instance, there are certain literal things [she said that] I've taken. The most specific example in the play is what she says about her husband being the best and telling the ladies about her husband. I've heard her tell that 50 times. So I tried to get the essence of her and I tried also to find a structure, a story that would have some dignity, since her end was tragic, although she didn't turn on gas. She did

---

[18] Everette Evans, "Review: Alley Captures the heart of Foote's 'Bountiful,'" *Houston Chronicle*, 8 April 2003.

turn on gas, but she didn't die from it. But in those days it was a constant concern of older people doing that, you know.[19]

Set in the summer of 1956, *The Day Emily Married* is a realistic play that tells the heartbreaking story of an elderly couple, Lee and Lyd Davis, and their thirty-eight-year-old divorced daughter, Emily, who is preparing for her second marriage.[20] Her fiancé is Richard Murray, an attractive and ambitious young oil field worker who has been helping out on the Davis's farm. Richard has developed a close relationship with Emily's father, Lee, who has made promises to set his future son-in-law up in a lucrative business after he sells the family farm. Richard tries to convince Lee to invest in a get-rich-quick oil venture with a man in Houston, but Lee wants to set him up with a steady job, that of overseer of his farm. Lee plans for the young couple to take over responsibility of the business and to move into the family homestead. He believes that the presence of the young couple in the home will enable him to rest from his labor and will be good for his wife, Lyd, who suffers from dementia and is unintentionally self-destructive.

Although Emily is reluctant, she does finally yield to her father's wishes, and a month after the wedding the reasons for her hesitancy becomes clear as the empowered Richard, who has become more and more disenchanted with Lee's manipulation, takes out his frustration on Jack Baker, a tenant farmer who owes Lee money, by forcing him to pay his debt or give up his land. Soon, Richard's relentless push for wealth and progress at any cost has Emily and her parents wondering about Richard's true intentions. Emily is caught in the middle of a confrontation between Richard and her father, which plays out in an all-too familiar way, bringing back painful memories of her first husband, Ben Lacque. Richard, who had known Ben, recalls that Ben

> used to slip into Houston on drunks every now and again after he was married, and he was full of how easy he had it, and of all the things you were going to do for him. Then one day, he turned up in town again, for good. He didn't have a job and he had very little money. What he had was all gone and after one good drunk. He said you had kicked both of them out and were paying their expenses and giving them fifteen dollars

---

[19] Robert Donahoo, "On The Day Emily Married: An Interview with Horton Foote," in *The Voice of an American Playwright*, 286–87.

[20] Horton Foote, *The Day Emily Married*, in *"Horton Foote: Getting Frankie Married— and Afterwards and Other Plays*, 1–76. Page references to *The Day Emily Married* in the text refer to this publication.

a week spending money until he got a job.... You knew he was a drunk before he married your daughter, didn't you?... You knew why Ben married your daughter, didn't you?... He married her because of all the promises you made to him. If you hadn't flattered him and encouraged him and led him to believe all kinds of things that you were going to do for him and with him, he would never have married her. (69–70)

During the argument, Richard reveals that he is actually no better than Ben Lacque and that the only reason he had married Emily in the first place was because of all the "assertions and promises" made to him (70). Lee tries to justify his actions, but his attempt to buy his daughter's happiness fails once again. Richard walks away from his commitment to Emily after securing a hefty financial settlement, and Emily, stunned by the confrontation, is left vulnerable, heartbroken, and lonely. Although Richard's actions are unjustifiable, Horton admitted that he had a "great sympathy" for the character because of the hard life he's had. "And in the middle of a most commercial, mercenary society, where oil was being discovered and people were getting rich and richer and richer, and again he wasn't prepared for much," Horton explained. "Although he did work, I think if [Richard and Emily] had been able to follow his plan that he would have stayed. I think he wanted to stay. But I'm not sure that his plan was wise. This guy he is putting all his faith in, this oil-well guy. He's such a type I've known all my life. I mean, they talk the best thing in the world, but then there are no guarantees but they tell you it's going to happen."[21]

There are similarities between Horton Foote's Emily Davis and Tennessee Williams's Laura Wingfield in that both exude a sense of innocence and emotional frailty that colors their actions. But unlike Laura, Emily displays a remarkably strong and self-reflective nature that, in the final scene, has her wondering "why a girl who has never really considered herself very attractive always felt she had to have a handsome husband" (71). As the play ends, Emily decides to leave home and to take up residence in an inexpensive apartment in Houston, where she can build a new life free from her parents' control. She finally decides to stop trying to become a social butterfly in her mother's image and to enter any new relationship she may have from a place of strength rather than desperate loneliness. Even though Emily assures her father that things will be all right and that they will all survive the disaster that has befallen them, deep down, Lee knows that he may never see his

---

[21] Donahoo, 297.

daughter again. Reflecting upon Emily's courageous decision to leave her home and begin a new life in Houston, Horton explained: "It's a very difficult problem for women, isn't it? I mean, they have to fight for identity. Particularly in those days. They weren't trained to do anything. They were dependent. And here she is. What she'll do: she'll go back to clerking or to being a hostess—some non-skilled thing, you know, because she's not trained. So, in other words, it's a wakeup call, to me. I am very much on the side of Emily."[22]

There is a good deal of comedy in *The Day Emily Married*, much of it coming from the character of Lyd Davis, Emily's mother, who grows more confused and alarming as the play progresses. Like many of Horton's characters, Lyd is emotionally paralyzed and frozen in the past, moving from one illusion to another. She clings to a collection of black and white photographs depicting her once large and prosperous family, who have long since passed away. Like Alberta Thornton and Cornelia Thompson, Lyd Davis yearns for a world that disappeared long ago and will never return. She continuously recalls the Harrison of her youth but admits that her father "wouldn't even recognize the town he was born in if he came back" (70). However, while Harrison has changed beyond recognition, Lyd adamantly refuses to sell the house that her great-grandfather built, even though it might save her daughter's marriage to Richard. When the curtain falls, the old woman expresses her fear of change and the heart-wrenching realization that she will soon die isolated and alone. Unconsciously failing to light the gas stove she has just turned on, Lyd speaks to Emily and Lee as if they could hear her:

> What's to happen to my house, Emily, when I'm gone, if you're not here to live in it? What'll happen, Emily?...What's to happen to my house, Lee? This house was built to last forever. My great grandfather built this house and he got the best bricks and lumber for miles around to put in here, because he said this was to last forever. His name was Robedeaux and he was in some kind of terrible trouble back in Virginia and he had to take his slaves and his wife and his children, and all he had, he had to sell, and move here. And when he came, he looked around and he was satisfied and he said, we're home, we can rest now. This is to be our home forever, and our children's home, and their children's. Our wanderings are over. But he was wrong, Lee. This was a place of rest to you and me. But Emily's wanderings are just beginning. (75)

---

[22] Ibid.

The production of *The Day Emily Married*, which opened for twenty-six performances on 5 August 2004, was directed by Michael Wilson and starred Hallie Foote as Emily, William "Biff" McGuire as Lee, James Colby as Richard, and Estelle Parsons as Lyd. The show was a big hit for Primary Stages and received excellent reviews from the critics, who noted that while the play seemed old-fashioned, Horton's story was told with great emotional authenticity by the cast, who captured the unbearable loneliness of the characters and the complexity of relationships within the Davis family. In his review of *The Day Emily Married*, Ben Brantley wrote: "Even at its most forced, *The Day Emily Married* emanates an infectious, eerily familiar melancholy that keeps pricking at the memory like a wandering melody. I can think of no other playwright who is as harsh in his sentimentality as Mr. Foote is. His plays may radiate the burnished nostalgia of sepia-tone photographs, but he insists on your feeling that there is more ice than fire in his glow."[23]

On 10 October 2005, the Quotidian Theatre Company of Bethesda, Maryland, presented the world premiere of Horton's *The Beginning of Summer* (1955), a sequel to the playwright's 1944 Broadway play, *Only the Heart*. Set in Harrison, Texas, during the 1940s, *Only the Heart* centered on the loveless marriage of the shrewd business woman, Mamie Borden, whose domineering nature drives her seventeen-year-old daughter Julia into marrying Albert Price, a young man she does not love. *The Beginning of Summer* picks up twenty-six years later, after Mamie has retired and convinced Albert, Julia, and their son Borden to move back to Harrison and live with her. In *Only the Heart*, Julia and Albert left Harrison and Mamie's stifling control to build a happier life in Houston, but when the couple moves back to Harrison their lives are once again filled with the bitterness and sorrow that had haunted them earlier as Mamie tries to control her children, Albert begins to drink heavily, and Julia resumes her adulterous behavior. The major conflict occurs when Albert catches Julia having an affair with his friend, Preston Murray, and threatens to kill him. While Albert decides that both Preston and Julia must die, he eventually comes to his senses and reconciles with Julia, who also realizes that she actually loves and needs Albert. In *The Beginning of Summer*, Horton explores the themes of violence, spousal

---

[23] Ben Brantley, "Theatre Review: The Suffocating Dust in a Household's Cozy Clutter," *New York Times*, 6 August 2004.

abuse, infidelity and materialistic greed while masterfully depicting the essence of a time, place, and people with accuracy and authenticity.

Shortly after the close of *The Day Emily Married*, Horton received a phone call from James Houghton asking if he would allow the Signature Theatre to do an Off-Broadway revival of *The Trip to Bountiful* in the fall of 2005. Houghton explained that he had been planning to stage a season of plays by August Wilson, but when Wilson died suddenly his estate was legally obligated to pull the rights, and the theater had to look for other options. Houghton, who decided to offer a season of "signature" works by playwrights whose plays had been previously performed at the Signature, wanted to showcase *The Trip to Bountiful* and to feature the renowned actress Lois Smith in the title role of Carrie Watts. Horton agreed to Houghton's offer without hesitation. He greatly admired the work of Lois Smith and had wanted to collaborate with her for many years, ever since he had seen her perform the role of Mrs. Campbell in *The Man Who Climbed the Pecan Trees* at the Ensemble Studio Theatre in 1988. In addition to featuring Lois Smith, the Signature production was to be directed by another Horton colleague, Harris Yulin, who had previously staged two of Horton's one-acts, *The Prisoner's Song* and *The One-Armed Man*, at the Ensemble Studio Theatre. The remaining cast members were Hallie Foote as Jessie Mae, Devon Abner as Ludie, Meghan Andrews as Thelma, Jim DeMarse as the Sheriff, and Frank Girardeau as the Harrison Ticket Man.

There was a sense of excitement and expectation permeating rehearsals for *The Trip to Bountiful*, and the show proved to be a rewarding experience for Horton, who was privileged to work with one of the finest casts he had ever assembled. He was especially thrilled with the performance of Lois Smith, who at age seventy-five dove into the role of Carrie Watts with great physical and emotional energy. Smith was equally thrilled to be working with Horton, whom she recalled "was in near-constant attendance at rehearsals and performances. His nourishing presence provided auspicious conditions for planting and growing seeds of character, trust, action, interaction, and event. I felt free to try anything…. In performance, at the end of the play, he would be there, speaking with me, watching the process, grateful as discoveries, changes, nuances, and differing emphases occurred."[24] Director Harris Yulin echoed Smith's sentiments about Horton:

> Horton was…an invaluable resource during rehearsals, an authority on feelings, furniture, history, clothing, any question that might arise. Most of all, he was there with us. He gave the proceedings an added measure of grace, a confidence in the authenticity of what we were doing, because if we weren't doing it properly then surely he would let us know. If you can image Chekhov in the rehearsal room while preparing for a production of, say, *Uncle Vanya*, you'll know what it was like having Horton there. He was tough minded, like Chekhov, and wasn't shy about expressing his misgivings about a direction or interpretation. On the other hand, one understood that he encouraged the search. One felt in his presence an approval of oneself, encouragement to experiment, and trust in one's ideas. He was a benevolent authority whose approval and delight were rewards of the highest order.[25]

The revival of *The Trip to Bountiful* was a major victory for the Signature Theatre Company as the theater was sold out on a regular basis. The production, which opened on 4 December 2005 at the Norton Theatre on Forty-second Street, was so popular that the run was extended twice, until finally closing on 11 March 2006.

Because of the show's popularity, there was a good deal of talk about transferring the play to Broadway and London, but a transfer never materialized. Horton and Houghton were told there were no Broadway theaters available to them. Wilborn Hampton believes that the actual reason the move to Broadway never occurred had more to do with New York theater politics than a lack of theater space. "The prominent Broadway theatrical producers had plays running for which they had Tony Award aspirations that season," Hampton explained. "If Yulin's staging of *The Trip to Bountiful* moved to Broadway, it stood a good chance of sweeping the Tonys—Lois Smith for Best Actress, almost certainly, but also for Hallie, Devon, and Yulin for supporting actress, supporting actor, and director, not to mention Horton himself and the play for best revival."[26]

---

[24] Lois Smith, "Untitled Essay," in *Farewell: Remembering Horton Foote, 1916–2009*, ed. Marion Castleberry and Susan Christensen (Dallas TX: Southern Methodist University Press, 2011) 195–96.

[25] Harris Yulin, "Untitled Essay," in *Farewell: Remembering Horton Foote,* 215–19.

[26] Wilborn Hampton, *Horton Foote: America's Storyteller* (New York: Simon & Schuster, 2009) 254.

Even though the production was excluded from Broadway, it nonetheless received a large number of prestigious honors, including a Lucille Lortel Award for Outstanding Featured Actress (Hallie Foote) and two Obie Awards: Outstanding Director (Harris Yulin) and Outstanding Revival (Signature Theatre). For her moving portrayal of Carrie Watts, Lois Smith won the Drama Desk Award for Best Actress in a Play, the Outer Critics Circle Award for Outstanding Actress in a Play, the Obie Award for Outstanding Performance by an Actress, and the Lucille Lortel Award for Outstanding Lead Actress. Ultimately, while the Signature production never reached Broadway, *The Trip to Bountiful* was performed with the same cast two years later (2008) at Chicago's Goodman Theatre. It became the centerpiece of a Horton Foote Festival organized by artistic director Robert Falls and was accompanied by productions of *The Actor*, *Blind Date*, and *Talking Pictures*.

Remarkably, more than fifty years after the play was written, *The Trip to Bountiful* moved audiences to laughter and tears while winning the admiration of a new generation of admirers who found Carrie Watts's desperate journey back to Bountiful personally inspiring and life-altering. Enthusiasts both old and young approached Horton after the show each evening to express their admiration and to tell him how the play had affected them. Critics also responded to the show with great respect and admiration. Ben Brantley lauded Lois Smith's portrayal of Carrie Watts in the *New York Times*, commenting: "I had never before realized how blue and bottomless her gaze is" and she "brings pure, revivifying oxygen to the role." Brantley also noted that what "this production provides that makes *The Trip to Bountiful* seem newborn is its artful counterpoint of the smothering, claustrophobic details of daily life and Carrie's barrier-melting faith in her destiny."[27]

While *The Trip to Bountiful* was playing at the Norton Theatre, there was another Foote play performing uptown at the Ensemble Studio Theatre (EST). The play was a revised version of Horton's poignant drama, *The Traveling Lady*, which traces Georgette Thomas's journey to begin a new life in a small Texas town after her husband is released from prison. She and her daughter, Margaret Rose, are taken in by locals, and when her husband, Henry, returns, the family and community are drawn into a chaos of lost love, heartbreak, and violence. Originally performed as the fiftieth-anniversary production of the play at Baylor

---

[27] Ben Brantley, "Theatre Review of *The Trip to Bountiful*: There's No Place like an Imaginary Home," *New York Times*, 5 December 2006.

University's inaugural Horton Foote American Playwrights Festival in 2004, *The Traveling Lady* was restaged by the American Actors Company at the Ensemble in March 2006. The production, which was directed by Marion Castleberry and starred Lynn Cohen as Mrs. Mavis, Margot White as Georgette, Quincy Confoy as Margaret Rose, Jamie Bennett as Henry, Stan Denman as Slim, Carol Goodheart as Sitter Mavis, Rochelle Oliver as Clara, Alice McLane as Mrs. Tillman, Frank Girardeau as the Judge, and Matthew Conlon as the Sheriff, was a triumph for the Ensemble Studio Theatre and enjoyed a brief but rewarding Off-Broadway run, receiving not only critical acclaim but also garnering, along with *The Trip to Bountiful*, a Drama Desk nomination for Outstanding Revival of a Play. Although neither *The Traveling Lady* nor *The Trip to Bountiful* won the award, Horton was given an honorary lifetime achievement award by Drama Desk for his contributions to American theater.

During Christmas 2006, Horton moved from his Horatio Street residence in New York to Pacific Palasades, California, to live with Barabara Hallie and Devon. He had begun to worry about financial security, and when apartment owners increased his rent to more than six thousand dollars a month, he saw no alternative but to pack up his belongings and move in with his daughter. He also sold off the last remnants of the primitive antiques and Early American art that he and Lillian had collected during their years together.

While living in California, Horton continued to write obsessively, and he was commissioned to pen two original screenplays: *The Great Debators* and *Main Street*. *The Great Debaters* was based on a true story about a championship debate team from Wiley College, an all-black school in Marshall, Texas, during the 1930s. Directed by Denzel Washington, who also starred in the film, the movie was produced by Oprah Winfrey's Harpo Films. After meeting with Washington and several former students of the college who shared their memories of the debate team, Horton was excited about working on the screenplay. However, his excitement soon turned to frustration when his agent, Barbara Hogenson, informed him that he would be one of four writers submitting a filmscript for *The Great Debaters* and that the final screenplay would combine pieces of all the versions. "I'm not putting anybody down who can do that, because some people are wonderful at it, but it just didn't interest me" Horton said. "I know Lori Parks, for instance [referring to the Pulitzer Prize-winning playwright Suzan-Lori

Parks, another writer on the script], and I kept looking for Lori Parks on the page but I didn't see her. I really did it as a tribute to Denzel. And those people I wrote about were my people. Our colors are different, but I grew up with them."[28] While *The Great Debaters* turned out to be an artistic success and fared well at the box office, Horton never felt comfortable with the project.

The second film Horton worked on was *Main Street*, an intriguing tale of an economically depressed small town (Durham, North Carolina) whose residents are thrown into chaos by the arrival of a stranger with a controversial plan to save their decaying hometown. In the film, Horton once again explored the fears and hardships associated with change, the necessity of letting go of the past, and the need to face an uncertain future with courage and integrity. The film was directed by Tony Award-winning director John Boyle (his film directing debut) and starred Ellen Burstyn as Georgiana Carr, a tobacco heiress who rents a vacant warehouse on Main Street to Texan businessman Gus Leroy, played by Academy Award-winning actor Colin Firth, who comes to town with the promise of a new business venture that will enliven the town's economy. As the citizen's embrace the newcomer, Firth's character, Gus, becomes involved in their professional and personal lives in a way they do not expect and which ultimately forces them to reevaluate the way they envision the world and the town in which they live. The cast, consisting of Burstyn and Firth along with Patricia Clarkson, Orlando Bloom, Amber Tamblyn, and Andrew McCarthy, give convincing and powerful performances; however, movie critics found the film's slow pace and focus on character development off-putting. Also, when *Main Street* was released in 2010, it lacked the funding necessary for proper distribution. Consequently, Horton's final screenplay remains a relatively unknown masterwork which deserves closer consideration.

In fall 2007, *Dividing the Estate*, Horton's comedy of family, money, power and greed, was staged by director Michael Wilson at Primary Stages Theatre in New York, fifteen years after the play was first performed at the McCarter Theatre in Princeton, New Jersey. The production opened for a brief run on September 27 with a star-studded cast that included Elizabeth Ashley as Stella, Gerald McRaney as Lewis, Arthur French as Doug, Penny Fuller as Lucille, Devon Abner as Son,

---

[28] Alex Witchel, "His Kind of Town," *The New York Times Magazine*, 19 August 2007, 28.

James DeMarse as Bob, and Hallie Foote as Mary Jo. *Dividing the Estate* was a major coup for Primary Stages, and the show garnered the attention of several producers who wanted to move the play to Broadway. Among them was André Bishop who, with Horton's approval, arranged for the production to open for a limited engagement at the Booth Theatre on 20 November 2008. The ensemble's outstanding performance and Horton's engaging script garnered a remarkable amount of popular and critical praise, earning for both the production and actress Hallie Foote Tony Award nominations in 2009. Although neither Hallie nor the production won a Tony, *Dividing the Estate* was a reminder of the distinctiness of Horton's voice in contemporary American theater. The play's universal themes of family struggle and survival in a world of moral and economic decline, its Chekhovian-like intrusion of past upon present, and gentle but acetic humor proved to be as timely and resonant in 2009 as they were when the comedy was first produced in 1989. Ben Brantley, critic for the *New York Times*, called the play "one of [Horton Foote's] masterworks" and proclaimed Hallie Foote's performance as one of "true comic genius." He praised the production as a whole, calling it "an ideally balanced ensemble piece, with acting that matches and magnifies Mr. Foote's slyly and acutely observant writing."[29]

As fate would have it, the Broadway debut of *Dividing the Estate* coincided with the collapse of the US economy in the fall of 2008. Almost overnight, theater attendance declined and Broadway shows began to close at a breakneck pace. However, in spite of the nation's serious economic depression, *Dividing the Estate* continued to draw large audiences. Producer André Bishop was eager to extend the play's run but his enthusiasm quickly turned to disappointment when the Shubert Organization announced that the Booth Theatre was no longer available and the show would have to close. Fortunately, Michael Wilson arranged to move *Dividing the Estate* to the Hartford Stage Company, where it experienced another successful run and concluded the company's forty-fifth-anniversary season in the spring of 2009. The only cast member not to make the trip to Hartford was Elizabeth Ashley, who had performed the role of Stella on Broadway. Ashley accepted a lead role in Tracy Lett's new play, *August: Osage County*, and was replaced by Lois Smith, who gave a stellar performance as the family matriarch. Later, Ashley

---

[29] Ben Brantley, "Review of *Dividing the Estate*: In the Midst of Family, Death, and Taxes," *New York Times*, 28 September 2007.

reprised the role when *Dividing the Estate* opened for a brief run at Houston's Alley Theatre on 12 October 2011 and later at the Old Globe Theatre in San Diego, California, on 14 January 2012.

During the run of *Dividing the Estate* at Primary Stages, Michael Wilson came up with the intriguing idea of staging the entire *Orphans' Home Cycle*. Wilson had first begun to think about producing Horton's nine-play masterpiece after seeing Peter Brook's Mahabharata in Avignon, Peter Hall's Tantalus in Denver, Tony Kushner's *Angels in America* at the Alley in Houston, and Tom Stoppard's *The Coast of Utopia* at the Lincoln Center. These productions, which were major artistic triumphs, convinced the director that epic dramas could, in fact, draw audiences to the theater. "There is nothing like being caught in the spell of a story that spans hours of theatrical storytelling," Wilson revealed. "What I find interesting is that rarely do we in America invest resources around an American playwright telling an American story. It's usually the Greeks or a British writer. In a way, this is Horton's American Odyssey and his search for a home."[30] Initially, when Wilson approached Horton about the project, the playwright wasn't confident that such a massive endeavor could be accomplished. But since he had for years dreamed of seeing the entire cycle performed together, Horton eventually agreed to accept the commission from Hartford Stage in December 2007. At age ninety-one, Horton began to condense the nine plays into three segments, each of which could be performed in about three hours. As a whole, the plays follow the twenty-six year journey of Horace Robedaux, based on the writer's father, from displaced child to struggling young adult to family patriarch. The first segment, *The Story of a Childhood* (1902–11), includes the plays *Roots in a Parched Ground*, *Convicts*, and *Lily Dale* and follows Horace in his formative years: the death of his father, the young boy's encounter with death on a convict farm, and his estrangement from his mother and sister. The second segment, *The Story of a Marriage* (1912–17), consists of *The Widow Claire*, *Courtship*, and *Valentine's Day*, and focuses on Horace's search for a wife and the rejections, betrayals, neglect, and temptations he encounters until he finds the restorative love of Elizabeth Vaughn, the daughter of Harrison's richest and most prestigious citizen. The final part of the trilogy, *The Story of a Family* (1918–28), is made up of *1918*, *Cousins*, and *The Death of Papa*, and depicts Horace's rise from orphan to successful

---

[30] Frank Rizzo, "Michael Wilson Knows What He Likes," *American Theatre* (May/June 2009): 24.

businessman to family patriarch. Along the way he struggles with the influenza epidemic of 1918, the loss of a child, and the death of Elizabeth's father, but in the end Horace and Elizabeth look forward to the future of their family and community.

Each of these segments was intended to both stand alone or be presented together, but whether taken as a whole or over three performances, Horton's saga of three families responding to the social, economic, and moral changes in a small Texas town is transformative. Horton remarked that it was "incredibly moving to see all of these plays from my years of writing come together into the theatrical cycle that I've always envisioned."[31]

The most significant challenge facing Michael Wilson in the early stages of pre-production was the overall cost of staging *The Orphans' Home Cycle*. The production required a total of twenty-two actors to play seventy roles and an estimated budget of more than $1.5 million, an amount that the Hartford Stage Company could not bear alone. Even though Wilson was concerned about raising enough private donations to stage the show, he never expressed his fears to Horton, who continued to shape and mold the work that would eventually be his final legacy and the culmination of a lifelong dream. While Horton wrote, Wilson began discussions with several regional theaters he believed might share the financial burdens of the production. Unfortunately, after the Alley Theatre and Lincoln Center, who were both experiencing the harsh effects of the economic recession, turned Wilson down, the director's enthusiasm plummeted, but he never gave up on the project. He had learned well from his mentor, Horton Foote, about the difficulties of funding artistic projects and the need to persevere through lean times.

By early January 2009, Horton had completed work on the first six of the cycle plays, so Wilson organized a reading of the plays at Lincoln Center. While listening to the actors read his plays, Horton finally knew that staging the entire *Orphans' Home Cycle* was indeed possible. "That's when he realized the cumulative power of the plays as they built through that day," Michael Wilson remembered.[32] After the reading, Horton returned to Hartford, where he proceeded to finish the cycle with deliberate speed. He had completed work on the final segment just

---

[31] Adam Hetrick, "Horton's 'Orphans' Home Cycle' to Play Hartford Stage and NY's Signature,"*Playbill*, 21 January 2009.

[32] Michael Wilson, interview by Marion Castleberry, 14 May 2013, New York.

before he passed away, ten days before the scheduled reading of part three.

Among those present at the Lincoln Center reading was James Houghton, who had committed himself and the Signature Theatre to the project. Houghton and Wilson immediately began discussions about how to unite their resources in order to effectively bring the cycle to the stage. Within weeks, they announced that *The Orphans' Home Cycle* would be co-produced by Hartford Stage Company and the Signature Theatre, with performances running at Hartford from 27 August to 17 October 2009, and at the Signature Theatre Company from 29 October 2009 to 11 April 2010. The three segments of *The Orphans' Home Cycle* would be presented on alternating nights in repertory, as well as a few one-day marathons, during which the three segments would be performed consecutively in the morning, afternoon, and evening.

Ultimately, Horton's final gift to the theater was an epic work with both personal and universal appeal, and its production was a miraculous and stunning achievement. One of the most impressive and skillfully written works in all of dramatic literature, *The Orphans' Home Cycle* is Horton's acknowledged masterpiece. Only one other American writer, August Wilson, had ever completed such an ambitious and unprecedented cycle project, and Horton had longed to mount a stage production of the entire work ever since he first penned the plays in the 1970s. Sadly, he did not live to realize his dream, but those of us who were privileged to see this remarkable production were awed by its power and beauty. For all of us, the cycle took on both personal and universal significance. In telling the story of his family, Horton told the story of America, and we were compelled to agree with Robert Duvall that Horton was the great American voice.

John Simon, writing for *Bloomberg News,* called the cycle "absorbing and uplifting," and noted that it was "suffused with Horton's almost uncanny humanity in portraying besetting hardships and hard-won victories, disheartening letdowns and dogged loyalties."[33] Horton's work would go on to win the Outer Critics Circle Award for Outstanding New Off-Broadway Play, the New York Drama Critics' Circle Award for Best Play, and a special recognition from Drama Desk to the cast, creative team, and producers of Horton Foote's epic *The Orphans' Home Cycle.*

---

[33] John Simon, "Horton Foote's 'Orphans' Home Cycle' Must Be Seen," *Bloomberg News,* 6 February 2010.

While waiting for rehearsals to begin for *The Orphans' Home* cycle, Michael Wilson mounted a production of *To Kill a Mockingbird* that incorporated elements of Horton's screenplay into the stage production. Starring Emmy Award-winning actor Matthew Modine as Atticus Finch, Hallie Foote as the grownup Scout, Devon Abner as Arthur Boo Radley, Olivia Scott as Scout, Henry Hodges as Jem, and Andrew Shipman as Dill, the play was a huge success for Hartford Stage Company. When *To Kill a Mockingbird* opened on 19 February 2009, it had the largest advanced sale of any show in the history of Hartford Stage Company and provided a chance for more than five thousand schoolchildren to see the poignant, truth-filled story of the Finch family. Matthew Modine recalls that even though Horton was usually at home working on *The Orphans' Home Cycle*, his spirit permeated rehearsals for *To Kill a Mockingbird*:

> In my performance...I had to find a way on stage to experience the struggle of Atticus Finch as he confronts a formidable moral dilemma. Michael Wilson, the director of *To Kill a Mockingbird* and the artistic director of Hartford Stage, had incorporated features of Horton's film adaptation into the stage production. I found my inspiration for playing the role of Atticus, not in Gregory Peck's performance in the film, but in Horton Foote himself. Horton was strong and stoic, and was always on high moral ground, with his goodness, his sense of humor, and his sense of duty and responsibility to family. When I went to hear him speak at Hartford Stage during a public talk hosted by Michael Wilson, I told Horton that I needed to look only to him for my inspiration for Atticus Finch. After Horton saw the first performance of *To Kill a Mockingbird*, he told me that it was a triumph.[34]

Sadly, after attending the performance, Horton began to suffer mental and physical complications from severe dementia. He had always feared that he might end up like his father, brother, John, and Aunt Loula, who spent their final days suffering from Alzheimer's. And by late February, Horton began to experience the symptoms of depression, memory lapses, confusion, sleepwalking, and hallucinations. He visited three doctors, all of who suggested individual treatments, but as time passed, Horton grew more confused and depressed. Barbara Hallie believed that her father lost his will to carry on after the doctors told him his condition was incurable, and in the end, there was nothing anyone could do to prevent him from succumbing to the disease. "He really didn't want to

---

[34] Matthew Modine, "Untitled Essay," *Farewell: Remembering Horton Foote*, 145.

live if he couldn't write," Barbara Hallie remembers. "Towards the end, I could see that that was the ultimate struggle for him, particularly in the last few months. It was getting harder to do that, and not being able to write was the one thing that really puzzled him. Not having the writing be effortless."[35] Horton Foote died in the early morning of 4 March 2009, ten days before his ninety-third birthday.

That evening, as the lights were dimmed on Broadway, the cast of *To Kill a Mockingbird* held a brief memorial for Horton and dedicated the show to their mentor and friend. Matthew Modine remembers: "I spoke to the audience that night and…said that everything in the theatre begins with the word, and that Horton's words will always live, because he left us a great legacy of language, and he left the wonderful characters he had created for actors and directors to work with. We expressed our gratitude to Horton for all his work in the theatre, and acknowledged his daughter Hallie, who despite her tremendous loss, performed on the night of her father's passing. Hallie was brilliant in the play, and in her words, 'It's what he would have wanted me to do.'"[36]

A few days later, Horton's body was cremated, and later, in April, his family flew to Wharton to bury his ashes in the Wharton cemetery. A small private memorial service was held at Horton's Wharton home, with more than fifty close friends and family members attending. As the mourners crowded into the tiny parlor and dining room of the house, Horton's children sang hymns and read from their father's memoir, *Beginnings*, and from Mary Baker Eddy's *Science and Health with Keys to the Scriptures*. Robert Duvall also read a touching letter he had written to the man who had been his closest friend for more than fifty years:

> Dear Horton,
> At this time I would like to say goodbye to you. I believe a goodbye is only temporary and that there is or will be a connection that is a definite continuation. A continuation to whatever is next. Something we don't really know until it is experienced. But I do believe these things are to be. I have greatly appreciated your friendship during these many years. I have warm feelings when I remember how you always expressed your sincere affection for my wife Luciana. I remember when Luciana first met you at the film festival in Indianapolis. She and I were both captivated by your spoken word as well as your written words. After hearing your

---

[35] Hallie Foote, telephone interview by Marion Castleberry, 6 January 2013.
[36] Ibid.

wonderful stories, she later said, "Bobby it's like listening to Hemingway." There are many wonderful memories for the both of us.

M.B.E. [Mary Baker Eddy] says, "Every individual fills his own niche in time and Eternity." You have certainly filled your niche here on earth and I am certain that you will continue to do so in your eternal life. You have blessed many people worldwide with your gifts and we all stand here today with gratitude and love for what you've given us and I thank you for that.

Your friend,
Bobby Duvall[37]

The family had planned to bury Horton's ashes that afternoon, but a Gulf storm had hit Wharton the day before, dumping buckets of rain on the area and flooding the cemetery. Fortunately, the following day brought clear skies and sunshine, and a small group of friends and family members returned to the house, where they each scattered a handful of Horton's ashes around the trees in the backyard, trees that had been planted there by Horton's father when Horton was a baby. Later, at the cemetery, everyone shared memories of their friend, and the children buried the remainder of their father's ashes next to the grave of their beloved mother, Lillian.

A month later, on 11 May 2009, the Lincoln Center hosted a public memorial for Horton in the Vivian Beaumont Theatre. More than seven hundred friends and colleagues—actors, directors, producers, critics, and playwrights—crowded into the space to pay tribute to one of their own, a gifted man of the theater and one of the most beloved artists to ever grace the stage. Throughout the memorial, Horton's children, Horton Jr., Hallie, Walter, and Daisy, took turns at the podium sharing their memories and stories of Horton, and reminding us all that he was a writer whose work was a testament to the American family and the human spirit. In addition, actors who had worked with Foote over the years performed monologues and scenes from his dramas. Roberta Maxwell and Estelle Parsons performed their respective final speeches from *The Carpetbagger's Children* and *The Day Emily Married*, and Elizabeth Ashley presented a cutting from *Dividing the Estate*. Matthew Broderick acted out a scene from *Valentine's Day* he had performed both on stage and screen, Lois Smith and Devon Abner revisited the ending scene of *The Trip to Bountiful*, and Hallie Foote concluded the

---

[37] Robert Duvall, letter read at the Horton Foote memorial, April 2009, from the personal collection of Gerald C. Wood.

performances with a touching monologue from *A Coffin in Egypt*. Among the playwrights on hand were Edward Albee and Romulus Linney, who were joined by directors Michael Wilson, André Bishop, Casey Childs, Harris Yulin, and James Houghton. Houghton, who had organized the event, was the last to speak. "I just have to say Horton's smiling somewhere because he'd have loved this afternoon," he remarked. "This is what Horton lived for. He had a love affair with the theatre for over eighty years, and those of us who were blessed enough to spend a few blips in that eighty years with him will live forever in those memories." Houghton concluded by saying:

> When Horton and I were trying to put together [*The Last of the Thorntons*], I went down to visit him in Wharton, and he walked me through a cemetery just jam-packed with family, distant relatives, second cousins, third cousins, and he was introducing me to every character in his plays. I remember that moment so vividly resonating with how that cemetery was full of life, full of the things that make a rich life. Several weeks ago, many of us gathered in Wharton to lay Horton to rest in that very cemetery. And, as you might imagine, the gods cooperated. There were torrential rains and black umbrellas and, practically, floods on the streets of Wharton. The funeral itself had to be delayed. But I walked that cemetery again before I left, and I thought of Horton in the good company of his characters.[38]

Fittingly, Houghton left the final words to Horton himself, who appeared to the audience via a video that Signature Theatre had recorded to mark the playwright's ninetieth birthday. "At ninety years, it's rather comfortable," he admitted. "I don't have the panic I used to get and think, 'Well, when is it going to happen?' At that time, I was very curious because I'd felt, in some ways, I was an off-horse, that I had this obsessive interest in the South—my South—but I thought, 'What would I have done if I had never had this? What would I have done?' And a lot of people would have said, 'Well you've been a bloody fool, you know. You don't give yourself to something as chancy as theater,' but I never—I never..." Horton doesn't finish his thought before the video suddenly cuts to him singing "Blessed Assurance," the hymn his mother and grandmother sang to him as a child:

---

[38] James Houghton, speech delivered at the Horton Foote Memorial, 11 May 2009.

Blessed assurance, Jesus is mine!
Oh what a foretaste of glory divine!
Heir of salvation, purchase of God,
Born of his spirit, washed in his blood.

This is my story, this is my song,
praising my Savior all the day long;
this is my story, this is my song,
praising my Savior all the day long.

The words of the old hymn were left hanging in the air, as if there was more Horton wanted to say but didn't. Suddenly, the audience arose from their seats giving Horton Foote one last sustaining ovation.

The indelible image of Horton singing "Blessed Assurance" continues to linger in the hearts and minds of those who loved him, assuring everyone that his words and stories will live on in perpetuity. But more than that, there was a feeling that Horton had personally acknowledged the spirituality of his life and work, and in singing the hymn he somehow reassured us that a greater, more comforting home awaited him. My wife Terri best summed it up when after the memorial she remarked: "Now I know there will be theater in Heaven because Horton is there."

"Things Have Ends and Beginnings."[39]

---

[39] Foote, *Genesis*, 95.

Conclusion

A Legacy

On 14 March 2016, Horton Foote would have celebrated his one-hundredth birthday. And he would have commemorated the event during one of the most active and rewarding decades of his career, one that saw a national award for playwrights established in his name, a foundation launched to promote his legacy and support the writing of young playwrights, and the resurgence of his works in theater productions throughout the nation. After Horton's death, *The Orphans' Home Cycle* played to appreciative audiences at Hartford Stage and Signature Theatre and *Dividing the Estate* performed in New York, Hartford, Houston, and San Diego—receiving a Tony nomination in 2009. In 2012, *Harrison, Texas*—consisting of Horton's one-acts *Blind Date*, *The One-Armed Man*, and *Midnight Caller*—ran for a month at New York's Primary Stages under the direction of Tony Award-winning Pam MacKinnon. The popular and critical success of *Harrison, Texas* set the stage for three more productions: the Signature Theatre's production of *The Old Friends* (2013), starring Hallie Foote, Lois Smith, and Betty Buckley; a film of the *The One-Armed Man*, directed by Tim Guinee, and starring Terry Kinney, John Magaro, and Charles Haid (2014); and the Broadway revival of *The Trip to Bountiful* at the Stephen Sondheim Theatre, for which legendary actress, Cicely Tyson, at age eighty-eight, won a Tony Award. Director Michael Wilson explained how the revival of *The Trip to Bountiful*, which was originally performed sixty years earlier (1953) at the Henry Miller Theatre (later named the Stephen Sondheim Theatre), was conceived:

> After Horton's death, there was something unfulfilled about our production of *Bountiful* in Connecticut. It is such a rich play, the kind as a director that you would love to return to again and again. So when Hallie approached me in 2011 and asked what I thought about the play being centered on an African-American family as opposed to a white family, I thought it was a marvelous idea. Carrie Watts would have to be played by someone with luminosity and legacy—someone like Cicely Tyson, whose performances in *Roots* and *The Autobiography of Miss Jane Pittman* made such an indelible mark on me in my childhood. We finally got the script to Cicely [and] as it turned out, Pete Masterson's film of *The Trip to*

Bountiful had made a strong impact on Cicely, as it had on me. Hallie, Cicely, and I met over dinner in September, and after a whirlwind six months, we were beginning previews at the Stephen Sondheim Theatre.

Everyone in our company feels that this is the moment to bring *The Trip to Bountiful* back to Broadway for the first time in sixty years. Our nation needs to experience this story. We need to consider the themes that Horton is exploring: that if we don't honor the past—the places, the people, the communities from where we've come—we are in danger of losing the very essence of ourselves. *The Trip to Bountiful* reminds us that as we strive to live in a high-tech world that is increasingly isolating and discombobulating from the constant motion and stimuli, if we can somehow stop and truly connect with our family legacy, we can bring ourselves "home" again, and with that re-found center, find the means to endure life's inevitable disappointment and unwanted change.[1]

As Wilson had hoped, the 2013 Broadway production of *The Trip to Bountiful* was brilliantly conceived and skillfully performed, capturing both the spirit and meaning of Horton's enduring masterpiece. The impressive cast, made up of Cicely Tyson, Vanessa Williams, Cuba Gooding, Jr., Condola Rashad, and Tom Wopat, gave stirring and powerful performances. Cicely Tyson's portrayal of Carrie Watts was especially moving as she portrayed the character's fragility, courage, and inner strength with remarkable honesty and authenticity. Her understanding of the spiritual nature of Carrie Watts's journey is best seen during the second bus station scene, a scene most often overlooked by actors and directors, when Carrie remembers the dances she attended as a girl in Harrison and then begins singing her favorite hymns. Thelma, Carrie's traveling companion, is initially mortified but before long she, and everyone else in the station, joins the old woman in musical praise, a tribute to God and Jesus and a final reclamation of who they are and where they belong. This moment was so inspiring that at almost every performance the audience insisted on joining Carrie Watts in song and then cheering her when she finally reaches the front porch of her crumbling old house. Cicely Tyson communicates the wit, the wisdom, the simplicity, and the spirituality of Carrie Watts like few actresses before her, and under the sensitive direction of Michael Wilson the production proved that Horton's story of Carrie Watts could not only

---

[1] Michael Wilson, "Director Michael Wilson on Dinners With the Foote Family & Falling in Love with The Trip to Bountiful," *Broadway.com*, 7 May 2013, http://www.broadway.com/buzz/169334/director-michael-wilson-on-dinners-with-the-foote-family-falling-in-love-with-the-trip-to-bountiful/.

transcend cultural and racial boundaries, serving as a mirror for the black experience of the 1950s, but it could also connect with a new generation of theater-goers seeking their own way home. The enormous success of the Broadway production of *The Trip to Bountiful* spawned a made-for-television movie of the play, which aired on Lifetime on 8 March 2014. Produced by Ostar Productions, the film starred Cicely Tyson, Blair Underwood, Vanessa Williams, and Keke Palmer and was directed by Michael Wilson. The movie is a beautiful and faithful rendition of Horton Foote's moving story.

Horton once told me the only thing he really cared about was that his plays would be performed after he died. If *The Trip to Bountiful* is any indication of how Horton's plays will be received in the future, I have no doubt that his work will continue to resonate with audiences for years to come.

For seventy years, Horton Foote committed his life to telling seemingly simple, yet profound stories of family and community with his own deeply felt sense of truth and integrity. There are only a few American writers of the past century—William Faulkner and August Wilson come to mind—whose reliance on a sense of place rivaled that of Horton Foote. Throughout his life, Horton carried a deep love and reverence for his home place, the small town of Wharton, Texas, and that powerful connection fueled his writing. The oral history of his family and his hometown of Wharton provided Horton with a treasure trove of plots and characters for his art and served as a valuable tool to explore the great mysteries of existence. As Gerald Wood and Laurin Porter have shown, Horton wrote "real fiction," works that consist of "thousands of things that did happen to living human beings in a certain part of the country at a certain time…things that are still remembered by others as single incidents."[2] However, Horton was not merely a local colorist nor was he sentimental about life in a small town. He believed that an artist must be a truth searcher, and that to arrive at truth he must fashion the history and stories of his region into plays with both personal and universal resonance. He used his Wharton materials to create the Harrison, Texas, of his imagination, and as Wood adds, "in order to meet the demands of his fictional place, he redesigned real stories so that they took the shape and nature of myth." He crafted them "into tales of going

---

[2] Flannery O'Connor, *Mystery and Manners*, ed. Sally and Robert Fitzgerald (New York: Farrar, Straus & Giroux, 1957) xiii.

away and coming home, grief and rebirth, freedom and fate, despair and healing."[3]

Horton was always foraging around in his ancestral garden, re-harvesting familial tales, examining them from many varied points of view, contemporizing them, breaking them down and interpreting them anew in an attempt to illuminate the beliefs and values embedded within them. He strongly believed in the power of story not only to enlighten individuals but also to tie a nation together by rediscovering its myths and legends, expressing its deepest ideals and aspirations, and reaffirming the significant connections between us all. Marian Burkhart has declared that, "Horton Foote has assessed American character, American myth, and American ambiance more accurately than just about any other figure in the American theatre."[4] In short, Horton believed that drama could be a healing force in the world, and during his career he touched the lives of more people than we can ever know.

With an amazing eye for the detail of characters' lives and the violence that lay beneath the ordinary surface of his creations, Horton captured the reality and significance of small-town America with a depth and honesty that will never be matched. While he repeatedly denied any conscious pursuit of ideas in his plays and films, even a cursory look at Horton's writing reveals his deeply spiritual view of human experience. The themes of his work are compelling and thought-provoking: the eternal search for home, the courage and resilience of some people in the face of unimaginable hardship and suffering, and the mysterious nature of family relationships. But Horton's real genius was in his ability to create authentic language and memorable characters. Horton was a master at translating the simple, stark vernacular and inconsequential small talk of Gulf Coast Texas into a language of transcendence. He allowed us to join him in witnessing ordinary folks—people we recognize, people we know intimately—at crucial moments in their lives. Their struggles intrigue us, and their ability to face heartbreak and sorrow with courage and dignity inspires us.

Not only did Horton record the lives and times of the inhabitants of Harrison, Texas, with realistic accuracy and detail, he also called attention to our national failures and shortcomings, to the loss of history,

---

[3] Wood, Introduction to *Selected One-Act Plays of Horton Foote,* ed. Gerald C. Wood (Dallas TX: Southern Methodist University Press, 1989) vi.

[4] Marian Burkhart, "Horton Foote's Many Roads Home: An American Playwright and his Characters," *Commonweal* (26 February 1988): 110–15.

community, and religious sensibility in twentieth-century American life. He wrote in reaction to the spiritual barrenness that he saw haunting our world. His characters, whether they know it or not, are all orphans driven by the need to connect with something beyond themselves: a home, a family, a community, or God. Horton's aesthetic is best defined by Robert Ellerman, who calls the playwright an "artist of spiritual transcendence":

> His characters are the conflicts of the soul struggling for inner peace. At the center of his plays is loneliness, loss, grief, courage, and love: the existential state of our common humanity. The elemental through-action of Horton Foote's world is Beckett's "I can't go on...I will go on." The conflicts between characters in a Foote play are rarely motivated by the egotism we label "success" and "failure." His creations are on a path of action which inspires all of the world's great religions. These men and women are seeking the experience we call God. To be enlightened, they are willing to face the divine nothingness of reality and the "infinite within" of the human spirit.... The theatre of the soul's imagination is the place to experience Horton Foote's transcendental art. To borrow from Eva Le Gallienne's tribute to Eleonora Duse, Horton Foote is our "mystic in the theatre."[5]

Horton's saddest characters—like Henry Thomas, Bubber Reeves, Brother Vaughn, Soll Gautier, Josie Weems—never come to understand the power of such benevolent attachments and often live out their lives in violent despair. On the other hand, Horton's strongest and most courageous characters—such as Carrie Watts, Mac Sledge, Horace Robedaux, Elizabeth Vaugh, Will Kidder, and Leonard Toliver— recognize their need for intimacy, forgiveness, and final sacrifice to life's divine mystery. Horton's commitment to such Christian verities as compassion, reconciliation, forgiveness, acceptance, and love for one's neighbor distinguishes his work from other writers and secures him a unique place in American theater.

While Horton never garnered the attention afforded other American playwrights, such as Eugene O'Neill, Arthur Miller, or Tennessee Williams, he has nevertheless been called the "greatest American playwright of the last century." Brooke Allen, critic for *The New Criterion*, explains:

---

[5] Robert Ellerman, Introduction to *Horton Foote: Collected Plays* (Lyme NH: Smith and Kraus, 1993) vi.

His work suffers from none of the limitations that have marred even the best of his peers. Eugene O'Neill had no ear for language, and was unforgivably self-indulgent in his refusal to edit; Foote seldom misplaced a phrase or an intonation. Arthur Miller delivered solid melodramas with neatly packaged moral messages, all totally lacking in humor. A view of life that does not include humor is an incomplete one. In Foote, as in Chekhov (with whom he is often compared), tragedy and comedy are not separate entities but are inextricably blended through all of life's trials. And where Miller was heavily didactic Foote was the opposite: nowhere in all his sixty plays and screenplays can one find a line as obvious or as nakedly declarative as Mrs. Willy Loman's famous "Attention must be paid.... Attention, attention, must finally be paid to such a person." Foote knew nobody talks like that. Tennessee Williams, a longtime friend and admirer of Foote's, knew it too, but his plays examined the pathological where Foote's turned to the universal.[6]

Horton was a remarkable man whose extraordinary talents were matched only by his deep and abiding humanity. One of his greatest virtues was his deep love and respect for people and his ability to look beyond the external façade of an individual to the emotional core of his or her being. He possessed a simplicity and directness that both charmed everyone he met and made all of us look at the hard truth about ourselves. He was the very essence of kindness, generosity, and grace. He was a devoted family man who loved his wife and children deeply, and those who knew him well and worked with him admired him as both a writer of immense talent and as a sensitive and loyal friend. During his lifetime he inspired people from all professions and walks of life—writers, directors, artists, students, teachers, and scholars. He was especially loved by actors, such as Lillian Gish, Geraldine Page, Robert Duvall, Gregory Peck, Jean Stapleton, Ellen Burstyn, and Lois Smith, who were privileged enough to embody his wonderful creations. While actors adored Horton, he loved and respected them. When working on a show, he was an inspiring and powerful presence and seldom missed a rehearsal or performance. The late playwright Romulus Linney recalled that Horton was once asked by a fellow dramatist what he imagined heaven might be like. Horton responded, "I think it will be like rehearsal."[7] That's how much he enjoyed the process of making theater,

---

[6] Brooke Allen, "Horton Foote's Staying Power," *The New Criterion* [London] (5 September 2012): 2.

[7] Romulus Linney, interview by Marion Castleberry, 20 October 2005, Waco, Texas.

of working with actors, and I, for one, am gratified to have had the opportunity to enjoy that process with him.

Whenever I think of Horton, I am always taken aback by the richness and longevity of his career, and I am emboldened by his courage to endure times of disappointment and economic hardship. Even in his darkest moments, when no one seemed to want to produce his work, Horton never forgot his calling; he never stopped writing; he never compromised his vision. He remained true to his original quest: to write a moral and social history of a small Texas town and its people. From the first play to the last, Horton remained true to his vision, compassionately depicting the joys and heartbreaks of small-town America with an impressive delicacy and understated intensity that was remarkable in its consistency.

If the true measure of a man is, in fact, defined by what he leaves behind, then Horton has left behind not only a rich and remarkable legacy of plays and characters well worth exploring but also a community of people tied together by their love for Horton, the man, and their respect for his truthful vision of the human condition. The world has been blessed and will continue to be blessed by Horton Foote's gentle and compassionate voice, his insight and wisdom, his honesty and integrity, and his incredible courage and grace.

As I reflect upon Horton Foote's career and writings, I am finally reminded of a passage from William Humphrey's *The Ordways*. The past "lives in that book of books," Humphrey wrote, "that collection transmitted orally from father to son of proverbs and prophesies, legends, laws, traditions of the origins, and tales of the wanderings of his own tribe. For it is this…feeling of identity with his dead which characterizes and explains the Southerner. In his time, he is priest of the tribal scripture, to forget any part would be sacrilege. He treasures the sayings of his kin…. If he forgets them, he will be forgotten. If he remembers, he will be remembered, will take the place reserved and predestined for him in the company of his kin, in the realm of myth, outside of time."[8] Horton always remembered, and because he did, his words will live on in perpetuity, testifying to the beauty, brutality, and mystery of life.

Now that the final curtain has fallen on Horton's extraordinary life and career, we who loved him know the applause for his work will go on forever and that he will continue to inspire audiences the world over for

---

[8] William Humphrey, *The Ordways* (New York: Alfred Knopf, 1964).

years to come. There is no doubt that Horton Foote's name will be recorded in the annals of American theater as one of the greatest, if not the greatest, playwright of this or any other generation.

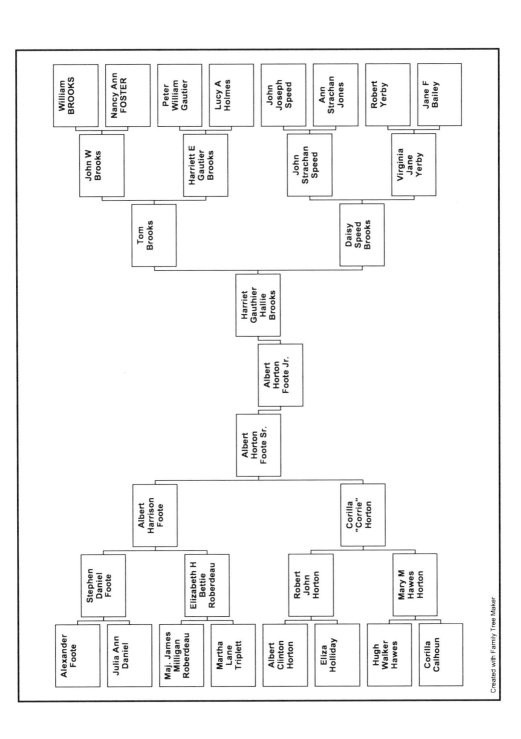

Created with Family Tree Maker

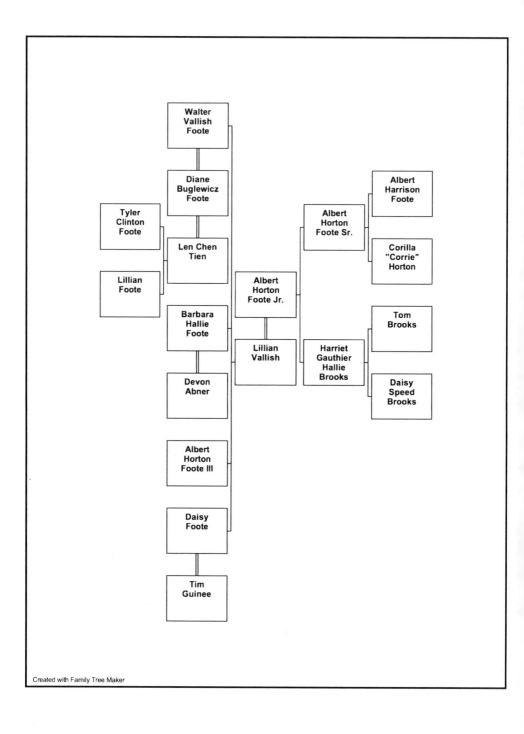

Walter Vallish Foote

Diane Buglewicz Foote

Tyler Clinton Foote

Len Chen Tien

Lillian Foote

Barbara Hallie Foote

Albert Horton Foote Jr.

Devon Abner

Lillian Vallish

Albert Horton Foote III

Daisy Foote

Tim Guinee

Albert Horton Foote Sr.

Albert Harrison Foote

Corilla "Corrie" Horton

Harriet Gauthier Hallie Brooks

Tom Brooks

Daisy Speed Brooks

Chronology

1916   Born 14 March 1916 in Wharton, Texas, to Albert Horton Foote and Harriet Gautier Brooks Foote

1932   Graduated from Wharton High School

1933–35 Studied acting at Pasadena Playhouse in California

1936–42 Worked as an actor in New York; trained with Tamara Daykarhanova, Andrius Jilinsky, Maria Ouspenskaya, and Vera Soloviova (1937–39); Joined the American Actors Company (1939)

1940   *Wharton Dance* produced by American Actors Company

1941   *Texas Town* produced by American Actors Company

1942   *Only the Heart* produced by American Actors Company at Provincetown Playhouse, New York

1944   *Only the Heart* produced on Broadway by American Actors Company, starring Mildred Dunnock and June Walker; Wrote briefly for Universal Studios in Hollywood, California; *Daisy Lee*, a dance play, choreographed and performed by Valerie Bettis; *Miss Lou, In My Beginning, The Lonely* (choreographed by Martha Graham), and *Goodbye to Richmond* produced at the Neighborhood Playhouse

1945   Married Lillian Vallish on 4 June 1945

1945–49 Moved to Washington, DC; taught at King-Smith School; wrote *Homecoming, People in the Show, Celebration, The Return, Themes and Variations,* and *The Chase*

1949   Returned from Washington, DC to New York City

1950–51 Barbara Hallie Foote born 31 March 1950; Wrote for *The Gabby Hayes Show* (also called *The Quaker Oats Show*); Ludie Brooks presented on NBC's *Lamp Unto My Feet* (1951)

1952   *The Chase* produced on Broadway by José Ferrer, starring John Hodiak, Kim Hunter, and Kim Stanley; Albert Horton Foote, III, born 7 November 1952

1952–64 Television plays presented by Philco-Goodyear Playhouse, Studio One, Gulf Playhouse, Playhouse 90, DuPont Play of the Month, and US Steel Hour include: *The Travelers* (1952), *Expectant Relations* (1953), *The Old Beginning* (1953), *The Trip to Bountiful* (1953), *The Death of the Old Man*

(1953), *The Tears of My Sister* (1953), *The Dancers* (1954), *The Oil Well* (1953), *A Young Lady of Property* (1953), *John Turner Davis* (1953), *The Midnight Caller* (1953), *The Dancers* (1954), *The Shadow of Will Greer* (1954), *The Roads to Home* (1955), *Flight* (1956), *Drugstore, Sunday Noon* (1956), *A Member of the Family* (1957), *Old Man* (1960), *Tomorrow* (1960), *The Shape of the River* (1960), *The Night of the Storm* (1961), and *The Gambling Heart* (1964)

1953   *The Trip to Bountiful* produced on Broadway by the Theatre Guild, starring Lillian Gish, Jo Van Fleet, and Eva Marie Saint

1954   *The Traveling Lady* produced on Broadway by the Playwrights Producing Company and Roger Stevens, starring Kim Stanley and Lonny Chapman

1955   Walter Vallish Foote born 4 December 1955

1956   *Harrison, Texas: Eight Television Plays* published by Harcourt Brace; *The Midnight Caller* and *John Turner Davis* produced by Sheridan Square Playhouse, New York City; Worked on first screenplay, *Storm Fear*, for United Artists; *The Chase*, a novel, published by Rinehart & Company; Moved from New York City to Nyack, New York

1959   Daisy Brooks Foote born 3 July 1959

1962   *To Kill a Mockingbird* produced by Alan Pakula and Universal Studios. Foote received an Academy Award for Best Screenplay, and the Writers Guild of America Screen Award for his adaptation of Harper Lee's novel. Gregory Peck won an Oscar for Best Actor; *The Trip to Bountiful* produced by Greenwich Mews Theatre in New York City

1965–66 *Baby, the Rain Must Fall*, screenplay based on Foote's original play *The Traveling Lady*, produced by Alan Pakula for Columbia Pictures, starring Steve McQueen and Lee Remick

1965   *The Chase*, screenplay by Lillian Hellman based on novel and original play by Horton Foote, produced by Sam Spiegel and starring Marlon Brando, Robert Redford, Jane Fonda, Angie Dickinson, and Robert Duvall; *Hurry Sundown*, commissioned adaptation of K.G. Glidden's novel, directed by Otto Preminger; Moved from Nyack, New York, to New Hampshire

1968   *The Stalking Moon*, commissioned screenplay, produced by Warner Brothers; *Tomorrow*, adapted from a short story by William Faulkner, produced by HB Playwrights Foundation, featuring Robert Duvall

1973–74 Musical adaptation of *Gone with the Wind* performed in London and Los Angeles; *Tomorrow*, film adaptation of William Faulkner story, produced by Paul Roebling and Gilbert Pearlman, featuring Robert Duvall and Olga Bellin (1973–74); Father, Albert Horton Foote, passed away (23 March 1973).

1974–77   Mother, Hallie Brooks Foote, passed away 19 February 1974; Wrote *The Orphans' Home Cycle: Roots in a Parched Ground, Convicts, Widow Claire, Lily Dale, Courtship, Valentine's Day, 1918, Cousins,* and *The Death of Papa; A Young Lady of Property* produced by HB Playwrights Foundation, New York City (1976); *Night Seasons* produced by HB Playwrights Foundation, New York City (1977)

1977–81   Adapted Flannery O'Connor's *The Displaced Person* (1977) and William Faulkner's *Barn Burning* (1980) for the American Short Story series on PBS television; *Courtship* produced by HB Playwrights Foundation (1978); *1918* produced by HB Playwrights Foundation (1979); *Valentine's Day* produced by HB Playwrights Foundation (1980); *A Coffin in Egypt* produced by HB Playwrights Foundation, starring Sandy Dennis (1980); Became member of the Ensemble Studio Theatre

1982   *The Roads to Home,* three one-act plays: *A Nightingale, The Dearest of Friends,* and *Spring Dance*—presented at Manhattan Punch Line Theatre, New York City; *The Old Friends* produced by HB Playwrights Foundation; *The Man Who Climbed the Pecan Trees* and *Blind Date* performed at Loft Theatre, Los Angeles, California

1983   *Tender Mercies,* starring Robert Duvall and directed by Bruce Beresford, garnered an Academy Award for Best Original Screenplay, a Writers Guild of America Award, and a Christopher Award for Horton Foote as well as an Academy Award for Best Actor for Robert Duvall. *Cousins* produced by Loft Theatre, Los Angeles; *Keeping On: A Drama of Life in a Mill Town,* teleplay produced for PBS's American Playhouse

1984   *Courtship* produced by Actors Theatre of Louisville, Kentucky

1985   Beginning of independent film production; *1918,* original screenplay based on *The Orphans' Home Cycle,* released starring Hallie Foote, William Converse-Roberts, and Matthew Broderick. Film shown at the Taormina Festival in Italy; *The Trip to Bountiful,* the film, was released, with Geraldine Page, who won the Academy Award for Best Actress. Foote nominated for the Academy Award for Best Screenplay Adaptation; *The Road to the Graveyard,* a one-act play, produced by the Ensemble Studio Theatre; *Blind Date, The One-Armed Man,* and *The Prisoner's Song* produced by HB Playwrights Foundation

1986   *On Valentine's Day,* original screenplay based on *The Orphans' Home Cycle,* released, starring Hallie Foote, Matthew Broderick, and William

Converse-Roberts. Official American entry in the Venice Film Festival, the Toronto Film Festival, and the US Film Festival; *Courtship*, screenplay based on *The Orphans' Home Cycle* play, released starring Hallie Foote, William Converse-Roberts, and Amanda Plummer; *Blind Date* presented at Ensemble Studio Theatre. The play was included in The Best Short Plays of 1988–89; *The Widow Claire* presented off Broadway at Circle in the Square Theatre, New York; included in *The Best Plays of 1986–87*; *Lily Dale* presented off Broadway at the Samuel Beckett Theatre, New York; *The Trip to Bountiful* shown at the Edinburgh Festival

1987   *The Story of a Marriage*, a five-part series based on *Courtship, Valentine's Day*, and *1918*, produced by PBS television for American Playhouse; Films honored at the Galveston Film Festival, Galveston, Texas

1988   *The Man Who Climbed the Pecan Trees* produced by Ensemble Studio Theatre; *The Habitation of Dragons* premiered at the Pittsburgh Public Theatre, directed by Horton Foote and featuring Marco St. John and Hallie Foote; Elected to the Fellowship of Southern Writers; *Roots in a Parched Ground, Convicts, Lily Dale*, and *The Widow Claire*, all part of *The Orphan's Home Cycle*, published

1989   *Dividing the Estate* presented at McCarter Theatre, Princeton, New Jersey

1990   *Convicts*, screenplay based on *The Orphans' Home Cycle*, released starring Robert Duvall and James Earl Jones; *Talking Pictures* premiered at the Asolo Performing Arts Center in Sarasota, Florida (performed at Stages Theatre in Houston, Texas, in 1991); *Dividing the Estate* performed at the Great Lakes Theatre Festival; *The Trip to Bountiful* performed by A.D. Players (Houston, Texas) and Zachary Scott Theatre (Austin, Texas); *The Man Who Climbed the Pecan Trees* published in *The Best American Short Plays* and presented at Applause Theatre in New York; *Of Mice and Men*, film adaptation of novel by John Steinbeck, released, starring Gary Sinise and John Malkovich; *The Trip to Bountiful* presented by Actors Theatre of Louisville, Kentucky, and New Harmony Theatre, Indiana; *Talking Pictures* presented by Stages Theatre, Houston, Texas

1992   Habitation of Dragons, TNT teleplay for Steven Spielberg Productions; *The Roads to Home* produced by Lambs Theatre, New York; *The Trip to Bountiful* presented at a theater festival in Perth, Australia; *Convicts, Courtship*, and *1918* presented by A.C.T. Theatre (San Francisco) as part of "A Great Day with Horton Foote" Celebration; Lillian Foote passed away in August.

1993   *Night Seasons* produced by American Stage Company, Teaneck, New Jersey; *The Trip to Bountiful* presented at TheatreFest (Upper Montclair,

New Jersey) and The Phoenix Theatre Company (Purchase, New York); *The Widow Claire* included in *The Best American Plays of 1983–1992*; 1994–95*Talking Pictures* (September 1994), *Night Seasons* (November 1994), *The Young Man from Atlanta* (January 1995), and *Laura Dennis* (March 1995) produced by Signature Theatre, New York; Brigham Young University hosted Horton Foote Festival of films and plays, Provo, Utah (Spring 1995); Received Pulitzer Prize for Drama for *The Young Man from Atlanta* (1995); *The Young Man from Atlanta* produced by Huntington Theatre (Boston), and Alley Theatre (Houston), directed by Peter Masterson, starring Ralph Waite and Carlin Glynn (1995); *Tender Mercies* published in *The Best American Screenplays of 1994–1995*; *The Young Man from Atlanta* published in *The Best Plays of 1994–1995*

1996   *Lily Dale*, film version of *The Orphans' Home Cycle* play, presented by Showtime on June 9, starring Mary Stuart Masterson, Tim Guinee, Sam Shepard, and Stockard Channing; Inducted into the Theatre Hall of Fame (22 January 1996)

1997   *The Young Man from Atlanta* restaged in January by Robert Falls, with Shirley Knight and Rip Torn, for Goodman Theatre, Chicago, and in March at the Longacre Theatre, New York; *The Death of Papa* produced by Playmakers Repertory Theatre, Chapel Hill, North Carolina, directed by Michael Wilson, and starring Ellen Burstyn, Matthew Broderick, Polly Holliday, and Hallie Foote; *Alone*, original teleplay, presented on Showtime and starring Hume Cronyn, James Earl Jones, Piper Laurie, Frederick Forest, Shelly Duvall, and Hallie Foote; *Old Man*, adaptation of William Faulkner's short story, produced by CBS Hallmark Hall of Fame, starring Jeanne Tripplehorn and Arliss Howard. The production received Emmy Award for Outstanding Writing for a Miniseries or a Special and the Christopher Award for adaptation; *Vernon Early*, radio broadcast for Chicago Theatre on the Air, starring Mary Beth Fisher, Frederick Forrest, and Hallie Foote

1998   *A Coffin in Egypt* produced by Bay Street Theatre Festival (Sag Harbor, New York), directed by Leonard Foglia and starring Glynis Johns; *Vernon Early* produced by Alabama Shakespeare Festival (Montgomery, Alabama), directed by Charles Towers and starring Jill Tanner and Philip Pleasants

1999   *The Death of Papa* produced by Hartford Stage (Hartford, Connecticut), directed by Michael Wilson and starring Jean Stapleton, Dana Ivey, Andrew McCarthy, Frankie Munis, Hallie Foote, and Devon Abner; *Farewell — A Memoir of a Texas Childhood* published by Scribners Press

2000   *The Last of the Thorntons* produced by Signature Theatre, New York,
       starring Hallie Foote, Estelle Parsons, Jen Jones, Mason Adams, and
       Michael Hadge; Received National Medal of Arts from President Bill
       Clinton; *The Carpetbagger's Children* produced by the Alley Theatre
       (Houston), Guthrie Theatre (Minneapolis), and Hartford Stage, starring
       Hallie Foote, Jean Stapleton, and Roberta Maxwell; *Beginnings*
       published by Scribner Press

2002   *The Actor* produced at the Royal National Theatre, London, England;
       The Carpetbagger's Children presented at the Mitzi E. Newhouse, Lincoln
       Center Theatre, directed by Michael Wilson and starring Hallie Foote,
       Jean Stapleton, and Roberta Maxwell; *Getting Frankie Married—And
       Afterwards* produced by South Coast Repertory Theatre, starring Nan
       Martin and Juliana Donald; *The Prisoner's Song* presented at the
       Ensemble Studio Theatre, directed by Harris Yulin and starring Mary
       Catherine Garrison, Tim Guinee, Marceline Hugot, and Michael Moran;
       Named "Visiting Distinguished Dramatist" by Baylor University, Waco,
       Texas, and joined Theatre Arts faculty

2003   *The Actor* presented at the ACT Conservatory (San Francisco); The
       fiftieth-anniversary production of *The Trip to Bountiful* presented by
       Hartford Stage and Alley Theatre, directed by Michael Wilson and
       starring Dee Maaske, Hallie Foote, and Devon Abner

2004   Inaugural Horton Foote American Playwrights Festival at Baylor
       University, Waco, Texas, March 3–6. The fiftieth-anniversary
       production of *The Traveling Lady* performed at the festival. The play was
       directed by Marion Castleberry and starred Margot White, Stan
       Denman, Jamie Bennett, Cynthia Sanders, Mary Jane Vandevier, Brenda
       Ballard, and Bettye Fitzpatrick; *The Day Emily Married* premiered at
       Primary Stages (New York City) in August. The play was directed by
       Michael Wilson and starred Hallie Foote, Biff McGuire, and Estelle
       Parsons.

2005   *The Trip to Bountiful* performed at the Signature Theatre (New York
       City) in November. The play, directed by Harris Yulin and starring Lois
       Smith, Hallie Foote, James DeMarse, and Devon Abner, received a
       Drama Desk nomination for "Best Revival" and a Lortel Award for
       "Outstanding Revival."

2006   *The Traveling Lady* performed at the Ensemble Studio Theatre. Directed
       by Marion Castleberry and starred Rochelle Oliver, Carol Goodheart,
       Alice McLain, Lynn Cohen, Stan Denman, Jamie Bennett, Matthew
       Conlon, Frank Girardeau, and Margot White. The play was nominated
       by Drama Desk for "Best Revival."

2007   *Dividing the Estate* debuted at Primary Stages. The play was directed by
        Michael Wilson and starred Hallie Foote, Devon Abner, Elizabeth
        Ashley, Penny Fuller, Pat Bowie, Arthur French, Maggie Lacy, Keiana
        Richard, Nicole Lowrance, Jenny Dare Paulin, James DeMarse, Virginia
        Kull, and Gerald McRaney. The production earned Foote an OBIE
        Award and an Outer Critics Award for "Outstanding Off-Broadway
        Play."

2008   Lincoln Center Theatre, in association with Primary Stages, presented
        Dividing the Estate on Broadway; The Goodman Theatre produced the
        Horton Foote Festival, featuring the production of four plays—*The Trip
        to Bountiful, Talking Pictures, The Actor,* and *Blind Date*; The Horton Foote
        Center for the Study of Theater and Film opened at Carson-Newman
        College, Jefferson City, Tennessee.

2009–11 Horton Foote died on 4 March 2009 in Harford, Connecticut, while
        writing a new adaptation of *The Orphans' Home Cycle* in three parts:
        "The Story of a Childhood," "The Story of a Marriage," and "The Story
        of a Family." Hartford Stage Company and the Signature Theatre co-
        produced *The Orphans' Home Cycle*. The cycle was directed by Michael
        Wilson and starred Devon Abner, James DeMarse, Hallie Foote, Bill
        Heck, Annalee Jefferies, Maggie Lacy, Stephen Plunkett, Pat Bowie,
        Leon Addison Brown, Justin Fuller, Jasmine Ami Harrison, Henry
        Hodges, Georgi James, Virginia Kull, Matt Mulhern, Gilbert Owuor,
        Jenny Dare Paulin, Bryce Pinkham, Lucas Caleb Rooney, Dylan Riley
        Snyder, Charles Turner, and Pamela Payton-Wright; *Dividing the Estate*
        was nominated for a Tony Award; *Main Street* premiered September
        2011, produced by 1984 Films and Annapurna Productions, directed by
        John Doyle, and starring Colin Firth, Ellen Burstyn, and Patricia
        Clarkson

2012–13 *Harrison, Texas—Blind Date, The One-Armed Man,* and *The Midnight
        Caller*—were produced by Primary Stages. The three plays were
        directed by Pam MacKinnon and starred Hallie Foote, Devon Abner,
        Mary Bacon, Jeremy Bobb, Alexander Candese, Andrea Green, Jayne
        Houdyshell, Evan Jonigkeit, and Jenny Dare Paulin; The sixtieth-
        anniversary revival of *The Trip to Bountiful* opened at the Stephen
        Sondheim Theatre. The production was directed by Michael Wilson and
        starred Cicily Tyson, Vanessa William, Tom Wopat, Devon Abner, and
        Cuba Gooding, Jr. Cicily Tyson was awarded a Tony Award for Best
        Actress; World premiere production of *The Old Friends* opened at the
        Signature Theatre. The play was directed by Michael Wilson and starred
        Hallie Foote, Lois Smith, and Betty Buckley.

2014   *The One-Armed Man,* a film version of Foote's one-act play of the same
        name, premiered at the SXSW Festival in Austin, Texas. The film,
        directed by Tim Guinee and starring Terry Kinney, John Magaro, and
        Charles Haid, was produced by Phillip Seymour Hoffman, Hallie Foote,
        Rex Camphuis, Ruben Garcia, Tim Guinee, and Bruno Michels; *The Trip
        to Bountiful,* an original television movie for Lifetime, aired on 8 March
        2014. The movie, directed by Michael Wilson, starred Cicely Tyson,
        Vanessa Williams, Blair Underwood, and Keke Palmer.

Bibliography

Alexander, W.F.S. *Last Will and Testament*, 30 March 1879. Wharton TX: Wharton County Courthouse.

Allen, Brooke. "Horton Foote's Staying Power." *The New Criterion* (5 September 2012): 2–5.

Ankor, Roy M. *Catching Light: Looking for God in the Movies*. Grand Rapids MI: Eerdmans Publishing, 2004.

Balcom, Louis. "Review: 'Daisy Lee' by Horton Foote." *The Dance Observer*, 15 February 1944.

Barr, George Terry. "The Ordinary World of Horton Foote." (PhD diss., University of Tennessee, 1987).

Benson, Sheila. "Horton Foote." *The Voice of an American Playwright*. Edited by Gerald C. Wood and Marion Castleberry. Macon GA: Mercer University Press, 2012.

Beresford, Bruce. "Memorial Essay." *Farewell: Remembering Horton Foote 1916–2009*. Edited by Marion Castleberry and Susan Christensen. Dallas TX: Southern Methodist University Press, 2011.

Borchard, Fredrika. "Horton from Wharton." *Houston Chronicle Retrogravure Magazine* (4 October 1953): 10.

Brian, Crystal. "'Be Quiet and Listen': *The Orphans Home Cycle* and the Music of Charles Ives." In *Horton Foote: A Casebook*. Edited by Gerald C. Wood. New York: Garland Press, 1997.

Briley, Rebecca. "Southern Accents: Horton Foote's Adaptations of William Faulkner, Harper Lee, and Flannery O'Connor." In *Horton Foote: A Casebook*. Edited by Gerald C. Wood. New York: Garland Press, 1997.

_____. *You Can Go Home Again: The Focus on Family in the Works of Horton Foote*. New York: Peter Lang, 1993.

Brown, Jared. *Alan J. Pakula*. New York: Back Stage Books, 2005.

Brown, Jeff. "The Making of a Movie." *Holiday*, 5 February 1966.

Burkhart, Marian. "Horton Foote's Many Roads Home: An American Playwright and His Characters." *Commonweal* (26 February 1988): 110–15.

Castleberry, Marion and Susan Christensen, eds. *Farewell: Remembering Horton Foote: 1916–2009*. Dallas TX: Southern Methodist University Press, 2011.

_____. "Remembering Wharton, Texas." In *Horton Foote: A Casebook*. Edited by Gerald C. Wood. New York: Garland Press, 1997.

_____. "Reflections on the American Theatre: A Conversation with Horton Foote." In *The Voice of an American Playwright*. Edited by Gerald C. Wood and Marion Castleberry. Macon GA: Mercer University Press, 2012.

Coe, Fred. "TV-Drama's Declaration of Independence." *Theatre Arts*, June 1954.

Malcolm Crowley, ed. *Portable Faulkner*. New York: Viking Press, 1974.

DeMille, Agnes. *Martha: The Life and Work of Martha Graham*. New York: Random House, 1991.

Davis, Ronald. "Roots in a Parched Ground: An Interview with Horton Foote." *The Voice of an American Playwright*. Edited by Gerald C. Wood and Marion Castleberry. Macon GA: Mercer University Press, 2012.

Donahoo, Robert. "On The Day Emily Married: An Interview with Horton Foote." *The Voice of an American Playwright*. Edited by Gerald C. Wood and Marion Castleberry. Macon GA: Mercer University Press, 2012.

Eddy, Mary Baker. *Science and Health with Keys to the Scriptures*. Boston: Christian Science Publishing, 1934.

Edgerton, Gary. "A Visit to the Imaginary Landscape of Harrison, Texas: Sketching the Film Career of Horton Foote." *Literature/ Film Quarterly* 17 (1989) 2–12.

Ellerman, Robert. Introduction. *Horton Foote: Collected Plays*. Lyme NH: Smith and Kraus, 1993.

Foote, Daisy. "Horton Foote: A Collector Remembered." *The Antiques Magazine* (5 March 2009) 8–10.

_____. "Memorial Essay." *Farewell: Remembering Horton Foote, 1916–2009*. Edited by Marion Castleberry and Susan Christensen. Dallas TX: Southern Methodist University Press, 2011.

_____. "The Pleasure and Pain of Doing like Dad." *New York Times*, 23 August 2012.

Foote, Horton. *A Young Lady of Property: Six Short Plays*. New York: Dramatists Play Service, 1983.

_____. *Beginnings: A Memoir*. New York: Scribner Press, 2000.

_____. "Dance and the Playwright." *The Dance Observer*, January 1944.

_____. *Farewell: A Memoir of a Texas Childhood*. New York: Scribner, 1999.

_____. "Flight." In *Television Plays for Writers*. Edited by Abraham Burack. Boston: The Writer, 1957.

_____. *Four New Plays: The Habitation of Dragons, Night Seasons, Dividing the Estate, Talking Pictures*. Newbury VT: Smith and Kraus, 1993.

_____. *Four Plays from The Orphans' Home Cycle*. New York: Grove Press, 1988.

_____. *Harrison, Texas: Eight Television Plays*. New York: Harcourt Brace, 1956.

_____. *Horton Foote: Collected Plays*. Vol. 2. Lyme, New Hampshire: Smith and Kraus, 1993.

_____. *Horton Foote: Four New Plays, 1988–1993*. Newbury VT: Smith and Kraus, 1993.

_____. *Horton Foote: Genesis of an American Playwright*. Edited by Marion Castleberry. Waco TX: Baylor University Press, 2004.

_____. *Horton Foote: Getting Frankie Married—and Afterwards and Other Plays*. Lyme NH: Smith and Kraus. 1998.

_____. *Horton Foote: Three Plays* [*Old Man, Tomorrow, Roots in a Parched Ground*]. New York: Harcourt Brace & World, 1962.

_____. *Horton Foote's The Shape of the River: The Lost Teleplay about Mark Twain.* Edited by David Dawidziak. New York: Applause Books, 2003.

_____. *Horton Foote's Three Trips to Bountiful.* Edited by Barbara Moore and David G. Yellin. Dallas TX: Southern Methodist University Press, 1993.

_____. Introduction. *Four Plays from The Orphans' Home Cycle.* New York: Grove Press, 1988.

_____. Introduction. *The Young Man from Atlanta.* New York: Dutton Press, 1995.

_____. "Notes for the Future," *The Dance Observer,* May 1945.

_____. *Old Man and Tomorrow.* New York: Dramatists Play Service, 1963.

_____. *Only the Heart.* New York: Dramatists Play Service, 1944.

_____. "Richmond, U.S.A," *New York Times,* 13 April 1952, sec. C.

_____. *Roots in a Parched Ground.* New York: Dramatists Play Service, 1962.

_____. *Roots in a Parched Ground, Convicts, Lily Dale, The Widow Claire: The First Four Plays of The Orphans' Home Cycle.* New York: Grove, Press, 1988.

_____. *Selected One-Act Plays of Horton Foote.* Edited by Gerald C. Wood. Dallas TX: Southern Methodist University Press, 1989.

_____. *The Chase.* New York: Rinehart and Company, 1956.

_____. *The Carpetbagger's Children and The Actor.* Woodstock NY: Overlook Press, 2003.

_____. *The Last of the Thorntons.* Woodstock NY: Overlook Press, 2000; New York: Dramatists Play Service, 2001.

_____. *The Orphans' Home Cycle.* New York: Grove Press, 1989.

_____. *The Young Man from Atlanta.* New York: Dutton Press, 1995.

_____. *Three Plays by Horton Foote* [*Old Man, Tomorrow, Roots in a Parched Ground*]. New York: Harcourt Brace, 1962.

_____. *Three Screenplays:* To Kill a Mockingbird, Tender Mercies, *and* The Trip to Bountiful. New York: Grove Press, 1989.

_____. *Tomorrow and Tomorrow and Tomorrow.* Edited by David G. Yellin and Marie Connors. Jackson: Mississippi University Press, 1985.

_____. *Vernon Early.* New York: Dramatists Play Service, 1998.

Foote, Horton Jr. "Untitled Essay," In *Farewell: Remembering Horton Foote, 1916–2009.* Edited by Marion Castleberry and Susan Christensen. Dallas TX: Southern Methodist University Press, 2011.

Forsberg, Myra. "Hallie Foote Relives Her Family's Past." *New York Times,* 13 April 1986, sec. 2.

Fraser-Cavassoni, Natasha. *Sam Speigel.* New York: Simon & Schuster, 2003.

Freedman, Russell. *Martha Graham: A Dancer's Life.* New York: Houghton Mifflin, 1998.

Freedman, Samuel G. "From the Heart of Texas." *New York Times Magazine,* 9 February 1980.

Goodman, Walter. "Review / Theatre: Marathon of One-Acts." *New York Times,* 14 July 1988.

Gottschalk, Stephen. *Rolling Away the Stone: Mary Baker Eddy's Challenge to Materialism*. Bloomington: Indiana University Press, 2006.

Griggs, John. *The Films of Gregory Peck*. Secaucus NJ: Citadel Press, 1984.

Guare, John. "My Trip to Bountiful," *Farewell: Remembering Horton Foote, 1916–2009*. Edited by Marion Castleberry and Susan Christensen. Dallas TX: Southern Methodist University Press, 2011.

_____. "Conversation with Horton Foote," *The Voice of an American Playwright*. Edited by Gerald C. Wood and Marion Castleberry. Macon GA: Mercer University Press, 2012.

Hampton, Wilborn. *Horton Foote: American's Storyteller*. New York: Simon & Schuster, 2009.

Hetrick, Adam. "Foote's *Orphans Home Cycle* to Play Hartford Stage and NY's Signature." *Playbill*, 21 January 2009. http://www.playbill.com/news/article/125468-Footes-orphans-home-cycle-to-play-Hartford-stage-and-NY's-Signature.

Hey, Kenneth. "Marty: Aesthetics vs. Medium in Early Television Drama." In *American History, American Television*. Edited by John E. O'Connor. New York: Frederick Ungar, 1983.

Hilder, Jeffrey. "Everlasting Grace." In *The Voice of an American Playwright*. Edited by Gerald C. Wood and Marion Castleberry. Macon GA: Mercer University Press, 2012.

Hopper, Stanley Romaine. *Spiritual Problems in Contemporary Literature*. New York: Harper & Brothers, 1952.

Houghton, James. "Untitled Essay," In *Farewell: Remembering Horton Foote, 1916–2009*. Edited by Marion Castleberry and Susan Christiansen. Dallas TX: Southern Methodist University Press, 2011.

_____. Introduction. *"Getting Frankie Married—and Afterwards" and Other Plays*. Lyme NH: Smith and Kraus, 1998.

Hubbard, Alan. "Untitled Essay." In *Farewell: Remembering Horton Foote, 1916-2009*. Edited by Marion Castleberry and Susan Christiansen. Dallas TX: Southern Methodist University Press, 2011.

Hudgins, Merle. "Albert Clinton Horton." Unpublished essay, 2009.

Humphrey, William. *The Ordways*. New York: Alfred Knopf, 1964.

Hunter, Mary. Foreword. *Only the Heart* by Horton Foote. New York: Dramatist Play Service, 1944.

Jewett, Robert. "The Mysterious God of *Tender Mercies*." In *Saint Paul at the Movies: The Apostle's Dialogue with American Culture*. Louisville KY: Westminster/John Knox, 1993.

Jilinski, Andrius. *The Joy of Acting: A Primer for Actors*. New York: Peter Lang, 1990.

Krampner, John. *The Man in the Shadows: Fred Coe and the Golden Age of Television*. New Brunswick NJ: Rutgers University Press, 1997.

_____. *Female Brando: The Legend of Kim Stanley*. New York: Back Stage Books, 2006.

Lee, Harper. "A Word." In *To Kill a Mockingbird: A Screenplay*. New York: Harcourt Brace & World, 1964.

Leuchtenberg, William. *The Unfinished Century*. Boston: Little, Brown and Company, 1973.

Martin, Carter. "Horton Foote's Southern Family in *Roots in a Parched Ground*." *Texas Review* 12 (Spring–Summer 1991): 76–82.

McLaughlin, Buzz. "Conversation with Horton Foote." In *The Voice of an American Playwright*. Edited by Gerald C. Wood and Marion Castleberry. Macon GA: Mercer University Press, 2012.

Mendell, Dean. "Squeezing the Drama out of Melodrama: Plot and Counterplot in *Laura Dennis*." In *Horton Foote: A Casebook*. Edited by Gerald C. Wood. New York: Garland Press, 1997.

Middleton, David. "Winning, Losing, and Compromising: The Screenwriter Contends for Personal Turf." In *The Voice of an American Playwright*. Edited by Gerald C. Wood and Marion Castleberry. Macon GA: Mercer University Press, 2012.

Modine, Matthew. "Memorial Essay." *Farewell: Remembering Horton Foote, 1916–2009*. Edited by Marion Castleberry and Susan Christensen. Dallas TX: Southern Methodist University Press, 2011.

Moore, Marianne. *The Complete Works of Marianne Moore*. New York: Macmillan-Viking Press, 1956.

Mosel, Tad. *Other People's Houses*. New York: Simon & Schuster, 1956.

Murphy, Mary McDonagh. *Scout, Atticus, & Boo*. New York: HarperCollins, 2010.

O'Connor, Flannery. *Mystery and Manners: Occasional Prose*. Selected and edited by Sally and Robert Fitzgerald. New York: Farrar, Straus and Giroux, 1995.

O'Quinn, Jim. "Eye of the Beholder." In *The Voice of an American Playwright*. Edited by Gerald C. Wood and Marion Castleberry. Macon GA: Mercer University Press, 2012.

Outlar, Nan. "Love of Writing Came Over Time," *Wharton County Journal-Spectator* 24 (September 1986).

Parish, James Robert. *Fiasco: A History of Hollywood's Iconic Flops*. Hoboken NJ: John Wiley & Sons, 2006.

Porter, Laurin. "An Interview with Horton Foote," *The Voice of an American Playwright*. Edited by Gerald C. Wood and Marion Castleberry. Macon GA: Mercer University Press, 2012.

_____."Memory and the Re-Construction of the Past: Horton Foote's Carpetbagger's Children." *The Horton Foote Review* (2005): 35–42.

_____. *Orphans' Home: The Voice and Vision of Horton Foote*. Baton Rouge: Louisiana State University Press, 2003.

_____. "Unpublished Interview." In *The Voice of an American Playwright*. Edited by Gerald C. Wood and Marion Castleberry. Macon GA: Mercer University Press, 2012.

Price, Reynolds. Introduction. *Courtship, Valentine's Day, 1918: Three Plays from the Orphans' Home Cycle*. New York: Grove Press, 1986.

Price, Reynolds. Introduction. *The Orphans' Home Cycle*. New York: Grove Press, 1989.

Reinert, Al. "Tender Foote." *Texas Monthly*, July 1991.

Rizzo, Frank. "Michael Wilson Knows What He Likes." *American Theatre*, May/June 2009.

Roberts, Edward Barry. "Writing for Television," *The Best Television Plays, 1950–1951*. Edited by William Kaufman. New York: Hastings House, 1952.

Roussel, Peter. "Profiles from Houston: Horton Foote," *The Voice of an American Playwright*. Edited by Gerald C. Wood and Marion Castleberry. Macon GA: Mercer University Press, 2012.

Roy, Morris J. *Behind Barbed Wire*. New York: Richard R. Smith, 1946.

Schneider, Alan. *Entrances: An American Director's Journey*. New York: Viking Penguin, 1986.

Schumach, Murray. "Hollywood's Roving Lady." *New York Times*, 5 January 1964.

Simon, John. "Horton Foote's 'Orphans' Home Cycle' Must Be Seen." *Bloomberg News*, 6 February 2010.

Skaggs, Merrill Maquire. "The Story and Film of Barn Burning." *Southern Quarterly* 21 (Winter 1983): 5–15.

Slawson, Judith. *Robert Duvall: Hollywood Maverick*. New York: St. Martin's Press, 1985.

Smeltsor, Marjorie. "The World's an Orphan's Home: Horton Foote's Social and Moral History." *Southern Quarterly* 29 (Winter 1991): 7–16.

Smith, Lois. "Untitled Essay." *Farewell: In Remembering Horton Foote, 1916–2009*. Edited by Marion Castleberry and Susan Christensen. Dallas TX: Southern Methodist University Press, 2011.

Sterritt, David. "Horton Foote: Filmmaking Radical with a Tender Touch." *Christian Science Monitor* (15 May 1986): 1, 36.

_____. "Let's Hear it for the Human Being." *Saturday Evening Post* (October 1983): 36–8.

Terrill, Marshall. *The Life and Legend of a Hollywood Icon*. New York: Triumph Books, 2010.

Thompson, Barbara. "Katherine Anne Porter." *Writers at Work: The Paris Review Interviews*. 2nd series. New York, *Paris Review* (Winter-Spring): 1963.

Underwood, Susan. "Singing in the Face of Devastation: Texture in Horton Foote's *Talking Pictures*," In *Horton Foote: A Casebook*. Edited by Gerald C. Wood. New York: Garland Press, 1997.

Watson, Charles S. *Horton Foote: A Literary Biography*. Austin: University of Texas Press, 2003.

Weales, Gerald. *American Drama Since World War Two*. New York: Harcourt Brace, 1962.

Williams, Annie Lee. *A History of Wharton County*. Austin TX: Van Boeckmann-Jones, 1999.

Wilson, Michael. "Director Michael Wilson on Dinners with the Foote family & Falling in Love with the Trip to Bountiful." *Broadway*, 7 May 2013. http://www.broadway.com/buzz/169334/director-michael-wilson-on-dinners-with-the-Foote-Family-&-Falling-in-Love-With-The-Trip-To-Bountiful.

Witchel, Alex. "His Kind of Town," *New York Times Magazine*, 19 August 2007.

Wood, Gerald C. "Boundaries, the Female Will, and Individuation in *Night Season*," *Horton Foote: A Casebook*. Edited by Gerald C. Wood. New York: Garland Press, 1997.

_____. *Horton Foote: A Casebook*. New York: Garland Press, 1997.

_____. *Horton Foote and the Theatre of Intimacy*. Baton Rouge: Louisiana State University Press, 1999.

_____. "Horton Foote at the American Actors Company, *Dance Observer*, and King Smith Productions: Nothing More Real than the Human Heart." *The Horton Foote Review*. Vol. 1. New York: iUniverse, 2005.

_____. "The Nature of Mystery: *The Young Man from Atlanta*," *Horton Foote: A Casebook*. Edited by Gerald C. Wood. New York: Garland Press, 1998.

_____. "Old Beginnings and Roads to Home: Horton Foote and Mythic Realism." *Christianity and Literature* 45 (Spring/Summer 1996): 359–72.

_____. "The Physical Hunger for the Spiritual: Southern Religious Experience in the Plays of Horton Foote." *The World is Our Home: Society and Culture in Contemporary Southern Writing*. Edited by Jeffrey J. Folks and Nancy Summers Folks. Lexington: University of Kentucky Press, 2000.

_____. "Variations on the Monologue: Brian Friel's *The Faith Healer* and Horton Foote's *The Carpetbagger's Children*," *The Horton Foote Review*. Vol. 2. Dallas TX: Southern Methodist University Press, 2009.

Wood, Gerald C., and Marion Castleberry, eds. *The Voice of an American Playwright: Interviews with Horton Foote*. Macon GA: Mercer University Press, 2012.

Wood, Gerald C., and Terry Barr. "A Certain Kind of Writer: An Interview with Horton Foote," *The Voice of an American Playwright*. Edited by Gerald C. Wood and Marion Castleberry. Macon GA: Mercer University Press, 2012.

Young, Stark. Foreword. *The Traveling Lady*. New York: Dramatists Play Service, 1955.

Yulin, Harris. "Untitled Essay." *Farewell: Remembering Horton Foote, 1916–2009*. Edited by Marion Castleberry and Susan Christensen. Dallas TX: Southern Methodist University Press, 2011.

Zeller, Bob. "An American Playwright: World Premiere of *The Habitation of Dragons*." *Playbill*, Pittsburg Public Theatre, 29 September 1988.

Index